THE SPICE OF LIFE

Also by J. N. Walton

Subarachnoid Haemorrhage. Livingstone, Edinburgh, 1956.

Polymyositis (with R. D. Adams). Livingstone, Edinburgh, 1958.

Essentials of Neurology. Pitman, London, 1961; 6th edition, Churchill Livingstone, Edinburgh, 1989.

Disorders of Voluntary Muscle (edited). Churchill, London, 1964; 5th edition, Churchill Livingstone, Edinburgh, 1987.

Brain's Diseases of the Nervous System. Oxford University Press, Oxford, 7th edition 1969; 9th edition 1985. (A 10th edition, which will be multi-author, is due to be published in 1993.)

Skeletal Muscle Pathology (co-editor): Churchill Livingstone, Edinburgh, 1982; 2nd edition 1992.

Introduction to Clinical Neuroscience. Baillière Tindall, London, 1983; 2nd edition 1987.

Oxford Companion to Medicine (chief editor). Oxford University Press, Oxford, 1986.

The Spice of Life

From Northumbria to World Neurology

JOHN WALTON
(LORD WALTON OF DETCHANT)

ROYAL SOCIETY OF MEDICINE SERVICES
LONDON · NEW YORK
1993

William Heinemann Ltd
Michelin House, 81 Fulham Road, London SW3 6RB
LONDON MELBOURNE AUCKLAND

First published 1993
Copyright ©Royal Society of Medicine Services Limited 1993

A CIP catalogue record for this book
is held by the British Library
ISBN 0 434 84156 0

Printed and bound in Great Britain by
Mackays of Chatham PLC, Chatham, Kent

Contents

To my wife, Betty,
with love and gratitude

Preface

While I accept that the title of this book will be regarded by some as a cliché, my life has been so full of variety that I could not think of a better alternative. After my retirement from the Wardenship of Green College in 1989, prompted by family members and friends, I began to collect and analyse some recollections and reminiscences of my personal and professional life, initially with the intention of preparing a typescript which would be circulated privately within the family. Indeed one version of the book will be handled in that way. However, some of those who were kind enough to read and criticize the early chapters persuaded me that a slightly shorter version should be presented to a wider audience. I have been exceptionally fortunate in my parents, my education, my wife, family and friends. Without the continual encouragement of Betty, my wife, the work would never have been completed; she offered invaluable comments and criticisms of each chapter as it emerged and regularly corrected errors when my memory played me false. I have also enjoyed the unfailing support of innumerable professional colleagues in the many different spheres of medicine and other activities in which I have dabbled over the years, and I have been loyally served by those who have worked with and for me in a manifold range of activities.

After some preliminary discussions with publishers with whom I had previously worked, I was delighted when my friend Howard Croft, Publications Director of Royal Society of Medicine Services Limited, and Richard Charkin of the Octopus Books division of Reed publishing (whom I had come to know well when he worked at Oxford University Press and when we collaborated over the Oxford Companion to Medicine) agreed to undertake the joint publication and marketing of the volume (under the RSM/Heinemann imprint). I am also grateful to the Leverhulme Trust for awarding me a two-year Emeritus Fellowship which enabled me to continue in my retirement to use the services of my long-serving secretary, Rosemary Allan. I also received a grant to cover other expenses involved in a concurrent study of the historical aspects of neuromuscular disease from the Wellcome Trust history of medicine panel. Rosemary has been a tower of strength throughout the gestation period and her immaculate preparation of the original manuscript made my task very much easier.

Her thoughtful and perspicacious comments upon parts of the book which were repetitious were also invaluable. I am also deeply grateful to Howard Croft for his helpful editorial comments which have, I hope, enabled me to amend the final version in such a way as to delete redundant material, to tighten up the text and to retain, in what I appreciate is still a lengthy work, those elements which he thought might be of interest to a wider audience than just my family and close friends. His associate, Yvonne Rue, has also helped enormously throughout the final production process.

I can only hope that in this tale, completed in my seventieth year, I have been able to convey something of the constant stimulation, interest and even excitement which so many varied activities, medical and non-medical, have aroused throughout my life. I appreciate that the book may contain in places a little too much detailed medicine and science for the lay reader, while for the medical reader some of my other commentaries may possibly be thought to be irrelevancies. But I have done my best in my descriptions and comments to achieve a reasonable balance between professional and other matters. I hope that the book will convey not just that sense of fulfilment which I have often (if not invariably) experienced but also, above all, the continuing aura of enjoyment, even at times of fun, which, for me at least, has enlivened so much of my life and work. This, like variety, is indeed the spice of life.

JOHN WALTON
Oxford
May 1992

CHAPTER 1

Early Years in Durham County

In 1988, armed with my birth certificate, my wife Betty and I set out to explore some of the haunts of my early childhood and to try to find the house where I was born. We knew that I was born at home and on 16th September 1922 in Rowlands Gill, Co. Durham, but the name of the house on the birth certificate could not be found in the street in Highfield which had often been pointed out to me by my parents when we had passed through the village many years earlier. We probably identified the correct one but nevertheless left the village with a sense of disappointment; we are both sentimental people and would have liked to be certain.

Rowlands Gill, though situated on the northern fringe of the Durham coalfield and harbouring an active and productive colliery until the early 1980s, is by no means a typical Durham mining village. It lies on the north bank of the Derwent River, a tributary of the Tyne, about eight miles from Newcastle, among some very attractive countryside and boasts many dwellings of well above average quality, some of which might indeed be classed as being slightly pretentious examples of the suburban or commuter-belt villa. The village is approached from Newcastle via Scotswood (of 'Blaydon Races' fame) and its bridge over the Tyne, then by a winding road climbing through the densely wooded valley of the Derwent reaching Winlaton Mill, a less attractive mining village just short of Rowlands Gill itself. The house which my parents bought when my father became an assistant master at Westwood Council School between Shotley Bridge and Medomsley was in the area of Highfield on the road which climbed steeply from the village, past the Methodist church, towards High Spen and Victoria Garesfield.

Close to Rowlands Gill on the other side of the Derwent, lying in attractive parkland, was the large Palladian style Gibside Hall, belonging to the Bowes-Lyon family, occupied in my childhood but largely demolished after the Second World War. However, its chapel, designed by James Payne and now lovingly cared for by the National Trust, still stands, its classical lines and cool, elegant interior creating an architectural gem which would no doubt delight the heir to the throne whose grandmother's family once owned it.

1

My father, Herbert, was born in the mining village of Allendale Cottages, the second of three sons, and spent his childhood in a two-roomed colliery cottage which, like all others in the village, had a kitchen cum living-room downstairs and a single large bedroom upstairs. There was a scullery at the rear with a small concrete-paved yard and coal house, and a gate leading on to a muddy back lane, on the other side of which were the earth closets or privies belonging to each of the homes. But in front of each house there was a long narrow garden, carefully cultivated, often adorned by a profusion of blooms in the spring and summer but with much of the area being devoted to home-grown vegetables. The village itself consisted of the colliery, in which almost all of its inhabitants worked (my grandfather, John Walton, began work in the mine in the last century at the age of 10 and worked there until retirement). There was one larger house in its own grounds occupied by the colliery manager on the other side of the road leading down to Westwood was the Wesleyan Methodist chapel. Here my grandparents worshipped and my father and his brothers spent many hours in their formative years attending Sunday services, Sunday school and various other church activities during the week. Westwood, a tiny hamlet, about a mile down the hill, provided the village school and a sports ground for village cricket and soccer. Allendale Cottages itself sat bleakly among open fields at the top of a hill facing down over the Derwent Valley, exposed to the cold northern and westerly winds in winter. The only trees in sight were those far below in the Derwent Valley and in the extensive wood between Westwood and Hamsterley Mill, known locally as 'Cuttythroat Wood' because early in the century a bank messenger was waylaid when walking there with a substantial sum of money; his body with his throat cut was found a day or two later by some villagers out for a stroll. My father often told me of the relative privations that he and his brothers endured in his early school years. When the soles of his only pair of shoes wore through after the daily walks to and from school, they often could not be repaired for lack of money, and brown paper was used to line the inside of the soles. Outer clothing, even in the snow-bound months (and this part of Durham still sees the snow much earlier than many other parts of the county) was also relatively skimpy. Nevertheless the family were well fed, happy and contented and practically all of their social life centred on the chapel.

My recollections of my grandparents are now relatively vague but I do remember the short, stocky figure of my grandfather, dressed, except on Sundays, in a shirt without a collar, heavy woollen waistcoat and trousers and stout boots. His bald head shone and he had a splendid Victorian-style moustache. On Sundays, however, out came his solitary dark blue suit, white shirt, tie and a pair of worn black shoes so that he could show due respect in the Lord's house where he sang with gusto and played a full part in the services. My grandmother was shorter still with her white hair drawn back into a severe bun; she wore a high-necked black dress with a white lace collar, thick stockings and buttoned shoes and always had a delightful twinkle in the eye. Her style of dress was invariable whatever the day or season; I cannot recall seeing her in any other clothes, but when she cooked (and how she cooked) a heavy apron almost enveloped her. The only addition to her dress was a black straw hat which was brought out for church on Sundays.

In the kitchen there was the coal fire, invariably blazing winter and summer, continually fed by the miners' free ration of coal. Water was heated in an open-topped boiler with a flat, iron lid to the right and on the left a black-leaded oven with a circular front which resembled the front of an old railway steam engine. A kettle stood constantly on a hob which was swung across the burning coals when tea was required. Out of that coal-heated oven came delicious Yorkshire puddings; there was always a succulent joint of meat with plenty of home-grown vegetables on Sundays, and home-made scones, cakes and bread at tea-time. My grandparents were kind, Christian people, and life-long tee totallers like my parents; I wish now that I had known them better. They both died before I was 10 years of age.

In 1987, as a part of our pilgrimage around north-west Durham, we went to Allendale Cottages so that I could revive memories of my early childhood and of visits to my grandparents, but were unprepared for the stunning shock we experienced. We should have been warned, as in the early 1970s a steward of the Allendale Cottages Methodist Church wrote to say that the church was to be closed and demolished; he sent me a brass plaque which had been installed in the 1920s to acknowledge the generosity of my father and his brothers who had paid for the installation of electric lighting in the church, previously lit by gas. As we drove up the well-remembered hill from Westwood and turned left into where the village had stood (the road sign for Allendale Cottages was still there), we were astonished to find a large open field with tall grass, rosebay willow herb waving in the sunshine and one solitary building, the former colliery manager's house, now a private residence surrounded by a small-holding. It was just possible to discern the outline of the streets and some foundations where the village had once stood, but almost no trace of the once-flourishing coal mine could now be identified and the entire village had been razed to the ground. In the eerie silence of the deserted site, we glanced nostalgically at the foundations of the chapel in which we had so often heard the lusty and enthusiastic hymn-singing of the miners and their families.

From the village school at Westwood, my father and his elder brother John (subsequently manager of the Co-operative Society store in Blackhill, near Consett) and his younger brother Ernest (who became a finance clerk with the now defunct but then prosperous Consett Iron Company) each obtained scholarships to the Consett Grammar School. My father made steady academic progress there and decided, after a few years, that school teaching was to be his career. All three boys showed some sporting prowess, and although my father was a competent soccer player and cricketer, hockey was his first love. For some years he he came close to county honours, becoming a Durham County hockey selector though never quite making the county team himself. In 1911, after passing the School Certificate examination, he enrolled at the Sunderland Teacher Training College where he spent the next two years. He obtained his teacher's training certificate without, I understand, serious difficulty, though he often told me that he was once arraigned before the Principal, having obtained 0% in an examination in psychology which, as he pointed out, was never his favourite subject.

While in Sunderland, like many others, he became increasingly apprehensive about the prospect of war and so enlisted in the embryo territorial force of the 7th Battalion, the Durham Light Infantry (DLI). His teaching career was not to develop before the war as in August 1914 he was, with several close friends, called to the colours with the DLI, being one of those who went to France early with his regiment as a young and untried second lieutenant. A few months later he was wounded by shrapnel, with injuries to his left thigh and left temple. For many years we kept his steel helmet with a jagged hole on the left made by the fragment which struck his temple; we often speculated as to what would have happened if the force of its impact had not been lessened. Soon he was back in the front line as a first lieutenant and later acting captain and company commander; but in 1916 he was again severely wounded by shrapnel from an exploding shell, this time receiving multiple wounds of which by far the most serious was to the abdomen; a piece of shrapnel pierced both walls of the stomach and lodged in the transverse colon. He then lay for several hours in 'no-man's land' before being retrieved by a stretcher party and taken to hospital. For some time, because of the inevitable peritonitis, it was thought that he was unlikely to survive and indeed, his parents were called to France to his bedside. But, miraculously, with the aid of skilful surgery and the rudimentary intravenous fluid medication then available, he ultimately made a good recovery but was nevertheless invalided out of the army with a 100% disability pension for life. As he said to me many years later and long before he died at the age of 77, that pension, supplementing his relatively meagre salary as a schoolmaster, was a great help in educating his children, each of whom, including myself, wished to become doctors.

My mother was christened Eleanor Watson Ward and was the youngest of 10 children born in Hebburn-on-Tyne where her father was a shipyard worker in the bustling industry of Britain's second greatest ship-building river after the Clyde. Two, or possibly three, of her brothers and sisters suffered from tuberculosis, from which they subsequently died, and her father, whom we never knew, died in his later forties or early fifties as the result of a shipyard accident. In her childhood my mother (who eventually lived to the age of 93) was regarded as being 'delicate' and as possibly suffering from a heart condition (some doctor had heard an apical systolic murmur). After her father's death, when the family faced serious financial difficulties, she was sent to live with an uncle in Rookhope in Weardale and spent there the formative years of her childhood, attending first the Rookhope village school and later, exceptionally, winning a scholarship to the Wolsingham Grammar School. Although she kept in intermittent touch with her mother, whom in later years we occasionally visited in her terrace house in Allendale village, where she was superbly cared for by her companion, Mabel, it was my mother's Uncle Nicholas and Aunt Mary whom she regarded as her true parents. In their stone-built terrace home in the main street of Rookhope she enjoyed a fruitful and happy childhood, centred first on the village school and later the grammar school some 10 or 15 miles away, but inevitably too upon the Methodist church as her family, like my father's, were staunch Methodists. Uncle Nicholas was revered by my mother as a scrupulously honest, intelligent, God-fearing and upright man of the Dales. He lost an arm during his working life in the lead mines of Weardale but continued to contribute effectively to his local community through many voluntary activities. He was my mother's great teacher and mentor from whom she learned a love of music, literature, and the countryside. Though Nicholas himself never benefitted from higher education, he became an avid collector of fluorspar and quartz and an able amateur geologist. Some of his writings on the geological characteristics of the lead mines of Weardale, written in beautiful, clear, copperplate hand, came into my possession many years later and are now lodged in the library of the Department of Earth Sciences of the University of Newcastle upon Tyne. Sadly, Uncle Nicholas died before I was old enough to remember him, but Aunt Mary lived on for many years. Often my brother and sister and I with our parents went to stay in the house at Rookhope in which she lived with her sister Emma. It had been created by merging two smaller houses so that there were several bedrooms and two separate flights of stairs. Although my mother's Rookhope childhood was a happy one, she regularly told tales about the lack of heating in the house and described how often, on rising in the morning, she had to break the ice on the water in the washstand bowl so as to wash before dressing to go downstairs into the main kitchen. This was the only room in the house to be heated by an open coal fire, save for the drawing-room where a fire was only lit on very special occasions when guests were to be entertained.

Although the holidays we spent there were invariably in the summer during school holidays, I too can remember how chilly it sometimes was and how striking was the Victorian style of its furnishings. Sometimes I was allowed to sleep in a four-poster bed with a feather mattress, which was comfortable and all-enveloping; all of us still had to wash in bowls set upon marble-topped washstands in each bedroom, supplied from tall jugs of cold water which were filled every evening. There was no flush toilet but an earth closet at the bottom of the garden. The most comfortable seats in the sitting-room were horse-hair sofas and chairs, and the room itself contained many ornaments of fluorspar and quartz, covered with glass domes, which Uncle Nicholas had collected so avidly. In Rookhope we enjoyed many delightful outings with long walks over the high moors towards Allenheads or on the low road towards Eastgate. Sometimes we even took a bus to St John's Chapel or to Stanhope and Wolsingham to visit relatives and friends, but more often we wandered around the disused workings of the now defunct lead mines or climbed the moors on the high road towards Edmundbyers. Sometimes, too, I was allowed to play snooker or billiards with my father in the Church Institute, and even to play tennis and bowls at the colliery recreation ground (the colliery was still functioning in those days). I also recall being asked, on one occasion only, to pump by hand the bellows of the organ of the Methodist Church; when the air ran out halfway through a verse of a lustily rendered hymn, I wasn't asked again. We had no car until my father acquired his first £100 Ford 8 in 1932 and often hired a small bus, or occasionally a large car, to transport us with all our luggage to and from Rookhope. More rarely we travelled by train to the terminus at Westgate and took a taxi from there to Rookhope, but that was a much more troublesome and expensive journey.

At Wolsingham Grammar School my mother was an eager and assiduous pupil; well into her eighties she could still quote verbatim much of the poetry she had learned in her childhood and often mentioned with pride that she was the only person, so far as she knew, in the village of Rookhope who actually learned a little French. English was, however, her first love and as her school career progressed she, like my father, was determined to become a teacher. Indeed, while at grammar school, she helped out occasionally as an unpaid pupil teacher at Rookhope School and soon recognized that she had a flair for this calling. Ultimately she, too, enrolled at the Sunderland Teacher Training College, where she met my father. Though they were friendly and although my father, as he told me in later years, made several tentative approaches to her, there was no hint, at least on her side initially, of romance. Indeed at the outbreak of the First World War she had become engaged to George Rivers who had also trained as a teacher and whose father was the colliery manager at Thornley in Co. Durham. He too joined the army at the outbreak of war but was killed on the Western Front in 1915. After my father had recovered from his wounds and had been invalided out of the army he again contacted my mother who had returned to Rookhope and was then teaching in the village school. By this time too, as the end of the war approached, my father had recovered sufficiently to be able to resume his teaching career and obtained a post as assistant master in Westwood School which he himself had attended in his childhood and which was just a mile away from his parents' home in Allendale Cottages. Despite the distance which separated them and the difficulties of getting from Allendale Cottages to Rookhope by public transport, my father made more and more frequent visits. These eventually led to engagement and to marriage in 1920, by which time they felt that with their combined income and savings they could just afford the purchase of a house in Rowlands Gill.

As was then customary, my mother gave up work soon after her marriage and devoted her considerable energies to becoming a competent whole-time housewife. No doubt it was she, much the more ambitious of the two, who encouraged my father to apply for school headships which intermittently became vacant in the neighbourhood; in due course he was successful and in 1923 was appointed headmaster of Pickering Nook School in Hobson Colliery, about four miles from Rowlands Gill. It was only many years later that I became aware of the remarkable system whereby headmasters of council schools (and no doubt of grammar schools also) were then appointed in Durham County. Such appointments were in the gift of the County Education Committee elected from the County Council and which then, as always in Durham, was controlled by the Labour Party. This was the case in most areas of the country where industries like mining and shipbuilding dominated the industrial scene. Although his parents had been Liberals, my father was a life-long member of the Labour Party, basing his beliefs upon the ideals of Christian socialism which were then so effectively nurtured within the Methodist Church, to which many Labour Party stalwarts of Durham County belonged. Among my father's friends and acquaintances were such notable Labour men as Sam Watson, Jack Lawson of Beamish and Willie Whiteley of Chester-le-Street. In my own early school years those Christian principles which sought to improve the lot of the working man, to achieve equality of educational and other opportunity and to provide support for those less well-favoured and fortunate appealed to me greatly. I could readily understand the source from which my father's deeply held religious and political convictions arose. In his later years my father became deeply concerned by the dramatic swing to the left which occurred in the British Labour Party in the late 1960s and 1970s with the increasing influence of Trotskyites, the Socialist Workers' Party and the Militant Tendency. He often said that the members and supporters of the early

Christian Labour Party would have turned in their graves if they had seen what had happened to the political body to which they had devoted their lives.

Be that as it may, appointments to school headships in Durham County were then, and for all I know may still be, subject to profound political influence. Nowadays it is often said in advertisements for appointments of many kinds that 'canvassing will disqualify', but in Durham canvassing was not only encouraged, it was indeed demanded. It was normal practice for all candidates for headships to visit and to be interviewed individually by members of the County Education Committee, almost all of whom at one time or another enquired about the candidate's political affiliation. In later years in Spennymoor I developed a great admiration for my father's senior assistant master and deputy head, Harold Brown, but knew that he would never succeed to the headship of a school in the county as he was a Conservative voter and enthusiastic supporter of the Tory candidate in the Spennymoor constituency. Perhaps it was this experience, and other evidence which seemed to me to imply an unfair and malign influence of the dominant Labour majority upon local affairs which persuaded me in grammar school and later in university to reject the political faith of my parents and to move in my own views some distance to the right. This was more than a simple reaction against my upbringing and environment; it was also a reaction in my student days against the domination of organizations such as the National Union of Students (and even of the British Medical Students' Association) by the Communist Party, many of those in the NUS, in particular, being Laski-trained at the London School of Economics. When I went as a delegate from medical school in Newcastle as a Durham University representative to the NUS conference in 1944, we, with the support of just one other university, conducted a filibuster and demanded a card vote over our wish to see retention of the university vote in parliamentary elections, to which all the other representatives at the conference were bitterly opposed. In retrospect, we could surely have chosen a more worthy cause to which to hitch our flag; nevertheless the most significant point, at a time when most students attending provincial universities lived nearby in the region, was that the solitary supporter of Durham was Cardiff. Other delegates could not fail to note that the two universities favouring a faintly right-wing line against the wishes of the majority came from the two major coalmining Labour strongholds.

But to return to my childhood, I was only a year and 10 months of age when my family moved in 1924 to the school house at Pickering Nook where my father for the first time became a headmaster. That school building, in grey stone with the multiple high-peaked gable ends and tall narrow windows so characteristic of Victorian architecture, still stands with the adjoining school house in which I spent so many formative

childhood years. The house was an integral part of the school buildings;
it had a reasonably large drawing room with one solitary window looking
out through the ornamental cast iron railings which adorned the front
of the school on to a road. Behind the drawing room was a large kitchen
and adjoining scullery with an old-fashioned black-leaded range and an
open coal fire with a kettle hob, like that in my grandparents' home. There
was space in the kitchen for a dining table, and upstairs there were three
bedrooms but, of course, no bathroom. There was, however, an outside
flush toilet across the concrete backyard next to the coal-house. We all
washed in turns at the kitchen or scullery sink, and when a bath was
required a galvanized iron bath was brought in from the scullery and was
filled with hot water from multiple kettles in front of the kitchen fire. Bath
nights then (often weekly and certainly not more than twice a week) were
something of a ritual. Behind our yard, separated from it by a high stone
wall, was the schoolyard and playground covered in tarmac in which the
hundred or more pupils then attending the school played regularly during
break periods and sometimes during the lunch hour. There was then no
such thing as school dinners, and everyone went home for a midday meal
before returning for afternoon lessons. Between the backyard and the
green wooden gate in another high wall which opened out on to the
pavement between the house and the road was a small patch of grass,
a tiny flower bed and a solitary tree which I regularly climbed in my
childhood, often sitting in its branches to watch the traffic going past.
Horses and carts, ponies and traps were the most common conveyances
and delivery vehicles were often horse-drawn but one did see occasional
lorries and motor cars. Although car ownership was increasing steadily,
cars were still an exceptional luxury and in the 1920s were rarely seen.

Early in my childhood I began to develop my lifelong passion for cricket
(which we could only play in the schoolyard or back street, usually with
a tennis ball and a wicket chalked on a stone or brick wall). But when
I was nine or 10, among my prized possessions were a small cricket bat,
an imitation cork cricket ball and three wooden stumps. I also began to
read with great enjoyment books by the great Jack Hobbs, starting with
Between the Wickets which I still have in my library. Indeed he became
one of my boyhood heroes, so much so that since neither Durham nor
Northumberland boasted a first-class county side, I supported his county,
Surrey, as indeed did my father. On one occasion we set up the stumps
in the flower bed in our tiny garden and my father took a photograph
of me in batsman's pose. I later sent this off with an essay of 50 words
on 'Why I like Grape Nuts' as a competition entry, winning, to my great
astonishment, a folding Kodak camera which I was to use for many years.

Hobson Colliery was a long, narrow, straggling place with almost all
of its buildings situated along one side of the road. Pickering Nook was
the name of the long terrace of colliery houses which stood next to the

school, ending at the Primitive Methodist church which we did not attend, as my parents were dedicated Wesleyans. They regularly travelled about a mile and a half to Tantobie on the road to West Stanley, almost always on foot, to attend the Wesleyan Chapel. However, in the late 1920s or early 1930s reunion between the Wesleyans and the 'Prims', as they were generally called, took place. It then became acceptable for us to go to the nearer chapel where I went to Sunday School and took part in plays and concerts, certainly reciting more than once and even, I believe, singing a solo (only once).

Hobson Colliery itself was then a large and thriving mine. At the far end of the village were several superior houses as one approached Burnopfield, next to the nine-hole Hobson Colliery golf course. In two such houses lived the colliery manager and the assistant manager whose son I came to know well at school and with whom from time to time I and some other boys used to ride bareback the pit ponies (locally called Gallowers, because they came from Galloway) when they were brought to the surface for fresh air and exercise and were for short periods relieved of pulling coal trucks underground. Close to the colliery was a large area of waste land pitted by landfalls over old colliery workings with, alongside, some crumbling old coke ovens where the boys of the village, including myself, frequently played and constructed secret hide-outs. It was here that at the age of eight or nine I was introduced by older boys, as we all were, to the mysteries and pleasures of cigarette smoking. By the time I was 9½ or 10, smoking had become a frequent secret indulgence encouraged, or at least not prevented, by a small shopkeeper with a tiny store in one of the back lanes close to our house who regularly ignored the law forbidding the sale of tobacco to minors. Once, indeed, when I must have been not more than 10 years old, my mother gave me a shilling (twelve old pence) to take a friend to the cinema at Burnopfield, about two miles away (of course we always walked there and back) with the intention that we should sit in the best seats, costing sixpence each. Wickedly instead we used sixpence to buy five Park Drive cigarettes and sat in the cheapest seats in the front of the cinema stalls which cost two-pence each, so that we even had some change. An unfortunate consequence of that expedition was that a few days later my mother noticed that I was scratching my head rather vigorously. Out came the fine-tooth comb and when I saw the head lice appearing on the newspaper with which she had covered the table I was violently sick and, in recognizing the retribution, determined not to make the same mistake again (later I learned that the cheap front stalls were almost always alive with the creatures).

Memories of my schooldays at Pickering Nook are now rather dim but I remember the soup kitchens provided in the school for the miners and their families during the General Strike of 1926; this must have been before

I was old enough to attend school myself but I have a clear recollection, curiously poignant, of doleful groups of people wending through the school yard. I also find it difficult to recall the names and faces of the boys with whom I played, apart from one John Henry Scott whose name lingers only because it was usual in those days to address one's friends not just by their first Christian name but by both, so that I was often addressed as John Nicholas. I clearly remember that my mother had a maid and helper who came to us at the age of 17 and remained with us throughout our period at Pickering Nook after my brother, Ernest, was born. Margery Taylor, who lived until 1990, often came to help my wife Betty when our own children were small many years later. We kept in touch until her death and she told me that she used to push me out in my pushchair at Pickering Nook and later did the same for Ernest.

It is always difficult to know just how much of one's recollections is based upon genuine visual or auditory memory and how much upon what one has been told subsequently by one's parents or has learned through seeing childhood photographs. The only two things I can remember clearly about my Pickering Nook schooldays are, first, that I learned that great hilarity had been aroused in the school staff room when I wrote in an essay that sometimes my father picked up my mother and carried her round the room. Secondly, I recall one of the assistant masters, the fierce but nevertheless kindly, Mr Nesbitt of the waxed moustache was on one occasion was so irate over the failure of the entire class to solve what he regarded as a straight-forward arithmetical problem that every child, including myself, received a single sharp blow from a cane on an outstretched hand. I can hear him now saying 'And you too, my boy, must take your medicine'! I wonder what present-day educators and the adherents of the Society to Outlaw Physical Punishment (STOPP) would have thought of this. But it didn't seem to hurt very much and I don't think that it had any real effect either as a deterrent or as an encouragement.

As for my parents themselves, they were very different people. My father was a quietly spoken and rather private man, often given to long silences but nevertheless articulate when he wished, and almost always cheerful. Throughout his life I can never recall seeing him depressed and only rarely angry, and then under extreme provocation. He was kindly, compassionate, but set himself high standards of behaviour and was scrupulously honest, a man of outstanding integrity. Throughout his life he was guided by his unswerving dedication to his Christian faith and his adherence to his Methodist beliefs. These led him to remain teetotal until his later years when, at a wedding, he would allow himself an occasional sip of champagne. After being severely wounded in the First World War he gained a great deal of weight and never again indulged in outdoor sport but became an exceptional snooker and billiards player in the Church Institute. He read comparatively little and was not a man of overt ambition, but he nevertheless devoted his energies to being a Society Steward and later a Circuit Steward in the Methodist Church and also a local preacher of above average ability. I found his sermons, while intellectually interesting, somewhat cold and lacking in inspiration despite his excellent command of English. But he inspired not only admiration and respect in his family, and among friends and pupils, but also love. He was one of those who, in school or in Sunday school, could quell an unruly group of pupils with a word or glance and never needed to raise his voice. Later he devoted much of his spare time to work in the National Savings Movement and later still, in Spennymoor, he was appointed a magistrate. Eventually, after retiring and moving to Newcastle, he became Chairman of the Gateshead Bench where I am told that his fairness and judicial skills won him widespread admiration.

In the home, my mother was clearly the dominant partner, but nevertheless their marriage created a thoroughly stable, warm and loving family environment. Above all, their shared belief in the benefits of education (and especially my mother's wish to see that her children had every conceivable opportunity to make the best of their abilities) was foremost and for this they would make any sacrifice. My mother's concern with educational achievement had its advantages but at times it could also be counterproductive. Her attempts to persuade her grandchildren to read aloud, to answer questions which she continually posed, or repeatedly to undertake some kind of intellectual task may have served as an irritant and may even at times may have created intellectual antibodies. For my brother, my sister (who was born after our move to Spennymoor) and me, however, her encouragement was unfailing. Whenever examinations approached everything possible was done to help us to work without interruption and with quiet reigning in the house. The radio was turned down, the warmest room was made available for quiet study and reflection, and my father was sent off to play billiards or snooker so that work could go on uninterrupted. Although she never returned to work after her marriage, she often hankered after her own early school-teaching days and did her best within the limitations of her own educational background to help us all with our educational tasks. Both she and my father never hesitated to deny themselves creature comforts or to make financial sacrifices (of which at the time we were unaware) to help us in our careers.

When later we had moved to Spennymoor and I attended, for one year only, my father's school at Middlestone Moor, the 11+ examination was taken in two parts. Part 1 was used as a screening examination to identify those who were thought to be potentially capable of passing Part 2 for grammar school entrance. It was only much later that I discovered that my performance in Part 1 of the examination would not normally have been sufficient to carry me through to the second part. My parents were prepared to mortgage their own financial future by borrowing money in order to send me to a private school at Barnard Castle if the need arose. However, the senior masters and mistresses at the school who had taught me felt that the result in my Part 1 examination was not a true reflection of my ability. They obtained the special permission of the education authority to allow me to sit Part 2, in which I was later told (if readers will forgive the immodesty) that I came out top of the district and so went on to the Alderman Wraith Grammar School.

Only later did I begin to recognize how little money my parents spent on things like clothes and holidays in order that their children should have every possible educational opportunity. Even when I obtained a County Major Exhibition on the results of my Higher School Certificate examination in grammar school, this came nowhere near covering the costs of my medical school training. At the time I did not realize how deeply my parents must have dug into such financial reserves as they possessed to give me a very generous allowance, more generous indeed than that received by many of my friends whose parents were much better off. When we came to have a family of our own, my mother was invariably willing to help out with looking after the children and even, on one occasion, without hesitation she travelled from Newcastle to London to help Betty when both of our daughters went down with measles when Betty was pregnant with our third child.

Perhaps one counterproductive attitude of my mother's was that in her determination to have the best she could afford for her family, she fed each of us as children on butter, cream, milk and eggs, all of which she felt would 'do us good', and even produced substantial dietary supplements such as Virol and halibut liver oil in the winter. The result was that all three of we children were substantially overweight and I was deeply embarrassed on being referred to by some friends as 'fatty'. Possibly this was one factor which led to my having a cholecystectomy for the removal of cholesterol stones at the age of 35. In later years not only I but also my brother, Ernest, and my sister, Mary, had to stick to rigid diets to remove the avoirdupois which we had each acquired in childhood and which caused us considerable distress during our schooldays. On going to grammar school, in my first two years I was invariably last or second from last in the annual cross-country race and Ernest had the same experience. By dint of taking a great deal of exercise and perhaps resisting the over-feeding in which we were encouraged in early childhood, I got my weight down sufficiently to be able to play cricket, soccer and tennis for the school and even to come in fourth in the senior cross-country race in my final year.

Another pleasurable feature of our years in Pickering Nook and Hobson Colliery was our family holidays at Wylam-on-Tyne with the Pattinson family. Thomas Pattinson, founder of the Tyneside firm of auctioneers and valuers, T. N. Pattinson & Sons Ltd, had originally been a miner but later began buying and selling belongings for his workmates from a horse-drawn cart. Gradually his business grew; he became an auctioneer and later an estate agent, and married Aunt Mary's sister, Jenny, from Rookhope with whom he eventually set up home in a beautiful detached house called 'Dalry' at the top of Elm Bank in South Wylam. Often we went to Wylam to have New Year's Day dinner, invariably with a succulent goose (a turkey was then considered appropriate for Christmas and a goose for New Year) in a splendid dining-room looking out over the valley of the Tyne towards the recreation ground in North Wylam. Later I was often invited to go and stay with Uncle Tom and Aunt Jenny by myself during school holidays and made friends with many local boys, including the Chaytors (Geoffrey subsequently became an ENT surgeon in Newcastle), Reavley Oswald and Bruce Pallett, whose father was a local general practitioner. Bruce was unfortunately paraplegic because when away at boarding school his girdle pain was misdiagnosed as being due to appendicitis and his appendix was removed. In fact it soon became clear that he had a tuberculous osteitis of the spine which rendered him paraplegic while he was recovering from the appendicectomy. I maintained a continuing friendship with Bruce in later years, especially when he opened a radio and television shop in Newcastle before eventually moving to the south of England where he still lives. Aunt Jenny was invariably kind and hospitable, Uncle Tom a little fearsome but nevertheless had a kindly smile often concealed by his luxuriant white moustache. He was probably the last person whom I remember always drinking from a moustache cup. The only unhappy conflict I had with the Pattinsons was after Aunt Jenny had told me that I could go to the paper shop in the village to buy a copy of the *Hotspur* (or was it the *Wizard* or the *Magnet* or the *Gem*?) and that I could ask them to put it on their account. Whether or not I misunderstood, I cannot really recall, but my parents were chastened to receive from Aunt Jenny when I had returned home after my holiday a bill for four *Wizards*, three *Hotspurs*, five *Magnets*, three *Gems* and possibly a number of other boy's magazines in addition.

Those childhood years were ones which I remember with pleasure and affection in a secure, loving family environment. I often wondered why it was that presents at birthdays and at Christmas were less lavish than those which other friends seemed to receive. It is only on looking back that I realize how difficult my parents must have found it to support the three of us through our lengthy education and what personal financial sacrifices they must have made. The pleasure which they so evidently demonstrated when we each achieved some academic success, graduated in medicine, married and had families in whose activities and achievements they shared was to them reward enough throughout their long and happy marriage. Sadly that ended when my father died of his second cardiac infarction at the age of 77 just a few weeks before our elder daughter, Ann, was to be married. And even though my mother had her first stroke on the day after my father's funeral, her pride in her family was the strongest motivating force throughout her life, fuelled by her unfailing Christian belief. Even when she became bedridden after a second major stroke a few years later, and before the last three grim years of her life, when she was unable to recognize any members of the family, she was always eager to have news of our activities and those of our children and grandchildren; her eyes lit up when some new and interesting development was reported.

The night before my father died our telephone in Gosforth was out of action. It was a cold, miserable, windy night and rain was pouring down; but as I had not spoken to my parents, then living in Wideopen, just north of Newcastle, for several days, I decided to go out to a telephone box to speak to them. I shall always remember, on asking my father how he was, his bright and cheery response in saying that he was fine; we had a lively and enjoyable conversation. The next morning, while at work in hospital, I was telephoned by the family doctor, Dr Derek Wilkinson, letting me know that he had died suddenly. I shall always be glad that I made the effort to speak to him; to him and to my mother I and all of the family owe a debt of gratitude that cannot adequately be expressed in words.

CHAPTER 2

Spennymoor

1931 was not a good year. There was a world-wide financial crisis, Britain went off the Gold Standard, the pound was devalued and Ramsay Macdonald formed a coalition national government. That act may in retrospect have seemed to be in the best interests of the country but nevertheless it was widely regarded at the time as being an act of betrayal of the Labour Party. Public servants, including the Armed Services, school-teachers and the police, were required to take 10% cuts in salary and in consequence there was a mutiny in the Atlantic Fleet of the Royal Navy and much unrest. My father learned that his school at Pickering Nook was to become a junior school only, and that his senior pupils would be transferred to Burnopfield. Since the size of the school roll determined the salaries of the headmaster and teachers, my father therefore faced a further drop in income and reasonably began to seek another school. Yet again the weary round of calling upon and being interviewed by members of the Durham County Education Committee began. Finally, after one or two unsuccessful forays, he was appointed headmaster of Middlestone Moor Council School near Spennymoor, about 20 miles from Hobson Colliery. A suitable house at 79 Whitworth Terrace, Spennymoor, about a mile and a half from the school, was quickly found (the purchase price was £200) and we moved to that address in 1932 so that my father could take up his new appointment. I enrolled as a pupil in his school, as did my brother. 79 Whitworth Terrace was one of a long line of red-brick two-storey houses forming a continuous terrace, with gaps every 20–25 houses allowing access to the back lane. Clyde Terrace faced us on the opposite side of the road so that the long approach to Spennymoor from Bishop Auckland and the west was lined on one side by Whitworth Terrace with Clyde Terrace on the other side, interrupted by the substantial grounds and Victorian pile of the vicarage.

Inside the house we had a reasonably spacious sitting or drawing-room and a dining-room and a kitchen on a lower level to the rear, with four bedrooms and a bathroom upstairs. The only form of heating was by coal fires, except in the bathroom where the exposed hot water tank (heated from a back boiler behind the kitchen fire), surrounded by a wooden rail for drying clothes, kept the temperature of the room above freezing.

17

Behind the large kitchen was a pantry, and a washhouse with a metal boiler encased in stone and another coal fire below, a large poss tub and stick for washing the clothes and an ancient mangle made of cast iron with an exceptionally heavy handle and large wooden rollers. This was where the Monday morning wash was carried out with the help of a daily maid, of whom we had many over the years, usually coming for about a year at a time after leaving school at the age of 14. Despite the financial problems of the early 1930s, my mother always seemed to have a maid who was responsible for laying in the fires, for helping with the washing and ironing, for dish-washing and for cleaning the house. Every spring there was a major ritual in that every carpet was taken up, carried out of doors and beaten with cane beaters, before being reverently relaid. Curtains also came down to be washed and ironed. That ritual, which also included scrubbing the floors before the carpets were relaid and wiping or washing down the walls and woodwork, was 'spring cleaning' and took place in April each year.

Behind the washhouse there was a garden with a small flower bed and grassy lawn interrupted only by the posts to which the washing line for drying clothes could be attached. And ironing was done, as I recall, with a flat iron which had been heated in the oven. At the end of the garden was the coal-house from which coal was carried some 15 to 20 yards into the house, and into which regular deliveries were made from a horse-drawn cart in the back lane through a hatch which was easily opened from outside. Regularly the coalman delivered five or even 10 cwt of coal without being asked to do so, and then trustingly sent in his bill. Next to the coal-house on one side was a tool-shed (which later became 'gang headquarters' for an unruly group of boys) with two doors, one opening out into the back lane and one into the garden, and on the other the traditional earth closet which was emptied into a Council horse-drawn wagon weekly and was regularly used only by the maid. The back lane was unpaved and often muddy and rutted, especially in winter. Beyond the lane were a low stone wall, a scattering of trees and open fields running down Whitworth Lane. To the right stood several gaunt pit heaps and, about three hundred yards away, a working coal mine close to the railway which then joined Spennymoor and Bishop Auckland.

It was my mother's belief, shared with many other British folk of the same vintage, that warm bedrooms were unhealthy. Each bed was well covered with sheets and blankets, and in the coldest weather Ernest, my brother, and I were sometimes allowed the luxury of a stone hot water bottle before retiring (rubber hot water bottles came much later). But even in the depths of winter the window was left open throughout the night to admit fresh air. On more than one occasion flakes of snow would flicker in through the open window between the curtains and would nestle on my bedspread or on the carpet. Only when one of us was ill and confined to bed were we allowed the luxury of a fire in the bedroom. Sometimes if the illness turned out to be influenza or no more than a severe cold, boiling water was poured on to Friar's balsam producing fumes which we would then inhale with a towel over the head. Alternatively a stone jar half-filled with a special type of medicinal tar was placed on the floor and a red-hot poker was plunged into it, thus filling the air with pungent aromatic fumes which were supposed to help clear the air passages (that distinctive olfactory memory remains vivid).

But these were happy days, with Ernest steadily growing in maturity though, being four years younger, he was usually too young to indulge in the leisure and sporting activities which I enjoyed; this was even more true of my sister, Mary, born five years after Ernest. The long gaps between our respective births meant that we never quite developed the close companionship which often emerges between siblings born closer to one another. Nevertheless my childhood was a happy and contented one, with kindly, caring parents, marred only by embarrassment about my obesity.

Spennymoor was then, and still is, a rather long, straggling town which must have grown by a kind of ribbon development. Its population in 1921 was 18,238, declined to 15,440 in 1935 when unemployment was running at 33 per cent, but grew again to 19,115 in 1961 and is now 20,600. Perhaps its most notable buildings were first the starkly elevated stone-built edifice of St Paul's Church with its square tower on the one hand and the Town Hall with its tall clock tower on the other. In Low Spennymoor there was then an active coal mine and a steel works, each still employing many men and producing substantial amounts of coal and steel from this area on the outskirts of the Durham coalfield. In King Street near the Brewery Field (home of Spennymoor United and next to a disused brewery) was the Spennymoor Settlement with a small private theatre and art gallery. Provided as a cultural centre for the community, it functioned effectively between the wars and afterwards. It nurtured the artistic talents of Norman Cornish, a former miner turned artist whose works became very popular throughout the North East. They were also admired by Mr Edward Heath who acquired several of his pictures when visiting the area as Prime Minister. Sid Chaplin, who, like Norman Cornish, received an honorary MA from Newcastle University, developed some of his writing talents through the Spennymoor Settlement and was a regular contributor, for example, to 'Penguin New Writing'.

The appearance of comparative prosperity demonstrated by some houses on the main street and buildings in the principal shopping area (though none of the shops was pretentious and many were one-man or one-woman businesses struggling to survive) stood in sharp contrast to the terraces of small, plain and often decaying homes behind the frontage on either side. There were also several small factories including Kenmir's furniture factory, numerous public houses and several non-conformist chapels (at one time there were three Methodist churches within two or three hundred yards). There was also a small elevated railway station and bridge crossing the main street; indeed for some years we used the station when going on holiday to Weardale or even when travelling via Newcastle to Wylam. And when I joined the Army after the war, I sent my trunk in advance by rail. However, this branch line from Durham to Bishop Auckland was clearly doomed as the traffic of passengers and freight became increasingly light, and eventually it was closed at the time of the Beeching axe. The rails were either lifted or cuttings were filled in and only traces of this once busy line survive.

Looking down from the hills to the east of Spennymoor was Kirk Merrington with its nine-hole golf course, and its charmingly simple Norman church standing high on a ridge. This is a landmark which can readily be seen still from the Durham motorway. To the west, Whitworth Lane passed Whitworth House, once occupied by the Shafto family (made famous by the 'Bobby Shafto's Gone to Sea' ditty) with its little private church and deer park, before dipping down a steep hill to the mining village of Page Bank and the River Wear. Middlestone Moor where my father's new school was situated, lay to the south on the road to Bishop Auckland. This again was a typical Durham mining village with row upon row of unprepossessing miners' homes and the Victorian school standing in a large concrete playground alongside its playing field which contained a single soccer pitch and a small cricket square. Apart from a single and grotesquely imposing public house and a working men's club, the village boasted no other buildings of note. Close by a road branched off to the little village of Binchester which, as its name implies, has some notable Roman remains, and from there continued to Byers Green, another mining village, beyond which were two secluded hamlets, one called No Place and the other Seldom Seen.

Even though Spennymoor and its adjacent towns and villages were dominated in the 1930s by outward signs of the coalmining industry such as pit heaps, and the winding engine wheels which lifted the cages were often etched in silhouette against the setting sun, there was much lovely country nearby. Down Whitworth Lane, attractive country walks towards the River Wear abounded, and if one ventured beyond Page Bank, one would eventually reach the lovely village of Brancepeth with its magnificent castle, championship golf course and attractive houses. Towards Merrington was an open area called 'the seven hills', a mini-paradise for sledging when snow came, as it often did in the winter; the walk through Tudhoe Village, with its stark but lovely hall, led down to an unspoiled stretch of the River Wear meandering through parkland. Hett village, near Croxdale, was also a delight to explore with its winding pathways through leafy glades, especially attractive on a spring morning. We explored many of these areas on rambles organized by the young people of the Central Methodist Church; a particularly traditional walk took place before breakfast on May morning. Only five miles away to the north was the solemn grandeur of Durham City with its magnificent cathedral and castle, its Palace Green, its narrow winding streets and that wonderful loop and sweep of the River Wear with unlimited opportunities for boating and picnicking which as a teenager I so often enjoyed with my friends. Hire of a skiff was exceptionally cheap and when three or more of us went together, our rowing became quite competitive.

To the south was the pleasant market town of Bishop Auckland, guarded by the attractive Bishop's Palace which houses the Prince Bishops of Durham. If one then ventured west through West Auckland and Staindrop, one would eventually reach Barnard Castle where the Bowes Museum, a veritable treasure-house of art, furniture and porcelain, is all too often neglected by those unaware of its magnificence or deterred by its relative inaccessibility. Close by, too, in Upper Teasdale were High Force, the highest waterfall in the United Kingdom, and the even more magnificent Cauldron Snout, while if one preferred architectural beauty, the grey splendour of Raby Castle, home of Lord Barnard and his family, was also a delight.

Hence although, as I shall later make plain, I regard myself as a Northumbrian (the ancient Kingdom of Northumbria stretched from the Forth to the Tees) and although lovely Northumberland is now my adopted county, I have a great admiration for, and loyalty to Durham. Its many delights both overt and relatively well hidden are all too rarely acknowledged and often escape the eye of the casual observer.

My recollections of the teaching I received in my brief sojourn at Middlestone Moor School are vague in the extreme, though my father's senior assistant master, Harold Brown, was a man of unflappable urbanity and an excellent communicator. I was always sad that he failed to achieve the headship which he so richly deserved, solely, as already mentioned, because he was a strong supporter of the Conservative Party. I now know that it was to Harold Brown's professional judgement that my father referred the decision about whether my poor showing in the Part I examination should be set aside, a decision which, as a man of integrity, he could not take himself.

And so in September 1933 I began in Form 3A of the Alderman Wraith Grammar School in Spennymoor, just in time to be interviewed by and then to witness the departure of the headmaster, Major Welch, MA, a martinet who ran the school with a rod of iron and of whom pupils and staff alike seemed to be in awe. He was succeeded by Mr William Sumner, MA, a cheerful, rotund bachelor whose approach was much less formal and whose informality and familiarity with staff and pupils alike was regarded by some as possibly endangering or detracting from his authority. Nevertheless he could be firm when necessary and later in my school career, when I needed his advice, I found him to be a wise and sensible mentor (though many girls, I fear, disliked him). I have always been sorry that for reasons which I now find difficult to understand, I never called on him after leaving school, perhaps because I was so caught up in all the excitement of university in wartime.

The Alderman Wraith Grammar School instilled in me a deep sense of patriotism and love of my country which has never left me, a delight in, respect for and love of the English language, and a horror of grammatical errors. To this day I cannot read (or even hear) a split infinitive without a sense of acute discomfort and am astonished to discover how many highly intelligent, well qualified medical students cannot distinguish between a simile and a metaphor, are unaware of the meaning of tautology and certainly do not know the difference between euphemism and euphuism. And am I alone in being irritated when even BBC announcers talk of drawring instead of drawing? I learned much English history and geography and also acquired a lasting admiration for English literature, so that even now I can still recite substantial tracts of Shakespeare and poems from masters like Milton, Keats, Tennyson, Francis Thompson and Masefield. I also read with pleasure and enjoyment works by Thomas Hardy, Thackeray, Dickens, George Borrow, Hilaire Belloc, G. K. Chesteron and George Bernard Shaw, to name but a few. While as a young adolescent, I discovered for leisure reading the *Gem*, the *Magnet*, the *Wizard*, the *Hotspur* and the like, I later graduated to the *Boy's Own Paper* and to Arthur Mee's *Children's Encyclopedia* before being introduced by my father to Sapper's *'Bulldog Drummond'* novels from which it was an easy transition to Francis Brett Young, Dornford Yates, Somerset Maugham, John Buchan and even Christopher Isherwood and Aldous Huxley all of whom, among others, became my favourites.

In Latin we studied Caesar's *Gallic Wars* (Book 1) and Virgil's *Georgics*; even though I found Latin descriptions of techniques of bee-keeping uninspiring, I am delighted that I learned the language as it undoubtedly helped me in my subsequent attempts to translate medical and scientific texts and papers written in the romantic languages. It has also been of great assistance in my efforts (only partially successful) to present short papers and speeches in Italian. And even now I cringe when I hear a senior and distinguished colleague say 'This data is . . . ' or 'This phenomena is . . .', or when another, in discussing medical education, talks of curriculi rather than curricula. I also waged a running battle (which I lost) with the Council of the Royal Society of Medicine during my presidency over the establishment of multidisciplinary forums. French, too, was sometimes tedious but more often a delight, and even though the teaching, as is usual in the UK, concentrated upon grammatical accuracy, I nevertheless learned to speak with a fair accent which years later was polished, reasonably successfully, when I had to lecture, deliver papers and make speeches in French. I regret that I never succeeded in mastering the language more completely and that I was always compelled to ask my hosts to translate a prepared script for me to read; and I also greatly regret that I never had an opportunity of learning German. Nevertheless, bus trips from school to Newcastle to see Shakespearean plays and even, in the old Stoll Theatre, productions in French of Molière's *Le Malade Imaginaire* and *Le Bourgeois Gentilhomme* stand out in my memory. Of those who taught me, I remember particularly Miss Cunningham in Latin, Miss McCaughey in French, Mr J. J. Egglishaw (a splendid teacher) in mathematics, Miss Midgely in history, Mr Noddings in geography and Mr Mitchell in music and art (in both of which he despaired of me as I had no artistic or musical talent, save for a reasonably good musical ear and the ability to sing in tune). My parents arranged piano lessons for me for almost five years, but in the end both I and my teacher were compelled to admit defeat as I found myself simply incapable of mastering the technique. But during these school years I began slowly to develop an increasing interest in music, much enhanced by my growing interest in Betty Harrison (of whom more later) whose tutelage had a profound influence. Of course I listened avidly to the dance music and jazz of Henry Hall, Carroll Gibbons, Geraldo, Ambrose, Harry Roy, George Scott Wood, Django Reinhardt and Stefan Grappelli (the Quintet of the Hot Club of France) and later Louis Armstrong, Duke Ellington and others. Indeed I still enjoy music of the 'swing era' and classical jazz. But slowly I graduated in my musical tastes through musical comedy and light opera (with a lasting delight in Gilbert and Sullivan) to the masters of symphony and later grand opera. And as more and more of my pocket money went on records, Tauber, Lehar, Anne Zeigler and Webster Booth gave way to recordings of symphonies and concertos.

But I must not forget my growing interest in the sciences as I much enjoyed chemistry, biology and physics, inspired in my senior years by the splendid teaching in chemistry of Mr Howard (who sadly died prematurely of leukaemia) and in physics of Mr G. W. Brydon who later became senior physics master at the Newcastle Royal Grammar School. Mr Brydon employed me as a part-time lab assistant when I was a sixth-former and this produced a little useful pocket money. So popular books on science by Lancelot Hogben and others were added to my diet of spare-time reading.

School was not all work and the annual school play was a notable feature of the calendar. These plays were produced and directed by a senior English master, Mr Standen, who, having been told by another teacher that I had certain declamatory skills, chose me from the Fifth Form to play Jack Absolute in Sheridan's *The Rivals* opposite Miss Lydia

Languish, played by an attractive and voluptuous sixth former. If that in itself were not sufficiently chastening and embarrassing, I also found myself fighting a duel with untipped rapiers against Harry Fleming, another vigorous sixth former who played Sir Lucius O'Trigger. On the first night of the performance the duel became so vigorous that as the point of my sword struck him in the midriff, the point of his caught me on the forehead above the right eye; when blood trickled down my face, my parents and others in the audience thought how clever it was and how very realistic it looked; only afterwards did I and they realize what might have happened if the blow had been an inch lower. However the production seemed to have been successful, so that a year later I was asked to play Hovstad, editor of the People's Messenger, in Ibsen's *An Enemy of the People*. The demanding part of Dr Stockmann was played by John Cowperthwaite, a second-year sixth-former from Ferryhill who, not surprisingly, had some difficulty in remembering his extensive lines. I much enjoyed seeing a new production of this rarely performed work in London in 1989. But I suppose that the pinnacle of my acting career (never subsequently repeated or emulated) came when, in my final year, I played Malvolio in an extract from *Twelfth Night* at the annual school Speech Day in the Town Hall and later in the same year (1940) took the part of Caesar in the quarrel scene from *Julius Caesar* but played in costume as if between Hitler and Mussolini. By this stage of my school career I had slimmed down and it was felt appropriate that I should be Hitler while a more rotund sixth-former took the part of Il Duce.

Many other leisure outings of various kinds were arranged from school, sometimes for large, sometimes for small groups. Whereas from Pickering Nook and Middlestone Moor respectively the entire school would go off for a day accompanied by staff in a fleet of old red Northern buses to somewhere like Whitley Bay for a day at the sea, from the Alderman Wraith the trips were rather more sophisticated and lengthy. Thus in 1938, I believe it was, we went to the Glasgow Exhibition, a kind of pre-war Expo; as we had to go there and back in a day, the trip involved an early start and a late return. I remember being as impressed by the buildings and by some exhibits almost as much as I was by Expo in Montreal many years later, but my most abiding memory of the day is that my brother Ernest managed to get lost. He was then a rather solitary, reflective youngster who wandered off by himself to view the exhibition but then forgot completely where the rendezvous point was where we were supposed to pick up the buses for the return journey. When I was informed that he had not returned I dashed around the exhibition site in a state of acute anxiety. Fortunately I found him sitting in the central police station waiting patiently to be collected. Hence the buses returned to Spennymoor a little later than originally envisaged.

Even more adventurous was the trip which some 60 or 70 fifth and sixth formers made to Paris under the auspices of the School Journeys Association in spring 1939. We stayed overnight in a hotel in London after travelling there by bus, and then continued by bus to the Channel ferry and onwards from Boulogne to Paris, staying in a decadent but reasonably clean hotel in the Rue St Jacques. We then congregated in Paris with boys and girls from many other UK schools. Among the many other delights we inspected were the Church of the Sacré Coeur in Montmartre, Napoleon's tomb at Les Invalides, Versailles, Fontainebleu, La Madeleine and the Conciergerie. In the Conciergerie a boy from Ferryhill, noting that virtually all of the young people around us were speaking French, said loudly 'There's nee bugger here speaks English'. Immediately one of the group in front turned round and said 'Thou canna speak it theeself, lad'; he turned out to be a British student from Newcastle then studying at the Sorbonne. We also enjoyed a visit to Notre Dame and the Left Bank, but perhaps the highlight was a circus performance in front of a large audience including approximately 1000 British school boys and girls. Among the acts was a Scottish pipe band which must have been astonished by the rapturous reception it received. Although many of us had been well aware of the Munich crisis of the preceding year and recognized that Europe was far from stable, our incurable optimism made our stay in Paris with tentative evening excursions into cafes in the Boulevard St Michel for a soft drink and a game of bar billiards, accompanied by a surreptitious smoke, all the more exciting. Little did we realize that it would be more than six years before there would be any prospect of returning to France; and few if any of us realized how devastating would be the storms that lay ahead.

After this brief and enjoyable interlude, I and the others in the fifth form were much too heavily occupied by working for the June School Certificate examinations (the forerunner of the GCE and of its successor, the GCSE). I worked extremely hard and my mother, as always, was immensely helpful in making sure that the dining-room was prepared so that I could work in reasonable comfort with a fire going throughout the evening. She would even get me up at 6.00 am when I felt that I needed some extra study time and never questioned my staying up late at night if necessary. The outcome was that I achieved ten passes at Grade A in the School Certificate and that the summer holidays at Whitley Bay and a brief spell at Allendale were among the most happy and enjoyable I can remember. Until, of course, September came.

None of us will ever forget 3 September 1939 when Neville Chamberlain in solemn voice announced on the radio to the world at large that Britain was at war with Germany. For one who was just under 17 years of age at the time, the announcement engendered a curious batch of emotions with elements of excitement and almost elation on the one hand coupled with an almost subterranean sense of dread and fearful anticipation on the other. But after the announcement, Spennymoor looked just the same; it was a warm, reasonably sunny day with blue sky flecked with cumulus cloud. We went to morning service as usual, and as we were leaving church the air-raid siren went. The reaction of the people around us was extraordinary. Some stood and looked at the sky in disbelief, others ran for the nearest point of shelter and security. I and other members of the family hurried up the main street to reach home, but even before we got there the all-clear sounded and, as everyone now knows, this was a false alarm.

Sport also played a major part in my school life. I possessed no athletic prowess even though in my last year, after shedding a substantial amount of excess fat, I managed to finish in the first six in the senior cross-country race. I also played soccer with great enthusiasm but not much skill (clumsiness was, I think, my major problem). Nevertheless in the first year sixth, playing at centre forward for the A team, I scored a couple of goals in the final trial and so played for the first team, initially at centre forward, later inside right, and then at half back during my last two years at school. We enjoyed several notable victories against other local grammar schools but never succeeded in defeating the King James VIth Grammar School at Bishop Auckland where the notable Bob Hardisty, one of the most oustanding amateur soccer players of his generation, later to captain the England amateur side, was a contemporary; he was so nimble and skilful that we could only stand and marvel at his prowess. Cricket, however, was rather different as this was my favourite sport and I played for the first team for four consecutive years, eventually opening the batting and being elected Vice-Captain in my final year. Although I managed a number of scores in the forties, I only achieved a single 50 and never aspired to the dizzy heights of scoring a century; however, in the one-day matches which we played no schoolboy of my acquaintance ever achieved that distinction. We did, however, defeat the King James VIth School at cricket several times since Bob Hardisty, though a useful performer, was never as outstanding at cricket as at soccer. Several times I put pen to paper to describe some of our sporting activities in the school magazine, The Wraithian. One such effusion entitled 'Boyhood's love of sport by a victim' now causes me acute embarrassment when I look at it again, and I cringed when it was quoted verbally and in the programme when I presented the prizes in the annual ceremony at the Spennymoor Grammar Technical School which was built in the 1950s behind Whitworth Terrace to succeed the by then outdated Alderman Wraith School. I was very impressed by the buildings, the leadership of the headmaster, Mr Cockburn, and the liveliness of the pupils (the head boy pulled my leg unmercifully in his speech of thanks). The old buildings of the Alderman Wraith School at the other end of the town, with its extensive sports grounds, continued to function as a secondary modern school. When passing by in 1990, we stopped to wander quietly around the buildings and grounds, so evocative of many childhood memories.

Of the many boyhood friendships I made, none were lasting. Roy Russell, a Presbyterian minister's son, was one with whom I became very friendly and we played cricket for the school together. He eventually became a banker. Others, including Raymond Hope, Roy Whillance (son of the local bank manager), Harry Hamilton and Derek Dodshon (whose father kept Tiplady's, a gentlemen's outfitters shop in Spennymoor High Street) were among those with whom I was involved in many typical boyhood pursuits. These included being chased by the local policeman more than once, especially when we set off fireworks in the centre of the roadway between Whitworth and Clyde Terrace (the traffic was light at the time). Often, too, we enjoyed together long bicycle rides into Weardale and even as far as the coast at Seaton Carew. A kind of bicycle speedway we constructed on dirt tracks in the colliery area was another favourite recreational pursuit. On one such occasion, in attempting a turn and skid at speed, I came down heavily on my left shoulder and fractured my clavicle; it was a greenstick fracture which healed but kept me off the cricket field for two or three weeks. Once, when playing soccer in the January mud, I fell heavily on my right wrist and fractured my right radius with another few weeks of restricted activity. Another friend was Chris Watson, whose family kept a large butcher's business in the centre of the town; they had a large yard behind the High Street. I remember with total clarity the deep sense of revulsion I felt when I saw there animals being slaughtered with a stungun; death was rapid, but as the gun was fired against the forehead of the unsuspecting animal and as it subsequently convulsed, I felt physically sick and decided that this was not something I wished to see again, even though death must have been instantaneous. In that yard we often played with powerful air-guns belonging to the Watson family; some was simple target practice but I also recall with a deep sense of shame that I occasionally potted at birds sitting on the chimney-stacks of surrounding buildings. But when I saw the pathetic bundle of feathers that had once been a beautiful blackbird lying on the ground because of my target practice, this was an activity in which I never indulged again. Yet another friend was the flame-haired Herbert Taylor, a bright but irascible character with whom I enjoyed many lively discussions which sometimes flared into violent, if transient, disagreement. While fighting, rarely serious, has always been a feature of boyhood, Herbert Taylor is the only person I can recall having knocked me down with a sharp and unheralded right uppercut in the school playground; but soon afterwards we were friends again.

Practical jokes were also a feature of school life. In the fifth form we succeeded in making and drying in the chemistry lab a preparation of nitrogen tri-iodide; we then scattered this behind the master's desk and in front of the blackboard just before a geography lesson to be given by the amiable Mr Noddings. As he walked to the desk, each time he put down a foot there was a little explosion. Eventually, with a trace of a suppressed smile, he stood behind the desk and said that he proposed to stand in one position throughout the lesson; he shifted his weight from one foot to the other and then produced the loudest bang of all. On another occasion, thought by us to be serious at the time but somewhat laughable in retrospect, four of us were summoned before Mr Sumner and received a long and stern lecture about the evils of immorality. We had been found by a master examining what would now be accepted as innocent and inaccurate drawings of naked women; but in that pre-war era this was regarded as a serious sin.

With only a few of the boys have I kept in touch. Roy Russell I later met when he was working in Lloyds Bank in Gosforth. Both Herbert Taylor and Derek Dodshon, after war service first in the artillery and then in the Durham Light Infantry, went to London at the end of the war and took degrees in psychology in the department led by the famous (subsequently notorious) Cyril Burt. Derek then decided to study medicine and did so in London before later emigrating to Australia where he went into general practice but eventually specialized in sexual counselling. He was, no doubt, drawn to Australia by the girl whom he married, the daughter of a notable Australian paediatrician whom he met while studying in London. Herbert Taylor became a schoolmaster and then a school counsellor and wrote several papers and a book on counselling. Living now in retirement in Norfolk, we met him by prior arrangement while attending the BMA Annual Meeting in Norwich in 1988 and enjoyed reminiscing about old times. Another notable figure, one year below in the sixth form, reading arts subjects while I was reading science, was Percy Cradock from Byers Green; he subsequently went to Cambridge to read English and later studied Mandarin Chinese before entering the Foreign Service. He became head of the British Legation in Peking during the time of the cultural revolution and later returned to Beijing as British Ambassador where he completed a distinguished period of service before being appointed, as Sir Percy Cradock, Foreign Affairs Adviser to the Prime Minister, Mrs Margaret Thatcher, at 10 Downing Street. During my period of office as President of the Royal Society of Medicine in 1985, he kindly gave an after-dinner talk at the RSM on China. It was a pleasure to see him again for the first time in well over 40 years and to reminisce about schooldays after his fascinating talk. Later, he was much involved in discussions with the Chinese government about the future of Hong Kong.

Even in a day school like the Alderman Wraith, an attempt was made to introduce a House system. Our Houses were Romans, Normans,

Angles and Saxons and we competed strenuously against one another in athletics, soccer, cricket, and even tennis. There was also a prefectorial system in that prefects appointed by the headmaster from the sixth form (and sometimes a few from the fifth) had some disciplinary authority over the younger boys, as did girl prefects over the younger girls. Our authority extended even to the giving of lines to younger boys guilty of minor misdemeanours. More significant breaches of the rules meant being reported either to the senior assistant master, Mr Peberdy, or even to the headmaster. Derek Dodshon and I were elected prefects in the fifth form, but when we entered the final year (the second-year sixth) two such prefects elected from the fifth form, namely Tommy Nichol and Keith Fleming, had already moved up into the sixth and told me publicly that they would propose me as Head Prefect. The normal procedure was that new prefects would be appointed from the first-year sixth alongside those of their number who had already been appointed in the fifth. This would be followed quickly by an election of a Head Prefect and Secretary to the Prefects from the total body of prefects both old and new. In the event, Mr Peberdy decided to go ahead with the election before the new prefects were appointed. It seemed at the time that he and the boys in the first-year sixth had all assumed that I would be elected. Clearly that assumption offended my colleagues in the final year and the result was that Derek Dodshon, for whom I myself had voted, became Head Prefect and I was elected Secretary. That came as a serious blow as I had genuinely expected to be Head; but I learned an important lesson about humility and recognized that no decision about election to office can ever be looked upon as a foregone conclusion (this was a lesson I had to relearn again many years later). As others told me later, I believe I took it 'on the chin' and Derek and I worked amicably together, along with the relatively small number of boys (including Herbert Taylor and Roy Whillance) who stayed on with us to take the Higher School Certificate and the much larger number of newly-appointed prefects from the first-year sixth, including Percy Cradock.

I spent my two years in the sixth form after the outbreak of war. We were continually beset by news of disaster after disaster, including withdrawal from Dunkirk and air-raids on our major cities, although Spennymoor and the nearby Durham Light Infantry depot at Brancepeth were never thought of as being prime military targets. In 1938, at the time of the Munich crisis, the school had been alerted to the possibility of air-raids to come and several air-raid shelters were built in a corner of the school playing field. We, as older boys in the fifth form, along with the sixth formers, helped in their construction and furnishing. One morning in the following winter (early 1939) an inspection revealed that the Elsan toilets which had been placed in each shelter and suitably charged with disinfectant fluid had been overturned so that each shelter reeked of disinfectant. Cries of vandalism went up until it was realized by a perspicacious master that a line around the walls showed that the shelters had all flooded after heavy rain and that the Elsan toilets had floated and overturned in the flood water. Fortunately the shelters, which remained throughout the war, were never needed and were only used for storage.

When war came, despite the pressures of school work for the forthcoming Higher School Certificate, I and many other boys felt on the one hand a sense of guilt at not serving in the Forces but on the other a recognition that we must complete our education. Nevertheless we nearly all sought some form of activity through which we could assist the war effort. I contacted the air-raid precautions organization at Spennymoor Town Hall. After applying unrelenting pressure, I was appointed as an air-raid warden at the ripe old age of 17 and was allocated to an Air Raid Precautions (ARP) post in Clyde Terrace where I was provided with a tin hat, a torch, a whistle and a hand bell and was included in a duty rota so organized as to fit in with my school work. I also proudly sported a military-style gas mask much superior to those which had been distributed to the civilian population. The post was soon equipped with a telephone, with buckets of water and sand and stirrup pumps to deal with the expected incendiary bomb attacks, and two whole-time wardens were appointed to man the post, one by day and one by night, at the princely wage of £3.00 a week. Apart from periods of day and night duty patrolling the streets, manning telephone boxes, looking at night for houses which were breaching the black-out regulations or for car drivers whose headlights had not been properly masked I and the other wardens were invariably required to muster whenever the air-raid siren sounded and to patrol the streets ringing our hand bells, warning people who might not have heard the siren that there was a possibility of impending air attack. Whereas a few German bombers returning from attacks on cities like Glasgow or industrial Lancashire occasionally jettisoned bombs in the countryside not very far from us (we heard very occasional explosions), Spennymoor and the surrounding towns and villages, including Durham, escaped unscathed. Even our solitary Searchlight Detachment (and the one anti-aircraft battery temporarily stationed in the town) had a very quiet time.

While I served as a warden, my father, being much too old for military service (and recalling that he had been invalided out of the DLI at the end of the First World War with a 100% disability pension for life) decided that he must do 'his bit' and so joined the Observer Corps (which later became Royal). An observer station was installed, suitably sandbagged and concealed, on the highest point of a pit heap close to Spennymoor Park. After a few lessons in aircraft recognition, he took his place on a rota with others, sometimes at night and sometimes at weekends so as not to interfere with his school duties duties. Memories of those days remain vividly etched in the mind. How avidly we listened to the radio broadcasts first by the rather querulous and ineffectual Neville Chamberlain but subsequently from the fierce, ringing and inspiring tones of the evergreen Winston Churchill. Radio talks by the Yorkshire writer and playwright, J. B. Priestley, seemed exceptionally inspiring, as did those of the Canadian Quentin Reynolds, especially during the Blitz which we were spared. And at weekends, after church, we always listened to songs by 'Our Gracie' (Gracie Fields) who also seemed to have an inspirational message, as did Vera Lynn who became 'the Forces' sweetheart'.

As the war moved into its second year, my long-cherished desire to become a doctor crystallized, a desire nurtured by my parents through adolescence to such an extent that when I said my prayers by my bed I prayed not only for the family but also, with prompting, that one day I might become a medical missionary. As soon as I had entered the second-year sixth, I approached the Dean of the Newcastle Medical School, Professor R. B. Green, applying for entry to the School in October 1941. In view of my academic record, I was told that my application would be accepted, subject only to interview. As the year wore on, despite the time and effort I devoted to working for my Higher School Certificate, I became increasingly restless and concerned about my failure to contribute effectively to the war effort, especially since being an air-raid warden in Spennymoor no longer gave me any sense of fulfilment when all the action was elsewhere. The decision of the school to create an Air Training Corps, commanded by Flight Lieutenant William Sumner with Flying Officer J. J. Egglishaw as second-in-command, in which I rose with somewhat indecent speed to the dizzy heights of Flight Sergeant, also gave no real satisfaction when the Battle of Britain was raging in the skies above us (though we saw only very occasional battles and few enemy aircraft). Hence when, in early 1941, a regular RAF Flight Lieutenant visited the school and interviewed all the boys of the second-year sixth with a view to recruiting potential RAF officers, I was sold on the idea, especially when he gave me a form in which I was duly attested as a suitable pilot/observer. He asked that I should travel to RAF Padgate to consider enlisting, with a view to flying either fighters or bombers, once I had completed my Higher School Certificate. Inspired by the prospect and potential glamour, as it then seemed, of flying Spitfires, I went home and told my parents that my long-cherished wish to become a doctor must now take second place and that I intended to join the RAF as soon as I had taken the examination. My father then telephoned Professor Green in Newcastle, who said that he wished to see me urgently for an interview. I explained to him that I had always wanted to be a doctor and had had every intention of going ahead with my application for entry to the Medical School (I had never even considered applying to any other university than

King's College, Newcastle, in the University of Durham, our local Medical
School) but that, in the light of the present emergency situation and the
country's need for pilots, I felt that it was my duty to enlist in the RAF.
I shall never forget the Dean's wise words. After a long discussion, during
which he explored my adolescent aims, objectives and even some of my
dreams, he said that the country certainly needed pilots but needed
doctors just as much. He said that he would do a deal with me; if I
accepted admission to the Medical School in October, he would arrange
for me immediately to join the University Air Squadron and to undertake
some RAF training, including perhaps some flying training. If at the end
of nine months in the Medical School I still wished to fly in the RAF,
he would release me even though, as a medical student, I would be in
a reserved occupation. He knew, as I did not realize then, that once I
had gone to the Medical School and had met many young men and
women in a similar situation to myself with similar ideas, I would become
so attracted by the course and by the prospects that lay before me that my
intention would waver and almost certainly subside, as indeed it proved.

And so, with that offer before me, I was able to concentrate that summer
upon the Higher School Certificate examinations in which I had chosen
to take pure and applied mathematics, chemistry and physics as principal
subjects, with biology as a subsidiary one, even though the standard
routine was to take either three principal subjects alone or two principal
and two subsidiary. In the event all went reasonably well, although the
necessity of having to go to the Darlington Grammar School for my
physics practical was chastening, despite the fact that Mr G. W. Brydon's
brother was physics master there. I made a complete mess of the practical,
having failed totally on an optical bench exercise to find an image which
would have enabled me to work out the refractive index of glass. To my
absolute astonishment, I obtained an A in physics and an A in pure and
applied mathematics (some time l..ter I discovered that if one performed
well in the papers, the examiners never bothered to mark the practical
examination!). Unfortunately my chemistry mark slipped to a B, perhaps
because in the last few months the teaching from dear Mr Howard, whom
I much admired, was less than rigorous, no doubt as a consequence of
his impending illness. My failure to obtain an A in chemistry cost me
a State Scholarship, though I did receive a county major exhibition which
relieved my parents of at least a part of the financial burden which would
otherwise have resulted from my being accepted for a five-year course.
I quickly learned, once the results had been published, that a State
Scholarship had gone to someone of whom I had been warned as a
potential rival, namely a Mr William Ross of the Durham Johnston
Grammar School who had obtained three straight As in his principal
subjects and who, like myself, planned to study medicine in Newcastle.
But that is another story of which more later.

In this chapter to date I have said very little about girls. The Alderman Wraith Grammar School was completely co-ed with as many girls among its pupils as boys. And indeed every class was mixed, so that from the beginning we came into contact with girls on a daily basis. Segregation at morning breaks, at lunchtime and later was in the first year or two almost complete as neither sex was particularly interested in the other, but as time passed the boys began to take an increasing interest in watching the girls in blouses and dark blue knickers doing physical training in the main school hall. In turn, some of the girls, who matured much more quickly, began to flaunt their emerging sexuality in a way that certainly concentrated the mind. Provisional and tentative pairings soon emerged, with even occasional hand-holding on the homeward walk or on the buses which took some pupils further afield to places like Ferryhill, Cornforth and Coxhoe. As matters moved on, tentative and clandestine assignations were arranged in Coia's ice-cream parlour in Cheapside or in Claughan's parlour, regarded by many as being significantly superior, further along the road. There were even some private forays into the countryside. Peggy Claughan, from my year, was one of my early heart-throbs and for a time I found it difficult to choose between her and Peggy Harle as the object of my tentative attentions, though it soon emerged that Peggy Claughan had too many admirers and that if I pressed my suit I would be only one of a crowd. And for a time I also looked with interest on the red-headed Jean Button whom I met at church, and from whom I stole a kiss during the rehearsals of a play. But as time went by, I began to look warmly, especially in the fifth form, upon the girl who regularly played the piano for prayers and hymns in the daily morning school assembly and who also, in that year, was the victrix ludorum in the School Sports Day. She won innumerable events including the high jump, long jump, 100 metres and 200 metres and possibly other events. But she, Betty Harrison, being a sixth former, at least a year older than myself, seemed far beyond the reach of an immature and callow fifth former, so that even the most tentative approach was inevitably rebuffed. But perhaps, to my astonishment, some hint of mutual attraction may have been sparked. Certainly nothing developed at school; she left at the end of the first-year sixth as Mr Sumner would not allow her to take music in the Higher Certificate (for reasons which are now obscure), but we continued to meet at the Central Methodist Church where she deputised for her father as church organist. One day, after a musical and social evening in the church hall, she suggested that I might carry her music and walk with her up the High Street to the house beyond the 'four lane ends' where she lived. As I have often said since, that was the beginning of the end and I have been carrying her music ever since, even though there were some unexpected problems ahead for us both.

Inevitably these comments lead on to the Central Methodist Church which was so much a part of my life and that of my family, as well as Betty's, during the years that we spent in Spennymoor. With my parents' strong Methodist background, on arrival at Spennymoor one of their first objectives was to find an appropriate church. Rosa Street, half way down the High Street on the left, was the closest, but for reasons which are not entirely clear to me, they chose the Central Methodist Church (possibly because it had been Wesleyan) as our place of worship. It was a gaunt but in some respects imposing building with a plain facade and a pseudo-Georgian interior on two levels, with a large balcony facing the communion rail and organ and spreading down either side of the church with at least four rows of pews on either side. Below, the central area of the church, with an aisle on each side, contained row upon row of hard, polished and uncushioned wooden pews, eventually reaching the communion rail with a raised central pulpit looking down on the assembled congregation. Above the pulpit was the splendid organ made by Harrison (no relation), the famous Durham organ builder, upon which Betty's father, Joseph Bell Harrison, as church organist, taught her the fundamental skills of musicianship, including the use of the pedals, building on her already well developed pianistic skills. We invariably attended church three times every Sunday, first for Morning Service, followed by Sunday School for we three children in the afternoon, and then back to Evening Service at 6.00 p.m. Although the church was then a major influence in my life and was often the source of happiness and even inspiration, there were times when the need to wear a dark suit, often with a black jacket, pin-stripe trousers and a dark tie to attend church three times, with total proscription on the playing of any kind of games on Sundays, caused me occasional rumblings of inward rebellion. Not only did the Methodist tradition make our household completely teetotal (my father said that if he had been a drinker he would not have survived the First World War), but we were never allowed to enter a shop on Sundays, to read Sunday newspapers, to play games or even ride our bicycles. It was also suggested that to read any book other than the Bible or one of the well-recognized classics was incompatible with proper Sunday observance. When in war-time we went for a short summer holiday to Saltburn-by-the-Sea in Yorkshire and my parents decided not to go to church on Sunday but to the beach instead, this came as a considerable shock; it heralded a degree of relaxation of attitude in our post-war life which we had never anticipated.

Another feature of church life in Spennymoor to which I became only very slowly accustomed and in which I was only allowed to participate once I reached 14 years of age, was attending the prayer meetings which often followed Evening Service on a Sunday. In the presence of a preacher or, more often, the minister, members of the congregation sat in silence until one or more was moved to pray aloud. I found these meetings forbidding, not least because of the protestations of devout Christianity which one heard declaimed in rounded tones by those whom one well knew fell far short of the Christian ideal in their everyday life. That some of those who prayed were devout Christians of the highest integrity there could be do doubt, but the contrast between the behaviour of some in the cloistered surroundings of a private prayer meeting and their everyday secular activity was so striking as to dismay an impressionable teenager. Nevertheless, church life brought many pleasures. There was an excellent church hall for the many social events throughout the year where we met, mingled and socialized with other young people of the neighbourhood. In addition, there was an excellent adjoining Church Institute where my father and I would frequently go during the week to play billiards or snooker. My father was an outstanding billiards player and a snooker player of above average competence, having honed his skills on a table in Consett where he went to grammar school, subsequently improving these at training college before the First World War. Whenever handicap events were arranged for knock-out billiards tournaments at the Institute, my father had a handicap of minus 10, while mine was plus 15 and I strove without any real success to emulate him. Nevertheless I achieved reasonable competence which helped me many years later in the Territorial Army and even in indoor sports competitions against the students of Green College in the 1980s. The church itself had a vigorous musical life, a large congregation and a flourishing choir in which at first I sang treble but soon, as an adolescent, transferred to the bass line with the fond belief that my voice had really deepened. As I now reflect in later life, it probably would have been much more appropriate if I had chosen to sing tenor. Public performance followed on public performance in those days, often with Stainer's 'Crucifixion' being offered at Easter and/or 'The Messiah' and other oratorios such as 'Samson', 'Elijah' and 'Judas Maccabeus'. Almost invariably Betty's father played the organ with her accompanying him on the piano. As time went by she graduated to playing the organ for major performances and I remember well the thrill of hearing her play for 'The Messiah' before a packed house with the many outstanding local soloists who seemed to be available in the area and who knew all the arias without ever requiring a score. Sam Martin of Ferryhill stands out particularly in my memory as an outstanding bass, as does Denis Weatherley who eventually won a national reputation much further afield.

Not all of our activities were strictly devout. Sitting in the choir on either side of the organ in the balcony, I can recall looking eagerly for a glimpse of Betty's knees as she swung her legs over the long organ stool in order to sit and listen to the sermon before returning to her musical duties. I also remember that we looked down almost directly on to the central pulpit where, on the Sunday before Palm Sunday (locally known as Carling Sunday) the bald head of the local preacher (who on more than one occasion was Sid Chaplin of Penguin New Writing fame) seemed an almost irresistible target for a young boy armed with a pea-shooter into which a carling (dried pea) could be surreptitiously introduced.

Sunday School in the early days was also well attended and was supervised by Betty's fearsome grandfather, a most stately and impressive figure with moustache and white goatee beard who ruled us with a rod of iron and from whom a single glance was all that was needed to produce total silence and attentiveness. Frankly we were terrified of Mr Harrison senior but eventually, through my burgeoning friendship with Betty, I came to know him better. Although he was something of a tartar and a traditionalist (who persuaded all of us in the Sunday School to sign the pledge and to foreswear alcohol for ever when we were about nine years of age) he shared with me an abiding love of cricket and a deep interest in literature. This was so, as I subsequently learned, despite the fact that he had never received a significant secondary education. In spite of this, he had established a flourishing bakery business in Spennymoor virtually from scratch, to which his son, Betty's father, eventually succeeded. His conservatism never allowed him to call Betty, christened Mary Elizabeth, anything but Mary as to him 'Betty' was an unacceptable modernism.

But memories crowd in not only of Sunday School, church services and oratorios, but of the many plays, musical concerts and other events which were mounted in the church hall over the years. At a time when I cannot have been more than 10 or 11 years of age, I found myself playing the bridegroom, suitably adorned and made up, in a play The Brahmin Marriage. Later still we performed excerpts from Gilbert and Sullivan and from various musical comedies, while in one notable concert Betty and her father brought the house down with a whistling duet of remarkable competence. Betty's sister, Joyce, had a good soprano voice, and her brother, Clifford, who joined his father in the family firm and to whom Betty was herself exceptionally close, was an outstanding baritone. On one occasion he won the second prize for baritone voice in the annual Newcastle Musical Festival. My own role in these activities bound up with the church varied from small parts in plays and other events to responsibility for props and stage management. Once during a dress rehearsal I was very much less than popular at the height of the performance for crawling beneath the stage and turning off the master switch for all of the lights so that the stage and hall were plunged into darkness. On yet another occasion, when as an intended practical joke I shoulder-charged Joyce's boyfriend, Colin Swonnell, off the platform, I was told in no mean terms by Betty that I was a bumptious and insufferable young man; but despite this she continued to see me.

In fact through our contacts in the church my parents, Derek Dodshon's parents and Betty's (the Harrisons) became good friends as my father was a society steward and later a circuit steward, as was Fred Dodshon. A succession of ministers came and went. One, the Revd Newbold, for reasons which are now obscure, came into open conflict with the lay officers of the church, including my father, Fred Dodshon and Joe Harrison, and an unfortunate period of confrontation ensured. With his departure all was happily resolved and the benign Revd C. A. Getliff from Buckie in Scotland arrived. We then had a period of stability despite the fact that his wife was a miserable pessimist who seemed convinced that Hitler and his invading armies would eventually take London, though she assured us that even when he did so, the war would not be lost. Later in the war we had the pleasure of having as minister the Revd 'Tot' Sloan, a former music hall comedian who had been converted to Christianity during his music hall career and before being ordained. He was a cheerful, witty, Puckish and entertaining man for whom as the years went by we began to have a very high regard. Often he led us on carol singing expeditions to the working men's clubs of Spennymoor and its environs where he enlivened the proceedings with some of his former music hall repartee, laced throughout the items of practical Christianity. He was also an effective, understanding and compassionate personal counsellor.

Throughout this period my relationship with Betty flowered; we shared many long walks and cycle rides together, particularly at weekends after cricket or football or after church or Sunday School, discussing the way of the world (and other things). Even though in several senses she kept me more or less at arm's length for some time and even though I went through an agonizing period of reappraisal when, for a few weeks, she seemed to be greatly taken by a khaki-clad private soldier from Brancepeth who began to attend our church regularly and even came to her for lessons in organ playing, I began to feel reasonably confident that our respective futures were bound up with one another, even though, early in the war, it seemed uncertain as to where the future would take us both.

Fortunately we shared many common interests, not least our love of sport and we played tennis together whenever we could. She was my musical mentor and educator and I in turn introduced her to my favourite authors. Some embarrassment inevitably arose as she, after leaving school, began to work part-time in her father's business while also studying and practising hard with Miss Thompson of Bishop Auckland for her Royal Academy of Music entrance examination. In consequence she began to earn a reasonable wage, while I, as a schoolboy with pocket money of 2/6 a week found it difficult to take her out or to be at all generous. When her birthday came round a single artificial silk handerchief or a 1/6 book by John Buchan was about all I could manage. But I eventually summoned up courage to take her to the cinema (best seats ninepence each) at Bishop Auckland to see Allan Jones in *Sweethearts* where after about an hour, rather self-consciously we held hands. Having been nurtured on regular Saturday morning matinees at the Town Hall, Arcadia or Tivoli Cinemas in Spennymoor (entrance twopence or even, at the Town Hall, two clean and unchipped jam jars) we soon became regular cinemagoers on Saturday nights and revelled in the delights of Nelson Eddy and Jeannette Macdonald and the dramatic contributions of Jean Harlow, George Arliss, Clark Gable, Spencer Tracy, Robert Donat, Madeleine Carroll, Boris Karloff and many more.

One other interest we shared was in driving. Betty's brother Clifford was a car enthusiast and before she was 17 she had already been encouraged to drive the family Ford V8 and other vehicles on private roads; in consequence she took her driving test soon after her 17th birthday and sailed through with ease (with, no doubt, a susceptible male examiner). Being 15 months younger, I was very envious while awaiting impatiently the arrival of my 17th birthday; I obtained my provisional driving licence on that very day and soon was driving the family Ford 8 (a very different car from the Harrison limousine) under my father's guidance. Six weeks later we went to Durham for my test where I thought I had performed creditably only to be told by the stern examiner that I had not 'achieved the standard required by the Ministry'. Afterwards he told me that on reversing I had simply used the mirror and had 'felt the car round by the kerb' instead of turning around to look out of the rear window. Returning shamefacedly to Spennymoor I could hardly bear to face Betty who could not resist mentioning this blemish on my record on appropriate occasions, even many years later. But her passion for driving resulted in her being recruited by the ARP organization as a volunteer ambulance driver in Spennymoor and her ambulance was garaged close to the 'four lane ends'. Hence when the air-raid warning sounded it was often easy for me as a warden to ring my hand bell outside her garden gate so that we could arrange an assignation at the garage.

Betty's father, who was a twinkling, upright man, much less forbidding than *his* father, and her mother, sister and brother seemed to approve of our relationship and even smiled upon us (fairly) benignly when we spent long periods talking before parting at the gate of their house late on a Sunday evening after church. Clifford had joined a Royal Signals unit in the Territorial Army before the outbreak of war and went abroad with the British Expeditionary Force but fortunately was one of those safely evacuated from Dunkirk. Betty herself, having obtained a distinction in Grade VIII in the music examination of the Associated Board of the Royal Schools of Music in 1939, was successful in her entrance examination and had enrolled as a student of the Royal Academy of Music in London with a view to beginning her course there in September 1939. Not surprisingly when war broke out her parents would not allow her to go to London. Hence she decided, in Clifford's absence, to work full-time with her father in the family business at Harrison's Bakery, with its two associated shops in Spennymoor High Street. But just as I had become restless early in the war while still at school, she herself began to share that same wish to contribute more effectively to the war effort and hence decided in early 1941 that she must enrol in the Women's Auxiliary (later Royal) Air Force. Her departure in June of that year for primary training in Gloucestershire and her subsequent posting as a clerk (special duties) to work underground charting the progress of German bombers, first in Leighton Buzzard and later in Corsham in Wiltshire, may well have been yet another factor which persuaded me to try to join the RAF instead of embarking upon my medical student training. But then, to my delight, having accepted the Dean of Medicine's proposal that I should after all begin my student career and having found lodgings in Newcastle at 22 Wingrove Road with a Mrs Kerr at 27/6d (£1.37½p) a week for full board (excluding lunches on Monday to Friday), I learned in September that Betty was being posted by the WAAF to undertake similar duties in an underground tracking station in Fenham and was in fact to be housed in a billet at 102 Wingrove Road! And so, as I started on my student career, our period of temporary separation was over and we both felt able to begin to rebuild our relationship.

CHAPTER 3

Medical School

Despite the fact that there was an hourly bus service from Spennymoor to Newcastle by the OK Bus Company, it never occurred to my parents that I should travel daily to medical school, as some few students did from as far afield as Bishop Auckland. They were insistent that even in war-time I should take full advantage of the educational and social opportunities offered by university life and, despite the expense, agreed from the outset that I should find 'digs' in Newcastle provided I returned to Spennymoor as often as possible at weekends. Mrs Kerr's boarding house at 22 Wingrove Road was not only inexpensive but was clean and comfortable and the food she served in her large dining-room was unexciting but substantial. On taking up residence I found that I was joined by three other 'fresher' medical students; this was a tall Victorian terrace house in which we each had a bedroom, but as was typical of British homes in those days, no form of heating was available in any of them. I had a small but adequate attic room and shared the bathroom with my three colleagues, Donald Webster from Stockton-on-Tees, Geoffrey Mellor from Esh Winning near Bishop Auckland (whose father, like mine, was a school-master) and Basil Poole from Middlesbrough. There were usually in addition three or four other 'lodgers', many of them commercial travellers who came and went after relatively short periods, whereas we students were the long-term residents. Also living in the house were Mrs Kerr and her husband and their mentally handicapped 35-year-old son, Douglas, as well as the family pet, a shaggy-haired mongrel, part-Collie, part-Labrador with a hint of other breeds as well. Douglas was generally quiet and ineffectual though occasionally given to spontaneous, unprovoked, prolonged episodes of cackling laughter. But both he and the dog became terrified whenever the air-raid sirens went, and more especially on those relatively rare occasions during air-raids when bombs fell within the vicinity of Newcastle or when the anti-aircraft batteries opened up along the Tyne. Neither Douglas nor the dog stopped shaking until the all-clear went. In fact Newcastle and Tyneside as a whole were spared the worst of the blitz. Although one attack destroyed the Forth goods station and a number of other stray bombs demolished a few houses and other buildings in Jesmond and elsewhere,

41

the centre of the city survived throughout the war virtually unscathed and none of us ever felt in serious danger. Whether or not the tar barrels which were placed at regular intervals along both sides of the Tyne and were then ignited at dusk to produce a pall of smoke which obscured the line of the river did actually mislead the German bombers we never really knew; certainly many bombs fell harmlessly in open countryside while heavy industry along the Scotswood Road and along the banks of the Tyne, as well as shipbuilding, were almost completely spared.

The major disadvantage of Mrs Kerr's boarding house was that the only three rooms which were heated were the kitchen, the dining-room and the drawing-room, all warmed by open coal fires. When we students wished to study in the evenings, we could choose to sit in the large drawing-room with our books and papers, trying to work while listening to the chatter of the non-student guests who often indeed tried to engage us in conversation, quite oblivious to our need for silence. Consequently we often retreated to our respective bedrooms where we each had a table and chair, but where in the absence of heat in the Newcastle winter the fingers and toes soon began to tingle even if one donned heavy sweaters, an overcoat and bed-socks under the slippers. The dining-room was no better as the fire was quenched as soon as the meal had been served. Of course the University library, with ample reading places, was open until 9.00 p.m., but it was over two miles away and if one went there straight from medical school in order to work, the choice lay between walking back to Wingrove Road for the evening meal and then returning to the library for not more than an hour or so, or alternatively missing the evening meal and paying for a snack in the Union in a brief break from study. We rarely took the latter course since as relatively impoverished medical students we objected on principle to spending money on food and missing a meal for which we had already paid as a part of our board and lodging. So more often we froze in our respective garrets while trying to concentrate on *Gray's Anatomy* or *Samson Wright's Physiology* or upon our own notes, even when it was almost too cold to write or even at times to hold a pen.

But when I speak of impoverishment, this was relative. My parents, who gave me £3.00 a week to cover my board and lodgings and all other expenses, were generous in comparison with many others. Geoff Mellor's parents treated him equally well but Donald Webster was much less well off and from time to time took part-time jobs as a lab assistant in the University to earn a little extra. And as Basil Poole was the only one of us who then drank alcohol, his forays to the local pubs sometimes left him so short by the end of the week that one or other of us often had to come to his assistance. But living expenses were remarkably low. For example, in the University Union at lunch-time one could obtain a substantial helping of shepherd's pie followed by Devonshire square and custard and a cup of coffee all for 1/-. Cigarettes (we were all fairly heavy smokers) also cost about a shilling for a packet of 20, and even medical books, of which we were required to buy relatively few, were reasonably inexpensive. Clothes in those days of coupons were worn until threadbare and, as I recall it, we rarely changed our shirts, underclothes and socks more often than twice weekly; my laundry was taken home or posted back to Spennymoor for my mother to do and to be collected or returned by post the following weekend.

We were fortunate in Newcastle to be taught in the then splendid facilities of the new Medical School built opposite the gates of the Royal Victoria Infirmary, first occupied in 1938 and opened formally by King George VI in 1939. This building, largely of red brick, and built partly through the generosity of Sir Arthur Sutherland, the Tyneside ship-owner, who made a major donation towards its costs, supplementing the funds provided by the University Grants Committee, was designed by Professor Edwards, the University's professor of architecture. It was nevertheless roundly condemned by many of his students who referred to the building disparagingly as 'the jam factory'; they were especially critical of the Doric columns which framed its main entrance and which had aluminium bases. Functionally, nevertheless, the Medical School was an attractive and convenient building in which to work, although it is interesting to note as one looks back from the post-war era that while it provided excellent lecture theatres, laboratories, a splendid dissecting room and all of the essential accommodation then needed for the teaching of anatomy, physiology, bacteriology and public health (the Professor of Pathology, Professor A. F. B. Shaw, stoutly and adamantly refused to move out of his hospital-based laboratories in the Royal Victoria Infirmary (RVI) into the new school), it did not provide any accommodation whatever for clinical specialties such as medicine, surgery and obstetrics and gynaecology. In those days it was not thought necessary to have offices, laboratories or teaching rooms for the clinical disciplines as the hospital and its wards were regarded by all teachers as being sufficient and appropriate for clinical teaching by honorary staff, some of whom were given honorary professorial titles without any stipend, offices or other facilities being provided by the University. For the first time in 1941 Newcastle took the revolutionary step of appointing a whole-time university clinical professor of child health, James Spence, with the aid of a major grant from the Nuffield Foundation, while Frederick Nattrass was appointed to a whole-time chair of medicine; both he and Spence were required to give up lucrative private practices in order to take up these appointments.

Although, as I have mentioned, the external characteristics of the new Medical School won few admirers, its facilities, including a capacious and comfortable common room and a well-appointed gymnasium in the basement, were more than adequate. Even the medical students of the day were less than enthusiastic about the external appearance of the new building and compared it unfavourably with the Victorian grandeur of its predecessor in Northumberland Road. One such, writing in the Durham University *Medical Gazette* of February 1938, said:

'Of beauty of design it has little. Every self-respecting building must be able to demonstrate its good proportions before being approved of by present-day pundits. The result is a dreary sequence of not altogether unpleasing, dull and unimaginative blocks of brick or stone. At their best they have dignity and a certain impressiveness; at their worst they resemble nothing so much as a large warehouse or barracks . . . if, as seems likely, we fail to impress the visitor by its external beauty, let us hope that the interior will give us greater comfort than our present cramped quarters now afford.'

In fact the latter hope was more than justified. Two interesting features of the School were first that in the light of his generous donation of £100 000 towards building costs (and a subsequent bequest), Sir Arthur Sutherland specified that the Faculty Room (soon called the Howden Room in acknowledgement of the outstanding services to the School as Professor of Anatomy for many years of Professor Robert Howden who edited *Gray's Anatomy* for longer than any other editor) should be a faithful copy in its ornamental plasterwork and panelling of that still extant in the principal room of the Bessie Surtees House on the Newcastle Quayside, the oldest surviving building in Newcastle. In fact the Howden Room, in which first as a student, subsequently as a member of staff and later as Dean I spent innumerable happy and also some tedious hours, never failed to impress the visitor. As I write, it is sad that following the move to yet another new Medical School opened in 1985 on a site behind the RVI, that historic room is no longer available to the Medical Faculty. However, I am glad that although that 1938 building has now been taken over largely by the Faculty of Agriculture of Newcastle University, the Howden Room has been retained with its original decoration as a room in which important University meetings can be held and in which, from time to time, visitors can be dined. Indeed it was a pleasure, tinged with nostalgia, to dine there as a member of the University's Research Advisory Panel in December 1989.

The second interesting feature, again specified by Sir Arthur, was that the ground floor must be floored throughout in wood-blocks (often highly polished and quite slippery and dangerous on occasion, particularly in war-time in the hours of black-out). And all the windows were framed in teak; Sir Arthur's bequest required that these teak windows should be scraped exteriorly and interiorly and treated with teak oil every five years. The solidity and quality of finish of the building is still such that it will plainly serve the University and its Faculty of Agriculture for many years to come, though it became clear in the 1960s that the building was no longer adequate to fulfil the manifold requirements of modern medical teaching and research and the needs of an expanding Medical Faculty. But many of the School's alumni, like myself, still have a great affection for our old academic home; we happily purchased and now proudly own copies of an outstanding watercolour painting of it produced by a notable physician and artist, Dr Alastair Brewis, during the 1984 celebrations which marked the 150th anniversary of the establishment of the Newcastle Medical School.

The turbulent history of the Newcastle School in the early years after its foundation and again in the period leading up to the Second World War has been related in many notable publications and especially in the sesquicentennial scrapbook published by Drs Gordon Dale and Fred Miller at the time of the 150th anniversary. In fact the teaching of medicine began in Bell's Court off Pilgrim Street in Newcastle in 1832 and the handsome doorway of that building was later transferred to the 1938 School in Queen Victoria Road, being installed near to the rear entrance in a basement corridor. One of the eight students who enrolled in 1832 was John Snow who had formerly been apprenticed to an apothecary, William Hardcastle of Benton. Snow it was who became famous not only for the contribution that he made to controlling an outbreak of cholera in the North East in 1831 but subsequently because of his seminal role in the practice of anaesthesia and his subsequent recommendation to remove the handle from the Broad Street pump in London in 1854 in the light of his well-justified belief that an epidemic of cholera occurring in that vicinity was the result of drinking infected water from the pump. His place in medical history was assured after he gave chloroform in 1853 and 1857 to Queen Victoria at the births of two of her children.

In 1834 the qualifications awarded by the Newcastle School were formally recognized by the Royal College of Surgeons and by the Apothecaries Hall in London and soon afterwards London University added its approval. Hence the formal establishment of the Newcastle upon Tyne School of Medicine and Surgery occurred in that year and the School moved to the Newcastle Barber Surgeons Hall, a handsome building with better facilities for dissection and for teaching. Unfortunately yet another move was soon necessary when the North Eastern Railway Company decided to demolish the Barber Surgeons Hall in order to make room for the Company's new buildings at the Manors; a new Barber Surgeons Hall and School of Medicine and Surgery was then constructed at Victoria Street, Westmorland Road, in 1851. Unfortunately a number of unseemly disputes then arose between the lecturers of the School and two separate competing groups were formed; only the minority group chose to occupy the Victoria Street premises; the majority moved temporarily to a house close to the Manors site, but soon obtained the lease of more capacious premises at 1 Leazes Terrace which was called Neville Hall and which opened in October 1852. The Neville Hall School negotiated an association with Durham University so that for the first time a formal university link was forged. In January 1852 this was formalized with the agreement of the Senate and Convocation of the University and the Medical School of the majority then became the Newcastle upon Tyne College of Medicine of the University of Durham. This School then obtained even more capacious premises in the old mansion known as Westmorland House, adjoining the Newcastle Literary and Philosophical Society in Orchard Street; when this new home of the Newcastle upon Tyne College of Medicine was occupied, Neville Hall was converted into a residential hostel.

As overtures from the rival School to the University which began in 1852 and continued until 1855 were rebuffed by Senate, it soon became clear that the continuing feud between the two organizations did a substantial disservice to the teaching of medicine and surgery in Newcastle. Eventually, through the good offices of Dr Greenhow who invited the warring factions to a dinner in Newcastle which was followed by placatory approaches from Dr T. E. Headlam, President of the College of Medicine, and from representatives of Durham University, a formal agreement was reached to merge the two Schools. Soon afterwards the staffs of the two institutions came together in the College and the premises on Westmorland Road occupied by the minority (usually referred to at the time as 'the Rye Hill group') were vacated. In 1862 the combined College had about 60 medical students and in 1867 the General Medical Council carried out its first inspection in Newcastle and reported that the examinations were 'satisfactory and to be noted especially for the practical character' but that the standard of the pre-medical examination was too low and did not include all of the required subjects. These deficiencies were quickly corrected and in 1870 an even more formal relationship with the University was agreed so that the College became the University of Durham College of Medicine; its teachers became professors and lecturers of the University and were represented on Senate. Unfortunately the School's troubles were not yet over and in 1883 the College received notice to quit its premises in Orchard Street, again because of the wish of the North Eastern Railway to enlarge Newcastle Central Station. With considerable difficulty the College found a site in what was then known as Bath Street (subsequently Northumberland Road) and the 6th Duke of Northumberland laid the foundation stone of the new College on 3 November 1887. That School was opened in 1889 and served the interests of the Medical Faculty with its expanding intake until the new building on Queen Victoria Road was occupied in 1938 and formally opened in

1939, almost exactly 50 years later. Subsequently the Northumberland Road School was taken over by the Sub-Faculty of Dental Surgery and functioned as the Newcastle upon Tyne Dental School from the 1940s until Newcastle's new Dental School was opened in 1978. The Northumberland Road buildings now form a part of the Newcastle Polytechnic.

In the meantime the clinical facilities available to serve the community at the old Newcastle Infirmary on the Forth Banks had proved outdated and inadequate and the teaching facilities available there for the growing numbers of medical students also became increasingly unsatisfactory. In 1897 the Freemen of the City gave the Governors of the Infirmary a site of eight acres on the Leazes as a free gift so that they could erect on that site a major new hospital. Funds were raised by public donation, including a gift of £100 000 from a Mr John Hall; the campaign eventually led to the building of the capacious Royal Victoria Infirmary (RVI) opened by Her Majesty Queen Victoria in 1906. It was in that building across the road from the Medical School that I received most of my clinical training, apart from the teaching and practical experience in obstetrics which was provided in part at the Princess Mary Maternity Hospital (about a mile away) and at the municipal Newcastle General Hospital (some two miles away).

Shortly before the new building was occupied in 1938, the history of the Newcastle School was yet again clouded by an unfortunate row which followed an attempt by the then President of the College of Medicine, Sir Robert Bolam, to dismiss the Professor of Bacteriology, Professor Hutchins; the history of 'the row' has been described *in extenso* by Ernest Bettenson, the first Registrar of Newcastle University and previously Deputy Registrar of the University of Durham. Many younger members of staff, feeling that Sir Robert Bolam's behaviour in the case had been autocratic if not despotic, sided with Professor Hutchins and among the most vocal of the opposition were James Spence and Fred Nattrass. Major differences of opinion regarding the management of the School, also highlighted during the campaign to raise funds for the new building, led first to an official enquiry into the affairs of the School of Medicine and later to a Royal Commission which recommended substantial administrative restructuring. A new Act of Parliament was eventually passed creating a tripartite University in which the Medical Faculty (including its Sub-Faculty of Dentistry) achieved a degree of independence within the University but was nevertheless a part of the newly-created King's College, Newcastle, of the University of Durham which grew out of the old Armstrong College of Physical Science. The second part of the University was the remainder of King's College excluding medicine, and the third the Durham colleges. The University continued to function under that tripartite structure until the University of Newcastle became independent of Durham in 1962 despite some spirited opposition from many in the Medical Faculty who wished to retain their traditional association with Durham (even though the latter for many years had had no practical significance). Since 1962 the Medical Faculty has retained a privileged position within the University of Newcastle by virtue of retaining most if not all of the statutes which it enjoyed as one of the three constituent bodies of Durham University.

The quality of the teaching we received in Newcastle was, I believe, exceptionally good. Not unnaturally, we all stood in awe of the Dean, Professor R. B. Green, who was also Professor of Anatomy, even though I well remembered his kindly and compassionate advice when I had seen him and had discussed with him my wish to join the Air Force before entering the School. He it was who gave us our first and memorable lecture on the anatomy of the human body, expounding certain basic principles, explaining the significance of his subject to the study of medicine and illustrating his talk throughout with rapid chalk strokes on the blackboard in a lecture theatre invariably known as the 'brain theatre' because, as I understand it, it was originally designed to allow students to dissect the human brain under supervision, though in fact it was only occasionally used for that purpose. We were all, of course, greatly amused and perhaps slightly shocked when at an informal freshers' tea party he regaled us with a racy talk, laced with spicy anecdotes, while attempting to persuade all of us not only to work hard and to enjoy our studies but at the same time to take advantage of the cultural, sporting and social opportunities which life in the Medical School and University provided. I well recall the story which he told us to illustrate the point; before the war a French visiting student came to the University to spend a year in the Medical Faculty and after a few weeks he, the Dean, interviewed him to see how he was managing to integrate into the alien culture of Tyneside. The visitor was in fact delighted with all that the University, School and City provided and said cheerfully to the Dean 'I 'ave, 'ow you English say, zee finger in every tart'.

Also notable and memorable was the anatomical teaching of the Reader in Anatomy who subsequently acquired a personal chair, John Short; his ability to draw anatomical diagrams using his left and right arms simultaneously with a piece of chalk in each hand was exceptional and greatly enlivened the subject. He, like Professor Green, was a chain smoker of cigarettes and we were not surprised many years later to learn that he had developed lung cancer but was one of the lucky few who survived for several years after a successful pneumonectomy. Yet another chain smoker of cigarettes who persuaded us, as did the Dean, to smoke throughout all classes, was John Secker, Lecturer in Physiology, whose practical classes with the inevitable frog-leg preparation and the rotating smoked drum introduced us to the elements of neuromuscular excitability.

Much later in the physiology course he taught the men, while a female lecturer taught the ladies (the sexes being segregated in different laboratories) the principles of physical examination of the cardiovascular, respiratory and nervous systems, where each of us was required to examine a colleague under his eagle-eyed supervision. Less memorable were the clear but dogmatic lectures of Professor David Burns, head of the Department of Physiology, in which department, rather curiously, we were also taught normal histology, each of us using the Watson service microscopes which we had been required to buy. My immensely supportive parents willingly provided the £25.00 necessary to buy the microscope, just as they had presented me with my first copy of *Gray's Anatomy*. Many years later, as an impoverished newly-appointed medical registrar in Newcastle, I sold the microscope in order to pay the deposit on a car.

Before going to Medical School we had all been regaled by schoolmasters and friends, some well-informed and some very much less so, about the potential horrors of the anatomical dissecting room where for the first time we would come face to face with dead human bodies. One unexpected problem was the necessity of buying laboratory coats in which to dissect and with which to cover our limited and vulnerable clothing. Unfortunately clothing coupons were required to buy white laboratory coats. But the Medical School offered a helpful solution, as white boiler suits could be purchased without them. Many of us bought these, though others of greater initiative and ingenuity acquired white coats from senior students and friends. In addition we all had to obtain black gowns, but in the janitor's office, presided over by the lordly Harry Rowe (who, as legend would have it, had been the Dean's batman in the First World War) there was a roaring trade in second-hand gowns. Some bought new ones but most, like myself, went for the second-hand and indeed we vied with one another to obtain the most tattered, disreputable and aged example. Gowns were worn for all lectures, 'sign-ups' (see p. 51) and examinations but otherwise there were no strict regulations relating to dress, though none of us ever then contemplated the possibility of attending lectures or indeed any classes of the Medical School without wearing a jacket and shirt with collar and tie. And when the time came for us to clerk on the wards some five terms after entering the School we were then compelled to buy white coats which were regularly laundered free of charge in the RVI laundry; underneath these coats a smart jacket and trousers (or preferably a dark suit) with collar and tie were regarded as essential.

Our first experience of the dissecting room turned out to be nothing like as fearsome as we had anticipated. This was a long, well-lit, airy room at the top of the Medical School, occupied by a series of clean metal tables upon which lay the bodies which the School had acquired for dissection purposes. Many years later when I became Dean I was the regular recipient of what were known to the secretaries as 'body letters' from those wishing to leave their bodies to the School for dissection. The supply was always more than adequate. From the beginning, the desiccated, embalmed human forms upon which we exercised our limited dissecting skills, previously nurtured somewhat inadequately in school zoology lessons, seemed to lack all sense and aura of humanity; even the pervasive smell of formalin was far from disturbing and was something to which one quickly became accustomed. Sixteen of us were allocated to each body, four on each arm and four on each leg. How we subsequently coped with dissection of the head and neck, thorax and abdomen I cannot now recall but I am sure that there was some well-defined system.

As I recall, there were about 80 of us who began our studies in October 1941, about 50 men and 30 women. In those days about a third of the year entered the School after a one-year course of pre-medical studies in the University whereas the rest of us were accepted on the basis of our Higher School Certificate examination results obtained after two years in a school sixth form, and were therefore about one year older than the pre-med entrants. Practically all of us came from some part of the North-East of England though one or two came from as far afield as Carlisle; but most were from the counties of Durham and Northumberland and the North Riding of Yorkshire; I cannot recall that any came from Scotland or the South of England. Not unnaturally, the year tended to divide itself into fairly well defined cliques. At the beginning those of us coming from a grammar school background, such as Bill Ross from Durham, Donald Webster and Basil Poole from Stockton-on-Tees, Geoff Mellor from Bishop Auckland and Bill Wood from Houghton-le-Spring, tended to congregate in one group, while those educated in public schools, like Alan Jenkins and Bob Dias from St Bees, Nigel Sprague and Fred Spencer from Durham and Rex Belas from Pocklington, came together in another. But perhaps the largest clique was that of boys from the Newcastle Royal Grammar School, of which there must have been at least a dozen in the year including John Noble, Bert White and Douglas Thomson. Whether or not the girls in the year formed cliques I cannot clearly recall, although many of them came from the Newcastle Central High and Church High Schools and already knew many of the RGS boys. They too tended, like the men, to club together within the first few months until a few male and female groupings slowly began to emerge.

It now seems curious in retrospect that often there was more than a hint of snobbery and inverted snobbery which coloured our attitude to one another. Whether intentionally or not, some of the public school boys were thought to look down on those of grammar school background, while our group in turn (some of whom never lost their local accents, though others worked hard to do so) categorized the public school products and even those from the RGS as snobs. The groupings in the dissecting room tended if anything to perpetuate these divisions and it took many months, even in some cases as long as two years or so, for these initial barriers to break down and for many of us to create friendships with those from different scholastic backgrounds.

Our laborious work in the dissecting room, at first performed with fumbling hands and not infrequently resulting in the inadvertent division of important nerves, arteries, veins or other structures which we were required to expose, was supervised by a group of lecturers and demonstrators in anatomy (most of the demonstrators were intending surgeons studying for the primary FRCS) who in turn every two weeks or so subjected us individually for about 20 minutes to a formal quiz, often over a prosected specimen of that part of the body which we ourselves had most recently dissected. These regular test sessions were known as 'sign-ups' and it was not possible to move on to dissecting another part until one had been satisfactorily 'signed up' on the previous one. Fortunately the allocation of students to individual lecturers and demonstrators was done on a random basis so that one did not always face the same inquisitor on each occasion. Most fearsome and universally feared by the students was Dr E. J. Field, Lecturer in Anatomy (who, many years later, became Professor of Experimental Neuropathology), a brilliant teacher but a fiercely impatient examiner and hard marker who set himself high standards and demanded these of his students. Apocryphally it was often said that students would be found praying on the stairs leading to the dissecting room on their way to an anatomy sign-up, saying 'Pray God I don't get E. J.'. Not only, of course, did we have such tests in anatomy but in both anatomy and physiology there were end-of-term examinations in the form of essay-type question papers, sometimes but not invariably supplemented by practical tests and *viva voce* examinations. There were many rapidly beating hearts when the marks obtained in these exams were exposed to public view on the Medical School noticeboard.

As time went by I began to realize that I was a member of a Medical School year in which there were many students who were exceptionally gifted academically. As the examination and sign-up results clearly demonstrated, there were at least ten capable of regularly achieving a mark of over 65%, regarded in the School as being of high second class honours standard, and at least two, or occasionally three or four, regularly achieving more than 75% or distinction standard. One of the latter was Bill Ross, son of the Durham City golf professional, a state scholar, formerly of the Durham Johnston Grammar School, and another was a Jewish refugee, Martin Menczer, a fiercely dedicated, ambitious and even at times slightly aggressive and combative student whose family had escaped from oppression in Austria during the Nazi era and had eventually settled in the North-East of England.

As the end of our first year in Medical School approached, it became clear to the four of us who lived in Mrs Kerr's lodging house in Wingrove Road that the working conditions were simply not satisfactory and would make it very difficult indeed for us to face the major hurdle of the second MB examination in anatomy and physiology which was due to take place in March 1943. Inevitably, therefore, we sought new lodgings; Donald Webster and I decided to move together and were fortunate in finding outstandingly comfortable and suitable accommodation with two maiden ladies, the elderly Misses Elliott at 21 Queen's Road, Jesmond, where we each had a comfortable and good-sized if unheated bedroom and a private combined dining and sitting-room with a coal fire, admirable for working. As we were the only two paying guests (for the very reasonable figure of 30s (£1.50) a week) these 'digs' could not possibly have been more ideal, despite the monotony of the simple, well-cooked evening meals with which we were regularly provided in rotation; we always knew that it was Tuesday when we were served toad-in-the-hole. I believe that Donald and I would have been happy to stay there for several years but unfortunately after about a year one of the strait-laced Misses Elliott came down at about 6.30 a.m. to put out the milk bottles and encountered us both returning from a Saturday night party. We were then requested to leave and eventually, with difficulty, found comfortable lodgings with Rex Belas, with whom we had become increasingly friendly, in Grosvenor Road, Jesmond, but at the increased cost of £2 weekly.

But before embarking on our second year of medical school, from the end of June to the beginning of October 1942 we enjoyed the first and only long vacation of the medical school course. This enabled me to see a little more of Betty, to have a family holiday with my parents and with Ernest and Mary, and perhaps to do a little more to allay those recurrent waves of guilt which still occasionally surfaced over being in a reserved occupation in war-time at a time when the war was still going far from well. First, like the rest of the men in the year, I attended Senior Training Corps (STC) camp, and secondly some 20 of us responded to a request for volunteers who were invited to work as navvies on an aerodrome under construction in Norfolk at a little village called Tibenham. The long and tiring coach journey to Norfolk was in retrospect hilarious, being enlivened throughout by the raucous rendition of the innumerable bawdy songs so beloved of medical students, many of which we had learned during our training in the STC (of which more later). Our accommodation at Tibenham in crowded dormitories in Nissen huts was primitive and the ablutions, toilets and showers even more so. On our arrival we were confronted by the fierce, tall, forbidding Cockney figure of the senior foreman employed by a London company called Burgess who were constructing the airfield. He told us in no uncertain terms that he would expect us to graft from morning to night, irrespective of blisters and aching muscles, alongside a group of some 40 or 50 young Irish and older London navvies who were the primary work-force. We were also told that the aerodrome was some three or four months behind schedule, that it was to become an American air base, and that the first American bombers were expected there in September.

Next morning, dressed in suitable working clothes (many of us improperly used our STC denims and Army boots in which to work) we were divided into squads, one of which, led by Doug Thomson, spent the entire four weeks pouring molten rubber into the cracks between the concrete slabs which formed the runways, while I and seven others, along with a group of navvies, were set on to dig drainage trenches along either side of the main runway. These trenches were having to be dug by hand as the mechanical digger had broken down. We were told that an area of soil 6 in. deep and 3 ft. wide had first to be removed at each side of the runway and in the centre of that 3 ft. area a trench 18 in. wide and 18 in. deep was to be dug into which drainage pipes, subsequently covered with loose stone and gravel, would be laid. For the first few days at least this unaccustomed toil resulted, as we had been warned, in blisters, aching backs and aching limbs, but gradually the work became more routine and less painful. Even if within the first few days our working hours from 8.00 in the morning till 5.00 or 6.00 p.m. left us capable of doing little more than to eat the ample but unexciting food (bangers and mash was the staple diet) with which we were provided, after a while an occasional foray to the solitary village pub or even, when we were released on a Saturday evening, to the Samson and Hercules dance hall in Norwich came as a welcome relief. After one such evening, having over-indulged, one of our number who many years later became a distinguished surgeon woke up with a hangover to discover that during the night, awakened no doubt by signals from a full bladder, he must have decided not to walk to the toilet but instead used one of his Wellington boots. After two weeks we were even fit enough to take on the young Irish navvies at soccer, a game which we won handsomely and in which I scored one of our three goals. Afterwards over a shandy, while our opponents including the foreman were downing pints repetitively, the foreman remarked sourly 'Well, you may not be able to graft, but at least you can play football'. What exactly our wages were I cannot now recall but I believe we were paid something like £3.00 a week with overtime on Saturday mornings and on Sundays.

Progress continued, however, to be unsatisfactory and so the company introduced a bonus system for those of us digging the drainage trenches. It was agreed that for every foot of trench over 30 ft. dug in a day, we would be given a one shilling bonus. Even I and some of the other students achieved 60 ft. a day in the first few days after the scheme was introduced, but as some of the younger Irish navvies were managing up to 120 ft., after about a week the scheme was hastily abandoned. For the first time I began to learn something of trade union attitudes since our Nissen hut was visited one evening by a deputation of three or four of the older London navvies who said that they were going to insist that the bonus scheme be abandoned as it set man against man; as some of those in the older age group found it difficult to achieve even the 30 ft. target they felt that they would be in danger of dismissal. Nevertheless, even after the bonus scheme disappeared, an average of 30 ft. of trench per man per day was regularly dug and by the time we left Tibenham after some four weeks the trenches were virtually complete. We also became fully aware for the first time of the deep divisions in Ireland between North and South. After some friendly but heated bar room discussions one of the young Irishmen said 'Give us back our six northern counties and you can have the whole Irish Army, millions of men'.

In March 1990 Betty and I, when driving to Norwich where I was to speak to the annual dinner of the consultant staff at the Norfolk and Norwich Hospital, took a brief diversion from our route to visit Tibenham where I was fascinated to see that despite much development, some of the original buildings including the village pub were still recognizable, as were the farm and the fields in which our Nissen-hutted accommodation had been provided 48 years earlier. Indeed two Nissen huts were still standing and being used for agricultural purposes, while some parts of the runway of the war-time airfield survived, surrounded by productive farmland. I understand that Tibenham functioned as an active US air base until shortly after the end of the war.

Returning to Newcastle to begin our second year, we were all aware that in the following March we would be faced with the second MB examination, that horrendous hurdle which our seniors told us was by far the most demanding examination of the medical course and in which there was usually a failure rate of about 20%. Certainly the colossal burden of knowledge in both anatomy and physiology which one was required to absorb and to be able to regurgitate at the time of the examination seemed increasingly fearsome as time went by. Indeed when we came to take a 'mock' examination in December 1942 I found myself in such a state of acute anxiety that on medical advice I was excused one part of the examination. At the time I thought that the disturbing symptoms I then experienced were of physical origin; only in retrospect did I realize that this was a severe psychological stress reaction which fortunately never recurred to anything like the same extent in my subsequent medical career. Even so, after a brief Christmas holiday at home, Donald and I returned to Queen's Road in early January 1943 and spent much of the next three months working night after night until 1.00 or 2.00 a.m., also (as a rule) on Saturday mornings and virtually all day Sunday. Only on Wednesday afternoons devoted to STC activities, Saturday afternoons for sport, and

Saturday evenings when we made our regular weekly visit to the cinema, were we allowed to break the routine. I doubt whether ever before or since I have studied with such unremitting intensity. Even though in the end I felt well prepared for the examination, anxiety again surfaced sufficiently to compel me to vomit up my breakfast in the basement lavatory in the Medical School on the morning before the final anatomy *viva*. In the end once the examination, which dragged on for nearly three weeks, was over, the emotional catharsis was substantial but was nevertheless muted by the anxious wait before the results were published. I was delighted to have achieved distinctions in both anatomy and physiology, as did Bill Ross and Martin Menczer, between whom the Stephen Scott Prize for the best results in the second MB examination was shared. By this time Bill and I, though clearly academic rivals, had become good friends, though neither of us ever achieved quite the same friendly relationship with Martin.

One prominent feature of our first few years in Medical School was the Senior Training Corps (STC) in which all male students who were medically fit were required to enrol. In the beginning we were provided with an archaic type of uniform belonging to the former Officers' Training Corps (OTC) and more suitable to the conditions of the 1930s. We wore peaked caps, a khaki shirt with tie, a jacket with brass buttons down the front and khaki belt, trousers which were rather like plus fours and puttees and boots. This uniform caused considerable embarrassment since we always wore it on Wednesdays and sometimes, when extra parades were called for, on Saturday mornings. Many of us were greatly embarrassed from time to time to be saluted by soldiers on the streets of Newcastle who, on seeing us wearing collars and ties, thought that we were officers. Soon, however, we were saved this embarrassment by being issued with standard battle-dress, gaiters, belts and army boots and a forage cap on which we proudly sported the cap badge of Durham University STC in the form of a bronze St Cuthbert's Cross. For the first two terms all medical students were required to enrol in the infantry unit in order to be instructed in the primary arts of soldiering. We drilled, we polished brasses and boots, were instructed in the use of the rifle and of the Bren gun; we shot on the rifle ranges at Ponteland and even on two or three occasions went on bombing parades in order to learn how to throw Mills bombs (hand grenades). We also learned a good deal about the habits and language of those Regular Army NCOs who were attached to the STC as permanent staff instructors. The stern but likeable Sergeant Gardner of the Durham Light Infantry had a characteristically limited vocabulary, exemplified by the occasion when Bob Dias turned up for a bombing parade without his tin hat; Gardner exploded by saying 'You, Dias, what the f...ing 'ell do you mean by coming on an f...ing bombing parade without an f...ing 'elmet—f... off'.

Most of us enjoyed this part-time training, even including the assault course exercises, scaling walls and other obstacles, with which we were regularly challenged. Indeed when after two terms we all took Infantry Certificate A and most of us passed with ease, I was invited by Major Vernon Brown (a friend and colleague of my father from the First World War) of the infantry unit to continue in that unit as a corporal for at least another term in order to take Infantry Certificate B, even though it was expected that all medical students would then transfer to the medical unit of the Corps for RAMC-type training. I then faced the somewhat paradoxical situation of having press-studs on my uniform to which I could attach my corporal's stripes when attending infantry training on Saturday mornings, before removing the stripes to be a private in the medical unit on Wednesday afternoons. My continuing infantry training must have been reasonably successful, including not only drill, weapon training and the like, but also intermittent study of such light evening reading as *Staff Duties in the Field*, as in June 1942 on the Palace Green at Durham, under the eagle eye of a major in the Highland Light Infantry, I was successful in the Infantry Certificate B examination which I was told would have ensured my admission to an Officer Cadet Training Unit if I had been intending to join the Army as many of the non-medical students did. Indeed it seems that my vigorous and stentorian drilling of an HLI sergeant through a strenuous bayonet exercise so impressed the examining officer that he tried, without success, to persuade me to give up my medical course in order to embark on officer training in an infantry regiment.

One other Corps duty was that on one evening every two weeks we were each allocated to teams of eight and were required to sleep in the Medical School and to undertake, in uniform, fire-watching duties. We all had our army-style respirators and steel helmets, while stirrup pumps, buckets of water and sand were conveniently distributed throughout the Medical School; we were each allocated specific stations in the building in the event of air attack. One evening, during one of the few sporadic air-raids on Tyneside, when some of us were watching the search-lights and the anti-aircraft barrage from the roof, Fred Spencer was somewhat startled by a loud clang and discovered that a piece of spent anti-aircraft shell had bounced off his steel helmet; Alan Jenkins, who had forgotten to bring his helmet with him, made a speedy retreat. Each fire-watching team was led by a member of the staff. Our leader was Professor Ernest Dunlop, the charming, erudite but prolix Professor of Bacteriology, throughout whose lectures we were sometimes compelled to ignore the factual content while waiting breathlessly for the end of each complex and flowery sentence. He spent most of the evening on fire-watching duty in his own office and laboratory and we rarely saw him. There was, however, one embarrassing occasion a little later in the war, by which time all air-raids on the North-East had ceased, when as a routine the fire-watching squad would go out to one of the local cinemas, leaving behind one member of the team to open the locked rear door of the Medical School when the absentees returned. On one occasion the standard arrangement failed and everyone, it seems, went either to the cinema, or to the pub; when we returned we found the building locked and virtually impregnable and were only able to obtain entry by alerting Professor Dunlop who came down to let us in and was both amused and understanding. Fortunately no disciplinary action followed.

Another interesting feature of our fire-watching evenings was that some of the girls in the year volunteered to man the main telephone exchange in King's College throughout the night; this led us to discover that there was a maze of underground tunnels carrying heating pipes through which it was possible, bypassing the boiler house, to make one's way underground from the Medical School to King's College and to the telephone exchange. These fire-watching evenings, of course, taught us a little about how to sleep on metal bunks with thin mattresses, between army blankets without sheets, and prepared us well for Corps camps which we subsequently attended in each of our first three summers in Medical School.

Mention of fire-watching reminds me of the notable Mr Herbert Bell who had, he believed, a personal reserved seat in the corner of the student common room which no other student was brave enough to try to annexe. Herbert Bell had served in the Army during the First World War and had been left a substantial sum of money by an aunt, in trust, from which he derived a regular annual income; the trust deed, however, required that that income would cease when he was no longer a medical student. He entered the Medical School in 1921 and after six or seven attempts at every professional examination, had finally succeeded by 1939 in passing every examination but the Finals. Eventually, after many unsuccessful attempts, his reserved occupation status ran out shortly after we arrived in the Medical School in 1941 and he was drafted as a whole-time fire-watcher in the centre of Newcastle.

But to return to the Corps, two summer camps stand out particularly clearly in the memory. The first of these was at Longhorsley and, being a keen young part-time soldier, I volunteered to go on the advance party which was involved with setting up camp, erecting tents and preparing the site for the influx of some 150 colleagues a few days later. I was detailed off to prepare a demonstration lay-out of carefully folded blankets, polished boots and blancoed equipment, etc., which everyone would subsequently be expected to emulate on regular inspections of our tented accommodation. Our Dean and Commanding Officer, Lieutenant-Colonel Green, seemed to have been sufficiently impressed by the demonstration to recommend me for my first stripe in the medical unit, but unfortunately confused my name with that of my good friend Geoff Mellor who was working equally assiduously in the cook-house, so it was he who became a lance-corporal rather than myself. My stripe came along just a few days later when the confusion of surnames was brought to the attention of the CO. While we certainly did some stretcher training, some field exercises and route marches and listened to several lectures, the detailed activities of the camp are now very vague, though I recall that Ian Bruce slipped out one evening to visit his girlfriend in Newcastle and, having missed the last bus, walked more than 30 miles back from the centre of the city to Longhorsley, with the result that he was not able to take any further part in the training in camp because of badly blistered feet. I also recall that after a particularly riotous evening party towards the end of camp, the student Regimental Sergeant Major, Maurice Brown, who had been a strict disciplinarian, found himself being deposited in a deep trench latrine; disciplinary action was quickly taken but did not subsequently prevent the two ringleaders (after a decent interval) from being promoted.

In the following year our camp was pitched in the splendid grounds of Belsay Hall; at that stage the 15th Scottish Division was stationed in Northumberland but was one field ambulance short. We were told proudly that if there were to be an invasion, we, as the Durham University STC Medical Unit, would form the third field ambulance. In acknowledgement of this onerous responsibility, the Deputy Director of Medical Services (DDMS) Northern Command, then Major-General Mitchiner, formerly of St Thomas' Hospital and of surgical fame ('Romanes and Mitchiner' was one of the larger textbooks we were recommended to read in surgery), later Sir Philip, decided to come and inspect us one Wednesday afternoon. It was arranged that the entire unit would fall in on the sloping road between the Medical School and the chemistry building of King's College and that we would then march past on Queen Victoria Road between the Medical School and the RVI, with a saluting base in the central bay of the Medical School. It was proposed that the unit would then go into the Medical School to listen to the General's lecture. The officers decided that Headquarters Company would turn into the front entrance but that, to avoid congestion, A Company would march beyond the Medical School and would turn left so as to enter through a rear entrance, while B Company would go in through the front and C Company again through the back. Unfortunately none of the senior NCOs had been told of the plan. In fact the march-past went smoothly and must have looked reasonably impressive with everyone, so far as one could see, marching efficiently and in step. Headquarters Company, led by the Commanding Officer followed by Captain Finlay, turned into the main entrance without difficulty, but then as A Company approached, Sergeant Pincius Roberts, a third-year student, showed his initiative by giving the order 'left wheel' from the rear of the company which smartly turned into the front entrance; blissfully unaware of this event, Captain Howard Tonge went marching on by himself to the great amusement of the visitors who were waiting to enter the RVI. Much was later said about this CMFU (complete military foul-up, to be distinguished from the less serious SNAFU or semi-non-adjustable foul-up).

In the event, the lecture by General Mitchiner was hilarious, Rabelaisian and utterly memorable. Some of his comments could not be quoted in a respectable publication but nevertheless we all remembered his stentorian comment to the effect that the job of a Regimental Medical Officer was not to go buggering about the battle-field in the hope that he would gain the posthumous award of a Victoria Cross, because if he did and he went puffing it about on his chest (we all recognized the *non sequitur* in that remark) he would have the pleasure of knowing that it was over the dead and mangled bodies of 999 of his comrades—'I've said it before and I'll say it again, the place of a Regimental Medical Officer is in his Regimental aid post'. It was, of course, that same General Mitchiner who in a crowded war-time train, sitting in a first class compartment, spied from behind his newspaper a young second lieutenant peering into the comparment and enquiring whether all the seats were taken, clearly noticing that one was occupied by an elderly lady and that on the seat next to her was a Pekinese dog. The lady in question said 'Of course, young man, all the seats are taken; Fifi is on the next seat, can't you see?'. Down came the newspaper in the opposite corner, revealing the maroon tabs of a Major-General who said 'Young man, throw the bitch out into the corridor, and that's an order', whereupon the young man picked up the dog, put it out in the corridor and sat down. After a pause, the paper again descended; 'Young man, you made a horrible mistake—wrong bitch!' Many other tales, of course, are told about 'Mitch' who became a legend in the Corps and in his own hospital, and I was greatly privileged to have been invited to give the Mitchiner Lecture at the Royal Army Medical College in November 1990.

The camp at Belsay was also notable for another memorable event. A group of us were out on an early morning route march and were returning to camp for breakfast along a road which ran very close to the officers' lines and officers' latrines, protected, of course, by standard army canvas. As we approached the camp the intrepid Sergeant Henry Robson saw to his right the Commanding Officer standing behind a canvas screen and, to the CO's discomfiture, gave a stentorian 'Eyes right'. The reaction of the Dean was unrecordable but nevertheless he returned the salute, clearly demonstrating his ambidexterity. The CO's comments were equally fruity when the Commanding Officer of one of the other field ambulances of 15th Scottish Division paid a morning call without receiving the expected courtesy of having the guard turned out; the student corporal on guard duty argued cogently that the visiting dignitary did not look as if he wished to have the guard turned out!

Many other aspects of STC duty were also memorable in retrospect. In my second year Geoff Mellor and I, who by then were both corporals, were sent to a hygiene course at the Army School of Hygiene at Mytchett in Hampshire where, exceptionally, we were given the privilege of living in the Sergeants' Mess despite having only two stripes and where we saw for the first time that extraordinary collection of demonstration field ablutions and latrines with which every medical officer became all too familiar during army service or subsequent service in the Territorial Army. But that course, too, lives in the memory if only because I still remember all the details of how to sterilize one's own personal water supply and of how to avoid schistosomiasis, while the outstandingly informative and entertaining lectures of Major McKenny Hughes, an entomologist from the British Museum, on mosquitoes and other insects were quite brilliant.

By the time we were in our third year, Geoff Mellor, Rex Belas and I and a number of others had been promoted to be sergeants, while Bill Ross had become our Company Sergeant-Major. We continued to enjoy our part-time military training which was regularly enlivened by the tall army tales of Sergeant-Major Harry Rowe, the senior janitor of the Medical School, and his colleague Sergeant Stan Tannatt, a former Guards sergeant who had transferred to the RAMC during the war and who had been posted to us as permanent staff instructor. In our third year I and a number of others decided to accept the opportunity of spending two weeks working on the wards of the York Military Hospital instead of going to annual camp, in order to obtain some direct experience of working alongside regular RAMC soldiers. My memory of those two weeks is curiously vague, though I remember one specific outing which taught me a hard lesson. As a good Methodist I was teetotal when I went to Medical School and did not taste any alcohol for about 18 months. I believe that it was at New Year 1942 when I paid a short visit to my aunt and uncle at Wylam that I was invited to a party at the home of Dr Pallett, whose son Bruce had become a good friend. During the party I was offered a drink and, like a good Methodist, asked for ginger wine; home-made non-alcoholic ginger wine had invariably been the Christmas and New Year drink in the Walton household. In fact I had one glass and then another, and then another, and started to feel distinctly elated. When I examined the bottle and found that this was Stone's ginger wine, not less than 20% proof spirit, I thought the ground would open and swallow me up, but nothing happened; afterwards I did tentatively have an occasional drink in the Union bar or elsewhere with my friends. But York is memorable because on one evening (having fallen even further) we went out to a local pub when duty was done and each of the four of us bought a round of pints of best Scotch Ale. After the four pints we walked back (in my case a little unsteadily) to our billet and in bed that evening for the first time ever I experienced a curious sensation of levitation and a feeling as if the ceiling were coming down to meet me. Even though I may occasionally have had a similar experience since and even though I imagine that my tolerance for alcohol may have increased somewhat with the years and with increasing girth, I learned that night that that particular consequence of inebriation was something to avoid.

As we became progressively more senior and as the demands of our clinical training escalated, so the Corps began to play less and less a role in our lives and by the time the final year came we were excused further part-time military service. After the horrors of the second MB, the next term spent in pharmacology and materia medica seemed a minimal commitment by contrast, though one could hardly regard as exciting the lectures on materia medica from Doswell Foggin who painstakingly plodded through the pages of the British Pharmacopoeia and said, for example, 'We now come to iron wire; no-one wants to eat that, so there's another five pages of the BP'. By this time, of course, we were all eagerly anticipating clinical training from which we had been studiously excluded until the first two years were over. The examination in pharmacology seemed a minor affair in comparison with what had gone before, but I obtained a distinction, as did Bill Ross and Martin Menczer. As the day approached when we would become dressers or clinical clerks in medicine or surgery, there was tremendous competition about appointments to individual firms, a problem which was finalized in a lordly manner by Percy Watson who combined the functions of Clinical Sub-Dean, secretary and students' guide and friend all into one from his poky office in the RVI.

I was fortunate enough to begin my surgical clerking with Mr (subsequently Professor) Norman Hodgson who, though not an outstanding surgeon, was an excellent if didactic teacher and whose love of medical students was legendary. Again and again he taught us the cardinal signs of inflammation and the characteristics one must know of every lump. I shall know to my dying day that one needs to know its situation, size, shape, consistency, surface, edge, relation to surrounding parts and condition of surrounding lymphatics. And I shall never forget the day on his firm when, after he had been examining an elderly gentleman with piles in the knee-elbow position, he took off his glove and handed it to me. I thought he wanted me to return the glove to Sister and I was about to do so when he said 'Walton, come here, what did Elisha do with Elijah's mantle?'. I said 'I don't know, sir'. He said 'Go and look it up'. I went to the library and found that Elisha took Elijah's mantle and donned it and therewith worked a miracle; I still don't quite see the connection. I think that he wanted me to examine the patient after him. Another vivid memory is of assisting the quietly spoken, gentlemanly and ever kindly John Brumwell in his bougie clinic (bougies, usually of metal, were used to dilate urethral strictures which usually, but not invariably, had resulted from previous gonorrhoeal infection). Many elderly gentlemen came along weekly or fortnightly to be dilated and we became quite skilled at passing these fearsome instruments. On one occasion George J..., a student in the year above, seeming to be about to pass a bougie, was asked by 'Daddy' Brumwell why he was holding it in a towel—'Because it's too hot to hold in my hand' was the riposte.

As we were undergoing our clinical training, often spending nights on reception and sometimes in the accident room, we were also learning pathology and microbiology. Pathology was never dull under the fiercely memorable eye of Professor Frederick Bernard Shaw who used to lock us into the lecture theatre at precisely one minute past the hour and then allowed his indefatigable chief technician, Albert, to unlock the door so that we would be released at one minute before the hour. The entrance and exit from the post-mortem room, too, were locked just after 9.00 and opened on the dot of 12.00 to make certain that the student audience was captive throughout. Goodness knows what the fire authorities of today would have thought of this; but his fierceness in his lectures, in his post-mortem teaching and in his so-called 'private hells' when he ranged widely over Egyptology, the history of medicine and pathology in such a way as to inspire his audience, concealed a gentleness and intrinsic sense of humour which occasionally shone through, as, when asked if he was any relation to *the* Bernard Shaw (his uncle) he said 'I *am* the Bernard Shaw'. He was ably supported not only by Ian Rannie and Rolfe Schade but also by Ginger Thompson who later moved to a chair of pathology in Cape Town and whose occasional exasperated response when receiving an incorrect answer to a question could easily be heard by everyone as the word 'preposterous' echoed round the PM room. At the same time, Ernest Dunlop lectured us on bacteriology, assisted by Alan Emslie-Smith who kept the bugs under strict control. The content of Ernest Dunlop's lectures was often splendid but they were delivered in such rounded and mellifluous phrases with so many qualifying clauses that one often lost the content while listening to the beauty of the English. Pathology, too, was greatly enlivened by that excellent book *Boyd's Pathology of Internal Diseases* upon which we all relied and which certainly is one of the best textbooks I have ever read. It, I am sure, enabled me yet again to pass the examinations in pathology and bacteriology with distinction at the end of the third year.

On the medical corridor there were, of course, many characters, not least dear Natty Armstrong who much later became Clinical Sub-Dean and who is still, as I write, eternally young and talking with authority about his favourite topic of inter-sex even into his mid-nineties. Sharing a female ward with him but each having a whole male ward (that anachronism had resulted from the financial sponsorship by the mining and ship-building unions, so that more beds were available for male than for female patients) was my own great mentor, Fred Nattrass, whose house physician, research fellow and friend I later became and to whom I shall refer later. His ward teaching was clear and logical, contrasting with the virtuosity and inspiration of James Spence whose lectures and classes in paediatrics were compelling, sometimes even electrifying. In obstetrics and gynaecology the dogmatism of Farquhar Murray, occasionally tinged with more than a note of crudity, stood in striking contrast to the flamboyant but memorable *obiter dicta* of Harvey Evers who later succeeded him in the chair and whose elegance of dress and behaviour was matched by the clarity and beautifully organized content of his lectures. As the verses for the House Concert in the RVI in 1947, penned by Peter Whittingham and others with music by him and by Roland Goodhead pointed out:

> 'My name is Harvey Evers,
> You may well recall my bow,
> In my Rolls Royce, my second choice,
> My suit from Savile Row.'

His nursing home, Fernwood in Jesmond, was known, of course, as 'The Golden Gates' and almost invariably he wore a bow tie; when he came to lecture to our year and found every man in his class wearing his tie in a bow, he was convulsed with laughter! But as we became more senior, for the first time it became possible for us to receive some of our teaching in the Newcastle General Hospital (NGH) as well as in the RVI, particularly in obstetrics and gynaecology; at the NGH Linton Snaith was also a most effective clinical teacher.

Midwifery clerking was especially memorable, first because we lived in a rather decrepit hut in the Princess Mary Maternity Hospital (PMMH) where there were so many holes in the plaster-board wall that it was an easy matter to pop an arm through the wall of the common room in order to drop carbide into the bath where an unsuspecting colleague was soaking. Secondly, it was challenging, even horrifying, to find on arrival at the Princess Mary in those war-time days that all anaesthetics for deliveries were given by students; nevertheless we quickly learned and even became skilled in anaesthetizing for forceps deliveries and Caesarian sections. There was also 'the district'. When a district call came in, two students would go by taxi to pick up the obstetrics bag on Jubilee Road and then, either by taxi or sometimes by bicycle, would go out together to carry out the domiciliary delivery. Usually a midwife was available to come along, but not invariably, and on more than one occasion one of a frightened pair of students in Byker would retire to the lavatory with

'Eden and Holland' (the standard textbook of obstetrics) before coming
out to offer whispered instructions to his partner. When anything went
wrong, we were supposed to call the resident surgical officer but
sometimes he was busy in theatre or occasionally could not be found.
On one well-remembered occasion it was too late to call him because one
student who had very long fingers had just carried out a vaginal
examination and had concluded that there would be a very long wait as
the patient was 'only one finger dilated'; to his horror a few minutes later
the baby's anus presented and he suddenly realized where his finger had
been; but even this breech delivery was successfully concluded, as was
another when the same student greatly impressed the mother by
informing her some time before the baby was born that the child would
be a boy as he was able to feel the genitalia. It was during my clinical
attachments to the PMMH and NGH in obstetrics that I first discovered
that I had dermatographia. Although I had been occasionally troubled
in childhood by urticaria and developed a mild atopic eczema in middle
age, I had never suffered from asthma or hay fever but discovered when
scrubbing up that if my skin was scratched with a blunt object it would
form a persistent wheal. When this was recognized by my friends, they
would sometimes scratch out an unmentionable word on my forearms
when I was due to do a delivery.

Our period of work at the Princess Mary was almost coming to a close
when VE night arrived. Cocktails, curiously manufactured by Stanley Way
in his laboratory, enlivened the party spirit. Of course it was absolutely
essential that we had a bonfire and wood was in rather short supply. The
owner of the broken-down and collapsing chicken hut in Jesmond, part
of which was collected by 'Black Jack D...' was, I suppose, justifiably irate
but eventually both he and the police saw the point and so too did the
magistrates who dismissed the case.

One outstanding feature of our medical course was the shortage of
qualified housemen in all the Newcastle hospitals due to the demands
of the armed services. At one time there were only six qualified housemen
in the RVI and all of the other house jobs were held by senior students,
though we were supported and supervised by Dr John Craig as a Resident
Medical Officer and by Mr Mac Stewart, a Resident Surgical Officer from
South Africa who was later succeeded by 'Taff' Evans. Practically all of
us had done at least three, and often as much as four or five months in
resident house appointments before taking the final examination. I worked
for four months in all as a student houseman in paediatrics under James
Spence and with Brenda Morrison and recall my growing confidence in
my ability to erect 'cut down' drips on babies, of which I had done some
10 before I qualified. But by comparison my expertise was somewhat
mundane when one listened to stories of students sewing up perforated
ulcers and removing appendices in Gateshead and elsewhere. While some

of this may have been 'line-shooting', there is no doubt that some such tales were true; as a year, we were thrust into a situation of increasing responsibility at a very early stage. I myself carried out a manual removal of placenta from a woman at the NGH who was suffering a major post-partum haemorrhage at a time when neither a midwife nor a qualified house officer or registrar was available, and I also cross-matched the blood and gave the blood transfusion. The experience we obtained at that time was clearly extraordinary; most of us were ready for it and most responded to the challenge under the supervision of the harrassed and overworked qualified housemen and resident medical and surgical officers.

But this superb clinical experience had certain disadvantages. I was a student houseman in the RVI with James Spence at the time of the professional examination in public health and medical jurisprudence and only had time to skim through my notes a couple of times and not even to open a textbook before the examination. Toxicology was then and still is something of a closed book, but the fates were kind and the only question on the paper relating to this topic was one on the general symptoms and signs of poisoning; little more than common sense was required in order to be able to devise a reasonably satisfactory answer. Yet again, to my absolute astonishment, I found that I came out of the examination with distinction in both subjects.

Once or twice before graduation and during the war there was great excitement when troop trains brought wounded from France to Newcastle and wards were cleared for wounded soldiers. Early in the war Grant and Bywaters had brought their MRC Unit to Newcastle to study air-raid casualties and defined the clinical characteristics of the crush syndrome with myoglobinuria due to extensive muscle damage; some early trials with penicillin were carried out in soldiers with infected wounds and I also well remember Frank Robertson's subsequent extensive MRC trial in which the value of penicillin in the treatment of subacute bacterial endocarditis was clearly established.

But throughout this period and despite occasional sojourns for days, weeks or even months as a resident in one of the Newcastle hospitals, our problems relating to digs escalated. Sadly, our delightful hosts in Grosvenor Road gave us notice because of the increasing problems being faced by the owner, a very pleasant haemophiliac schoolmaster whose wife found it increasingly difficult to cope with his problems and with student lodgers. We did, however, part on excellent terms. But good lodgings were exceptionally difficult to come by and eventually I, with Rex and Donald, sought an appointment with the then Rector of King's College, the amiable and charming Lord Eustace Percy, and explained to him the problems that we as medical students in war-time were facing in identifying suitable accommodation. We had noted that the Stephenson

Hostel originally endowed in Eldon Place specifically for the use of medical students, had been taken over by army cadets seconded for periods of special training to the University, while of course appreciating the need for the University to help in such training. Eventually, after listening carefully and sympathetically to our problems, Lord Eustace was able to free some rooms in the principal men's hostel at Henderson Hall in Heaton, into which with a sigh of relief Donald, Rex and I moved with several other medical students including our good friends Basil Roebuck and Jim Oldfield. Henderson Hall was a happy haven for us all for the last 18 months or so of our course. While the food was of typical canteen standard and while we sometimes came into conflict on disciplinary issues with the Warden, Major Vernon Brown (who was a considerable martinet), our problems in relation to accommodation were now behind us and we were able to settle down without too much distraction to enjoy the rest of our time at medical school.

I suppose that student politics was much the same then as now; but we had an independent Medical Sub-Council of the Students' Representative Council (SRC) of King's College and every alternate year the President of King's College SRC was by statute a medic. Sometimes we engaged in conflict with the parent KCSRC over financial allocations to the medical student bodies and were ably supported by Mr Curry, registrar of the Medical School. Nevertheless, on the whole relationships were harmonious and I served first as Secretary of the Medical Sub-Council and then in my final year as its President. After much persuading, the Dean allocated to us a room in the Medical School which was subsequently occupied by student officials. We scoured Newcastle seeking second-hand desks and chairs at reasonable prices in order to provide the officers of the SRC, the Medical Society and the Athletic Union with a haven of quiet refuge in which they could conduct their representative activities. We also had one or two brushes with authority when Peter Dickinson as President and I as Secretary organized questionnaires on student health and on medical education in response to the Goodenough Report and produced detailed analyses of student opinion which we later presented to the Dean. I like to feel that this was one of the first steps towards the subsequent initiation of an effective and in some respects exemplary student health service in Newcastle; perhaps, too, those faltering reports may even have led eventually to reorganization of the curriculum. The Dean was far from pleased when in our reports we dared to include pronouncements on such matters as the appointment of full-time professors and the duties and responsibilities of deans. Nevertheless he agreed to establish for the first time a Staff/Student Committee which continued to meet reasonably amicably for many years afterwards and which was ultimately followed by student representation as of right on the Medical Faculty and on other committees.

I think I can also justifiably claim that ours was the year which initiated the Newcastle spearhead attack upon the then Communist-dominated British Medical Students' Association (BMSA). The President (David Pyke, subsequently to become Registrar of the Royal College of Physicians of London) and its Secretary, John Rich, were both at that time (in David Pyke's case, only briefly) Communists. One or two of our predecessors had been known to go to BMSA meetings in London as official delegates from Newcastle without actually attending the meetings, but in our last two years we mounted a filibuster at the Annual Meeting and captured two places on the National Executive; in my final year I became Treasurer. This was my earliest contact with the BMA, with which I was associated later in many different capacities. For many years Newcastle continued to play a prominent role in BMSA affairs and a year or two after us Denis Cook became the first Newcastle President. I was rather sad to learn in the 1970s that a student whom I interviewed and admitted to the Newcastle Medical School when I was Dean, Cynthia Brook, who also became President, presided over the dissolution of that organization which merged with other health students to become the Health Students' Group of the National Union of Students (NUS) thus effectively forfeiting the identity it had taken many years to establish. Cynthia was totally sincere in her wish that medical students should not be represented by a body which many others thought to be elitist, but her worthy objectives of harmonizing with other health students were never fulfilled. Now, however, through the Medical Students' Group of the BMA and the young National Association of Medical Students, it begins to look as though a phoenix is arising from the ashes.

Even though we worked pretty hard, not only for examinations but in hospital, with a degree of responsibility for patient care which can hardly ever have been equalled subsequently by medical students, and even in those war-time days of rationing and at times when the war seemed to be going badly with losses in the air and at sea, we somehow managed to find plenty of opportunities to enjoy ourselves. There were parties in the Union, in flats and boarding-houses and hostels throughout Jesmond and Heaton, with the usual hops and occasional formal dances at the Old Assembly Rooms (affectionately known as 'The Old Ass') or in the Sutherland Hall. I remember especially the night when a certain student, now a well-known surgeon, had to be pulled dripping from the static water tank behind the Union before being admitted as an emergency (? appendicitis) overnight to Ward 19 until his clothes dried, and the occasion when two of the largest rugger-playing students of the year became esconced on top of the rotating door in the entrance to the Medical School following a dance and refused to come down. Perhaps one remembers most of all Finals Night when a number of name plates belonging to consultant members of the staff in Jesmond were borrowed and when the mob were finally tracked down by police car to Henry Robson's home in Fenwick Terrace.

The police were extremely civil and were quickly pacified when the cause of the revelries was explained, but they were somewhat less impressed when, suitably reassured, they returned to their car to find that Alan Jenkins had let down the tyres.

Sport also played a very important part in the life of the School. Indeed medical student sport reached its zenith in war-time when the rugby team ran off on several occasions with the Northumberland Senior Cup, the cricket team was almost invincible in competition with other college and university sides, and even the soccer team put up a good showing in the Northern Alliance. I myself was always an enthusiastic, if not very competent, performer on the sports field, except possibly at cricket which was for many years my abiding passion and in which I occasionally achieved something worthwhile. I well remember the soccer trial for freshers in our first year when the Medicals freshers, with Geoff Mellor and me at full-back and Howard Scott at centre-half, defeated a team of King's freshers 9–0. Jimmy Oldfield's performance at right-half was so outstanding that he was immediately drafted into the senior soccer side. Subsequently I had a few games for the first team but was a regular for the second team and ultimately became secretary of the soccer club and captain of the seconds for two seasons. Unfortunately a relatively minor but troublesome injury to one foot prevented me from playing soccer throughout the whole of one season; but I was still able to run and enjoyed, as an alternative, playing hockey. We also played tennis occasionally at Henderson Hall or in Leazes Park, but cricket dominated my summer-time interest and I was a regular for the Medicals first team from my second year onwards. I shall never forget the freshers' cricket trial where I scored a few runs and the captain of cricket, Nigel Wood, himself an RGS boy, asked me for whom I had played; when I said Spennymoor Grammar School his attitude was a bit dismissive. Nevertheless I made the team as No. 11 choice and some two weeks later came the annual match against the staff. The staff turned up one man short and Nigel, who seemed extremely senior to a young fresher still tentatively feeling his way, said 'You, boy, go and play for the staff and our first reserve can come into the team'. The captain of the staff was Stanley Way, the gynaecologist, who asked me what I did; I said that I sometimes opened the batting, so he put me in to open the batting for the staff. After I had scored 25, with one six off Peter Dickinson's bowling, David Salkeld, the vice-captain, who was an outstanding all-rounder and played for Northumberland County, came up to me and said 'This crowd hasn't come to see you bat; they've come to watch the staff. The next ball I bowl you will be on your middle stump; miss it, or I'll see that you never play for Medicals again'. In retrospect I ought to have had the strength of my convictions, but I did deliberately get out (if not to the next ball) and often regretted doing so in later years. As time went by, however, relationships with the senior students and with those from different cricketing backgrounds steadily matured; indeed, among my close cricket-playing friends were Bert White, a useful all-rounder, and Alan Jenkins whom I remember scoring an immaculate century in the Grey Cup match against Durham Colleges. That was something I never achieved though I did have several scores in the thirties and forties and one fifty for Medicals and was invited to play a solitary game for the University against Edinburgh after being chosen as first reserve. The University side, with seven medical members, had celebrated rather too well the night before and our opening fast bowler (subsequently a distinguished surgeon) ran up to the wicket and fell flat on his face and was unable to deliver another ball.

Throughout our time in Medical School, socializing inevitably led to burgeoning relationships between some men and women in the year which ultimately resulted in several successful marriages. Indeed there were many attractive girls in our year. Perhaps the most striking was Jean Arkle, daughter of the senior ophthalmic surgeon to the RVI, Mr J. S. Arkle. She was admired by many and vigorously pursued by some of the men but their ardour was cooled when she became engaged to Mike Norman, a few years above us—but that relationship faded when he was in the Army and Jean ultimately married Peter Mitchell who became an obstetrician in Tynemouth. When we were living in Wingrove Road and Betty, in the WAAF, had a billet in the same street, she suggested one night that we should make up a party and that I should bring along two of my friends with two of hers on a blind date. The evening was uproarious. Geoff Mellor and the girl with whom he was paired got along well but their relationship soon foundered. However, Basil Poole and Corporal Chris Fisher were immediately attracted to one another and although their relationship was at times stormy, it lasted throughout medical school and they eventually married.

As for Betty and myself, things went along smoothly and even after she left the Air Force to return to Spennymoor to run the family business after her father's death, we met regularly, either in Newcastle or Spennymoor. Newcastle was possible for her since she had the full use of the family Ford V8 and a reasonable supply of petrol coupons for business purposes. We enjoyed some outings into the country, either on foot or on bicycles, sometimes went to the theatre (invariably in 'the Gods'), and she also continued to develop my musical education so that we began to attend occasional symphony concerts which continued in a somewhat desultory manner throughout the war in the Newcastle City Hall. With the full approval of our families, we became engaged on my 21st birthday and spent a short celebratory holiday together (in single rooms, of course) at the Dale Hotel in Allendale. As time went by, some of the frustrations consequent upon a long engagement began to surface and in 1944 when Derek Dodshon, who by then was in the Army and had been transferred from the Royal Artillery to the Durham Light Infantry, came back slightly wounded from D Day, matters came to a head. Unknown to me, Derek had always admired Betty and, at a time when I was working exceptionally hard for examinations and in hospital appointments, I had much less spare time. I later learned that Derek's pursuit of Betty in Spennymoor was relentless and eventually, without my being fully aware of all of the circumstances, she and I met in Newcastle and had a blazing row when she handed me back the emerald and diamond engagement ring for which I had scraped together some £18 some two years earlier. I tried to return the gold signet ring which she had given me at the time of our engagement but she refused to accept it; of course I stopped wearing it but later began to do so again and still do. I cannot deny that I was bitterly hurt and even the relationship between the Waltons and the Harrisons in Spennymoor became cool with unfortunate things being said on both sides. I still had my work and sporting interests; nevertheless I did try, on the rebound, to establish relationships with one or two nurses and on another occasion with one of the girls in our year, but none of these worked out or seemed even marginally rewarding.

In my spare moments and late at night, after working, I continued to read innumerable novels from pens as varied as those of Leslie Charteris (the 'Saint' novels), Dorothy L. Sayers, Russell Thorndike, Somerset Maugham, Francis Brett Young, Winifred Holtby, Hugh Walpole and many more. Indeed my thirst for literature, both light and serious, has always been insatiable and I cannot contemplate a long journey by train or by air without adequate reading material. By that time I had also become deeply interested in medical history and in Sir William Osler, whose biography by Cushing, as well as his personal writings, I had read with enormous enjoyment. I started a wall newspaper in the Medical School to try to interest my fellow students in medical history. I also wrote articles for the Students' Medical Gazette on Osler and on Sydenham. Professor Pybus, the retired Newcastle surgeon, was a noted bibliophile; a bachelor, he had applied virtually all of the substantial sums that he earned from his private practice to the purchase of books and accumulated a magnificent collection of incunabula and of other early medical books which now resides, as the Pybus Collection, in the Newcastle University Library. In some respects the collection challenges in its breadth and content the magnificent library of Osler himself, now in the McGill Library in Montreal. Pybus had some three or four first editions of Vesalius, a copy of one of Harvey's works with Harvey's own handwriting in it, and innumerable other treasures. Because of my growing interest in medical history, I had been introduced to him and on more than one occasion he invited me to go round to see his book collection; about a third of his books were on shelves but many of the remainder were piled on the floor in the rooms of his house where he lived in solitary splendour with only an ageing but tolerant housekeeper to care for his needs. Later I became a member of the 'Book Club' in Newcastle which subsequently was renamed the Pybus Club for the study of medical history. My reason for interjecting these comments is because one of my embryo relationships with Jessie, an attractive RVI nurse, foundered suddenly when at short notice I 'stood her up', choosing to accept an invitation from Pybus to see his books rather than to take her to the cinema.

Eventually it seems that Betty realized that she might have made a mistake and broke off her relationship with Derek; I soon recognized, too, that my feelings for her had in no sense diminished. Nevertheless I was so bruised that when she wrote to me suggesting a meeting, I wrote back saying that I could not see that it would serve any useful purpose. But without my knowledge she wrote to Donald and to Rex who invited her to Henderson Hall where eventually, after much persuasion, I agreed to see her. Once we had met I was again bowled over and after a few frosty moments and a good deal of frank talking, we soon took up again where we had left off.

It is extraordinary to recall how casual we often became in war-time about the hazards of enemy action. When I was due to go to London as a delegate to a three- or four-day meeting of the BMSA (I believe it was its annual conference in 1944) I asked Betty whether she would like to come with me so that we could have some evenings together in the theatre or at concerts; she readily agreed and so we stayed in the rather seedy Avondale Hotel in Bloomsbury where she had a room at the top of the hotel and I another at the other end of the building. I believe that each of us would have felt some comfort in being together but in those conventional days it was something we never contemplated or at least dared to suggest, even though we were there at a time when the attack on London by the V1 (buzz bombs) and the V2 rockets was continuing. Throughout the night one could hear, either when in bed or when sitting in the theatre, the intermittent crunch of explosions in different parts of the metropolis. Looking back, it is extraordinary that her mother seemed to feel no apprehension about allowing her to join me in London when fatalities were occurring from enemy attack every night. In the event, we saw some memorable performances of plays by Noel Coward and Terence Rattigan which I think nurtured our subsequent love and enjoyment of theatre; we particularly remembered the playing of Roland Culver.

As the medical course proceeded, we learned that we were to be allowed to qualify in a special war-time course six months shorter than the normal five-year curriculum and were told in good time that our final examination would take place in December 1945 instead of in the following June. Yet again this meant that much work was concentrated into a relatively short period, but no doubt our extensive clinical experience and responsibilities stood us in good stead. Soon it seemed that my love of clinical medicine enabled me to overtake in some academic respects others like Bill Ross and Martin Menczer who had excelled in the preclinical course. Although we all suffered serious apprehensions as finals came nearer about whether or not we would be able to recognize a presystolic murmur and while we all spent longer than the normal hours in the wards talking to and examining the many willing patients who were always glad to oblige 'the young doctors', in the event the final examination did not prove to be such a horrendous hurdle as some of us had anticipated.

It was, however, arduous enough with a series of written papers, a gap of about two weeks while these were marked and then a 'long case' and a series of 'short cases' in medicine, surgery and obstetrics and gynaecology, stretching out over almost a two-week period and followed by a series of vivas in each of the principal subjects. The papers, as I recall it, were pretty straight-forward and all went relatively smoothly in my clinical examinations in medicine and surgery. I was much more apprehensive about obstetrics and gynaecology, which were not my favourite subjects, but was greatly reassured after examining my two patients (one obstetric and one gynaecological), on meeting the houseman in the centre of the ward as I was waiting for the examiners; she whispered in my ear 'Did you get that transverse lie, that leucoplakia of the vulva and that cervical polyp?'. I had in fact identified these problems but nevertheless was greatly reassured to have that hint which enabled me to face the examiners with much greater confidence. When the time for the vivas came, paradoxically, obstetrics was easy because the examiners were somewhat unguarded in leaving the marks exposed in front of them on the table; I found that I had scored 80 in the papers and also in the clinical, so that when they asked a long series of questions about the physiology of the human reproductive cycle, it seemed as if they were simply going through the motions. But my assurance was somewhat blunted when an invigilator who shepherded us from one set of tables to another said 'Watch out for the surgeons, they're going to hammer you'. In the event, after a straightforward discussion about gallstones and their operative treatment when, fortunately, the relevant pages of 'Bailey and Love' seemed to flash by as memory engrams, I knew that all would be well when the external examiner, with a straight face, passed me a smooth kidney-shaped stone, clearly retrieved from some seaside beach, as indeed I told him.

Feeling rather limp, I met my friends in the School café knowing that we were faced with at least an hour-long wait on the ground floor of the Medical School while the examiners' meeting worked out the marks and made their decisions. The sense of fearful anticipation was invariably heightened by the policy, which has, I understand, continued virtually unchanged up to the present day, of having the names read out seriatim by the Registrar of the Medical School. Mr Curry was a dear man whose dedication to the interests of medical students was absolutely total. Nevertheless the spine tingled, the pulse rate increased and the palms became more and more moist as one heard him say, as he looked down on us from the stairs, 'University of Durham, Medical School, King's College, Final Examination for the Degrees of Bachelor of Medicine and Bachelor of Surgery. The following have satisfied the examiners'. But when he then said 'With first class honours and distinction in medicine, surgery and midwifery—John Nicholas Walton' my knees went weak and I almost collapsed. I was barely able to hear him read out the six names of those, including my friends Alan Jenkins and Geoff Mellor, who had received second class honours with distinction in one or two subjects, let alone the names of the others who had passed. Sadly there were some, well known in the year, who had achieved well academically in the past, including Denis Whitehouse, who failed the examination. In those days failure to identify a major cardiac murmur, for instance, meant failure in medicine, and failure in a single subject meant a fail in the entire examination. Denis ruefully admitted the next day that he had totally missed the diagnosis of myxoedema in his 'long case' in medicine. Curiously, a similar thing happened a year later to Alan Horler who subsequently became a most distinguished physician and eventually President of the Medical Defence Union. Many years later the structure and regulations of the final examination in medicine were modified so as to make it impossible for a single error to have a similar result; we also began to take account of the continuous assessment of students throughout their clinical years so that those who had consistently performed well would not fail the final examination as a result of one mistake when under considerable stress. The result came as an enormous comfort and relief to me, and was coupled, not unnaturally, with a great sense of pride.

As I have already mentioned, our celebrations that night went on into the small hours, after I had telephoned Betty in Spennymoor and arranged to meet her the following day. When the traditional photograph of the graduates was taken in front of the Medical School, they all insisted on placing me in the centre of the front row among the ladies. When our degrees were conferred in King's Hall a week or two later by the Chancellor, Lord Trevelyan (the great historian) I was deeply touched when the members of my year, despite being advised that applause was appropriate only when everyone had passed through, insisted on clapping vigorously when I shook the Chancellor's hand. No experience can ever quite compare with the time when one graduates in medicine, even though the euphoria which success engenders is often followed by a sense of anticlimax with reactive flattening of the affect for a few days before one begins to face up to the problems associated with clinical work and the acceptance of professional responsibility.

Having, as we all did, joined the BMA and the Medical Defence Union, we then looked forward to our first house appointments with only a brief break over Christmas and New Year before being due to begin work in the RVI in mid-January 1946. But so short of money was I that immediately after Christmas was over I arranged to do a three-week locum appointment in general practice for Dr Pallett of Wylam who had not had a holiday for some years and who welcomed the opportunity of a break—but of this more later.

I suppose that every medical school 'year' believes that it has a personality of its own, but I think I am justified in believing that the class of '45 was in some respects exceptional. Most of us came from the north of England and many decided to settle and to work in that area where our roots were. But others travelled widely and some settled overseas. We first came together again for a reunion 20 years after graduation when I organized a weekend celebration in Newcastle. This was such a huge success that since then we have met (those of us who have survived) at 25, 30, 35, 40 and 45 years and have all agreed that our final reunion will be the 50th in 1995 (*Deo volente*). Many friendships made during the course have lasted. Perhaps my closest friends were Donald Webster (who was my best man when I married in 1946 and whose best man I was when he married Betty Lawson of our class a few months later), Rex Belas from Middlesbrough and Basil Roebuck who lived on the floor below us at Henderson Hall. My friendship with Alan Jenkins, one of my cricketing buddies, burgeoned when he and I were the respective house officers of Fred Nattrass and Natty Armstrong in the RVI in 1946, and I was his best man later in that year when he married Dr Rita Hedley. Personality traits, I suppose, last throughout life. I confess that I have always had a somewhat tidy, obsessional mind, sometimes, according to my family, excessively well-organized in that I have often tried too rigidly to compartmentalize my life by setting aside specific periods for work and for organized leisure, with little flexibility. And they still tease me unmercifully about my wish to be early in order to catch trains and planes and often deliberately dawdle as they see signs that my inner tension and restlessness are escalating. Donald Webster, who ultimately became a psychiatrist, was in some respects equally obsessional though in a rather different way. When working in the evening at Henderson Hall we would often break off at about 10 o'clock to have tea in one or other of our rooms. My room was regularly used and so was that occupied by Rex, but on the rare occasions that we were invited into Donald's room he made us welcome by spreading newspaper over the bed and over the floor so that none of the detritus of our evening snack should sully the splendour of his domain. Basil Roebuck on the floor below, by contrast, was ethereal and dreamy in his approach and would often break off from work in order to play Rachmaninoff (with considerable skill) on the hall piano. His room was invariably untidy; when he went to bed he would leave a trail of clothing across the floor on the way from the toilet and bathroom. I suppose we were rather puerile but once when he entertained a girl friend in his room we wrote on a large placard and dangled it outside his window so that they could both read the words 'Stop it, Basil'! He was not amused. The diminutive Rex Belas, a rugger fly-half and competent swimmer whose father was a surgeon in Middlesbrough, was a man of ebullient and irrepressible humour who still pulls my leg unmercifully to this day. Rex went into general practice in Middlesbrough before deciding that, like Donald, he would wish to practise psychiatry; he then took up a series of junior hospital appointments with Donald at St Luke's Hospital. Then being, like myself, a keen part-time soldier (he was for some time RMO to a Territorial Green Howard battalion) he eventually decided to join the Army and after postings in Germany, Singapore and Hong Kong, rose to become Colonel Belas, Command Psychiatrist to Northern Command. As he lives now in retirement in Catterick Village, we often get together to share ribald reminiscences but above all to play very competitive games of golf (for £1.00 a time) where at the moment honours (and our bank balances) are reasonably even.

Sad to say, we lost all too many members of our year relatively early. One whom we hardly had time to get to know was killed in a hit-and-run air-raid on Tynemouth in 1941. Charlie Johnson died tragically in a Mosquito crash after graduation while serving in the RAF. Jimmy Arkless, while in the Army in Germany, suffered a minor injury in a game of football and insisted that another member of our year, Bert White, who was serving in the same unit, should give him an injection of anti-tetanus serum, as a result of which, to everyone's horror, Jimmy died of anaphylactic shock. Joyce Dixon died suddenly of subarachnoid haemorrhage shortly after qualification, and sadly one of our number committed suicide in the second year. Victor Franks (known by the soubriquet of Boris because of his alleged resemblance to Boris Karloff) was known to have mitral stenosis and survived only long enough to practise medicine for a year or two after qualification. Much later three members of the year died from cardiac infarctions and two from cancer, and each year we learn sadly of the loss of yet another valued colleague and friend.

Of the members who survive, most are now retired. Four in the United States have held chairs of paediatric pathology, public health (Fred Spencer), rheumatology and family medicine (Maurice Wood) respectively. Martin Menczer, who later changed his name to M. Menser Martin and who had a distinguished research career at Hammersmith, became a professor of paediatric endocrinology at Georgetown University in the United States, Denis Whitehouse worked in paediatrics at Johns Hopkins, and Basil Roebuck became a consultant psychiatrist in North Carolina. Maurice Moore became a consultant radiotherapist in Canada and Edwin Smith a consultant in the same specialty in Australia. Bill Ross went into radiotherapy almost immediately after graduation and eventually became the distinguished head of the Regional Radiotherapy Centre in Newcastle, from which appointment he was elected President of the Royal College of Radiologists; he continues to give distiguished service as the Secretary of the Conference of Royal Colleges and Faculties. Some 50 members of the year entered general practice in Great Britain, four-fifths of them in Northumberland, Durham and North Yorkshire. Of these, one may single out John Noble of Ashington who became prominent in BMA politics and was for a time Chairman of the Representative Body. Henry Robson became a lecturer in anatomy at Loughborough before entering general practice. Edwin Clarke was consultant neurologist at Hammersmith before relinquishing neurology for the full-time study of medical history (a series of notable books came from his pen), and two members of our year became osteopathic physicians—Phil Hogg in Newcastle and Jack Davidson in London. Some 15 members of the year held consultant posts in Great Britain, three in anaesthesia, two in ear, nose and throat surgery (including the notable Desmond Dawes), one in pathology (George Graham at Dryburn Hospital in Durham), two in psychiatry, one in general surgery and urology (Jimmy Oldfield at Middlesbrough), one in radiotherapy, one in radiology, one in venereology (Basil Schofield, at one time Chairman of the Society for the Study of Sexually Transmitted Diseases), one in ophthalmology (Douglas Thomson of Cheltenham), one in orthopaedic surgery (Peter Robson of Newcastle) and one in cardiology. Many of the men married girls in the same year who joined them in practice, but many of the other ladies in the year who married outside the profession did not practise for many years, if at all, though some few eventually returned to part-time work. Bill Wood became a notable figure in the pharmaceutical industry and was largely responsible for the development of the British polio vaccine before giving up that work to become a business tycoon in the City of London. My friend Alan Jenkins had an extraordinarily varied career. After being house physician to Natty Armstrong while I was HP to Nattrass, he decided to become house officer in neurosurgery with Fred Rowbotham at the Newcastle General Hospital before joining the Navy. At the time he was determined to train as a neurosurgeon but on returning from naval service, by which time he and Rita had a child, he discovered to his horror when taking up a demonstratorship in anatomy in order to work for his primary FRCS, that he would not be able to proceed to the final FRCS examination as he had not done a house officer post in general surgery. After much heart-searching, he and Rita decided that they could not contemplate that prospect and hence he entered general practice in Gateshead. After some years they decided to emigrate to Australia where in Maffra in Victoria he not only developed an outstanding general practice but also began to do some part-time neurosurgery. Eventually he returned to the UK on sabbatical leave to work again with Rowbotham and under John Hankinson's tutelage became skilled at stereotaxic surgery for the treatment of parkinsonism; he also wrote an excellent MS thesis on acoustic neuroma. On his return to Maffra, for some years he practised part-time stereotaxic surgery while continuing as a GP, before being chosen by Squibb as the Director of their pharmaceutical services in Australia; subsequently he became, before his retirement in Australia, Medical Director of Squibb USA.

I have often wondered how we compared with present-day medical students. We were probably about as hard-working (sporadically) and about as keen and as conscientious as the students of today. Perhaps war-time and the positions of responsibility into which so many of us were thrust as students made us mature a little earlier, but I doubt if this difference would stand statistical scrutiny. We probably needed to know a good deal more anatomy and physiology but very much less biochemistry, endocrinology, medicine, surgery and basic science in the broadest sense than a student needs to know today. We could be rebellious against authority when we thought it necessary and just as vociferous in the defence of students' rights or just as bawdy or boisterous or bibulous when the occasion arose. Today the men dress very differently but frankly I do not believe that the genus medical student has changed very much in the last 50 years.

CHAPTER 4

Hospital Houseman

The stress of finals and of the few days of celebration that followed now behind us, we all set about preparing for our 'house' appointments. I think that some of my erstwhile colleagues in the Department of Child Health had assumed that I would be applying for the Spence house job and Brenda Morrison, the formidable registrar, was very surprised to find that I did not do so, not having even put it down as one of my four choices. When she confronted me and asked my reasons, I had to admit that I had been told by my friend Denis Whitehouse, who had also done a short student house job in child health, that he had been promised one of the available jobs by Prof. Spence, and I thought that a mature Oxford graduate called Rolfe would get the other. In the event Denis unexpectedly failed the final examination, but since all applications for house appointments had had to be submitted earlier, I had put down as first choice the professorial house physician's appointment in medicine with Professor Nattrass at the Royal Victoria Infirmary (RVI) and was very glad that I did so as my experience in that post proved invaluable. Nattrass, though lacking the virtuosity and much of the charismatic aura which invariably surrounded James Spence, was a superb mentor, clinical teacher and supervisor.

However, before taking up the appointment in mid-January 1946, and feeling very impoverished despite some money that I had won through various prizes, I took the opportunity of working for three weeks as a locum for Dr W. B. Pallett in general practice in Wylam-on-Tyne. This was my first and only continuous period in general practice, an experience which I look back upon with very great pleasure. Dr Pallett was a single-handed GP who had not had a holiday with his wife during virtually the whole of the war. Bruce, his paraplegic son, had become a close friend of mine and we had also got to know well his sister, Doris, an actress who performed regularly at the Newcastle Playhouse and who occasionally played minor parts in films, including that of Highland Mary, allegedly Robbie Burns' true love, in a film about his life. Although my experience of emergency medicine and particularly of emergency paediatrics gained as a medical student probably stood me in good stead, I faced the prospect of single-handed general practice with some trepidation. In the event, so far as I can tell, there were no disasters during the weeks that I lived in the Pallett household. Their home was a solid, spacious, Victorian stone house in extensive grounds with stables and garaging. The surgery was, of course, a part of the house and I was astonished to find that while there was a desk and chair for the doctor, along with two chairs upon which the patient and a friend or relative could sit, nowhere in the surgery was there an examination couch or a treatment area. If one wished to examine a patient this could only be done by taking him or her through into the drawing room to examine them on the couch. There was, however, a well-stocked dispensary which I found pretty alarming, never having had the experience of dispensing drugs or of making up concoctions. Fortunately it was not difficult to count out tablets of sulphonamide or aspirin and there were many prepared containers (Winchester bottles) of cough mixtures and other panaceas which one simply poured into a medicine bottle and labelled as seemed appropriate. Fortunately, in view of my inexperience, I was not confronted with the vast range of drugs and medications now available and, equally fortunately, there was an excellent chemist's shop in the village where prescriptions could be dispensed if I felt in any way out of my depth. I was also concerned to discover the very limited equipment available in the surgery and in the doctor's Gladstone bag which I regularly took out on my rounds. Indeed it was only with great difficulty that I managed to locate a single rubber glove with which to carry out rectal or vaginal examinations, and hence I was compelled to buy more from the local chemist.

Morning and evening surgeries throughout the week seemed to pass uneventfully and I cannot recall any major crises, though one experience of having to shave a scalp in order to sew up some extensive and rather dirty scalp wounds resulting from a cycle accident greatly alarmed me; nevertheless healing took place by primary intention. Much more vivid in my memory are some of the house calls, including one made in Dr Pallett's reliable but ageing Wolseley motor car to an outlying farm north of Wylam which one had to approach by about a mile of unpaved farm road through several gates in the snow. That particular farmer showed all the classical signs of lobar pneumonia; it was a delight to see the way in which he responded to sulphonamides and we (I and the family) greeted the crisis with great relief, after which he made a rapid recovery. Equally memorable was the effort of having to cope with status asthmaticus in a council house in Throckley where ultimately there was a very satisfactory response to a slow injection of subcutaneous adrenaline which, when oral ephedrine had failed, was virtually the only effective remedy then available. Being a GP for that brief period also taught me a little about the problems which general practitioners often faced in trying to obtain a hospital bed for a patient. I became quite irate on the telephone in trying to persuade a recalcitrant surgical registrar at the RVI that I had a patient with severe acute appendicitis who needed urgent admission. The repetitive response of 'no beds' was heard even then. Only on one occasion, faced with a middle-aged miner who had become jaundiced and in whose case I was uncertain as to whether I was dealing with infective hepatitis or obstructive jaundice, did I have to resort to sending the patient unannounced to the RVI accident room, having failed to persuade a medical registrar of the need for a an emergency admission.

Perhaps my most abiding memories of my brief sojourn in general practice relate first to the realization that one rapidly became the trusted adviser and confidant of people in many different walks of life and of very varying personality. I could see very readily how a GP could become in many respects the hub of a village community. My experience then with so-called 'panel' patients and with those not covered by any form of insurance, who therefore had to be billed for all services, brought home to me how great was the need for a more comprehensive national health service available to the entire population. All too often one saw a child with a perforated appendix who had been dosed with castor oil for abdominal pain by a doting but impoverished mother because two-pennorth of that oil was cheaper than the doctor. But I was also greatly struck, even in a relatively affluent household, as Dr Pallett's was, by the primitive nature of the facilities and equipment then provided for medical practice. There was no way in which I could have done a red or white cell count or measured the haemoglobin even if I had wished, and no microscope was available to examine a specimen of urine. Certainly there was a small sterilizer for boiling up syringes and the few other instruments available for stitching up wounds, etc., but the absence of an examination couch and of finger stalls, etc., struck me as alarming. Even this was not quite so disturbing as was the practice in Newburn-on-Tyne where subsequently I did, some two to three years later, occasional evening surgeries for an elderly doctor. In his surgery there was a desk and a chair upon which the doctor sat but no seat was available for the patient who simply stood by the desk while describing his or her symptoms, being then offered a prescription and/or certificate before being dismissed. As a result of major advances in medicine and medical science, but more particularly through the growing recognition that general practice is a specialty in its own right, now justly requiring a formal period of vocational training before one can become a principal in the NHS, the quality and nature of general practice has improved out of all recognition in the last 45 years. Even in 1946 I could see what enormous rewards in a cognitive, emotional and intellectual sense could potentially be derived from general practice with close involvement in the life and work of a restricted community. It is not surprising that many of our most dedicated, able and intellectually gifted medical students now choose in the 1990s to enter general practice vocational training once fully registered. And I trust that the essential gate-keeper function of the GP in the British health care system will be preserved for all time. This system, whereby it is exceptional for a patient to consult a specialist without first consulting his or her GP, who then advises upon the specialty and specialist to whom the individual should be referred for further advice, is infinitely preferable to that followed in many parts of the United States and in some other parts of the world where patients consult specialists direct, often to their ultimate detriment. The recent growth in family medicine training programmes in the United States pays due testimony, I believe, to the recognition by teachers in that country that their health care system, and particularly their system of specialist reference, leaves much to be desired.

And so by the time I took up my house physician appointment with Professor Nattrass on Wards 9 and 15 at the RVI I felt that I had already acquired some experience in accepting clinical responsibility, but soon I began to recognize just how arduous, demanding and at times almost terrifying the life of a house officer could be in those days in a busy general hospital. The open wards of the RVI were typical Nightingale-style, with no more than two, rarely three, side rooms on each. Each ward had a total of 28 beds, but for historical reasons based upon the contributory system introduced by the local mining and shipbuilding communities, there were twice as many male as female wards, so that Ward 9 was an all-male medical ward and Ward 15 (the female ward) was shared between the two senior physicians, Professor Nattrass and Dr C. N. Armstrong, to whom Alan Jenkins became house physician. The unit was staffed by Professor Nattrass himself with Dr R. B. Thompson as first assistant, Dr Hewan Dewar, newly returned from the Forces, as registrar, and Dr Frank Robertson, who was then doing some research on the treatment of subacute bacterial endocarditis with penicillin, as a research fellow and supernumerary registrar. I, as house physician, was responsible for clerking all the 28 male and 14 female beds; in other words, I had to look after some 42 patients at the best of times, but since whenever we took emergencies they had to be accommodated in so-called 'centre beds' down the middle of the ward, I often had up to 60 patients for whom I was personally responsible at any one time. Emergency take or so-called 'receptions' in those days rotated around the four medical firms on a weekly basis so that one had three weeks during which patients were supposed to be admitted from the waiting list or from the out-patients for investigation, while in one week one was on call 24 hours a day for seven continuous days. As there was then no formal rota system, this meant that seven whole days were spent within the hospital and the wards, often with very little sleep, and during that period one literally never saw the outside world. Even in the three weeks between reception periods, if one wished to leave the hospital, this could only be done by arranging for the house physician on call to stand in, in case some emergency situation arose on one's ward. Fortunately Alan Jenkins and I developed an increasingly close friendship and an arrangement between us which did allow us from time to time to leave the hospital for brief periods, even if whole week-ends off were virtually unknown. Frequently, too, after a reception period it took several days to be able to 'clear' beds to receive 'cold admissions' and often in the few days before receptions one had to be sure of keeping beds vacant to receive the emergencies who were sure to come. Another problem was the standing arrangement whereby if a patient, say with diabetes, under the care of one firm, developed an emergency complication, then that patient had to be admitted not to the firm on reception but to the firm with which he or she was previously registered. Hence there was a continuous trickle of emergency admissions even during 'off reception' periods. In one record day I admitted to Wards 9 and 15 14 emergencies in the course of 24 hours, and in one never-to-be-forgotten week on reception 62 patients in all were admitted to my wards for the emergency care of a wide variety of illnesses.

The range of clinical experience obtained in those days was immense. Bronchopneumonia, asthma and other respiratory infections were common and I also saw occasional cases of lobar pneumonia; sulphonamide was the standard treatment as the shortage of penicillin even then meant that it was reserved for the most severe cases and especially for patients with staphylococcal endocarditis, septicaemia or other seriously life-threatening disorders. We often admitted patients with meningitis, usually meningococcal, pneumococcal or due to haemophilus, but with a sprinkling of cases of tuberculous meningitis which was then, of course, a universally fatal affliction. Professor Nattrass would instruct one, having confirmed the diagnosis of tuberculous meningitis by CSF examination, that the patient should be sedated heavily and confined to a side-ward until the disease reached its inevitably fatal termination. Poisoning, too, was not uncommon, although the agents employed were often very different from those seen nowadays. Some individuals used barbiturates and/or anti-convulsants but many more attempted suicide with the head in the coal gas oven and others even did so by swallowing corrosives such as bleach or powerful antiseptics like Lysol. The horrifying after-effects which one observed in the latter type of case included severe oesophageal strictures which often followed an unsuccessful suicidal attempt. I also learned quickly to recognize the remarkable alkalosis and cyanosis which resulted from a heavy aspirin overdose. Perhaps somewhat curiously in a traditional coal-mining and shipbuilding area where the massive consumption of Newcastle brown ale or other local brews was a traditional week-end occupation, I cannot remember seeing many of the neurological and other complications of alcoholism, but we did admit many patients with haematemesis and melaena from duodenal ulcer and occasional cases of cirrhosis of the liver with oesophageal varices. Rheumatic fever was also not uncommon (though more often on the children's than on the adult wards) and many patients came into hospital in cardiac failure from rheumatic heart disease.

Looking back, it is remarkable that we then had so little effective treatment for many of these disorders. For heart failure, digitalis in the form of digitalin or Nativelle's granules (not then digoxin) and mercurial diuretics were the standby, but sometimes when there was severe ascites as a complication, one was compelled to insert a drain into the peritoneal cavity. I became pretty skilled at draining pleural effusions, just as I also learned how to deal with a pressure pneumothorax in emphysematous patients. Lumbar puncture, too, became a regular procedure and although one could send the CSF sample to the laboratory for a cell count and for culture, it was the custom to examine the CSF in the side-room, to carry out a cell count using a Neubauer counter, to try to identify the nature of the cells present, and also on occasions to carry out a Gram stain in the hope of identifying the organism, especially at week-ends, since emergency laboratory services were rudimentary. Blood grouping, too, was carried out by the houseman, as was cross-matching of the blood obtained from the blood bank for transfusion; often I found myself transfusing a patient with a severe haematemesis and melaena in the middle of the night.

With respect to 'cold' admissions, of course, we saw a good deal of malignant disease, though the bronchogenic carcinoma epidemic had not yet begun to peak. I learned to recognize the cardinal features of intracranial tumours, but as soon as a patient suspected of having such a lesion was identified he or she was quickly transferred to the neurosurgical department under Mr Rowbotham at the Newcastle General Hospital. Subarachnoid haemorrhage and cerebral haemorrhage were, however, invariably treated conservatively as no angiographic facilities were then available. In view of the Prof's major interests, I also began to recognize some major neurological disorders and clearly recall a minor diagnostic triumph when I recognized a half-cape of dissociated analgesia in his living-in housemaid who had been thought by him for some years to be suffering from disseminated sclerosis. In fact she also had a craniovertebral anomaly and was shown to be suffering from syringomyelia, for which the treatment in those days was radiotherapy. Goodness knows in retrospect how it came to be thought that that was an effective treatment. One other curious feature was that it was generally believed in neurology that disseminated (now multiple) sclerosis could be harmed by lumbar puncture; hence I was strictly forbidden by the Prof. to carry out the procedure in any patient in whom that diagnosis was suspected. Myelography was never done at the RVI and I now shudder to think how many patients with undiagnosed spinal tumours there were in the North East carrying a diagnostic label of disseminated sclerosis, which was generally thought then to be by far the commonest cause of progressive spastic paraparesis at any age. Another disorder which we often saw was status epilepticus, as at that time the only anticonvulsants which were widely available were phenobarbitone and phenytoin. The standard treatment for status epilepticus was intramuscular paraldehyde which, despite the unpleasantness of its smell and of its route of administration, as the dosage had to be substantial, was often remarkably effective.

Not infrequently, too, we saw major complications of diabetes, not least diabetic coma which was invariably treated with intravenous saline and progressively increasing doses of insulin; no-one seemed to know much in those days about the importance of electrolyte imbalance in such cases. Hypoglycaemic coma was yet another common cause of admission but was usually rapidly controlled by intravenous glucose. Severe iron-deficiency anaemia was also common and I saw several classical cases of the Plummer-Vinson syndrome. On the other hand, we also identified many subjects with pernicious anaemia and subacute combined degeneration of the spinal cord, for whom the standard treatment then was regular injections of crude liver extract. Dr Charles Ungley, one of the other senior physicians at the RVI, was a world expert on pernicious anaemia and was subsequently much involved in work leading up to the identification and isolation of vitamin B_{12}; he was one of those primarily concerned in the clinical trials of treatment, in collaboration with Professor Latner of the Department of Clinical Biochemistry and Dr Lester Smith of Glaxo Laboratories. In those days, too, we often saw classical neurosyphilis, both tabes dorsalis and GPI, as well as occasional cases of taboparesis; to observe a tabetic crisis was a most distressing experience. Once these patients had been identified, then they were normally transferred to the Department of Venereal Diseases at the Newcastle General Hospital for treatment. Even then most were still treated with arsenical preparations, often with mercury and iodides, and occasional patients with GPI still received malaria treatment, since the efficacy of penicillin as the sole treatment of syphilis was still not fully accepted; but the situation was soon to change dramatically as it became apparent that that drug alone was by far the most effective remedy.

Perhaps one of the most difficult lessons of all for a young doctor to learn was how to organize one's time and how to survive and function effectively with the minimum of sleep, rest and relaxation. Although the medical students on the ward kept their own notes, it was the houseman's responsibility to write up the history and physical examination as well as the investigations carried out on all cases and also to write prescriptions in the record. All too often after a flood of admissions, I found myself writing up my notes at 2.00 or 3.00 a.m. Students helped with taking blood samples, with examing urine and stool specimens, but yet again the houseman was responsible for checking the findings. Accommodation in the residence was then strictly segregated according to the sexes, with the men's residence half way down the long main corridor of the RVI on the right. Our individual rooms were sparsely furnished with hospital-type metal bedsteads, a single wardrobe, dressing table, desk and chair, and a bathroom and toilet shared between five or six, while the female housemen lived in separate accommodation above the main entrance at Peacock Hall, so named because traditionally the wallpaper decoration of the entrance hall had been for many years adorned with peacocks. Although there was a telephone extension in each bedroom, it was a rule that the telephone should not be used to summon housemen after midnight and if emergencies arrived or developed, then a porter was dispatched to waken the houseman on call. Not infrequently, on a reception week one would get to bed at 1.00 a.m. or there-abouts, to be wakened for an emergency admission at 3.00; slipping back into bed at about 4.00 a.m., one would then be wakened yet again at 5.00 or 5.30, so that sleep was almost invariably savagely interrupted. There was indeed one occasion when I was told that after having been awakened three or four times during the night, I was eventually summoned to Ward 9 to see a patient with a haematemesis at about 5.30 a.m. Customarily one would simply pull a sweater over one's pyjamas and slippers and cover these with a white coat before going to the ward. Apparently I examined the patient, took blood for grouping and cross-matching, put up a blood transfusion and then went back to bed and had no recollection of having done so the next morning. I cannot now but be astonished at the fact that we all seemed to be able to cope so well with chronic sleep deprivation and fatigue which was at times overwhelming but were nevertheless capable of functioning, I believe, reasonably efficiently. However, the treatment which we had at our disposal and the procedures which were mandatory in clinical practice in those days were exceptionally limited compared with those now involved in complex modern medicine. I am in no doubt that the working hours of junior hospital doctors must be greatly reduced to avoid the appalling stress and fatigue to which we in our time were subjected and which many of them nowadays experience in a setting of infinitely more complicated and demanding clinical practice.

Even though our accommodation was relatively primitive, we had a reasonably comfortable common room in the residence and a well-appointed billiard room to which we could repair for a game of billiards or snooker when there was time available for relaxation. Food, though plain, was on the whole well cooked and ample, and it is interesting that a plentiful supply of free beer (as well as soft drinks) was traditionally provided in the housemen's dining-room. By and large, however, meals were an exceptionally hurried affair and, as dinner was traditionally served between 6.30 and 8.00 p.m., those house officers who were on reception or involved in long surgical lists had to make do with the cold meat and salad which was left out to be consumed when one had a spare moment. On the wards themselves there was always some food available if one was seriously pressed, and there was also the ubiquitous coffee invariably simmering on the stove. Hospital coffee was then a most curious drink, made by putting coffee grounds into a pan and covering them with milk, then allowing this to simmer throughout the day. As one invariably consumed three, four or more cups a day, it is not surprising that I and others, despite the pressure of work, gained a good deal of weight. There was also a traditional break during the Prof's morning ward round at which we all retreated with him and Sister into her room for the coffee ceremony. All of us in those days smoked cigarettes and the Prof. never carried any with him, so that as soon as one of us took out a cigarette case he would rise and a predatory hand would stretch forwards towards the case for his ritual morning cigarette, for which he always said 'Thank you very much'. Considering that we as housemen were paid the princely sum of £50.00 a year (19/2d. a week) plus keep, there were no doubt some who felt that the regular supply of cigarettes for one's chief was something of a financial burden, but he was so kindly, generous and considerate a man in other ways that everyone accepted his little habit with good humour.

The daytime routine then consisted of out-patient clinics with students present on two mornings a week, in which one assisted the Prof. by taking a history and examining a patient and then presenting the clinical findings to him so that he could make up his mind about the diagnosis and management before dictating a letter to a secretary in the next room. On the other three mornings there was a teaching ward round when either I as the houseman or one of the students presented the clinical features of each patient as we slowly worked out way around the wards. Afternoons were generally spent in admitting and examining ward patients, in note-taking and in carrying out investigations and sometimes in helping with the research projects of the first assistant or registrar. I became especially interested in Frank Robertson's trial of penicillin treatment for subacute bacterial endocarditis and also helped R. B. Thompson in some of his earlier work on leukaemia, so that I became quite experienced at obtaining and staining samples of blood and bone marrow and in recognizing primitive white cells. For a time, indeed, I considered the possibility of following him into haematology, but gradually found myself increasingly attracted by the demands and complexity of neurology, despite the fact that in those days we had very little in the way of effective treatment and were still indeed treating

Parkinson's disease, for example, with tincture of stramonium. But despite my growing interest in neurology and despite a suggestion from Prof. Nattrass that I might consider applying for the house officer post in neurosurgery with Rowbotham at the Newcastle General Hospital, paediatrics was still my first love. Having resolved the misunderstanding which had arisen between James Spence and myself at about the time of the final examination when I had thought that he might be preferring Denis Whitehouse to myself as a potential paediatrician, I applied for and was appointed to his house officer post and indeed found myself working on Wards 8 and 16 with Denis as my colleague as he had successfully passed the final examination at his second attempt in June. The pressure of emergency admissions went on continuously. Since all so-called medical and surgical paediatric cases came into the children's wards (with the exception of those requiring ENT surgery, which still went to the ENT department on Ward 3) these wards were continually 'on reception'. However, I was no longer faced with a full week of unremitting emergency duty since, as there were two of us (one primarily responsible for Ward 8 and the other for Ward 16 in rotation), we were at least able to work a kind of one-in-two rota, and as the registrar, Brenda Morrison, a woman of enormous energy and single-minded devotion to her work, was almost invariably there, responsibility could be shared more effectively.

In paediatrics I renewed my acquaintance with emergencies in neonates and young infants, became familiar yet again with the management of severe infantile gastroenteritis and respiratory infections, but also extended much further my knowledge of surgical emergencies such as intussusception and acute appendicitis. We also saw a great many children with burns and, under Brenda Morrison's tutelage (as she was doing some research on this topic and subsequently published a notable paper in Clinical Science) I learned how to estimate the loss of fluid and plasma in such cases and found that the formula which she herself had devised relating to fluid and protein replacement appeared to be remarkably successful. However, we were not able to devise any universally effective method of dealing with the toxic shock phenomenon which often occurred in such cases, nor did we have available any uniformly effective method for dressing the burns in order to prevent secondary infection. A brief experience with the so-called Bunyan bag method of continuous hypochlorite irrigation soon convinced us that this was not a viable method despite the enthusiasm engendered by Commander Bunyan, a dentist then studying for a degree in medicine who was resident in Newcastle and had been admitted as a medical student after leaving the Navy.

Perhaps my most abiding recollection of this period is of the extraordinary charisma and at times electrifying personality of James Spence, whose ward rounds, often attended by many visitors from elsewhere in the UK and from overseas, were universally exciting, despite some of his unusual ideas. When he received his wholly deserved knighthood, the *Lancet* said of him that his flow of ideas, always arresting and often strangely right, made him one of the most valuable members of our profession. I recall especially the tale which subsequently became legendary and was from time to time embroidered, of the occasion when a child with severe croup had been sent from the accident room to the ante-room of Ward 8 where, beside his agitated mother, he was sitting upright in obvious respiratory distress with a severe expiratory stridor while awaiting admission. Sister and Brenda Morrison both became alarmed lest we might inadvertently have brought into the ward a child with laryngeal diphtheria, as that condition was still occurring from time to time in the North East. In the midst of an agonized *sotto voce* discussion as to what might and should be done, James Spence, who happened to arrive at just that moment, walked imperiously into the day-room, glanced at the child and then slapped him heartily on the back, whereupon a pea shot out of his mouth and his breathing immediately became normal. Turning to mother without a flicker of an eyelid, Spence said 'Mother, your child will get well' and walked out again with slow and equally imperious gait. On yet another occasion I remember him having a consultation with Rowbotham over a child with what Spence had no doubt was a neurological disorder requiring surgical treatment. The exact details of the case are now obscure but in his characteristically languid voice Spence said 'Ah, good morning Rowbotham. I've just asked you to come along to see this case of (let us call it, after Groucho Marx) Hackenbush's syndrome'. Rowbotham said 'Well, Spence, that's very interesting, but how do you know this is Hackenbush's syndrome?', to which Spence riposted 'The diagnosis is obvious with these clinical features'; Rowbotham, however, persisted in saying 'Yes, Spence, but what makes you so certain?', to which, in an even more languid tone, Spence riposted 'When I see you going along the corridor, I say 'There goes Rowbotham'!'.

So many memories continue to crowd into consciousness and I think that my 12 months as a house physician in the RVI were amongst the most demanding but yet at the same time the most professionally fruitful and formative of my career. On one particular week-end when Brenda Morrison, unusually for her, took a day off to visit distant relatives, Denis Whitehouse was off duty and I was all alone virtually in charge of the ward when the eight-year-old son of a senior orthopaedic surgeon, who was at the time away from Newcastle, was admitted with obvious meningitis. Not unnaturally, his wife was anxious and asked that her son should be seen by the professor, but he could not be contacted by telephone. Hence I found myself doing the lumbar puncture, examining the CSF and staining it for bacteria. When it was impossible to discover any bacteria in a smear of a centrifuged deposit, I felt reasonably convinced that the diagnosis must therefore be one of meningococcal meningitis, particularly in view of the acuteness of the illness. I therefore gave sulphadiazine and penicillin and am glad to say that the boy made a speedy and uninterrupted recovery. Not every experience was as happy and I well recall the total feeling of impotence and indeed despair which I experienced when, despite setting up an emergency blood transfusion in the day-room, a child suffering bilateral femoral fractures in a road accident died before our eyes, solely as a result of massive loss of blood into the tissues of both thighs.

Brenda Morrison was, of course, an excellent teacher and mentor with an unrivalled experience of emergency paediatrics. Being single and totally devoted to her work, she very rarely left the premises and taught me a great deal. Nevertheless she herself had some emotional problems, in part related to the sense of guilt that she often expressed over the fact that her much-loved sister was a chronic invalid housed permanently in a ward in the Newcastle General Hospital. During the time that I was a house officer, Brenda on several occasions poured out her worries and anxieties to me late into the night. On one occasion my anxiety about her escalated to such an extent that I felt I had no alternative but to contact the professor; Sir James came in in the early morning to listen to the tale and counselled her superbly. I was not surprised to learn a year or two later that Brenda had forsaken paediatrics and had taken up psycho-analysis in which she later had considerable success.

It was, I believe, my clinical experience first in medicine with Fred Nattrass and later in paediatrics with James Spence, Brenda Morrison and others that taught me the vital importance of communication in the doctor/patient relationship. I learned how crucial it was, even when heavily pressed, to be able to talk to patients in simple, understandable language about the nature of their illnesses and to be able to communicate sensitively with their relatives. Talking with the recently bereaved is never easy and is a problem which all doctors find to be a tremendous challenge, but this was something that we were compelled to learn quickly, not only by example but also by experience. On the rare occasions that I saw Professor Nattrass talking to relatives of a patient who had died or who had to be told that a loved one was suffering from a progressive and incurable illness, I was greatly impressed by his calm and pragmatic approach which, despite the lack of emotional overtones, invariably seemed to have a calming and, paradoxically, even a reassuring effect. James Spence's approach was often more dramatic, but when faced with an emotional crisis he could easily discard the languid and even faintly bored tone of voice which all too often characterized his general comments, particularly in the latter years; he too could provide great comfort and support to parents even in the most distressing circumstances. His out-patient clinics were a joy and much of his experience in that setting was subsequently crystallized in the paper he wrote on the art of the consultation. Nowadays many would criticize his approach to the parents of a child with Down's syndrome in that he would never reveal the diagnosis at the outset unless asked directly whether the child was 'a mongol'. His belief was that the parents should slowly come to terms with the nature of the child's affliction and that the full truth of the situation should be slowly revealed over a series of consultations instead of at or shortly after birth. There was something totally compelling about his personality which shone through his consultations and seemed invariably to persuade the patients and students who were avid listeners and observers of the process that they were sitting in the presence of genuine greatness.

Three other people who impressed me greatly during the time I spent in paediatrics were first Donald Court, who had come to Newcastle as first assistant in the department, the gentle, scholarly and compassionate Fred Miller, and a visiting Greek paediatrician, Spyros Doxiadis, who subsequently became very eminent in his own country, becoming Professor of Paediatrics in Athens and later Minister of Health. Donald Court it was who first interested me in research; indeed while I was a student houseman I told him one day that I was very concerned over the fact that intravenous drips which one had erected with the greatest possible care (it was then customary to cut down on a foot vein in infants and to cannulate the vein in question in order to administer intravenous blood or fluid) tended to slow down and stop if not carefully observed every half hour or so. He suggested that I should set up a research project to investigate this phenomenon, which I did. I looked at the pressure of fluid in the chamber intervening between the drip bottle and the metal clip which controlled the rate of flow through the rubber tubing; I examined different flow rates and watched drips running into an empty container over several hours and on one occasion even overnight. I proved that even in the absence of any resistance from venous pressure, 'drips' did slow down and stop, presumably because of some inherent problem with the controlling clip and not due to any failure in technique. I eventually reported my findings in a paper which I wrote while a student but which was published in the *Lancet* shortly after I graduated. I shall always be grateful to Donald Court for the way in which he guided my faltering hand in this project and helped me to construct a reasonably scientific paper from my initially somewhat disorganized jottings.

Of course life in the house during that year was not all work and we did have some off-duty periods. Several memorable parties occurred, though we were rarely off duty long enough to indulge in cricket or organized soccer and only managed a very occasional week-end game of golf at Ponteland. Fresh air and exercise were therefore at a premium but high spirits invariably enlivened the occasional house parties. Many of us took part (first as students, later as housemen) with enthusiasm in the annual house concert at Christmas 1945 and 1946 when the music provided by Roland Goodhead and Peter Whittingham, with the support of Ken Pickworth, was quite outstanding. A number of acting talents previously dormant came to the surface and impressed both the staff (even those who were lampooned) and those patients who attended. Roland Goodhead was a consummate musician who subsequently went into general practice in Newcastle but also became a member of the musicians' union and wrote successful summer shows, many of which were produced at seaside resorts around the country. Peter Whittingham demonstrated equal pianistic virtuosity and he and Roland together were largely responsible for producing several successful King's College rag revues at the Palace Theatre in Newcastle, one of which featured the never-to-be-forgotten satirical song, 'Gay old city on the Tyne' (the initial adjective did not mean then what it does now). Peter Whittingham subsequently entered the Royal Air Force and had a distinguished career at the RAF Institute of Aviation Medicine; he also married Ann Nattrass, one of Fred Nattrass' daughters, who went into general practice in Farnborough.

High spirits resulted in several memorable episodes such as the occasion when a few members of the men's house stole up into the ladies' residence late one night, armed with screw-drivers, and removed all the lavatory seats. On another occasion an old and somewhat decrepit Austin 8 was driven down the half-mile long central corridor of the RVI. That corridor from the men's residence was indeed so lengthy that it was quite usual when setting out to do one's night round to approach the ward by bicycle. On one occasion I, for a dare, succeeded in leaving the residence on a bicycle, ascending the stairs and doing a circuit of Ward 16 in the Children's Department quietly at about 1.00 in the morning, returning to the residence without getting off the bicycle. On yet another occasion, golf balls were driven from the flat roof of the housemen's residence after a party in the general direction of King's College, and Lord Eustace Percy, the Rector, was somewhat surprised the next morning to find his room with two broken windows and with a couple of golf balls on the carpet. I believe that he suspected the direction from which they had come but, so far as I know, nothing was ever proved and no formal action was taken. After one party a well-known senior resident surgical officer who subsequently joined the honorary staff of the RVI and had a most distinguished surgical career, was called before the fierce House Governor, Dr A. W. Sanderson, after he had learned that fire hoses had been turned on in the housemen's residence late at night. The offender was told in no uncertain terms that never again would he receive an appointment of any kind in the Royal Victoria Infirmary. Another notable evening was when the other RSO, then known as 'Taff' Evans, an excellent surgeon with a severe stammer, who later had a distinguished career in cardio-thoracic surgery in South Wales, had passed his Fellowship. The celebrations were so riotous and he imbibed so excessively that eventually he was put to bed with two walking plasters and a (non-functioning) drip attached to one arm; his comment when he woke with a sore head the next morning was that he thought he had gone to bed with his boots on but then realized that he didn't have any boots. He it was, too, when being assisted by a member of our year, a house surgeon who did not have skilful fingers in the operating theatre, said 'Sister, boil me up a bloody gun; I want to shoot L ...'. Once, when he was trying without success to locate a surgical registrar by telephone, he said 'Get me Mr Edington. You can't find him? Then get me Mr Thompson. You can't find him either? Then send for Rutherford Morison! (the distinguished but long-dead Newcastle surgeon).

Throughout my year of residency I did manage to see Betty from time to time but only very rarely had the opportunity of going to Spennymoor for a day or a week-end. Much more often she drove up to Newcastle in the family V8, never during reception weeks but on other occasions perhaps once a week so that we could snatch an hour or two together and go out for a walk to get the limited exercise that was then possible. Despite the fact that we were pretty impoverished (though she was earning a reasonable salary from the family firm where she continued to work even after her brother returned from the Army and took over the business) I continued to be very short of money, though our pay as house officers during the second house job was increased from £50 to £100 a year—38/4d. a week. We had now decided that in view of my impending recruitment to the Forces at the end of my house officer year, we should certainly marry, even though we knew that a long period of separation lay ahead, particularly in view of the fact that Betty had reapplied for entry to the Royal Academy of Music and had been accepted to begin her course there in October 1946. It was then regarded as very unusual for a resident house officer to marry; indeed this was generally frowned upon by many senior consultants who felt that no young man should be diverted from his professional duties and training at such an early stage by marital responsibilities. Nevertheless, when in fear and trepidation I approached James Spence and told him that we planned, subject to his agreement, to marry at the end of August 1946 and then to take ten days' holiday to go on our honeymoon, he was extremely kind and understanding and I well recall him saying 'How sweet'.

And so, in in the midst of all my hectic medical life, we arranged to marry at Jesmond Methodist Church on 31 August 1946, to have our reception afterwards at the Gordon Hotel in Jesmond and then, through Betty's inspiration, to have a 10-day holiday on a package tour (the first to be arranged after the war) in Norway, sailing from the Tyne on the SS Jupiter. She had noticed a tiny advertisement in the *Daily Telegraph* indicating that these holidays were beginning. I had carefully protected the £50 that I had won on the final examination (the Hare Phillipson Prize for achieving the best result in the examination) and was thus able to cover the cost of our honeymoon, since ten days in Norway, including transport from Newcastle and all meals in a charming hotel at Oystese on the Hardanger Fjord, cost £22 per person so that I had just a few pounds left over for spending money. All of our friends and relatives were extremely generous, but the range of presents then available in days of rationing was very limited, though I remember that my colleagues in the house at the RVI clubbed together to buy us a Pyrex dinner set. Most notable was Betty's brother Cliff's generosity to us since, on his return from the Army, he decided to buy a new car and allowed us to have his 1934 Morris 8 open tourer for £100 (it was worth much more); this was my parents' generous wedding present to us. Some of our friends gave us individual gifts which were, I think, far more expensive than they could reasonably have afforded, and yet others, including our wealthy 'uncle' from Wylam, was rather less generous than one might have expected, sending us a cheque for £10, while his eldest son, who later in the family firm of auctioneers and estate agents was exceptionally kind and helpful to us, met Betty one day in Bainbridges in Newcastle and said 'Oh, I've just bought your wedding present'. He handed to her with great ceremonial a leather-backed clothes-brush, needless to say of good quality, but not perhaps as lavish a gift as we might have anticipated from that quarter.

One major problem at that time was that clothing, like many other items, was still rationed. Betty borrowed her sister's wedding dress but we all had to club together to produce some coupons so that she could have one or two outfits in her 'trousseau'. Donald Webster was my best man and we hired morning suits from a company called City Stylish in New Bridge Street in Newcastle. I had no black shoes at the time and had to borrow some from Frank Hudson in the residence. In those days one privilege which housemen enjoyed in the RVI was that the porters used to clean our shoes which we left outside our rooms at night. I am told that when Betty and I knelt down at the communion rail in Jesmond Methodist Church during the wedding ceremony, which was attended by many of our family and friends, the number of Frank Hudson's room was clearly chalked on the soles. Fortunately, as some of my colleagues were kind enough to mention, the same number was not chalked on Betty's soles. The ceremony itself passed in something of a blur but the reception afterwards at the Gordon Hotel was a splendid occasion, even though, as my parents still adhered to their staunch and strict teetotalism, the toasts were drunk in orange juice.

One potential hitch had seemed likely to cast a blight on the day. Basil Roebuck had obtained house appointments at Darlington Memorial

Hospital as his parents lived there. He and I and Rex and Donald had had several discussions before the wedding and on one occasion, after the usual banter and leg-pulling which invariably went on between those of us who had lived together in Henderson Hall, Basil uncharacteristically took offence and telephoned to say that in the light of what we had had to say about him, he thought it would be inappropriate if he turned up at the wedding. In fact we had all arranged a couple of days' holiday before the event; Donald, Rex and I planned to meet at my parents' home in Spennymoor and then to travel up to Newcastle on the morning of the wedding to change in a room set aside at the Gordon Hotel. When we got to Spennymoor, because we were so distressed about Basil's decision, my mother insisted that we should drive to Darlington to see him and to persuade him to change his mind; in the end he relented and spent the night with us in Spennymoor so that we four were able to drive to Newcastle the following morning. One of Betty's bridesmaids, Lil Ashton, an old school-friend of hers (my sister Mary was the other), also travelled up that morning to join her and the proceedings went without a hitch although Clifford was rather distressed that we had not found time to clean the car which he had so kindly made available to us. After the reception, when we were driven off by Rex to the ship at Tyne Commission Quay, with tin cans, confetti and festooned streamers all around us, I realized for the first time just how dirty the car had become, but this did not detract from the pleasure and excitement of the occasion. Cleaning cars seemed in those days to have, for a busy houseman, very low priority.

One problem which I faced in relation to the honeymoon was the lack of any respectable clothing in which to go away. I had hardly noticed the fact (or perhaps I ignored it) that during my houseman year and particularly while working in paediatrics, I gained weight steadily and became frankly obese. This was not unrelated to the fact that we drank a great deal of milky coffee and ate well in the residence, but in addition every night in the children's ward the night nurses made ice-cream in the fridge from baby food such as Ostermilk and Trufood. It is horrifying to consider just how much cholesterol I must have consumed; by the time we were due to go away on our honeymoon the only sports coat which I had simply would not meet, and as there were no coupons left in the family for me to buy any additional clothing, I also had a little difficulty in getting into such trousers as I had which were in reasonable condition. Nevertheless, the honeymoon was a delight and the sea on leaving the Tyne was pretty calm. We ate an excellent evening meal on the boat but afterwards, as Betty was concerned about possible seasickness, I gave her a tablet of hyoscine hydrobromide, which was then the recommended prophylactic, with the result that almost immediately after dinner when we retired to our cabin she went fast asleep.

Another abiding memory of the sea voyage was the food, the like of which we had never seen in wartime. Fish cooked in butter, abundant eggs, meat and fresh fruit, including bananas, were available, and of course the Norwegian breakfasts with a selection of cheeses, cold meats, pickles and various salads were extraordinary; we ate superbly. We called briefly at Stavanger where we explored the town for an hour or two and then sailed on to Bergen, a lovely city and an old Hanseatic port with extremely attractive buildings around the quayside and rising steeply on the hills around the harbour. It seemed to have suffered very few ravages as a result of the war; while staying there for one night we met Helen Mowinkle, an English girl from Spennymoor who had married a Norwegian shortly before the war and who told us something of the privations they had suffered during the German occupation. However, she added wryly that being liberated by the British paratroopers was not a totally unmixed blessing as there were frequent fights with the Norwegian men who tried to protect their womenfolk against the depredations of the liberating army. It was nevertheless remarkable how Norway seemed to have returned to normal in just one year after hostilities ended.

Next day we drove by bus through the mountains and along the fjords to Oystese, a charming and peaceful little village on the banks of the Hardanger Fford. The Oystese Hotel was a delightful hostelry with comfortable rooms, sitting on the edge of the fjord with its own private beach and a boat which we could borrow to row across to the islands. The weather in early September was variable but we had several superbly sunny days and explored the local countryside with the fruit orchards, the mountains, lakes and quiet roads; I cannot imagine a more idyllic setting for a honeymoon. The hotel was far from full, the propietor and his wife were charming and were continually persuading Betty to sit down at the piano in the drawing-room after supper to play Grieg. Ever since we have remembered and enjoyed Grieg's piano music and particularly 'Wedding Day'. Trips to Ulvik and Alvik by bus added to the pleasure of a wonderful eight days and, like many North Easterners, we have always felt a very close affinity with Norway and its people. Indeed some 26 years later when I was invited to lecture at the new medical school in Tromso in northern Norway, we again took the boat from Newcastle to Bergen and hired a car so as to spend two or three days in Oystese reviving old memories; we even stayed in the room next to the one which we had had on our honeymoon and the hotel seemed very little different from what it had been in 1946. That particular visit was followed by a memorable meander up the coast by steamer to Tromso, pausing in the beautiful towns of Trondheim (with its superb Chopin museum), Aalesund, Bodo, and many more. I well recall Betty awakening me in our cabin at 4.30 one morning to point out through the porthole a rock adorned by a large globe indicating that we were crossing the Arctic Circle. She also had the privilege during that trip, when out with some of the wives of members of the Tromso Medical Faculty, of playing the organ in the splended Arctic Cathedral which looks down over that city.

No sooner, of course, was the honeymoon over than I was back into the throes of my houseman duties in paediatrics at the RVI and Betty was preparing to leave home to begin her course at the Royal Academy. But before doing so she figured in a series of celebrity concerts in Spennymoor Town Hall where she played some two-piano works with J. E. (Teddy) Cooper and also accompanied, among others, the soprano, Joan Hammond. Earlier that year she and her mother had decided to leave Spennymoor and move to Newcastle, and they bought an attractive bungalow, 'Morest', in Manor Avenue in Benton, into which they moved just six weeks before the wedding. Hence we were able to see each other much more often and there was a haven there to which I could retreat when off duty. Nevertheless, it was an enormous wrench when three weeks after being married we were parted and she left for London where she found, through friends in the Methodist Church, pleasant lodgings with the family Richards at 143 Woodwarde Road in Dulwich. Though the accommodation was comfortable and convenient for her in several respects, in that the family possessed a reasonable piano upon which she could practise, nevertheless, in view of rationing, home comforts were relatively few; food, though ample, was unexciting and had to be supplemented by twice-weekly visits to the British restaurant in Dulwich Village. And in the winter that followed, Betty told me how difficult it sometimes was to practise in the drawing-room when the only heating consisted of an open coal fire which, as she put it, was occasionally refreshed by spoonfuls of coal; her abiding memory that year was of the cold, particularly as the 1946–47 winter was one of the coldest in living memory.

Her discomfort was somewhat compounded when we discovered in January 1947 that she was pregnant, no doubt because we had been less prudent than we had intended when she came back to Newcastle for the Christmas vacation and when we were able to spend a few hours together in my off-duty periods. Though we were naturally delighted, this was something we had never intended as I knew that I was going into the Forces and she had intended to take the GRSM (Graduate of the Royal Schools of Music) examination after three years at the Academy, by which time we knew that my military service would probably have been completed. Slowly but surely, however, we all came to terms with the situation and Betty's mother was splendidly cheerful about it, even though she shared our disappointment that Betty would not be able to complete her course at the Academy as we had all hoped. Despite the nausea associated with the first few months of pregnancy, she made very good progress both with piano, under the tutelage of Reginald Paul, and with her singing under May Blythe. One or two minor public performances followed and after my house appointment ended at the end of January 1 was able to travel to London to stay with her for a few days in Dulwich, where I greatly enjoyed hearing her sing some solos at Barry Road Methodist Church and some duets with Marian Studholme, who at that time was a student at the Royal College of Music and who later had a prominent career with the Sadlers Wells and English National Opera Companies. I greatly enjoyed Betty's rendering of 'In Summer Time on Bredon' and her subsequent private recording of 'Softly Awakes My Heart' from 'Samson and Delilah' by Saint-Saens, and of a number of piano pieces including 'Le Petit Âne Blanc' by Jacques Ibert and of 'Mouvement Perpetuel' by Poulenc. That much-loved and scratched 78 recording is still in our possession, as is the later recording she made of 'Oh Rest in the Lord' from Mendelssohn's 'Elijah'.

Social activities in 'the house' were not totally confined to parties and high jinks, though, as already mentioned, we had little time for sport apart from a very occasional foray to the Ponteland Golf Course where I played once or twice with my father's old hickory-shafted clubs. When we were able to enjoy some brief relaxation, a few of us from the residence often went to Brough Park to watch the Newcastle speedway team and were even occasionally called upon to give first aid in the case of injury to the riders, among whom the Lloyd brothers, Sid Littlewood and Charlie Spinks, the Australian, were then prominent. In retrospect, I find it difficult to see what it was that interested us in speedway as our enthusiasm for that sport soon waned, but at the time it seemed to be an enjoyable relaxation. Betty, too, before going to the Academy used to enjoy it, but our pleasure was substantially blunted on one occasion when we came out after the meeting to find that the car, our little Morris 8 which had a simple, plain, flat ignition key, had been stolen. Fortunately it had been taken by a straight-forward joy-rider who abandoned it in Gateshead later that night and it was returned to me none the worse at the RVI the following day. Occasionally, too, we went to St James' Park to see Newcastle United, a team which I have supported keenly ever since, though usually from a substantial distance since football violence reared its head. James Spence himself was a great enthusiast and had played for the University in his student days. So successful was he as a soccer player that at one time Portsmouth Football Club tried to sign him on professional forms and he often said to me with a twinkle that he wondered what his career might have been if he had accepted that offer. On one occasion in the winter of 1946–7 he asked Betty and me to go with him to watch a Second Division game and we stood in the crowd opposite the main stand, swaying backwards and forwards with the movement of the 40,000 or so others who in those days customarily attended home matches. The crowd was singularly well behaved, especially since Newcastle defeated Newport County by the record score of 13-0 and Len Shackleton, recently signed from Sunderland, laid on a sparkling performance which James Spence remembered long afterwards and often referred to as a highlight. Less often we were able to spare an hour or two to go to the cinema (often the Haymarket, close to the RVI, where in the circle a limited number of double seats were available specifically, it was alleged, for young lovers). Very occasionally we ventured into 'the gods' at the Theatre Royal to see a play or occasionally an opera, and Betty continued to nurture my musical education by taking me to an occasional symphony concert at the City Hall. Even then the Hallé Orchestra and the London Symphony and Philharmonic Orchestras used to visit Newcastle, while many plays were tried out in Newcastle and other provincial cities before going to the West End, while at the Newcastle Playhouse in Jesmond Dene a repertory company was then flourishing and Dame Flora Robson sometimes performed there. Indeed there were four active theatres in Newcastle, with variety of better quality at the Empire and of much lower quality at the Palace at the foot of St Thomas' Street near to the RVI, where the student rag revues were regularly performed once a year. Slowly but surely I began to develop a taste for serious music and opera and much enjoyed hearing Betty playing the organ, as she often did for practice, in the City Hall.

Slowly, then, my 12 months as a houseman drew to a close and towards the end of my time in child health I received, as expected, my 'call-up papers' from the Army, confirming that I would be joining the RAMC in early 1947. Several of us went together to a medical examination at York Military Hospital where I recall being utterly horrified to discover that I weighed 15 st. 6 lb. fully dressed, though in other respects my examination was satisfactory. Even then it seems that the message failed to get through and, so far as I can tell, I made no effort to lose weight, so that the army uniform I had made at Downey's tailors in Grey Street in Newcastle was pretty capacious and my father's First World War Sam Browne belt was only just adequate to encircle my girth. Why it was that I made no attempt to diet at the time is now a mystery, but at least in the month or so after completing my house job and awaiting my military service I did manage to have a little relaxation and even to enjoy some sport, though this was heavily restricted by the fact that across the entire country in February and March 1947 the temperature rarely rose above freezing point and the streets, roads and fields were blanketed with snow. Our good friend Donald Webster had by then married his long-time friend and classmate, Betty Lawson, and had decided to make a career in psychiatry. Having been found medically unfit for military service because of a minor skin problem, Donald obtained a post at the Cherry Knowle

Mental Hospital at Ryhope, near Sunderland, and one evening when Betty was home from London we went to visit there, driving from Newcastle on roads which were icy and covered with packed frozen snow. On being compelled to brake while travelling through Low Fell, the little Morris 8 turned completely round twice in the road but fortunately without hitting another vehicle or any obstruction; afterwards I recall that with my pregnant wife by my side I drove with exceptional care. Yet another journey between Spennymoor and Newcastle stands out in my memory that winter because the frozen snow had become rutted and had broken up in places into deep pot-holes, to such an extent that the journey throughout was immensely slow and hazardous and, we had thought, likely to be very damaging to the springs and suspension of the little car, but it chugged on manfully and never let us down.

Finally, then, having received all my documentation and having provided myself with a service dress uniform, shirts and the other specified requirements, paid for from the modest but adequate uniform allowance available to new Army recruits, I was commanded to report to the RAMC depot and training wing at Church Crookham, Hants, to begin my military service, along with a number of my colleagues from the year, though some, like Rex Belas, had done only one house job and had joined the Army six months earlier. After spending a single night with Betty at the Richards' home in Dulwich on the way, I reported on the specified date to Crookham and set out to try to become a soldier.

CHAPTER 5

Military Service

I suppose that my training and experience in the Senior Training Corps (STC) made me much less apprehensive about the prospect of military service than I would have been without it. Indeed that powerful sense of guilt which I had felt in my early years as a medical student about not serving in the wartime Forces strongly reinforced the keen sense of anticipation with which I looked forward to joining the Army proper, despite my inevitable concern about the enforced continuing separation from my pregnant wife so soon after our marriage. Those of us called up in early 1947 were still given emergency commissions; National Service came some three years later and the wartime state of emergency had not yet been formally concluded. As virtually all of the newly-qualified doctors who were recruited into the RAMC in those days had had STC experience, we found it easier to understand and comply with military discipline and procedures than would otherwise have been the case. Nevertheless, the weather in early March 1947 removed some of the gilt from the gingerbread as the country was still blanketed in snow and ice. When we arrived at the RAMC Depot, then situated close to the village of Church Crookham in Hants (the Army School of Hygiene was then at Mytchett and the Depot moved there a few years later) we were each allocated a bed, small bedside locker and wardrobe in large, open Nissen huts, heated somewhat inadequately by central coke stoves with stove pipes passing through the roof in the traditional manner. The ablutions and toilets were even colder, but at least there was a reasonably plentiful supply of hot water in the washbasins and showers. The food was adequate and there was a comfortable officers' mess with billiard room and bar in which we could relax in the evenings when training was over.

Whereas most of us had purchased our service dress uniform, with brown boots and shoes, before arriving, we were all issued with battle dress, sets of webbing, including gaiters (which had to be 'blancoed' regularly), and black army boots with the usual metal studs on the soles. The hazards associated with drill on the barrack square in dangerously icy conditions caused us all some amusement as we slithered and slid to the great annoyance of the senior NCO permanent staff instructors whose language was at times as choice as that we remembered from our

DLI instructors in the STC. The difference, of course, was that since we were all officers, however 'green', they included a token (and at times grudging) note of respect; 'Pick up your bleeding feet' or 'Keep in bleeding step—sir' was heard all too often. Nevertheless, with regular drill, an occasional route march and early morning physical training in the gymnasium, I think we all gradually became much fitter than we had been when virtually confined to hospital and lacking exercise over many months. We also enjoyed numerous lectures from well-motivated and well-trained NCO instructors, as well as from RAMC officers, both senior and junior, on such issues as hygiene in the field, tropical medicine, the structure of the Army medical services, and the like. On one occasion we were even required to subject ourselves to the matrix test as a speedy test of intelligence. So far as I know, most of us performed adequately, though the exact results were suppressed; it nevertheless leaked out that one distinguished surgeon who had joined the Army rather later than most came out as being fit for the unarmed pioneers.

The Commanding Officer then of the Training Wing at the Depot was Lt Col W. J. Officer, RAMC, while the CO of the Depot as a whole was the almost legendary Brigadier Glyn Hughes, whom it was alleged, during the retreat to Dunkirk, found almost intact an infantry battalion which had lost most or all of its senior officers. It is said that he tore off his RAMC badges and insignia and took command of the combatant unit, which he led with outstanding bravery and competence over the next few days. We saw, however, comparatively little of him but were regularly lectured by Lt Col Officer whom I later came to know well and to respect when he had advanced to Major General and when I was serving in the Territorial Army. At the time, however, he did seem a little stuffy and, while the comment may have been made tongue in cheek, I recall especially a talk that he gave us on 'Being an officer and a gentleman' where he explained that we were all doctors and must, of course, serve the Army in that capacity but nevertheless must learn to behave as officers as well. His most memorable comment was that many young officers asked him how they should address their batmen; he suggested that one should address one's batman as one would address one's second footman, whereupon one of our number stood up and said 'May I ask a question, sir?'. 'Yes, my boy' was the response. 'Sir, I never speak to my second footman'. To the CO's credit, he, like the assembled company, burst into laughter.

During the month of preliminary training we visited the Army School of Hygiene at Mytchett where we saw yet again, as Geoff Mellor and I had done during our sojourn there when in the STC, that splendid display of field hygiene equipment, with the remarkable variety of latrines which every RAMC officer probably remembers better from his or her preliminary training than any other aspect of military life. From the administrative standpoint, we were taught a little about Army accounting procedures (but very little); most of what we learned concerned our own banking arrangements. I was surprised, and not a little distressed, to learn that as a lieutenant, while I would receive a salary far greater than that I had been paid as a houseman, I was not allowed to receive marriage allowance until I reached the age of 25. This struck many of us who were married as being a peculiar and archaic Army regulation; I understand it was rescinded a few years later. Apparently it was then thought that young officers should be discouraged from marrying until they were at least 25 years of age.

In the third week at Crookham, while undertaking early morning PT, we were all instructed to run backwards in the gymnasium as fast as we could; in doing so, I tripped over a mat which had been left on the gymnasium floor and landed heavily on my right arm. Immediately I felt pain and discomfort in the 'anatomical snuff-box' of the wrist and both I and Ramsay Horler, who was with me at the time, thought that I had probably fractured my scaphoid. I was sent to the Cambridge Military Hospital at Aldershot where I saw a Major (RAMC) orthopaedic specialist who took an X-ray which showed no fracture and diagnosed a sprained wrist; my wrist was strapped and I was sent back to duty, but I found stretcher-bearing exercises very painful over the course of the next few days. Towards the end of our month of preliminary training we were all gathered together to be told what our subsequent postings would be. Since Betty was expecting our first child, I had applied for a compassionate posting to the UK or to Germany, as had several of my colleagues. In characteristic Army fashion, we learned that all of the married men had been posted far afield (my posting was to South East Asia Command) while most of the single men were posted to the UK or to Germany. I well recall the comment in the letter I received from AMD1 which said that 'owing to the exigencies of the service' my request for compassionate posting could not be granted.

After a riotous farewell party, we all went home before taking up our respective postings. I was given 14 days embarkation leave and returned despondently to Newcastle to greet Betty and her mother and to stay with them in Manor Avenue as by this time Betty had reluctantly decided that because of her pregnancy she must abandon her course at the Royal Academy of Music. But my right wrist continued to be painful and slightly swollen. I knew, as I had been taught as a student, that sometimes a scaphoid fracture does not show up on the first X-ray. Hence as soon as I could, I went to the RVI and consulted Ian McIver (then an orthopaedic registrar, who subsequently became a consultant neuro-surgeon at the Newcastle General Hospital); he took a further X-ray which clearly demonstrated a crack across the centre of the scaphoid. The arm then went into plaster, but this in no way impaired our enjoyment of those two weeks of leave since spring had arrived at last and the snow and ice had disappeared. Hanging over us still was the cloud of my impending departure to South East Asia; after bidding Betty a tearful farewell I returned to Crookham, this time to a transit camp to await my transport overseas. However, the medical officer in charge took one look at my arm in plaster and concluded that I was not fit to go on the draft to SEAC; he produced a certificate to the effect that I should not travel to SEAC but would be fit to resume full duties in about 10 weeks. I therefore sat around for a few days in Crookham awaiting instructions, having telephoned Betty with the good news. There was very little to do, but I struck up a friendship with the officer who had the next bed to mine in camp, Lt Bernard Tomlinson, a pathologist from the Birmingham area who had also returned to the Depot to await an overseas posting. I was delighted several years later when Bernard was appointed Director of the Institute of Pathology at the Newcastle General Hospital, where he subsequently made an outstanding career in neuropathology and became a close friend and colleague, receiving the CBE for his work in neuropathology and as Chairman of the Medical Advisory Committee of the Newcastle Hospitals; later he moved on to become Chairman of the Northern Regional Health Authority and of the Joint Planning and Advisory Committee of the Department of Health as Sir Bernard.

My friend Ramsay Horler was also with us and there was one hilarious occasion when he and I took out a boat on the Basingstoke Canal on a lovely afternoon but each made the mistake of putting one leg in the boat as we cast off its moorings, leaving the other on the bank. Our legs slowly spread wider and wider apart as the boat drifted out towards the centre of the canal, with the result that we both returned to camp later very wet indeed. After a few days of rather desultory inactivity, I was suddenly called before the Adjutant who said to me cheerfully 'There's not much point in your hanging about here, is there? You may as well go home on unposted leave'. Eagerly I packed my kit, picked up my railway warrant and said goodbye to my friends (Ramsay Horler had just learned that he was shortly to leave for East Africa but Bernard Tomlinson was still uncertain as to where he would be going) and, having telephoned Betty to warn her of my impending arrival, set off home. I then enjoyed an idyllic 11 weeks in Newcastle with Betty on full pay, with no communications whatever from the Army. Paradoxically, it turned out that my fractured scaphoid was not as bad as had originally been thought; after another 10 days back in Newcastle the plaster came off; my wrist was quite painless and has indeed remained so ever since.

I cannot recall exactly what we did within those weeks, though I know that we indulged our interest in music and in the theatre, attending concerts and theatrical performances, that we took long walks (and occasional drives, despite petrol rationing) in the country, visited friends and were even able to hold a party at 'Morest' for some of our colleagues who were still in Newcastle, with Betty's mother's indulgent help and support. We also paid several visits to my parents and friends in Spennymoor. By this time Betty and her mother had decided that the old Morris 8 tourer had seen better days and so they traded it in and bought an Austin 8 saloon (BPY 871) which was more comfortable, particularly in cold weather (although car heaters were still virtually unknown). In that car the three of us set out early one day to visit Betty's sister, Joyce, and her husband, Colin, who were then living in Sheffield. Unfortunately the car, which had been running beautifully but which was six years old when they bought it, broke down at Bramham. The AA man discovered that a bevel on the crankshaft which, as it turned, drove the petrol pump, had worn; by the simple expedient of removing the gasket between the pump and the crankshaft casing, the car functioned quite well again and we completed the visit without any further untoward events.

We also found time to visit Bruce Pallett at Wylam; he now had a girl friend and we enjoyed some fine meals together at a farm run by a Mrs Murray near Heddon-on-the-Wall where one sat in splendid isolation in a wooden hut in the centre of a field, capable of seating only four or at the most six people around an old pine table. The food was carried across the field from the farm house but always arrived piping hot and was of outstanding quality. I did virtually nothing medical in those few weeks and simply enjoyed the lengthiest holiday that I have ever had before or since. The possibility of doing some writing or of thinking about a modest research project never crossed my mind; I suppose that I excused my indolence by the fact that I had no idea when I would be recalled to the colours! In mid-June 1947 the weather was at its brilliant best; one of the worst winters in living memory was followed by a stunningly beautiful hot summer, even in the North East, and I managed to fit in a few games of cricket with G. C. Slade's XI, a group of medics who had come together to play occasional friendly matches in the Newcastle area shortly after the end of the war. Geoff Slade was himself an outstanding cricketer who played for Medicals in wartime and for Northumberland County, and whom I once saw carve out a flawless century at the County Ground. I also managed a game or two for County Club second team on his introduction. George Mallen, the Secretary of the Northumberland County Cricket Club, was a most capable administrator, if a little inflexible in his attitude, though much admired and loved by those who played for the various Club teams. On one occasion, when we were having a net at County Club (this must have been considerably earlier, possibly when I was a houseman) a young officer appeared in Australian air force uniform and asked whether he could join in at the nets. George said of course that he could do so; when he saw him batting with great confidence and skill and then bowling at a very lively pace, to the discomfort of several of us, George went up to him and said 'You're a pretty useful performer, young man. Would you like to play for the second team on Saturday?', to which Keith Miller (for that is who he was) replied 'I'd like to, but I'm afraid I'm playing in the Victory Test at Lords'.

As that glorious summer meandered on, realization dawned that the Army must surely recall my existence before too long. I rarely dream but both Betty and I well remember that on waking one morning I told her that I had had a vivid dream to the effect that I would receive a telegram asking me to report in 24 hours to an airfield in Norfolk. Why an airfield and why Norfolk I cannot imagine, unless this was something to do with my wartime experience of working as a navvy at Tibenham. Remarkably enough, I did receive a telegram a week later, giving me 24 hours to report to the ADMS Embarkation at Southampton. As I had no idea of the significance of that particular appointment, we both of course assumed that I was again destined for an overseas posting. Hence, after more tearful farewells, recognizing that our baby was due some two months later (fortunately Betty was exceptionally fit throughout the latter months of her pregnancy) I set off by train and eventually reported, as ordered, at the old Southwestern Hotel in Southampton. After meeting the DADMS, Major McPhail, he took me in to meet the ADMS (Embarkation), Colonel 'Tossie' Thompson (late RAMC), a cheerful, rubicund figure, who explained that his office and staff were responsible for running the hospital ships and troopships of the British Army (at least from the Army standpoint, as all such vessels were staffed in a maritime sense by the Merchant Navy, whereas all of the administrative details relating to their military function were in the hands of the Army). He also explained that he was responsible for providing the medical administration at the UK ports from which these ships sailed and to which they returned. By that time Tilbury was about to close as a trooping port and Liverpool had already done so, and the only ports in the UK which still handled military traffic were Southampton in England and the Clyde ports and Leith (near Edinburgh) in Scotland. After a somewhat quizzical appraisal he then said 'You look as though you're a young man who can stand on his own feet and accept responsibility—I'm therefore going to send you as Embarkation Medical Officer (EMO), Scottish Ports, stationed in Glasgow, to replace Captain Charles Rolland' (who later became a physician in Carlisle and whom I came to know well) 'who's due for demobilization in two weeks. Here's your rail warrant to Glasgow via Newcastle; no doubt as the week-end is approaching, you'd like to stop off briefly at home before reporting to Movement Control Headquarters at Kirklee Camp, Great Western Road, Glasgow, on Monday or Tuesday next week, where you can arrange to take over from Captain Rolland'. There ensued yet another telephone call to Newcastle, greeted by Betty with a combination of astonishment and delight; after a further bout of frenzied repacking, I and my heavy baggage embarked yet again on the train via London to Newcastle, where we enjoyed an emotional week-end together before, very early on Monday, I set off for Glasgow, arriving at Queen Street on a cold, grey, misty day, one of the very few to blight that glorious summer. Glasgow in those days, on a drizzly, overcast morning, was not a particularly appealing sight; but it was a city which, as I came to know it, I began to enjoy and for whose people I developed an increasingly high respect and affection as they often reminded me of the Tynesiders and natives of Durham county among whom I had been brought up.

On reporting to the Major in charge of Movement Control, I found that no Army accommodation was available and that I would be living out on the 'lodging list'. A room had been found as a temporary arrangement in the Lukyns Hotel on Winton Drive, a small and beautifully clean private hotel where the proprietress, Mrs Clark, soon began to look on me rather maternally and allowed me the indefinite use of a small but comfortable attic room at an inclusive rate (including breakfast and dinner) well within the range I could afford on my Army lodging allowance. And since by September 1947, when my birthday came, I was at last entitled to receive marriage allowance, for the first time I was beginning to feel reasonably secure financially and was able to transfer an adequate sum monthly to Betty's account in Newcastle to contribute towards her living and other expenses. Nevertheless, we both realized the extent to which we were dependent upon her mother's generosity. It seems curious now that the thought that she might come to join me in Glasgow in a rented flat never seemed to occur to us, partly, I believe, because her mother was enthusiastic about the prospect of having Betty at home with the baby for as long as I was in the Army. And this decision must also have been facilitated by the fact that after a week or two in Glasgow I soon realized that the pressure of work was far from great and that it would be possible to return to Newcastle for the week-end every two or three weeks. Indeed I also quickly recognized that with a leave entitlement of 21 days per year in addition to public holidays (my unposted leave did not count towards that allotment which, as the Army repeatedly told us, was a privilege and not a right) I would have no difficulty in taking 7–10 days leave in Newcastle at the time when the baby was due, as indeed I did.

Charles Rolland was extremely helpful and produced a very comprehensive briefing document about the duties of an EMO to Scottish ports. In the hutted camp at Kirklee on Great Western Road (long ago replaced by a block of flats) were the staff of Movement Control (Royal Engineers) and my own staff consisting of a staff sergeant, two privates (RAMC) and two privates (RASC) who were drivers. Staff Sergeant Ball, whom I came to admire greatly, was a most effective chief clerk and general factotum who, after the initial tutelage from Charles Rolland, guided me through the mysteries of part 1 and part 2 orders, the keeping of an imprest account and the handling of the manifold Army documentation with which, as the head of a small sub-unit, I continually had to deal. I was most impressed to find that on my desk in my spacious office there was one ordinary telephone with an outside line but also two other phones, one a direct line to the ADMS in Southampton and yet another a direct line to the War Office. I also had a substantial safe in which I kept cash, regularly withdrawn from the bank against my imprest account in order to pay the men; here too I kept my precious railway and other warrants.

My duties as EMO involved obtaining the standard 'scale' of medical stores and equipment from Cowglen Military Hospital with which to equip the medical facilities of the troopships which berthed in the Clyde or the few that came to Leith. We were also required to collect the 'scale', carefully accounted for, from incoming ships and to check this against the documentation which the Senior Medical Officer (SMO) of the ship and his staff provided for us, to make certain that there were no discrepancies. In addition, on receipt of appropriate signals we were required to disembark in appropriate ambulances or other vehicles (obtained from the local RASC) invalids or the injured or wounded and to see that they were appropriately received at Cowglen or at some other military hospital which offered the specialized facilities that they required. I quickly learnt the documentation and the procedures and the work was not arduous as the traffic was no longer heavy. We had one three-ton truck available for transporting stores and a utility van (a standard Army 'tilly') in which I travelled with my driver but which often, after obtaining appropriate permission, I drove myself, particularly on the longer journeys to Leith or elsewhere. Staff Sergeant Ball also had a 500 cc Norton motor cycle of which he was inordinately proud and one day in camp he proudly invited me to 'try her out'. I had never ridden anything more powerful than a 250 cc machine owned by Rex Belas, and that only briefly, but felt that if I refused I might 'lose face'. But as I mounted the beast tentatively, let in the clutch and touched the throttle, she roared off head-on into the wall of a static water tank. Fortunately I escaped injury and the front forks were straightened relatively inexpensively; I'm glad to say that the Staff/Sgt tactfully refrained from ever mentioning the incident and I believe our relationship was unimpaired.

Quickly I gained familiarity with the docks along the Clyde, including Govan, the Gorbals, King George V, Gourock, Greenock and the Tail of the Bank, to all of which we went from time to time in the course of these duties. One other responsibility was to join the Merchant Navy Chief Officer, the SMO and other appropriate personnel on tours of inspection of all troopships in order to be satisfied before they left port that the galleys, dining facilities, latrines, bathing facilities and medical sick bays were appropriately equipped, clean and of a good standard. This all too often involved the hazard of drinking cheap duty-free gin or whisky at the insistent hand of a senior Merchant Navy officer or of an SMO (RAMC) and a brisk trade ensued in duty-free cigarettes, much sought after by those like ourselves on shore. Staff Sergeant Ball and I at this particular time were each smoking somewhere between 20 and 25 cigarettes per day, as indeed were most of those medical and other officers and other ranks with whom we came into contact. Soon after arriving in Glasgow I was amused to find that one item on the equipment 'scale' on each ship which was expendable and did not have to be accounted for was a carton which contained several gross condoms. It took me some time to discover that if we had problems, for example, with our vehicles, the standard tip which Staff Sergeant Ball used to offer to the senior NCO at the RASC depot at Maryhill Barracks in order to obtain a replacement vehicle was a round dozen of these items. Medically I found very little to do as there were Army medical officers who held sick parades in Cowglen, but every two or three weeks I was called upon to do week-end duty for Army personnel falling sick while on leave in Glasgow. I then saw something of the degrading poverty and sordid living conditions which existed in some of the old tenements and particularly in 'single-ends', where sometimes a family of six occupied a single room, in the Gorbals. I also had occasionally to examine and treat Army personnel who had fallen foul of the law while on leave and who were being housed, if only temporarily, in Barlinnie Prison. I recall even now the deep sense of shock, almost outrage, which I experienced on seeing for the first time the horrifying crudity of the cells in that institution. I found a soldier, clearly suffering from a severe hangover after being arrested for being drunk and disorderly the night before, lying on a thin mattress on top of a bare stone platform in the floor of a starkly cold cell with virtually no other furniture apart from a single sanitary bucket in the corner for slopping out the next morning. That left an indelible impression and made me realize that even then the British penal system was still dominated by Victorian values.

Returning to Glasgow on many occasions since, I have been greatly impressed by the redevelopment programme of that city, the European City of Culture 1990, in which the mean, decaying, rodent and insect-ridden tenements have disappeared to be replaced by modern dwellings, and the gaunt riverside buildings of the old dockland where, despite their forbidding appearance, I spent many happy hours, have been replaced and restructured. It is nevertheless sad that what was then a vigorous and thriving shipbuilding river has seen such a decline in its commercial viability over the succeeding years. Even then, of course, drunkenness was rife and one was regularly advised never to venture into George Square or under the arches nearby on a Saturday night for fear of violence; horrifying stories were told of the razor gangs who allegedly prowled the streets, while absenteeism and rampant Trade Union power were beginning to have those dire effects upon Glasgow industry which subsequently came near to destroying it. Nevertheless, the magnificent stately Victorian buildings of Glasgow University such as the Bute Hall, many of the municipal buildings such as Kelvin Hall and the attractive if austere architecture of Kelvinside, along with the beauty of the surrounding countryside, made a lasting impression, offsetting the inner city squalor which in those days scarred the city and its reputation.

With work being as light as it was, opportunities to explore the surrounding countryside as far as Loch Lomond and the Kyles of Bute abounded; I managed an occasional game of cricket with an army side but never received any invitations to play golf. Nevertheless, I continued to develop my musical interests by attending occasional symphony concerts and by going to the theatre, but having been such a vigorous supporter of Newcastle United, I perhaps enjoyed most a week-end visit to a football match, either at Ibrox Park to see Rangers, to see Partick Thistle playing at Maryhill or to watch Queen's Park in the vast arena of Hampden Park. On one occasion there the tannoy in a stentorian voice requested Lieut J. N. Walton, Embarkation Medical Officer (Clyde) to make his way to King George V dock in order to deal with an invalid unexpectedly requiring disembarkation from a troopship.

One interesting experience arose when we learned from ADMS(E) that a ship (the 'Eastern Prince', run by the Prince Line of Furness Withy) was being prepared to come to Leith to repatriate a large number of Polish invalids who had asked to return home. They had all served in the Polish Army in the UK during the war; some were housed at a Polish military hospital in Inverary and some at another such hospital at Taymouth Castle, Aberfeldy. Accompanied by a Captain (RE) from Movement Control, I visited the two hospitals, examined and documented the invalids and categorized them appropriately according to the accommodation available on the ship, while he made arrangements for their transportation by train to Leith where they would be embarked for the journey to Poland. This proved to be a fascinating, if complex, exercise, but also gave me, with my RE colleague, the opportunity of an exceptionally pleasant few days driving our respective utility trucks to Inverary (up the long haul of 'Rest and be Thankful') and on through the Trossachs to Aberfeldy. It was from him that I learned on our first evening together of the extraordinary Scottish drinking custom of 'whisky and a chaser' (i.e. a dram followed by a pint of bitter). I am glad to say that despite the obvious anxiety of Colonel Thompson, who came up from Southampton specifically to see the exercise, everything went like clockwork to his evident satisfaction, though a slight problem did arise over my decision, perfectly proper as he agreed on medical grounds, to confine patients with open tuberculosis to restricted accommodation on the ship. The patients in question protested that they had never been similarly isolated in the hospitals from which they came, and I imagine that once they sailed the isolation broke down; nevertheless, with the Colonel's approval, I stuck to my guns during the embarkation process.

Also living in the Lukyns Hotel was a P & O captain, Captain Sidney French, and his wife with both of whom I became very friendly. He was living in Glasgow while his ship, the SS 'Chitral', was being refitted for its civilian post-war role, having previously served as a troopship. We went on several outings together and kept in contact for many years afterwards. From Captain French I learnt much about the sea and the Merchant Navy which held me in good stead in my subsequent service, as did my experience of inspecting the many different ships which came to the Scottish ports. While the Frenchs were in Glasgow, Sidney's elder brother, who had been Commodore of the P & O line, had died in Australia and all his clothing was sent to Glasgow in a trunk. Among the items it contained were a complete set of evening dress tails and a morning suit. Since Sidney French already had his own, and since he thought that his brother was about my size, he asked me one day tentatively whether I would like to buy these items. As they fitted me very well, I was delighted to accept his offer and so obtained evening dress (with two white waistcoats) and a morning suit (with black waistcoat) for the princely sum of £5.00 each. Even though both garments were made by Gieves in Savile Row in 1935, they are still in excellent condition and I wear them regularly on appropriate occasions (even to Buckingham Palace), never having felt the need to replace them.

Fortunately, as the time of our baby's arrival drew near, things became relatively quiet in Glasgow and I decided to begin my week of privilege leave the day before the baby was due. Arriving back in Newcastle in keen anticipation, we looked at each other that day, and the next, and the next, but nothing happened. Betty was very fit, if large. After four or five days of anxious anticipation we deliberately went out for long and vigorous walks in the country and even for several rides in the car across a very bumpy road in Gosforth Park. As I told Professor Harvey Evers, with whom I had become very friendly, we could not afford the luxury of having the baby born in Fernwood, his private nursing home then colloquially known in Newcastle as 'the Golden Gates', but had arranged with another of our distinguished teachers, Linton Snaith, that he would deliver the baby at the Newcastle General Hospital. As my week of leave drew to a close, we both became increasingly despondent, but when I telephoned Staff Sergeant Ball in Glasgow he said that things were very quiet and such items as I was required to deal with personally could be sent to me by post in Newcastle. I therefore stayed on for another few days, telephoning him daily, and eventually, some nine days after the due date, Ann arrived. Linton Snaith had left on holiday when labour began but Betty was safely and happily delivered of our daughter Ann after a labour greatly eased by gas and oxygen. Betty shared a double room with Josie Yeates, wife of Mr W. K. Yeates, subsequently to become a distinguished Newcastle urologist. They enjoyed together a lively and at times hilarious week sharing in the delights and problems associated with the nursing of their respective first-borns. With a deep sense of pride and delight in my new daughter, whom we had decided to call Elisabeth Ann, I returned to my military duties in Glasgow but was still able to return regularly to Newcastle for week-ends to share in the pleasures of parenthood.

As time went by it became increasingly clear that military traffic in Scottish ports was declining and in early 1948 Colonel Thompson agreed that medical services in the Scottish ports should be closed down. I therefore moved to become EMO Southampton, working in a hut in the New Docks area with a Lt McKinnon (RAMC) who soon afterwards married Barbara Corlett, a member of my medical school year, then training in Southampton in surgery. Many years later I met the McKinnons again when they went into general practice together in Coxhoe in Co. Durham.

Southampton was an attractive city, though it had suffered considerably in the blitz. Nevertheless its Civic Centre had survived, as had several of its main thoroughfares and excellent shops and its leafy and extensive common, close to the main built-up area, over which one could wander at leisure. Arriving in Southampton on 7 March, I found that yet again I was required to live out on the lodging list and found a comfortable room (without food) in a Victorian terrace house owned by a Mrs Judd on Hills Lane for 35/- (£1.75p) a week. However, I was required to walk over a mile each way for breakfast and dinner, to the officers' mess in the hutted transit camp on the common, an activity for which, in that cold, wet spring, my enthusiasm soon waned. Happily the kindly Mrs Judd soon took pity on me and after a few weeks offered to give me breakfast and an evening meal. My lodgings were close to the Southampton FC football ground, where on one occasion I saw the local team rousingly defeated by Newcastle United with a superb display (including two goals scored with typically electrifying bursts by Jackie Milburn). The work in Southampton was quite interesting but lacked the variety, freedom and flexibility of Glasgow as one was working directly under the eagle eye of the colonel and his efficient DADMS, Major McPhail, who subsequently became a consultant anaesthetist at Hexham General hospital. The work was similar in character to that in Glasgow but the ship traffic was much heavier. I became familiar with such beautiful former liners as the 'Andes' and 'Andorra' of the Royal Mail Line, several former P & O and Union Castle liners, and on more than one occasion was able to board the 'Queen Mary' and 'Queen Elizabeth' as they sailed imperiously into Southampton, having by then been relieved of their wartime trooping duties and having revived the transatlantic liner traffic. Troopers such as the 'Empire Ken', 'Empire Test', 'Empire Halladale', 'Dunira' and 'Dilwara' regularly came and went, usually from the Middle East and occasionally from the Far East. There were also two sole surviving army hospital ships, the HS 'Oxfordshire' and the HS 'El Nil', which, together with the old HMS 'Maine', the only remaining naval hospital ship which spent most of its time in the Mediterranean, provided all of the sea-borne hospital services which the armed services still required. As I met the SMOs of each of the troopships, who regaled us with tales of their fascinating visits to exotic ports in the Middle and Far East and in East Africa, I began to find my work in Southampton increasingly mundane and felt that I would be unhappy if I completed my Army service without some experience, however brief, of foreign parts. On 21 March I had to return to Glasgow to supervise the disembarkation of the 'Empire Halladale' (under the watchful eye of Lord Wavell who had a personal interest in the disembarking regiment) and called at home for a stolen week-end on the return journey. As it was clear that the SMOs of troopships frequently did well for leave at the end of their lengthy voyages, Betty agreed that I should seek a ship. Although at the beginning of March 1948, after 12 months' service, I had received the routine promotion to Captain with a little boost in pay, the possibility of further promotion to Major as an SMO was also attractive in our straitened financial circumstances. And so I began to make a habit of reporting to the Colonel and to Major McPhail early on a Monday morning before beginning work and saying 'Sir, may I have a ship?'. After a few weeks, enlivened temporarily by three games of cricket at the Southampton sports centre where I played for the RAMC and scored 22, 28 and 46 (including three sixes and five fours—the bowling was pretty poor), I was summoned to the Colonel's office on 12 May and was delighted to be offered the post of Second-in-Command of HS 'Oxfordshire' which would be sailing for the Middle East in about two weeks' time. Naturally I jumped at the chance, snatched a delightful week's leave with Betty and Ann, who was growing rapidly and becoming more interesting each week, and then reported on 23 May to the HS 'Oxfordshire' in the Old Docks at Southampton ready to undertake my new duties.

The 'Oxfordshire' was a splendid old ship of 1910 or 1911 vintage which, owned by the Bibby Line, had plied her trade as a combined cargo and passenger liner between Britain and the Far East. She was a vessel of some 5500 tons displacement, with a single tall central funnel bearing the insignia of the Bibby Line. As Second-in-Command I had a cabin on the starboard side of A deck, its door and window shielded, as were all the cabins and port-holes along that deck, by a canopy which protected us from the sun's glare. The cabin had a good-sized desk, an excellent wardrobe, a comfortable bed and good drawer and cupboard space with a single washbasin providing hot and cold fresh water, so that at once I felt completely at home. I hastily visited the stores at RVH Netley to be provided with standard issue khaki drill tropical uniform, with long stockings, two pairs of shorts and two pairs of thin long trousers and three bush jackets, as well as badges of rank to go with my new-found distinction as a major. One of my first decisions after being promoted major was to grow a moustache, as all too often other officers used to say embarrassingly 'Doesn't he look young to be a major!'. When asked why I've kept the moustache ever since, I've always said 'Because I'm attached to it!'.

In a nautical sense, the ship was staffed by British officers of the Bibby Line; the Captain was a fearsome ex-RNR officer of strong views but an excellent sailor, as was the rather prim First Officer from London, an excellent card player but not much of a socializer. The Second Officer was a huge, cheerful Yorkshireman (remarkably, a school friend of Rex Belas) known as 'Tiny' Howard, about 6 ft. 3 in. in height and weighing about 18 stone, who became a close friend. There was also a clutch of engineers, a couple of radio officers and several stewards, including two cabin stewards whose prime duty was to look after the officers and their cabins and to run salt water baths for us whenever requested (only the Captain and the Commanding Officer were allowed the luxury of bathing in fresh water). The deck and engine crew were all Goanese, and kept the ship immaculate; the daily ritual of washing down the decks and the other ritual of applying red lead and paint to all blemishes whenever we were in port seemed to be second nature, and in consequence she gleamed, as did all of the brasswork which was lovingly polished every few days.

On the Army side, the ship was commanded by Lt-Col J. B. Bishop (RAMC) who only had another four months or so to serve before demobilization and with whom I subsequently corresponded occasionally when, after leaving the Army, he became a medical officer at Broadmoor, having previously had some limited experience in psychiatry. He was an interesting and studious bachelor who did comparatively little and left the running of the ship largely to me, though he was always available for advice whenever necessary and had regular consultations (usually over gin or whisky) with the Captain to discuss affairs of state; but very few orders or instructions of moment resulted from these regular consultations. I found it embarrassing when he asked me to conduct his annual medical examination as I found that he had a minor neurological problem which plainly exlained his slightly unusual gait which I had originally attributed, clearly erroneously, to the fact that he had spent much of the last 18 months at sea. When I tried to downgrade him to P7 in the newly-introduced

Pulheems system, he remonstrated so vigorously that, having realized that his Army career was almost over, I upgraded him again to P2 while feeling a few pangs of conscience in doing so. The other RAMC officers on board were Captain McMin (graded physician), Captain B. O. (Bryan) Scott (graded surgeon) and Captain Frank Goodwin (general duty officer); in addition, we had a dental officer, Captain G. L. Howe (RADC). Our Army complement also included eight nursing officers, QARANC, of whom one, the Matron, Major Robertson, a former hospital senior sister from Glasgow, presided over her chicks with kindly but magisterial efficiency. In later years I lost touch with Captain McMin but Bryan Scott, after leaving the Army, was compelled to give up surgery because of a minor but troublesome skin problem and eventually achieved an outstanding career in physical medicine and rheumatology at the Radcliffe Infirmary, Oxford, where we met again and shared many reminiscences when I moved to Oxford in 1983. Frank Goodwin at first entered general practice in the Birmingham area but later became a consultant accident surgeon and we also met on several occasions later, as recently as 1990. Geoffrey Howe, the dentist (of whom more later) disappeared from my ken for a few years until he turned up in Newcastle as the newly-appointed Professor of Oral Surgery, having had an outstanding career in London. Subsequently he moved back to London to become Dean of the Eastman Dental School while at the same time carving out a distinguished career in the Territorial Army and eventually rising to become the first dental officer (to the best of my knowledge) to command a Territorial General Hospital, namely the 217 (London) General Hospital (TA). Later still, he went to Hong Kong as the Professor of Oral Surgery and as the Foundation Dean of the new Duke of Edinburgh Dental School in Hong Kong University. And for many years after leaving the Army I received intermittent letters from one of the more senior nursing officers, Captain Elaine Scholte, who had assiduously kept in touch with many of those who served on the 'Oxfordshire' and regularly kept me up to date with the news.

The ship was pretty well equipped as a hospital according to the medical standards of the day. There were four open wards below decks (two medical and two surgical), each with over 60 beds, and forward in the bows, just above the other ranks' sleeping accommodation, was a male psychiatric ward with two fully-equipped padded cells. Wards for officers and females were on B deck and there was also a sick bay for the crew. Our total bed complement was 352. There was a well-equipped operating theatre with a wide range of surgical instruments, even including some suitable for neurosurgery, and reasonably up-to-date anaesthetic equipment was also provided. However, since we had no specialist anaesthetist on board, it fell to the lot of the physician and GDMO to give anaesthetics on those rare occasions when surgical operations were needed; Bryan Scott's diary of the time he spent on the 'Oxfordshire' reveals that while at sea he carried out no fewer than 19 emergency surgical operations, including, for example, appendicectomies and an ischiorectal abscess among others. There was also a well-equipped MI room which was Frank Goodwin's domain and in which he looked after the medical needs of the 60 or so RAMC other ranks, as well as the Merchant Navy members of the ship's crew who required medical attention.

The discipline and welfare of the RAMC personnel was supervised by a formidable Regimental Sergeant Major (RAMC) of long service who had seven other sergeants to assist him, including a sergeant pharmacist, a chief clerk and a series of senior male nurses, one to each ward, who in turn supervised the work of the junior NCOs and private soldiers, some few of whom were clerks and orderlies but most of whom were nursing orderlies and worked on the wards. We also had a female physiotherapist employed by the Red Cross but treated in all other respects as a member of the Army; she had a small treatment room below decks; there she offered radiant heat, short-wave diathermy and massage but there was little room for exercise. The ship also boasted a barber's shop and on A deck, looking out over the bows, there was a comfortable officers' mess for Army and Merchant Navy officers, with a well-equipped bar. Below decks there was an adequate sergeant's mess and a canteen and recreation room for the men.

When at sea, and tobacco and alcohol were out of bond, cigarettes could be bought at 50 for 1/8d (8p), a double gin was 4d (2p) and a double whisky 6d (2½p). Soft drinks such as lemonade and tonic water were as expensive as spirits, and beer was slightly more so. Beer was also available in the men's canteen and galley area, but only in restricted quantities. And the food on board was of a standard incomparably better than that to which we had all become accustomed in wartime and in the strictly rationed post-war years. Large helpings of meat, supplies of butter, eggs, cream and a wide range of fruit and cheeses seemed to be available virtually without limit. None of this helped to control my still substantial obesity, and again I find it strange that I did not recognize the need for restraint in relation to my food intake. In the light of my upbringing I remained reasonably abstemious with regard to alcohol, even though when at sea few nights passed without the evening ritual of a pink gin or gin and french before dinner, and one, or occasionally two drinks over cards or during a cinema show (provided on alternate evenings) in the mess. In those days, too, none of us recognized the potential medical hazards of cigarette smoking and I would regularly get through a round can of 50 Senior Service within, at the most, two days. There were also some curious customs of which one became aware only gradually. On sitting one evening before dinner with the Captain and the Colonel and on ordering three pink gins, I noted that their drinks before the angostura bitters was added were crystal clear, while mine was faintly yellow; on enquiring from the barman as to why this was so, I was told that it had always been the custom to provide Gordon's gin (thought by some to be marginally superior) for the Captain and the Colonel, with Booth's gin (with its characteristically faint yellow tinge) for all other officers. On one occasion, too, when we were about to enjoy a game of cards after dinner (bridge and poker alternated with the cinema shows in quiescent periods, and, having played only a few games beforehand, I was quickly introduced by some experts to the mysteries of Culbertson, the one and two club conventions, the forcing two, Yarboroughs and the like) the Captain offered me a drink and, when I asked for a pink gin, he almost exploded. He made it quite clear that in the naval tradition, when on board ship, 'a gentleman drinks gin before dinner and whisky afterwards'.

My duties on board, as carefully explained first by the ADMS and later by the Colonel, were first to run the orderly room, to publish part 1 and 2 orders, to look after the imprest account and to pay the troops, and secondly, as something of an after-thought, to be responsible for the medical care of the officers, the females and the mentals, whom I subsequently discovered to be the most difficult groups of patients to handle in that descending order. I was also nominated as Entertainments Officer. Fortunately when, in late May 1948, I first went on board the 'Oxfordshire' and checked the medical stores, the dangerous drugs and the other appropriate items before signing a 'handing and taking over' certificate so that my predecessor, a Canadian Major RAMC, could go on leave before being demobilized, I discovered first that the RSM was an experienced old hand, if a trifle condescending in the first instance to someone whom he clearly regarded as an upstart major. Subsequently I believe that we achieved a greater feeling of mutual respect, with even some friendly banter. The chief clerk, Sgt Bailey (later a sea-going purser) was also exceptionally able and, having been on the ship for almost a year, knew the orderly room procedure to a T. Without his help I should have been in much more serious difficulty.

On 30 May, while preparing to sail we were told that our expected trip to Port Said to embark British sick and wounded remaining in the Middle East, as well as German POW sick and wounded, was to be extended in that we would first sail for Port Said and would then go on to Haifa in order to cover events leading up the final evacuation of Palestine. We also heard a disturbing rumour that the demobilization of my particular group of officers, originally planned for December 1948, might be postponed because of the volatile international situation. 1 and 2 June passed in a haze of frantic last-minute activity, taking on money, stores and the like, and dealing with all of the last-minute administrative chores. Never having been abroad save for the brief school journey to Paris in

1939 and our honeymoon in Norway in 1946, I could not suppress a feeling of excitement at the prospect of a Mediterranean voyage, though this was tinged with a minor sense of apprehension as these were the days at the height of the troubles in Palestine when the Irgun Zvei Leumi and Stern gang were at the height of their activities and when only recently two British sergeants had been murdered by Jewish activists. We had also heard of the two 'battles of Haifa' earlier that year in which, in their efforts to keep Jews and Arabs apart, British troops had suffered several casualties. But the sense of adventure prevailed, especially as we sailed down Southampton Water on the early morning of 3 June, passing that magnificent Victorian pile of the Royal Victoria Hospital, Netley, and also passing the Queen Mary which was coming in to dock at the time, before skirting the Needles and heading off into the open Channel. Since the ship was sailing empty for the Middle East, we were all substantially under-employed and as Entertainments Officer I organized several panel games broadcast over the public address system and based upon 'Twenty Questions', that popular radio programme of the time hosted by Stuart Macpherson. We also had a concert which fell a little flat for lack of talent despite the intense amusement engendered by the performance of a stoker who sang and accompanied himself on the guitar and was so excruciatingly awful that his act was riotously funny. But perhaps one of the activities best enjoyed by the men was 'housey housey' (now of course known as bingo), the only form of gambling officially allowed in the British Army at the time. On the evening that we sailed I felt it was right to join the RSM and several other NCOs, with the men, to play 'house' in the men's mess below decks in the bows of the ship. As luck would have it, a force 9 gale blew up in the Channel that evening even before we had turned into the Bay of Biscay. As the game proceeded I began to feel, after an excellent dinner, rather queasy and sadly ended up, without due warning, by bringing up my dinner all over one of the tables. Plainly I had not yet found my sea legs, but the NCOs and men were very understanding and this shaming event did not seem to impair our subsequent relationship. Fortunately, never again, even in much worse weather, did I ever have a similar experience during my sea-going career.

As we sailed through the Bay of Biscay on Friday, 4 June, the weather steadily improved and by Saturday, 5th, we were for the first time able to sunbathe on the deck, from which we had an excellent view of Cape Finisterre. The following day was equally glorious and we were surprised how close we sailed to the shore around Cape St Vincent, topped by a beautiful white monastery and lighthouse. A large school of porpoises was now playing regularly around the ship and dolphins regularly came up to gambol around the bows where it seemed that they were almost scratching their backs. On the Sunday we passed through the Straits of

Gibraltar with the awesome grandeur of the Rock on our port side, and next morning had an excellent view of the Sierra Nevada rising to almost 12,000 ft. and still snow-capped. Passing the Galatea Islands to the port side, we could see the coast of Algeria on the right and after passing Cape Bon and Pantelleria to starboard, we then sailed on into the open sea, eventually arriving off Port Said on Sunday, 13 June.

I suppose that my most abiding memories of my first outward voyage related first to the enormous variety of seascapes which one encountered and which taught me a deep respect for, and love of the sea, each of which have stayed with me. Secondly, I became increasingly familiar with Army routine and with the responsibility of administering a larger military unit than any to which I had been accustomed previously. Pay parades for the men, the drafting of part 1 and part 2 orders (first done by my chief clerk, carefully checked by myself and then taken for approval to the Colonel), the detailed accounting relating to my imprest account, regular inspections of mess rooms, of the wards and of the men's sleeping quarters all settled into a familiar routine and there was plenty of time left to gaze at the passing ships and scenery, to watch the occasional flying fish (particularly at dusk), to marvel at the Mediterranean sunsets, to delight in the ubiquitous dolphins and porpoises, and to look forward to one's first sight and experience of Egypt.

My first sight of Port Said was not particularly exciting as we sailed for some distance along a rather ugly breakwater, but soon we saw the statue of Vicomte de Lesseps, the designer and constructor of the Suez Canal, and docked opposite the lighthouse, a situation providing a view of the harbour and of buildings along the sea front, including the impressive store of Simon Artz. No sooner had we docked than we were surrounded by the inevitable swarm of 'bum-boats' selling leather goods and many other items; and we were much impressed by the skill with which young children dived successfully for coins dropped into the murky harbour water. Within the first hour or two many of the men and some of the officers were swayed by the pleadings of swarthy gentlemen, many adorned by a fez but masquerading under such splendid Arabic names as Geordie Smith, Jock McNab and others, and made a number of purchases. Once we had tied up to the dock and the gangplank was down, Egyptian port officials, customs men and the port medical officer came on board, to be swiftly followed by the EMO (Port Said) whom I was delighted to recognize as my old friend Captain Maurice Wood, a member of my medical school year, who told us that because a state of war was apparently existing between Egypt and Israel and because we were due to sail for Haifa, there would be no shore leave for other ranks but only for officers. This was a decision which I had to explain to the assembled other ranks; it must have come as a considerable disappointment to those who had never been to the Middle East before, but they took it with good grace.

Although I had an opportunity of going ashore with Maurice Wood and of meeting his wife, Erica, for a drink at their flat, and was also able to do a little shopping, two unfortunate experiences which taught me a sharp lesson stand out in my memory as the most notable experiences of my first visit to Port Said. One possibility which naturally interested the officers and men on board was that we might be able to take home some food, still heavily rationed in the UK. And the officers in particular were interested in the possibility of buying bottles of spirits since although drinks were freely available in the bar, whole bottles were not for sale. Soon after we had tied up at the dock, a man came to the gangplank wearing an official NAAFI cap. The Sergeant Major and I were together and he asked us whether we would like to order some tinned salmon and other foodstuffs to take home. He brought an official NAAFI printed list of tinned goods with prices and said that he would not wish to have any money now but that if we cared to take orders from the officers and men, he would come back and collect the orders and the money a few hours later. This seemed a reasonable suggestion; but just as he was about to depart he asked *sotto voce* whether we wished to have any whisky for the officers' mess and the sergeants' mess. Both the RSM and I jumped at this suggestion; he went on to say that in order to get the whisky out of bond, he would need to be paid for this now at 10/- (50p) a bottle. I therefore gave him £3.00 for a bottle each for the officers and the RSM (who as an older soldier should have known better) gave him £4.00 for a bottle each for the eight members of the sergeants' mess, and off he went; not surprisingly, we never saw him again and no tinned food was bought. My second experience about which old hands should have warned me was that on shore, walking with two other officers, I and they were suddenly confronted by a swarm of small boys waving newspapers fiercely in front of our faces. It was only when we had succeeded in chasing them away that we discovered that our fountain pens were missing from the top pockets of our bush jackets. This was a well-known trick; confronted with a similar experience, old soldiers would regularly cover their breast pockets with their hands and wait until the youngsters disappeared. They did not, however, have any easy answer to the alternative approach employed by some small boys seeking to polish one's shoes. If told to run away ('Imshi' was the appropriate Arabic term) the riposte would be 'If I don't black your shoes, I'll black your bloody trousers'. And the inevitable invitations to sex shows and to sample the pulchritudinous offerings of various ladies surfaced around every corner. Otherwise my first experience of Port Said was relatively uneventful, save for the fact that in the oppressive heat of the night (90° F at night, up to 100° by day) I left the port-hole in my cabin open, to find next morning that the arm which had been exposed on top of the single sheet with which I covered myself was covered in mosquito bites, though fortunately these must not have been malaria-carrying.

Next afternoon, having taken stores, fuel and water on board, we left for Haifa in a shade temperature of 95° F, arriving there at 5.30 a.m. on Tuesday, 15 June, and anchored in the inner harbour. This large harbour, surrounded by high breakwaters and with a narrow entrance, was then exceptionally attractive and the view of the city shimmering in the heat, rising up to the heights of Mount Carmel, was equally beautiful, despite the evidence of unrest within. The harbour was crowded with shipping, mostly freighters but with an occasional troopship, including our old friend the 'Eastern Prince'. Half way up the mountain we got an excellent view of the Bahai shrine, glistening white in the brilliant sun, and intermittently we could see the magnificent Carmelite monastery near the top of the mountain as scattered cumulus clouds drifted languidly by. There was, however, little time to stand and stare as our duty on this brief visit to Haifa was to embark 156 patients, 60 of them surgical and several post-operative, from Haifa Military Hospital and to transport them back to Port Said where they would move on to BMH Fayid in the Canal Zone. In no time the ship was swarming with senior officers, including sea transport officials, the EMO and several officers from the Brigade of Guards and from the Highland Regiment. However, after we docked, the embarkation process, for which I, the RSM and the chief clerk were largely responsible, was quickly completed, the stretcher patients were bedded down and those who were ambulant, having been allocated beds and lockers, were free to stroll around the ship. By 2.00 p.m. we had cast off and were on our way back to Port Said, passing two illegal immigrant ships which had been arrested by the Navy and from which we received clamorous protests and obscene gestures from those immigrants who were still aboard. Our journey back to Port Said was a leisurely one through a superbly beautiful tropical night, illuminated by brilliant moonlight which gave the sea a magnificent transparent sheen. We sailed at only about 8 knots and few, if any, medical problems arose to disturb the tranquillity of the voyage; even the few psychiatric patients and officers for whom I was responsible were calm and required no further attention after my evening ward round. The journey was slow because we had been warned that if we arrived at Port Said before dawn, we would be fired upon by the Egyptian port artillery.

We arrived in Port Said at 6.30 a.m., to be visited again by the EMO. By 4.00 p.m. disembarkation of all patients was complete and they were on their way by hospital train to BMH Fayid. Shore leave was then granted for all ranks and I had a pleasant evening dining with Maurice and Erica and also met two other members of our year (Doug Thomson who was doing ophthalmology at BMH Fayid, and George Graham who was trooping in the Middle East). More shopping followed with a relaxing visit to the Officers' Club the following day and I bought a leather grip, a 'pouffe' and an Axminster carpet to take home on instruction from Betty and her mother since carpets were virtually unobtainable in the UK at that time. The use of Maurice's EMO's launch came in very handy. Ill-feeling surfaced between the officers and other ranks when, without warning, the Egyptians stopped all leave for other ranks on Thursday, 17 June; hence most of the officers spent Friday on board, though some of the more adventurous, with a group of NCOs and men, took out lifeboats for a rowing race around the harbour. On Saturday some of us went ashore again and this time visited the officers' shop where I bought some sheets and a pair of cricket boots with crepe soles since my own buckskin boots in the UK had seen better days. In fact those canvas boots from Port Said lasted me through my subsequent cricketing career and I last wore them for two matches against the students of Green College in Oxford in 1989, which must say something for the quality of the boots available in those days.

At 5.00 p.m. that afternoon we sailed again for Haifa, having been warned that we would be required to evacuate all of the staff, stores and the few remaining patients from Haifa Military Hospital and to provide medical cover during the final evacuation of all British troops. At 5.50 a.m. on Sunday, 20th, we anchored off Haifa alongside HMS 'Troubridge' and noted an outer cordon of naval ships ringing the area outside the harbour. A cruiser, HMS 'Phoebe' (known, of course, as the 'Honourable Phoeb' in the light of a popular radio programme of the time) was busily dashing around in and out of the harbour supervising the traffic and demonstrating the consummate seamanship of its crew, since by this time the Jewish pilots and tug captains were becoming increasingly reluctant to handle British military traffic. Eventually we again entered the harbour, where searchlights continually swept the area throughout the night and small craft plied backwards and forwards, largely staffed by marine commandos and naval frogmen looking for limpet mines which it was felt some of the Jewish activists might have wished to attach to British ships. In the harbour were several British troopships awaiting the evacuation of those troops who remained on shore, including the 'Empress of Scotland' (Canadian Pacific), 'Eastern Prince', 'Empire Test', 'Ocean Vigour', 'Orduna' and 'Georgic', which anchored sufficiently close to us to allow those troops on board to engage in banter with our own personnel. 'Get your number dry' frequently echoed across the water. Also in the harbour were two American destroyers and one large American troop carrier, carrying American troops who were there as observers of the evacuation. That particular vessel caused our own troops and those aboard the 'Georgic' some amusement when, having watched HMS 'Phoebe' pull astern into the harbour and then swing to port in order to sail out through the harbour entrance at an increasing rate of knots, the clumsy large

American troop carrier attempted the same manoeuvre without the aid of tugs and struck the harbour wall, tearing a hole several feet long in her bows. The cheer that went up from the decks of the 'Georgic' echoed from the hills for several seconds.

While awaiting the final evacuation, Tuesday 22nd and several days which followed were comparatively free days ('Z' day of the final evacuation was postponed twice) and all of us not on duty were allowed ashore, though we were all required to wear side arms and six nervous and somewhat hesitant medical officers who had not previously handled army issue pistols were provided with these and with ammunition; so off we went to explore Haifa and to visit the Haifa Military Hospital, which was about to close. Though British troops were much in evidence, so too were male and female soldiers of the Haganah (the army of the Jewish State), many of whom looked surly and even trigger-happy, and some momentary consternation arose when one of our number, claiming that he had handled a pistol before, loaded his with five bullets and pulled the trigger to bring one 'up the spout', only to hear a loud explosion and to see a hole in the ground; he had mistaken the direction in which the chamber of a Smith and Wesson revolver rotates on pulling the trigger. After a brief visit to the restaurant on Mount Carmel (called Prost, colloquially known as Prossies) most favoured by the British Army officers, we visited the Carmelite monastery at the top of the mountain, where I was astonished to find that the monk who had been there for 20 years and who showed us Elisha's tomb, spoke English with a broad Geordie accent and told me that he came originally from Longbenton. We also discovered that no fewer than 600 Arab refugees had sought sanctuary in the monastery and often wondered what happened to them later.

We returned to the ship in good time to meet the officers of 40 marine Commando (commanded by Lt Col Houghton, RM) who had been patrolling the harbour and its environs and whom we had come to know well. We had invited them on board for a drinks party and a game of skittles. The evening passed in something of a blur (though we won the skittles) and some of the marine commandos were far from steady when going ashore in their launch, but insisted that we should join them for a return 'batting party' in their tented Mess the following evening. That too went well, though as our launch was returning us noisily and in exuberant if unmusical voice to the ship, the chief engineer fell in the drink but was quickly fished out and proved none the worse for the experience.

On Wednesday, 23rd, we watched in oppressive heat (95° F) large numbers of troops being embarked on the various troopships, and the harbour began to clear as several such vessels moved out. Some of us also had time, after completing our administrative duties, for a visit to a local beach for a swim and a game of football. The following day, however, was exceptionally busy as we took on board all the officers and other staff of the Haifa Military Hospital, together with a few remaining patients and all of their stores, including one ton of contraband opium which had been discovered hidden in the grounds of the hospital shortly before the evacuation. As the process proceeded, the RASC Operating Battalion and Movement Control personnel, along with General Macmillan, the GOC, embarked on the 'Empire Test' in the harbour to supervise the on-going evacuation. The American ships left on the 27th. Activity in the harbour and the search for limpet mines continued and on the nights of Monday and Tuesday, small depth charges were dropped in the harbour regularly throughout most of the night to foil any potential attacks on the shipping, so that we had relatively little sleep as every time one of these went off the ship shook from stem to stern. Considerable excitement and not a little dismay resulted from the news that three Cromwell tanks had been hijacked by Jewish activists, but one of these was eventually recaptured and the other two were immobilized by rocket-firing Typhoons.

Z Day, the day of the final evacuation, was Wednesday, 30th June, and we were instructed by the GOC to man a launch with one medical officer, two NCOs and six nursing orderlies, all to be fully armed and equipped with emergency medical equipment, stretchers, dressings and the like, to stand by the dock and to give medical cover until such time as the last troops had embarked. By this time HMS 'Triumph', the aircraft carrier, had arrived off the port and more planes began to circle the harbour area. Privately I had asked the Colonel whether I might be the MO on the launch, but he insisted that this would be inappropriate for the 2 i/c and Bryan Scott as the ship's surgeon undertook that duty. He had an excellent view of the evacuation (also watched by Count Bernadette's UN peace delegation); first came a Guards regiment who were embarked on the 'Eastern Prince', carrying unfurled colours, followed by the staff of 35 Field Ambulance RAMC, again carrying their flag. Tanks and bren carriers were then embarked, and the last troops to leave were 40 Marine Commando who embarked on an LST, while the tanks and carriers were evacuated by two LCTs. Brigadier Maxwell had a few words with our medical party in the launch as the last troops climbed aboard their respective vessels and then left himself, to be greeted as he sailed out to his troopship by a 16-gun salute from HMS 'Phoebe' and a fly-past by 16 fighter planes which Bryan Scott believes were Spitfires (but which I said in a letter to Betty were certainly Typhoons), flying first in line astern, then in line abreast, and finally in formation. In fact everything went smoothly with no shots being fired and even the Haganah troops who quickly moved into the dock and harbour area as the British left lost their previously surly expressions and many allowed themselves a smile, while a few even waved as we departed.

In the afternoon we were on our way again to Port Said with on board a gaggle of brigadiers, colonels and senior RAMC officers. Major Tony Batty Shaw, the physician whom we evacuated from the Haifa Military Hospital, subsequently became a good friend as a distinguished senior physician at the Norfolk and Norwich Hospital and a great Oslerian. We also later got to know well Captain Hugh Mackay, the anaesthetist, who went into general practice in Birtley in Co. Durham. Almost 40 years later to the day, when Betty and I went to the BMA Annual Meeting in Norwich in 1988 to see Sir David Innes Williams installed as President of the Association, four of us—Bryan Scott from Oxford, Tony Batty Shaw from Norwich, Hugh Mackay from Birtley and myself—met at the reception for a mini-reunion and recalled those stirring events of 1948.

Arriving early on 1 July at Port Said, our distinguished guests were quickly disembarked with their equipment and we prepared on the 2nd to take on board over 310 patients coming up by train from BMH Fayid, including a large number of British sick and wounded but also 80 German POWs who were segregated in one of our wards, along with a number of officer and female patients and six German generals including Field Marshal von Brauchitsch, former head of the German General Staff, and Colonel General Strauss. Embarkation of the patients and their distribution to the various wards seemed again to go very smoothly, but little did we then imagine the problems we would encounter on the return journey to Southampton. One of the duties of our dental officer (since his dental duties tended to be very light) was to look after the exchange of currency on behalf of the patients. On the arrival of the military train he was presented with a large bundle of Egyptian currency and a complete nominal roll of the patients with the amount of currency which each had handed in for exchange listed alongside each name. It was his responsibility to meet the port cashier, to exchange the money in bulk and then to disburse the individual sums in sterling to the patients on the return voyage. Two days out from Port Said, Geoffrey Howe came to me with a long face and explained that he was £100 short. Having signed for the bulk amount, and while recognizing that the only reasonable explanation was that the port cashier had made a personal profit on the transaction, he had, I suppose, no valid excuse as he should personally have checked carefully the rate of exchange before accepting and signing for the money. However, such a mistake by a young and financially inexperienced officer can readily be understood. I had no alternative but to provide the money from my imprest account and to hold a court of enquiry of which of course I, as 2 i/c, was President. This was an arduous challenge as I had never sat on a court of enquiry before, but fortunately the appropriate Army manuals were available and in the end the court seemed to go quite well. Eventually, long afterwards, Geoffrey Howe told me that after much negotiation with the powers that be, having first been asked for £50, he was eventually required to pay £5.

I have more personal reasons for remembering Geoffrey Howe on that voyage. A few days after leaving Port Said, when I was eating a delicious steak at dinner, I heard a loud crack and discovered that one of my teeth, in which a root filling had been inserted some years before in Newcastle, had split down the middle. Geoffrey's attention was prompt, but sadly, when he attempted to remove the tooth, the crown came away leaving a deeply embedded root behind. As he said at the time, perspiring slightly, this kind of thing never seemed to happen to Joe Snooks but always to the CO or the Second-in-Command. In the event, he had no alternative but to give a full mandibular block and to dig for the root, which was eventually extracted with difficulty. As, however, the socket was clearly infected, he inserted a pack and told me to remind him to remove this about a week later. The pain soon eased and I was not conscious of the presence of the pack until we arrived in Southampton after our Hamburg trip, when I suddenly reminded Geoffrey that it was still in, by which time he had already packed up all his dental equipment preparatory to going on leave. Nevertheless he was able to unpack and sterilize a pair of forceps with which he removed, as he thought, the pack and smartly disappeared. I followed on leave to Newcastle some two days later, at which time my jaw had begun to swell and throb and so I went to Newcastle Dental Hospital where the residue of the pack was removed and the socket quickly healed. This was an event about which I was able to remind the Professor of Oral Surgery in Newcastle on suitable occasions in later years.

My second major problem on the otherwise uneventful return journey to Southampton was that, without any warning, one of our female psychiatric patients squeezed herself through an open port-hole in her cabin and, despite the fact that the alarm 'man overboard' was quickly raised and that the ship turned round, no trace of her was found. Several experienced sailors told me that when women decided to commit suicide in this way, they were usually successful, but that men often changed their minds on striking the water and were picked up (as we were to discover later). In the Army in those days, psychiatric patients were classified as PP (meaning psychotic) or PN (meaning psychoneurotic) and were also graded by the evacuating medical officers as being suitable for open or closed accommodation. In closed accommodation they were under continuing surveillance by nursing orderlies, but in open accommodation no such restrictions were imposed; the lady in question, the wife of an officer, was clearly classified as 'PN open'. Doug Thomson, as officer in charge of the hospital train from BMH Fayid, had warned us of the problems we might encounter with a manic-depressive wife of a major but she gave us no difficulty, and the lady who disappeared had seemed mentally stable. Yet again, however, a court of enquiry under my Presidency had to be held, and once more the findings of that court, too, were confirmed by higher authority in due course. Mention of this psychiatric classification reminds me that during embarkation in Port Said a soldier being evacuated was weeping profusely; a corporal looked at his label and, noting that he was classified PN, said 'Don't cry, mate—you'll be OK; it's those PPs that we can do nothing for'. He made this remark oblivious of the fact that the officer standing in line immediately behind, who was seriously depressed, was classified PP.

Medically, my duties were not particularly arduous. I did morning and evening ward rounds on the officers', female and psychiatric wards and only encountered one other major problem. One British officer was suffering from terminal secondary cancer. He was in considerable pain but this was generally relieved by opiates. To save him the necessity of having regular injections of morphine, I prescribed an appropriate heavy dose of tinct. opii, suitably diluted. One evening the sergeant pharmacist came to me with ashen face and pointed out that by an appalling mistake he had dispensed for the patient tinct. opii in 10 times the prescribed dose, having made a mistake about the dilution. When in fear and trepidation I went along to the ward he was sleeping normally and next morning, the patient sat up, smiled and said 'That was a wonderful draught you gave me last night, doc. I've had the best night's sleep I've had in months'. I suppose that that experience taught me a lesson about the tolerance which develops in patients receiving regular medication with powerful analgesics.

On this section of the voyage, too, no other serious problems arose with the psychiatric patients and none of the schizophrenics, for example, required heavy sedation or needed to be held in one of the padded cells. This was perhaps just as well since, quite unbeknown to me and, I believe, to the Customs, the walls of the padded cells were detachable; a syndicate of psychiatric orderlies had detached the walls and had lined them with flat tins of Senior Service cigarettes which were eventually removed, as I learnt some time later, once the ship had been cleared by Customs in Southampton. The German generals, too, presented no problem; they were solemn and relatively uncommunicative, but since most of them were classified as invalids on the basis of having had a previous cardiac infarction or some other condition of which the acute stage was long past, little medical attention was required.

On arrival in Southampton, the disembarkation process with transfer by Captain McKinnon, the EMO, of the patients to appropriate military hospitals was quickly concluded, stores were again taken on board and, within 24 hours, we set sail for Hamburg where we were to disembark the German POWs and were to pick up for return to the UK British invalids from The British Army of the Rhine (BAOR). Even this brief and somewhat stormy voyage was not uneventful since, as we sailed down the Elbe, one of the German POWs, again classified as 'PN open', threw himself over the side but was quickly picked up by a cargo ship following astern. One could perhaps understand his motivation as we later learned from his friends that his wife had run off with another man and that he was being repatriated to the Russian zone. A third court of enquiry was held and once more its findings were subsequently confirmed.

As we approached Hamburg down the Elbe I felt a sense of incredulity that destruction wrought by air attack could be so total and comprehensive. Dock after dock consisted of no more than a mass of rubble and broken machinery; and as we reached our moorings close to the centre of the city, devastated buildings could be seen to every side. No experience before or since has ever made me appreciate so vividly the horrors of war. Perhaps a visit with Betty to Auschwitz when I was lecturing in Poland many years later brought home to me fully the ultimate savagery of man's inhumanity to man; nevertheless that first sight of Hamburg was a tremendous shock. Our short stay there passed in a blur of activity with disembarkation of the Germans, followed soon afterwards by embarkation of the British patients, but we did have sufficient time to visit the Army Officers' Club, 'The Four Seasons' (which we revisited when attending a congress in 1985 to find that it had been restored to even more than its pre-war glory as a splendidly luxurious and expensive hotel). A brief visit to a rather sordid night club followed where, as in all of occupied Germany at that time, cigarettes served as currency. On our return journey to Southampton with a full complement of British patients aboard, I was kept much busier since the psychiatric ward was full. There were several seriously disturbed schizophrenic patients on board, at least two of whom had to be restrained in the padded cell as the only drugs available for sedation were, on the one hand, a number of barbiturates and, on the other, intramuscular paraldehyde which was extensively used throughout the voyage. When in Southampton disembarkation was again completed, we were visited by Colonel Thompson who brought the news that once all administrative details had been finalized, we could all go on 10 days' leave. He also confirmed that the HS 'Oxfordshire' was now to be decommissioned and that I and the colonel on our return would be required to complete the decommissioning process. He then said that he thought I had done a splendid job on the voyage (despite the three courts of enquiry) and in the light of that performance he was going to appoint me as Second-in-Command of HS 'El Nil', the only remaining hospital ship in the British Army, which would be sailing again for the Middle East in about three weeks' time.

And so, after a splendid 10 days at home with Betty, her mother and Ann, who had matured greatly in the eight weeks I had been away, I returned to Southampton to deal with the rather boring dispersal of stores and medical equipment from the HS 'Oxfordshire' and to handle the mass of documentation which the decommissioning of a hospital ship required. Of the events of the next seven or eight days only one stands out in my memory and related to the contents of the pharmacy. While the range of drugs then available was minimal when compared with those found in a hospital pharmacy today, nevertheless, once the dangerous drugs had been taken on charge by the chief pharmacist at the Royal Victoria Hospital, Netley, I told him that I was planning to pack up all the remainder and send them to him. His reaction was, I suppose, predictable. He said that if he was compelled to take on charge, for example, large bottles which had originally contained 1000 tablets of 3 g of sodium amytal or other similar remedies, and that if these bottles had been opened, he could not accept them as to do so would mean that he would have to count every individual tablet in order to add these to his departmental manifest. His reaction and that of his Major Quartermaster, to whom I expressed concern, was that I should throw all the opened bottles of drugs into the harbour. I was so outraged by this suggestion that I consulted Colonel Thompson, on whose advice I eventually crated up all the remaining contents of the pharmacy and took them by 3-ton truck to Netley when I knew that the chief would be at lunch. Having obtained a receipt from a junior NCO, I beat a hasty retreat but never learned what ultimately happened to those stores.

And so, having said a sad farewell to the charming old 'Oxfordshire', I moved over to the HS 'El Nil', now in port, and introduced myself to the CO, the short, wiry, balding, bespectacled and moustachioed Colonel R. D. Davy, a delightful man with a tremendous twinkle and a charming wife who was staying with him on board while the ship was in port. I soon learned that even though he was in his early sixties and looking forward to retirement from the regular service, he was nevertheless a redoubtable opponent at deck tennis and an extremely competent soldier with an extensive knowledge of King's regulations and of the RAMC. Clearly he would be a splendid teacher and mentor if any administrative problems arose. The 'El Nil' herself was, like the 'Oxfordshire', a pretty ancient craft, having been built in Germany before the First World War. She was taken over by Britain in reparations after the armistice and for some time was used on passenger services in the Baltic. In the 1930s she was leased to the Egyptian government and for a time served as King Fouad's private yacht before reverting to Britain when war broke out in 1939; she seemed, however, to have retained an innate affection for Egypt and the Canal Zone since whenever in the subsequent months she broke down or needed major repairs, this almost invariably happened in the vicinity of the Canal Zone with some consequential unexpected delays to our voyages and some unexpectedly lengthy sojourns in the Middle East.

Again, however, my personal cabin was a comfortable and attractive one on A deck, next to that of the Colonel, and yet again our dining facilities, food, lounge accommodation and bar were excellent. On the open deck aft there were facilities for deck tennis and other deck sports, with plenty of room for sunbathing on the boat deck. In addition to Colonel Davy and myself, the other officers included a graded surgeon, Captain Carr, a graded physician, Captain Leslie Doyle, a jovial Irishman who subsequently became a consultant physician in the Manchester area and whom I later met many times, and another Irishman, John Rogan, the GDMO who was responsible for the medical care of the other ranks and the crew. The hospital section of the ship was well equipped and the accommodation with 452 hospital beds was in many ways similar to that on the 'Oxfordshire'. However, the 'powers that be' had suddenly realized that it was not very cost-effective for a ship like the 'El Nil' to sail out to the Middle East empty apart from its RAMC and QARANC personnel and crew. It was therefore decided to bring some of the wards into use as dormitories for officers travelling out to the Middle East; hence on our next two voyages we functioned as a troopship for officers on the outward journey and at least had some administrative tasks to undertake even if there was very little medical work to occupy us. However, my dormant and immature talents as Entertainments Officer were tested to the full in arranging 'Any Questions?', quizzes and concerts and must have been reasonably successful as one brigadier suggested that I should give up medicine and join the BBC, advice which I took with a pinch of salt.

My principal recollection of our first voyage on the 'El Nil', beginning in August 1948, was of the oppressive heat in Port Said with the temperature hovering around 96–100° F. And as a boiler broke down and needed three days of work, we were able to swim at the Plage des Enfants at Port Fouad and I bought yet another carpet. I also enjoyed another excellent dinner with Maurice and Erica Wood whose Arab servant, Abdul, cooked a magnificent meal on two primus stoves (when we spent Christmas in Port Said on a subsequent voyage, he cooked a turkey with all the necessary trimmings for an English Christmas dinner with the same primitive equipment).

Having disembarked our officer passengers on arrival, we took on board from the Fayid hospital train 386 British and German invalids and sailed for home four days later. By this time the port cashier in Port Said whom we had met to our cost on the previous voyage had moved on and our dental officer was more carefully briefed, so that no problem arose in currency exchange on the return voyage. On this occasion, too, we called at Grand Harbour, Valletta, Malta, in order to embark 23 patients and to refuel but were prevented from going ashore by the determination of the sturdily independent Captain Clark of Furness Withy, a crusty old salt who never seemed content while in harbour and only relaxed at sea. In consequence, though the ship was surrounded in Malta, as in Port Said, by the usual swarm of bum-boats, we were not allowed even an hour or two of shore leave in that beautiful port and were only able to gaze longingly at the ramparts of the Castle of the Knights of St John and at the attractive streets winding upwards from the harbour. Probably, too, the Maltese lace which we bought from the bum-boats was not of top quality and almost certainly we paid far above the normal price for those examples of Maltese workmanship which many of us acquired. This voyage was in fact comparatively uneventful and certainly there were no untoward administrative events. I did, however, have the unusual experience of treating a German officer patient with cerebral malaria with quinine injections; fortunately he recovered.

Back in Southampton after our usual Hamburg foray, we were then told that the ship would turn round very quickly to do exactly the same trip again; after I had completed the necessary administrative chores the Colonel told me that as it was a weekend I could have a 36-hour leave. After telephoning Betty, I dashed for the station and was just in time to catch an overnight train from Kings Cross to Newcastle. Recognizing that there were no sleepers and that I would inevitably be tired out if I did not get some sleep, I settled down in the corner of a first class compartment and took 3 g of sodium amytal. Although I slept only fitfully at first, I must later have lapsed into a deeper slumber because when I opened my eyes the train was passing through Berwick-upon-Tweed. When eventually we arrived in Edinburgh, I guiltily telephoned Betty to say that having slept through Newcastle I would not after all be with her until lunch-time on the Sunday. This meant that we only had that afternoon and evening together before I had to set out on my overnight return journey. Ever since in similar circumstances I have always carried a portable alarm!

After another almost identical voyage, enlivened by two games of football against the MN crew and a Tank Corps unit in Port Said, both of whom we beat 2–0, we did have a slightly longer period of leave and, in addition, through the kindness of Betty's mother, she was herself able to come to Southampton to spend three days with me on the ship in port. This was a delightful interlude as it was the first time that she had been able to leave Ann, who by now was very active and almost, but not quite, walking, so that Mrs Harrison felt that for three days or so she could cope.

We set out on our next voyage on 14 December with 197 officer passengers, anticipating that it would follow the same routine. By this time the surgeon, Captain Carr, had been demobilized and had been replaced by Captain Harry Links, a surgeon of great energy and initiative who, not surprisingly in view of his entrepreneurial skills, subsequently established the extremely prosperous Links private clinic in Edmonton,

Alberta, Canada. I make particular mention of his entrepreneurship because he had discovered that in Hamburg there was an aquarium which stocked neon fish (they are rather like goldfish but are phosphorescent and glow in the dark) which were bred in another aquarium in the eastern zone of Germany. On arrival in Hamburg Harry went ashore with a very large metal water container and 1000 cigarettes, with which he would then purchase about 300 of these fish (for three cigarettes each); he would then bring them aboard and keep them warm with the radiant heat apparatus from the physiotherapy department. Then, as the proud possessor of an import licence, he would walk off the ship in Southampton and take them to Hamleys in Regent Street where he sold them for about 10/- (50p) each, with consequently a very substantial profit on each voyage despite a modest mortality among his piscine passengers. My only 'coup', very modest by comparison, was the discovery of a NAAFI shop in Port Said where one could buy fresh Egyptian eggs and on one voyage I preserved 200, bought very cheaply, in 'Oteg'; they lasted for well over a year in Newcastle.

As we approached Port Said on our third such voyage on the 'El Nil', we received news that was not totally unexpected. It was confirmed that those of us who had anticipated serving in the Army for less than two years were being required 'in view of the exigencies of the service' to continue for three months longer, so that our long-awaited demobilization would be delayed. I cannot recall what emergency prompted confirmation of the decision but I well recall the dismay which Betty and I felt as we had continued to hope that my demobilization might still occur late in 1948 and now realized that I would not be out of the Army until April 1949 at the earliest. I also learned with some alarm that during my absence at sea she, encouraged by her mother, had found a three-bedroomed semi-detached house at 42 Benton Lodge Avenue in Newcastle which, admittedly with her mother's financial support and a modest contribution from what I had saved from my major's pay, she bought in my absence, despite the fact that there was no certainty that I would have a job to return to in Newcastle when I left the Army. The purchase price was £2550, and I felt that we could just afford the monthly payment of £11.13.4 on a 90% endowment mortgage, in addition to the £3 weekly I then gave Betty for housekeeping. As I said in a letter, to rent a furnished flat would cost us at least £3 weekly! Despite my apprehension, I could not conceal a sense of pleasure and pride that at last we had a home of our own, even though it was sparsely furnished with such few items as Betty's mother could spare and with the very limited amount of utility furniture which newly-married couples were then entitled to buy on furnishing 'dockets'. At least we were able to buy a bed, a wardrobe and a dressing table, and a cot for Ann's bedroom, while Betty's Bluthner boudoir grand piano which her father had bought for her 21st birthday, was installed in solitary state in our drawing room on the delightful embossed Indian carpet which I had taken home from Port Said, while a functional but less attractive English Axminster, also bought in that port, eventually concealed the bare boards of the living room floor. Later still, yet another Indian carpet was obtained in Aden; it, and its fellow from Port Said, still give good service in the respective homes of two of our children. Sadly the two English Axminsters (one bought for Betty's mother), which plainly in retrospect were not of good quality, became threadbare within some 20 years and had to be discarded.

The second piece of news that we learned after arriving at Port Said at midnight on Christmas Eve was that we were to undertake an extended voyage via Aden to Mombasa in East Africa and onwards to Mauritius. The Army had recruited many young Mauritians to undertake guard duty around British military installations in the Middle East and some 200 of them had developed various medical conditions which necessitated their repatriation. Some of our regular officer passengers were not amused when Colonel Davy published a Part I Order which said that on arrival in Port Said officer passengers would line the rails on the port side and would sing 'Hark the herald angels sing' while warrant officers and staff on the starboard side would sing 'What wondrous music fills the midnight air'; but most, I'm glad to say, chuckled.

After disembarking our passengers very early on Christmas Day and after enjoying a riotous Christmas, partly on board (where the officers served Christmas lunch to the men) and partly in the evening with Maurice and Erica Wood at their home (even though Erica had her first baby on Boxing Day), we embarked our Mauritians and set sail through the Canal. Interestingly, of the 200 Mauritians, 72 were diagnosed as being psychiatrically ill and, of those, some 59 were labelled as hysteria. Being responsible, as always, for the care of the psychiatric patients, I did not face the challenge of looking after them with total equanimity. In the event they caused no problems and I could only assume in retrospect that the label of hysteria should really have been changed to one of homesickness as none of the people in question, who spoke Creole but who could understand my rudimentary and halting French, developed any major psychiatric manifestations during the voyage. They were indeed cleaner and better behaved than many British troops. One patient, a tailor, mended my clothes and darned my socks and several asked to be photographed with me before the voyage ended. There was, however, one notable medical incident during the voyage. As we sailed down the south Indian Ocean towards Mombasa, one Mauritian invalid who had undergone three laparotomies in hospital in the Middle East for severe abdominal pain (first for suspected appendicitis, then for suspected gall bladder disease) but with completely negative results, became confused and Leslie Doyle noted that he had some loss of sensation in the legs with absent reflexes. He asked me whether we could look at him together as he knew of my interest in neurology. When we found that he was passing very dark urine of port-wine colour, the penny dropped and we realized that we were dealing with a case of acute idiopathic porphyria which the physicians and surgeons who had dealt with him at BMH Fayid had failed to recognize; the attack on board ship had been precipitated, as so often happens, by his having been given a nocturnal barbiturate. The memory of that incident stayed with me and helped me to diagnose the condition on several occasions later.

Sailing through the Suez Canal was a memorable experience. I shall always remember my first sight of the impressive Anzac memorial close to the RAMC base depot at Gebel Maryam which we subsequently came to know better, just as one could not fail to be impressed by the expansive lake area around the port of Ismailia, before one rejoined the Canal to sail on to Port Tewfik where we had a few hours ashore to explore its palm-lined streets and attractive boulevards before taking on stores at Adibaya and then setting sail down the Red Sea. Fortunately, as this was late December, the area was not as oppressively hot as it would have been in the summer. We had heard harrowing tales of heat exhaustion cases occurring there when soldiers and even some officers failed to take appropriate precautions, and a colleague from Newcastle, Captain Harold Lake, later told us of his experience as a medical officer on a landing ship tank (LST) which lost its rudder in the Red Sea and began to circle aimlessly in a temperature of over 110° F with no air-conditioning, before eventually being rescued and towed into port by a naval tug.

The voyage past 'The Brothers' in the Red Sea and then the 'Twelve Apostles', before passing through the 'Gates of Hell' into the Gulf of Aden and onwards to Mombasa was uneventful, the sea being calm throughout. It was enlivened by the CO's decision, aided and abetted by several long-serving senior NCOs, to hold a formal 'crossing the line' ceremony for the initiation of those of us who had never previously crossed the Equator. A canvas swimming pool was hastily rigged on the deck aft and the old soldiers who conducted the ceremony under the watchful eye of the CO, himself dressed as King Neptune, somehow managed to garb themselves in outlandish costumes (one staff sergeant made a most impressive Zulu with spear and shield). We who had never crossed the line, including the nursing officers (fortunately all of us had brought swimming costumes on the voyage) were ceremonially ducked and later given formal certificates to acknowledge our participation in the ceremony.

We were most impressed by our first sight of Mombasa with its splendid beaches and palm-lined streets, though the few of us who were taken by road for a brief visit to the medical centre at the Army Camp at

McKinnon Road, between Mombasa and Nairobi, were much less impressed on learning that that camp had the highest incidence of malignant tertian malaria and of cerebral malaria of any British military installation in the world. Fortunately, after leaving Port Said, we had all taken our anti-malarials regularly and no member of the crew or of the military personnel succumbed. It was a pleasure to find that the EMO in Mombasa was Captain Ramsay Horler, another old friend and member of our year, whom we were able to entertain briefly on board before we restocked the ship, took on board a few military passengers and some more Mauritians and sailed for Mauritius, 'the pearl of the South Indian Ocean', passing Madagascar, with a glimpse of Diego Suarez Bay, en route.

Mauritius was then, and presumably still is, a truly magical island, ringed by coral lagoons, gleaming white beaches and with an impressive range of mountains cutting across the centre of the island and dividing it in some respects so precisely that the climate is remarkably variable. While the sun is shining brightly from a cloudless sky on one side of the island, a tropical storm might be flooding another area on the other side of the range. Port Louis was not itself a particularly attractive town but the capital, Curepipe, high up on a plateau towards the mountain range, where I was taken by Captain David Scott, the EMO, was much more so. With my interest in neurology nurtured by Professor Nattrass, I could not help reflecting that Charles Edouard Brown-Séquard, the great British/American neurologist, had been born on Mauritius as the product of a union between an American sea captain, Captain Brown, and a French planter's daughter, Mme Séquard. The island had enormous charm though beneath the surface all was not so glamorous and John Rogan much later told us that in a single night ashore a stoker from the ship had succeeded in acquiring syphilis, gonorrhoea, scabies, soft sore and crab lice. After disembarking our invalids, we had sufficient time in the two days that we spent in port to visit the Jardins de Pamplemousse and to take a picnic at Grand Bay, which was then a magnificent semi-circular deserted beach, protected from the incursion of sharks by a coral reef. Swimming in the crystal-clear water of the lagoon, in which it was easy to see below the tropical fish and the enchantingly sparkling many-coloured coral dotted about on the sandy bottom, was a wonderful experience, and we all wished to return one day in a different capacity, though as yet for myself that hope has never been fulfilled.

Our return journey to Mombasa was enlivened by the fact that we embarked as passengers the band of the King's African Rifles who had played for a ceremonial occasion on the island and were returning to their headquarters in Kenya. They played for us on several occasions ('Colonel Bogey', extracts from 'The Student Prince' and many other familiar pieces were included in their repertoire) and indeed did so on deck as we sailed into Mombasa. They were 45 keen young black musicians, with an average age of 17, whose enthusiasm far outweighed their musicianship and, as one of our number wryly remarked, 'This lot wouldn't make much of an impression at the brass band festival at Belle Vue'. Nevertheless their presence added greatly to the pleasure of our peaceful return voyage.

Equally peaceful at first was the journey back from Mombasa to the Middle East, with 30 British invalids on board who were being repatriated. As we approached the Gulf of Aden I exchanged greetings with my old friend of Glasgow days, Captain Sidney French, whose SS 'Chitral', outward bound, passed us to starboard. But as we approached the 'Gates of Hell' our boilers began to play up yet again and we were compelled to call at Aden for water and oil and temporary repairs. A 24-hour stay gave us the opportunity of visiting the Crater district and of seeing the famous tombs and reservoirs allegedly built by the Queen of Sheba, as well as huge bones thought to be a part of dinosaur skeletons. I also bought another beautiful embossed Indian carpet and the RAF entertained us briefly in their officers' mess. Unfortunately as the ship approached Suez it became increasingly clear that we had another major problem not just with the boilers but with a broken propeller blade; her homing instinct had surfaced again and we were told that we would need to spend at least a week in dry dock there for urgent repairs. Our invalids and the nursing officers were transferred by train to BMH Fayid and we male officers, leaving only a skeleton staff on board, were transported by road to the RAMC depot at Gebel Maryam to spend a few days under canvas since in dry dock all of the ship's toilets became unusable.

I had never realized before just how perishing cold it could be in January in the Egyptian desert alongside the Canal; the temperature in the middle of the night often fell below freezing so that we all required masses of blankets to keep us even reasonably warm. Another problem was that the Egyptian population were becoming increasingly restive about the presence of British troops, so that arms were again issued to all officers leaving the camp in the vicinity of the Canal Zone. Many tales were told at the time about the ingenuity of the local inhabitants. One Egyptian driver of an Army truck had driven off the road into the Canal allegedly, as he said, to save the vehicle from being stolen; he claimed he had been attacked by bandits armed with automatic weapons. When a line of bullet holes was discovered in his cab, he was feted as a hero until a local village dignitary revealed that he had fallen asleep at the wheel and had borrowed a drill to bore the holes. The camp itself was ringed with a high wire fence but on one occasion some of the locals managed to avoid the Nubian guards. Having cut through the wire, they entered the camp during the night and completely stripped two officers of all of their belongings while they were asleep. These two unfortunate gentlemen woke up to find nothing left in their respective tents apart from the beds upon which they were sleeping. Fortunately we officers from the 'El Nil' escaped that fate.

While at Gebel Maryam we did have the opportunity of visiting BMH Fayid and of making a preliminary assessment of the patients whom we would be repatriating to the UK and of another batch of German POWs. We were also allowed a train trip to Cairo with an overnight stay at a rather seedy establishment called the Victoria Hotel. This gave us time to visit some of the sights of the city, including the famous mosque, and above all to see the Pyramids at Gizah. When we arrived at the Pyramids after enjoying a leisurely lunch at the Mina House Hotel, we were immediately attacked by a swarm of dragomen who virtually lifted each of us bodily into the air, some trying to get us on to a camel, others on to a horse. When calm was restored, I found myself sitting on a horse, while some of the others were on camels. The photograph subsequently taken of our group was of admirable quality, and when delivering the Telford Memorial Lecture in Manchester in 1990 I was surprised to find that Leslie Doyle had surreptitiously prepared a slide of it for projection during my introduction. The first sight of those Pyramids and of the Sphinx is, of course, breathtaking and their sheer magnitude and grandeur will always induce a sharp intake of breath. That sense of awe is rapidly followed by a feeling of astonishment that monuments of this magnitude and scale could conceivably have been built simply with the aid of hordes of slave labour so many centuries ago. When Betty came with me on a Swan Hellenic cruise in 1989, the impact upon her was as great as that which this spectacle had had upon me so many years earlier. As we wound our way back from the Pyramids towards our transport, some of us decided that we would try to achieve a little more speed from our respective steeds. But when I slapped the horse which I was riding on one flank, the dragoman said to me plaintively 'Hey meester, my horse called Charlie Chaplin; he very good horse, but meester, you no slap Charlie Chaplin, he pregnant'.

Eventually the news came through from Port Said that the ailing 'El Nil' had been repaired and was now seaworthy and so we re-embarked at Suez, only to find that we faced a further two or three-day delay as an Italian tanker had broken down and had blocked the canal. Eventually we arrived in Port Said at 10 p.m. three days later, but despite the late hour we embarked 300 patients and Maurice Wood worked like a Trojan. Even now, the delays were not over as he told us that the ports of Tobruk and Tripoli had just been reopened and that we must call there as well as in Malta and Gibraltar for more patients. Tobruk was unexciting save for the wrecks of the Italian cruiser 'San Giorgio' (which had been removed from the harbour entrance) and the SS 'Ligorna'. We took on 15 patients there and another 25 in Tripoli, where concrete blocks which had been sunk by the Germans across the harbour entrance had just been removed. The wreck of an Italian hospital ship was lying on its side in the harbour but nevertheless the city, with its long curving promenade, its gleaming white buildings and its lovely classical opera house, looked beautiful in the sun. A short visit to what the Port Medical Officer called 'a lemonade factory' led to us each receiving some gifts of exotic Italian liqueurs. During our usual brief stop at Malta, I was enormously impressed by the sight in port of the battleship HMS 'Vanguard', the pride of the Royal Navy, and we also paid a brief fraternal visit to the only other remaining hospital ship afloat, the HMS 'Maine'. This, my last voyage, was only slightly marred by the fact that after returning from Hamburg in a Force 10 gale, I met an excessively rigid customs officer in Southampton to whom, as usual, I declared all of my purchases with perhaps the exception of a few trivialities. For the first time I was charged £20 customs duty on my Indian carpet, so lovingly purchased in Aden, and £30 on that bought in Port Said; he even charged me duty on some more British-made sheets which Betty had asked me to buy in the officers' shop in Port Said to help in furnishing our new home.

By this time (early March 1949) I was becoming increasingly anxious about my subsequent career, recognizing that we were now burdened with a mortgage, that my relatively lavish Army pay as a major (which had by now risen to about £1000 a year, including all allowances) would soon be coming to an end and that I had no job to which to return. Since such trivial capital sums as I had managed to save during my service had all been absorbed in the purchase of the house and our few items of furniture, apprehension mounted and was not greatly allayed when I went to see Prof. Nattrass and various other physicians at the Royal Victoria Infirmary, to be told that a medical registrar post was about to be advertised but that there would inevitably be, apart from myself, several more senior candidates of greater and longer experience, some of whom had served as graded medical specialists in the Forces. This anxiety over my future had clouded to some extent my last and longest voyage on the 'El Nil', but during our brief stay in Southampton before our final trip to Hamburg, I learned from Betty that the interviews for the registrar appointment were being held on a date when that voyage would have been completed and when it was virtually certain that I would be able to take leave in order to meet the committee. I travelled home in fear and trepidation which was not lessened when I discovered that of the five candidates short-listed, I was the only one to have had no experience other than my two house officer posts and my Army service. But in the end I was deeply gratified (and much relieved) that the committee chose me for the appointment. So I returned to Southampton to complete my last few weeks in the Army, during which Colonel Davy, who was due for demobilization at the same time, and I completed the process of handing over the ship to our successors. Feeling at last secure in the knowledge that I had an appointment to return to which would begin immediately after my demobilization, that I had a pleasant, if sparsely furnished, home in which my wife and daughter were now happily installed, I completed the demobilization process, said goodbye to those friends and colleagues with whom I had enjoyed so many fascinating experiences, and returned to Newcastle to face the future as a medical registrar on the princely salary of £400 per annum.

CHAPTER 6

Medical Registrar

In view of my limited clinical experience during my two years in the Army, and since I had only opened a medical textbook on very rare occasions (for reference purposes) throughout that period, I faced the prospect of a return to continuing clinical responsibility with considerable apprehension. During my short demobilization leave, I read quickly through a few chapters of Conybeare's 'Medicine' and also slipped down to the RVI to attend one or two clinical meetings, but nevertheless anticipated my first ward round with the formidable Dr Alan G. Ogilvie ('The Og' or AGO) with some anxiety. Curiously, I felt less concerned about working for the legendary Henry George Miller, then still known locally as Henry 'Gorgeous' Miller. After leaving the RAF Medical Branch at the end of the war, he had gone back to Queen Square to polish up his neurology before being appointed assistant physician to the RVI in about 1948. Fortunately, also serving on the 'firm' was a mature post-service registrar, Dr Ian Spencer (later to become a consultant physician in Tynemouth), who, despite being a prisoner of war in Germany for several years, had built up a considerable store of clinical experience; he proved to be an outstanding mentor and teacher. In fact integration into civilian medicine and into the life and work of a teaching hospital proved easier than I had expected and before long I felt myself completely at home in attending ward rounds, undertaking emergency duty, assisting in the out-patients, carrying out follow-up clinics (including special clinics for asthma and for diabetes) and even in teaching medical students—a task which every registrar was then required regularly to undertake.

The students were an extraordinarily mixed bunch, with many varied backgrounds. Between half and two-thirds of them had come into medicine directly from school, as I myself had done, but the remainder were men (and a few women) who had served in the Forces in various capacities during the war and who had been given the opportunity, on post-service grants, of studying medicine after demobilization. Most of these were ex-officers in their thirties and some had notable wartime records, such as F. A. Haddock (known to his colleagues as 'Fin'). He had had a distinguished career in occupied France where his alleged relationship with a countess who lived in the chateau where for a time he took refuge greatly enhanced his reputation (whether or not the story had a grain of truth or was totally apocryphal is still uncertain). Later 'Fin', with whom I kept sporadically in touch, went to Grimsby as a general practitioner but subsequently made a much greater national reputation as an abstract painter in oils, as F. Aldridge Haddock. Equally memorable in his own way was J. F. S. T. McClory who supplemented his grant in order to maintain his wife and family by working in the evenings and at night as a taxi driver from the Central Station while continuing to study medicine. He was a very able golfer, against whom I played on more than one occasion in the staff v. students annual golf match; he also had a private pilot's licence and after graduation won several flying competitions for light aircraft, as well as joining my Territorial Army unit where we shared many interesting experiences (of this more later). Once he himself was established in general practice in the West End of Newcastle, he insisted that his wife, despite her family responsibilities, should study medicine. Eventually she entered the Newcastle Medical School, graduated without difficulty and joined him as a partner. Another lively, even ebullient, character who stood out from the crowd, was A. H. Grabham who had come directly from school and who, after training in Newcastle, later became a consultant in Kettering and ultimately chaired the BMA Council during my Presidency before becoming, as Sir Anthony, the distinguished Chairman of the Joint Consultants' Committee. One of the most outstanding students whom I taught during my time as a registrar was J. B. (Jack) Foster, a man of considerable brilliance and the intellectual leader of his year. He too was an excellent golfer with a single figure handicap; his questioning in our clinical teaching sessions demonstrated to the full his lively, inquisitive mind and kept me on my toes. Henry and I were delighted when he chose to train in neurology after National Service in the Royal Navy. I remember well and much enjoyed the sometimes far from respectful inquisition to which these lively student groups subjected me and their other teachers. After one such group had spent several weeks on 'the Og's' 'firm', they were kind enough to present me with a whip as a parting present.

That experience engendered in me a love of clinical teaching at the bedside which has lasted. Ever since I have obtained great enjoyment and professional satisfaction from being able to discuss with under-graduates or postgraduates, or both, clinical history taking, physical examination and differential diagnosis based upon the pathophysiological analysis of clinical problems. Indeed I still enjoy the exercise of being presented with the clinical history of a patient whom (with his or her agreement) I can then examine before discussing the possible diagnoses which come to mind on clinical evidence alone, before being presented with the results of any tests which have been performed and which may confirm or refute my suggestions. This 'blind' assessment of clinical problems is something which I have done regularly in many different parts of the world and which I hope to go on doing from time to time (as I tell my colleagues) until I am invariably proved wrong. I think it is invaluable for young trainees to see in this way into the mental processes of an experienced clinician. It is not, of course, for me to say, but I believe from such feedback as I have received over the years that clinical teaching has always been one of my fortés. I believe, too, that the more one sees of medical practice the more one comes to recognize that whereas clinical expertise can be developed and honed through guidance, example and experience, there are nevertheless some highly intelligent doctors who find this clinical analytical process exceptionally difficult. But others who regularly take what often seem like unjustifiable short-cuts (such as Henry Miller) demonstrate an intuitive brilliance and a 'feel' for clinical diagnosis and management which is inborn and generally reliable, though clearly fuelled by past experience ('this is something I have seen before and therefore recognize').

The heavy load of clinical responsibility which I carried as a registrar with 'the Og' and the many out-patients and in-patients whom I saw undoubtedly helped me to sharpen my skills in diagnosis and management in general or internal medicine. And I believe that I was able to acquire and develop, and thus to be able to teach, a clinical method based upon a pathophysiological analysis of symptomatology and signs, while bearing in mind the importance of emotional and physical inborn characteristics and of environmental influences. Everyone who loves clinical medicine and possesses some diagnostic expertise develops a kind of medical sixth sense allowing him or her to discard the irrelevant, to recognize the significant and to be able quickly to collate a constellation of clinical phenomena into a coherent whole. Perhaps it was such an inherent trait which enabled me within a few weeks of arriving on 'the Og's' firm to reach a correct diagnosis in a patient whom Henry Miller invited me to examine with the kind of wicked twinkle in his eye which I subsequently recognized as implying that he expected to catch me out. Although I had never seen the condition before, when I spoke to the 13-year-old girl in question and found that she had a striking and unusual slurring speech, as well as inco-ordinate movements of the limbs, and when on examining her eyes with an ophthalmoscope I saw the sudden golden flash of a ring around the cornea (due to the deposition of copper), something stirred in the mists of memory leading me to recognize that she was suffering from Wilson's disease (hepatolenticular degeneration). The patient was subsequently given appropriate treatment with penicillamine, with very great benefit, and in later years I continued to see her in one of my neurological clinics. Eventually she became a nursing sister and a mother, as the condition had been diagnosed and treated sufficiently early. The outcome in her brother, not previously known to be affected, who had no neurological symptoms but conspicuous liver enlargement, was also very satisfactory.

On yet another occasion I was greatly puzzled by the problems presented by a lady in her forties who came into hospital with a history of curious episodes in which she developed throbbing headache and a racing pulse and perspired profusely. On straightforward examination we could detect nothing abnormal, but soon after admission a paroxysm occurred in which her pulse rate went up to 160 per minute, she was drenched in perspiration and her blood pressure rose to over 250 mm Hg systolic. Investigation confirmed our suspicions that she was suffering from a phaeochromocytoma of the adrenal and this condition was the subject of my second scientific publication in *The Lancet*, in which I described the clinical features, diagnosis and management of the condition with particular reference to this lady's case. Perhaps I may be forgiven for quoting a third experience which made a lasting impression. Since, as the Og's registrar, I was often required to take his asthma clinic, I was called urgently to the RVI physiotherapy department to see a lady physiotherapist was thought to be having a severe asthmatic attack. I found her panting deeply and rapidly with a flushed face and rapid pulse, complaining of tingling around the mouth and in the hands which were cramped in the 'main d'accoucheur' position; she was surrounded by solicitous colleagues saying 'Use your diaphragm dear'. When I insisted they leave us alone, firm but sympathetic exhortation quickly terminated the attack which, as I later learned, had been precipitated by a broken romance. This helped me later to recognize easily the classical features of hysterical hyperventilation (which, of course, it was).

Writing has always given me particular pleasure despite the recognition, confirmed by others, that I have at times a tendency to prolixity which is difficult to curb (one kind colleague once suggested that John Walton had written more than he had read). Having written on Osler and Sydenham for the students' *Medical Gazette*, I later wrote, with Alan Jenkins, a paper for that journal on anaemia in pregnancy, based upon our experience with some patients whom we had each seen as housemen, but my two papers in *The Lancet* on intravenous infusions and phaeochromocytoma were the first to appear in national and international publications. There quickly followed a short report in the *British Medical Journal*, written jointly with one of our house officers, Dr Norma Lill (later Dr Norma Forster), in which we reported two cases of bleeding Meckel's diverticulum. Despite my leaning towards neurology, an interest nurtured increasingly by Henry Miller, yet another fascinating clinical problem began to exercise my interest as a result of my treating over about two years a girl of 17 who had aplastic anaemia and for whose regular blood transfusions I found myself responsible. This was long before the days when continuous intravenous lines and other modern sophisticated techniques of obtaining access to the venous system were devised and bone marrow transplantation was, of course, unheard of. Pat had had many transfusions before I began to look after her; many veins had been damaged and some indeed had thrombosed. We never discovered the cause of her aplastic anaemia and in the end I resorted to many different tricks in order to give her blood, including on more than one occasion transfusion into the external jugular vein, because of the inaccessibility of those in the limbs. Fortunately the intervals between her transfusions became longer and longer and she eventually began to make her own blood again. Ultimately she recovered completely and married, though she was never able to have children; she had experienced such menorrhagia in the early days of her illness that eventually Dr R. B. Thompson advised us to irradiate her ovaries to stop her menstrual periods.

My interesting and rewarding experiences with this patient encouraged me to study as intensively as I could all of the patients with aplastic anaemia who had been admitted to the Royal Victoria Infirmary over a 10-year period; many of them had been under the care of another assistant physician, Dr T. H. (Tom) Boon, with whom I wrote a paper describing our joint experiences. I use the term literally as I wrote out the entire text, the case histories and the references in longhand and gave them to Tom Boon's secretary for typing; how it happened she could never explain, but my precious manuscript, produced by many hours of labour, disappeared. Eventually I had to start again from scratch from my notes and jottings, as photocopying was unknown in those days and it had never occurred to me to make a carbon copy. This was a lesson learned and I hope and believe that the paper was much improved at its second writing; certainly the editor of the *Quarterly Journal of Medicine* accepted it with alacrity and I was much impressed and encouraged (the feeling wore off in later years) by the flood of reprint requests I received from many parts of the world.

As the weeks and months fled by, I developed an increasing regard and respect for 'the Og', though he was a man of unusual personality who sometimes used an extraordinary medical shorthand, never easy to interpret; and his distractibility and absent-mindedness sometimes led him into amusing and memorable indiscretions. He had a wickedly Puckish sense of humour which always enlivened our contacts, but his innate kindness and generosity to patients and to staff in all grades belied the aura of fierceness engendered by his gruff and sometimes stentorian voice. With his red hair, beetling eyebrows, heavy features and muscular frame, invariably attired in brown tweed and brown shoes to match his colouring, some patients were at first frightened of him but soon recognized the kindliness beneath the formidable exterior. Students were less ready to recognize these saving graces and found his clinical experience impressive but his teaching much less so as it was often so disorganized. I once heard him ask a student if the cardiac apex beat was systolic; neither I nor the hapless student ever came to know what he meant. Examples of his medical shorthand abounded; once after examining a patient he turned to the houseman and said 'You'd better do them and, if they're up, split them'. This meant that the patient needed a white cell count and, if the total count was raised, a differential count. On another occasion, turning to me he said 'You remember the man in bed 9 from Blyth with the leg—get his notes'. After learning the principles of his code, only very rarely were we stumped. As he had a deep and abiding interest in chest diseases, we often watched him examining patients' chests and paled at the vigour with which he, as a former athlete of note, carried out percussion; the thuds often echoed round the ward, though few, if any, patients ever complained. Not infrequently we saw him applying a stethoscope to the chest wall and looking at the end of the instrument with puzzlement when he found that he could hear nothing, for the good reason that he had not put the earpieces into his ears. Once he came to hospital and completed half his ward round with the two ends of his tie hanging loosely around his neck before anyone dared point out that his dressing had been incomplete. On yet another occasion he appeared wearing one black and one brown shoe—and when again this was hesitantly drawn to his attention, he said with a twinkle 'Do you know, I think I have another pair like that at home'.

But 'the Og's' experience of emergency medicine was unrivalled and recognized as such by many of his colleagues and by general practitioners. One GP colleague said that he knew how excellent a clinical opinion Dr Ogilvie usually gave and would have called him out much more often in consultation were it not for the fact that whenever he had done so, he invariably had to go back to explain to the patient what AGO meant. 'The Og's' emergency experience was undoubtedly enhanced by the fact that, even in his later years, when his 'firm' was on reception he would invariably come to his wards late at night to see the patients who had been admitted during the day; all of us, housemen and registrars, were expected to be on parade. On one never-to-be-forgotten occasion, an elderly gentleman had come in complaining of bleeding per rectum. We had examined him and were unable to identify the source. 'The Og', wishing to carry out a rectal examination, arranged for screens to be placed around the bed and invited the patient to lie on his left side while Sister provided the glove. After inserting his finger, and while gazing out of the window, he said loudly 'Oh, dear me' and we could not think what we could possibly have missed. On removing the finger he turned to Sister as he handed her the glove and said 'Oh dear me, another seven years bad luck—I've just seen the new moon through glass'. Fortunately, the patient, as well as the staff, saw the joke and he then turned to the patient and gave him a kindly explanation, this time very clearly, about what the appropriate management of his problem would be. Another patient in the out-patient department was, however, much less impressed when, after describing some symptoms suggesting that he was having difficulty in passing urine, 'the Og' said 'Can you start all right? Can you stop all right? Can you reverse?—Oh, I'm sorry, I was thinking about my car'. His distractibility was further exemplified by the occasion when he walked to hospital from his home in Brandling Park, Jesmond, spent the morning working and then not being able to find his car in the hospital car park at lunch-time, he telephoned the police and reported it stolen, whereas it had, of course, been parked outside his home all morning. And on a ward round in our female ward he came across a strikingly attractive lady sitting up in bed and said 'Ah yes, this must be one of Dr Miller's patients' and moved on; she was, but we were never sure just how he could be so certain, despite the growing reputation that Henry Miller was acquiring in private practice in the locality.

Christmas time on Wards 13 and 10 was also very lively and, without fail, 'the Og' always came in on Christmas Day to carve turkey for the patients. Housemen, registrars and their families were required to watch (a 'three-line whip') before repairing to sister's room for drinks, coffee, mince pies and Christmas cake (and the distribution of presents to the staff); I still treasure several books which 'the Og' and Henry gave me. Bearing in mind AGO's innate clumsiness (despite his athleticism, his erstwhile skill as a long-distance runner and his continuing interest in fell-walking and beagling, he was strikingly maladroit) he invariably borrowed a waterproof apron from one of the operating theatres to protect his clothing while carving. More than once the turkey ended up partially on his lap or even on the floor under the vigorous thrust of the carving knife which he applied with obsessive intensity, all the while with protruding and oscillating tongue. Even in the midst of these celebrations his wit shone through, as in the case of a man who had been admitted on Christmas Eve, having over-indulged, with an acute exacerbation of a peptic ulcer, for which in those days the appropriate treatment was a nasal tube and a slow drip of milk into the stomach. Looking at him sadly and shaking his head, 'the Og' said 'Oh Sister, look at that poor fellow in the corner, not able to have any Christmas turkey; speed up his drip, please, speed up his drip'.

These and innumerable other tales enlivened my association with Alan Ogilvie—a kindly man, a delightful mentor, a strong supporter of all his junior staff, he was also generous to a fault. When any member of the 'firm' succeeded in passing the MRCP examination, he invariably organized a dinner for the successful individual and spouse in Tilley's, then the best restaurant in Newcastle, with Henry and Eileen Miller and other members of the 'firm'. I remember clearly more than one such riotous occasion, especially that after I myself passed the examination in 1950. Betty, too, enjoyed these events; after her initial fear of 'the Og' she learned to like and respect him as much as I did, though she always felt somewhat swamped by the towering presence of Henry

Miller who, despite his reputation as something of a ladies' man, was so dominant a personality, with such an extraordinary flow of sparkling and mordant wit, that many people, and women in particular, seemed perpetually overawed in his company. Coming, as we both had done, from the relatively cloistered lower middle class background of Spennymoor, we had neither of us been much exposed to rapid, erudite and witty conversation, and it took Betty many years before she felt comfortable in Henry's presence. I too could not help but feel a little suppressed by his extraordinary and versatile personality. Often then and for several years afterwards, whenever I attempted to best him in conversation or to cap one of his fierce and outrageously funny quips, I found myself coming off second best. Sometimes, indeed, in striving to manufacture an appropriate response, I found that I had been painfully, and not at all amusingly, sarcastic to a degree which I had never intended. But on the rare occasions when I or anyone else did succeed in getting the better of an argument, he invariably roared with laughter and insisted on telling other people about it. And he was always ready to extol the diagnostic triumphs of his junior staff, particularly if and when they succeeded in detecting something which he had failed to spot and which either changed the diagnosis or significantly altered the patient's management. The only young doctor in whose case that particular principle faltered was one of our housemen, Anthony Ashcroft, who regularly clerked and examined patients whom Henry had seen in private practice or on a domiciliary consultation before arranging admission to the RVI. In those days it was customary, whenever possible, for the houseman and the registrar to meet the consultant each morning at the entrance to the hospital. It is said, perhaps apocryphally, that Dr Ashcroft would regularly say to Henry 'Good morning Dr Miller. You remember that case you sent in last night as a 'so and so'; what a pity that you missed (the specific feature) which strongly suggests that the diagnosis is 'so and so''. We often said that this little habit was what resulted in Anthony Ashcroft making a distinguished career in general practice rather than hospital medicine, though I believe that this was always his intention.

To return to 'the Og' and his MRCP dinner parties, he often regaled us as the night wore on with his years of early struggle when, as an honorary registrar in the RVI, he eked out his living by doing evening surgeries for GPs and child welfare clinics in the area (which gave him a tenuous attachment to the Department of Child Health). His delightful wife, Grace, was however, rather prim and proper, and on one occasion when 'the Og' was roaring on about how they lived in a single room above a fish and chip shop, she said with clear evidence of outrage, 'But Alan, it was a very *nice* fish shop!' Alan Ogilvie was one of those unforgettable characters who used to abound in British medicine; perhaps the undergraduate and postgraduate education which has moulded those of us of comparable age today has ironed out those quirks and facets of personality which made people like 'the Og' and Henry so memorable. When after two years I left 'the Og's' firm to begin research with Fred Nattrass, AGO wrote me a charming letter in which he said 'In years to come when I look back with parkinsonian stoop and tremor upon my years at the RVI, I shall be able to say 'Sir John Walton was once my registrar''. I thought that he was guilty, as so often, of gross hyperbole but was nevertheless greatly touched. After retiring from the RVI and after writing a distinguished work on chronic bronchitis based upon his long experience of this condition in Northumberland and Durham, he moved permanently, with Grace, to the cottage they had long owned at Thropton, near Rothbury in Northumberland, where he could continue to indulge his many interests, all countryside-based. Sadly when, in his late seventies, I saw him as a patient, he was beginning to develop those manifestations of neurological disease which ultimately led to his having to be admitted to a long-stay hospital where I saw him more than once and where, despite the effects of his illness, his charming twinkle and lively chuckle still shone through; even in the last few months of his life flashes of reminiscence and recognition continued to surface.

Henry was, without question, one of the most remarkable figures in British medicine of the age. When I first knew him, he was relatively slim and was gradually building up a huge private practice in general medicine, but more particularly in neurology and in psychiatry, in the North East. He regularly dressed in black jacket, grey waistcoat, pinstriped trousers and carnation in the buttonhole, though after a few years he came to recognize that attire which might be regarded as de rigeur in Harley Street did not necessarily impress as much in Geordieland. Such recognition probably dawned after the occasion when he came with retinue, including myself, to Ward 13 to see his patients; as he approached the bed in which one of them was lying, the Geordie in the next bed took one look at him and said 'Ee, what a toff—I wonder what he wears on Sundays?'. The more I worked with him, the more I came to admire and respect his intuitive diagnostic skill and his remarkable ability to handle some difficult clinical problems. True, there were occasions when his inevitable quips were wounding rather than funny, and a few patients found his rather cavalier and seemingly casual approach offputting and even offensive, though most adored it. None, however, could fail to be impressed by the sheer magnetism and overweening personality of the man and, as I came to know him better, I came to admire him more and more, despite the inevitable annoyances and irritations. He, like the Og, was incredibly generous and would, for instance, every year take me and a colleague (often Robert Orton from the Department of Psychiatry) to the annual BMA meeting in his car, which he drove with typical verve and abandon. In the early days on the 'firm' he went through a phase of buying Jowett

Javelins one after another (two, at least, were 'pranged'). On our way to such a meeting in Harrogate we stopped characteristically to enjoy a huge meal (which he had ordered by telephone in advance) at the George Inn at Wetherby. Having taken the wrong road in or near Ripon, he found himself by mistake entering the driveway of an imposing residence which, we believe, was that of the Bishop of Ripon who seemed to be holding a garden party. Fortunately the drive was semi-circular with an entrance and exit; Henry, with typical verve drove straight through, his tyres spraying gravel, while the Bishop and his guests looked on in astonishment.

Often Henry would take me out with him on a private domiciliary consultation which frequently led to my having to help him in the management of patients with, for example, haematemesis, either in the Saville Nursing Home in Jesmond or in some other appropriate private ward such as that of the Leazes Hospital (the private wing of the RVI). While Henry's knowledge and experience in neurology was well-recognized, he was nevertheless practising then as a general physician and once had three private patients with cardiac infarction in the Leazes. Hewan Dewar, who had been appointed assistant physician at the same time and whose principal interest was cardiology, met Henry in the Leazes one day and, in my presence, said 'Good gracious, Miller, I see you've got three patients with cardiac infarction in the ward; what do you know about cardiac infarction?', to which Henry riposted 'Nothing, but I know a great deal about Jews'. The management of haematemesis in a private nursing home in Jesmond was by no means easy. It inevitably involved taking a blood sample for cross-matching, collecting matched blood from the transfusion service, and then erecting a drip. At the Saville Nursing Home I discovered that there was no such thing as a drip-stand and in one particular case (the alcoholic managing director of a major Tyneside company) the only way in which the drip could be made to function was by bringing in a hall stand upon which the bottles of blood could be hung alongside the patient's bed. Soon the position was put right by obtaining a proper drip-stand, but as I expostulated to Henry, there were better situations and circumstances in which such emergencies could be managed, though the nursing staff were outstanding.

These experiences led Henry to recommend me as a transfuser to Harvey Evers for whom I often performed similarly before Wertheim operations or other major gynaecological procedures at Fernwood, which was Harvey's private nursing home just down the road from the Saville. Both Henry and Harvey were very generous and each invariably paid me fees for these tasks which helped me to eke out the miserable income I was then receiving from the RVI. These extras certainly contributed towards keeping the wolf from the door, as did the fact that because of my previous interest in, and experience of, paediatrics, I was nominated by James Spence to carry out fortnightly child welfare clinics in Dinnington Colliery Welfare and in Stannington by the Northumberland County

Council (the first held in a cricket pavilion, the second in a back room of the 'Howard Arms' public house). Even though these activities occupied one afternoon a fortnight at a time when I was supposed to be a whole-time registrar, 'the Og' and Henry both approved, particularly since 'the Og' had done exactly the same himself in his registrar days. An afternoon session in a child welfare clinic from 2.00–4.00 paid the princely sum at that time of £2 10s. per session. But even an extra £5.00 monthly made a major contribution to the failing family finances. Eventually, however, the great day came in late 1949, more than a year after the establishment of the National Health Service, when I learned that as from the date I had been appointed I had been graded as a registrar and Ian Spencer as a senior registrar. My salary therefore jumped from £400 per annum to £775; there was even some substantial back-pay which helped a little towards paying off the growing overdraft.

Henry, of course, was not only an able general physician and outstanding neurologist but also a competent psychiatrist. While in the RAF he had obtained a Diploma in Psychological Medicine, though this was a qualification that he subsequently suppressed. Nevertheless I learned much from him about the manifestations of depressive illness in particular and often admired the way in which he handled some difficult psychiatric problems. Once he was called to Hexham General Hospital to examine a scion of the nobility who had suffered a fracture-dislocation of the spine in a riding accident and who allegedly was refusing to stay in bed. As the injury was to the dorsal region and was unstable, and as the patient had no evidence of any weakness or numbness in the legs, it was clearly important to prevent spinal cord damage. Henry arrived and after listening to the history and following a pretty cursory neurological examination, which confirmed the absence of signs, he turned to the patient and said 'I understand that you're keen to get up and walk around', to which the patient replied 'Yes doctor'. Henry said 'Well, you're a racing man and knowledgeable about odds. If you get up and walk about, there's a 50:50 chance that you'll be OK, but there's a 50:50 chance that you'll be paralyzed in your legs and lose control of your bladder and bowels for the rest of your life. I reckon that odds of evens are pretty good and, if I were in your position, I would do exactly the same. So off you go—get up and walk around', to which the patient, with a shocked expression, said 'Oh, I don't think we should take any risks, doctor'; after that there was no trouble. But Henry's psychiatry, which he regularly described, to the chagrin of some of his psychiatrist colleagues with whom he often came into sharp conflict (especially when he insisted on writing articles about psychiatry) as 'neurology without physical signs', was sometimes rather superficial. Whenever he felt himself out of his depth he always called upon Robert Orton of the Department of Psychological Medicine, then newly established under Professor Alexander Kennedy, a man of not dissimilar personality with whom Henry developed a splendid love/hate relationship built on mutual respect.

One of my first objectives after becoming a medical registrar was, of course, to pass the MRCP examination since that, after my discussions with James Spence, was my prime purpose in accepting the appointment, at least at the outset. This, after the day's work in hospital was done, regularly involved long hours of studying books and journals, often until 1.00 or 2.00 a.m. Betty was exceptionally tolerant and understanding, particularly since, as in my student days, we tried to keep weekends relatively inviolate, though there were regular ward rounds on Saturday mornings and Henry often visited the hospital on Sunday mornings as well. Nevertheless, there was some time for family outings into the country and we had also decided that it was time we had a second child. In 1950 we were delighted when Betty fell pregnant again and Judy was born in October of that year. By the end of 1949 I felt myself reasonably well prepared to face the rigours of the examination and so presented myself in London in early 1950. The papers, even including the translations from the Latin and French which were then included, were reasonably straightforward, even if many of the questions, as was then common, were phrased so vaguely and broadly as to leave one considerable flexibility in answering them. Though I felt some distress at having overlooked one obvious disease (erythema nodosum) in a question which asked what skin diseases might be due to tuberculosis, I nevertheless felt reasonably confident. When next day I presented myself at King's College Hospital for the clinical, to be examined by Macdonald Critchley and R. V. Christie, I was suitably chastened to find on being introduced to the patient whom I was supposed to question, examine and diagnose in 30 minutes flat, that he began by saying 'No spik English'. Fortunately he turned out to have a spastic paraparesis and it seems that I was able to discuss the differential diagnosis sensibly. One of my colleagues encountered a young lady of exceptionally histrionic personality and hysterical mien who had weakness of one arm and leg and he was uncertain as to whether this hemiparesis was organic or emotionally determined. Seeking to elicit the plantar response (the Babinski reflex of elevation of the great toe on stroking the sole is a safe indicator of organic disease) he found that the big toe on the affected side had been amputated and swore that the examiners had done it on purpose.

In those days marking in the MRCP examination gave 100 marks for the papers, 100 for the clinical, and 80 for the so-called pathology viva, with 20 marks left over for the final viva. The papers were written in the Old Examination Halls in Queen Square, where the pathology viva was also held, while the clinical examinations were carried out in various hospitals throughout London and the final viva took place in the old buildings of the Royal College of Physicians of London in Trafalgar Square. The pass mark was 66%. If one achieved 200 marks, therefore, after completing the pathology viva, no final viva would be required, but no candidate was told this in advance. In order to allow the examiners time to mark the papers, there was a 10–14 day interval between the papers and the clinicals on the one hand and the pathology viva on the other, and one had to await a letter from the College letting one know whether or not the first hurdle had been successfully surmounted. If one received a thick envelope, this meant failure as it would contain instructions about how one might present oneself for a retake, whereas a thin envelope usually meant success. The thin envelope eventually came to Benton Lodge Avenue, telling me simply that if I presented myself at the Examination Halls on such-and-such a date at an appropriate time, my examination would be continued. In the pathology viva one was first directed to a table with two examiners to be shown various pathological specimens, X-rays, electrocardiographs and clinical photographs and to be questioned on these. It was then the custom to move to a second table with another pair of examiners for a further 15 minutes. Things began pretty well as the first clinical photograph I was shown was of an infant's legs demonstrating severe distal erythema and swelling. When, in the light of my experience with James Spence, I remarked that this was probably Pink disease, the examiner, with a broad smile, said 'Yes!' very loudly. After this good start, things went along quite steadily until at the end of my period at the second table the examiner handed me an electrocardiogram. When I said 'Left bundle branch block' his response was 'What!', but I quickly corrected myself to say 'Paroxysmal ventricular techycardia', at which he smiled and said 'Quite right, my boy'; the bell rang and I went away feeling quite good. I stayed overnight in London at the old Cranston's Waverley Hotel in Southampton Row, beloved of northerners; in those days one could rely upon the post and, having given the hotel address at which I could be contacted, the following morning I impatiently awaited the letter saying whether or not I had been successful. Yet again my slip of paper came saying that if I would attend at the College that afternoon, my examination would be continued.

And so I went into the library under the eagle eye of the head porter who had in front of him a complete list of the names of the candidates and who, I believe, knew full well whether some would get a long final viva and others none at all. As luck would have it, the Persian doctor in front of me must have required several marks to achieve a pass as he had a final viva lasting some 30 minutes while I sat in fear and trembling awaiting my fate. When eventually I was called into the Censors' Room, the President eased himself from his chair, looked at the other Censors sitting on either side of the table, walked the length of the table; shook me by the hand and then said 'Please sit down, Dr Walton'. He then walked with leisurely gait back to the far end of the table facing me, took his seat and said 'Any questions, gentlemen?'. When the response was nil, I knew that I had achieved the pass mark without a viva, but subsequently wondered why it was that those of us in that position should be subjected to the agony of waiting when everyone involved in the examination process knew that we had already passed. Nevertheless I was so relieved that when I moved into the next room and Miss Cook, the College Secretary, said 'That will be 30 guineas, please' I paid up with good grace despite the inevitable hole that this sum, together with travelling expenses to and from London and hotel charges, etc., had made in the family budget. Amusingly the Persian doctor in front of me, who had just succeeded in passing the examination at his eleventh attempt, was sitting in the office, still perspiring and expostulating that he hadn't expected to pass and that the Embassy would now stop his grant and insist upon his returning home. That hurdle successfully completed, I stayed in London for another day in order to have the diploma conferred and met Dr John Webb from Oxford, like myself relatively recently returned from the Services, who was next in line and whom I subsequently came to know as a close friend first when he was a paediatric registrar in Newcastle and much later when he followed Donald Court as Professor of Paediatrics. I later learned that 39 candidates passed the examination from an initial entry of over 400.

Having obtained the MRCP, and bearing in mind that by then I had been qualified almost five years, my next objective was to obtain an MD as soon as possible. After consulting Henry Miller and in view of my growing interest in neurology, I decided that I would write a thesis on subarachnoid haemorrhage. I therefore set out to analyse from hospital records the clinical features of all of those patients with subarachnoid haemorrhage admitted to the RVI over a 10-year period from 1939 to 1949. Fortunately the notes written by house officers and students were pretty extensive, as were the results of CSF examination and other tests, though at that time cerebral angiography was unknown in Newcastle. However, many of the patients who had died had undergone post-mortem examination and records and slides were also available in the Pathology Department, so that there was ample material with which to work. I identified some 312 cases; since this was long before the analysis of information by computer became feasible, and since, having tried a simple card indexing system, I was not particularly enamoured of the technique which enabled one to select cards from a large number by putting a metal rod through one or more perforated holes, I set out to create a huge chart upon which the different aspects of the clinical features of the condition and the investigative findings were each carefully tabulated in longhand. Later, however, in order to analyse the findings numerically I did transfer the data on to other punch cards which could be mechanically sorted in the Hollerith machine (presumably a precursor of today's computers) which had just been installed in the RVI Records Department. I also arranged, after consulting each of the consultants under whom the patients had been admitted, to contact the general practitioners of all of the patients who had been discharged from hospital, in an effort to identify those who were still living and those who had died. In the case of the latter, the GPs, to whom I sent stamped addressed envelopes (at my personal expense) were extremely helpful in letting me know the nature of the fatal illness, as far as they were aware. Subsequently I wrote to all of the survivors and invited them to attend for examination to assist in my research programme. Some had moved, some had even gone abroad, but with persistence I was eventually able to trace all but two of the surviving patients, so that the follow-up data proved to be remarkably complete.

Yet again, long hours of evening and night-time work continued in analysing all of the data. Eventually, after a solid three-month period in late 1951 (after I had moved to the Department of Medicine) during which, apart from weekends, I worked pretty consistently after supper from about 7.30 or 8.00 until 1.30 a.m., my thesis was written and subsequently typed (again at considerable personal expense) in their spare time by some secretaries whom I had got to know (through my work in EEG interpretation) in the Department of Psychological Medicine. Betty, bless her, despite her increasing domestic responsibilities with two young children, took all the cards upon which I had listed the individual references and carefully put these into alphabetical order so that a list of several hundred references could eventually be typed. Once it was submitted I waited in keen anticipation to hear the outcome. Later I learned that Professor Nattrass had been the internal examiner and Sir Charles Symonds from Queen Square the external. Both provided enthusiastic reports and so eventually in 1952 I was able proudly to wear the scarlet and palatinate purple gown of a Doctor of Medicine of Durham University at an impressive and memorable degree ceremony in Durham Castle in the presence of Betty and her mother and my parents. Our daily help, the totally reliable Mrs Young, happily agreed to look after Ann and Judy for a part of the day.

Even at that busy time, life was not all work. Betty and I, with her mother, regularly attended Jesmond Methodist Church and we joined the badminton club and tried whenever we could to play there weekly. After playing a few desultory games of cricket for Slade's XI, I decided, with the connivance of Alan Jenkins and a number of other friends who were working at the RVI and in the area, to establish a cricket club to play friendly fixtures and which we called the Victorians (of which I shall say more later). Seeking too, in our continuing impoverished state, for sources of additional income, I was very receptive to an approach from Robert Mowbray, who by then was a physician in Durham City (having unsuccessfully competed against Hewan Dewar and Henry Miller for one of the two consultant jobs at the RVI); Robert had become Commanding

Officer of the No. 1 Northern General Hospital (TA), situated at Fenham Barracks, and was looking for a physician to join the unit. Having much enjoyed my experience of the Army, and while recognizing that joining the TA would mean one evening a week of attendance, occasional weekends of training and two weeks at camp in the summer, Betty and I eventually decided that the benefits and potential income would make this very well worth while and hence I accepted. Subsequently I served with great pleasure and considerable enthusiasm for the next 16 years (see Chapter 12). Some of the funds which I derived from that source and which also came from the sale of my Watson service microscope, which I no longer needed, went towards the purchase of a new Ford Prefect motor car to replace the ageing Austin 8 previously bought by Betty and her mother and which had given us such excellent service. The necessity of having a new car was heightened when I learned from Professor Nattrass that he wished me to join his unit to undertake some research into muscle disease, research which would inevitably involve substantial travelling in order to visit patients and their families.

Soon after I returned to Newcastle from the Army it did at last dawn upon me that I must do something positive about the obesity which had developed apace while I was a houseman and which had not abated during my Army service, no doubt largely as a result of the excellent cuisine we had enjoyed aboard ship. I still weighed over 15 stones (220 lbs) and Betty regularly pointed out to me how breathless I became when trying to play vigorous games with my agile daughter. I also discovered very quickly that I had become much more ponderous in my movements on the cricket field and badminton court. And so, by dint of severely restricting my fat and carbohydrate intake (I have never had sugar in tea or coffee since then), I succeeded in losing 2½ stone (35 lbs) in just over two months and ever since have fluctuated between about 170 and 180 lbs. I must admit that this weight loss was a great relief. I was able to move much more easily and my enjoyment of sport was much enhanced.

Unfortunately in the summer of 1949 I discovered that I had developed, quite insidiously, a swelling in my left groin which I recognized at once to be a left inguinal hernia. Although it was only intermittently painful, did not prevent me from playing cricket and had only a limited nuisance value, I recognized that it would at some stage require an operation. And then later that summer when trying to bowl quickly in a cricket match at Close House (bowling was never my forté) I twisted my right knee and developed a painful effusion. This settled with rest but a few weeks later the knee locked when I was running and I was unable to extend it fully. The realization then dawned that I had torn a medial cartilage; later the joint continued to lock occasionally, often after sudden turning movements and often at very inconvenient moments. While I soon learned that I could usually unlock it by kneeling down, flexing the joint fully and then externally rotating the leg and foot, the unlocking process was not always easy, so that clearly another operation was in prospect. Fortunately in the spring of 1950 I was able to persuade Mr J. K. Stanger to remove the torn cartilage and Mr G. Y. Feggetter to repair the left-sided hernia under the same anaesthetic so that I had two operations for the price of one! The discomfort and inconvenience of having a painful right knee and left groin at the same time was something I had not considered too carefully and I was mildly alarmed on recognizing that I had a small area of deep vein thrombosis in the right calf soon after the operation. But the worst was soon over, I was quickly up and about and able to start physiotherapy; progress was then rapid, I was back to work in three weeks and able to open the batting for the Victorians in six.

Family holidays in those days were something of a luxury. While I was in the Army Betty had rented a small cottage on a windy hillside above Garrigill in Cumbria where she took her mother and Ann for a week. Fortunately they had good weather, which was just as well because although the cottage was charmingly situated with splendid views over the village and the surrounding moorland, water had to be carried in buckets from a standpipe across the road, the toilet was an outdoor earth closet and the rooms were lit with paraffin lamps. And milk was fetched from a nearby farm. But despite Ann's persistent sleeplessness they enjoyed the week, so that in September 1949 we took the cottage again for a week. While we loved the tranquillity and stark grandeur of the Cumbrian hills and moors, the weather was intermittently cold, there were frequent showers and relentless wind, so that we vowed that we would try to seek future holidays in a location with greater creature comforts. Fortunately my newly acquired additional source of income from the TA allowed us in September 1950 to try out the Beadnell Hall Hotel which we found to be a charming and comfortable family hotel (Ann settled quite well and Betty, well advanced in pregnancy, found the temporary relief from domestic chores a joy).

By this time, after much agonizing and heart-searching, and after several consultations with Professor Nattrass and Henry Miller, I had firmly decided that I must, admittedly with some reluctance, turn my back on paediatrics in order to train in neurology (while nevertheless hoping that paediatric neurology would fall within my ambit).

Yet another interest emerged within these fruitful two years. Having been something of a student politician in the Students' Representative Council and in the BMSA, I was interested to learn that the British Medical Association (BMA) had established a Registrars' Group to represent the interests of all junior hospital doctors and particularly those in the registrar grades. Having joined the BMA on graduation, I occasionally attended meetings of its Newcastle Division and was not surprised to be approached by the Secretary and by Weldon Watts (who later became

BMA President) inviting me to establish a regional Registrars' Committee in Newcastle. I did so willingly, with the enthusiastic support of many registrar colleagues including Ian Spencer, Christo Strang, Malcolm Thompson and many more. We had quarterly meetings to discuss issues of importance to junior hospital doctors; we also held an annual dinner at which we invited speakers like James Spence and Henry to regale us with their experiences. Eventually I found myself representing the Newcastle Division on the Central Committee of the Registrars' Group at BMA House, to which I went two or three times a year. The organization was then led by R. M. (Sam) Forrester, later a consultant paediatrician in Lancashire, who soon invited me to join the Executive, so that I began to acquire some modest national responsibilities.

The registrars at the RVI also held regular clinical meetings and ward rounds in the evenings to discuss difficult or interesting clinical problems, and in these V. H. (Vin) Allen, Tom Grimson, Christo Strang, Lionel Carstairs and Alan Horler were prominent. I well recall on one such round being invited to comment on a young woman with lymphocytic meningitis who happened to have one extensor plantar response and of whom I casually enquired as to whether there had been a sick dog in the household, to which she responded immediately and positively. I only raised that question because I had just read an article in *The Lancet* about canicola fever presenting in this way, and to my amazement that turned out to be the correct diagnosis. It is upon such serendipitous events that clinical reputations sometimes depend.

During these two years of exciting clinical experience and opportunity with 'the Og' and Henry, AGO also established lunch-time discussion groups in a side room off Ward 13 at which we and other registrars, including Christo Strang, presented short prepared papers. On one such occasion Christo had been smoking a pipe, which he had laid on the desk. 'The Og', presiding, absent-mindedly picked it up, lit it, contentedly smoked it for the rest of the meeting and then took it away. Weeks later at another seminar it was 'the Og' who left the pipe on the desk and departed; we at once turned to Christo saying 'There's your chance— pick it up, he'll never remember'. Christo's hand stretched out to pick up the pipe when the door flung open and in marched 'the Og' saying 'Where's my pipe, where's my pipe?'; he took it and again disappeared. We believe that he continued to smoke it until eventually it wore out, or perhaps until he himself, after being injured in an unfortunate car accident, gave up smoking completely. When eventually he retired, many of us, including Henry, Christo, Ian and others who had worked on the 'firm', gave him a testimonial dinner at which we formally presented him with what had been known on Ward 13 as 'The Line Book' in which many of his most notable and even outrageous sayings and some of his eccentricities had been recorded for posterity. He was embarrassed but also delighted and left for Thropton with that same delightful chuckle and twinkle which had endeared him to us all.

Having now been confirmed by Durham University as a research assistant in the Department of Medicine with Professor Nattrass, I moved over to Ward 9 as from the end of March 1951, but almost immediately went, as he had arranged, for the first three months of the appointment to work at the National Hospital, Queen Square, in order to learn something about clinical electrophysiology, including EEG studies but more particularly electromyography. To leave behind my wife and two young children (Judy was still only six months of age) was a considerable wrench but in a sense it revived for us some memories of my Army service. Betty never hesitated in agreeing cheerfully that I should accept the appointment of which that short period of work, training and experience in London was a necessary part. Despite the inevitable strains it would impose, she recognized how important it was to my future career. She was particularly pleased that our friends the Richards in Dulwich, with whom she had stayed when a student at the Royal Academy, willingly agreed to house me at very reasonable cost. And since I was now to be paid £1000 per annum, we felt more confident about our financial future, even though I knew that I would lose at least temporarily the perks derived from helping Henry and Harvey Evers in private practice which had supplemented my registrar income.

CHAPTER 7

Research Assistant

I have often explained how it was that Professor Nattrass came to persuade the University to establish a research assistantship in his department in order to investigate muscular dystrophy, a topic in which he had not previously had a specific interest. Dr C. N. ('Natty') Armstrong had collaborated in the late 1930s with Dr Freda Herbert of the Department of Chemical Pathology in a clinical trial of treatment with glycine in muscular dystrophy; that trial, like so many before and since, proved the treatment to be ineffective. In 1950, a man living in Low Fell, Gateshead, whose son had 'pseudohypertrophic' muscular dystrophy and whose wife was becoming progressively crippled with Parkinson's disease decided to try to establish a lay association in order to raise funds for research. Some of the publicity which he achieved in the national press was a trifle unsavoury and headlines such as '£1000 to anyone who can save my child' abounded. But though his efforts to establish a national association foundered, he received many letters in response to these articles and among them were five from the parents of patients who had been diagnosed as suffering from muscular dystrophy but who had recovered, or had at least failed to deteriorate to the extent and as rapidly as had been suggested by the diagnosing physician. Copies of these letters were sent to the then Ministry of Health in London, where they were handed to Dr (many years later Dame) Albertine Winner, who felt that the evidence was sufficiently interesting to warrant further investigation. Accordingly, she showed the letters to two senior physicians on the staff of the National Hospital, Queen Square, each of whom said that if the initial diagnosis in these cases had been one of muscular dystrophy, it must have been wrong; they suggested no further action. Despite this rebuff, and inspired by the same determination and dogged persistence which she demonstrated throughout her subsequent distinguished career in the Department of Health, Dr Winner brought the letters to Newcastle and showed them to Fred Nattrass. He, to his everlasting credit, felt that the story was one which warranted further study and hence sought financial support through the University and from the Department of Health in order to establish the research post which I subsequently held. His motivation may not have been totally unrelated to the fact that the diagnosis in one of the cases had been made by himself and in yet another

161

by James Spence. Nevertheless, while the primary objective of the new appointment was to study those patients who had so unexpectedly recovered from what had seemed to be a progressive and incurable neuromuscular disorder, he suggested that it would also be useful to survey all the patients with muscular dystrophy and related neuromuscular conditions whom I could identify in the Northern Region as a secondary objective. He also decided that it would be necessary for me to acquire some expertise in the rapidly developing field of electro-myography (EMG) and therefore arranged for me to spend my first three months in the appointment in London, partly at Queen Square in Bill Cobb's Department of Clinical Neurophysiology, but partly also in Phillippe Bauwens' Department of Physical Medicine at St Thomas' Hospital which had acquired a considerable reputation in the EMG field. He felt, too, that it would be invaluable for me to be exposed to some of the outstanding neurological teachers on the staff at Queen Square, so as to develop further my clinical knowledge and diagnostic expertise.

Much excited, therefore, by this new opportunity, I set off by train to London at the beginning of April 1951, while nevertheless feeling some anxiety about leaving Betty and Ann and Judy, then aged three years and six months respectively, though it was reassuring that Mrs Harrison was still living nearby. We had also been fortunate in identifying Mrs Polly Young, a near neighbour who lived at 11 Benton Lodge Avenue, who came to help with the domestic chores and housework on two mornings a week and whose unfailing kindness and selfless help and support for relatively little pay proved of enormous benefit to us during our early years of married life, and indeed much later. Not only did she turn out to be a capable domestic help but her husband often helped in the garden in his spare time. Mrs Young herself was for many years our regular babysitter and became so much a friend that she adamantly refused to accept money for babysitting, even on those occasions when she looked after the children for a few nights in order to allow Betty and me to go off together on some expedition or other. Long after she no longer worked for us, she was available not only as a 'sitter' but also as a temporary custodian of our successive dogs whenever the need arose. Inevitably, therefore, she and her husband were honoured guests at subsequent family weddings and even, after her husband had died, at a party we gave for all of those who had worked for me as secretaries, for Betty in the home and for both of us in our garden, when I celebrated my knighthood in 1979.

Despite that support, those three months, fruitful and exciting for me, imposed a considerable strain upon Betty, not least because Ann, always a rather poor sleeper, reacted to my departure by waking up almost hourly throughout the night to demand reassurance. Our GP, Bob Martin, was kindly; we took paediatric advice and ultimately, with reluctance at first but later in despair, we tried a number of increasingly powerful sedative drugs but none made the slightest difference. To be awakened sometimes six or seven times during the night, and never less than on three or four occasions, often left Betty dropping with fatigue, and even when I came home, as I did, every two weeks or so for a short weekend to help out, there was little time for enjoyment or relaxation. It is all too easy to recognize why some parents, faced with similar problems, have exploded into rage and have physically injured their offspring. But despite everything, Betty was immensely supportive and saw the period through without mishap, recognizing the importance that this experience in London would have in relation to my future career. Fortunately Judy, though possessing at times a fiery temper and showing occasionally from early in life that kind of fierce reaction to frustration which is accompanied by stentorian howling and repetitive banging of the hands and heels on the floor, slept very much better. Nevertheless I can recall later, on the very rare occasions when she did wake in the early hours, kneeling or sitting by her cot in our small and freezing cold front bedroom, holding her hand through the cot rails as the early morning trams went clattering down Benton Park Road. James Spence had once said on a teaching round that when a woman becomes a mother, she secretes a new hormone which results in her requiring much less sleep than before; I am sure he said it with tongue in cheek, and Betty later told him in no uncertain terms that the idea was nonsensical. I can certainly vouch for the fact that no such phenomenon occurs in fathers. But the joy we derived increasingly from our two daughters, so very different in personality, far outweighed these problems which must surely have been shared before and since by innumerable young couples.

My living accommodation in London, through the outstanding kindness of the Richards, was already familiar and I quickly settled in the room which Betty had previously occupied at 143 Woodwarde Road. The only disadvantage of living in Dulwich, close to that delightful village with its splendid picture gallery, park and other amenities, was the problem of travelling by public transport to Queen Square. Each day I would walk about half a mile to Dulwich library to catch the No. 12 bus which meandered through Peckham and Camberwell Green to the Elephant & Castle, where I could then take a tube, subsequently arriving, with one change, at Russell Square. All in all, the journey took about 45–50 minutes and it was then that I realized some of the advantages of living elsewhere than in the metropolis with its horrendous commuting problems which have continued to worsen since those days. Londoners who have never experienced life in Newcastle and its environs simply cannot conceive how infinitely superior is the quality of life in the North East when compared to that in the metropolis.

Professionally, my experience at Queen Square was invaluable. Being classified as a clerk, I was free, when my other duties allowed, to attend

out-patient teaching sessions and ward rounds in order to sit at the feet
of some of the great men of twentieth century British neurology. Of the
senior members of staff, Critchley was invariably entertaining, suave,
elegant, accurate and lively, even if he gave, perhaps through a degree
of innate shyness, more than a hint of aloofness; when questioned he
invariably looked almost startled but nevertheless, after a pause,
responded crisply and appropriately. Elkington, too, was clinically
efficient but rather cold and distant, and I cannot readily recall anything
of note which he taught me. Carmichael was calm, pragmatic,
physiological in his approach, and thoughtful, if rather deliberate. Most
deliberate of all, however, was J. Purdon Martin, whose ward rounds
were punctuated with long periods of painful silence, justifying fully the
epithet which has been applied to many other similarly uninspiring
teachers of 'shifting dullness' as one moved from bed to bed; nevertheless,
his knowledge of extrapyramidal disorders was original and encyclopaedic.
Denis Brinton struck me as being an exceptionally nice man to whom one
could always talk on equal terms, but his teaching was not particularly
inspiring, whereas Michael Kremer, almost as suave, elegant and polished
in his approach as Critchley, was an outstandingly sharp clinician with
that kind of insight into the nature and significance of clinical phenomena
which identifies the great diagnostician. Sadly, in out-patients especially,
his apparent lack of compassion and somewhat cavalier management of
patients were occasionally distressing, though I was told by those who
worked with him closely that in the privacy of the consulting room he
was very kindly and understanding. Denis Williams, the flamboyant,
oozed Welsh charm but at the same time was still so much immersed
in a continuing, if waning, interest in electroencephalography (EEG) that
I saw little of his clinical expertise; later I came to respect him greatly as
a most able consultant in the widest sense. Larger than life, at least in
personality and flow of language, was Sir Francis Walshe, who, somewhat
like my friend and mentor Henry Miller, could never resist the sharp,
incisive and at times wounding comment which, however clever, witty
and memorable, must nevertheless have regularly left emotional scars
upon those with whom he came into conflict. I shall never forget his
comment about neuropsychiatry being 'that hybrid which, like the mule,
has neither pride of ancestry nor hope of progeny' (though the recent
birth of a foal, unexpected but now well authenticated, to a mule has
effectively demolished the scientific basis of that remark). In meetings
his criticism could sometimes be devastating, as indeed could be his
speedy demolition of views unguardedly expressed by young clerks or
house officers trying to make their way in neurology. Most notable was
his comment upon a paper on polymyositis delivered by a London
colleague, to which Walshe responded by saying 'Dr X has taken us out
into the wasteland of muscle disease and has made us partners to his

own confusion'. But the sheer brilliance of his discourse and even of his repartee left an indelible impression. Paradoxically he was not a good clinical neurologist and all too often, perhaps through carelessness, perhaps through lack of innate clinical skill, he was led into error. He often gave a clinical demonstration on a Saturday morning in the lecture theatre at Queen Square but, unlike most of his colleagues, did not trouble to see any of the patients being demonstrated beforehand. Once when, with consummate showmanship, he discussed the history and carried out a relatively superficial examination on a patient and concluded that the individual was suffering from a proximal myopathy, the young Australian registrar was so shocked by the inaccurate diagnosis that, as the patient lay on a trolley waiting to be wheeled out of the room, he walked past the recumbent patient's protruding feet and gently stroked each sole, eliciting clear-cut bilateral extensor plantar responses. That evidence of bilateral pyramidal tract disease, clearly invalidating Walshe's diagnosis, did not pass unnoticed by the great man who turned to the Australian in question and said, in front of the audience, 'A young man with his eye on the future would never have done that'.

Walshe was the senior physician on the same firm as Swithin Meadows, an exceptionally competent clinical neurologist who was often taken surreptitiously around the ward by the housemen after the great man had passed by in order to correct his all-too-frequent diagnostic errors. Yet another notable figure was M. J. (Shaun) McArdle, perhaps the most obsessional of all the Queen Square physicians, to whom time seemed irrelevant and who often spent interminable hours studying and examining a single patient. Technically he was brilliant and his ability to dissect clinical features caused by, for example, lesions of individual peripheral nerves or roots, was unparalleled; but by the time the denouement was reached, clerks and house officers alike had often lost interest, not so much from boredom, as his demonstration of clinical skills was invariably arresting, but simply through exhaustion. It is said that Hugh Garland, the well-known Leeds neurologist, when in the Army in India, travelled at night to take up command of a general hospital; arriving at 3 a.m., he found lights on in the out-patient department where McArdle was apparently charting the visual fields of a grumbling soldier whose neurological condition was far from urgent. Garland himself was not free from eccentricity; moving to another hospital as CO, he entered the gates riding royally in a carriage and pair, having transported the carriage and horses in a military train. But in those weeks at Queen Square McArdle taught me a great deal of value in my subsequent studies of neuromuscular disease.

Towering above them all, however, was the great Sir Charles Symonds. He was one with whom it was always possible to discuss the details of a clinical phenomenon and, unlike some of his colleagues, he never seemed in the least affronted if his *obiter dicta* were challenged; indeed he seemed to enjoy it—'Interesting question!' he would say. Never before or since have I come across a physician with such a remarkable ability to dissect and analyse the details of a clinical history in a way which, in over 90% of cases, led him to draw the correct conclusions about the nature of the patient's illness. Invariably, however, the final brick in the diagnostic edifice was drawn from a prodigious clinical memory and an unrivalled experience of clinical neurology. 'Charlie', as everyone called him (behind his back) was an incomparable clinician, but despite the enormous respect and admiration in which he was held, there was perhaps here, too, a hint of shyness, even aloofness, which meant that few younger colleagues, however well they came to know him, seemed to achieve closeness to him as a person. And he seemed to have a blind spot about psychiatry, often failing to recognize, or at least to appreciate, the significance of symptoms which were emotionally induced. Nevertheless, generations of neurologists from the UK and overseas owe him a very great debt for the way in which he tutored them in the principles of clinical neurological diagnosis.

While clinical neurology remained my first love, my main purpose in going to Queen Square was to develop some degree of electrophysiological expertise. Despite my grade A passes in both HSC physics and mathematics, I have virtually no knowledge of electronics and decided that while I was learning the techniques of clinical EMG and EEG, it was important that I should at least understand something of what went on inside these machines. Hence I set out in my spare time to try to learn about the principles of the thermionic valve and of push/pull amplifiers, etc. I also read such texts as I could acquire on the EMG and EEG, including Cobb and Parr's magnum opus. Bill Cobb was very helpful and arranged for me to attend most of the regular EEG course which was then in progress, partly in his department and partly at the Maudsley Hospital, where I got to know Professor Denis Hill. He was a fine man with whom I was much more closely associated years later at the General Medical Council but who at that time was carrying out some important fundamental work on the EEG in temporal lobe and related forms of epilepsy.

EMG work at Queen Square at that time was relatively restricted in scope and, as Bill Cobb freely admitted, he was not especially interested in it; indeed that aspect of his department's work did not begin to flower until a little later when Roger Gilliatt, who had been appointed to the staff and who was later joined by Robin Willison, took over responsibility for developing those clinical neurophysiological techniques, including EMG and nerve conduction velocity measurements, which have subsequently been performed so effectively at Queen Square. So for my EMG training I was largely dependent upon Phillippe Bauwens at St Thomas' and his senior registrar, A. T. (Tony) Richardson. Bauwens, an elegant, bow-tied, bachelor doctor of Belgian extraction, was still much enamoured of strength duration curves as a method of detecting partial denervation, a technique which quickly fell into disuse, though I learned it under his tutelage. While he was also a competent electromyographer, it was probably from Tony Richardson, under whose supervision I at first carried out many EMGs, that I learned the finer points of the technique, and after a few weeks I was thought to be sufficiently competent to be able to carry out such examinations unsupervised. But even when I returned to Newcastle at the end of the three months, I had not developed any expertise in measuring nerve conduction velocity, as that method was still thought, incorrectly as it turned out, to be limited in its scope and diagnostic value. It was also Tony Richardson (who had developed a simple meter to analyse the EMG recording and to determine what proportion of the wave-form was made up of waves occurring with a frequency of less and more than 250 per second) who interested me in the potential diagnostic value of frequency analysis which I determined to study on my return to Newcastle. For the uninitiated, diagnostic electromyography involves the insertion of a needle into a muscle and recording of its amplified electrical activity, first on the screen of a cathode ray oscilloscope and secondly as a sound in a loudspeaker. Usually the visual tracing demonstrates features of diagnostic importance but there are, on the other hand, occasions when the sound that is recorded either when the muscle contracts or when it is at rest and the needle is moved within it, is also important diagnostically. The method is especially helpful in determining whether weakness of a muscle is due to disease of the muscle itself (a myopathy) or of its nerve supply (denervation); and there are various other EMG phenomena which can be recorded either from resting muscle or during contraction, which help to distinguish between many neuromuscular diseases.

I certainly worked very hard in those three months and I believe that in consequence I became reasonably competent in interpreting EEGs, and in electromyography; but I have to confess that I never mastered the principles of electronics to anything like the extent that I had hoped. In moments of introspection, whenever I have tried to analyse critically such expertise as I possess, I have had to recognize first that I am seriously lacking in practical skills and that, for instance, I could never personally have built or serviced electronic equipment, in the way that some colleagues did. Similarly I have never been any good at motor car maintenance. These deficiencies are not solely the result of clumsiness and lack of manual dexterity, to which I freely admit (in the Walton household, there are jobs that are done well and jobs that are done by me); but I have never understood why, having achieved some success in mathematics and physics in my school days, I never mastered electronics or statistics which some colleagues found easy. And whenever I have tried in the course of my research to design a piece of equipment to perform some simple scientific task (involving, for example, the measurement of muscle power), I have found this beyond me. Moments of insight also convince me that I have a remarkable ability to forget some information that others find easy to retain. I now have no idea of the principles underlying, for example, differential and integral calculus, and even find it difficult on looking at a table of logarithms to recall the purposes for which they are used. Many years ago, when my son Christopher asked me how to calculate a square root from first principles (at that time I invariably used a slide rule) I was totally unable to recall how this should be tackled. Yet simple mental arithmetic comes easily; I have no difficulty in remembering many important historical events and dates and items of geography, and can still quote from memory long sections of poetry which I learned at school. Even my schoolboy Latin and French have made it relatively simple for me to read parts of medical texts in the romantic languages such as Spanish, Portuguese, Italian and Roumanian, while a gift for mimicry has helped me to imitate accents with reasonable skill and to lecture in French (once or twice even in Italian). I can also remember without having to refresh my memory the verses and tunes of many hymns and songs, including 'Geordie' folk songs which I learnt in my childhood or adolescence. But quite soon in my medical research career I realized that I did not possess the fundamental scientific ability to make a career in laboratory work and that I would always be dependent upon others if my equipment for EMG, etc., went wrong, just as I would be compelled to enlist the help of expert statisticians whenever necessary.

Those three months at Queen Square, interrupted only by short weekends in Newcastle with Betty and the children, were not all work. I had the pleasure of meeting various overseas doctors including Arthur Schweiger from Melbourne, Henry Barnett, Charlie Drake and Oscar Kofmann from Canada and Hal Gregg from Los Angeles, whose remarkable 'faux pas' at the one party for clinical clerks held at the National Hospital during that period was especially memorable. As a handsome, eligible bachelor he was surrounded by a group of secretaries and EEG technicians who were teasing him about his unmarried state. One said 'Hal, why don't you marry a nice English girl . . . for example, what about so-and-so?'. When Hal responded by saying 'Oh, no, her fanny's too big for me' he was greatly taken aback by the shocked silence which followed. Only later did understanding dawn when we pointed out that whereas 'fanny' in the USA meant the backside, in Britain it meant the female genitalia! I also managed a number of forays into 'the gods' at Covent Garden and at various West End theatres and went to a few concerts (this was the wrong season for the Promenaders), thus continuing to develop the spare-time interests which Betty and I had so much enjoyed when time (and money) allowed. But having managed to slim down substantially during my medical registrarship, I ate only very light lunches and breakfasts and, with the plain but ample evening fare which Mrs Richards provided, I kept my weight under control and returned to Newcastle eager not only to spend more time with the family but also to launch myself into my research projects and to get back to the cricket field with my colleagues of the Victorians who were already enjoying a successful season (Chapter 10).

By the time I returned to Newcastle, the Stanley Cox EMG equipment which we had agreed to purchase was installed in one of two laboratories on the medical corridor at the RVI, in rooms previously occupied by the Records Department. The latter was now totally rehoused in the former consultant staff dining room and library. On the advice of the chief electronics technician whom Professor Kennedy had now recruited to service EEG equipment in the Department of Psychological Medicine, the room in which I was to do my EMGs was screened electrically. From Department of Medicine funds I was provided with a desk, a patient's couch and a second desk for a part-time secretary/technician who was appointed to help in my EMG work and research (Joan Molyneux, usually known as Mrs 'M'). In the laboratory next door, R. B. Thompson was pursuing haematological studies, and George Smart, recently returned to Newcastle as Reader in Medicine, had also installed there a research assistant (Dorothy Charlton, later Murchison) who was helping in some of his biochemical and endocrinological work. George was a great help and mentor as he possessed that electronic and statistical expertise which I lacked. Whenever problems emerged in either field I could turn to him and be sure of obtaining appropriate advice and support.

While I was preparing to get my muscle research under way, I was also completing my M.D. thesis on subarachnoid haemorrhage and several papers derived from it. However, I now set out to try to track down all of the clinical information I could find, first about the patients who had allegedly recovered from muscular dystrophy, and secondly about all of those with muscular dystrophy and related disorders who could be traced through the records of the RVI and the Newcastle General Hospital (NGH). It soon became clear that this alone would give information quite inadequate for a full survey. I therefore wrote to all of the physicians, paediatricians and orthopaedic surgeons throughout the region explaining the objectives of my research and inviting them to allow me to contact and, wherever possible, to see patients with neuromuscular disease under their care. As I had expected, this initial approach yielded no more than a 60% response; hence more correspondence and telephone calls followed, often succeeded by visits to long-stay and general hospitals throughout the region in order to see and examine the patients who had been identified. In the meantime I had collected together and analysed such literature as I had been able to identify in the University Library about muscular dystrophy. I was particularly impressed by the work of Julia Bell in *The Treasury of Human Inheritance*, by studies carried out by Dr Frank Tyler and colleagues in Utah, and by a relatively recent survey of muscular dystrophy in Northern Ireland carried out by Professor A. C. Stevenson. Inevitably these publications led on to many more, and gradually I built up a picture of what seemed clearly to be a state of relative confusion in relation to the classification of the muscular dystrophies. Some classifications then current were based solely on clinical and descriptive criteria, and others on genetic information. It seemed to me that no serious attempt had been made to marry the two approaches and I therefore concluded that I should try to achieve a revised classification based upon both clinical and genetic criteria.

I also obtained without difficulty the case notes of the patients who had been alleged to have recovered, then traced and arranged to visit them, one in Northumberland (Professor Nattrass's case), one in Durham (the patient diagnosed by James Spence), one in Bristol, one near Doncaster and another in Penn in Buckinghamshire. As I saw more and more patients referred to me from physicians and paediatricians throughout the region, it emerged that some patients, especially in childhood but also in adult life, who had been thought to have a muscular dystrophy because of weakness of shoulder and pelvic girdle muscles had clinical evidence suggesting inflammation of the skin and connective tissue strongly suggesting the presence of an inflammatory disorder of skin and muscle rather than a primary muscular dystrophy. As my work progressed, I became increasingly convinced that an inflammatory disorder of muscle, polymyositis or dermatomyositis, could sometimes mimic muscular dystrophy and that it must often have been misdiagnosed as such. In some such patients the disease appeared to remit spontaneously (though this was uncommon) while in others it tended sometimes to burn itself out, leaving the patients with a greater or lesser degree of disability. In most, however, the condition was subacutely or rapidly progressive and could not be controlled except by treatment with cortisone or other related steroid drugs. Nevertheless, on the basis of retrospective and current clinical evidence I strongly suspected that at least three of the patients who had allegedly recovered from muscular dystrophy had probably suffered from this inflammatory disorder, while the others clearly had a benign non-progressive myopathy and not muscular dystrophy. Being excited by these findings, and feeling that the first objective of my research was satisfactorily concluded, I therefore wrote a paper on 'Recovery from "muscular dystrophy"' and presented this to Professor Nattrass for his consideration, suggesting that we should submit it jointly (as he had been the initiator of the project and I had consulted and kept him informed of progress throughout) to the journal *Brain*. A week or two later he called me into his room and was clearly concerned. He explained that having just been elected President of the Neurological Section of the Royal Society of Medicine, he had been invited to give the customary Presidential Address which, by custom, would be published in 'Brain'. He asked my permission to use this paper for that address, making it clear that if he did so my name could not unfortunately remain on the paper as a co-author. While not unnaturally I was initially somewhat taken aback, as I felt that the work it described was largely mine, nevertheless the Prof., for whom I had developed an increasing regard, had clearly been the prime mover, so, of course, I could not but agree. In the event, the opening sentence of his lecture and of the published paper paid a warm tribute to me for the work that I had done in making its publication possible.

In view of the training I had received in EEG interpretation at Queen Square, Professor Nattrass had also arranged an informal attachment for me to the newly opened Department of Psychological Medicine which had been established in the old Dental School at the RVI under the direction of that remarkable extrovert Professor Alexander Kennedy. In those halcyon days of university expansion, Kennedy had persuaded the University to provide him not only with a reader and two senior lecturers but also with four lectureships, three or four secretaries and about four technicians, two of them working in electronics. I was never totally clear as to where all the money came from, but the department was certainly lively. As Kennedy himself had had some interest in the EEG before coming to Newcastle, he decided that one lectureship should be held by an individual who would supervise the EEG service in the RVI; he also established a small sub-department at St Nicholas Hospital with a technician and modern equipment. J. W. (Sandy) Osselton ('Os'), who had a degree in electronic engineering from Newcastle and whose mother was a consultant anaesthetist at the RVI, was appointed to the post and with Joan Farrall (who later married a lecturer in psychological medicine, James Gibbons, subsequently Professor of Psychiatry in Southampton), established a very effective EEG department. This supplemented that created a few years before by Mr Rowbotham at the General Hospital where all of the EEG work was done by one solitary technician, Barbara Longley. While initially Kennedy himself interpreted some records, I soon found myself involved in regular interpretation sessions with Os and Joan (and later with Barbara). While I soon recognized the limitations of the technique, I believe that the EEG in those days made a major contribution to the diagnosis not just of epilepsy but also of intracranial lesions, since Newcastle as yet had no specialized neuroradiological services. We also published a number of papers on this topic, including one on the EEG sequelae of subarachnoid haemorrhage and yet another, with Leslie Kiloh (who had recently forsaken neurology to become first assistant in psychiatry in Kennedy's department), on the EEG changes seen in pernicious anaemia and subacute combined degeneration of the cord. Our results were presented at several meetings of the EEG Society, and even on one occasion at an EEG conference in Brussels where, having had my paper translated into French by Joan Emmerson, the Newcastle medical librarian, I was able to present my findings in that language; apparently my gift of mimicry stood me in good stead as the paper came over quite well, but I had a frightful problem with the rapid-fire questions which followed. Even Henri Gastaut from Marseille, one of the masters of the EEG, and W. Grey Walter from Bristol who had been a leading light in founding the EEG Society in Britain were complimentary. For about three years I served on the Council of the EEG Society and attended regular meetings in London, but inevitably as I was drawn more and more into EMG work and other means of investigating neuromuscular disease, the time available for EEG work, and indeed my interest in the subject, declined. Its limitations as a diagnostic technique became increasingly evident as we became more and more dependent upon neuroradiology. Nevertheless, for many years I did continue to help with interpretation both at the RVI and NGH, though Leslie Kiloh assumed increasing responsibility for the service before leaving Newcastle to take up the Chair of Psychiatry in Sydney, Australia.

Alexander Kennedy was a man of remarkable personality; a huge man physically, he looked like a boxer and had indeed been an amateur pugilist in his youth. He was a competent psychiatrist, a compelling and inspiring teacher, and was so much 'larger than life' in all respects that he had an astonishing ability to persuade university and hospital administrators alike to shell out funds when some new project or even a fad caught his interest. His showmanship shone through, first when he bought some spectacles which allegedly focussed at about 4 ft., so that in delivering a lecture he could stand back from the podium and give every impression of spontaneity while in fact reading a text set out in front of him. His public demonstrations of hypnotism in student lectures and to the Students' Medical Society were memorable, if a little alarming to those subjects who so readily succumbed to the force of his personality. Like our senior orthopaedic surgeon, Gordon Irwin, he had a penchant for embroidering and elaborating upon his past experiences, though it seemed likely that his tall tales contained at least a grain of truth. He claimed not only to have been a boxer but also to have had some hair-raising experiences during his military service in occupied Yugoslavia, and also said he had been a racing driver. The distinguished Herbert Jasper, head of the EEG department in Wilder Penfield's laboratory at Montreal, told of meeting Kennedy when he was a young trainee on the west coast of America and agreeing with him that they would share the drive back to eastern Canada in Herb Jasper's car. Jasper, being properly suspicious of Kennedy's ebullience and extroversion, insisted at first on doing all the driving. After being constantly bullied by Kennedy he eventually allowed him to drive, despite his sense of alarm at his insistence that Jasper was not treating the vehicle properly but that he, as a former racing driver, would show him how to get the best out of it. Jasper says that eventually he fell asleep in the passenger seat but suddenly awoke as the car tilted, before ending up on its roof at the side of the road on which Kennedy had taken a curve at an impossibly high speed. Fortunately neither was injured and damage to the car was slight; they continued their journey with Jasper at the wheel, despite Kennedy's protestations that the proper thing to do after such an accident was to get right back behind the wheel and to drive again in order to restore confidence. Whatever one felt about the strict historical accuracy of some of Kennedy's taller stories, he did a great deal for psychiatry in Newcastle and built up a large and vigorous department with an admirable programme of undergraduate and postgraduate teaching (including the introduction of a Newcastle Diploma in Psychological Medcine with a part-time day release course for trainee psychiatrists throughout the region, in which both Henry and I taught the neurology). When eventually, after innumerable achievements and after recruiting some very able psychiatrists to the Newcastle clinical service at the RVI, NGH and St Nicholas, Kennedy took up the Chair of Psychiatry in Edinburgh, he left a fine department with an impressive range of facilities upon which Martin Roth, his successor, was subsequently able to capitalize.

In addition to my EEG interests, I began to provide a diagnostic service in EMG, not only for patients in the Newcastle hospitals but also from other parts of the region, and soon found myself at first offering one afternoon of diagnostic EMG services, and subsequently two. Even then I quickly found it difficult to cope with the demand which was no doubt increased by the invitations I received to talk about the EMG to the Regional Association of Physicians and in postgraduate centres throughout the region. I also published some simple teaching papers in the *Newcastle Medical Journal*, then still being published as the organ of the Newcastle upon Tyne and Northern Counties Medical Society. Remembering my wish to introduce automatic frequency analysis as a diagnostic refinement with particular reference to the diagnosis of primary muscle disease, I borrowed from the Post Office an audio-frequency spectrometer which, with the aid of Mr Stanton, chief technician in the EEG Department, and Mrs M, I was able to hitch up to my Stanley Cox EMG equipment. It gave me a continuous simultaneous read-out of a detailed analysis by frequency of the EMG tracings which I was recording. Fortunately the camera provided with the audio-frequency spectrometer took excellent cine films from which still photographs could readily be obtained. Sadly the camera which the Stanley Cox company produced for my EMG machine itself never functioned, so that I was unable to photograph my EMG traces and did not have the skill to be able to devise a method of doing so.

My first task with the audio-frequency spectrometer was to define the normal range of frequencies obtained on recording from a selected number of muscles during minimal, moderate and full voluntary contraction. I recruited many volunteers, largely medical students (including Tony Grabham, who still remembers the experience with distate), technicians and nurses, and a few medical colleagues from different age groups to help with the task. Though some were chastened on seeing the bipolar needle electrodes which had to be plunged into several muscles, they soon discovered that the investigation was not too unpleasant. Thus we were able to build up a substantial body of control data to define the range of normal frequencies before I embarked upon a comparable study in patients with muscular dystrophy. Soon a clear and significant difference emerged between the dominant frequencies of the EMG interference pattern in patients with muscle disease on the one hand and normal subjects on the other. My findings were eventually published in the *Journal of Neurology, Neurosurgery and Psychiatry*. Later a much more sophisticated range of new and refined techniques of analysis were devised, not least by Robin Willison and his colleagues at Queen Square. One later publication was kind enough to call the method 'Walton's frequency analysis of the electromyogram'.

As my work on the muscular dystrophies continued to develop, several points became increasingly clear. The first was that the condition which had traditionally been called pseudohypertrophic muscular dystrophy was not properly identified as such, as enlargement (often true hypertrophy rather than pseudohypertrophy) of individual muscles could be seen in any of the different forms of dystrophy. Slowly my views began to crystallize about the clinical and genetic classification. Clearly there was a severe and relatively rapidly progressive form of muscular dystrophy occurring in males and inherited by an X-linked or sex-linked mechanism as it was passed on by apparently unaffected female carriers and manifest in half their sons, while half their daughters could themselves prove to be carriers. These patients often showed striking enlargement of the calves and sometimes of other muscles as well; most first had difficulty in walking at about the age of three and became confined to a wheelchair at about 10 years of age. Very few in those days survived beyond the age of 16 or 17 years of age and died from respiratory or cardiac failure in a tragically crippled state. I also recognized, though not as clearly as did Professor Becker of Freiburg, that there were some patients in families showing an identical mode of inheritance in whom the condition was similar clinically but ran a much slower and more benign course, with survival into middle life. However, I did not then characterize this Becker

X-linked variety as precisely as Becker had done. After discussing the problem at length with the Prof, we decide to call the severe disease the Duchenne type to acknowledge the early clinical descriptions of Duchenne de Boulogne who first fully described it in the latter part of the 19th century, especially since we could not think of a satisfactory descriptive title.

I was also satisfied that one could readily separate out a group of patients with a characteristic facial appearance who were unable fully to close the eyes and lips and had a pouting appearance of the lips, often called the tapir mouth. They also showed selective weakness of some muscles around the shoulder girdles and to a lesser extent in the lower limbs, often involving elevation of the feet. This was clearly the facioscapulohumeral variety first described by Landouzy and Dejerine which is inherited by an autosomal dominant mechanism. The most striking feature of this variety was its remarkable clinical variability, in that within the same family there might be some patients in whom the disease was relatively rapidly progressive, causing severe disability, whereas in others it was so benign and restricted in its effects that the patient was unaware that he or she was affected, or was at least unprepared to admit it. One member of an extensive family, for instance, who had had clear evidence of facial weakness in his teens was still working as a miner at the coal face, despite severe weakness of his pectoral and biceps muscles, in his late fifties.

Different again from the Duchenne and facioscapulohumeral types were other patients without facial involvement, in whom the disease normally began in adolescence or adult life, either in the shoulder or in the pelvic girdle muscles, with eventual spread to involve the other; in them the condition ran a much more benign course, often with survival to a normal age but nevertheless with progressive disability and usually recourse to a wheelchair in middle life. Family studies in these cases clearly indicated an autosomal recessive mode of inheritance and we decided to call the condition limb-girdle muscular dystrophy. I quickly learned from these studies of patients and their families how important it was in any genetic study to examine all available relatives, as in the facioscapulo-humeral families especially I identified many individuals not previously known to have been affected. I also found that even in the Duchenne families, occasional carrier mothers of affected boys did show signs of slight muscular weakness, though at the time the significance of this finding escaped me. And while I was collecting and analysing all this clinical information using the same Hollerith punch-card system in the RVI Records Department which I had used for my work on subarachnoid haemorrhage, I also identified many families of patients with dystrophia myotonica or myotonic dystrophy, as well as many others with infantile spinal muscular atrophy (Werdnig-Hoffmann disease).

My studies also helped me to confirm that polymyositis, which I began to see more and more often, could be clearly distinguished from muscular dystrophy on clinical, electromyographic and other grounds. Hence I also collected material about this condition and dermatomyositis with a view to subsequent publication, becoming increasingly impressed as I did so with the interrelationship which often existed, especially in childhood, between weakness and inflammation of muscle on the one hand and involvement of other tissues such as skin, lung, heart, kidneys etc. in patients with what subsequently came to be known as mixed connective tissue disease. All too often one found that a minor Raynaud-type phenomenon, difficulty in swallowing and shiny, thin skin on the tips of the fingers, with injection of the nail-beds or even calcification over bony extremities had been overlooked even by some very experienced doctors who had sent along patients thought by them to have muscular dystrophy but who proved to have polymyositis with minimal skin changes. Another feature which impressed me greatly was the diagnostic importance of recognizing the way in which in muscular dystrophy individual muscles were involved selectively and became weak and wasted at a time when others were bulky and powerful. Involvement especially of the brachioradialis muscles of the arms was often a striking feature which stood out.

As my training in human genetics had been rudimentary in my student days, and despite the knowledge I had gleaned from reading works such as those of Julia Bell, I clearly needed more expert advice and so consulted Dr Ursula Philip of the Department of Zoology at King's College, whose support and interest in my project was unflagging. Even though she was essentially a beetle geneticist, her knowledge of genetic principles was profound and she undoubtedly helped me to avoid many fundamental errors. It was at her suggestion that I began to explore the possibility of linkage between the genes responsible for the various forms of muscular dystrophy on the one hand and known human markers on the other. In one interesting family, I discovered evidence of crossing over between red/green (deutan) colour blindness on the one hand and what I then thought to be Duchenne dystrophy on the other (though I subsequently realized that in this family, in which most affected individuals survived into middle life, the disease was actually the Becker variety). This led ultimately, with the expert mathematical assistance of Dr C. A. B. Smith of the Galton Laboratory, to a publication in what had previously been called the *Annals of Eugenics* but was then changing its name to the *Annals of Human Genetics* under the inspired editorship of Professor Lionel Penrose, whom I came to know well. On receiving a paper I had submitted with a view to publication, he insisted that when I was next in London I should call to see him at the Galton Laboratory to discuss its content. This was the first of many such contacts which I enjoyed over the years

as my work on the genetics of the muscular dystrophies progressed. The
care and attention he took in helping to revise these publications was
invaluable. Both he and Dr Philip thought it would be helpful to carry
out blood grouping studies in all of my dystrophy families. Since the Blood
Transfusion Unit at the Newcastle General Hospital was unable to cope
with the number of samples involved, I contacted Dr R. R. Race at the
Lister Institute and he kindly agreed to handle the material for me. After
much driving around the Northern Region, I was able to collect blood
samples from many patients and their relatives; our findings were again
published in the *Annals of Human Genetics*. As we had expected, no
evidence of linkage emerged, but in at least one Duchenne family the
blood group studies showed that two affected boys within a single sibship
had almost certainly been born to the same mother but must have had
different fathers. This gave additional support to the premise derived from
inspecting pedigrees to the effect that the condition was passed on by
the female line. A few years later, when I worked again at Queen Square
and identified a young woman in the east end of London suffering from
Duchenne dystrophy who also had Turner's syndrome with an XO
chromosome constitution (see Chapter 9), I was able to provide the final
link in the evidence which confirmed irrefutably the X-linked recessive
inheritance of the disease.

But as my work on neuromuscular disease proceeded, I began to
recognize that there were several serious gaps in my knowledge and
experience. First, I knew that I did not have the knowledge or technical
skill to be able to pursue those biochemical studies which I felt would
be essential if the nature of the dystrophic process was to be more fully
elucidated. I therefore determined to do what I could to bring to Newcastle
a biochemist who could help in such studies. Freda Herbert had by now
retired as head of the Department of Chemical Pathology and Professor
Albert Latner had replaced her. He was a vigorous, thrusting individual
who had some interest in the subject but had neither the time nor the
staff and facilities available to help in such research. However, we did
carry out and publish a limited study of ribosuria in the muscular
dystrophies, refuting a transatlantic claim to the effect that this was a
useful diagnostic test. I also became involved in some studies of the
skeletal changes in the muscular dystrophies with Charles Warrick of the
Department of Radiology, and these too were published. Ian Rannie and
Professor Duguid (who by then had succeeded Bernard Shaw in the Chair
of Pathology) were also very helpful but it was clear that neither they nor
any of the other members of staff in that department had had experience
of interpreting muscle biopsy sections; it was therefore clear to me that
I must find a means of acquiring experience in muscle pathology.

For some time George Smart, who had previously worked in the United
States for a year on a Commonwealth Fund Fellowship (these subsequently

became the Harkness Fellowships) had encouraged me to investigate the possibility of going to America in order to develop further my research skills. I made extensive enquiries and was strongly advised to go to the Massachusetts General Hospital (MGH) in Boston to work with Raymond Adams, who recently had left Denny-Brown's unit at the Boston City Hospital in order to establish his own department at the MGH. That intention was greatly enhanced by the recent publication, with Denny-Brown and Pearson, of his outstanding book on *Diseases of Muscle*, based largely upon their studies of muscle pathology. And since I also wished to develop and extend my diagnostic skills and clinical experience in general neurology, it seemed to me that to spend a year at Queen Square before going to Boston would extend my neurological experience, while also giving me additional opportunities to pursue my research interests. My appetite for clinical neurological experience at Queen Square had been whetted by the time I had spent there in 1951. Both Professor Nattrass and James Spence (a Nuffield Foundation Trustee) favoured that proposal, as did Betty, first because if it succeeded our children would be a little older and more mature before we went to America; secondly our friends the Richards from Dulwich had told us that they were planning to sell their house and to move to the south coast in retirement, but would be very happy for us to rent their home furnished during the year that we proposed to spend in London.

I therefore applied for a two-year Nuffield Foundation Travelling Fellowship in order to spend the first year at Queen Square (where I proposed to extend my clinical and genetic studies of the muscular dystrophies and other neuro-muscular disorders and also to investigate the 'floppy infant' syndrome in which I had become increasingly interested). I proposed to spend the second year with Raymond Adams in Boston, learning about muscle pathology and carrying out further studies on the dystrophies and inflammatory diseases of muscle. The interview itself, in the beautiful surroundings of Nuffield Lodge in Regent's Park, was a considerable ordeal but seemed to go quite well. However, a week or two later I learned that while my application for a fellowship had succeeded, I was to be granted one year only on condition that I went to America in October 1953. The Queen Square component had not been approved and hence we had at once to unscramble our provisional arrangements. Fortunately the Dean in Newcastle, the long-serving R. B. Green whom I remembered so well from my student days, in consultation with Fred Nattrass, agreed that I would after all be able to go to Queen Square on my return from overseas and offered me the King's College Travelling Fellowship in Medicine which had not been awarded recently and which could be held in abeyance until 1954. And the kindly and long-suffering Richards agreed that although they were going ahead with their move to the south coast, they would let their

Dulwich home furnished to other tenants for 12 months so that we would be able, as we had hoped, to live there for a year from October 1954 before they eventually disposed of it.

At last everything seemed to be set fair, apart from a single major snag. Before being able to take up the fellowship (the interviews were in May and it was due to begin in early October) I had to have a positive acceptance from Ray Adams, to whom I had written several times enclosing a curriculum vitae and outlining my plans; the response was a stony silence. Fortunately I learned that Edwin Bickerstaff from Birmingham had recently worked with Ray. On the telephone he told me that Ray, despite his outstanding and sterling qualities, was never a reliable correspondent who invariably delayed responding to letters and sometimes failed to answer at all. In the end I had no alternative but to invest in a transatlantic telephone call (a pretty major undertaking in those days) to Ray's secretary, the formidable Miss Eulalia F. Grzebieniowska, who said that Dr Adams had verbally agreed to accept me. She eventually persuaded him to send the formal acceptance letter required by the Foundation so that after months of anxiety, all was well.

One very sad and unexpected event marred these otherwise happy months. Betty's mother had enjoyed, on the whole, very good health and we saw her regularly; she delighted in her grandchildren and helped out whenever she could, though she was perceptibly ageing. We gradually became aware that she was suffering occasional tightness in the chest on exertion and her general practitioner, Dr Robert Martin (formerly an outstanding registrar in medicine at the RVI) confirmed that in his view she was suffering from mild angina, but felt that this did not demand specific treatment. Mrs Harrison was, not unnaturally, somewhat apprehensive about our intention to go to America for a year and then to spend another year in London as she had become accustomed to having Betty and the children nearby. She was, however, cheered by the fact that her elder daughter, Joyce, her husband, Colin, and their daughter, Angela, had returned from Sheffield to Newcastle and had bought a house nearby in Gosforth. One morning in January 1953 she met Joyce in Fenwicks in Northumberland Street to do some shopping and collapsed suddenly with severe pain in the chest. She was taken by ambulance to the RVI but regrettably was pronounced dead on arrival. This tragic event was, of course, immensely distressing to the whole family; its effect upon Betty was devasting as she had been exceptionally close to her mother and had now lost both her parents, one at 56 and the other at 67 years of age. It took her, indeed all of us, some time to recover but we soon found ourselves fully occupied in making arrangements for the sale of Mrs Harrison's bungalow, 'Morest', and for the disposal of her belongings. We, with Joyce and Clifford, divided her furniture and household effects amicably between us. As a result, we were at last able to complete the furnishing of our home in Benton Lodge Avenue. And when Mrs Harrison's estate was settled, each family received about £3000, so that for the first time in our married life we were able to pay off our debts and even had some capital behind us. In view of the expenses which would inevitably be involved in our projected trip to America and our subsequent year in London, this bequest was a godsend. As I told Betty, without her mother's generosity during her life and after her sadly premature death, we would have faced serious financial difficulties.

There then followed a feverish round of activity. For reasons which we cannot clearly recall, we had decided not to let our house in Benton furnished, even though we knew that I would be returning after two years to my post as a research assistant. We therefore sold our house, invested the proceeds in a building society account, and put our limited furniture and other belongings into store. The Nuffield Foundation arranged for us to travel to New York tourist class on the French liner 'Liberté' and paid the return travel costs for the four of us. In view of British Government currency regulations which allowed us to take no more than £5 per head out of the country, they gave us $300 in cash for out-of-pocket expenses and paid for a hotel room for us for one night in New York, after which we would be on our own. The total sum available for the fellowship was $3600; the remaining $3300 was deposited in a banking account in Boston in my name, and upon that we were expected to survive for the 12-month period.

Correspondence with Ray Adams' secretary, Miss G. (as everyone called her) then ensued but it soon became clear that to identify appropriate furnished accommodation in Boston would be neither easy nor cheap. Fortunately, through our contacts in the Methodist Church we were told of a young Methodist minister, the Revd Don Sapp, who lived just outside Boston and who generously found a furnished apartment for us in a three-storey frame house in Hyde Park, Massachusetts, at a rental of $100 a month, which we felt that we could just afford. Not only, therefore, did we have a place into which we could move after our arrival, but he and his wife, Rocky, agreed to meet us at Boston Station and to put us up for one night before we took over the tenancy. Since we knew that we would soon be facing the rigours of a Boston winter, followed by the stifling, humid heat of a New England summer (about which we had been fully apprised) we did our best to put together appropriate clothing, both heavy and light, suitable for all seasons, recognizing that we would not have adequate funds to buy clothes for ourselves or for the children in America. We also bought (in second-hand stores) two very large cabin trunks as we also had to provide linen, towels and a limited range of domestic utensils for the apartment. Our luggage was therefore substantial and had to be sent in advance by rail to the French Line depot in Southampton. How we planned to get it to Boston on arriving in New

York remained a mystery but we felt confident that we would muddle through.

Our time in Benton Lodge Avenue was a period of excitement and delight, certainly in a professional sense as my clinical experience grew and my research expertise and interest burgeoned. With the help of the ever-present Mrs Young, we managed some limited socializing, though eating out (except when invited by others) was almost out of the question. We did a little entertaining (including one never-to-be-forgotten evening when we entertained Henry and 'the Og' and their wives and when they insisted that Betty should play the piano for them afterwards—Henry, I believe for the first time, began to realize that this girl who had been so silent and overawed in his presence had talents and hidden depths). We managed an occasional visit to the theatre (in the upper circle) and to concerts (in the cheapest seats). Ann, after interview, was eventually accepted for admission to the Central High School Junior School in West Avenue, Gosforth, and we were even able to send Judy on a couple of mornings a week to a local nursery school, allowing Betty a few hours of freedom. I continued my regular appearances for the Victorians Cricket Club which now had an extensive range of fixtures, usually played on either a Saturday or Sunday and on one evening weekly. Sometimes, after an enjoyable game and a session afterwards in the pub, I was rather later in returning home than I had intended; it was then that Betty used to wear what came to be known between us as her cricket face. We also managed, as petrol rationing eased, occasional outings at the weekend into the country with the children and with Mrs Harrison. By this time my parents had moved to a house in Lilburn Gardens in South Gosforth, so that we also saw them more often. When our house in Benton Lodge Avenue was sold, they gladly agreed that we could spend some time with them before leaving for the great adventure.

During this period, family holidays were relatively brief but nevertheless enjoyable. In 1952, having again attended Territorial Army camp (Chapter 12), I had made sufficient money as a major medical specialist to be able to afford to go back to Beadnell Hall Hotel in early September. On the beach in the beautiful west-facing harbour of Beadnell we renewed our acquaintance with many friends from Newcastle, including Austin and Peggy Laws and their children who were of comparable age to ours. We were fortunate to have good weather and made the best of the sea, sand and sun and of relief from the kitchen sink, as the food at Beadnell Hall, provided by Hector Hall and his acolytes, was of very good quality. We were impressed by the extraordinary appetite displayed by two-year-old Judy who somehow managed to polish off everything that was placed before her with no evident short- or long-term ill-effect. These holidays gave us a great affection for the magnificent Northumbrian coastline between Amble, Druridge Bay, Craster, Beadnell, Seahouses, Bamburgh,

Holy Island and Berwick-upon-Tweed. Henry Miller, who by then had a holiday home in Middleton Hall, near Belford, and who often came to Beadnell to swim, commented that the only thing wrong with Beadnell was the sight of Natty Armstrong (who also had a home in Beadnell which he still owns at the age of 94) in bathing trunks. We all riposted that the huge Mephistophelean figure of Henry, who by then was showing clear evidence of the excessive weight gain which marred his later years (even when wrapped in a huge towelling robe) was even more repellent. And as I told him once as he wallowed in the shallows like a stranded whale, these efforts stood in striking contrast to the elegant swimming stroke of his wife Eileen, who had been a champion swimmer in her youth.

Fortunately, before we left I had managed to complete, and Fred Nattrass had finally approved, our magnum opus on 'The classification, natural history and treatment of the myopathies'. I had submitted it, after at least three drafts had been painstakingly corrected with much retyping by Mrs M., to Lord Brain with a view to publication in the journal *Brain*, of which he was then editor. He accepted it with very complimentary comments and hence I left for the States knowing that it was in the press and that I had with me enough illustrative slides and papers to enable me to talk, if I were asked to do so, on the classification of the muscular dystrophies and on many different aspects of subarachnoid haemorrhage. I still felt a little apprehensive about our financial prospects and hoped that some lecturing engagements might emerge, even though the exchange visitor visa which I had been given as a travelling fellow strictly precluded formal employment in the United States.

CHAPTER 8

Our American Adventure

On 6 October 1953 we said a tearful farewell to my parents and to Betty's sister and family at Newcastle Central Station and set off by train to Southampton where we due to embark on the SS 'Liberté' of the French transatlantic line. In view of the currency regulations then in force, we had with us just sufficient in the way of sterling funds to buy sandwiches on the train and to spend one night en route at the Cora Hotel in Woburn Place in London where we managed one night, including dinner and breakfast, in a room with a double bed and two single beds for just over £10.

Embarkation on the 'Liberté' with emigration and customs formalities quickly completed was an exciting experience for us all. We were travelling tourist class, which was not the cheapest mode of travel, and although our cabin was relatively small, we had four comfortable berths and a porthole, even though we were on E deck. There were four classes of passengers—first, cabin class, tourist and steerage (steerage cabins were below us, and below the water line)—each of them carefully segregated with their own blocks of cabins and dining and other relevant accommodation. Our dining facilities were more than adequate and the food was good. I am sure that we managed to take through the emigration procedures rather more than the £20 which was strictly allowed and we had also been allowed to buy some vouchers in francs, as only French currency could be used on board ship (even so we did not have sufficient funds to be able to buy any alcohol even at duty free rates). Limited deck space was available for tourist class passengers and we managed to reserve some deck chairs and rugs. For October, the weather in the first two days of the voyage was exceptionally good and the sea calm; hence we were able to sit and read on deck while keeping a weather eye out for the activities of Ann, aged six, and the mischievous Judy, aged three, who were continually on the move exploring such parts of the ship as were open to them. On one day in the central Atlantic when the sea was rough, Judy quietly vomited up her lunch but showed no other obvious evidence of distress, and as a family we escaped the worst hazards of mal de mer. Indeed the voyage was generally uneventful, apart from the occasion when Judy, drinking a glass of orange juice, managed to bite a perfect semicircle out of the glass and quietly deposited the portion removed on the tablecloth without apparently suffering any injury. Unfortunately, however, as we put back our clocks and watches one hour each night, by the time that we arrived in New York the children were waking between 2.00 and 3.00 in the morning; all our ingenuity was exercised in keeping them quiet by reading books and playing games in the cabin, etc., while waiting impatiently for breakfast. We were amused to find that an elderly couple who shared our table, each of whom spoke with strong Yorkshire regional accents, responded to my enquiry as to whether this was their first visit to the USA by saying that they had lived there for over 30 years and had just made their first return visit to relatives in Yorkshire. I soon learned that those emigrating to another country after 14–16 years of age usually retained the accents of their childhood. Our cabin steward, who spoke good English with a very strong accent but who found our French equally amusing, was charming and co-operative throughout until our arrival in New York when the relatively few francs that I was able to offer him as a pourboire seemed so much less than he had hoped for that his attitude changed dramatically, despite my attempts to explain to him British currency regulations and our financial problems.

Few experiences can compare with arrival in New York by sea on a clear, sunny, autumn day. Shortly after breakfast we sailed past the Statue of Liberty and Coney Island into the East River and watched entranced as the astonishing panorama of Manhattan Island unrolled in front of us. Because of what we had told her and the photographs she had seen, even Ann was able to identify some of the most notable landmarks, including the Empire State Building and the Chrysler Building. As we moved slowly and majestically into our berth on the East River we noted with a strong sense of patriotic pride the even more majestic Queen Elizabeth preparing to sail on her return journey across the Atlantic. The Nuffield Foundation had arranged for us to be met by a representative of the English Speaking Union and we were due to be accommodated overnight in a downtown hotel at the Foundation's expense. Our first problem was to arrange for our heavy trunks to be sent on to the Boston apartment which we had reserved in advance. Happily, in the disembarkation area we soon identified a representative of 'Railway Express' who speedily arranged for our trunks, once cleared through customs, to be despatched to Boston. However, that arrangement cost 30 of my precious dollars, so that already we began to look upon the future with considerable financial apprehension.

The immigration and customs formalities in New York were then frankly disgraceful. We stood, as the Americans say, in line for almost two hours watching each bunch of passengers being interrogated, with cases and trunks being opened by customs officers. Not unnaturally the children, who were pretty short of sleep, became increasingly impatient and Judy

above left
The photograph taken by my father which, with my essay on 'Why I like Grape Nuts', won me a camera in 1930.

above
With Ernest and my paternal grandparents, Allendale Cottages, 1930.

left
My parents (1931)

Our home at 79
Whitworth Terrace,
Spennymoor, as it was
in 1990.

Middlestone Moor
Primary School (my
father's school) as it was
in 1990.

Myself (on the right) as
Hovstad, editor of the
People's Messenger in
Ibsen's *An Enemy of the
People* at Spennymoor
Alderman Wraith
Grammar School in
1939.

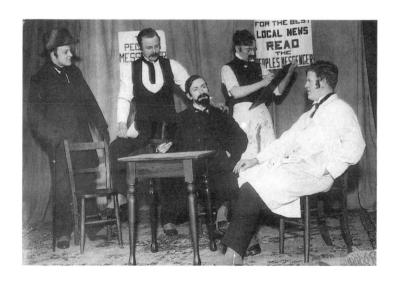

Betty as a WAAF, 1941.

Myself as an Air Raid Warden,
Spennymoor, 1940

With Alan Ross, Bill Ross, Geoff Mellor, Ken Woolas, Harry Simon and Basil Poole as fresher medical students in Leazes Park, Newcastle, 1941.

Graduation, 1945. Myself, Donald Webster, Rex Belas and Basil Roebuck from left to right.

The Royal Victoria Infirmary, Newcastle.

As a houseman at the RVI. *Front row* (from left): Jean Arkle, Bill Ross, A. N. Other, 'Taff' Evans (RSO), John Craig (RMO), Jean Mitchell, John Walton, Eileen Cameron, Rex Belas. *Middle row:* Desmond Dawes, A. N. Other, Martin Menczer, Rachel Cameron, John Noble, Jim Oldfield, Bob Dias, George Hindson, C. Rolfe. *Back row:* George Graham, Frank Hudson, Alan Jenkins, J. Bulstrode, Geoff Mellor, Paul Tanner.

With Frank Goodwin on board H.S. 'Oxfordshire'.

At the pyramids at Gizah with (from left) Captain Carr, our physiotherapist, our dental officer, Captain Rogan and Captain Doyle (myself astride 'Charlie Chaplin').

The Victorians CC at Bamburgh. *Back row (from left)*: B. McCulloch, J. Borthwick, P. H. Dickinson, T. Bird, D. Walker, E. Cox, A. N. Other. *Front row:* L. C. Harris, A. C. Jenkins, A. N. Other, J. N. Walton, A. R. Horler.

The Regional Neurological Centre, Newcastle General Hospital (from the brochure produced for the opening ceremony).

With Sir Richard Attenborough
(and Rupert Bear) at the Muscular
Dystrophy Group Annual Branch
Conference, London, 1989.

About to drive in as
Captain, Bamburgh Castle
Golf Club

in particular a little fractious. The immigration officers were, when we reached them, extremely civil; I was amused on presenting, as one had to do in those days when awarded an exchange visitor visa, the chest X-ray required as part of US Government policy; the immigration officer said 'Ah, a professor!'. Before being granted visas through the American Consulate in Edinburgh Betty and I each had to have blood samples taken for Wassermann reactions to exclude syphilis. I (though not Betty or the children) had also been fingerprinted and had been compelled to sign a form to the effect that I had at no time even been a member of, or had supported, the Communist party. There was a curious anomaly about exchange visitor visas as these allowed only a single entry into the United States. When much later Betty and I were able to visit Canada, we were astonished to discover on returning to the United States via Detroit that I had to go through the paraphenalia of obtaining a new visa; this did not apply to her as she had a standard visitor's visa. We then learned the amusing tale of another British visitor like myself who went to the States on a similar travelling fellowship to work in Detroit and who, as part of his clinical duties, had to undertake a weekly out-patient clinic across the bridge in Windsor, Ontario. Each week he had to obtain a new visa to allow him to return to his Detroit apartment and to his wife and family. The US immigration officers on the bridge got to know him well after the first week or two and were able to bypass most of the red tape, but many pages of his passport were quickly filled with the relevant documentation.

We still had to face the customs officers in New York and more and more of those awaiting clearance began to complain. Eventually the senior customs officer came to life and said 'Let's get these damn kids outa here'; he gave us priority, so that after almost three hours of waiting we eventually got through. The man from the English Speaking Union took us by taxi to the Windsor Hotel, a rather seedy and run-down establishment not far from Times Square, hardly the most salubrious part of New York. Nevertheless, the city did not then have the unsavoury reputation for urban violence which it later acquired. In the few hours we had available we walked the streets without any feeling of apprehension, gazing in total wonderment at the urban landscape since the skyscrapers were even more impressive than pictures had led us to expect. Conscious, however, of the need to preserve our US currency, such sightseeing as we did was largely on foot. After walking for an hour or two and after looking at the Empire State Building from below, we reluctantly decided that $1.25 each to go to the top of the building (10/- as we translated it) was more than we could afford. Nevertheless, as by now we were a little footsore and weary, we decided that we could probably afford a taxi back to our hotel before the evening meal. It was only afterwards in our hotel room, when I was counting the dollars I still possessed, that I discovered to my horror that I had given a taxi driver a $10 note thinking that it was $1 and that he had not pointed out the error. Next morning, when we were all refreshed by sleep despite the cacophany of New York traffic throughout the night, I was much more careful in the taxi to Grand Central Station (rail tickets to Boston had also been provided by the Foundation) in working out exactly what the fare, with a modest tip, should be.

Riding in comfort (coach class) in the clean and well-appointed coaches of the New York and New Haven Railroad (a well-known Bostonian was alleged to have remarked that the only decent sight in New York was the terminus of the New Haven Railroad) we gazed in delight upon the New England scenery as it slid by, and in particular upon the glorious fall colours of the foliage, especially the maple trees. Another amusing feature of the journey, particularly when in Connecticut and Rhode Island we came close to the sea, was to note the British names of many of the places through which we passed, though many appeared, in relation to the respective locations of their namesakes in Great Britain, in what we regarded as the wrong geographical order. American railways then, long before their subsequent sharp decline in quality, cleanliness and efficiency as domestic air travel burgeoned in the continental United States, were to us a revelation. Being accustomed to the run-down British railway system in the postwar era and the oldfashioned facilities at our mainline stations such as Newcastle and Kings Cross, the huge, echoing, cavernous grandeur of Grand Central Station, bestriding Fifth Avenue and other streets, made a tremendous impression, as did the swiftness and smooth comfort of the journey and all of the diverse catering facilities aboard. Throughout, the children sat goggle-eyed gazing out of the window in delight.

On arriving in Boston, we were much relieved to be met by the Rev. Donald Sapp, the American Methodist minister whom we had contacted in advance through Methodist friends in the UK and who was then undertaking a period of postgraduate study and training in Boston. Quickly he whisked us out into his large six-cylinder motor car, with ample room for all our cases in what we soon learned to call the trunk rather than the boot, and we set off along the complex highways through the centre of Boston, travelling in urban conditions at what seemed to us a remarkable speed, to stay overnight with Don and his wife, Rocky, in Peabody, Mass., about 20–30 miles north of the city. The Sapps could not possibly have been kinder to our by now weary and travel-stained little group. They fed us superbly, the children were soon in bed, and we were able to learn from Don something of the arrangements which would enable us to move into the apartment which he had found for us in Hyde Park. Our most abiding impression of that evening, after a lifetime spent in houses without central heating, was of what then seemed the almost oppressive heat of the Sapp residence, which Don and Rocky explained was kept constantly, day and night, at a temperature of 72°F by thermostatic control.

Early next day Don took us to Hyde Park on his way to college and introduced us to our landlady, Miss Glenn Russell, who showed us the apartment which was to be our home for much of the next year. Hyde Park was a populous suburb some seven or eight miles from the centre of Boston and must clearly have been a prosperous upper middle-class area in the early part of the century. By now it was slightly down-at-heel but still respectable, though many of the large family homes had been converted into apartments, as had the former Russell family home into which we moved. It sat about two-thirds of the way up Fairmount Avenue, which swept up a steep hill from the main shopping area of Hyde Park. This was an attractive tree-lined road where the fall colours, especially of the maples, shimmered in the autumn sun in an ambient temperature in the low seventies, even though this was mid-October. The house itself was a late 19th century frame house, covered in dark brown wooden cladding with a huge garage and a large open grassy yard containing such amenities as a barbecue and lots of shrubs but very few flowers. Glenn Russell gave every evidence of joviality and kindness; a slightly corpulent middle-aged spinster wearing a peaked baseball cap, a heavy plaid jacket and tartan trousers, she first struck us as being almost a caricature of the loud travelling American.

Our apartment was on the second floor (American) or first floor (British). We had a small kitchen, a living room of reasonable size (about 14 ft. × 12 ft.), a bedroom which was slightly smaller with two single beds and a range of wardrobes and chests; the bathroom was well appointed with a shower, and the kitchen was also well stocked with a huge refrigerator and waste disposal unit but no dishwasher (this was not something we had expected as nobody of our acquaintance then possessed one); indeed we ourselves had never enjoyed the luxury of a refrigerator in our Newcastle home. Betty and I, we learned to our surprise, were to sleep in an unheated sunroom porch. Glenn pointed out that the sunroom would be comfortable but would get very cold in the winter without heating; she therefore provided us with extra bedding and even with two pairs of bedsocks! Later as the Boston winter revealed its true colours, the garden was blanketed with snow and ice and the temperature plunged below zero, we used to undress in the living room, don warm pyjamas and bedsocks and leap into bed with two hot water bottles. And apart from the night in April when the glass roof leaked and rain dripped on to us and soaked our bed, we survived without too much discomfort.

Our first priority after moving in was to obtain food and other provisions; Glenn drove us into Hyde Park in her huge Dodge station wagon, to the A & P supermarket, a stunning experience for we British who had never seen the like before. After parking in an enormous carpark, we picked up a trolley and entered a store which looked about the size of Newcastle Central Station and had a bewildering display of goods on its innumerable counters. Our financial anxieties were heightened as Betty examined the labels and translated the prices into sterling; everything seemed to cost half as much again, or sometimes twice as much as in the UK. Meanwhile the children stared in wide-eyed wonder at the shelves when not tearing around the alleys to the discomfiture of other shoppers. Even though Betty felt that she had been less than prudent in some of her purchases, we were now able to eat. After a snack lunch we began to assess our position and prospects more calmly. We decided that we must plan expenditure very carefully, with $100 a month going on rent, a maximum of $100 a month on food, etc., thus leaving $100 a month for all other expenditure including telephone, electricity and other bills. After unpacking everything we had brought with us (our four heavy trunks had arrived and could be stored in the capacious loft above the garage, which was full of accumulated Russell family junk), one of our first priorities was to try to lessen the oppressive heat in the living room and in the children's bedroom. The radiators could not be turned off and the windows were firmly occluded by exterior storm windows which in the summer were replaced by fly screens. A ladder was quickly located in the garage and I was able to unscrew and remove two of the storm windows so that Betty could, as she put it, get some fresh air into the place. What this did to the fuel consumption we never enquired; indeed after a few weeks, as the ambient temperature fell sharply, we became so acclimatized to American interior temperatures that the storm windows were quickly replaced.

We were delighted to find that we had pleasant neighbours in the apartments above and below us. Above us lived a kind and friendly divorcee, Mrs Virginia de Burgh, while on the ground floor were Dr Lyman Hale, a resident in thoracic surgery from Boston City Hospital, and his wife Neva, along with their two children of comparable age to Ann and Judy and with whom they were soon playing in the yard. Fortunately the children soon became sufficiently aware of the hazards of traffic on Fairmount Avenue that after a while they were able to play out in the unfenced yard without causing us undue concern. After completing his residency Lyman Hale eventually went into the mission field and worked for many years in a mission hospital in Korea; we have exchanged Christmas cards and messages with the Hales ever since.

Our landlady, Glenn Russell, much given to the use of florid and unparliamentary language, was nevertheless exceptionally kind in our first few months. We soon learned that she was regarded locally as 'a character' and, despite her somewhat hirsute, unglamorous, masculine appearance, was generally thought to have an eye for the opposite sex.

Being in her early or mid-fifties, I was surprised to overhear her tell Betty that she (Betty) must never feel jealous if Glenn were to help me out in the garden or in the house or car since she was determined to be helpful to her British guests because of all that our country had done in the Second World War. Perhaps she thought of herself as being attractive to men, but that was a thought which would never have crossed my mind. However if we were in need of some additional item to help us in the kitchen or in the apartment, she would rummage around in her treasure trove in the garage loft, almost invariably finding something appropriate from the Russell family store. And she often drove Betty to the A & P supermarket; we soon learned that public transport was minimal as everyone in the neighbourhood had a car of some kind. Even though Betty could take a bus to the foot of Fairmount Avenue, it was a long haul up the hill with the two children (Judy still sometimes needing a pushchair) with heavy bags of groceries. But the prospect of having a car of our own seemed no more than an impossible dream as we were struggling to survive on such money as we had left in my account with the First National Bank of Boston. I was indeed astonished to find that Hyde Park bus drivers were earning a basic $5500 a year, very much more than the Foundation was able to offer to us foreigners to support ourselves over a twelve-month period. Nevertheless, we did manage to afford an ageing second-hand black and white television set which we bought for $25.

I also had to find a means of getting to the Massachusetts General Hospital (MGH) by public transport, and eventually found I could do this by walking to the bottom of Fairmount Avenue, by catching a bus to the subway station at Mattapan and then travelling by subway to a station close to the MGH. Once I got there the departmental secretary, Miss G., could not have been more helpful, though I learned later from a senior resident, David Poskanzer, that her rather cool and distant initial attitude was largely based upon the fact that I arrived wearing a dark suit and waistcoat, which made her feel that I would prove to be a stuffy and stand-offish Englishman with whom she would be unable to achieve a rapport. But this barrier soon broke down and we became good friends, so that she did everything that she could to smooth my way. Raymond Adams, the Prof. (everyone called him Ray behind his back but not to his face) was more practical and forthcoming than his erratic correspondence had led me to expect. I told him that I hoped to acquire experience in neuropathology and especially in muscle pathology under his tutelage, and also wished to broaden my clinical experience. He found a desk and filing cabinet for me in a laboratory used by his department in the old Bullfinch Building of the MGH and introduced me to the weekly programme of teaching activities. He himself, following the usual American system, as chairman of the department was on 'service' (i.e. responsible for ward patients) for only two months in the year. In the other 10 months other members of staff of the university department, as well as attending neurologists, took the ward rounds and supervised the care of the in-patients, though the primary responsibility for their management lay with the residents. Ray, however, presided whenever he could over the grand rounds in the old Ether Dome of the MGH from 10.30–12.30 on Thursday mornings and regularly attended the brain cuttings which were run by E. P. Richardson, Jr. (head of neuropathology) in the Neuropathology Department on Tuesday afternoons at 4.00. Those brain cutting sessions were normally followed by a diagnostic slide interpretation session after a light evening meal in the canteen. That session, starting at about 7.00, commonly went on to about 10.00 p.m., after which one had to find one's way home (which in the winter months was quite an expedition). Ray also made available to me an excellent teaching collection of slides with accompanying explanatory notes; this had been prepared for Harvard medical students to use in their teaching course in neuropathology. It struck me at once that if medical students in a four-year medical course, however intensive, were required to learn everything included in those notes and slides, they must have been exceptional people. Even though I knew that Harvard students were the cream of the American intelligensia, it seemed to me that the content of the course was far and away greater than any medical student could be expected to absorb. I was not therefore surprised to learn later that, under Faculty pressure, the course had been substantially curtailed despite Ray's appointment to the Bullard Chair of Neuropathology and against his spirited resistance. His personal dedication to, and love of, the subject had led him to offer what was virtually a three-month intensive postgraduate course, certainly not appropriate for undergraduate medical students. Nevertheless, from my standpoint the collection could not have been more admirable, and through studying the slides and notes and Greenfield's *Neuropathology* I slowly but surely began to acquire some expertise in neuropathology and more especially in recognizing pathological changes in muscle.

The Tuesday evening slide sessions were a joy. Pearson Richardson would seek out each week a set of slides of two or three interesting cases, each demonstrating certain salient neuropathological changes. Seven or eight of us, including Ray, Maurice Victor (the associate professor), Betty Banker (whom Maurice subsequently married), Lowell Lapham (later neuropathologist in Rochester, New York) and various residents in neuropathology, neurology and neurosurgery (including at one time Harry Webster, Peritz Scheinberg and Al Heyman) would each sit in the laboratory with a microscope and would pass the slides to one another, making notes, and subsequently being invited by Pearson and Ray to discuss what we had seen and to attempt a differential diagnosis. I soon found that when sections of muscle and nerve were presented, I was able relatively quickly to master the important diagnostic principles, but with sections of brain and spinal cord my learning curve was slower. Nevertheless, I recall with pride an occasion when everyone, including Ray, after studying a series of brain sections had concluded that the case was probably one of encephalitis but had taken the matter no further; however, I had found scanty inclusion bodies in neurons and glia and had concluded that the case was one of what was then called inclusion body encephalitis (now known as subacute sclerosing panencephalitis). Such minor diagnostic triumphs contribute much to one's enthusiasm for a subject and stick in the memory much more clearly than do the infinitely more common failures to recognize obvious pathological changes. Nevertheless, even in the depths of that exceptionally severe Boston winter when I found myself trudging up Fairmount Avenue in brilliant moonlight, my breath freezing into rime on my chest, in deep glistening snow frozen so hard that it squeaked as one walked upon it, Betty said that however late it was (and often it was approaching midnight by the time I got home) I was invariably bubbling over with excitement because of the evening's scientific experience.

The brain cutting sessions were also thrilling. Years later in Newcastle I tried hard to model our comparable sessions upon those I had experienced at the MGH. A resident or attending neurologist would first be invited to give the detailed clinical findings in a case and this would be followed by a presentation of the results of investigations, including relevant EEG and neuroradiological studies, for example, and a clinical discussion. Then Pearson would cut the fixed brain or would, where appropriate, dissect out intracranial aneurysms, etc., under our gaze before passing around brain slices, again with the requirement that we would individually be asked to comment upon what we saw as being the principal abnormalities. It was upon such clinicopathological correlations that I based much of my subsequent practice in neurology, just as it was also moulded by the grand rounds in the Ether Dome. Here again, the clinical findings in a patient would be presented and when, as nearly always happened, the patient had given permission and was present, Ray would demonstrate the salient physical signs. Then, before any results of tests were discussed, he would invite each of us (the residents, myself and others) to comment upon the findings and upon the potential diagnosis before he himself would conclude with that kind of masterly, detailed summary for which, throughout the United States and indeed throughout the world, he was becoming justly famous. Finally the results of tests, if any, would be revealed and we would learn how right (or wrong) we had been. When eventually I had my own department in Newcastle, I tried to organize our Friday morning clinical meetings on similar lines.

Another unusual feature of neurological practice at the MGH (at least to British eyes) was that almost all of the neurologists did some neuropathology, while all of the neuropathologists, like Pearson Richardson, saw patients, shared in the ward service and also had private patients of their own. But what struck me as very odd was the arrangement whereby all out-patient clinics for new patients were held by the residents, with an occasional attending neurologist, but none of the senior members of staff such as Ray himself, Miller Fisher who had just arrived from Montreal to work on cerebral vascular disease, Maurice Victor or Pearson Richardson ever attended these clinics. All in-patient ward consultations on other services were also fulfilled by residents rather than by senior members of staff. Admittedly, when a resident was faced with a problem which he or she found insoluble in out-patients, they would admit the patient to hospital for a senior colleague to examine; and whenever they were confronted by a problem on another service which they were unable to elucidate, they would arrange for the patient to come to grand rounds or to be seen by Ray or Maurice or another senior neurologist. Nevertheless, this policy struck me as being at variance with that which dominated British medicine at the time and which still, I hope, prevails. As Sir James Spence said in his article 'The art of the consultation', 'Out-patient medicine should be practised by the most senior rather than by the most junior members of the profession as it is in that setting that many of the most difficult decisions have to be made'. The other problem of which one immediately became aware was that of cost, and of the huge bills which could quickly accumulate for in-patients in particular, when the daily cost of a bed seemed horrendous to a Briton nurtured by the NHS, and every item of investigation or service was added up on what seemed like a cash register in perpetual motion. Despite insurance which covered many patients but by no means all, I recognized that in the USA, unlike Britain, one then had to ask not just 'What is best for the patient?' but also 'Can the patient afford it?'.

I was also quite impressed by the quality of the work done in the EEG department, upon which the care of patients with epilepsy was largely based under the supervision of Robert (Bob) Schwab. Yet another staff member in that department was Dr John Abbott, whom I met in an elevator at the MGH a few days after arriving in Boston. He was wearing a tie in the exact colours of the Royal Army Medical Corps and, to open conversation, I asked when he had served in the RAMC; he replied 'I've never had that honour' in what seemed an impeccable Oxford accent. I later learned that John, to whom EEG interpretation was no more than a hobby, was an 'old Bostonian', thought by many to ape British speech and manners, who made his living as a psychiatrist. Yet another distinguished individual working in that department was Dr Molly Brazier, whose seminal contributions to human neurophysiology and to the history of her subject became increasingly well known; she eventually moved to work in California. Bob Schwab, in addition to his interest in epilepsy and the EEG, also looked after the myasthenia gravis clinic and had published many papers on that topic. Despite the comparative excellence of the EEG service, I fear that electromyography in the MGH was then appallingly bad. Sometimes an EMG was recorded with an ink writer on EEG paper and a report was issued saying that no fibrillations were seen. Whoever produced the report should have recognized that an ink writer on paper was simply incapable of registering fibrillation, even if such were present. Equally unsatisfactory EMG examinations were carried out in a rather desultory manner on primitive equipment in the Department of Physical Medicine; my urging that a proper EMG service should be introduced came to nothing. However, I was delighted to learn that a few years later Robert Young established a very satisfactory diagnostic service in EMG and nerve conduction velocity studies.

Another who often attended neurological departmental meetings and conferences was the neuropsychiatrist, Mandel Cohen, whose views on neurological topics, often couched in semi-philosophical vein, were always arresting, if eccentric, and invariably worthy of attention. Two other distinguished figures, especially in neuropathology and neuroanatomy, were first Charles Kubik, still an attending physician though long retired from the post of senior neuropathologist, and secondly Paul Yakovlev. Dr Kubik had an incredible memory for specific neuropathological changes which he had identified in individual cases over the many years that he had served at the MGH, while Dr Yakovlev's extraordinary collection of whole brain sections stored in the Harvard Medical School provided a major facility for neuroanatomical and neuropathological scholars. He too had extensive clinical experience and wrote a fascinating paper on paraplegia-in-flexion of cerebral origin which read very persuasively, though I cannot convince myself, after reading it more than once, that I have ever seen such a case. He also told us of a study he had carried out once when working in a Boston mental hospital where he had invited patients to volunteer to go with him on a route march. Before doing so, he examined them all neurologically and found that 1% had extensor plantar responses; after one hour of steady walking, 6–8% had extensor plantar responses, and after two hours the percentage went up to something nearer 20%. He thus concluded that physiological exhaustion of the corticospinal (pyramidal) tracts, and not just structural change in these pathways, might sometimes produce this physical sign.

The quality of the neuroradiological service at the MGH was high, though I had few personal contacts with the neuroradiologists. However, I came to know well the distinguished neurosurgeons working there at the time, namely James White (whose work on pain was internationally known), William H. (Bill) Sweet (who had trained and worked in Britain with Geoffrey Jefferson and others during the war) and Tom Ballantyne. All three were skilful surgeons in the Boston tradition but they were also interested in research. It was even suggested that at times Bill Sweet's professional life was so dominated by his interest in measuring cerebral blood flow or in carrying out other physiological observations during his operations that he was in danger of overlooking the primary purpose of the surgical treatment upon which he had embarked. Despite their excellent surgical skill, I was surprised that the results of operations upon intracranial aneurysms at the MGH were sometimes less good than those which I saw at the Newcastle General Hospital a little later in the hands of people like John Hankinson and Robin Sengupta. I have no idea why this was so, as the surgical expertise, the quality of the anaesthesia and the nursing care seemed exemplary. I particularly remember one young patient who had had an operation for a middle cerebral aneurysm which had left him with a severe hemiplegia. Maurice Victor, in examining him, deployed one of his highly personal tests to try to demonstrate dysarthria (slurring of speech); he said to the patient 'Say "There's no place like the Massachusetts General Hospital"', to which the patient replied 'I'll say it, doc, but I don't think it'.

Because of its growing reputation, the MGH department had no difficulty in recruiting residents of outstanding quality. Among those whom I saw in action at that time were H. de F. (Harry) Webster, later of Miami and then NIH, Pierre Dreyfus (who later became chairman of department at Davis, California) and David Poskanzer, of whom more later. The neurological ward on the 11th floor of the White building (White 11) was a happy and lively place—occasionally in the evenings when work was done we went upstairs to the penthouse to relax and sometimes were entertained by a young Harvard mathematics don who played the piano and sang in his distinctive voice and style the songs which later made him famous; his name was Tom Lehrer.

Soon after my arrival Ray Adams arranged for me to go each Saturday morning to the clinical demonstrations supervised by Dr Derek Denny-Brown at the Boston City Hospital. The 'City' was then a huge decaying mausoleum of 3000 beds; being funded totally by the city, which found it to be an increasingly demanding financial 'running sore', it had become, I fear, a down-at-heel, grim institution. Denny-Brown's appointment to the James Jackson Putnam chair led to the departure from Boston of Houston Merritt, whom many had expected to be appointed in view of his many original contributions, including his introduction of phenytoin as a treatment for epilepsy. Houston moved to the New York Neurological Institute, where he later became chairman and director of neurological services and continued to develop an outstanding national and inter-national reputation as one of the leaders of American neurology. Despite the many years that he worked in the United States, Denny never lost his strong English accent with only a faint hint of a New Zealand twang; he was generally regarded as a strict disciplinarian, even in some respects a martinet. Legend has it that the residents at the City would hold regular ward rounds under the senior resident in order to practise how the tyros should present patients and even how they should hand the chart (the notes, in English parlance) to Dr Denny-Brown. Hence, while he inspired respect and indeed admiration in his staff and colleagues, this was tinged with fear as he could, on occasions, be extremely irascible. And clarity was never a striking feature of his written work. Indeed some of his most original papers were notable not least for the obscurity of the language in which they were couched. One such, written while Denny was on the staff at Queen Square, before he moved to Boston, inspired Francis Walshe to say 'That was an interesting paper you just published in *Brain*, Denny; when is the English translation coming out?'. At one Saturday conference a patient who had a painful ophthalmoplegia was demonstrated, and Denny, who invariably discussed the diagnosis without calling upon other members of the audience, concluded that this was a case of the Tolosa-Hunt syndrome, for which he proposed treatment with mercury and iodides. I felt unhappy that he had failed to consider in differential diagnosis the alternative possibility of an aneurysm in the cavernous sinus and so had the temerity to raise this possibility at the end of his discussion. Although he was courteous, he was far from pleased at having his diagnosis questioned, however tentatively. When I returned to the MGH at the end of the morning (we always worked on Saturday mornings and often quite late into the afternoons) the telephone lines had been buzzing and several residents told me that some junior staff at the City had telephoned to find out who this guy Walton was who had dared to argue with Dr Denny-Brown.

Denny's second-in-command was a most able clinician and neuropathologist, the gregarious Joe Foley who moved a few years later to establish a fine department of neurology at the Cleveland Metropolitan General Hospital, taking with him Dr Simon Horenstein, also a fine clinician, and being joined there for a few years by Dr Richard Johnson (now Professor and Chairman of Neurology at Johns Hopkins) and later by Maurice Victor (who, with Betty Banker, also moved to Cleveland to establish a second outstanding neurological service alongside that led by Joe). Although Denny's first love was clinical neurophysiology and he performed neurophysiological experiments until late in his professional career, he was also interested in muscle disease and was co-author with Ray Adams and Carl Pearson (a former chief resident at 'the City' who had by then moved to Los Angeles) of the book *Diseases of Muscle* which I had read avidly from cover to cover, being the first major treatise on the subject. Shortly before I arrived, Denny had postulated that the primary abnormality in muscular dystrophy was a failure of the muscle cell to regenerate and had presented work supporting this hypothesis at a meeting of the American Neurological Association. It seemed to me and to Ray that this was something worth investigating (as mentioned previously) and hence I completed in Boston an experimental project which showed that human dystrophic muscle was capable of regenerating but that the regeneration seemed to be abortive. As a courtesy, Ray suggested that I should take my slides to show them to Denny as my stay in Boston drew to a close. By this time I had got to know Denny well and our relationship had become quite friendly. Nevertheless, when I showed him the slides derived from my experiments, he was furious, suggesting that I had no business to be working on this as it was his problem. This curious quirk of personality in an otherwise kindly and likeable man and outstanding clinical scientist may well have meant that Denny's national reputation was less unblemished than it would otherwise have been; many colleagues felt that he was excessively secretive and protective of his own experimental results and that he was less willing to give credit to the ideas and research results of his juniors than were many others like Ray Adams. Nevertheless, I came to like and admire Denny greatly and shall always regard him as one of the great figures of twentieth century American neurology, from whose department many outstanding leaders of the specialty continued to emerge.

After giving several short seminars on the results of my research on subarachnoid haemorrhage and muscular dystrophy, Ray told me that the American Neurological Association was to meet in Atlantic City and that a paper on muscular dystrophy was to be given by Dr Frank Tyler of Salt Lake City. He arranged for me to be invited to be an official discussant of Dr Tyler's paper and suggested that in the five minutes allotted I should try to present my work on classification. I found a very cheap hotel in Atlantic City and Ray was good enough to cover my travel and to entertain me to meals during the meeting. This included a memorable visit to Hackney's Restaurant at the end of the Broad Walk where Alaskan king crab was the favoured dish and where one was draped in a huge plastic gown, like an operating theatre apron, in order to be able to cope with this particular delicacy. My discussion of Tyler's paper aroused considerable interest, to the effect that I was invited by two heads of departments, Russell DeJong from Ann Arbor, Michigan, and Augustus Rose from Los Angeles to visit their respective departments in order to lecture on my work. And Frank Tyler himself insisted that if I were to succeed in travelling west, I should also call at Salt Lake City. In the Mormon community there, where polygamy had been the rule in earlier generations, he had been able to study some extraordinary pedigrees of families with facioscapulohumeral dystrophy. I was also approached by Dr Ade Milhorat of the American Muscular Dystrophy Assocation who told me that if I subsequently wished to seek some financial support for my work, I must certainly apply to the MDA. I had not previously been familiar with the research grant system either in the

UK or in the USA, but this too came as a great encouragement. Two other papers presented at the meeting also interested me greatly. One related to work done by Dr Donald McEachern in Montreal, with Dr Milton Shy, on what they called menopausal muscular dystrophy, a muscle syndrome developing in middle life which sometimes remitted. Yet another paper was presented by Dr Lee Eaton of the Mayo Clinic (subsequently famous for his work with Ed Lambert on the Lambert-Eaton myasthenic syndrome often seen in association with cancer). He talked about polymyositis and it at once occurred to me, in the light of my Newcastle experience, that so-called menopausal muscular dystrophy was probably a form of adult polymyositis.

As I had taken to Boston some records of the patients with polymyositis and dermatomyositis whom I had studied in Newcastle, I decided, with Ray's agreement, to go through the MGH records and to follow up the patients with these conditions who had been seen in his department. We were ultimately able to collect a series of 50 such cases with full clinical and pathological data; it was upon this material that our joint monograph on polymyositis, published in 1958 by E. & S. Livingstone of Edinburgh, was based.

After a week or two, the strangeness of our new surroundings and the sense of unfamiliarity began to wear off and we settled into a happy domestic routine, even if this was still dominated at times by continuing financial anxiety. Nevertheless we were exceptionally prudent about all expenditure, to the extent that every day Betty made me peanut butter sandwiches to take to work at the MGH and my lunch consisted of these sandwiches together with a 5 cent bowl of soup and a 5 cent cup of tea.

We were so grateful to our Methodist friends that we soon contacted the minister of the Hyde Park Methodist Church, the Revd Gilbert Taverner and his wife Bette, who made us very welcome and with whom we have kept in contact ever since. Indeed they have stayed with us both in Northumberland and in Oxford and Gil even wrote a poem about our Northumbrian retreat which, appropriately framed, now hangs in the entrance hall of 'The Old Piggery' (of which more later). We became regular attenders at Sunday morning service; Betty joined the choir and on several occasions sang various contralto arias from 'The Messiah' and other oratorios, much encouraged by the enthusiastic young organist who was a considerable musician. The church, though of wooden construction, was in its interior design, with a gallery and rows of pews facing a central pulpit with the organ behind it, so reminiscent of the chapels of our childhood that we quickly felt at home. Gil was also a considerable preacher whose sermons were sufficiently intellectual to be stimulating, sufficiently clear and down-to-earth to be readily understood, and sufficiently declamatory when necessary to be inspiring. We still had a tendency to convert dollars into sterling and were much chastened on one occasion when he thundered about the iniquity of hearing the sound of coins (rather than dollar bills) being offered by members of his flock as the weekly collection was taken. I was somewhat amused to discover, having been brought up under the strict temperance rules of the British Methodist Church, that temperance was not required of the American methodists but that ministers were forbidden to smoke (perhaps the 'powers that be' were clairvoyant about the health hazards of smoking?).

Having been advised by the Nuffield Foundation to contact the British Consulate in Boston, largely as a courtesy, I did so quite early in our stay and found the Consul, Allon Barker, to be a delightful person. He quickly recruited me to give a talk after dinner to the Victorian Society, a substantial group of native Americans and British expatriates who met quarterly in the premises of the Harvard Club. In one corner of the room was the 'Stars and Stripes', in another the Union Jack and after dinner there was a joint toast to the President and the Queen. My talk on the National Health Service evoked a lively discussion, not all of it hostile, even though US public opinion, inspired by the skilful propaganda of the American Medical Association, was then firmly opposed to 'socialized medicine'. It was through that meeting that I came to meet John Allan May, a columnist for the *Christian Science Monitor*, undoubtedly the best Boston newspaper, and was also invited early in the summer of 1954 to turn out with him and several other expatriates (including one who sported an Oxford Authentics cap) for the British Consul's XI against the Windsor Cricket Club which played weekly on Dorchester Plains and had been playing regular cricket in Boston for over 25 years. Their entire playing strength was then black and of West Indian origin, their excellent equipment was all imported from Britain, and their enthusiasm (and that of their supporters, often with calypsos and steel bands) was unrestrained. My first appearance was undistinguished; after scoring a couple of singles I vainly tried to hook a short, fast, rising ball which came off the top edge and was easily caught by the wicket keeper. As I walked from the wicket disconsolately, the West Indian umpire said 'Man, you ought to know better than to try hookin' until you have your eye in'! But in a return match a couple of weeks later I was in the runs and I, with John Allan May and one or two others, made occasional guest appearances for the club throughout the summer. In 1955 when I was working in London I was delighted, when playing for Dulwich second XI, to meet John Allan again, playing for Oxshott in Surrey.

One immediate problem we faced was that of arranging schooling for Ann who had completed a year at the Central High Junior School in Gosforth. We knew that children in the US did not begin Grade School until they were six years of age and felt that she might be required to start again from scratch. But after she was interviewed by the headmaster of the attractive modern school in Hyde Park, 200 yards away from our apartment, he tested her reading and to our delight agreed that she should join the second rather than the first grade. Ann enjoyed school though she was sufficiently British to ask whether she really ought to pledge allegiance to the US flag every morning as all schoolchildren were then required to do. But she did show some continuing evidence of insecurity with regular wakening during the night and a habit of repeatedly calling out 'good night', anticipating a response, before she eventually settled down to sleep. Judy, apart from occasional oubursts of rage when frustrated, seemed generally very happy though to our surprise she totally refused to be separated from us and to join Sunday school, as Ann regularly did whenever we went to church.

The Adams family were exceptionally kind and offered us generous hospitality, as indeed they did to all foreign visitors, from the first day we arrived. They lived in a wonderful old huge frame house on Adams Street in Milton. It had 15 rooms, five bathrooms and was surrounded by 3½ acres of land where they kept a dog, a cat and a horse, and two ageing motor cars. Ray's policy was to buy a new car, virtually to ignore maintenance and to run it until it eventually collapsed from neglect or exhaustion. Parked outside their very large garage was yet a third vehicle, a vintage Buick, about 15 years old, which had regularly been loaned to overseas visitors but which had finally developed a serious oil leak which rendered it virtually unserviceable, though it could be driven for a mile or two if the oil was regularly replenished. Soon after we arrived Ray offered us the use of that car, as it had been used by Henri van der Eecken from Belgium who had left shortly before we arrived. In the beginning, however, I felt that I must decline his generous offer, if only for financial reasons, despite the inconvenience of being without a vehicle in a city with a very limited public transport system. Ray's attitude towards all types of domestic activity was frankly unworldly and his home and family were presided over by his efficient but rather daunting wife, Elinor, who not only ruled the four children, Billy, Mary, Carol and Sarah, with a firm hand but who paid the bills and handled all aspects of home administration. It is alleged that she even put money in Ray's pocket each day before he went to work, otherwise it was likely that he would never pay attention to such mundane issues. Ray, nevertheless, despite his total dedication to neurology and neuropathology and the long hours which he spent until late at night in his huge and superbly appointed library writing endlessly papers, chapters and books on those pads of lined yellow paper still seen in every American hospital and university, was a considerable handyman. He invariably rose at about 6.00 a.m. to work in the garden, to feed the horse and to do other tasks around the house. For example, he and his teenage son Billy painted the entire exterior of the house at least once and even replaced a part of the roof. Although one might have assumed that an Adams family living on Adams Street in Milton, in a very well-heeled residential area, might be members of an old Boston family (the street was named after John Quincy Adams of presidential fame), Ray's background was quite different. He had been born and educated in Portland, Oregon, where his father was a railway worker. Elinor told us that Ray took up many types of menial employment to raise enough money to see himself through college and medical school. They met in university where he was reading medicine and she languages. The principles of thrift which governed his early life clearly persisted when we got to know him, even though he was earning a very substantial salary as a professor of Harvard Medical School and was, like all Harvard professors, allowed to do sufficient private practice to no more than double his income, which he could readily achieve on one, or at the most two half days a week. Just as his domestic life and finances were under Elinor's control, so his professional life at the MGH was handled with consummate efficiency by the indefatigable Miss G. Her experience was such that many residents jokingly said that she had learned so much neurology that a consultation with Ray Adams cost $50 while one with Miss G. could cost $25 for the same diagnosis! Ray's thrift and dedication to New England values were such that he had an enormous vegetable garden and fruit garden which he and Elinor cultivated with the help of the family; their deep freeze was full of frozen strawberries and other delights gleaned from the garden. There was also an acre and a half of lawn which he cut every week in the summer with a hand mower.

After a few weeks in Boston, our initial 'honeymoon period' with Glenn Russell began to fray at the edges, despite her initial kindness and generosity, as the quirks of her unusual personality became more evident. Next to our apartment on the same floor there was another, with a single bed/sitting-room, bathroom and tiny kitchen which she had reserved for her own use but which was formerly occupied by her niece. The main thermostat controlling the central heating was in that apartment and we were told by Neva Hale that as the autumn and winter approached, Glenn would regularly turn down the thermostat in order to save heating costs. This did not disturb us, having been accustomed to much lower temperatures, but the Hales found that their kitchen sometimes became uncomfortably cold so that even in November the temperature sometimes fell to about 50–55°F. One day in late November we were invited to join the Adams family in Milton for tea and Elinor collected us in their large Plymouth station wagon. When Elinor drove us back to Hyde Park we were horrified to find fire engines outside the house. In the Hales' kitchen there was an old, round, metal stove with a chimney pipe passing through the wooden wall. Neva had lit the stove, which had overheated and had set fire to the wooden wall. Their kitchen wall, and ours immediately above, were severely damaged and there was a hole in our kitchen roof so that the room was unusable. Fortunately our living room and bedrooms had survived relatively undamaged, apart from the effects of smoke. And the contents of our refrigerator, including some precious penicillin suspension which I had brought from England 'just in case', survived. Until the worst of the smoke damage was overcome and some cleaning and decoration had been completed, Elinor insisted that Betty and I and the children should move into their home, where we spent an exceptionally happy week and further cemented our relationship with the Adams family before returning to Hyde Park. With some reluctance, Glenn then agreed that we might use the tiny kitchen in her own apartment so that, with some inconvenience, we were able to live in our own apartment while repairs, which took several weeks, were completed. Needless to say, the stove from the Hales' kitchen was removed. The only bright spot arising out of our fire was that I had taken out an insurance policy to cover our belongings while in the USA. As the insurance company was an international one, an assessor came along and eventually gave us $150 for smoke damage, which supplemented our meagre financial reserves.

One day in early December Ann came home from school with a severe sore throat and high temperature. This was clearly an infected sore throat and so I gave her some of our precious hoard of penicillin, but when after 48 hours her temperature had climbed to 105°F my nerve gave out. Betty consulted Elinor by telephone, who arranged a visit from her family general practitioner (there were still some GPs in Boston in those days), Dr Tudor, who pointed out to me not only the inflamed and engorged tonsils but also the strawberry red tongue, the circum-oral pallor and the bright red rash typical of scarlet fever. Happily, after increasing the dose of penicillin (we had to buy some more, but Dr Tudor refused to send a bill and only reluctantly accepted a modest gift) Ann quickly recovered. Fortunately, throughout the rest of our stay we had no further medical problems, which was just as well as I was ineligible for Blue Cross and Blue Shield insurance; if any major medical disaster had intervened, we would have been in serious trouble. And while we had always intended to have a third child, we clearly could not contemplate having one born in Boston in view of the high cost of maternity services. But we soon discovered that in the USA blood donors (apart from those giving blood voluntarily through the Red Cross) were paid, and both Betty and I registered as donors at the MGH. I, being group O Rh negative, gave four pints of blood during the year at $25 each, but since Betty's group was AB Rh negative, her blood was worth $50 a pint because of its comparative rarity.

Christmas in Boston was both a surprise and a delight. In wartime in the UK Christmas decorations and lights were limited, except indoors; even afterwards only an occasional outdoor tree was illuminated, such as that presented annually by the Norwegian government to the city of Newcastle which was decorated and displayed in the Central Station. In

Boston, by contrast, even in Hyde Park and less affluent areas, innumerable lights and many ingenious decorations were on display out of doors, illuminating not only the houses but also trees in many yards, while the centre of the city was lavishly decorated, particularly in the main shopping areas. Wreaths of holly were seen on almost every door. In the garden of one house near Hyde Park there was a stunning display of glittering artificial reindeers and sleighs which delighted the children. Having been invited by Ray to go with him to the meeting of the Association for Research into Nervous and Mental Disease in New York in early December, I had an opportunity of seeing the lavish decorations on Park and Fifth Avenue and in major stores such as Saks and Macy's and the illuminated reindeers and sleighs which still appear each year at the Rockefeller Center, close to the outdoor skating rink. Hyde Park Methodist Church also celebrated Christmas superbly, but above all we recall yet again the remarkable hospitality of the Adams who, having already entertained us to lunch with turkey on Thanksgiving Day, insisted that we should join them on Christmas Day, along with several other overseas visitors and junior staff. We recall that delightful day with pleasure and gratitude.

As the New Year dawned we realized that we must try to acquire a car. We had controlled our expenditure carefully and had managed to make a few supplementary sums through blood donation and the windfall of our insurance claim; Ray's offer of his elderly Buick still stood, but it was now so decrepit that it would not last much longer. I therefore scoured Boston for a cheap and reliable vehicle and eventually, in Dorchester, came across a delightful man of French-Canadian origin called Bill Picot, who was a gem. After scratching his head and looking around his used car lot, he spotted a 1941 six-cylinder Dodge coupé which, though old by American standards and with 89,000 miles on the clock, seemed modern to us, with fluid drive, independent front suspension, a steering wheel gear change and a working heater and radio, as well as four good tyres. After a test drive, she seemed just what we wanted. Bill offered her at $100 precisely, provided he could take Ray's old Buick in part exchange. We therefore went together to Adams Street and towed the Buick to Bill's lot. Before I could take delivery of the Dodge, however, there remained the small problem of acquiring a US driving licence as British licences were not then acceptable in the US. This involved some intensive swotting of the local driving regulations, followed by a driving test. Glenn Russell was good enough to allow me to practise in her large estate car (known, of course, in Boston as a station wagon); it felt at first as if I were driving a tank. Eventually I went to Dorchester for my test and was surprised to learn that while I was to drive with the examiner by my side, the owner of the car was required to sit in the rear seat throughout. The examiner asked me about 15 questions, including some about the school bus law in Massachusetts and the definition of a soft shoulder, and tested my visual fields, visual acuity and colour vision. We then spent some 40–50 minutes driving around the streets, doing emergency stops, U turns, starting on hills and executing all the other manoeuvres which I had remembered from my previous test in the UK. At the end, by which time I was perspiring profusely and feeling deeply anxious, the examiner turned to me and said 'Well John, you've passed'. The sense of relief was enormous and with my precious licence I proudly went to Bill's to collect our car. A week later Betty, not to be outdone, insisted on taking her test and so, while Carol Adams looked after the children, we went off to Dorchester together and I sat in the back seat keenly anticipating her ordeal, about which I had briefed her fully. The examiner asked her one question, she drove a hundred yards down the road, did a U turn on his instruction and came back to where we started from within three minutes flat, to be immediately offered her licence. This confirmed my view about the advantages conferred on women by having a male driving examiner.

The car, which we christened Josephine, was a delight and brought a new dimension to our lives. For the first time we could take the children into the country at weekends, though I quickly discovered that Josephine's thirst for oil, as Bill Picot had warned us, was substantial. Nevertheless, I bought an eight-gallon can cheaply from Sears Roebuck and kept it in the boot (sorry, trunk) and fed her a quart of oil every couple of days; with that nourishment, she ran like a dream. We explored the woods and countryside around Route 128 and occasionally visited one of the famous Howard Johnson establishments where the children quickly developed a taste for American ice cream, though they were not particularly enamoured of the large number of exotic varieties on offer and usually stuck to something simple. The only real problem about Josephine was that of insurance. Having paid $100 for her, I was horrified to find that the insurance (which also covered registration and number plates) would cost me $112 for the year for third party cover only. Many months later, after Josephine had given us sterling service and just before we were due to return home, I sold her to a Harvard medical student for $100, including the remainder of my insurance to the end of the year. I had forgotten that the car was still registered in my name and when we went to live in Dulwich I received no fewer than six parking tickets from the taxation authorities in Boston which I hastily posted back to my student friend; whether he ever paid or whether I would have had to pay the fines if I had tried to renew my Boston licence was something I never discovered.

Despite the new dimension which Josephine brought to our lives, all was not sweetness and light. One day Ray Adams rang us up and asked whether Betty and I would like to go to a concert by the Boston Symphony Orchestra for which he and Elinor had subscription tickets but which they were unable to attend. When he also said that their daughter Carol would be happy to babysit, we gladly accepted the offer and I arranged to collect the tickets. I drove up the incline of the curving driveway to the Adams' house, turned around in the large courtyard by their garage and pointed the car down the drive ready for the return journey. Josephine's handbrake was not perhaps as efficient as it should have been, but I put the car into gear and went to ring the door bell. As I stood awaiting a response, to my horror I saw Josephine slowly moving off and gathering pace as she approached the end of the driveway where traffic was flashing backwards and forwards on Adams Street. To my great relief, the left-hand front wing struck the stone gate post and she came to a juddering halt. Goodness knows what might have happened if she had cleared the broad gateway and reached the busy road. As the crumpled nearside wing was now resting on the front wheel, Josephine was plainly crippled and had to be towed by Ray backwards up the drive to be parked outside the garage until we could get the long-suffering Bill to come and collect her for repair. Fortunately the damage was slight and the wheel unaffected; and although the wing always looked rather battered, the repair cost us just $25 and our precious car was again serviceable. I should have realized that putting a car with fluid drive in gear did not hold the engine; so the next thing I did was to make sure that the handbrake did its job.

The next problem which arose with the car was in late January, after a typical violent Boston snow storm blew up in the afternoon. I went to the MGH parking lot to find that almost 18 inches of snow had fallen within a few hours. Virtually every car was covered and unrecognizable so poor Josephine sat there for about 10 days until the thaw set in and she could be retrieved. Not unnaturally, she protested at that experience by failing to start, but a colleague used the standard American technique of driving up behind with his much newer vehicle and giving me a push so that we got her away. I set off to drive back to Hyde Park, only to stall at a traffic light and to find that the battery was still completely flat so that she was again immobile. In the din of the traffic flashing by on either side Josephine lay silent, unperturbed and unresponsive while the cacophony of impatient horns from behind mounted in intensity. Eventually another neighbourly commuter recognized my plight and gave me another push and so I drove directly to Bill's to buy the new battery she obviously needed.

Another pleasure which a car made possible was when the Adams arranged for us to become temporary members of a country club in the tree-lined hills above Route 128 at Lake Ponkapoag (an Indian name which means 'the sleeping Indian maiden'). There we spent many happy hours in the late spring and summer, lazing in the sunshine and swimming in the clear cool lake.

As the months sped by Ray arranged for me to give one or two talks to local medical societies for generous honoraria so our financial anxieties eased and we occasionally managed a restaurant meal and especially enjoyed visiting the legendary Durgin Park restaurant near the harbour. This old restaurant was the favoured haunt of the Boston meat traders. Its decor was plain and simple with crude wooden benches and tables and a standard menu which consisted simply of large and luscious steaks, followed by traditional Indian pudding, all cooked superbly and served under the ugly unadorned light bulbs which dangled irregularly from the ceiling. In the spring, on a glorious fresh and clear New England day, we drove to Plymouth to see the monument and other memorabilia commemorating the arrival of the Mayflower and the establishment of the Plymouth Bay colony. We also visited the nearby railway museum where we were treated as honoured guests when I mentioned that I had spent many childhood holidays in Wylam, the birthplace of George Stephenson. There, too, we rode around the cranberry bogs in open wooden coaches on a narrow-track railway installed by the cranberry magnate and railway enthusiast who had planned the museum. Naturally we also visited Concord and Lexington and sites of the early battles of the revolutionary war, reviving such knowledge as we possessed of early colonial and American history and seeing the homes of such notables as Thoreau and Louisa M. Alcott. Invitations to lecture in Philadelphia and Baltimore allowed me to take Betty and the children (during the Easter school holidays) to explore those cities (with a short stay in Washington). I gazed in admiration on Osler's old wards at the Philadelphia General Hospital (then about to be demolished) and upon the famous picture of him teaching in the hospital grounds. This is now displayed in the entrance hall of the University of Pennsylvania Hospital close to which many of the university buildings and the splendid library are architecturally so reminiscent of some Oxford and Cambridge colleges. In Philadelphia, too, we saw the usual tourist sights on Independence Mall, including the Liberty Bell and the Declaration of Independence, which I noted had been signed by one George Walton. The bus trip which we took also called at the Betsy Ross house; neither Betty nor I knew who Betsy Ross was, but Ann, having attended school, was horrified at our ignorance and explained that she was the lady who designed the first American flag. Washington in the early springtime was also a joy even though the cherry blossom was not yet out, and we revelled in seeing the Washington Monument, the White House, the Jefferson and Lincoln Memorials, the Capitol and the museums, as well as the simple colonial elegance of Mount Vernon, George Washington's home, as it looked proudly down over the Potomac river. And we were touched when a middle-aged lady who served us in a Washington store took one look at Judy and said 'Gee, a brown-eyed blonde; ain't that sumpin?'. So on we went to Baltimore where our host was Dave Clark, internationally famous for his work in paediatric neurology, who hospitably housed the four of us in his lovely old stone farmhouse in the beautiful Maryland countryside where his wife (and their English bulldogs) made us most welcome. The children were fascinated by the slave house at the bottom of the garden. The Johns Hopkins Hospital reminded us irresistibly (in an architectural sense) of the RVI in Newcastle and I was greatly privileged to meet Dr Frank Ford and Dr F. B. Walsh, legendary doyens of paediatric neurology and neuro-ophthalmology.

Yet another travelling opportunity was in the offing as I had been invited to visit Montreal, Toronto and Ann Arbor and had reluctantly decided that I must do so alone as Ann was back in school and we could not afford another trip with the children. To our amazement Ray, learning of this opportunity, spoke to Elinor who without hesitation agreed to look after Ann and Judy during the week we would be away. And so we took the night sleeper from Boston station to Montreal, waking in time to see a little of Vermont from the train windows before we arrived. To my delight, the great Wilder Penfield himself greeted us and seemed to enjoy my talk on subarachnoid haemorrhage, while Bill Cone and Bill Feindel treated us to the exceptional whisky sours of the McGill Faculty Club, Herb Jasper gave us a delightful dinner at his home and Francis McNaughton (that gentle, courteous but exceptionally able neurologist who was generally known because of his openness and total integrity as St Francis) showed me some patients. The snow was only just disappearing from the streets and we were amused to see, close to the Scottish baronial grandeur of the Royal Victoria Hospital and McGill University, that milk was still being delivered on the slopes of Mount Royal by horse and cart. Even then the French-speaking influence of Quebec was becoming obtrusive and was particularly noticeable during the brief time we had available for sight-seeing.

After the short train journey to Toronto, we were met by my friend Barney (H. J. M. Barnett) whom I had got to know well during my earlier sojourn at Queen Square. He and his delightful wife Kay insisted that we stay with them despite the fact that the arrival of their third child was imminent. Ward rounds at the Toronto General and at Mount Sinai with Oscar Kofmann followed, and I again trotted out my standard talks on subarachnoid haemorrhage (in which the senior neurologists, Drs Hyland and Richardson, were very interested and upon which they had written one of the classical papers) and muscular dystrophy. Toronto struck me as an exceptionally vigorous medical centre and as a vibrant expanding city; we were much impressed by the mixture of stately traditional and modern urban architecture and the spacious downtown area. Ever since those days, Barney and Kay have been among our closest friends.

Between Toronto and Detroit, on our way to Ann Arbor, we managed a single night in a simple hotel in Niagara Falls, Ontario, and were suitably amazed, despite our anticipation in the light of photographs, by the sheer grandeur of the Falls, particularly as seen from the Canadian side. The area was heavily populated with hotels and apartment blocks and we were mildly surprised to discover that there was a major highway running alongside the Horseshoe Falls, having been brought up in the north of England where one had to walk some distance through woodland or across the moors to see modest waterfalls like High Force or Cauldron Snout. The experience of entering the tunnel which takes one behind that immense wall of water is stunning. Later, in Ann Arbor, Russell DeJong told us the tale of Fritz Buchthal, the distinguished Danish neurologist and neurophysiologist, who had, like us, come to Niagara Falls late at night and had booked in at his hotel. Next morning he rose early and walked on to the bridge across the river to the American side, only to find that he had forgotten his passport and he was not therefore allowed to enter the USA; when he turned round and tried to re-enter the Canadian side, the same problem arose. To make matters worse, he had forgotten the name of his hotel where he had left the passport in his baggage. When I tackled Fritz a few years later, he told me that the story was true but that fortunately he soon identified the name of his hotel from a list produced by an immigration official, so that all eventually was well.

Ann Arbor offered another contrast as that delightful city, though relatively modern, had an aura like that of a British university town, being dominated by faculty buildings, dormitories, libraries and other elegant, late 19th century or early 20th century edifices. Cities like Ann Arbor, Durham (North Carolina), Chapel Hill, Winston-Salem and Princeton, to name but a few, each dominated by their respective universities, convey to me a feeling of academic peace and tranquillity which stands in striking contrast to the noisy, garish bustle of some of the larger US cities, despite the excellence of their universities and hospitals. I have often told my American friends how comfortable Betty and I always feel in small-town America, by contrast with big-city America, despite the many pleasures we have enjoyed in places such as Boston, New York and San Francisco.

Yet again, despite my youth and lack of seniority, Russ DeJong and his colleagues, including Martha Westerberg, Ken Magee and Eddie Kahn, treated us royally. As I lectured yet again on muscular dystrophy and subarachnoid haemorrhage the huge audience of staff and students seemed very appreciative and laughed, it seemed, more than politely at English jokes, even including expressions like 'batting on a sticky wicket'. Russ and Madge DeJong who, like the Barnetts, later became close and dear friends, also put us up in their delightful home on Harding Avenue. On our riotous second evening the tears came to their eyes as I regaled them with some Tyneside dialect and stories, including one about Geordie blowing the candle out, and as Betty at the piano and I performed some old Tyneside songs.

We telephoned Elinor several times during the trip and were relieved that all was well; Ann had even been persuaded to stop calling out 'good night' repeatedly when trying to fall asleep. Nevertheless we were thrilled to see them again and they us when we disembarked from the sleeper in Boston to find them waiting with Elinor.

For financial reasons, this was as much travelling as we could manage to do together, but as 1954 wore on and my work progressed, Ray generously arranged through some friends for me to lecture in Salt Lake City, Grand Junction (Colorado), Reno (Nevada), San Francisco and Los Angeles. I was thus able to spend about 12 days travelling to the west as the lectures in Grand Junction and Reno (where there were few senior medical visitors) would each offer honoraria of $150, while more modest sums would also be available to cover expenses in the other centres. As I flew into Salt Lake City on a DC3 of Frontier Airlines, a stewardess saw me taking photographs through a window and invited me to sit in the front with the Captain. I had an excellent view of the flats around the Great Salt Lake and also of the city itself, including the renowned Mormon Temple and Tabernacle, as we came in to land. I found that I was billed to give not just one lecture but two, on the same day that Dr William Dameshek, the haematologist, was visiting Max Wintrobe's department of medicine. The morning was therefore taken up with three solid hours of lectures, one by myself on subarachnoid haemorrhage, one from Dameshek on haemolytic anaemia, and a third hour, with only a brief break, by myself on muscular dystrophy in view of Frank Tyler's interest. The audience was remarkably patient and, as far as one could judge, wakeful throughout, but I did feel that perhaps we were overgilding the lily. Nevertheless Wintrobe, Tyler and Len Jarcho, the neurologist, were very hospitable and Dameshek kindly referred to a lecture delivered by 'a sparkling coal from Newcastle'.

Frontier Airlines then carried me on to Grand Junction, Colorado, where I was met by Dr Hall, formerly a resident with Ray and now chief physician to the Veterans Administration (VA) Hospital in this small city of some 25,000 inhabitants. The hospital itself was well appointed and several consultations were arranged on the first morning, but in the afternoon I was driven by Dr Hall around the Colorado National Monument with its extraordinary variety of stone formations, surrounded by cactus-ridden desert and scrub, so characteristic of what one had seen in innumerable cowboy films. That combination of stone monuments and canyons lives in my memory as one of the most remarkable sights of the United States, though never quite challenging the sheer magnificence, grandeur and scale of the Grand Canyon which I first saw many years later. My lecture to the VA Hospital on subarachnoid haemorrhage was due that evening and, as we returned, we found members of staff and of the local medical society gathering in the hospital hallway. The secretary came forward with a sheepish look to say that there had been an unfortunate error in that the dinner arranged before the lecture was not available as the cooks had expected to provide it the next evening. The society put its collective heads together and concluded that the best thing to do was to go to the President's for a drink. We piled into a flock of cars and drove two or three miles to his house, where his wife was putting the children to bed but nevertheless, as American wives do, soon coped manfully with this unexpected emergency and quickly served us all with cocktails. After an hour or so of convivial chat, it was decided that we should go to Smokey Joe's restaurant for a quick meal before my talk. As the steaks and more liquid refreshment were consumed, a floor show began and clearly occupied the attention of many society members. The secretary, however, inserted a spanner in the works by saying at about 8.30 p.m. (my lecture had been due at 8.00) 'Don't you think it's time this guy was giving his lecture?'. Even though I heard a surreptitious 'Aw, shucks' from a few of the gathering, we nevertheless returned to the hospital and its lecture theatre where, to the secretary's horror (I often wonder if he kept his appointment) the projection stand was empty. Another member immediately said 'That's no problem—I live two minutes away and I'll get my own projector'. In no time at all he was back with a black box which he set on the projection stand and opened up, to find that it was his wife's electric sewing machine. At last a projector was procured and my talk, which I tactfully cut short, was given more than an hour late to a somnolent audience; nevertheless the $150 was still handed over before I left for Reno, Nevada, the next morning.

Yet again in Reno it was the VA Hospital at which I gave my talk. That hospital had no difficulty in recruiting high-quality medical staff, many of whom came to Reno to work for a few months while achieving the residential qualification necessary in order to get an easy Reno divorce. Things have changed since then since divorce has become simpler in other parts of the US. Reno was then the gambling capital of America and Las Vegas, though growing rapidly, had not yet taken over. Never having been much of a gambler, I still felt that I should see some of the sights, including Harold's Bar where the entire bar counter was covered in silver dollars. After a few desultory insertions of quarters into some fruit machines, I decided not to chance my arm at the roulette table and went back to my quiet hotel before flying on next day to California.

San Francisco was a stunning visual delight. Its white buildings, many designed in the Spanish style, nestling on its multitude of hills and overlooking its beautiful harbour, made an instant, almost incredible impression. My host was an old friend of Ray's, Dr Knox Finlay, who had a very lucrative practice and who lived in a gracious home on Pacific Heights, usually referred to locally as 'Nob Hill'. He and his wife were effusively kind and took me for drinks and dinner at 'The Top of the Mark' in the Mark Hopkins Hotel, then the best in San Francisco. Next day I met Professor Robert Aird, chairman of neurology at the University of California Hospital (SF) who, with his wife Eleanor, subsequently became lifelong friends. Again I trotted out one of my standard talks, with the agreement that the other one would be given at the VA Hospital next day. Among others whom I met was a Dr Van Meter who had received much national publicity as he believed that he could cure muscular dystrophy with a mixture of amino acids and with whom I agreed firmly to disagree. Also working there was Donald Macrae, a Scottish graduate trained at Queen Square, revered by his colleagues in San Francisco as an outstanding clinical neurologist and teacher. A car journey to the Airds' home in Mill Valley followed, passing the lovely village of Sausalito which perched on a cliff-side overlooking the sparkling Pacific. We also found time to visit the famous Californian redwood forest on Mount Tamalpais (where a car could be driven through a gap in the trunk of one monster tree) and to drive over the stately red Golden Gate Bridge. Fortunately on that day it was not wreathed in the swirling fog which so often blights the San Francisco skyline. Another highlight was a flight in Knox Finlay's personal private plane which he used each week to travel to a clinic in northern California and in which, after taking off to my surprise from the San Francisco International Airport, we swooped low over the bay and over the island of Alcatraz and Golden Gate Bridge before flying inland to see the remarkable fruit-growing area of the central valley of California, before inspecting the San Francisco skyline. Of course in San Francisco a ride on a cable car is a 'must' and everyone is shown that extraordinary street lined with flowers through which the road winds steeply in a series of sweeping curves. And we also went to Fishermen's Wharf (still in those days unspoilt) where we ate abalone steaks in Joe de Maggio's restaurant. This wholly memorable visit made me feel, as I still do, that San Francisco, like Sydney, Rio de Janeiro, Cape Town and perhaps Marseille, is one of the most scenically lovely cities in the world.

So on I went to Los Angeles to be met by Hal Gregg, the young American neurologist whom I had met at Queen Square in 1951 when he uttered at a party the memorable double entendre which I have mentioned in an earlier chapter. Hal kindly accommodated me at his bachelor apartment in Beverley Hills, close to the University of California Hospital (LA) where I was pleased to meet for the first time Carl Pearson, co-author with Ray and Denny of *Diseases of Muscle*, the book which I had so much admired. Carl was continuing to work on muscle disease, though his principal specialty was rheumatology rather than neurology.

Carl and his wife Gloria later became good friends of ours. My third (and most senior) host was Augustus (Buck) Rose, a tall, jovial American with a delicious southern accent which he had retained despite being trained in Boston and giving long service as head of the department in LA. He had achieved a considerable international reputation but had also acquired a huge private practice, numbering many movie stars including Spencer Tracy and Judy Garland among his patients. When he kindly invited me to dinner at his home, along with Hal Gregg, Carl Pearson and others, we strolled around the elegant leafy streets of Beverley Hills; the first person we encountered, also stretching his legs around the area, was his neighbour Mr Louis B. Mayer, Chairman of MGM Studios, who invited us both to visit his studios next day. This experience was remarkably evocative of many cinematic memories. There, for example, were sets including the Andy Hardy house from which Micky Rooney had made so many films, Mrs Miniver's home from the notable wartime movie starring Walter Pidgeon and Greer Garson, and many more. And on an indoor set a film called 'The Emperor's Daughter' was being shot starring George Sanders, with his typically sardonic British grin, and the still delectable Esther Williams, more familiar, of course, in a bathing suit but this time dressed in period costume. Hal also pointed out the homes of many other famous stars and the forecourt of Graumann's Chinese Theatre on the ugly and decaying Hollywood Boulevard where one can see in cement the footprints of many great screen stars of yesteryear, including such people as Jean Harlow and Wallace Beary.

Only two minor problems marred my visit. The first was that in Hal Gregg's bachelor apartment breakfast consisted simply of a cup of black coffee. Having been nurtured on good English breakfasts, my stomach complained steadily throughout the morning while I was seeing patients and lecturing. His huge refrigerator contained nothing at all and there was no bread, butter, fruit or milk, let alone breakfast cereal which would have filled the gaping void. The second problem was my return flight by four-engined Constellation direct from Los Angeles to Boston. As we climbed over the Rockies, the pilot announced that there was a problem with one engine but that this would not prevent us from flying on to Denver where we would refuel; a little later, however, he announced that a second engine was about to shut down and that we had no alternative but to return to LA, where we eventually landed at the second attempt in a typical thick LA smog. We took off a few hours later in another plane but the experience was not exactly enjoyable.

In late May 1954 Ray was invited by a Mexican doctor to see the Mayor of Mexico City. The financial reward of that consultation, rumoured to be well into four figures, led the Adams family to decide that as the children were growing up, this might be their last opportunity of taking a family holiday in Europe. They decided to leave in mid-June and to return in mid-September and generously invited us to look after their home while they were away. Our relationship with Glenn Russell had by now deteriorated further because of some of her unsympathetic actions and at times offensive statements, so that we were barely on speaking terms. When we told her that we proposed to accept the Adams' offer and must therefore break our one-year lease on the apartment, she told us that she would sue us for the three months' outstanding rent. We had consulted a lawyer at considerable expense who confirmed that our lease was legally binding. Fortunately in the end we were able to settle out of court by paying half of the outstanding rent.

We helped to plan in detail a journey for the Adams family around England, Wales and Scotland as they had decided to buy a British car which we arranged for them to obtain (a Ford Consul) from a dealer in London. We also recommended hotels in various places they were due to visit, including Newcastle where my parents met them and where we also paid for them to have a dinner as our guests at Tilley's, still the best restaurant in Newcastle. They were very touched when they arrived there after seeing some of the glories of north Northumberland and Hadrian's Wall to see that the Stars and Stripes and the Union Jack sat proudly on the centre of the table which had been reserved for them. As dedicated yankees, they were a little less impressed when, as they entered, Tilley's string quartet, which played throughout evening meals, broke into the strains of 'Dixie', more appropriate to those coming from south of the Mason-Dixon line.

Ray had arranged for their horse to be looked after during their absence, but we still had the dog and the cat and they soon became part of the family. The only problem arose when one morning a powerful and unpleasant smell pervaded the entire establishment. We discovered that the ginger tom cat had killed a skunk which he had proudly deposited on the back doorstep; the smell took some considerable time to eliminate. Looking after the house was no problem, though Betty was amused to find when the Adams left that they had no keys for either the front or the back door as break-ins in that part of Boston were then unknown and no-one ever bothered to lock their homes. Living in that lovely house, despite the absence of air-conditioning, with daytime temperatures which often rose into the nineties with comparable levels of humidity, was a wonderful experience. It was so large and airy with lofty ceilings that the heat rarely seemed oppressive and the fly screens which covered all the windows allowed us to open them wide so that some air was always circulating. There was an excellent piano in the hall upon which Betty could practise, and we could always go to Lake Ponkapoag for a swim if and when the heat became too stifling. We were also able for the first time to do some entertaining as the money I had earned from my lectures and from a couple of chapters which I had written at Ray's request for

Harrison's *Textbook of Internal Medicine* at last made us feel that we had some funds in reserve. We therefore invited many of the members of the department, including the Fishers, the Pearson Richardsons, Maurice Victor, Betty Banker and many others to a cocktail party for which we made large quantities of punch based on a combination of Merrydown cider, white wine and a touch of brandy with soda water and fruit; it all seemed to go magnificently.

We had by now transferred our decrepit television set to Ray's library (as the Adams refused to have a set) where we occasionally became immersed in traditional TV programmes, including 'I Love Lucy', 'Sergeant Bilko' and many of the popular 'soaps', but where we were also impressed by the Shakespearean productions, usually starring Maurice Evans, the British actor long domiciled in the United States. We also watched avidly the 'Mile of the Century' at the Commonwealth Games in Vancouver that year in which Roger Bannister beat John Landy. Not only were we able to entertain Boston guests but we were in turn entertained ourselves by the Richardsons, Fishers and others. We also discovered that our old friend Peter Dickinson from Newcastle had come to work for a year in surgery in Chicago, while Griff Owen, another old Tyneside friend who graduated about two years after me and who in later years became Second Secretary of the Medical Research Council, had married Ruth, a young American doctor whom he had met while she was working briefly in London. He had come to spend some time in Philadelphia where they were setting up home. Indeed Griff and Ruth sent us a card giving us their new address and telephone number; on receiving it I immediately telephoned them, to discover to my embarrassment that their dispatch of the cards had been somewhat premature as I had disturbed them on their wedding night! Both Griff and Ruth and Peter Dickinson enthusiastically responded to our invitation that they should spend a few days with us in the Adams house in Boston during the summer, not least because I told Peter that I would be able to arrange for him to play cricket with the British Consul's XI and this was something he simply could not resist. We told neither Peter nor Griff that the other would be coming and had a most enjoyable reunion over the few days that they spent with us, as well as an excellent game of cricket where both Peter and I were fortunately in the runs. We also took them to Provincetown, that lovely unspoilt colonial town at the tip of Cape Cod with its own Town Crier where we swam and enjoyed the beach before having a delightful meal in the Provincetown Inn. Unfortunately, perhaps because of the clams which I consumed with great enjoyment, I was acutely ill on the return journey and have avoided that kind of shellfish ever since (though clam chowder never had the same effect).

Just as Betty continued to pursue her musical interests, especially through the church, and just as we heard the Boston Symphony Orchestra or the Boston Pops under Arthur Fiedler whenever we could spare the time and afford to do so, we did not ignore our sporting interests. On one occasion we went to the Longwood Cricket Club (where cricket vanished years ago to be replaced by tennis) to see the US national doubles championship where, among others, we watched Ken Rosewall and Lew Hoad. Unfortunately the cost of playing golf was beyond my pocket, but I became quite enthusiastic about basket ball and baseball (though never ice hockey) and went several times to the Boston Garden to watch the Boston Celtics who were enjoying a run of success with Bob Pusey of national fame being one of the stars. Indeed when, with Ray, I went to the ARNMD meeting in New York we also saw the Celtics playing at Madison Square Garden. And with Miller Fisher I went several times to Fenway Park to watch the Boston Red Sox from the 'bleachers', so called because these seats were exposed to the unremitting and blazing sun, chewing popcorn like everyone else and drinking Milwaukee beer such as Pabst Blue Ribbon or Schlitz. The great star of the Red Sox then was Ted Williams and I could never quite overcome the shock of seeing a photograph of his X-ray on the front page of the Boston Globe after he had broken his clavicle; this public exposure of matters medical was something which was then quite unfamiliar in the UK. It was Ted Williams who some years later, being moved by the plight of a young child with cancer, established what became known as the Jimmy Fund after the boy's name. This produced vast sums of money with which a major cancer research unit was established at the Boston Children's Hospital. There I came to know well the paediatric neurologists, Bronson Crothers and Randolph Byers, later to be succeeded by Charles Barlow.

During that summer I received further invitations to lecture and paid brief visits to the New York Neurological Institute, where I met the great Houston Merritt and that outstanding clinician Carmen Vicale, and to Chicago (as a kind of return visit to Peter Dickinson) where I was greeted by the outstanding neurosurgeon, Percival Bailey, and the famous paediatric neurologist of the University of Chicago, Douglas Buchanan, an emigré Scot. I also met for the first time, and was hosted by, a young English neurosurgeon who was working at the University of Illinois, John Hankinson, whom later we were delighted to recruit to Newcastle.

One of the problems about caring for the entire Adams establishment was cutting the lawn with the old hand mower; this normally took much of my spare time from Thursday night to Tuesday morning. We also tended the strawberry beds and planted out the new runners, as well as collecting the fruit and vegetables which we packed carefully and, where appropriate, packed them into the huge deep freeze. That deep freeze contained not just Thanksgiving and Christmas turkeys, but as the summer wore on we had frozen about 62 quarts of strawberries and many other items from the garden. While I continued as enthusiastically with my research and academic work, Betty and I nevertheless worked so hard in the garden that by the end of summer we were both very fit. Every now and then there were, of course, torrential downpours with a rapid growth of weeds, again requiring much hard labour to restore respectability to the garden. On 31 August (our wedding anniversary) I mentioned to Betty over breakfast before setting out for hospital that it was a frightful morning. The wind was howling and the rain coming down in sheets, rather like a particularly bad English day. However, as I set off in Josephine I was astonished to find as I went through Milton and Dorchester and on to the John J. Morrissey Parkway along the coast towards the MGH that there were almost no cars on the road, while at this hour of the morning the road was normally choked. The wind had become exceptionally strong and waves were cascading on to the roadway, so we were clearly in the middle of a severe storm. When I got to the MGH the residents said 'What are you doing here?'; on saying that I'd come to work, they responded 'Haven't you heard about the hurricane?'. Unfortunately we had not listened to the radio and had not realized that Hurricane Carol, one of the most powerful tropical storms ever to approach the New England area, was due to strike Boston that day. In haste I returned to the car and drove home through the teeth of the storm, feeling increasingly fearful that the car might be blown off the road. Fortunately, though I saw many fallen telegraph poles and broken electricity and telephone cables as well as fallen trees and much other damage, the main road to Milton was just passable. But I was compelled to park Josephine at the foot of the driveway which was totally blocked by fallen trees. The telephone wires were down, as were the electricity cables, and I found Betty with the two children apprehensively watching an enormous tree close to the back door of the house which seemed to raise its roots from the ground and lean towards the house as each powerful gust struck it. Fortunately it survived and by the time I got there the worst of the storm had abated. Later that day and early next morning as we surveyed the devastation, having found some candles with which to find our way around, we discovered that 11 trees had fallen though none had struck the house and in this regard, unlike many others, we were lucky. We were at once faced with the problem of the deep freeze (all around us, barbecues were quickly held as people emptied their freezers). Once the roadways were clear, I scoured Boston for dry ice and eventually found a firm still selling this in Cambridge. With the aid of a new supply bought every 48 hours, I was able to keep the freezer going for the 10 days that we were without electricity. I also spent many hours in the garden and driveway cutting off branches and hauling them into the centre of a field for a subsequent bonfire, but as I could not cope with the largest tree trunks, there was no alternative but to call in a tree surgeon; fortunately one of Bill Picot's sons was in that business and helped us clear up the worst of the mess. We sent a cable to the Adams telling them that the house was undamaged but later learned that they were astonished to receive it as by then they were in Germany and the devastation wrought by Hurricane Carol had not even made the principal German newspapers.

Very soon I was again going regularly to work and clearing up the garden in the early mornings and late evenings, but we were now alerted to the prospects of future storms and watched the television regularly. The strongest gusts recorded in Carol had been up to 160 miles an hour and the steady wind velocity in the area at one stage had been 110. Ten days after Carol, Hurricane Edna struck with fearsome force from a different direction, though she was never quite so fierce as Carol. This time I stayed at home throughout the storm and recall very clearly the eerie period of relative calm as the eye of the storm passed over us and as the winds abated, only to become violent again from the opposite direction. This time we were prepared and lost only six more trees, while electricity was lost for only three days. Soon we were back virtually to normal, though when the Adams eventually returned in mid-September shortly before we were due to leave for England, they found huge piles of logs carefully stacked in many parts of the garden and were shocked by the yawning gaps where some of their favourite trees had once stood.

During the summer of 1954 after the Adams had left, I heard again from Ade Milhorat, then the *eminence grise* of the Muscular Dystrophy Association (MDA), and from Bob Ross, its Executive Director, that in view of my contributions to the subject, they would welcome an application from me for a research grant to support my work on my return to the UK. In the meantime I had corresponded with Professor R. B. Green, still the Dean in Newcastle, to confirm that the King's College Travelling Fellowship in Medicine which he had offered me was still available so that I could spend a year at Queen Square as arranged. Unfortunately, however, while the money available was regarded for tax purposes as a scholarship and was therefore tax free, the total was only £1000. Despite the very reasonable rent of £6 6s. 0d. weekly which the Richards proposed to charge us for their home in Dulwich, we knew that we would run into debt if that were the only income I had to cover our stay in London. We were anxious not to make further substantial inroads into the diminishing capital sum left to us by Betty's mother as we knew that we would need that in order to buy another home when we eventually returned to Newcastle. I therefore applied to the MDA for support of two specific research projects, one a further survey of the clinical, genetic, electromyographic and histological aspects of the muscular dystrophies based upon studies of patients seen over the last 10 years at Queen Square. The second related to a study I had hoped for some time to carry out of infants and children suffering from the 'floppy infant' syndrome;

this was much in need of clarification, especially in view of the confusion which already existed in the literature between infantile spinal muscular atrophy (Werdnig-Hoffmann disease) on the one hand and amyotonia congenita (Oppenheim's syndrome) on the other. Many paediatricians used the two terms as if they were interchangeable, even though Oppenheim had originally suggested that the syndrome which he described was benign, while Werdnig-Hoffmann disease was invariably fatal. By correspondence I was able to agree with the Dean of the Institute of Child Health, Dr Newns, and the then professor, Alan Moncrieff (a close friend of James Spence) that I would be able to carry out this work at Great Ormond Street and that Dr Basil Kiernander (who was in charge of the physical medicine department and of the EMG services) would be willing to offer me the facilities of his department.

I was, incidentally, distressed to learn from Henry Miller during my stay in the US that James Spence had been found to have a carcinoma of bronchus (he was a heavy smoker of full-strength cigarettes) and died a few months later. His premature death was an irreparable loss to Newcastle and world medicine; we were all delighted when, a few years later, the decision was made to call the Chair of Child Health (then occupied by Donald Court) the James Spence Chair.

But I digress. Before leaving the US at the end of September, I learned with much relief that my application to the MDA had been successful and that I had been awarded a grant of $7500 for the following year. This would enable me first to supplement my scholarship grant by £300, and secondly to employ a secretary in London, while covering all the relevant postal and other research expenses which would plainly be incurred in carrying out the surveys which I planned. Happily, too, Dr Carmichael's administrator and the Medical Research Council agreed to handle the grant on my behalf, so that all seemed set fair for me to continue my work on returning to the UK.

We look back upon our time in Boston with enormous affection, despite the fire, the law suit, the hurricanes and the problems with the car. The kindliness and generosity we were shown were outstanding and the travel opportunities I enjoyed and in which Betty and the children sometimes joined me were uniformly exciting. Above all my academic work, the clinical experience and the training in neuropathology which I enjoyed had an indelible and incalculable effect upon my career. Ray's teaching, firmly based on pathophysiology and on clinicopathological correlations as well as on his long experience of clinical practice was beyond praise. And Betty and I laid the foundations of many professional and social relationships from which we profited greatly in later years. Indeed we were all tearful, Betty particularly so, when we left, while at the same time keenly anticipating our return to the UK. Shortly before leaving I was offered an assistant professorship of neurology at Peter Bent Brigham Hospital at $15,000 a year, plus private practice, and admit that it was only after considerable heart-searching that I decided to refuse. The ties of home, country, the English countryside, cricket and so many other features of British life pulled very strongly so that I turned down the offer, despite the recognition that I would be returning to the UK on a salary miniscule in comparison to what Boston would provide.

A splendid farewell party was given by Ray and the department, after which we had another one-night stay in New York at the Tudor Hotel close to the United Nations, slightly less seedy than the one in which we had stayed on our arrival. With much of a day to spare, we saw the 'Rockettes' at the Radio City Music Hall and when considering whether or not to go to the top of the Empire State Building to see the view we said 'Oh sure, no problem; it's only a dollar 25'; this now seemed infinitely less than when we had converted it to 10/- at the time of our arrival.

We sailed again on the 'Liberté' for our return journey with just enough dollars to keep us going throughout the voyage, to be able to afford a rather more generous tip to our steward than on the outward journey, and to be able to cover the sterling costs of our transport and accommodation overnight in London before taking the train to Newcastle.

CHAPTER 9

Queen Square and Back to Newcastle

Our return journey on the 'Liberté' was marred only by the minor inconvenience of finding that we would disembark in Plymouth. This meant that we would then face the long and tiring journey from Plymouth to Newcastle via London as there were no convenient cross-country trains in those days. Fortunately disembarkation was speedy and efficient. We had no problems with the customs and were quickly able to arrange with British Rail for our heavy trunks to be delivered later to Woodwarde Road in Dulwich. But first we were anxious to get back to Newcastle to see the family and to finalize the administrative arrangements relating to my travelling fellowship at Queen Square.

The train journey was memorable because of the incredible green of the October countryside as we rattled by, contrasting with the brown sunscorched countryside of the US to which, despite the torrential rain which accompanied the hurricanes, we had become accustomed. I also remember with amusement that as we ate lunch on the train the children avidly devoured apple pie and custard with recollection and enjoyment, as custard (hardly a gourmet's delight) was virtually unknown in America. After another overnight stay at the Cora Hotel in London, there followed the five-hour train journey from King's Cross to Newcastle, where my parents met us at the station for a joyous reunion. Credit cards were then unknown and I did not possess a British cheque book so our accounting was pretty accurate; having changed our dollars into sterling, we arrived with £2 5s. 10d. between the four of us.

There followed a few hectic days of planning and reorientation. Fred Nattrass, Henry Miller and the Dean were very helpful and so too was George Smart, as Reader in Medicine by then firmly established. Our family and friends were much amused by Ann's striking American accent which had been nurtured in school but which vanished totally in under six weeks. We decided that we must replace our car, especially since the pre-war Ford 8 which my parents had been running had finally collapsed. We therefore gave them our Ford Prefect which they had used during our absence, and became the proud possessors of a new Ford Consul which we thought would be more suitable for the journeys we hoped to make between London and Newcastle and to other parts of the country during the next year.

And so, after a few happy and fruitful days in Newcastle including a visit to Spennymoor and a reunion with Betty's brother and sister and some of our friends, we loaded up the car and set off for Dulwich, a journey which then, on the old A1 with only very occasional stretches of dual carriageway, took over eight hours. Although the traffic was much lighter than that of today, it was still sufficient to make the journey less than pleasurable. As we painfully crawled through the traffic jams in Darlington, Doncaster, Newark and Grantham (quite apart from the crawl which ensued on reaching the outskirts of London) the children became increasingly impatient and irritable and we determined that this was a journey which we would undertake as infrequently as possible.

It was with considerable relief that we eventually reached the familiar surroundings of Woodwarde Road where the Richards, bless them, had erected a wooden garage in their back garden, partly for our benefit but partly because they had decided that once we had lived in the house for a year, they would sell it and a garage would clearly enhance its value. Despite the fact that the house had not been refurbished or modernized, so that we lived for the next year surrounded by Victoriana in a home heated only by open coal fires (the one in the kitchen also heated the water) we soon made ourselves comfortable, having brought with us from Newcastle a couple of electric fires to produce much-needed supplementary warmth in the winter. We also splashed out some of our remaining capital to buy a Prestcold refrigerator and a Thor automatic washing machine similar to that which Betty had used in the Adams' house in Boston. Such luxuries were things which the Richards (despite his position as a senior executive officer in the Civil Service) had never contemplated possessing, just as it had never crossed their minds to own a car. That old refrigerator, bought in 1954, continued to give us excellent service until 1989 when we left it behind in the basement of the Warden's lodgings at Green College. It may still be working somewhere in the college, but the washing machine, which followed us through two homes in Gosforth, eventually died and had to be replaced in the mid-1960s. But we still use Betty's mother's Hoover vacuum cleaner bought in 1935.

One of our first tasks was to see Ann settled into school and she was enrolled at Dulwich Hamlet Primary School, close to Dulwich Park and the magnificent Dulwich College picture gallery which we came to know well. She soon settled, though at first she was academically a little behind some other children of her own age, not, I believe, because of any inadequacy of the American educational system of education but simply because it was different; nevertheless, she quickly caught up with her peers. Judy, however, was still at home so that Betty did not have the opportunity of returning to the Royal Academy. Soon after we had settled in London we learned from the Newcastle Central High School Junior Department, which Ann had attended before we went abroad, that Judy would have to go there for an interview and test with a view to entry in September 1955. Hence yet another slow train journey to the north and an equally slow return followed. Judy fortunately restrained her intermittent firebrand tendencies and behaved, it would seem, angelically; we learned with relief a week or two later that she had been accepted. Our only concern was to be confident of affording the fees, but as those were about £60 or £70 per annum for each of the girls, this did not seem likely to be too serious a burden.

At Queen Square I joined Dr Carmichael's neurological research unit. As agreed with Dr Newns of the Institute of Child Health, I was able to examine the records of all children diagnosed as 'amyotonia congenita' at the Hospital for Sick Children, Great Ormond Street, while Dr Basil Kiernander with the full agreement of Paul Sandifer, the senior paediatric neurologist, offered me a small office from which I could carry out that work. Indeed from the accommodation point of view I was afforded a surfeit of riches as Dr Carmichael also obtained a room for me in the building which was being taken over from the Royal Institute of Public Health and Hygiene. I was able to house there not only my growing collection of manual records and microscopic sections brought back with me from Boston (as well as a new microscope I bought with my MDA grant) but also the secretary whom I was able to appoint through that grant.

Not only did I find Arnold Carmichael to be an able and pragmatic teacher and mentor, but others in his unit, including Pat Merton and George Dawson, could always be relied upon for sound physiological advice, as could John Bates and Martin Halliday. Peter Nathan and Marian Smith, that indefatigable duo whose applied anatomical studies made such a major contribution to neurological knowledge, especially in relation to spinal cord function, were also splendid colleagues and advisers. Working on the unit with me as temporary research fellows were J. A. (Iain) Simpson from Glasgow and Norman Geschwind from Boston. Iain later became senior lecturer in neurology in Edinburgh before being appointed to the foundation chair in Glasgow, where his work on myasthenia gravis brought him well-deserved international recognition, while Norman Geschwind returned to Boston where he eventually succeeded Denny-Brown in the James Jackson Putnam Chair of Neurology and became a world expert on aphasia, other disorders of speech and higher cerebral function. Iain, now retired, is indulging his long-term interests in music and violin playing and sailing on the Clyde, but Norman died suddenly only a few years ago at the height of his powers.

While I soon became immersed in my prearranged research programme, I was still able from time to time to learn again in ward rounds and conferences from that distinguished team of neurological masters who were on the staff at Queen Square. The clinical diagnostic expertise of

Sir Charles Symonds continued to be unparallelled, the meticulous analyses of Sean McArdle continued to amaze (if one had time to watch the painstaking process), Macdonald Critchley's erudition continued to stimulate, and Francis Walshe's mordant wit still excited, while the quiet, compassionate, sound and accurate doctoring of Swithin Meadows was, as always, refreshing. But among these and the other giants, Carmichael ('the boss') had good reason to hold his head high as he was a fine clinician whose practice was based upon profound physiological knowledge and considerable expertise in pathophysiological analysis. I learned much from him in out-patients and on his ward rounds and was gradually allowed much greater freedom in out-patient consultation under his increasingly limited supervision; this tutelage further increased my growing neurological knowledge and experience. If 'the boss' had a fault, it was that he found writing extremely painful (every word a drop of blood, as he said). He therefore published far less than he could and indeed should have done, so that some of his most important original observations never saw the light of day in print. But he was a kindly, if at times stern critic whose comments upon work produced by his juniors were invariably trenchant. When I showed him two papers that I was hoping to publish on the floppy infant syndrome arising out of my work at Great Ormond Street, he said sharply 'Stop shuffling the clinical pack of cards and do some decent investigative work!'. Nevertheless, it was with his encouragement and on his introduction that I offered my first paper to the Association of British Neurologists in Cambridge in April 1955 when I presented my analysis of the clinical and pathological findings in over 50 cases of polymyositis—material upon which my 1958 monograph published with Ray Adams was based.

At Queen Square I got to know well James Bull of the Department of Neuroradiology who gave me some exceptionally wise and helpful advice. He also taught me the technique of transcutaneous cerebral angiography which I helped to introduce on my return to Newcastle. However that expertise, painstakingly learned and invaluable in an experiential sense, soon decayed as an able neuroradiologist, Gordon Gryspeerdt, was appointed and my services in that regard were not required. James Bull taught me one very important lesson. While in Boston I had offered my monograph on subarachnoid haemorrhage based on my MD thesis to Charles C. Thomas and to Harvard University Press, each of whom turned it down for publication. On returning to the UK I was advised to approach Charles Macmillan of E. & S. Livingstone, who was immensely encouraging and agreed to publish it. I made the mistake, however, of sending him the text and illustrations together, without having the latter checked by experts such as James Bull. It was only when the galley proofs came through that I realized that the reproductions of the radiographs left much to be desired. I had not then recognized the importance of careful trimming of illustrations to an appropriate size and of discarding irrelevant marginal detail. Charles Macmillan was very reasonably distressed to find that the blocks of several illustrations had to be remade in the light of James Bull's advice, and wrote me a rather testy letter while accepting the necessity for change. As he said, 'We may not make much profit, but at least we'll have had the satisfaction of producing something of good quality'. His prediction about profit proved more true than he or I had imagined. In those days Livingstones did not pay royalties but published most medical textbooks on a profit-sharing basis. Even though the book eventually sold about 1400 copies, I learned that it would not be in profit until 1500 had been sold, so that the income I received from it was precisely nil. Charles Macmillan had agreed to take on our joint monograph on *Polymyositis* even before the sales figures for *Subarachnoid Haemorrhage* were known. It sold rather more copies and eventually, some five years after publication, I received a cheque for my share of the profits, being £2 3s. 4d., as did Ray Adams (I never heard his reaction). That cheque having been received, both books were promptly 'remaindered' and removed from the market. Since then the archaic system of profit sharing by authors has, so far as I know, vanished. The system was excellent for those who wrote student or nursing texts which proved to be bestsellers, but was infinitely less satisfactory in relation to specialized monographs. Nevertheless, I shall always be grateful to Charles Macmillan for the start he gave me in medical publishing. Since then I have much enjoyed the relationship I have achieved with his successors at E. & S. Livingstone (subsequently Churchill Livingstone) and with many other medical publishers, not least Oxford University Press.

Others whom I came to know well in the neurological research unit were Martin Halliday, an able clinical neurophysiologist, and Alec Elithorn who was doing some important research on the physiological effects of anxiety. My interest in the EEG as a diagnostic method had waned slightly as I recognized the increasingly restricted role of this technique in mainline neurological diagnosis and management, despite its value in studying the various forms of epilepsy and in diagnosing obscure disorders like subacute sclerosing panencephalitis. However, my interest in the EMG continued unabated and, in consequence, I came to know well Roger Gilliatt, newly appointed to the staff, whose work on nerve conduction velocity was beginning to bear fruit, and subsequently Robin Willison who in Bill Cobb's department ultimately established an outstanding diagnostic service in EMG, nerve conduction and related techniques. He was sufficiently interested in the work I had done on automatic frequency analysis of the EMG to develop a more sophisticated automated technique of counting 'turns' in the EMG record, a method which added precision to the diagnosis of primary muscle disease.

In pursuit of my principal research objectives I first identified 91 patients with various forms of muscular dystrophy in 31 families who had been seen over the preceding 10 years at the National Hospital. I was able to trace them all and to examine them in the hospital or, where necessary, in their own homes (one extensive trip around Norfolk, Cambridgeshire and Essex was particularly memorable because of the kindness, hospitality and willing collaboration of the local general practitioners and of the patients and their families). That scientific excursion yielded interesting clinical and genetic information about family relationships in the Fens. The village of Manea was especially fascinating as there was a cluster (often called in medicine a genetic isolate) of patients with muscular dystrophy in that small community where there was evidence that intermarriage had been common, thus resulting in a far higher incidence of the disease there than in the general population. It also gave me the opportunity of visiting Hempstead in Essex where William Harvey was born and where a memorial to him, dedicated by the Royal College of Physicians of London, is still faithfully tended in the village church. That same village was also the home in the last century of the highwayman Dick Turpin, he of the famous ride on Black Bess to York. Memorabilia relating to that other village notable are suitably arrayed in the principal village pub.

It was especially interesting to see at Queen Square several patients in whom a diagnosis of muscular dystrophy had been made on what turned out to be unsatisfactory clinical and investigative evidence. Thus I found several patients with polymyositis in whom effective treatment was given (confirming my Newcastle experience) and there was yet another patient, thought to have muscular dystrophy, who had lost 4 in. in height over the preceding three years even though muscular weakness was her most prominent symptom. She proved to have hyperpara-thyroidism with an associated myopathy and her condition too was effectively treated. It seemed to me that one potential disadvantage of a single-specialty institution such as Queen Square was the absence of a member of staff with extensive experience in general internal medicine. I was glad to learn some years later that that deficiency was corrected by the appointment of my friend Sir George Smart as physician and endocrinologist to the hospital when he moved from Newcastle to become Director of the British Postgraduate Medical Federation in London.

During this period I also identified yet another patient thought to have muscular dystrophy who also had striking fatiguability, suggesting myasthenia, but her weakness was only partially responsive to neostigmine and its analogues. Iain Simpson, Norman Geschwind and I wrote a joint paper describing the clinical and investigative findings in her case under the title of 'benign congenital myopathy with myasthenic features'. Almost certainly she had one of the rare forms of congenital myasthenia which have been so clearly reported and analysed recently by Andrew Engel of the Mayo Clinic and his colleagues.

In one family with a well-documented and extensive pedigree demonstrating transmission of Duchenne muscular dystrophy through several generations (invariably through the female line) I found a female patient with the disease. Before I could fully examine and investigate her, I postulated that perhaps this had resulted, as seemed theoretically possible, because her mother, an obligate carrier, might have married a man upon whose X chromosome a mutation had occurred. In fact the explanation turned out to be quite different, because when I examined the patient in the East End of London, I found that she was indeed female and had classical Duchenne dystrophy but also had Turner's syndrome (ovarian agenesis), a disorder of development in which the morphological female has only a single X chromosome. In other words, in the XO female, as distinct from the normal XX female, the effects of a recessive gene on the single X chromosome became clinically manifest. This was the first such case reported in the world's literature, but within the next few years two further such reports appeared. My further studies of the muscular dystrophies, again with the invaluable help of R. R. Race and Ruth Sanger of the Lister Institute in blood group typing and with the invaluable advice on genetic issues of Dr C. A. B. Smith of the Galton Laboratory, eventually led to a further publication in the *Annals of Human Genetics*. Again this was preceded by long, detailed, hilarious and at times almost Rabelaisian discussions with Lionel Penrose who with his usual meticulous attention (interrupted only by outrageous asides) went through the manuscript line by line before being satisfied that it was fit for publication.

Meanwhile my follow-up study of over a hundred infants and children seen at Great Ormond Street with the 'floppy infant' or 'limp child' syndrome also prospered. Here again the follow-up data I obtained were virtually complete. In the end I concluded that most of the patients previously diagnosed as 'amyotonia congenita' were in fact suffering from spinal muscular atrophy, sometimes of the severe and fatal Werdnig-Hoffmann type but more often from what was later called type 2 as the affected individuals showed severe continuing disability but with prolonged survival. There was a second substantial group of patients in whom the floppiness and limpness of the limbs with developmental delay proved to be due to many different conditions (including, for example, congenital heart disease, metabolic disorders, mental retardation, and atonic cerebral palsy) and in whom the hypotonia was therefore symptomatic but not due to a primary neuromuscular affliction. Finally, there was a relatively small group of patients with a syndrome of what I called benign congenital hypotonia, in some of whom slow spontaneous recovery occurred as they grew older, while in others some weakness persisted. I thought that the latter group was suffering from a benign congenital myopathy, while recognizing that the nature of the condition was obscure. Subsequent work has clarified greatly the nature of many forms of benign congenital myopathy, but nevertheless it seemed to me that my survey had helped to clarify the so-called amyotonia congenita syndrome. Publications describing the results of this work appeared in the *Lancet* and in the *Journal of Neurosurgery and Psychiatry*.

Our year in London passed by busily, happily and profitably. Ann was happy in school, Judy was maturing rapidly, Betty was able to indulge a little in her musical interests and I found time to play some cricket for Dulwich. When both the girls went down simultaneously with severe attacks of measles, my mother came down to London at short notice in order to help out. Socially, we managed an occasional evening at the theatre or at a concert, but more especially enjoyed family outings at the weekends when we explored parts of London and the surrounding countryside which we had never previously seen. Whipsnade was especially popular, as was the London Zoo, and our exploration of the Leith Hill and Box Hill areas. But time after time the girls, nurtured in the North East, would say as we drove through the almost interminable streets and outer suburbs, 'Daddy, when are we going to reach the really deep country?'. Dulwich was, and still is, something of an oasis between Peckham and Camberwell to one side and Streatham and Croydon to the other.

Other diversions included a two-week holiday in a Newquay guest-house in Cornwall arranged by Betty's aunt who lived in a bungalow on Lusty Glaze Beach where we had our first (and only) experience of surf-boarding. On the way we saw Stonehenge, Salisbury, Wells, the Cheddar Gorge and Wookey Hole, among other delights; the journey was marred only by the interminable traffic queues on the Exeter bypass and by a minor accident when sombody ran into the back of our car on Porlock Hill. Fortunately no-one was injured, and equally fortunately, the damage to our car was not sufficient to interfere with our journey. The weather was good in that lovely summer of 1955 but while we also visited the beautiful villages of Polperro and Mevagissey, as well as King Arthur's Seat at Tintagel, we vowed never to return to Cornwall at the height of the summer season as the crowds and the traffic were intolerable. This experience contrasted strikingly with the comparable beauty but sparsely populated areas, never overrun with tourists, to which we have become accustomed in our beloved Northumberland and Durham. Even so, this was a time when we could take the children to the Tower of London to see the Crown Jewels and to Hampton Court and its maze without standing in an interminable queue. We also managed a delightful weekend in Stratford-upon-Avon, staying at the old Swan Hotel and visiting Shakespeare's birthplace and the other standard tourist sights. Fortunately, too, by now Ann seemed to feel much more secure and at last slept better without the hourly awakening which had caused us both such chronic fatigue. Having vowed not to add to our family while in the US for financial reasons, we now decided that the time had come to have a third child and were delighted when Betty became pregnant that summer.

Knowing that we were due to return to Newcastle that autumn, our next objective was to find a home in which we could become properly installed before our third child was due in February 1956. There followed the usual weary routine of contacting estate agents but our good friend Leslie Pattinson of Thomas Pattinson & Sons was most helpful. On brief visits to Newcastle we saw a few houses, but eventually during the summer we learned that Mr H. S. Thorne of the Newcastle Students Bookshop, whom I had come to know well, was proposing to sell his Victorian house in Dilston Terrace in Gosforth. He was formerly manager of the medical section of Waugh's bookstore in Ridley Place but, feeling that he was not advancing professionally, he set up his own bookshop in Percy Street, close to the RVI and to the University; this was an instant success. He was a very kindly, if precise and obsessional man, with a hint of fussiness but an invariable willingness to listen and to advise. Unfortunately his life had been irrevocably scarred through the death of one of his two sons, a paratrooper who was killed at Arnhem. From that day Mr Thorne always wore a black tie and never recovered from the blow. His other son, Harold, took over the business after his retirement.

His double-fronted house in Dilston Terrace was not well situated, as it looked down on the electric railway from Newcastle to the coast close to South Gosforth station and was separated from the grassy cutting by only a footpath and a fence. Hence one could not approach the house at the front by car, though there was a double garage at the rear to which access was from an unattractive cobbled back lane overseen by the gaunt brick walls of the coalhouses and other outbuildings of Dilston Terrace on one side and the equally grim Victorian Rectory Terrace on the other.

While the house was surrounded by small areas of lawn and flower beds in which bluebells grew in profusion, along with a few trees, its frontal appearance was not very attractive either. There was a green wood and glass Victorian porch, the steeple-like gable ends were protected by ornamental Victorian woodwork, and heavy, lowering bay windows both up and down sat on either side of the front porch. Inside, however, was a very attractive panelled hall and wide staircase, on the half landing of which there hung an enormous, heavily-framed oil painting which seemed to be a copy of a painting by Claude. The wide staircase led to a spacious landing and there were four bedrooms, two very large and two much smaller, close to the reasonably well-appointed bathroom and toilet. Downstairs there were large, square, well-proportioned dining and drawing rooms on either side of the hall, with high ceilings and well-preserved ornamental plasterwork around the central lights and cornices, while to one side at the rear there was a pleasant breakfast room with excellent cupboard space, and on the other a very large kitchen with three separate pantries but with an old-fashioned Meridian range and open coal fire. There was, of course, no central heating, but nevertheless the house seemed in many ways ideal for our purpose and, as the asking price was just £3000, we rapidly closed the deal. Two other huge oil paintings virtually covered one wall of the breakfast room from floor to ceiling. One was an oil of King George V. Mr Thorne offered to give these to us but we felt them to be too overpowering so they went to the Laing Art Gallery where, so far as I know, they may still be stored. In the dining room was a superb Georgian mahogany break-front bookcase, 10' 6" in width and in excellent condition. Mr Thorne said that it would be impossible for him to take that bookcase, which he loved, to his bungalow in Belford and asked if I would like to buy it. Being something of a bibliophile, I said that I would love to have it but felt that I could not possibly afford it after buying the house; when his response was that he was thinking of £50 I was barely able to conceal my amazement and accepted at once. That bookcase, now my pride and joy, as Betty's Bluthner piano is hers, has followed us through each of our homes and now sits resplendently in the former drawing room of the Oslers in 13 Norham Gardens, Oxford.

Five Dilston Terrace proved to be an invaluable interim home for us for the next eight years, though we knew that its location was far from ideal. Having been built by the builder of the terrace for his own occupation in the late 19th century, it was the only detached house in a terrace and some of the other terraced houses were clearly in decline. After moving in we installed some gas radiators and managed to keep reasonably warm. In the eight happy years we spent there, we nevertheless felt somewhat isolated from many of our friends and colleagues most of whom were living in rather more salubrious and easily accessible areas of Jesmond or Gosforth. Betty's third pregnancy was not quite as easy as her first two as she was troubled in the last few weeks by a good deal of sciatic pain. Eventually, however, Christopher arrived a few weeks early in February 1956 at Ashleigh Nursing Home (Linton Snaith was there for the delivery this time) and we were delighted to have a boy to complete our family.

The last few weeks at Queen Square passed in a flurry of activity, what with the completion of my clinical surveys of patients, the writing up of my results and the preparations involved in helping the Richards to sell their house in Dulwich. My parents were again very helpful and happily accommodated the four of us for a few days while we completed our removal, which went very smoothly, and there was very great satisfaction in again having a home of our own. It was also a pleasure for the first time in two years to be reunited with our furniture and other belongings which had been stored following the sale of Benton Lodge Avenue during the time we had been away.

Returning to my old appointment as a research assistant in the Department of Medicine in Newcastle at a salary of under £1500 per annum did come as something of a let-down as I had been in some ways lionized during my trips around the US. I suppose that the reaction was very much less than it might otherwise have been if I had returned directly to Newcastle, as my sojourn at Queen Square had helped to reattune me to British traditions and the British medical hierarchical system, even though I found this at times somewhat chafing and restrictive. It struck me as extraordinary that American neurologists coming to Queen Square, even some of outstanding seniority and distinction, were then treated as clinical clerks and were sometimes even required to pay a fee to attend ward rounds and out-patient clinics and demonstrations. They mixed in the graduate students' room in the basement with young embryo neurologists from the Third World and from elsewhere in the UK who had come at their own expense to be clerks, usually in the hope and anticipation that they might ultimately be appointed to house officer posts to further their neurological training. I was particularly struck by the fact that Russell DeJong, who had come to Queen Square on a six-month period of sabbatical leave from his prestigious chair at Ann Arbor, was treated in the first instance, despite his seniority and distinguished authorship of a major text on the neurological examination, as was any other clerk. When I complained to 'the boss' and said that in my view the institution was doing itself no good by treating distinguished Americans in this way, he agreed that the place had always been somewhat traditional, stand-offish and rigidly conventional. In the end, however, he did invite Russ to take some ward rounds and to participate in discussions and in the teaching programme, though not, in my view, before time.

Gradually things began to change and as people like Roger Gilliatt became progressively more senior, they involved overseas visitors much more in their research activities and no longer banished them to the clerking periphery. Nevertheless, I became aware while at Queen Square that the stance of the Institute in a changing international neurological scene caused some resentment and concern. For a time, indeed, the American Board of Psychiatry and Neurology withdrew recognition of periods of training spent at Queen Square as qualifying candidates to take the examinations of that Board. Recognition was later very properly restored, but in the succeeding years Henry Miller and I were touched and amused to find that with the very different approach that we ultimately followed in Newcastle in our department of neurology, up to one year in our training programme there was approved by the American Board.

Carmichael's research unit, though perhaps never quite as productive of original work as the MRC would have hoped, was in some respects the jewel in the hospital's research crown. The system whereby the senior consultant staff (and those more junior as well) spent part of the week as consultants in a London teaching hospital and only part in Queen Square (in addition to the extensive private practice in which practically all of them indulged) meant that time for research was at a premium and some members of staff did virtually none at all. It is indeed remarkable that, for example, Critchley did his outstanding work on aphasia and the parietal lobes, that Symonds and Meadows continued to contribute seminal clinical papers to the literature, and that Walshe's philosophical and at times even physiological musings continued to flow freely from his fertile pen.

However, at a time when neurological research was being increasingly nurtured in laboratory-based disciplines and when scientific tools were beginning to be applied more intensively to the study of clinical phenomena, Queen Square to some extent stood still. Indeed it was this which led Henry, wickedly provocative as ever, to refer in one notable lecture to Queen Square as 'one of the great silent areas of neurology'. Even the excellent original observations of Hallpike and of his colleagues in the neuro-otology research unit, after an initial highly productive period, seemed eventually, if only temporarily, to lose some momentum, though the straight-forward, conventional and perhaps uninspired but nevertheless original neuropathological studies of Blackwood and Mair ground steadily on. Unfortunately, despite my urging, they could not be persuaded to establish the exciting type of brain cutting session to which I had become accustomed in Boston, and certainly slide interpretation sessions in the evenings were thought to be out of the question. Hence those many neurologists from elsewhere, both young and old, who passed through the hospital and institute had relatively little exposure to, and experience in, neuropathology, while the able John Cumings in the Department of Chemical Pathology, himself very productive in research, was involved very little in the Institute's teaching programme. As a cradle, therefore, of world-wide teaching and practice in clinical neurology Queen Square was outstanding and had a well-deserved international reputation, but as a fountain-head of neurological research in the UK it lagged progressively behind until the energy and industry of younger members of staff such as Roger Gilliatt began to reverse the trend. Today, as I write, the Institute of Neurology has deservedly received an exceptionally high grading from the British Universities Funding Council because of the outstanding quality of the research which has been and is being undertaken in its laboratories in the new building of Queen Square House and in its wards and departments. Although the MRC neurological research unit closed many years ago, the Gilliatt tradition of promoting research and the lively inspiration and leadership of John Marshall, David Marsden, Alan Davison, Ian McDonald and Anita Harding, to quote but five examples of the many people involved, have ensured a secure place for Queen Square in international research in the basic and clinical neurosciences.

While I was working at Queen Square it emerged that London University had eventually decided to establish its first ever academic appointment in neurology, a readership at Queen Square, with the implied hope and prospect that if the appointment were successful it might well evolve into a chair. While I felt a strong sense of loyalty to my alma mater and still felt myself to be a committed North-Easterner, I nevertheless concluded that I must apply for the Queen Square post as such academic appointments were then very rare (indeed the senior lectureship in Edinburgh to which John Marshall, originally of Manchester but also Queen Square trained, had been appointed shortly before was virtually the only other such established university post in the specialty in the UK). Professor Nattrass was very supportive despite the comparatively junior post I was still holding and told me that he had been asked to be an external assessor (with Professor Charles Stuart-Harris of Sheffield) on the appointment committee. The field was a strong one, including John Marshall, Peter Nathan and Iain Simpson, and although my interview went well I was not surprised when John Marshall, already a senior lecturer of consultant status, was appointed. A month or two later the vacancy which his departure from Edinburgh had created was advertised and again, after considerable thought and after seeing the facilities available at the Northern General Hospital, I submitted an application which was yet again unsuccessful as Iain Simpson was appointed. I have never quite forgiven the University of Edinburgh for failing to write to the unsuccessful candidates, including myself, until 10 weeks had elapsed following the interview (John Stanton, the local candidate, had already telephoned me to say that Iain had been appointed); even then the administration was so discourteous as to send a rather scruffy cyclostyled letter with a facsimile signature, clearly intended for unsuccessful applicants for all manner of appointments, with the title of the post 'Senior Lectureship in Neurology' typed in. I made certain later when I myself was involved in University matters that a courteous signed letter would be sent to those whose applications for all academic appointments had not succeeded. Despite my inevitable disappointment (these were the only posts for which I ever applied unsuccessfully), I looked forward keenly to taking up life in Newcastle again.

Returning to Newcastle as a research assistant, to find myself yet again being required in the out-patients to see and examine patients and to present them to the professor who made the decisions and wrote the letters was somewhat chastening as I had gradually acquired increasing responsibility in the United States and even to some extent at Queen Square. Nevertheless, I still had much writing to do and many research loose ends to tie up. I quickly restored the service in electromyography which had been largely in abeyance during my absence, and also returned to work in the EEG department with J. W. (Sandy) Osselton. Throughout this period my clinical experience grew and matured and my interest in neuromuscular disease never wavered. My research grant from the Muscular Dystrophy Association of America was renewed and now offered me not only a salary for a research secretary but also that of a research assistant, along with running expenses. Room was found for my research secretary in the Medical School in accommodation then occupied by George Smart and other colleagues of the Department of Medicine; but as I was a research assistant myself, it was thought inappropriate for me to employ a personal research assistant, at least until I had achieved a more senior appointment. Fortunately Professor Nattrass told me that plans were well advanced for the establishment of a Department of Neurology in the RVI in a neurological ward (with a limited number of neurosurgical beds for Mr Rowbotham). This would be Ward 6, formerly a male surgical ward, which was being converted into single and double rooms in order to accommodate patients of both sexes. I also learned that a consultant appointment in neurology was planned, along with a university first assistantship. The intention was that Henry Miller should be appointed to the consultant post and that, hopefully, I would be prepared to become his first assistant. Everything went (surprisingly) according to plan and in the spring of 1956 Henry Miller was appointed as the first consultant neurologist to the RVI. I was then appointed to the university first assistant post at a slightly enhanced salary and we were able to open the unit. In the meantime, Fred Nattrass had reached retirement age and was succeeded in the Chair of Medicine by George Smart. One of my last responsibilities in the Department of Medicine was to arrange the Prof's farewell dinner, a memorable occasion when his past and present house officers, registrars and other colleagues presented him with some fine bird-watching binoculars (he was a very distinguished ornithologist) which he later used to very good effect in Africa where he worked for two years as Professor of Medicine in the Ibadan medical school.

For the first time I was now able as a first assistant (temporary lecturer) to appoint a research assistant on my MDA grant and recruited Dr Peter Leyburn, a very intelligent and able young senior house officer with an honours BSc in physiology who seemed to me to have the appropriate background to be able to help in the EEG and EMG work and to carry out some specific research projects under my supervision. As he had a very severe stammer it seemed that perhaps laboratory-based and clinical research, rather than clinical practice, might be his forte. We were also fortunate to attract to our registrar post a research assistant from Iain Simpson's Edinburgh department, Dr Andrew Lenman, already experienced in electromyography.

While Henry and I began to build up a rapidly expanding clinical clientele and to establish an undergraduate and postgraduate teaching programme, Peter and I managed to complete some projects relating to the treatment of myotonia and the results of two controlled clinical trials were subsequently published in *Brain*. Henry and I both recognized that there would ultimately be a need for a consultant post in clinical applied neurophysiology in Newcastle and hoped that Peter Leyburn might ultimately succeed to that appointment. In the end he decided that he would much prefer a career in psychiatry and later worked successfully as a consultant at St Nicholas Hospital in Newcastle for many years.

The 20 beds on Ward 6 were shared between neurology and neuro-surgery, though for much of the time there were many more neurological than neurosurgical patients in the ward. A limited neuroradiological service had been established at the RVI to complement that which Gordon Gryspeerdt and his colleagues were providing at the NGH, but the theatre facilities available for neurosurgery at the RVI were limited. Although the energetic and ebullient John Hankinson from Wylie McKissock's unit at Queen Square had recently joined the Rowbotham neurosurgical team at the NGH and had sessions at the RVI, neurosurgery never prospered in that hospital. After Mr Rowbotham's retirement a few years later Ward 6 became a wholly medical neurological ward and all neurosurgery was based at the NGH. We were very fortunate in our staff on Ward 6 and the 18 months that I spent there as first assistant were happy and productive ones, not least because of the very large number of patients I began to see, through which my clinical experience steadily grew. The nursing sister in charge of the ward, Dorothy Blenkinsop, ran a first-class team and later went to Dryburn Hospital, Durham, as Chief Nursing Officer before becoming the Regional Nursing Officer at the Regional Hospital Board in Newcastle, ultimately receiving the CBE for her distinguished services. We were also fortunate to be able to recruit senior house officers of outstanding ability. One was Dr John Wilson, a local graduate (whose father had followed mine as headmaster at Pickering Nook School). We hoped that he might establish paediatric neurology in Newcastle in due course and so arranged for him to spend some time with Paul Sandifer at Great Ormond Street. His training must have been very effective as he was eventually appointed to the consultant staff of that hospital as a successor to Paul. Another was Dr Donald Irvine, son of an Ashington general practitioner and another Newcastle graduate. Dr Irvine followed his father into general practice, as had always been his intention. Ultimately he became a member of the Merrison Committee on the Regulation of the Medical Profession, later Chairman of the Council of the Royal College of General Practitioners, and subsequently was appointed to the General Medical Council where he is now giving distinguished service as Chairman of that body's Committee on Professional Standards. Yet another most able senior house officer was a member of my own medical school year, Douglas Thomson, who had trained in ophthalmology, having worked both in Oxford and in Newcastle. Recognizing that he needed the FRCS qualification, and having without difficulty passed the primary examination, he then, despite being married with a family, decided that he needed wider experience and more opportunity for study than his senior registrarship in ophthalmology allowed. He therefore took a six-month senior house officer post with us in neurology (which, as he told me later, helped him very greatly in dealing with neuro-ophthalmological problems in future years). Then for a few months more he made the sacrifice of giving up work completely in order to study whole-time. Having been successful in the examination he was soon appointed to a consultant post in Cheltenham where he had a distinguished career in his specialty before retiring in 1988.

As my clinical responsibilities grew, Henry and I decided to establish a regularly weekly clinical meeting at which we would discuss important and interesting clinical phenomena in the presence of the patients provided, of course, that they gave their permission. Invariably they did so (in all of my years in clinical neurology, I only once recall a patient refusing to have her condition discussed at a clinical meeting). We always impressed upon our students and junior staff the importance of handling the discussion in front of an audience compassionately and sensitively, and I believe that we usually succeeded. Certainly the Friday clinical meetings have continued to be a regular and important feature of Newcastle neurology and a vital part of the postgraduate teaching programme. Later, when I was appointed as a consultant to the General Hospital, we organized the meetings on a friendly but competitive 'home and away' basis, alternating them weekly between the RVI and the NGH and making certain that the staff of the other unit did not know in advance what problems were to be discussed. Hence those working in one hospital could challenge the clinical knowledge and expertise of those from the other, beginning with the juniors and later inviting senior members to conclude the discussion. These meetings were generally based upon the 'grand round' experience from which I had profited so much in Boston. So far as I can judge, the very large number of doctors who passed through the Newcastle unit over the years found them an invaluable teaching experience. In later years a careful record was kept of the patients whose cases had been discussed and it is planned that this will eventually lead to a publication by David Bates, Niall Cartlidge and others.

Henry's principal research interest was multiple sclerosis (MS). When working as a general physician he had written extensively about the collagen or connective tissue disorders and later conducted several interesting clinical studies of encephalomyelitis which led to the publication of some important papers in the *Quarterly Journal of Medicine*. It was therefore natural that he should become interested in MS. Soon after the unit was established he obtained a research grant from the local branch of the MS Society in order to pursue several clinical studies of the disease. I helped him to collect and analyse some of the relevant literature with particular reference to the mental and psychological manifestations of the disease. However, as he recognized, my own interest in neuromuscular disease meant that there was little prospect of my being able to devote much of my time to MS research and so he invited Dr Kurt Schapira to join him in his work. Together they carried out some population studies of the incidence and prevalence of the disease in the northern region; much important work on this disease and its epidemiology and management has subsequently been published from the RVI unit.

An important consequence of intensive clinical practice is that one is for ever learning new lessons. While I was Henry's first assistant, seeing many out-patients, I perhaps failed to recognize that there are times when one may become so involved, almost subconsciously, in trying to promote the interests and welfare of one's patients that a hint of irrational advocacy may creep in. I remember one young girl with epilepsy who seemed to be responding well to anticonvulsant treatment and whose attacks were reasonably controlled but who had a number of behavioural problems which her mother attributed to mismanagement in her school. There was a suggestion of victimization by her peers and it was suggested that she was being excluded from her class and was being sent home unduly often on account of her disability at a time when it seemed to be under satisfactory control. Without thinking too deeply, I therefore wrote a letter to her headmistress, one which I soon recognized with hindsight was intemperate though it was one which I enjoyed dictating. I ended it by saying that unless the position could rapidly be corrected, the school would have failed not only this patient but also the community. Not unnaturally, the headmistress was incensed and contacted the Director of Education who, in turn, having known Henry for some time, wrote to him. In consequence I found myself on the receiving end of a well-deserved and well-justified wigging. Later I visited the school and found that while there were undoubtedly faults on both sides, the patient's behaviour had at times been such as to demand action from her teachers; clearly her mother's version of events had been very biased and I had not tried to assess both sides of the case, as I certainly should have done, before firing off a foolish letter. The headmistress graciously accepted my apology, the child's behaviour and management were greatly improved; this was another lesson learned.

There were three other cases which taught me an important clinical lesson during my time as first assistant. The first related to a man who was a close friend of some relatives of mine; he was admitted to Ward 6 with symptoms clearly indicating vascular disease of the brain stem. Soon after admission he improved and we sent him home. It was only when I was examining his notes in order to dictate a discharge letter that I found his blood count, showing clearly that he was suffering from polycythaemia vera (a gross excess of red cells in the circulating blood). This condition, which often causes vascular symptoms because of increased viscosity or sludging of blood, had clearly caused his symptoms. Quickly we brought him back to hospital and gave him appropriate treatment. Somewhat to my chagrin, we later learned from our relatives that they and others had been greatly impressed by the diagnosis. Little did they know that we had overlooked the true state of affairs when he was first in hospital.

A similar event occurred in the case of the wife of a senior professor of Newcastle University; she was admitted with general symptoms of malaise and lassitude along with troublesome headaches. We investigated her fully, as we thought, but for some time were unable to identify the cause of her condition. It was only after about two weeks that I found an X-ray report in her notes; this had been filed by one of the ward staff. Gordon Gryspeerdt had pointed to some areas of translucency in the X-rays of her skull which at once suggested that either she was suffering from multiple myeloma, a disease of the bone marrow, or from secondary deposits of cancer in the skull. In fact we had overlooked for some time the X-ray changes; when they came to our attention we soon found that she was suffering from multiple myeloma for which again effective treatment was soon given.

Yet a third example related to a young man in his thirties who was admitted complaining of weakness and numbness in all four limbs. He had been to see his dentist for multiple extractions under general anaesthesia; after recovering from the anaesthetic and leaving the dentist's surgery, when standing at a local bus stop he developed tingling in all four extremities and soon had difficulty in walking. Within a day or two the symptoms had worsened and his doctor sent him to us as an emergency. When I examined him I found evidence of spinal cord disease with severe loss of position and joint sense in all four extremities, brisk tendon reflexes and extensor plantar responses, pointing to a lesion in the cervical spinal cord. As his X-rays did demonstrate some evidence of intervertebral disc degeneration in the neck (with central protrusion of discs shown by myelography) it seemed logical to suggest that while he was anaesthetized and his neck was hyper-extended in the dentist's chair, his spinal cord had been contused. At this time the final examination in medicine was taking place and the registrar from the professorial unit asked us whether we had any patients who might be used in the examination. This young man readily agreed. He therefore went up to Ward 9 where a candidate examined him, after taking a careful history. When the examiner came to discuss the patient's case, the student mentioned the possibility of a cervical cord lesion but also raised the question as to whether subacute combined degeneration (SCD) of the spinal cord in association with vitamin B_{12} deficiency might not enter into the differential diagnosis. The examiner smiled, feeling that this was a far-fetched suggestion in the light of the history, but said 'Well, let's see what the blood count showed'; when he found that this demonstrated a macrocytic anaemia, he was dumbfounded (as was I). In fact the patient did prove to be suffering from SCD, which we had never suspected in view of the history and which was later confirmed by bone marrow examination and vitamin B_{12} estimation. Not surprisingly, that student achieved honours in the examination.

These three clinical cases taught me the crucial importance of examining regularly and repeatedly all of the results of investigations which came through to the ward. We subsequently made sure that these were never filed in the patient's records without being examined by the ward staff.

During my time on Ward 6 I also enjoyed my first domiciliary consultation. A senior medical student came to me one day and insisted that I should go out with him to Bedlington to see his father-in-law, about whose condition he was very concerned. I pointed out that I was not a consultant and was not supposed to do any such consultations, but under pressure agreed to go with him and examined the gentleman in question, who fortunately turned out to have an eminently treatable condition which responded very well to treatment. That experience, however (needless to say carried out without fee) taught me the importance of domiciliary consultations in the presence of the general practitioner (who was present and with whom the student, Paddy Ivory, subsequently went into practice). I much enjoyed such consultations and did them for many years after ultimately being appointed a consultant.

Another amusing series of incidents enlivened clinical life on Ward 6. I came across a family of patients with a form of periodic paralysis. One affected member, a North Shields trawler skipper, regularly had attacks when returning from the sea and after selling his catch. He would then repair to the nearest pub and would consume several pints of Newcastle Brown Ale, as a result of which he became both physically and metaphorically paralysed. Recognizing that it was probably the potassium in the beer which caused this, we gave him chlorothiazide to promote potassium excretion and his attacks were controlled. His nephew, also affected, though less severely, was a bus conductor who found himself unable to collect fares on the top deck of his double-decker bus when an attack came on. His attacks were controlled by the same treatment until his general practitioner said it was very old-fashioned to take chlorothiazide and gave him chlorothiazide-K (with added potassium) until we pointed out the error of his ways. A year or two later, David Poskanzer from Boston (who published the details of this family with David Kerr) investigated the effects of Newcastle Brown Ale on the serum potassium, using himself as a control; after four pints he (Poskanzer) became comatose while the patient (who was accustomed to the brew) was relatively unaffected.

In the midst of this hectic clinical activity, during which time I strove to keep my research interests alive with Peter Leyburn's help, I had not totally forgotten my medico-political interests. Indeed on returning from the United States to work at Queen Square my former colleagues of the Registrars Group of the BMA had re-elected me chairman of the group and I represented the registrar interest on the Central Consultants and Specialists Committee. There I came to admire the successive chairmen Dr Rowland Hill and Sir Thomas Holmes Sellors under whom I served, while Dr R. D. Lawrence (of diabetic fame) and the well-known surgeon Mr Lawrence Abel regularly incited me to attack my seniors on behalf of the registrars ('Give 'em hell, boy'). Even then we were much exercised by the numerical relationship between registrar posts and prospective consultant vacancies ('the ratio') which still exercises the interest of that committee today. But after my return to Newcastle and as my clinical and research commitments continued to develop, it became increasingly difficult for me to attend meetings in London and eventually therefore, with some reluctance, I resigned. I knew, too, that there was every likelihood (or so I hoped) that I would soon be appointed as a consultant as plans to create such an appointment at the NGH in order to begin to offer a regional neurological service were well advanced.

I was also delighted when Professor Nattrass and I were approached, at the instigation of Sir Harry Platt, the Chairman, by the organization then known as the Central Council for the Care of Cripples with the suggestion that we should establish within it a group of individuals for the support of patients with neuromuscular disease and their families. The Executive Secretary of the Council, Miss Drury, was helpful and supportive and seconded Mrs Joan Vincent, a member of her staff, to help us establish the organization. With the aid of a distinguished Medical Advisory and Research Committee which we soon recruited and of which Professor John Cumings of Queen Square became the chairman, the organization grew steadily. Its aim was to bring together patients and their families in many different parts of the country who wished to develop a friendly link between those suffering similar afflictions; it also proposed to raise funds for the support of research. Thus the Muscular

Dystrophy Group was born and, about two years later, broke off from the Central Council for the Care of Cripples to become independent with Joan Vincent as its first Executive Secretary. But of this and of my extra-professional interests I shall say more later.

One troublesome medical problem intervened during my time on Ward 6. For some time I had suffered troublesome attacks of upper abdominal pain, particularly in the upper right quadrant, often coming on after a heavy meal and particularly after rich, fatty food. I recall especially one wedding reception when, after eating too many rich vol-au-vents and other pastries, I had a sharp severe attack which laid me low for an hour or two. Curiously, most such attacks came at weekends, lasted for no more than one or two hours and quickly recovered, so that they did not interfere significantly with my professional life. On one occasion, however, in San Francisco between lectures, when we were in the US, I had an exceptionally severe attack and had to rest on a couch in the consulting room of one of the doctors for a few hours before being able to resume my professional activity. In the late summer of 1957 I had one exceptionally severe attack which lasted for almost 24 hours and which led Betty to call our general practitioner, Dr Bob Martin, who at once diagnosed gall bladder disease. I had suspected that that was the diagnosis myself but, as many doctors do, had postponed taking action as the attacks had been so intermittent and relatively brief in duration until this last and most severe one occurred. X-rays subsequently confirmed that I had some cholesterol gall stones (no doubt due to my earlier over-indulgence in ice cream made with baby food on the paediatric wards) and the Professor of Surgery, Andrew Lowdon, had no hesitation in recommending a cholecystectomy. Henry Miller was not particularly pleased at the prospect of losing his first assistant for a few weeks and at first a little grudgingly but then with his typical sardonic smile agreed that I must have the operation, provided I could be back at work in two weeks! I chose to have it done between the Christmas and New Year holidays in order to disrupt the work of the ward as little as possible. The operation went smoothly, I was up and about in 48 hours and was even able to walk down the RVI corridor, as a patient this time, to watch the annual Christmas Revue. I was back to work in under four weeks, so that the flow of professional activity continued relatively unabated.

At last the great day dawned when, after the Regional Hospital Board had completed all of the necessary negotiations, the consultant post of a neurologist at the NGH with regional responsibilities was established in late 1957, and in February 1958 I was interviewed and appointed. So at last, approaching 36 years of age, I had achieved the permanent career post upon which I had set my heart. I was allocated four beds in Ward 27 (Mr Rowbotham's ward) in the neurosurgical department at the Newcastle General Hospital and was given facilities to hold two out-patient clinics there, one an open clinic for general practitioners and another a closed clinic for consultant reference only. I was also allocated 14 beds in the Chester-le-Street General Hospital, some 10 miles from Newcastle, where there were no neuro-radiological facilities. It was recognized that I would have to move patients backwards and forwards between Chester-le-Street and Newcastle in order to take advantage of the specialized investigative facilities which only the Newcastle unit could provide. I was also required to carry out fortnightly closed out-patient clinic sessions (again for consultant reference only) at Dryburn Hospital, Durham and also in alternate weeks at the North Ormesby Hospital in Middlesbrough on Teesside, in order to begin the task of developing a regional service. Fortunately I was also given two nominal sessions at the RVI in order to maintain a link with Ward 6; that link allowed me access to the private ward in the Leazes Hospital at the RVI since, on Henry's advice, I had decided to accept the new appointment on a part-time basis, which would allow me to spend two half-days a week in private practice. It was clear that this would prove to be an exceptionally busy and demanding appointment with much responsibility and travel and I recognized that in consequence my research interests might, at least for a time, have to take a back seat.

And so, my happy days as first assistant at the RVI came to an end. That first assistantship then proved, and has proved since, to be an invaluable training post, comparable to a senior registrarship in many respects but also carrying university teaching and research responsibilities. Since I vacated it many distinguished neurologists from Britain and overseas have passed through the appointment. Andrew Lenman followed me and ran the EMG service for a time before going to Dundee as a consultant. For a time Henry and I worked out an exchange arrangement with Ray Adams' department so that Lenman was succeeded as first assistant by David Poskanzer from Boston; he in turn was followed by Jack Foster, our own Newcastle graduate who, having decided to train in neurology, had been a houseman at Queen Square. Yet another Boston exchange followed when Jack, with his wife Jennifer and their baby went to the MGH to work with Ray, while Richard Johnson came to Newcastle to hold the first assistantship. Dick Johnson subsequently carried out some important research in virology in Australia and in the United States before moving to Cleveland, subsequently being appointed to the Eisenhower Chair of Neurology at Johns Hopkins Hospital in Baltimore, an appointment which he still holds with great distinction.

Perhaps I may include one final personal postscript to this chapter. Henry and Eileen had for some time rented a very beautiful apartment in Middleton Hall near Belford in Northumberland, within easy reach of Beadnell where Betty and I and the family had enjoyed many family holidays, and only some four or five miles from Bamburgh where we had begun occasionally to play golf together. Henry entertained us and the children on several occasions in his lovely country retreat where on Sundays he often, with some locals and professional friends with country cottages in the area, attended what he wickedly called 'morning service' at noon in the bar of the Lord Crewe Arms in Bamburgh. He suggested that we should explore the possibility of finding a cottage on the Greenwich Hospital Northern Estates, of which he was a tenant. Accordingly I wrote to George Thomson, the receiver and agent, asking whether anything was available. On the very day of my consultant interview, I received a letter offering us the rental of Ivy Cottage, Detchant, a semi-detached cottage which had been vacant for six months and which was available at a rent of £76 a year. A few days later Betty and I and the children drove up to Detchant on a cold, snowy February morning. Although the cottage was cold, miserably neglected and had clear evidence of damp with a huge stain in the main bedroom covering a large part of an outside wall, we were nevertheless charmed. This had been an old stone farm labourer's residence but had been modernized after the war. It had a bathroom, kitchen, living room and three bedrooms, an attractive, if badly neglected, garden and superb views over Kyloe Woods and down towards Holy Island. While such capital as we had possessed from Mrs Harrison's estate had rapidly dwindled, and while saving had continued to be impossible on the salary I had been earning, we were in no doubt that Ivy Cottage was for us and clinched the lease immediately. Fortunately we were able to buy some furniture which was shortly to be discarded from house officers' rooms in the RVI, along with some bedside lockers and old ward chairs (for which we paid a shilling each). These, once cleaned and painted, gave us good service for several years. Other furniture was bought cheaply in a saleroom at Crawcrook owned by the Pattinsons, and in no time at all we had a sparsely furnished but nevertheless comfortable and reasonably warm country cottage to which we could retreat and from which we could enjoy the glory of the sea and the hills and all of the other delights of north Northumberland.

There followed innumerable happy weekends and family holidays at the cottage with many visits from friends and colleagues. Over the years the rent rose only gradually but our attempts to buy were continually rebuffed. However, Greenwich Hospital did decide to sell Detchant Farm and its new owner offered to sell to us a somewhat derelict but structurally sound stone building on the other side of the road from Ivy Cottage. This was known as 'The Old Piggery' as it had accommodated pigs for some years after being originally constructed to provide wash-houses for tenants of the cottages. We accepted the offer eagerly (the locals thought we were crazy). Eventually we converted the building into a delightful home which was later extended three times and we moved in in 1977, continuing to rent Ivy Cottage for the family for a few more years. From half an acre of open field Betty created a lovely garden. *Of course*, we decided to keep the original name.

CHAPTER 10

My Sporting Life

I am not certain how or why I became so deeply interested in sport, both as a participant and as a spectator, but this must surely have had something to do with my home environment. My father was a reasonably competent soccer player and cricketer in his youth but at school he concentrated on hockey, at which he was an above average performer. My mother, by contrast, had no sporting interests and never tested her competence in any form of sport because she was regarded on medical advice as being 'delicate' in childhood. It was no doubt my father's inspiration which kindled my enthusiasm for cricket, soccer, snooker and billiards. Before I was nine or 10 years of age he encouraged me to handle a cricket bat and ball and often we would rise at 5.30 a.m. when a test tour was taking place in Australia to listen to the ball-by-ball commentary on the radio. Whenever we could, we saw local cricket teams play and often while on holiday we would travel considerable distances to watch the Durham County cricket team, of which the redoubtable all-rounder Jack Carr was then so notable a member. For a special treat we would travel to Leeds for one day of a test match, where I once saw an outstanding partnership between Wally Hammond and Joe Hardstaff and also had a glimpse of the great Don Bradman, who unfortunately did not on that occasion make a very large score against the redoubtable bowling of Kenneth Farnes and Hedley Verity. Later, when the family moved to Newcastle, my father was a regular Newcastle United supporter, as was I (when I had the time); he always carried a large wooden block wrapped in brown paper on which he would stand at the back of the paddock in front of the main stand in order to get a better view of the game. In later years I sometimes joined him and was fortunate enough, through a friend, to be able in the 1950s to go to the FA Cup Final at Wembley and to see Jackie Milburn's two magnificent goals which defeated Blackpool despite the wizardry of the great Stanley Matthews.

As my schooldays progressed, my enthusiasm for sport escalated though I soon recognized that I was neither as nimble nor as agile as many of my peers; whether I realized that this was at least partly due to my obesity resulting from my mother's dietary beliefs, I cannot now say. Nevertheless insight did dawn as I recognized that on the soccer field

I was inherently rather clumsy and not very fast. However, I persevered and in my last year at Middlestone Moor Council School made the school soccer team at right full back; there may have been an element of nepotism (as my father was headmaster). Clearly I was placed in a position where it was thought that I might do least damage. My efforts at the Alderman Wraith Grammar School were in the first few years no more distinguished, but in the fifth form I did ultimately achieve the first house team (the Saxons) which won the house championship. However, as I eventually slimmed down my performance improved, and when in the school trials I scored two goals from centre forward I felt sure that I must have achieved my ambition of playing for the school. However, those seniors with greater perception than myself recognized my lack of innate ability and selected me at inside right for the second team. In the sixth form, now much slimmer and fitter, I astonished everyone, not least myself, by leading the annual cross-country race for a few miles and eventually coming in fourth. And at last I was selected for the first team, for which I appeared regularly for the next two years, though the captain decided that I should revert to right full back instead of playing in the forwards.

On going to medical school, therefore, I put my name down for the first soccer trial. On the second Saturday of term the final year dignitaries who ran the team (including Charles Routledge, a dental student, who later had a distinguished cricketing career, playing regularly for Northumberland) decided to field a team of freshers against a similar team from King's in a search for new talent. I was at right back with Geoff Mellor on the left, Jimmy Oldfield at right half and Howard Scott at centre half, and as I mentioned in Chapter 3, we defeated King's by the resounding margin of nine goals to nil. Jimmy, a consummate performer, was immediately selected for the first team while the rest of us were chosen for the seconds. Eventually, however, I managed to play many games for the firsts, though I was never consistent enough to be awarded my colours. Among the stalwarts of medical soccer were Wilf Jack (later a notable general practitioner in Consett) and Willie Walker (later Reader in Haematology in Newcastle who became nationally famous for his work on haemolytic disease of the newborn). Perhaps the highlight of my playing career was when, playing at right half, I scored a goal against the Netherton Approved School from about 40 yards; as the ball curled into the top left-hand corner of the net, well out of the reach of the goalkeeper, I thought it would be improper to confess that this had been intended to be a pass to our forwards. Unfortunately in one match I suffered an injury (as I recall it, undiagnosed) to my right foot which did not affect my ability to run but made it difficult for me to kick the ball; so for a year I relinquished soccer and played several enjoyable games of hockey for Medicals, recognizing then that mixed hockey (male and female) can be a very dangerous game as one endeavours to avoid the whirling sticks of hearty, enthusiastic, Amazonian females. After graduation soccer took a back seat, though I played a few games in the Army in Glasgow and Southampton and in the Middle East, while recognizing (and perhaps unconsciously suppressing) the fact that my increasing obesity was again beginning to affect my performance adversely.

Cricket was, however, my first and most durable love. As I said in Chapter 2, I read avidly the writings of Jack Hobbs and that great man became my schoolboy hero, to the extent that I became an avid supporter of Surrey County Cricket Club (from a distance) and have supported them to this day since first class cricket is not played in Northumberland or Durham (as I write, Durham's first class status has just become a reality in 1992). While I tried hard to bowl, I soon realized that I would never do so with more than limited competence, though in later years I was occasionally used as a change bowler for the Victorians and even once took five wickets against Charlie Naylor's XI (Charlie Naylor was the Records Officer at the RVI whose cricketing skills, however, along with those of his colleagues, fell far short of his administrative ability and of his enthusiasm for the game). My personal performance was put into perspective first by the fact that we dismissed the opposition for 26 runs, and secondly by our irreverent wicket keeper who remarked loudly that it was incredible that such innocuous 'straight up and down stuff' should take so many wickets. On yet another occasion, when I was captaining the Victorians and put myself on for one over only to allow our opening bowlers to change ends, I delivered a rank long-hop which the batsman hooked into the safe hands of mid-wicket, an event which inspired Freddie Herbert to remark audibly from the slips that an extraordinary thing about the game of cricket is how often piss takes wickets.

Realizing, therefore, that such ability as I possessed lay in batting, I worked hard at my technique with such coaching as I was able to find in Middlestone Moor and Spennymoor. In the fourth form at the Alderman Wraith I played regularly for the school second XI, being then promoted to opening batsman in the first XI in the fifth form and being awarded my colours for 1939–41. When I last played against the Green College students in 1989 I was still able proudly to wear my white AWS cap with these dates emblazoned in blue on the peak. Fortunately despite the moth holes it has acquired over the years, the cap just, if only just, held together. I loved school cricket; in the first year sixth I became secretary of the club and in my final year vice-captain. We played against many schools in Durham County, including the St James VIth Grammar School at Bishop Auckland where two able cricketers, Charles Elmes and Bob Hardisty (later captain of the England amateur soccer side) were outstanding. Although I achieved one 50 and several 40s I soon recognized that the greatest flaw in my game was an innate nervousness which often made it difficult to get started, as well as a fundamental impatience which so impaired my concentration as often to tempt me into indiscretion at a time when I thought I might be about to achieve a big score. These problems certainly impaired my early performances for the Middlestone Moor Cricket Club, which had taken over the ground of the Spennymoor club, the latter having become defunct during the war. Middlestone Moor played in the Mid-Durham Senior League and when I was about 14 I turned out occasionally for the first team and later played more regularly. I recall particularly playing against Ferryhill and going in fifth wicket down to face a redoubtable league bowler called Turnbull who seemed able to swing the ball in both directions. As I walked to the crease, the fielders, seeing a young boy taking guard, gathered round in a menacing circle but soon retreated when I hit the second ball back over the bowler's head and out of the ground for six. In that same match I gained further kudos by taking a catch from Ferryhill's star batsman above my head one-handed close to the boundary, and as years went by my fielding steadily improved. One problem which, however, concerned me throughout was that I never learned to throw a cricket ball any distance, even though close to the wicket my throwing was pretty quick and accurate. As my colleagues in the Victorians concluded, this made me into a specialist gully fielder so that I was never required to throw from the outfield.

Cricket in medical school was also a delight and we managed to defeat many local sides, largely because most of the outstanding local cricketers of less than mature age were serving in the Forces. I mentioned earlier the occasion when in my first year I was ordered to play for the staff against the students; that performance at least ensured that subsequently I played regularly for Medicals and achieved some reasonable scores, though never reaching the standard of some of our outstanding performers like Nigel Wood and Bert White (formerly of the Royal Grammar School in Newcastle) and Alan Jenkins (of St Bees) who scored an immaculate century for Medicals against the Durham Colleges in the Grey Cup. That cup was awarded for annual matches between the three sections of Durham University (the Medical Faculty including dentistry, King's College, and the Durham Colleges). We won the cup several years running, at the same time as the Medicals Rugby Union Football Club was carrying all before it in Northumbrian competitions. We even defeated several outstanding Army sides, including one we played against at Morpeth and which boasted two former Minor Counties cricketers among its number. Our fast opening bowler, Desmond Dawes, had an extraordinary delivery in which he seemed, as his arm came over, to bring the ball from somewhere behind his left ear. This so surprised the opening batsman for the opposition (a major who, it was said, had played for Dorset) that he allowed the first ball to remove his middle stump. The victim was later heard loudly complaining in the pavilion by enquiring

'Who was that peculiar bowler?' On one solitary occasion I was selected for a Durham University side to play against Edinburgh as first reserve to travel. As we travelled north on the eve of the match and were royally entertained by our hosts, one of our number so over-indulged as to be incapable of performing next day so that I managed at last to play for the University. Sadly the weather later intervened and the match was eventually rained off as a draw.

After graduation, I joined County Club but as a houseman had so little time to play that apart from one or two occasional games for the Second XI, I was unable to play regular cricket. Occasional games followed during Army service, but when I returned to Newcastle and played a few times for Slade's XI I and several friends soon decided that we must establish a club to arrange more regular friendly fixtures; so the Victorians was born. The story of this club has been told in the book entitled *Northumberland's Non-League Cricket Clubs* by B. D. R. Stevens, published by the Smith Print Group of Newcastle upon Tyne in 1978. I became founder secretary and we invited past and present members of the medical and dental staffs of the RVI and Dental Hospital to join us. The club was in difficulty, largely for financial reasons, in its early years but I, with some affrontery, approached all the senior members of the medical, surgical and dental staff of these hospitals to become members and to subscribe towards the cost of buying club equipment. Many responded eventually, so that at last we were established. In our first season we arranged several fixtures against local clubs, all played away from home; often we had to beg or borrow equipment belonging to the home team. For example, when we played against Burnopfield Cricket Club we were loaned bats and pads and were resoundingly defeated, largely through a storming innings played by a rotund Mr Milburn (locally referred to as 'that aaful skelper, Milborn') whom we learned was the father of Colin Milburn, later of Northants and England.

In our second season F. I. Herbert, the plastic surgeon, a splendid left-arm bowler who had played for Durham County and for Benwell just prior to the war, joined us, as did Stafford Maw, a senior registrar in ophthalmology who came to Newcastle from Dunfermline where he had been a regular member of the Forfarshire county side. We arranged an extensive fixture list with matches against many country sides in Northumberland such as Bamburgh, Matfen, Belsay and Etal. However, with Freddie and Stafford and with other stalwarts like Donald Heaton, Tom and Angus Bird, Ramsay Horler, Ron Howd, Peter Dickinson, Hugh Davison, Alan Jenkins and others, we also felt strong enough to challenge some powerful local sides, including Gateshead Fell, North Durham, Morpeth, County Club and South Northumberland. Each of these turned out friendly sides against us, including several first team members, along with others who normally played for their second elevens. Unfortunately

Freddie Herbert, whose bowling was still impressive, played for only two seasons (possibly because we dropped too many slip catches) but the dentist W. M. M. Robson of Gateshead Fell, another outstanding bowler, did play from time to time.

One less auspicious occasion in the early years was when we arranged a match against Ryton; they, anticipating that players like Stafford Maw and Freddie Herbert would be in our team, arranged a special game in their holiday week and turned out a Tyneside Senior League select against the Victorians. Unfortunately we could not field our strongest team and N. Calder of Greenside scored 50 against us within the first 20 minutes of the innings, though Dr Donald Veitch of Consett managed with his accurate swing bowling to take a few wickets and in the end we faced a total of 180 for 6 declared. Unfortunately, against a strong bowling side we fared poorly and were dismissed for just over 90 runs, of which I was fortunate enough to score over 20. I think that the crowd that turned up at the ground felt they had not had their money's worth; one memorable remark of a spectator was always remembered by the Victorians—'Aall claethes and nee strokes!'.

Nevertheless, we had some notable victories against Gateshead Fell and even County Club and South Northumberland and many close matches against local friendly teams like St George's Rovers. We had now been allowed to use the Medical ground at Heaton for our home games, had our own equipment and prospered with as many as 30 fixtures per year. We also played King's Old Students XI and had regular games against teams from St Nicholas' Hospital and St Mary's Hospital, Stannington, as well as memorable matches against Blagdon on that tiny but fascinating pitch in the grounds of Viscount Ridley's Blagdon Hall. These delightful games, sometimes on weekday evenings, sometimes on Saturday or Sunday afternoons, were always followed by a period of carousing with our opponents in some nearby hostelry. Sunshine, white flannels, green turf, tea in the pavilion, and a pint or two afterwards—these are 'the stuff that dreams are made on'—even if a late return home sometimes found Betty wearing, especially after a difficult day with the children, her 'cricket face' (Chapter 7).

Perhaps our finest hour was in 1951, some six weeks after I had had my right internal cartilage removed and my left inguinal hernia repaired, when we had a Wednesday afternoon fixture against the Durham Colleges XI and took along one of our strongest sides. We won the toss and W. B. Robertson and I opened the batting. We were mildly surprised to find a large crowd at the ground and were amused to hear from the spectators comments about their 'demon bowler'. I took first strike and the bowler in question disappeared in the direction of the sight screen, came hurtling up to the wicket, his arm came over, there was a loud whistling sound and my stumps lay in a heap on the ground. Fortunately our umpire,

Donald Auld, had had the great presence of mind to shout 'no ball'. This was a very straight and very fast full pitch. Eventually we put on about 50 for the first wicket, but then Robertson and I were both clean bowled by a man bowling slow left-arm at the other end. When I came into the pavilion I told my friends that this was the fastest bowler I had ever seen and was greeted with ribald laughter; but it turned out that I was not very far wrong as he was Frank Tyson, then an undergraduate at Durham University, who graduated a year later, went to Northants and subsequently, as everyone knows, to Australia. On that day John Webb, formerly a regular for Oxford Authentics and then a paediatric registrar in the RVI, scored over 80 not out and the Victorians ran up 200 for 4 wickets. Frank Tyson never forgot that occasion, so that I wrote to our former Victorian, Alan Jenkins (not only a competent bat but a teasing slow right-arm bowler), who had emigrated to Australia, telling him that Tyson was going to Australia with the MCC. As a result Alan was appointed official doctor to the England team during the tour and was later Frank Tyson's best man when he married in Australia; they have remained close friends. These are experiences which Alan can perhaps attribute to playing for the Victorians.

Another highlight was in the late 1950s when, through the good offices of Mr Bruce McCulloch, a Newcastle orthopaedic surgeon who was for several years a regular, we undertook an Easter tour beginning with a match against Berwick-upon-Tweed and then playing in Dunfermline against the Forfarshire XI. One difficulty we faced was that we depended largely for membership on registrars in medicine and dentistry who often moved around the country to take up consultant posts and so our team changed regularly from year to year. Nevertheless, people like Roy Gray, Alan Horler, Callum Stark, Roger Finney and Griff Owen were regulars and many visiting doctors from South Africa, Australia, the West Indies, India and New Zealand, like Len Harris, Dick Willing and many others, played from time to time.

Also memorable was a match against Bamburgh Castle Cricket Club when Crewe Dixon was in full flight on that splendid pitch in the shadow of Bamburgh's magnificent pile and when our bowling was opened by Ramsay Horler, whose fiancée Ann, to whom he had just become engaged, came along to watch. After the opposition had scored a good many runs, Ramsay clean bowled one batsman and had a second caught in the slips next ball. Everyone clustered round the wicket in anticipation of a hat-trick. Ramsay sent down a quick, short ball which rose rapidly and struck the batsman in an unmentionable place; as he collapsed to the ground, his bat flicked backwards and knocked off a single bail and one of our fielders at silly mid-on appealed. This is the only hat-trick I can recall from the Victorians' history but it wasn't greatly appreciated by the Bamburgh players and relations were for a time a little strained.

Another regular player who joined us later, even though he had no medical or dental qualification, was Duncan Murchison, now Professor D. G. Murchison and Pro-Vice-Chancellor of Newcastle University. He qualified a little tenuously because his wife worked as a scientist in the RVI. Duncan played some remarkable innings but was often a little irascible. I remember well the day when he felt that he had been run out by myself in a match at Etal; on leaving the wicket he turned round every five or ten yards on his way back to the pavilion to glare, and when he eventually got there I am told that he threw his bat almost horizontally across the room so that it struck the rear wall with a resounding thump. When some time later I was dismissed and returned to the pavilion myself to say cheerfully 'There was never a run in it, Duncan', his riposte was unmentionable.

During the time I spent at Queen Square in 1954–5 and as we were living in Dulwich, I joined Dulwich Cricket Club which proved, as I had not known before, to be a famous club and something of a nursery for Surrey cricketers. It was also a place to which former Surrey county players of distinction often returned in middle-age. Among these was Jack Parker, the famous Surrey all-rounder who, because of the war, never achieved the number of performances for England which might reasonably have been anticipated in view of his record. He proved to be an incredibly kind and friendly man and an excellent coach; at least on one evening a week I practised in the nets in Dulwich and learned a great deal from him. In consequence I played a few games for the Dulwich first team, but it was then so strong that although I took a few catches and scored a few runs, I soon asked to be allowed to play for the lesser sides and much enjoyed a very fruitful season. One match between Dulwich 2nd XI and Oxshott in Surrey was the occasion of a pleasant reunion with John Allan May, formerly of the *Christian Science Monitor* with whom I had played in Boston.

In the late 1950s and early 1960s, the Victorians went from strength to strength and we began to use for some home matches, in addition to Heaton, that beautiful ground at Close House near Wylam, which we shared with the Wimpey team. Dr G. F. G. Woodman of Morpeth, an outstanding bat and wicket keeper who had had several county caps, became a regular Victorian, and Dr B. W. T. Ritchie, an excellent and aggressive bat, played whenever he could manage to escape from his prior commitment to the Borderers. I remember with great affection some wonderful matches, superb comradeship and poignant memories. Having served as secretary for many years, after I became a consultant, because of professional and other commitments my appearances inevitably became fewer and I had to hand over secretarial responsibility to others. Happily, the club later decided to make me President, following Mr Stanley Way, Professor F. H. Bentley and Mr L. H. Lake. On one occasion only, in the late

1960s in a season when I played only four matches, I scored 57 against County Club and achieved another substantial score against Bamburgh, finding myself at the annual dinner, to my astonishment, to be at the head of the club batting averages for the first and only time.

The Victorians is one of those clubs which often seem to be teetering on the brink of disintegration. Ultimately, after the halcyon days of the 1950s and 1960s, its programme was reduced to one of Sunday fixtures, but it continued to enjoy the use of fine facilities and had some loyal and capable cricketers; to the best of my knowledge, it is still in existence.

In the 1970s, by which time we had arranged an annual golf match between the neurologists at the RVI and those at the NGH, it was decided to have a similar annual cricket match for the 'Neurology Ashes', a cup having been generously presented for the occasion by a drug company. This pleased me as the first golf match had elicited a circular from Jack Foster inviting participants to play in the first game for the Walton Trophy. Having thus been driven to buy one fairly expensive silver cup, it was good to find that someone else was prepared to provide the second. The first match took place on the ground at St Nicholas Hospital in the mid-1970s and Jack Foster, who captained the NGH team, invited me to open. I did so against the steady right arm bowling of Peter Fawcett, then a registrar at the RVI (now consultant in clinical neurophysiology) and in my first over, playing forward, there was a perceptible click and the ball ended up in the safe gloves of David Bates behind the wicket. While I was tempted to expostulate that I thought the ball had touched my pad rather than my bat, I accept that perhaps I was wrong and so departed with an ignominious duck. However, we had fielded only ten men so that as the game continued and the wickets tumbled, our opponents kindly agreed that I should bat again as last man in. I did so, only to drive the third ball firmly into the hands of mid-off. This is the only time that I ever achieved the distinction of scoring two ducks in a single innings. This made me wonder whether it really was time for me to hang up my boots; but I realized that having begun for the first time to wear bifocals, these were no good for cricket as the ball went out of focus at just the wrong moment. Hence I bought some distance glasses with plastic lenses and in the next few seasons scored a fair number of runs, thus putting the ignominy of that occasion behind me.

On another notable occasion at Close House, the Faculty of Medicine challenged the Faculty of Arts and won a resounding victory. John Webb (then back in Newcastle as Professor of Paediatrics) and I enjoyed a useful stand for the second wicket, which brought back happy memories of Victorian days. There were many other useful performances from the medics, not least from Grimley Evans and from George Alberti who insisted on batting with verve and abandon but with a smouldering pipe firmly clenched between his teeth throughout.

As the years passed my appearances became increasingly intermittent and desultory, though I also played fairly regularly for the medical staff against the students in Newcastle when the annual fixture was intermittently revived. Indeed in my last year as Dean of the Medical School in 1981 I was invited to open the batting for the staff, whereupon their opening fast bowler, reviving memories of Tyson, took an immensely long run and came tearing up to the wicket with a view to delivering what seemed likely to be a very fast ball. Not having held a bat for over a year, I faced him with some apprehension, but as he reached the wicket he brought his arm over gently to deliver a slow half volley which I happily hit back over his head for four; the cricket then took on a more serious note. The fact that he had already consumed about four pints of Newcastle Brown Ale before the game began may have done something to impair his performance and I was able to score over 20 runs on what I then thought might well be my last game of cricket.

When I then left Newcastle in late 1983 for Green College, Oxford, having played my last game in the RVI v. NGH confrontation, I felt that my cricketing days were really over, but not so. My predecessor as Warden, Sir Richard Doll, himself a keen player in his younger days, had established the tradition of having an annual match between the college fellows and the students and it was made clear that I would be expected to play in summer 1984. I was fortunate not only to score some runs, including a few boundaries, but also to pick up a couple of sharp slip catches. As a result I was invited to play for a medical staff team (the Radcliffe Ectopics) against the medical students on a brilliantly sunny day on a hard, fast pitch owned by Brasenose down by the Thames. Having told the captain, Derek Hockaday, that it would perhaps be appropriate for me to bat at about number 6, I was horrified when the first four wickets tumbled against the accurate fast bowling of the students for 25 runs. Hence I found myself going in to bat with the opening bowlers still in full flight. But as I leant forward on the first ball I received and watched it go smoothly past the bowler for two runs, my confidence returned, the runs began to flow rather better and in the end our score was respectable.

Clearly news of this particular game got about on the Oxford grapevine as in no time at all I was asked by Hugh Sinclair to play in his renowned annual match for the Oxford doctors against the lawyers and was soon asked also to turn out for Oxford against the Cambridge Medics. After much thought, I declined both invitations, being anxious not to become involved in what seemed pretty serious cricket at a time when I was in my sixties and knew that my ability to play fast bowling was rapidly declining.

Although I continued to play annually against the Green College students until my last year as Warden (1989), always with enjoyment,

I finally decided that at 67 the time had come to retire gracefully from the cricketing scene. While the fellows' side at Green College, with such stalwarts as Jeff Burley, Wattie Fletcher, Jeff Aronson, Keith Hawton, Ken Fleming and others, invariably performed well and only lost against the students once during my term of office, the fact that I dropped three slip catches in 1989 before successfully picking up the sharpest chance of all, strengthened my resolve. But I was cheered by scoring 11 not out before retiring so as to attend a concert in Burford where our daughter Judy was singing. At least now, as a member of MCC (after waiting many years, I was finally elected in 1984) I can at times indulge in the joys of spectatorship; the recent improved performances of the England team have revived my interest, which flagged a little a few years ago.

Despite my almost obsessive love of cricket, I also enjoyed some other sports. Betty was a competent tennis player and played for the school; after playing with her several times I eventually achieved a fair level of competence and also played for the school, though tennis was never taken very seriously by the Spennymoor boys. Later she and I often played together, and after enduring the ordeal of having our game assessed by committee members spent a few happy years as members of Gosforth Tennis Club, close to our home in Beechfield Road. Later we much enjoyed playing on the all-weather courts at Green College. I also took up squash in my forties and for a few years the members of the Department of Neurology got together to play weekly at the University Squash Club in Northumberland Road on winter Wednesday evenings after work. Enthusiasm for that game later waned after I learned of several colleagues who had torn Achilles tendons on the squash court. When my son Christopher, aged 15, began to beat me regularly, I decided that that was the time to give up, though I did play occasionally until the late 1970s at the Gosforth Squash Club where Dr Roland Freedman, our GP, was a formidable opponent. But that club, where I retained my membership until we left Newcastle, had excellent gastronomic as well as sporting facilities.

In my youth, again with my father's inspiration, I was also in danger of becoming addicted to snooker and billiards. Often we went together in the evenings to the Church Institute. As I mentioned in Chapter 1, my father was a most able performer. Billiards was then much more popular than it is today. I played regularly in the annual billiards knock-out competitions while still at school and was eventually good enough to be given a handicap of +15, though my father was playing off −10. This meant that he had to score 10 points before he began to contribute points towards the ultimate target of 200 whereas I was given 15 points start. My father won the cup several times but I never progressed further than the semi-finals. After leaving Spennymoor I played occasionally at medical school but never regularly. Nevertheless, these skills were not totally lost and I played from time to time in the Territorial Army and even later at Green College. In each of my years of Wardenship the fellows defeated the students in the indoor sports competition (snooker, darts, table tennis and bar football). Table tennis was another game at which both Betty and I became reasonably good and for several years we had a table in our studio room on the top floor in Gosforth.

With my upbringing and education, I never took part in field sports and was far too impatient ever to enjoy fishing. Apart from riding pit ponies bareback as a child in Hobson Colliery I was not interested in riding, though I occasionally rode on trips overseas, as during a meeting on muscular dystrophy research in Arizona. Range shooting with both rifle and pistol was something I much enjoyed during my service in the Senior Training Corps and later in the Territorial Army, and for a time I was quite successful at small bore shooting on indoor ranges. However shooting for game has never appealed and I must also confess that horse racing, both on the flat and over the sticks, leaves me cold. One visit only to the Northumberland Plate at Gosforth Park convinced me that this was a sport which I could never find inspiring. Motor racing, too, is something that I have enjoyed occasionally without catching the 'bug', and in the TA I became quite interested in map reading exercises and rallying, but never sufficiently to wish to take up the sport seriously.

As a family we took up skiing when Betty and I were both in our forties and went in two successive years to Norway, but soon found that despite our preliminary training on an artificial ski slope in Newcastle we were both too nervous and I especially was too clumsy ever to become proficient, though the exhilaration and vigorous exercise of cross-country skiing was something which we both enjoyed. The family regularly recall the occasion when we were trying to practise downhill skiing on thin frozen crust on top of powdery snow; my skis went through the crust and as I attempted to get up I dug a deeper and deeper hole from which, with pipe in mouth, I eventually extricated myself with the utmost difficulty. Unfortunately that particular scene is faithfully recorded on cine film, even though a little less than clearly as the camera which Betty was holding shook continuously because of her laughter. After those two Norwegian adventures, apart from a very occasional foray at ski de fond in Switzerland when we visited our daughter Ann and her family in the winter, we decided that skiing was not for us, though the children continued in the sport and all became pretty competent.

My thirst for sport in general would alone have justified the purchase of our first television set in 1953. Whenever time allows, I watch avidly much of the sport on television (with the exception of horse and motor racing) and when, for instance, athletics, cricket or golf are shown, I am glued to the set. And Betty is virtually incapable of indulging any other interest than watching tennis during Wimbledon fortnight and feels herself deprived if taken away from the television for any reason. Fortunately we have had the privilege since moving to Oxford of going to Wimbledon three times, on one occasion in the Royal Box, through the good offices of our friends the Bachmanns (Larry Bachmann, a visiting fellow of Green College, is a member of the All England Club and a former film producer for MGM in Hollywood; despite the fact that he is no longer in the first flush of youth, he continues to be an excellent tennis player).

However, in recent years the game which has occupied my sporting interest to the exclusion of most others has been golf, despite the frustration it has engendered as I have struggled, usually without success, to achieve reasonable competence. I first tried my hand at the game in my early teens at Spennymoor Golf Club, a small nine-hole course attractively situated near Kirk Merrington, with six holes on one side of the road and three on the other. Sadly neither the course nor the cheerful wooden clubhouse survived after the war. In the 1930s it was a flourishing little club where, with the aid of my father's hickory-shafted clubs, I took a few lessons from the professional, Sid Hyde, who divided his attentions between Spennymoor and Bishop Auckland. Soon, with a few friends, I was hacking my way around, becoming familiar with the driver, brassy, spoon, mashie, mashie-niblick and niblick and, of course, the putter. Golf balls could easily be acquired at low cost from the small boys who swarmed across the course and railway line along which several holes ran. Often balls disappeared from the fairway when the owner was unsighted and were subsequently offered for sale by cheerful urchins. While I never acquired a handicap in those days, I was fascinated by the game, though it had to take second place to cricket. Nevertheless a few of us as students and housemen did play an occasional game at Ponteland; but I did not take it up at all seriously until I was in my forties when my cricketing skills began to decline and as the time available for sport became much less. The fact that we had by then acquired our Detchant cottage, close to Bamburgh Castle Golf Club, heightened my resolve to tackle the game again. Whereas Betty and I had played a little together on the much less demanding course at Seahouses (then nine holes) during some of our Beadnell holidays, our decision to join Bamburgh was prompted when, in the early 1960s the Cruddas family who owned the land upon which the course was situated withdrew their longstanding embargo on Sunday golf.

In the 1960s I also applied to join the Northumberland Golf Club at Gosforth Park where there was a substantial waiting list. My former CO in the Territorial Army, J. V. (John) Todd, Durham County golf champion in five successive years before the war and still an outstanding performer (later he became President of the English Golf Union), kindly nominated me and Jack Foster seconded the nomination. I thought it would take a few years to reach the top of the list but was pleasant surprised to find that about 12 months later I was offered membership though the entry fee and subscription were a little alarming. I then paid £25.00 a year for membership at Bamburgh and Betty £20.00, whereas at Gosforth Park the entrance fee was £150.00 and the first year's subscription, including Betty, was also £150.00. Ladies were not then able to be members of the club and, so far as I know, the situation has not changed; they were nominees of their husbands or of another male family member and their playing hours were greatly restricted. There was also a rule whereby ladies could not enter the clubhouse by the front entrance, which led directly into the men's bar, but had to go round to the rear to the ladies' entrance; it was also a rule that they must not cross the front verandah of the club but had to use the path between the clubhouse and the eighteenth green. Elderly male members justified this rule by claiming that if ladies walked along the verandah, those men sitting out in the sun to watch the golf would regularly have to stand up and sit down again. This rule eventually disappeared during Jack Foster's captaincy when he ceremonially accompanied his wife Jennifer across the verandah; even before then other citadels had begun to crumble in that after club dinners ladies were allowed not only into the mixed lounge bar but also into the men's bar. The club was then also rather stuffy and traditional in other ways. I nominated my friend Austin Laws for membership, seconded by Dr George Anderson, and only subsequently learned that he was not elected solely on the grounds (I was then told) that although he was a well-known pharmacist who had been chairman of the Northern Division of the Pharmaceutical Society, the committee turned him down because he served behind his own counter!

As my clinical work expanded and my practice grew, there was still relatively little time for golf though I did have some enjoyable games, usually with medical colleagues, and regularly played in the annual staff v. students golf competition. My performances in the early days were abysmal but gradually improved, so that occasionally I participated in some notable victories. Indeed on one occasion, having been invited by the late Mr Hedley Whyte to play in the annual doctors v. lawyers golf match at the Alnmouth Golf Club at Foxton (an all-day event with four-balls in the morning and singles in the afternoon) I managed, with Ian Rannie (the Professor of Dental Pathology) to win our morning four-ball and then, to my astonishment, found that I was the only medical winner in the afternoon singles. It is my erratic performances which have made the game at once so pleasurable and so infuriating. I have never been able to reduce my handicap below 17, if only because there are very few medal rounds in which my card has not been marred by one or two disastrous holes. By contrast, I much enjoy Stableford competitions and match-play, as I have often surprised myself by having four or five successive pars and even a few birdies before yet again destroying a card by lashing a couple of consecutive drives out of bounds. As in cricket, my inability to keep calm and to concentrate over long periods has invariably impaired my performance. My good friend Dr Jack Phillips, the former captain and secretary of Bamburgh Castle Golf Club, never hesitates to remind me (and even, on public occasions, others) of the time when I took 11 on the first hole at Bamburgh (182 yards, par 3) after hitting four consecutive drives with a three iron out over cover point on to the beach. I have never been able to play a single bad shot and then to relax and concentrate in order to repair the damage; one bad shot is almost invariably followed by another and another, and it takes two or three holes to settle down again. Nevertheless I have many happy and abiding memories of the game, as of the notable occasion when, during TA camp at Mytchett, near Aldershot, I played around the nine-hole officers' course with John Todd and beat him 3 and 2 off level. The fact that he was spraying balls in all directions, including at least two which went over the fence into the heavily-protected grounds of RAF Farnborough (where stress tests on many secret aircraft developments were carried out, including those on the ill-fated Comet airliner) may not have been totally unrelated to the fact that he had had five double gins before we began. And in later years the annual golf matches for the Walton Trophy between the RVI and NGH neurologists at that superb championship course at Brancepeth Castle, a few miles from Durham, were also memorable. A gloriously indiscreet after-dinner speech made by Bernard (later Sir Bernard) Tomlinson stands out in the memory, as does the occasion when the Rabelaisian behaviour of two of our non-playing members (one of whom later became a distinguished professor of neurology in the United States) resulted in us being ordered by the irate secretary to clear the dining room; and our invitation to return to Brancepeth in the following year was also withdrawn. Fortunately this transient misunderstanding was soon resolved and the matches are still played there regularly.

I had always fondly imagined that if I played the game more often my competence would improve and my handicap would inevitably come down. In the 1970s, when I played regularly at Bamburgh, I often came near to winning but yet again my temperament intervened. Once when playing with Jack Phillips in the Challenge Cup I stood on the seventeenth tee and Jack said 'Keep it up, John. Two fours and the pot's yours!'. I knew that I had been playing unusually well but when I suddenly realized that playing, as I then was, off a handicap of 22, I needed only two fours for a net 62, up came my head, two consecutive drives soared out of bounds into the cornfield on the right and I did exactly the same on the eighteenth hole, ending up with a pair of eights. Nevertheless, to my surprise, I did win Captain's Day during the year that dear old Harry Birkett, the retired schoolmaster from Bamburgh, was captain (1977) with a gross 84 (net 62). Two strokes were then taken off my handicap, yet another two came off in the following year, and then another, so that at last, playing off 17, I felt that I had a respectable handicap for the first time.

In August 1978 on a warm sunny day (inland at Detchant) I went down to the club to seek a game, only to find that the sea fret (the 'haar') was rolling in so that visibility was very poor. Nevertheless, the course was just playable and the three men (Gerald Baker, Harold Gilbert and Derek Grant) on the first tee invited me to join them. We tossed for partners and I took the first drive, which for once I struck cleanly with a three iron; the ball soared in the general direction of the green, though because of the mist we did not see it finish. My partners insisted it would be on the green but I thought it would be over the back, which is where I went to look when we got there, only to be summoned back by Gerald who showed me the ball nestling in the hole! And so, as I have often said since, I achieved a lifelong ambition, further enhanced in 1986 when, playing at Frilford Heath near Oxford (where I became a member on moving to Green College) I had another hole-in-one at the short eleventh on the Red Course, playing with John Webb (who by then had retired to Lechlade). Strictly, as we were playing winter rules on temporary greens, this second effort barely counted, but as we both saw the ball roll into the hole, I still regard it as my second hole-in-one.

As Betty and I began to play much more at Bamburgh (where in 1966 she won the Runciman Cup off a handicap of 36, to find that her handicap in consequence came sharply down) we began as the children grew older to involve ourselves more and more in the social activities of the club. We even came in fourth in the annual mixed foursomes. The following year, when she set out to defend the cup, 13th August 1967 was exceptional. The rain was torrential, the temperature plummeted and there was a howling gale on the very day when the club had erected a marquee in the car park to hold its annual barbecue. Despite her waterproofs Betty almost froze and was quickly drenched to the skin, so that when she eventually returned to Ivy Cottage like a drowned rat, an immediate hot bath and a large whisky dispensed by 11-year-old Christopher in front of a blazing fire were the order of the day. Not surprisingly her enthusiasm for golf in bad weather conditions rapidly declined from that day onwards. I too played with Jack Phillips later and only just succeeded in getting back to Ivy Cottage as the roads were flooding and that from Detchant to the A1 was almost a river with water several inches deep. Nevertheless, we braved the elements and went back that evening to the barbecue in our Austin Princess; as the monsoon continued unabated, the floods became even worse and many friends were marooned. Dr W. Lyle Brown and his wife, attempting to return to Fenton, had to abandon their car at Crag Mill level crossing where it stalled in 18 inches of water. We too were compelled to leave our car at

Detchant lodge and to walk back the half mile to our cottage through water
6–12 inches deep and in the continuing rain, so that we were both soaked
for the second time that day. Never since have we experienced comparable
weather and flooding in north Northumberland.

In the early 1970s I was invited to join the Bamburgh committee, I
imagine because of my administrative experience and certainly not
because of golfing prowess. Soon I found myself Chairman of the House
Committee and we raised sufficient funds to see through many much-
needed improvements and extensions to the clubhouse. And in 1978 I
was delighted to be asked to become the Captain for the succeeding year.
Fortunately the Captain's duties in Bamburgh are relatively seasonal and
based almost wholly on weekend activities so that I did not feel that this
responsibility would be incompatible with my professional work. Two
weeks after my hole-in-one at the first, I drove in in front of the customary
large audience and, after composing myself suitably, fortunately produced
a respectable drive just to the left of the green. I was especially delighted
to be Captain in the year when the club celebrated the 75th anniversary
of its foundation in 1904. This was an exciting year, not least because of
the many social events which we were able to introduce, but also because
of the friendly matches which we played against other Northumberland
sides. I especially enjoyed that against the Northumberland Golf Club
at Gosforth Park where the Vice-Captain and I resoundingly defeated
Jimmy Hilton, the Captain of the Park, and his colleague (for once my
putting was magical). On 3rd January 1979 the Berwick Advertiser had
a large headline on its front page which read 'Her Majesty's New Year's
Honours List'. The opening story ran as follows:

'A Tweedmouth skipper has been awarded the O.B.E. in the New
Year's Honours List for his services to the fishing industry, while the
captain of Bamburgh Golf Club has been knighted.'

That cutting is one of my treasured possessions.

Later the committee generously invited me to become Chairman,
succeeding Douglas Souter, and I held that appointment for two enjoyable
but demanding years between 1981 and 1983 when I left Newcastle for
Oxford. Finally, in 1989, after the death of Lord Armstrong whose family
had been closely associated with the club for very many years (he had
been President for as long as I could remember) and following the
resignation of Mr Stanley Armstrong, who was President for just a year
but then felt that because of his age and inability to travel he must
relinquish the appointment, I was elected President, an appointment
which I am still honoured to hold.

Though the game has given me tremendous pleasure and even
sometimes genuine relaxation, when the sheer fury of the sliced drive,

the shanked iron shot or the missed two-foot putt has not intruded too severely, my first reaction on being approached by the editors of the Newcastle Medical Students' Gazette in 1979 to write an article on 'Exotic Golf Courses I have Known' was to say that I felt unable to do justice to the topic since I knew so few exotic courses. But when I began to think of some of those where I had played over the years during professional visits to many different countries in each continent, I thought that perhaps after all there might be something interesting to say.

Golf in the United States can be an extraordinary experience depending upon where one plays and at what time. Staying in Englewood Cliffs, New Jersey, while lecturing in New York a few years ago with Dr Callum Stark, late of Newcastle, we decided to play early one Sunday morning on the local course. The only way of doing so was to get up at 5.30 a.m. to drive to the club in order to pay a green fee and book a starting time; this proved to be at 9.10 a.m. We therefore spent the next three hours having breakfast and reading the huge Sunday paper until our turn came. Our starting number was hung on a board and the rules required that we two must play with those whose numbers came next on the board. We had a delightful round with a New York surgeon and the Vice-Chancellor of Mount Sinai University, even though, typically, the round took some five and a half hours.

One of the most irritating aspects of American golf is the total obsession of one's American colleagues over the completion of every hole, holing out every putt even when the hole has been irrevocably lost. I recall particularly the occasion we played nine holes on a delightful course in Carefree, Arizona, where I was attending a conference at the Carefree Inn, and where two American organizers of the conference invited Betty and me to join them. The course was closed for two hours every morning and every evening at about sundown to allow it to be watered, as otherwise the grass would have disappeared in the heat of the Arizona desert. We played just after dawn, first in order to have a game before the meeting began, and secondly because at midday the temperature rose to well over 100° Fahrenheit so that golf would have been uncomfortable. Perhaps the fact that we beat our American friends by four and three over nine holes added something to the pleasure. 'How many is that, George?'. 'I'm 10, how about you?'. 'I've taken 11!'.

A few years later, when teaching at the Bowman Gray School of Medicine in Winston-Salem, North Carolina, I played with a neurological colleague, Jim Toole against the Dean and Associate Dean on the magnificent championship course of Tanglewood. This was where a distinguished graduate of Wake Forest University, Arnold Palmer, learned his golf. Perhaps my most striking memory of that course, in the rolling North Carolina countryside, was of the tree-lined fairways and of the huge bunkers filled with silver sand, one of which was said to cover almost a quarter of an acre. Curiously, American bunkers are often much more shallow than most of those we see in the UK, and therefore represent nothing like the hazard posed, for example, by those devised by the Royal Society of Edinburgh Golfers at Muirfield.

I also recall with pleasure rounds at the Duke University course in Durham, North Carolina, in Lansing, Michigan, in Toronto, in Hamilton, Ontario, and at the Rolling Hills Country Club in Los Angeles with Joe Van der Meulen, but perhaps a game even fresher in my memory was one in June 1980 at the Key Biscayne Club in Florida, close to the Sonesta Beach Hotel where a one-week conference on neuromuscular disease was being held. This is a combined inland and seaside course where one is often required to drive over lakes, pools or streams on to plateau greens or narrow fairways. Playing with an Australian against two American colleagues, including Paul Larson, the Dean of the Louisiana School of Medicine from New Orleans (who once spent two years in neurology at the NGH and who is still a Newcastle United supporter), we chalked up a substantial victory for the Commonwealth not unrelated, I am sure, to the fact that my Australian colleague had a handicap of three. Perhaps one of the most notable memories of the round was that the exchange rate of the pound against the dollar was then so favourable that the green fee, plus hire of a bag of clubs, the purchase of six golf balls and the hire of an electric cart shared between two cost each of us £12.50: a remarkable bargain by anyone's standards!

Perhaps even more memorable was a round I enjoyed with three neurological colleagues when visiting Buenos Aires in Argentina. They invited me to play at the BA Jockey Club, a club established by British capital when Argentina had a large and thriving British community. This was one of the most luxurious and huge clubhouses I have ever seen. I played, of course, with borrowed clubs; as we drove up to the main gateway of ornamental wrought iron, a uniformed attendant met the car, opened the boot and removed the clubs; we then drove in and changed in the superbly appointed accommodation. When we walked out to the first tee four small boys were waiting as caddies with the four sets of clubs. Though none of them spoke English, communication was not too difficult (I signified my choice of club by holding up the appropriate number of fingers) and was much more satisfactory than when I played with Betty during a short holiday in Tenerife in the Canary Islands a year or two later, where again we had two small boys as caddies. This was a particularly disastrous round on a rather hot day and I could see that my caddy was unimpressed, to such an extent that after four or five holes he took out one of the clubs from the bag he was carrying on my behalf and started to hit a ball of his own in order to show me how to do it.

There must indeed be something about the Spanish influence which has a malevolent effect upon my game, since in Barcelona in 1973, during the World Congress of Neurology, I had a thoroughly disastrous round (including three successive balls in a lake) at the Royal Barcelona Golf Club and retreated in shame after a resounding defeat by a local professor of neurology. Fortunately, we entertained him in Newcastle some time later and retrieved a little lost respect in a round at Gosforth Park. After the round in Barcelona he presented me with a tie of the Royal Barcelona Golf Club, which I still wear, but which was hardly justified by my performance. Perhaps it was the heat as I played equally badly a few years later in Bali in Indonesia.

I think there is something very special about golf in the Caribbean, just as there is about golf in Australia. In 1969 after lecturing in New York, Durham, Miami and New Orleans and afer a delightful final dinner at Antoine's on the Sunday evening, knowing that I had to be in London for a meeting of the Medical Research Council on the following Thursday, Betty and I drew a line on the map from New Orleans to London and noted that this passed almost exactly over the Bahamas. This seemed to be too good an opportunity to miss and so we managed three days of relaxation in Nassau on the way home. There is nothing particularly beautiful about the Nassau Golf Club, though it is pleasantly situated close to the sea on the one hand, with palms, lakes and well architectured holes on the other. But the most striking feature of golf in that environment, particularly in September, is the tendency for clouds to appear from nowhere and to disgorge torrential tropical downpours lasting for only 15 minutes or so, two or three times in a round. This took little away from the enjoyment of the game because if one is lightly clad when temperatures are in the high 80s and low 90s, clothes quickly dry and the damp greens begin to hold the pitches a little better. But within a very short while in the blazing sun they dry out and the ball runs like lightning once again.

Far more attractive, but equally vulnerable to the vagaries of the weather are the many beautiful courses on the superb, friendly and relaxing island of Bermuda, where again we managed to have a few days on the way back from a conference in Montreal in 1978. But if you ever go to play at the Royal Mid-Ocean Golf Club, at Port Royal or at any of the others, take a pocketful of golf balls, since there are so many beautifully situated holes, both long and short, where one drives over tongues of the ocean and where, lost in admiration at the view, the tendency is to lift the head and to top the ball which disappears for ever beneath the waves.

Perhaps my most lasting memories of Australia where in 1971 we played on the Royal Adelaide and Royal Perth courses, are first of the eternal flies which swarm in myriads and which require the essential equipment of a fly-spray to cover oneself from head to foot every few holes. And there is the never ceasing background cacophony of parakeets and particularly of the kookaburras, which in Adelaide in particular seemed to feel that it was appropriate to laugh every time I played a bad shot. In 1981 we had the pleasure of returning to Australia and look back with great pleasure upon playing on the attractive little Tambo Valley nine-hole course near Omeo in Northern Victoria. This beautiful little course carved out of pine forest lies deep within hilly country alongside the Tambo River. Playing late one evening as dusk was falling, an emu walked across the fairway on one of the holes, and on the next fairway three kangaroos sat and watched dispassionately from the sidelines as we moved by. After Betty and I subsequently enjoyed the memorable experience of travelling across Australia by the Trans-Australian Railway from Melbourne to Perth (largely because there was a radar strike on the internal airlines) golf at Lake Karrinyup was very different; this championship course with a magnificent clubhouse almost approaching the standard of that in Buenos Aires was memorable not least for the fact that we completed 18 holes in a temperature in the mid-nineties, but only with frequent pauses for liquid refreshment. Our Australian hosts, the McKellars (with splendid Scottish accents despite having lived in Perth for 30 years) were kind enough to allow us to halve the match on the 18th green, which made the event particularly memorable and lessened our chagrin a little at not having been able to clear two (or was it three?) lakes between us during the day.

What a contrast it was to play on the bare burned course on Rottnest Island off the coast of Perth, where the greens (so-called) consist of oiled sand which has to be scraped flat every time before one putts out. But we didn't really go to Rottnest just to play golf, since the island itself with its salt lakes, its hills and magnificent beaches and lagoons, its ospreys and its quokkas (a small marsupial found nowhere else in the world) carried so much fascination that the golf was virtually an irrelevance.

Why have I concentrated so much upon exotic golf courses overseas? There are so many delights for the golfer in the UK. Scotland is superb; even if one leaves aside the holy of holies at St Andrews, as well as Muirfield, Carnoustie and Troon, the sheer magnificence and scenic beauty of Gleneagles, the calmer but testing delights of Rosemount, Taymouth Castle, Boat of Garten and Southerness are fascinating. So too is the tiny little course created almost on a postage stamp at Gairloch, where on the first tee it is wise to aim well to the right; otherwise there is a chance that a well-hit drive may strike the large tree situated just to the left of centre and may end up, as my ball did, some 50 yards behind the tee. The hazards of that course, where the fairways of several holes cross one another add a little to the zest, particularly if one is playing in the constant light rain (a 'Scottish mist') which is all too often a feature of the north-west of our island. And in my beloved North-East the challenges of Brancepeth, Gosforth Park and Foxton, for example, are difficult to beat.

Even since I wrote that article, my golfing experiences at home and abroad have increased. Having discarded my father's hickory-shafted clubs (which we later had cut down for Christopher), I bought a set of Nicoll irons and woods very cheaply from Weldon Watts, a member of the Park who had been a single handicap golfer in his early days but who had been compelled to give up the game. Later I replaced these with a second-hand set of Dai Rees woods and John Letters irons, which gave excellent service for many years. However, when I was BMA President from 1980–82 and when Betty and I went to the BMA Clinical Meeting in San Diego in California in the autumn of 1981, the exchange rate of the pound against the dollar was still favourable. Right next door to the Town and Country Hotel where the meetings took place and where we stayed, was the Stardust Golf and Country Club where Betty and I played two enjoyable rounds (I also played at Torrey Pines); we found that in the pro shop run by the genial Cliff Crandall clubs were being sold on a special offer; I bought a complete set of Cobra woods and irons for the remarkable sum of £150 (or rather its equivalent in dollars) and these are still in excellent condition. Living, however, the divided life that we now enjoy in retirement so that I spend part of my time in Detchant and part in Oxford, I now need a set of clubs in each location. I bought at a very good price from Stan Long at Gosforth Park an excellent set of irons made by John Letters but carrying a Swedish name, which had been ordered by a Swede who had never called to collect them. To these, for use at Bamburgh, I have now added three metal 'woods' which certainly give greater distance.

Recently I have been able to play on many other courses overseas, not least that at Stresa in northern Italy with its outstanding scenic views, and with our daughter Ann, her husband Ian, and their two children on courses at Evian on Lake Geneva, at Divonne and most recently at Bonmont, the country club of which they (the McNeil family) have now been members for some years. After being sent to Switzerland by Chase Manhattan Bank for an initial three-month period in 1976, Ian eventually found himself permanently established there and the McNeil family have lived in Geneva and its surroundings (now in the village of Founex in Vaud) for 16 years. Bonmont is a relatively new course in the grounds of an abbaye, with a superbly appointed elevated clubhouse from which, when the weather allows, one has magnificent views across the lake to Mont Blanc. It is a long and challenging course with many water and other hazards; remarkably we have been able to play golf on three consecutive Christmas and Boxing Days when it might reasonably have been expected that Switzerland would have been snowbound. Our daughters, Ann and Judy, showed no interest in golf as children or teenagers, but when Ann became engaged to Ian, he had decided to give up his rugby interests and to turn to golf, to which he became totally dedicated; eventually he managed to get his handicap down to 7. Inevitably, Ann decided that she must play the game and succeeded in reducing her handicap to 12; for three years she was captain of the ladies' club at Bonmont. Not unexpectedly, the enthusiasm for golf was passed on by Ann and Ian to their children; Drew, now 19 and a student at Durham University, has a handicap of 5 and plays for the University, while Victoria, now also a student at Durham, is equally enthusiastic and has reduced her handicap to 15.

With my retirement from the Wardenship of Green College at the end of September 1989, I had fondly hoped that my forays to Frilford Heath for an occasional game of golf would become more frequent, but as yet that hope has not been fulfilled, though I still manage to play fairly frequently at Bamburgh. Each year I play at the Royal East Berks against Ewan Page, Vice-Chancellor of Reading and former Pro-Vice-Chancellor in Newcastle, with a return match at Frilford. And at least two or three times a year I challenge my old medical school friend Col. Rex Belas (late RAMC) either at the Catterick Garrison club near his home or at Bamburgh. The stake of £1.00 enhances the pleasure—honours at present are fairly even. In one unforgettable round at Frilford I played with Sir Raymond Hoffenberg (formerly President of the Royal College of Physicians and now President of Wolfson College, Oxford) who once played for South African Universities with a handicap of 3, with John Webb, my occasional golfing partner and former Victorians cricketer, and with Sir Roger Bannister, the Master of Pembroke and first four-minute miler. He would be the first to accept that his prowess on the golf course does not approach his former athletic distinction and sadly on that day he so wrenched his lower back as to be incapable of venturing out on to the course again for many months. In our occasional four balls we invited George Adams, former Professor of Geriatric Medicine (and a single figure handicap man) to join us. When discussing the serious matter of money, I mentioned casually that when I played Jack Phillips at Bamburgh we usually played for 50p on the first nine, 50p on the second and 50p on the match. The name rang a bell and I soon discovered that George and Jack had been together at a Naval Hospital in Alexandria during the war and hadn't met since. So a delightful reunion (with golf, of course) was arranged in Oxford. But I haven't quite forgiven George, in writing a year or two later to Jack sending his apologies for not being able to attend Jack and Joan's golden wedding celebrations in Bamburgh in 1990, for saying that in one match in which I played with him against Sir Raymond and John, my golf was 'a mixture of Arnold Palmer and Houdini'.

Unfortunately in summer 1990, having for the first time fulfilled my lifelong ambition of being a spectator at the Open Golf Championship (at the old course at St Andrews and won by Nick Faldo) I developed, through over-vigorous and over-prolonged walking, a plantar fasciitis and calcaneal spur which restricted my golfing activities so that in that year I was unable to play in any competitions at Bamburgh and had to hire a motorized buggy to get me round the course. Fortunately, as I write, the condition has recovered and I intend to play more in the future. Who knows, perhaps I might even succeed in again reducing my handicap, which has steadily risen to 20 over the course of the last few years. An interesting sideline of our visit to St Andrews was that we were able, through the good offices of our friend Harry Carpenter (whom we came to know well through his help in the work of the Muscular Dystrophy Group of Great Britain and Northern Ireland) to visit the BBC complex where we watched and listened to the work of the commentators, including the redoubtable Peter Alliss.

Despite all of the disappointments and frustrations with which the game of golf can be associated (particularly when one is an indifferent and temperamental performer), it has given me enormous pleasure. Golfing around the world helps one to see wonderful country, to meet fascinating people and, incidentally, to learn a degree of patience and perseverance in trying to cope with the many different and unexpected hazards which beset one's game. But to be strictly honest and not, I hope, too parochial, when I write not just about challenging golf courses but of pure scenic and natural beauty, I believe that there is nothing in the world to compare with the succession of views that one experiences from the course of Bamburgh Castle Golf Club, culminating with that superb vista from the 15th tee, from the Cheviots in the west, across to Berwick and Budle Bay in the north and down over Bamburgh, Seahouses, Beadnell, Coquet Island and Dunstanburgh in the south. True, a former captain Eddie McDougle said 'It isn't windy at Bamburgh when the ball stays on the peg on the 15th tee'. Nevertheless, from that heavenly location, as Wordsworth said on Westminster Bridge, I cannot help but conclude whenever I play that 'Earth hath not anything to show more fair'.

CHAPTER 11

Consultant Neurologist

No experience can quite compare with that of beginning work as a consultant in the British National Health Service (NHS). At last, after years of training, of recurring anxiety about future prospects coupled with a pervasive sense of insecurity, realization dawns that one has finally achieved an appointment secure to retirement age. The first decision I had to make was whether to accept the post on a whole-time basis, then being paid a salary but being unable to do private practice. If general practitioners called me out on domiciliary visits I could be required to undertake these but would not be paid for them save for a refund of travelling expenses. The whole-time contract also precluded any payment being made for travel between home and hospital, though it would be possible to claim expenses for journeys between individual hospitals. That was just as well as my contract required me to undertake out-patient and in-patient work at the Newcastle General Hospital (NGH), a closed out-patient clinic (for consultant reference only) at the Royal Victoria Infirmary (RVI), and similar closed clinics fortnightly at the North Ormesby Hospital, Middlesbrough (45 miles away) and at Dryburn Hospital, Durham (about 18 miles from Newcastle). If, however, I chose a maximum part-time contract, I would be paid nine-elevenths of the full-time consultant salary but could also spend two half days a week in private practice, while devoting nine half days to NHS work. I would also be paid a fee for each domiciliary consultation and could claim travelling expenses between home and my principal hospital.

After consulting Henry Miller, whose private practice was becoming legendary, and being conscious of the financial constraints under which we had lived for so long, I opted unhesitatingly for a maximum part-time contract while recognizing that this would inevitably erode time available for research into neuromuscular disease. In retrospect, I am sure my decision was right. Although my research output was inevitably curtailed, the clinical experience I gained in ten years of part-time private practice was very rewarding professionally. Such practice offered adequate time to assess all aspects of the clinical problems which came my way from all echelons of society (in the North East one was just as likely then to be invited to see in private consultation a miner on the one hand or a member of the aristocracy on the other). And the resulting income meant that almost for the first time since graduation we were able to afford a few of the luxuries of life which we had denied ourselves for many years—new clothes for ourselves and the children, gramophone records, books, items of antique furniture, and even a few works of art were slowly acquired. We also began to attend concerts, to go to the theatre and occasionally, when time allowed, to eat out with greater freedom than we had ever done in the past.

Of course private practice did not come quickly or easily. All newly appointed consultants entering such practice went to the local BMA office and had cards printed for circulation to local general practitioners. The accepted convention was that one could say once only that Dr X was now available for consultation, giving an address and telephone number but no other information. It was not thought ethical to mention a specialty. Whereas before the war many Newcastle consultants had consulting rooms in private nursing homes, such as the Windsor in the grey Georgian grandeur of Windsor Terrace or in the gaunt Victorian four-storey houses of Sydenham Terrace (soon to be demolished to make way for road improvements) which then overlooked what was euphemistically called the Great North Road leading from the Haymarket to Gosforth. In the 1950s fashions changed and most consultants began to see private patients in their own homes, largely because of tax advantages (conducting a business from one's house allowed one to claim relief on a proportion of the standing charges on the residence, such as heat, light and telephone and the like, and one could also employ one's spouse as a secretary/receptionist).

While the situation of 5 Dilston Terrace was not ideal, in that patients had to park some distance away before walking along the path between the terrace and the railway to reach our front door, we converted the dining room into a combined study/consulting room. My desk was bought at an auction room in Crawcrook for £4 10s. (I still use it) and an examination couch was appropriately curtained off in a corner. On consulting afternoons (which later extended into the evenings) the drawing room became the waiting room. Invariably Betty was faced with the problem of keeping the children quiet in either the living room or kitchen during consulting hours. In the first year or two she was also my receptionist and was thus able to hone her observational skills. A common problem in private neurological practice was depressive illness as it was thought by many to be more respectable to see a neurologist than a psychiatrist; often she came into the consulting room after a patient had left to say that the one she had just shown into the waiting room seemed to be 'another depressive'.

Bearing in mind Henry Miller's popularity in the local community and his consulting expertise, practice grew slowly, though it soon emerged that his rather cavalier and slapdash approach, his joviality and mordant wit, which often surfaced even in a clinical setting, went down well with many patients but offended others. After a while I told him, not wholly in jest, that I could make a satisfactory living out of patients who had refused ever to go back to see him again! I also found that Henry then charged three guineas for a 45-minute consultation, so I decided to charge four; when he learned this, he immediately put up his fee to five guineas. We then cried truce and continued with that differential for some time until inflation compelled us each to increase our fees steadily in later years. And when Jack Foster entered the lists, a similar leap-frogging was repeated.

Although we spent eight happy years in Dilston Terrace and found the house comfortable and convenient, and well within our financial means, it soon became clear that we must eventually move. Living in a rather isolated detached Victorian house in a terrace which was somewhat in decline had disadvantages, not least because of lack of vehicular access to the front door and also because of the unattractive back lane along which one approached the house by car. This also made it difficult to entertain, as guests had to park some distance away. Without wishing to sound snobbish, though our neighbours in the terrace were pleasant Newcastle folk, none were from a professional or academic background similar to ours, so that we found that we had little in common. Nevertheless we did do some entertaining and I particularly remember one occasion when Ruth and John Hankinson came for supper in the kitchen; John's eagle eye spotted a list hanging on the door which specified sums to be deducted from the girls' pocket money as penalties for various misdemeanours. They included items such as 'To leaving my clothes all over the bathroom floor—2d.', 'To not tidying up the bedroom before I go to school—2d.', 'To bothering Daddy the moment he comes in through the door—2d.', etc., etc. To this list John wickedly added 'To getting in the family way—6d.'.

After about seven years we decided to look for another house in Gosforth. Several we saw were attractive but had significant disadvantages, even including some in Elmfield and in Graham Park Road. We learned from our friends the Strangs that houses in Beechfield Road, where they lived, rarely if ever came on to the market and were almost always sold by private arrangement. Christo Strang told us that Joe Atkinson, a local shipowner, proposed to sell his house at number 9 and suggested that we should telephone him, which of course I did. Negotiations moved swiftly and were very friendly, although there was a minor hiccup when I offered £8,750, a figure lower than he had anticipated; we eventually settled for £9,100 and 'Holmwood', 9 Beechfield Road, was ours. We moved in summer 1963, little realizing that this was to be the home in which we were to spend 20 exceptionally happy and fruitful years.

Beechfield Road can properly be regarded as one of the most desirable roads in Gosforth. It has only twelve houses, bordered at one end by a delightful open green space and at the other by North Avenue which carries local traffic. The street was an ideal location for the riotous street parties held later to celebrate the Queen's Silver Jubilee and the marriage of the Prince of Wales.

Our new home, though semi-detached, was very spacious with four good-sized reception rooms—a breakfast room, a small dining room and two much larger rooms, one of which was our drawing room and the other became my study/consulting room. Remarkably, Gosforth society in those days was so conservative that we were told quietly afterwards that people in Beechfield Road would only sell their homes to 'WASPS' (White Anglo-Saxon Protestants). Seriously, it was suggested that if we had not passed scrutiny Joe and Meta Atkinson would not have sold us the house; this was something of which we were quite unaware at the time. The kitchen and breakfast room needed some reconstruction, some work was required in the five first floor bedrooms and we eventually installed a second bathroom for our guests. On the top floor there was a billiard room, another bedroom and a boxroom, and we had a charming walled garden with a terrace, as well as a double garage. One important deficiency was that there was no central heating, so that before we moved our old friend Harry Durham from Gateshead undertook a good deal of interior work including the installation of a central heating system with a boiler in one of the now redundant coalhouses. I was a little sad, because of my love of billiards and snooker, that Joe Atkinson gave away his old billiard table (which *was* in poor condition). However we converted that room into a studio in which in subsequent years the children held many memorable teenage parties (of which more later). Another attractive feature was that the Atkinsons had built a sunroom at the rear, opening off the dining room, and in that delightful conservatory-like structure we spent many happy hours. I was also able to install a desk, telephone and appropriate cupboards in part of the dining room where my part-time secretary, Mrs Dodds, could work. Hence once we had moved Betty was largely (except in the evenings) relieved of her receptionist duties, though there were still many telephone calls with which she had to deal.

But before we could move there remained the not insignificant problem of selling 5, Dilston Terrace which had suited us well but which was not everyone's 'cup of tea'. We advertised it for sale at £5,500 and were delighted when a newly-appointed orthopaedic surgeon and his wife came to see it and were so pleased with the accommodation that they decided to buy it on the spot. A couple of days later, however, they had obviously had second thoughts, probably because of the inaccessible front entrance, and withdrew from the deal. There followed a few anxious weeks until finally the newly-appointed Secretary of the Newcastle YMCA came and found it to be just what he wanted, though the selling price had eventually to be reduced to £4,500. Rather foolishly, we left behind the huge oil painting on the landing, which we thought was a copy of a Claude and for which we could find no room in Beechfield Road. Several years later we saw a photograph of the painting in an art magazine; it had apparently fetched a substantial sum in an auction at a Newcastle gallery. We were a little less knowledgeable then about art than we subsequently became.

Being on the staff of both the NGH and the RVI, I had the right to admit patients to private wards in either the Leazes Hospital at the RVI or Ward 21 at the NGH. Nursing homes still existed in Newcastle but were in decline because of the few modern facilities they could provide; the Jesmond Nuffield Hospital was built several years later. I soon decided that in order to offer the care and attention which private patients needing in-patient investigation required, they must be admitted to a hospital where a full range of investigative facilities was available and where, in an emergency, my junior staff would also be available to help. As Henry had done when I was his registrar and first assistant, I regularly paid fees to my junior staff involved in clerking and investigating such patients under my supervision. Much later, after the Regional Neurological Centre opened in 1962, we were able to use up to four beds in single rooms on Ward 30 (the neurological ward) for private patients. This was an inestimable boon as one was then geographically whole-time on one's own ward looking after NHS and private patients together. It was a sad day in the 1960s when Mrs Barbara Castle, Secretary of State for Health in the Labour Government, under pressure from trade unions, decided to try to exclude private patients from NHS hospitals. Ultimately there was only one private bed in the NGH, one in the RVI and one at the newly-built Freeman Hospital. This policy more than any other resulted in a tremendous upsurge in private hospital development throughout the UK. It had a seriously detrimental effect upon the NHS not just because of loss of income but also because those consultants who practised privately and in the NHS were compelled to treat their private patients elsewhere. In larger centres of population this inevitably eroded the time that some spent on their NHS duties. As I write, I have been delighted by the efforts now being made in many centres to reintroduce private wards and investigative facilities into NHS hospitals so that the consultants who so wish can again be geographically whole-time. When the Castle edict had had its full effect, we were faced with the ridiculous situation that I, by then a whole-time academic with a chair in neurology, was unable to accept patients referred to me for investigation and treatment from countries overseas, since very properly by law such overseas patients coming to the UK specifically for medical reasons (except those from the EEC) were required to pay the full cost. I even had to refuse patients referred from the United States as it would have been inappropriate to admit them to a Newcastle private hospital which could not offer facilities for investigating fully patients with obscure neuromuscular disease. That policy also had a serious effect upon the funding of some clinical academic departments as full-time academics with clinical consultant contracts who were by convention unable to charge fees for personal gain had nevertheless been able to arrange for such fees to contribute to departmental funds.

Another fascinating component of consultant practice was the arrangement under which any general practitioner (GP) could call out a consultant listed by the Regional Hospital Board (as it then was) as being available for domiciliary consultation. As my clientele of GPs increased, I began to do more and more of these. These visits gave me an excellent insight into the standards and methods of family medicine but also revealed clearly the strengths and weaknesses of the many GPs whom I came to know through these contacts. I continued to do 'domiciliaries' until I was awarded a personal chair in 1968 and about 98% were carried out with the GP. Indeed I usually refused unless the GP intended to be there, even though we each recognized that the consultant's day and that of the GP are different. The consultant is often free in the early evening after completing his hospital work, but this is the time when the GP often begins his evening surgery. Nevertheless, save in the most exceptional circumstances I never went out on a domiciliary consultation alone. These visits, though time-consuming, were exceptionally rewarding. I learned a great deal of emergency neurology and certainly refined my diagnostic and management skills. Each visit in 1958 paid four guineas plus a few pence a mile for travel. At the end of each month the forms, appropriately completed and signed by the GP, were posted to the headquarters of the Regional Hospital Board and the fees and expenses were added to one's monthly pay chit. There was then a regulation that consultants could only be paid for a maximum of 200 domiciliary consultations per year. Presumably this was introduced to prevent abuse of the system, but it was irksome as after two or three years I was regularly completing more than the maximum. When in February or March I was called out on a return journey of some 60 or 70 miles recognizing that no fee would be payable, my sense of duty, however well-developed, frayed a little at the edges. Once in mid-March I struggled to reach Wolsingham in Weardale over snowbound roads late at night but of course did not hint to the GP that this visit would not attract a fee.

Many such consultations were, however, memorable for different reasons. I was called out by Alan Jenkins to a modest flat in Gateshead lying beneath a viaduct across which trains from Newcastle to London regularly thundered by. The man of the house had been to a Saturday midday drinking session and had returned home to sleep it off, only to be awakened by the piercing whistle of a train passing by his window. Jumping, startled, out of bed, he tripped over a carpet and fell face forwards into a Victorian armchair, jerking his head backwards and immediately losing the use of all four limbs. Somehow his wife manoeuvred him into the living room where we found him spreadeagled in a chair, still almost immobile and also complaining of loss of sensation in the limbs. In another chair was the mentally-handicapped daughter, gurgling and squealing repetitively, and in a corner a large television set going full blast. When I asked if that might be turned off, the wife said 'Please forgive me, doctor, but I daren't turn it off because she (the daughter) screams whenever I do'. Despite the challenging circumstances, it was evident that the patient had suffered a contusion of the spinal cord due to acute hyper-extension of his cervical spine; in the end he made a good recovery.

Soon afterwards I saw a similar case in a young woman who had very long hair and who worked at a cable-making factory in Birtley. Her hair became loose from under her protective cap and caught under a cable she was feeding on to a rotating drum. She was dragged over the drum, striking her forehead on the ground and immediately losing the use of her limbs. Not unnaturally she was acutely distressed, and when seen at a local hospital she was thought in the casualty department to be hysterical and was sent home. Her GP doubted this diagnosis and asked me to see her; again the physical signs clearly indicated cervical cord contusion and yet again recovery was complete within a few days.

Probably the longest journey I ever did for a domiciliary consultation was to Great Ayton in North Yorkshire (a round trip of some 120 miles) where Dr Waldie (a GP who was much esteemed by his colleagues) asked me to see a young woman who worked in a bakery. One of her tasks was to go to the bakery early each morning and to light the ovens before other staff arrived. On one occasion it seemed that the gas had not been turned off properly the night before; when she inserted a taper there was a loud explosion and she was flung across the room, fortunately without suffering severe burns but merely some singeing of her hair and eyebrows. This acutely distressing experience led to her being admitted to a Teesside general hospital where she was heavily sedated with barbiturates, only to become seriously confused; she was therefore transferred to the local mental hospital where the barbiturates were withdrawn and she was given chlorpromazine. Gradually she improved, her physical injuries healed and she was discharged, but was then found to have severe difficulty in walking and Dr Waldie found her lower limb reflexes to be absent. As the out-patient clinic which I then held at the North Ormesby Hospital in Middlesbrough was open only to patients referred from other consultants, Dr Waldie invited me to see her at home and I found that she had an acute polyneuropathy. The history suggested that her confusional state had been precipitated by barbiturates, and when I learned that she was passing dark urine, the colour of port wine, it seemed likely that she was suffering from acute idiopathic porphyria and on admission to hospital in Newcastle so it proved.

Only once in my 10 years of domiciliary consultations did the GP and I find, sadly, on reaching the patient's home that he had died shortly before we arrived. And once only, too, by which time we had acquired a second family car (a secondhand Ford Popular for Betty) did I arrive at the house of a somewhat up-market GP driving Betty's car rather than my own, to be met by his pained comment that we would visit the patient in his car rather than in mine. Only then did I realize that consultants lost face, whatever the social status of the patient, if one arrived in a motor vehicle thought to be inappropriate to one's consultant role. While in later years I managed through the good offices of our friend Joe Patrick of Birmingham to graduate to an Austin 3-litre Princess saloon (costing, I recall, £1,400), I never owned or even aspired to, the Bentley or Rolls Royce then popular in the consultant world, especially in London but also on Tyneside (Henry Miller drove two or three Bentleys during his consultant career). Mr Rowbotham, too, had a large antiquated Rolls Royce, while Alexander Kennedy at one stage had a Bentley and even George Smart, the whole-time Professor of Medicine, had a 12-cylinder Lagonda, while Harvey Evers of 'the Golden Gates' ran through a succession of brand-new Rolls. Rowbotham it was, of the fallible memory, who went out on a consultation with Alan Jenkins; after taking a brief surgical history he invited the male patient to remove his clothes and to lie on the bed. He then realized that he had left his ophthalmoscope in the Rolls and excused himself in order to collect it. As Alan Jenkins watched from the window, he saw Rowbotham climb into his car and drive away, leaving both doctor and patient bemused. History does not relate whether or not the consultation was ever completed.

Another memorable consultation was when I was called out by Roland Goodhead to see a boy of 17. He telephoned me at 2.00 p.m. as I was beginning an EMG clinic at the RVI; I agreed to meet him at 4.15. It was as well that I had agreed to see the patient after an interval of just two hours. When I arrived at the house in Fenham, Roland told me that the boy had gone to his local grammar school normally that morning but had soon begun to have difficulty in writing with his right hand, which also became numb. Gradually the weakness extended to involve the whole of the right upper limb and soon afterwards affected the left arm and hand. Nevertheless he was able to cycle home despite further weakness now developing in both legs. Dr Goodhead thought at first that this might be poliomyelitis and wondered whether to send the patient to the isolation service at Walkergate. However, finding sensory loss as well as weakness puzzled him, which is why he sought my opinion. By the time I saw the boy he was almost totally paralysed in all four limbs and was beginning to have difficulty in breathing. There was also loss of sensation on the limbs and trunk, indicating either an acute polyneuropathy or a transverse spinal cord lesion. We called an ambulance at once and had him admitted to the RVI where he went immediately into intensive care, requiring respirator support because of his ascending transverse myelitis (as his condition proved to be). Slowly over the next few months he made a very satisfactory recovery, eventually returning to school. Later he went to university with only a relatively minor residual disability. Such dramatic events certainly mould one's experience and influence one's subsequent management in neurological medicine.

Also memorable for very different reasons were the many consultations which I carried out with Dr 'Skem' Hutchinson of Amble (of whom more later), a remarkable eccentric and well-known 'rough diamond' who more than once found himself practising without a motor vehicle as his elderly and decrepit Ford Prefect had broken down yet again. His nickname 'Skem' arose in medical school when he played soccer at outside left for Medicals. In Geordieland a 'skemmie' is a pigeon and on one occasion a spectator was heard to remark loudly about 'Yon skemmie gannin' doon the wing'; the name stuck. Several times after meeting him I found myself left sitting in my car while he visited two or three successive houses, thus completing his own programme of visits before we eventually reached the home of the patient whom he wished me to see. He was largely responsible for the fact that one year, at a time when Betty and I tried to go with the children to Detchant most weekends, I did not have a single Sunday over a six-month period when I was not called out to see at least one patient. Once when I was away but Betty and the children were at Detchant the telephone there rang at 2 a.m. She stumbled downstairs to be greeted by a stentorian Geordie voice saying 'Is he in?'. Rather coolly she responded, recognizing the voice, that I was in London, to which Skem replied 'It's the Captain he came to see six weeks ago with the stroke; he's got better from that but he's been to the races and has fallen and hurt his knee—listen, you can hear his screams!'. Quickly and even more coolly she advised him to call a surgeon.

Despite the unremitting pressures of this form of practice, the experience gained, the friendships forged and the insight achieved into GP/hospital relationships were invaluable. True, there were rare occasions when a domiciliary consultation was used as a poorly disguised subterfuge in order to achieve rapid hospital admission. Much more often such consultations were used by GPs to confirm their own diagnosis and management and to reassure the patient's family that everything necessary was being done. Less often, the GP was genuinely perplexed and uncertain as to whether or not hospital investigation and treatment was needed. Often, as in the case of patients suffering a severe sensory or motor aura of migraine where the possibility of stroke had been raised, it was possible to avoid hospital admission so that the consultation fulfilled its principal objective. I have been surprised to be told that recently the 'domiciliary' has been used more often as a means of admitting a patient to hospital and that few are now carried out by consultants with the GP. This, if true, is a sad development; both I and my GP colleagues profited from these consultations from which we both learned a great deal.

A curious feature which everyone beginning practice recognizes is the extraordinary periodicity with which requests come for your clinical services. Both in private consulting practice in one's rooms and in domiciliary work, calls come in clusters interrupted by quiet periods, sometimes so prolonged that as both Henry and I agreed, you begin to wonder whether (a) the telephone has broken down, (b) the population is becoming neurologically more healthy, or (c) the clients (i.e. the GPs) have at last got wise to your inadequacies. Often I came home late and took a sideways glance at my appointment book sitting by the hall telephone, noting that the afternoons in the following week were still vacant; on other occasions there would be a veritable flood so that I would find myself consulting from 2.00 p.m. until 8.30 or 9.00 in the evening, just as sometimes one would be asked to do three or four domiciliary consultations in a single day.

Another interesting commitment which also grew slowly was my medico-legal work which I was able to continue on a limited basis even when I became an academic and gave up private work. Whether it involved preparing reports for solicitors, insurance companies or government departments, it was something I much enjoyed, not least because it was one of the few sectors of clinical practice which could be regarded as a pure intellectual exercise as one did not have to take account of the patient's interests. As time went by the fallibility in that respect (if I may say so) of some colleagues became evident. Some psychiatrists especially seemed to feel that when asked to report upon a patient claiming damages for symptoms alleged to be the after-effects of an industrial accident, they should identify themselves with the patient's interests; in consequence they sometimes grossly overstated the plaintiff's case. However hard one tried to explain to colleagues that all such reporting (irrespective of whether one was acting for the plaintiff or the defendant) must be totally objective and impartial, there were some who found it difficult or even impossible to accept that principle.

I now recognize, however, that in the early days there were times when I slavishly accepted the plaintiff's case without exploring as fully as I should have done the genuineness of his or her complaints. In a few such cases in which I presented expert evidence in court on behalf of the plaintiff, subsequent events plainly revealed that I had been wrong in accepting his or her complaints and related disability at their face value and in attributing these to the effects of the accident. In one case at York Assizes where I was on one side (for the plaintiff) and Henry on the other (acting for the insurance company) I was taken aback when Rudolph Lyons, QC, opened my cross-examination by saying 'You are the assistant physician in neurology, Dr Walton, and you claim that this man's symptoms are genuine and his disability severe, whereas the physician in neurology, Dr Miller, will say later that he is an out-and-out malingerer'. That was not quite what Henry intended to say; nevertheless, he was convinced that the man's complaints were being greatly exaggerated in a desire for material gain. The plaintiff won the case and was awarded substantial damages, but subsequent events showed that his disability was neither as severe nor as permanent as I had thought. In another case in London, after three long days in the Law Courts during which I averred that the plaintiff, a young sailor injured in a car accident, was so disabled that he would never work again, his case was argued so effectively by James Miskin, QC (subsequently Recorder of London and later still a judge) that he too won substantial damages. My subsequent follow-up of the patient (who came from South Shields) showed that he improved remarkably and the hemiparesis which had seemed so severe and disabling troubled him relatively little in the successful career he later carved out in business.

These and other similar experiences subsequently made me take a long, hard look at comparable cases. I believe that my opinions became progressively more dispassionate and that I was not as often misled as in the earlier years. Nevertheless I felt that in his challenging Milroy lectures on accident neurosis Henry Miller substantially overstated the evidence which suggested to him that the post-traumatic or post-concussional syndrome was largely emotionally determined. However, I believe that I became relatively skilled in recognizing those manifestations which were often labelled as hysterical (due to subconscious motivation) but which were related to malingering (i.e. conscious motivation and desire for material gain). They included, for example, sensory loss in a limb ending sharply in an upper border at the knee or shoulder and weakness so gross that attempts, for instance, to grip with the allegedly affected hand produced no perceptible effect despite a florid display of apparent effort, often accompanied by straining and groaning. Spurious contractures (fingers curled irresistibly into the palm) were also easy to recognize.

My interest in the EEG also led to my being consulted at times by the late Dr Ian Pickering, the Chief Medical Officer of H.M. Prison Medical Service, about prisoners at Durham gaol, among them many murderers, who were advancing epilepsy as a potential defence. Despite a few relatively well-documented cases in the literature, I could never convince myself that any patient whom I saw had committed a crime of violence during an episode of epileptic automatism. I did, however, give evidence for the defence in the case of a lorry driver who had had two accidents within a week, in each of which he had inexplicably failed to brake before colliding with another vehicle. He claimed to have had no recollection of the few seconds before each impact. Between the two incidents his girlfriend described him as having two transient episodes of impaired consciousness. When his EEG recorded during barbiturate-induced sleep with sphenoidal electrodes in place demonstrated temporal lobe spikes, it was clear that he was having minor attacks of temporal lobe epilepsy. He was acquitted of the charges of dangerous driving but lost his licence. His epilepsy was subsequently controlled by anticonvulsant drugs.

One pleasure associated with medico-legal work was that in court one had to pit one's wits against intelligent and experienced barristers. This intellectual game (for such is what it often seemed) was an enjoyable battle of wits. One had to learn, often by hard experience, the techniques commonly employed in cross-examination in order to be ready, not for the next question, but for the one which lay two or three questions ahead. I regularly crossed swords with such worthies as John Cobb, QC, and Henry Scott, QC—the one quiet, reflective and persistent, the other sharp, combative and aggressive, but each very effective. I remember Henry Scott, for example, attacking on behalf of the plaintiff a senior neurological colleague who claimed that the patient's post-traumatic symptoms were spurious. In response to three successive questions—'You say this man's symptoms are imaginary?'; 'In other words, he is telling lies?'; 'And so he is committing perjury?'—the hapless consultant answered 'Yes' without qualification and so in the eyes of the court lost credibility.

As I grew in experience, so did some of my barrister friends from the North East, including Roderick Smith, Humphrey Potts and, notably, Peter Taylor; all later became High Court judges and Peter, as Lord Justice Taylor, is now Lord Chief Justice, famous in his profession most recently for his report on the Hillsborough football stadium tragedy. He and I have shared many after-dinner platforms, exchanging jokes, medical and legal niceties and friendly banter; at the annual dinner of the Newcastle upon Tyne Medico-Legal Society, he was compelled to leave early to catch the night sleeper as he was prosecuting in the Jeremy Thorpe case and said on leaving that he had to go to Minehead 'to see a man about a dog'!

To return briefly to the issue of malingering, an important lesson derived from a case in which Henry Miller was the fifth or sixth consultant invited to report upon a man alleged to have become totally mute as a consequence of a minor head injury. Various diagnoses had been offered, including schizophrenia. Henry saw the patient in his rooms in Jesmond and was unusually solicitous in offering afterwards to drive the patient and his wife to the Central Station so that they could catch the train to

Manchester. Before doing so he telephoned Dr Colin Brown (then his registrar, now a consultant neurologist in Norwich) and asked him to board the train with the patient and his wife, to get off at Durham and then to report his observations. Colin had no difficulty in entering the same compartment as the patient whom he had identified as Henry escorted them to the train. The patient had remained mute throughout the consultation but as the train crossed the Tyne he turned to his wife in Colin's presence and said 'Well, I think that went all right, didn't you?'.

An experience which angered me arose when in the late 1950s, in preparation for the Annual Meeting of the BMA which was to be held in Newcastle, I and Griff Owen were invited to plan and produce a series of closed-circuit medical television programmes which were being transmitted in colour by an American team. This team, sponsored by a major US drug company, had arranged a preliminary canter by producing a similar series of programmes during meetings in London commemorating the 300th anniversary of William Harvey's death. Griff and I and our wives were invited to spend a few days in London to see the programmes. The hospitality was exceptional in that Betty and I were accommodated at the Connaught Hotel and Griff and Ruth at Grosvenor House. While we were in London I was telephoned by a firm of solicitors for which I had prepared reports, notifying me that I was required at Newcastle Assizes in the middle of the week. I had no alternative but to fly from London to Newcastle, only to find that soon after I reached court the case was dismissed, as liability could not be proved. Next week, by which time we were back in Newcastle, the same firm again called me to the Assizes, but this time, in the light of my evidence, the plaintiff was awarded substantial damages with costs. When I later submitted my two accounts, I included in that relating to the first case the additional costs of return air travel from London to Newcastle. My account in the second case was much less; the solicitors telephoned suggesting that as the first case had been lost, I should switch my bills from one to the other. Indignantly I refused, and also refused ever again to see any cases for that firm.

Gradually, as my national and international commitments increased, it became more difficult for me to be able to guarantee a court appearance and hence my medico-legal practice declined. Indeed when I became Professor of Neurology and later Dean, I told the solicitors and insurance companies who had previously instructed me that I could no longer agree to appear in court, even at a fixed hearing arranged well in advance. Nevertheless, for some years I was regularly invited, for example, by the National Coal Board and the National Union of Mineworkers to report on appropriate cases, with the agreement that my report jointly commissioned by the two organizations would be binding on both parties. Thus I continued to enjoy some limited medico-legal work, and also enjoyed serving on the Newcastle Medical Appeal Tribunals until eventually I moved to Oxford in 1983.

However, private, domiciliary and medico-legal practice was very much a secondary part of my professional life in view of my primary commitment to develop clinical neurological services in Newcastle alongside those being provided by Henry and his colleagues at the RVI, and to develop a regional neurological service. To that end, as mentioned in Chapter 9, I was provided with four beds in Mr Rowbotham's ward, Ward 27, at the NGH and shared the services of his senior house officer. I was also, through the good offices of Robert Mowbray, provided with 14 beds in a redundant surgical ward at the Chester-le-Street General Hospital. The plan was, that with the assistance of medical SHOs from Tom Grimson's wards at Chester-le-Street, I would admit patients for initial assessment at Chester-le-Street and would then shuffle them backwards and forwards to and from my four beds at the NGH whenever they required specialized neuroradiological or other investigations which Chester-le-Street could not offer. I held a single-handed out-patient clinic for new patients only (an open clinic for GP reference) in the old and decaying out-patient department at the NGH on Monday mornings and a follow-up clinic in the same setting on Saturday mornings. I then drove fortnightly on a Monday afternoon (eating a sandwich in the car) to North Ormesby Hospital, Middlesbrough, to see patients referred by other consultants, while on alternate Tuesday afternoons I would do the same at Dryburn Hospital, Durham. On Wednesday afternoons I saw out-patients in a closed clinic at the RVI, and held ward rounds at Chester-le-Street on Tuesday and Friday mornings, leaving the early part of Tuesday mornings, Wednesday mornings and Friday afternoons for ward rounds at the NGH and in-patient consultations on other wards (often these had to wait until the evenings). Alternate Monday and Tuesday and each Thursday afternoon were my consulting times at home. In between these commitments I was expected to fit in some EMG work (though Andrew Lenman at the RVI had taken over much of that service) and some EEG interpretation sessions both at the RVI and the NGH. There was then no medical student teaching in neurology at the NGH but nevertheless Henry asked me to contribute to the neurological lecture programme so that several times a year I gave a 9.00 a.m. lecture in the Medical School and also did some postgraduate and undergraduate teaching about twice a term by giving clinical demonstrations in the old basement lecture theatre at the RVI. Research inevitably took something of a back seat, though there was a little time in the evenings and at weekends to follow up these interests.

Clinical secretarial services were provided on a part-time basis by Dorothy Aynsley from the NGH typing pool; the Hospital Secretary let me have an office in splendid isolation in a storage area above the ophthalmology out-patient department. That office was inconvenient and used very little; after about two years I gave it up and did most of my clerical work on a dictating machine at home or at the RVI, where my research secretary Shirley Whillis, employed under my MDA grant, was working. I also appointed as a research assistant David Barwick, newly returned from the United States, who followed Peter Leyburn and soon acquired expertise in EMG and EEG while also helping with various clinical and genetic projects and with my out-patient practice at the NGH. In the beginning Shirley (who later married Rob Uldall, a neurological SHO on Ward 6) did my limited private practice correspondence, for which I paid her extra, but as that practice grew I eventually employed a part-time private secretary two half-days a week. She used my consulting room and desk at Dilston Terrace on days when I was not consulting as we were not able to offer her a place in which to work when I was seeing patients, so Betty continued as my receptionist until we moved to Beechfield Road.

A major problem of the first few years was the growing burden of travel, necessitated not only by my statutory clinical commitments and growing domiciliary practice but also by the increasing number of consultations I was asked to carry out in innumerable regional hospitals. Invitations from consultant colleagues to see with them patients in locations as far afield as Ashington, Sunderland, Shotley Bridge, South Shields and Tynemouth came frequently, if somewhat irregularly, and almost always my closed out-patient clinic at Middlesbrough was complemented by requests from physicians like Guy Warnock of Stockton-on-Tees to see a patient with him on my way home; and an occasional similar call at Sedgefield often meant that my return to Newcastle after a morning seeing out-patients at the NGH and an afternoon seeing more at North Ormesby was greatly delayed. Often I got back to Newcastle between 8.00 and 9.00 p.m. after various calls on the way, only to be greeted by Betty at the door asking me to have a quick snack but not to put the car away as there was a domiciliary consultation somewhere in the vicinity. Once I got back to Gosforth at 9.30 p.m. and turned round immediately to go to Birtley with Dr Ron Howd to see an elderly man who was paralysed in both lower limbs due to an anterior spinal artery thrombosis.

Visits to Chester-le-Street and to Dryburn imposed similar pressures as there were often in-patients to see at both hospitals, while Frank Robertson and Geoff Ismay occasionally asked me to go on from Durham to Bishop Auckland to see various neurological cases. By 1960 or 1961 I calculated that I was seeing personally more than 50 new patients each week in numerous locations; despite strenuous attempts to cope with the increasing load, my out-patient waiting list at the NGH grew to over six weeks, even though I saw regularly 12 or 14 new patients every Monday morning. Inevitably I could provide little more than a screening service;

many patients had to be admitted to hospital because of sheer lack of consultative time in which to offer a proper assessment. To my great regret similar pressures upon diagnostic services in neuroradiology and in clinical neurophysiology meant that one was never able, as I would have wished, to provide a patient with a full range of appropriate investigations during a single visit. This uneconomical system meant that the load of work escalated, as if a patient required, for example, an EMG or related studies, that had to be arranged a few weeks after the out-patient consultation. Then the patient had to be asked to return to the follow-up clinic to discuss the results of the tests and consequential recommendations about management. If investigations such as angiography or myelography were needed, there was no alternative to hospital admission. With only four beds available, however, a myelogram often had to be booked several weeks in advance. Occasionally this policy, inevitable because of lack of time, beds and junior support, meant that there was little time after admission to review the need for the test; sometimes I felt that it was not after all necessary in view of findings which had emerged between the original consultation and admission.

When a patient seen on a domiciliary consultation had a problem requiring urgent admission, I was sometimes compelled, if only temporarily, to exceed my quota of four beds and often returned to hospital in the late evening to reassess the situation, commonly in consultation with one of my neurosurgical colleagues, among whom John Hankinson became a close and valued friend. I remember with pleasure and profit the many interesting and exciting clinical situations in which we collaborated and the many patients from whom, with his exceptional surgical expertise, he removed benign intracranial or spinal tumours. I also recall many cases of parkinsonism in which his abolition of disabling tremor through stereotaxic surgery was often so complete and dramatic. In one Sunday morning postgraduate course for GPs in which I discussed the medical treatment of parkinsonism, and he the surgical, one older GP, increasingly wide-eyed as the tale unfolded, said 'Do you mean, Mr Hankinson, that you make a hole in the skull and that you then pass a cannula into the depths of the brain before you inject a freezing solution?' John's response was typical; 'It's a living', he said! Nevertheless, we both soon recognized that even when physical improvement after the operation was striking, it carried a risk of impairing memory, drive, intellect and personality, having in some patients a leucotomy-like effect which had not been fully documented previously. This led us to seek full psychological assessment in all such patients prior to operation, especially if a bilateral procedure was likely to be needed.

We also learned to our cost how detrimental to a patient's own interests may be the effects of a relentlessly importuning and obsessional personality. I was consulted by a retired naval officer who was complaining of troublesome and intractable intercostal neuralgia (sharp intermittent pain around the chest wall). I tried several combinations of analgesic drugs, freezing sprays, a Pifco vibrator, local anaesthetic and later phenol injection of relevant intercostal nerves, each time with temporary improvement but invariably followed by relapse. Eventually John Hankinson, whom I consulted, divided four intercostal nerves on the appropriate side, extending above and below the primary site of pain. Again the patient had a few weeks of relief but yet again the pain returned. He pestered us continually to do more and yet more, until in the end, perhaps unwisely in retrospect in an ageing individual with evidence of arteriosclerosis, John was persuaded to operate on pain pathways in the spinal cord by carrying out an anterolateral spinal cordotomy. All seemed to go well but 48 hours later a spinal artery thrombosis ensued, rendering the unfortunate patient permanently paraplegic.

I owe much to John Hankinson for his dedication and expertise, for his devoted treatment of those patients of mine who required neuro-surgery; we enjoyed a long and fruitful professional relationship, not just in practice but also in postgraduate teaching and research, until I left Newcastle in 1983 shortly before his retirement. In spinal surgery, not least in the treatment of children and adults with spinal dysraphism, I enjoyed a similarly close relationship with Laurie Lassman and much later with Ram Kalbag and Robin Sengupta, while Gordon Gryspeerdt, Arnold Appleby, Keith Hall and later Vic McAllister gave us all an impeccable service in neuroradiology.

We were very sad that in latter years our relationship with G. F. (Freddie) Rowbotham deteriorated. As he approached the age of 65 it became increasingly clear that he had no intention of retiring, whereas we all knew that retirement at that age was an absolute rule in the NHS, certainly in Newcastle, and we wished to plan for the future. When we raised the issue tentatively with Dr R. H. M. Stewart, the Senior Administrative Medical Officer of the Regional Hospital Board, he confirmed that Mr Rowbotham, like everyone else, would retire at the usual age. When GFR was informed accordingly, he was shocked and asked with whom Stewart had discussed the matter; when he learned that among others Henry Miller, John Hankinson, Andrew Lowdon (Professor of Surgery and Dean of Medicine) and I had been consulted, he refused to speak to or even to acknowledge any of us from that day onwards.

Of my clinical experiences during these exciting years much more could be said, but I became increasingly convinced that while driving 20 to 25,000 miles a year, still trying to keep abreast of research in neuromuscular disease, and while accepting occasional invitations to lecture elsewhere in the UK and abroad, it would be impossible for me to continue under such unremitting pressure indefinitely. I therefore raised with the Regional

Hospital Board the question as to whether a second consultant neurologist appointment could be created as well as one in clinical neurophysiology. In those halcyon days when the Health Service was still expanding, both requests received sympathetic attention, though it was clear that there would be no room for an additional consultant or junior medical staff in the regional neurological service until the long-awaited Regional Neurological Centre was built. This major development had been contemplated for many years and was in an advanced stage of planning when I was appointed in 1958. The department of neuroradiology, presided over by the charming and meticulous Gordon Gryspeerdt, had already been built as the first phase and the new block as planned was to have 120 beds, 30 for neurology and 90 for neurosurgery (the latter including an eight-bed overnight stay and intensive care ward). In addition, there was to be a suite of operating theatres with a large EEG department immediately adjacent on the ground floor. However, there were no plans to include any space for electromyography or for research. The plan provided for a T-shaped building with out-patient facilities, radiology, theatres, EEG department and the admission ward on the ground floor, and four 30-bedded wards above one another along the front of the building. The north wing of the T ended at the second floor and contained workshops, changing rooms for the theatres, the records department and a conference room, etc.

By now my research grant income, not only from the Muscular Dystrophy Association of America (MDA) but also from the Muscular Dystrophy Association of Canada (MDAC) and from the Muscular Dystrophy Group of Great Britain (MDGGB) was increasing but the research workers employed under these grants were still dispersed around various sites in the RVI and Medical School (see below). My clinical research registrar, David Barwick, spent much of his time at the RVI in the EMG lab, while helping me with clinical work at the NGH; my research secretary, Shirley Whillis (who was succeeded by Rosemary Allan after Shirley married Rob Uldall in 1960) worked on Ward 6 at the RVI. Geoffrey Pearce, a research fellow in histopathology and electron microscopy, worked first in the J. H. Burn Research Laboratories at the RVI and later (with our newly-purchased electron microscope) in association with the Demyelinating Diseases Unit headed by E. J. Field in Framlington Place. Dr W. H. S. Thomson, a research biochemist also recruited under my research grants, was offered space in the first instance by Professor Albert Latner in the Department of Chemical Pathology. I hoped to add a research neurophysiologist to the team and had already identified as a potential candidate a former neurological SHO at the RVI, Dr Alan McComas. When sufficient funds became available to employ him after he had acquired a PhD in London, Professor Harper, head of physiology, kindly appointed him (paid from my research funds) as a temporary lecturer in his department, pending a possible move later to the NGH.

There followed several meetings with the Regional Hospital Board and its Research Committee, presided over with skill and expertise by the Dean of Medicine (still the long-serving Professor R. B. Green). I was able to persuade the Board to modify its plans for the Regional Neurological Centre and to add on to the north wing two floors of research laboratories, including facilities for histology, histochemistry, electron microscopy, neurophysiology and neurochemistry (as well as a combined office/laboratory for myself and a room for Rosemary Allan). This would make it possible to bring together all the people working on research into neuromuscular disease whom I had recruited under my various grants.

One major problem remained—that of equipment. As plans for the modified Regional Centre were finalized and the contract was ultimately let, estimates of cost based upon standard Regional Hospital Board formulae were derived for equipping the building with beds, furniture, EEG machines and the like. With my research colleagues we put together a substantial list of research equipment which we wished to see added. This included many expensive items such as ultracentrifuges, spectrophotometers, cryostats and microtomes, etc. Fortunately our need for an electron microscope had been fulfilled well in advance of completion of the centre since an application which I had submitted jointly with Dr Pearce to the Polio Research Fund (subsequently the National Fund for Research into Crippling Diseases) had been successful. We had already purchased and had installed a Siemens instrument in the basement of 13 Framlington Place. Nevertheless, when the Regional Hospital Board examined the potential bill for equipment they found this to be £35,000 over the original estimate, wholly due to the addition of equipment for research in neurophysiology, neurochemistry and experimental neuropathology. Somewhat shaken by this estimate (the capital cost of the entire building was £330,000) and not having encountered a similar situation before, they therefore referred the research equipment to the Region's Research Committee which decided to invite independent external referees to comment. While it may seem remarkable in retrospect, the secretary of the committee consulted me about whom to nominate as referees. In neuropathology I suggested Professor Blackwood at Queen Square and Professor Dorothy Russell at the London Hospital, in neurochemistry Professor John Cumings at Queen Square, and in neurophysiology Professor (later Sir) Andrew Huxley who was already becoming interested in the work of the MDG. Each referee scrutinized the list, congratulated the Regional Board upon its research programme and even made some additions so that, to our delight, all our requirements were approved and we could look forward to the opening of the building in 1962 with confidence.

Happily, the Regional Board also agreed to the appointment of a neurological registrar and two senior house officers, while the appointment of a second neurological consultant, who would also have major consultative sessions in Sunderland, along with a few beds in that city, was also approved, so that at last some relief from my increasing clinical load was in sight.

And so the great day dawned in November 1962 when the Regional Neurological Centre was opened by Sir Harold Himsworth, Secretary of the Medical Research Council. At last I was able to feel that I had adequate clinical facilities to be able to fulfil my regional responsibilities. The beds in Chester-le-Street were retained for rehabilitation purposes and as a back-up to our expanded facilities at the NGH. My first registrar was Dr John Balla, a young Australian who had worked with my friend Arthur Schweiger in Melbourne and who subsequently returned to that city as a consultant; he later became Postgraduate Dean in Hong Kong and made a considerable reputation in postgraduate neurological education. He was succeeded a year later by Dr John Pearce, formerly an SHO with Hugh Garland in Leeds. Later he became one of my clinical research registrars before returning to Leeds as a senior registrar and ultimately being appointed consultant neurologist in Hull where he has had a distinguished and productive career. John Pearce was followed in turn by Dr Peter Hudgson who, like John Balla, came from the Schweiger stable in Melbourne; when he moved into a research post in 1965, Ron Joffe from Johannesburg became registrar, to be followed by Walter Bradley (of whom more later) in 1966.

David Barwick, too, moved up to the NGH to supervise the work of the EEG department while continuing his programme of research under my supervision. Later he moved into a newly established senior registrar post in clinical neurophysiology before becoming our first consultant in that specialty, a post in which he has given and continues to give outstandingly loyal and dedicated service. Soon afterwards Jack Foster, who had spent some time on 'the house' at Queen Square before returning to Newcastle as first assistant in neurology, was appointed as the second consultant neurologist to the NGH in order to share the clinical load and to give a consultative service in Sunderland. So for the time being our team was complete. In the research labs we now had Alan McComas in charge of experimental neurophysiology, Ron Pennington (who had succeeded W. H. S. Thomson) in neurochemistry, and Geoffrey Pearce supervising work on muscle pathology, histochemistry and electron microscopy.

CHAPTER 12

Research Director and Professor of Neurology

Despite my escalating clinical commitments and my extensive travelling, my interest in neuromuscular research continued unabated. Slowly the number of staff employed on research in the Regional Centre grew. I was able to appoint a succession of clinical research fellows from the UK and overseas, each with registrar status and each making a part-time contribution to the clinical work of the unit. John Pearce, with Ron Pennington, did some excellent work on serum creatine kinase activity in muscular dystrophy and the other neuromuscular diseases and presented this work superbly at a meeting of the Association of Physicians. Alan McComas not only did some first-class work on recording from sensory neurones in animals (and in man during John Hankinson's stereotaxic operations) but also completed several important projects in the neuromuscular field including, for example, intracellular recording from skeletal muscle in patients with myotonia and periodic paralysis. Later he devised a technique of motor unit counting in the extensor digitorum brevis muscle of the foot, an original method which has subsequently been refined by himself and others and has proved invaluable in studies of neuromuscular function in human subjects. It may have been certain deficiencies in the original technique, and the probability that some patents to whom he applied it who were thought to be suffering from muscular dystrophy actually had spinal muscular atrophy, which led him to draw the erroneous conclusion that muscular dystrophy might be due to a primary defect of the motor neurone. Nevertheless, his espousal of this 'neurogenic theory' inspired many important neurophysiological studies of neuromuscular disease. After he, along with Ron Pennington, had been appointed to the external scientific staff of the MRC (see below) we were disappointed to lose him when a few years later he accepted the Chair of Neurology at McMaster University in Hamilton, Ontario, where he has had a distinguished career.

Ron Pennington came to us from the Rowett Research Institute in Aberdeen. Soon after arriving in Newcastle he followed up the distinction of being an editor of the *Biochemical Journal* by being elected a Fellow of the Royal Society of Edinburgh. He did some outstanding work not only on serum enzyme activity in the neuromuscular diseases but also studied, with a succession of research assistants, protein metabolism in skeletal muscle in muscular dystrophy and the other neuromuscular diseases, with particular reference to the role of proteinases.

Geoffrey Pearce, who came from Professor Glees' department, established our programme of research in tissue culture on the one hand and ultrastructural studies of neuromuscular disease on the other. He also published some important work on the changes observed in skeletal muscle in dystrophic humans and in dystrophic mice of the Bar Harbor strain. Later he elected to become a consultant neuropathologist to work with Bernard Tomlinson at the NGH. Our work on the electron microscopy of muscle and nerve was then taken over first by Peter Hudgson, formerly registrar in neurology. Then in 1972 we were joined by Dr Michael Cullen, trained with Professor Pringle in Oxford; his work on insect muscle fitted him well for the research post which we offered him. The work which he reported with our chief technician, John Fulthorpe, in 1975 on the earliest ultrastructural changes observed in muscle biopsy sections obtained from cases of preclinical Duchenne dystrophy led to a major breakthrough in understanding the process of fibre breakdown in that disease. They showed in unfixed specimens of skeletal muscle and later in plastic-embedded sections stained with toluidine blue, that dystrophic muscle demonstrated focal areas of hypercontraction, sometimes involving only a small segment of a fibre in transverse section but sometimes the whole fibre, thus producing the waxy hyaline fibres seen so strikingly in transverse sections of dystrophic muscle examined under the light microscope. They also demonstrated a high concentration of calcium in these hypercontracted areas and postulated that the plasma membrane of the muscle fibre had become defective, allowing calcium to enter and to activate calcium-activated neutral proteases which digested the fibre. Pennington had in parallel shown these enzymes to be increased in concentration in samples of dystrophic muscle. In the same year Andrew Engel with Dr Mokri at the Mayo Clinic demonstrated with the electron microscope small deficiencies in the plasma membrane of these diseased fibres, giving strong support to this hypothesis. In 1987, when the gene responsible for Duchenne dystrophy was discovered and the missing gene product, dystrophin, was shown to be an important component of the muscle fibre membrane, these observations made 12 years earlier by Cullen and Fulthorpe were vindicated as revealing the nature of the process leading to muscle fibre breakdown.

As our work expanded it became clear that the group of laboratories in the top two floors of the rear wing of the Regional Centre would be inadequate to house the full team of workers whom we all envisaged would be needed to pursue our research with vigour. After Geoffrey

Pearce had succeeded in keeping dystrophic as well as normal human muscle alive in culture for some weeks (American workers had been culturing dystrophic muscle successfully for some years but this was the first time this had been done successfully in the UK) I reported this development at a meeting of the Newcastle branch of the Muscular Dystrophy Group, quite unaware that a reporter was present. These results were mentioned in a local newspaper, picked up by the nationals and then by the international media network, all of whom concluded, despite what we had said, that this was a major breakthrough. For days the telephone wires hummed, not least between my office and those of the MDA and MDAC; after a while the furore died down when the true significance of our findings became clear. My American colleagues and paymasters, who had often experienced overstatement by the media, were very understanding and supportive; but the publicity had one important effect in that soon afterwards the MDG received from some London lawyers a cheque for £50,000 from an anonymous donor, specifying that the sum should be spent on muscular dystrophy research in Newcastle under my supervision.

By this time the MDG (see Chapter 9) was making increasing headway, having become independent under Joan Vincent's direction. An effective National Council of parents and other interested laymen was established, as was a Scientific and Research Committee under the chairmanship of Professor John Cumings from Queen Square. Professor Nattrass was Chairman of the Group and National Council and I was the first Honorary Secretary. One member, Joe Patrick, a successful Birmingham businessman and founder of Patrick Motors, had a son, Andrew, who had died of Duchenne dystrophy. He established with a major capital sum the Patrick Trust which produced an increasing income, much of which he passed on to the Group to support its research programme. A quietly spoken, self-effacing but perspicacious and eternally kind man, he was one of the pillars of the Group's fund-raising activities in its early years and could always be relied upon whenever the Group found it difficult to fulfil any of its objectives. His surviving son, Alexander, who has carried on the family business and the tradition, followed his father on the National Council. As current Vice-Chairman of the Group he has been even more munificent in supporting the Group's research and patient care programme and in establishing the Joseph Patrick Memorial Trust in order to provide appliances and other patient aids such as, for example, electric wheelchairs for those unable to obtain them from the State. The Group made Joe Patrick an honorary Life Vice-President for a few years before his death, while Fred Nattrass became honorary Life President when he relinquished the chairmanship and I succeeded him in that office in 1971. The Group's earliest rented premises in Borough High Street in London soon proved inadequate and its headquarters, first in an old converted school in Macaulay Road, Clapham, and now in newer and more extensive premises nearby have been called Nattrass House.

Sadly after only a few years in office Joan Vincent died and Margaret Duval succeeded her. No UK charity can progress, particularly in fund-raising, without the support of some glitterati of stage and screen and of other notables including, whenever possible, royal patrons. Mrs Duval had family connections in the film business and invited the actor Richard Attenborough to host an event held in aid of muscular dystrophy research at a hospital in Carshalton where several young boys with Duchenne dystrophy were living. Richard Attenborough (Dickie to his friends) often recounts how deeply he was affected by seeing those cheerful young people in wheelchairs. Afterwards, on returning home, he saw his son kicking a football on Richmond Green and realized how fortunate he was not to have a child with dystrophy. He telephoned Mrs Duval and said that if there was anything he could do, she had only to ask; so began an era which ultimately led to Sir Richard's (as he now is) appointment to the Presidency of the Group. Despite the innumerable good causes with which he has been concerned, he has been indefatigable in his support of this charity and it is through many of his unremitting efforts that the Group's income has grown steadily. Later he was instrumental in persuading HRH Prince Philip, Duke of Edinburgh, to become Patron.

Ultimately Mrs Duval herself retired to be replaced by the cheerful, hard-working and energetic Hugo Walford and under his guidance the Group continued to prosper. Then in 1973 Paul Walker, Executive Director for 19 years, was appointed. His extraordinary energy, his efficiency, his tireless pursuit of the Group's interests throughout the length and breadth of the country and abroad and his ebullient advocacy of the Group's work, combined with an exceptional entrepreneurship, made the Group into one of the most effective and successful of the 'second-line' medical charities in the UK with an annual income, as I write, of about five million pounds. But the Group has also owed much of its success not only to the innumerable fund-raising activities organized from headquarters but to the dedicated work of the many branches throughout the United Kingdom which still succeed in raising about half its income. Haig Gudenian, a distinguished journalist, was for many years chairman of the Group's Management Committee and deservedly received the OBE to acknowledge these services. Sadly he died several years ago but was succeeded by the equally efficient and dedicated Lloyd Brooks, also the Group's treasurer. The Group was also very well served not only by John Cumings, the long-serving chairman of its Research Committee, but by Sir Andrew Huxley, the distinguished physiologist and Nobel Prize winner who succeeded him and only relinquished the post when he became President of the Royal Society. Professor Joe Smith of Birmingham followed him for a while and I then assumed the chair, but was myself succeeded by Professor Peter Lachmann, the outstanding Cambridge immunologist who in turn resigned on being elected President of the Royal College of Pathologists. The present chairman is Professor Arthur Buller, formerly professor of physiology in Bristol and later Chief Scientist at the Department of Health, who, after retiring from the latter post, was for several years the Group's immensely capable Research and Development Director.

In late 1964 the Group was faced with the decision as to how to spend the anonymous donation it had just received with conditions attached; with the advice of my colleagues I submitted to the Research Committee and National Council a proposal that we should build, adjacent to the Regional Centre (unfortunately with the consequential loss of many car parking spaces) a block of muscular dystrophy research laboratories with two floors, including an animal house, an animal operating theatre, facilities for electromyography (not previously available at the NGH) and additional rooms for histochemistry, histopathology of muscle and nerve, tissue culture and experimental neurophysiology. While my neurosurgical colleagues at the NGH (and others) had to be persuaded of the importance of this development, and while there were initially some objections from the adjacent Maternity Unit, the plans were eventually accepted and the Group awarded a grant of £32,000. The Hospital Management Committee agreed to cover the cost of services and maintenance, so that the project went swiftly ahead.

The official opening was on Wednesday, 9 March 1966; it had been intended that Dickie Attenborough would perform the ceremony but at the last moment he was prevented from doing so by filming commitments overseas so that Haig Gudenian officiated. David Barwick had now become senior registrar in clinical neurophysiology and had been followed as a clinical research associate by Dr David Gardner-Medwin, while Dr K. F. A. Ross had joined us in 1962 as a senior research associate in order to take over the tissue culture work from Geoffrey Pearce. Keith Ross was a most able, if mildly eccentric, cell biologist and an expert on phase contrast and interference microscopy, on which topic he had written with a colleague a definitive monograph. Ron Pennington, too, had been joined by Dorothy Park (subsequently Dorothy Hart-Mercer), while Alan McComas had recruited the first of a series of PhD students, Dr Sahib Mossawy from Iraq (who even in the midst of the Gulf crisis of 1990–91 sent us a Christmas card from the Department of Physiology in Baghdad in which he had worked since leaving Newcastle).

Our research programme continued to expand but in 1966 the MDA, while agreeing to continue support at the existing level, felt unable to offer additional funds and the MDAC, after supporting us for eight years, notified us that because of a change in policy and shortage of income, they would no longer support work outside Canada. I therefore applied to the Medical Research Council (MRC) for a project grant as the funds then being raised by the MDG were insufficient to support an expanded programme in Newcastle. Indeed in 1966 the Group's total expenditure spread over three principal research centres (Newcastle, Queen Square and Glasgow) and in funding 12 project grants elsewhere was £83,000. To my surprise, I was invited in May 1966 to give a lunch-time talk on our research programme to the MRC's Clinical Research Board. After a lengthy discussion and many searching questions (not least from Professor Alastair Currie of Edinburgh, with whom I subsequently served on Council and who became a good friend) it seemed that the talk was well received. The Council awarded me a grant to cover the salaries of two medically-qualified research assistants (Peter Hudgson and David Gardner-Medwin), one chief technician, two senior technicians, one technician and one secretary, with up to £1,000 per annum to pay for chemicals, animals, food, photographic materials and travelling expenses for patients. It was awarded for five years from 1 October 1966 and later became a formal programme grant which was renewed twice, from 1971–76 and from 1976–81, so that financial support for our programme was again secure. [See Appendix, p. 318.]

Yet again, however, as my colleagues developed and extended their work, even our new laboratories became increasingly overcrowded. We concluded that it would be feasible to build an extension on to the Dystrophy Research Laboratories so as to rationalize our facilities and to provide more space for the new research fellows who were joining our team, and some limited laboratory and desk space for the many visiting fellows who were coming to Newcastle from different parts of the world. The MDG gave us a grant of £38,000 for the capital costs of the extension and in 1970 the new accommodation was opened, this time by Sir Richard Attenborough. We took advantage of his visit to organize a major fund-raising ball at the Mayfair Ballroom at which he and Sheila were guests of honour and which raised a substantial sum for the Group. It had also become clear that in addition to our ageing Siemens Elmiskop I high resolution electron microscope, we needed a lower resolution instrument for our ultrastructural studies; in 1968 the MDG gave us a grant to purchase a Zeiss EM9 machine which was an invaluable supplement to our facilities.

While I shall describe in Chapter 14 some of my experiences when lecturing and teaching overseas, in 1969 I had an experience which demonstrated that morality pays. Professor Victor McKusick, head of medicine and an internationally renowned clinical geneticist, organized a conference in Baltimore on inherited diseases of the neuromuscular system and invited me to deliver a paper, to which I readily agreed. I had just arrived there when I received a telephone call from Professor Labe Scheinberg (with whom I had worked three years earlier) asking me to go to New York to see a wealthy patient who was suffering from motor neurone disease but who wished to have a second opinion. Unfortunately the timing of my visit did not make this possible. However, the patient and his wife flew down to Baltimore and took a suite in the best hotel where I saw him in a consultation which lasted about one and a half hours. After I had confirmed the diagnosis, discussed the management and commented upon current research, the patient asked me to name my fee. Having just been awarded a personal chair in the University of Newcastle, I had relinquished private practice and had a whole-time contract; hence I said to the patient and his family that my contract did not allow me to receive fees. In saying so I had a feeling that perhaps I should remove my halo and polish it, but I left the patient and his family on excellent terms even though I had not been able to offer any really effective treatment; unfortunately, too, his condition was in an advanced stage and it was clear that he did not have long to live. In 1971 to my astonishment I received a warm and generous letter from the patient's widow enclosing a cheque for $10,000 and offering similar donations in each of the next two years to support research into motor neurone disease.

By this time David Barwick had been appointed as consultant in clinical neurophysiology while retaining three sessions in clinical neurology. David Gardner-Medwin had left to become a senior registrar in paediatrics with a view to becoming a consultant paediatric neurologist, and Walter Bradley, who had done some admirable experimental studies in muscle and nerve as a clinical research associate, had been appointed as a Wellcome Senior Research Fellow in Clinical Science. Dr J. B. Harris, who had joined us in 1967 in order to work with Alan McComas in neurophysiology had had a distinguished record of research in Bradford on the pharmacology and toxicology of the neuromuscular system. We had also recruited Margaret Johnson from the Department of Microbiology in Newcastle as a research associate in order to supervise our work in histochemistry. It seemed that the MRC had been pleased with the progress reports we had submitted, as in 1973 my supplementary application seeking a capital sum of £26,000 to replace our Siemens Elmiskop I electron microscope was successful and a Siemens 102 instrument was soon installed; the old machine was bought by Bernard Tomlinson for research use in his Institute of Pathology where the single machine then available for diagnostic work in microbiology was heavily committed. I had also submitted to the MRC in late 1969 a proposal to establish an MRC Unit for research into neuromuscular disease in our Muscular Dystrophy Laboratories, while suggesting as an alternative that if that application were unsuccessful Drs Pennington and McComas, key members of the team, might be offered external scientific research staff posts. The latter proposal was preferred by the Clinical Research Board which offered them each permanent appointments and went on to renew our programme grant for five years from 1971. A few years later, Alan McComas accepted the foundation chair of neurology at McMaster University, Hamilton, Ontario, but Ron Pennington held his MRC external staff appointment in Newcastle until retirement.

In 1974 a further small (and final) extension to the laboratories was added. This time we did not need to call upon MDG funds as a good friend and benefactor, the late Lionel Jacobson of Newcastle (originally Managing Director and Chairman of Jackson the Taylor and later of Montague Burton) gave us a substantial capital sum from the Ruth and Lionel Jacobson Trust; other sums came from various north-east charities and yet a further substantial figure was added by Joe Patrick of Birmingham. These, along with the unexpected American benefaction, allowed us to cover the cost of the extension which provided yet more accommodation for research associates and visitors and for the Group's national occupational therapy adviser and a family care officer.

As my commitments in Newcastle in clinical work, teaching and research continued to escalate, I was compelled to relinquish my responsibilities at Durham and Chester-le-Street which were taken over by Jack Foster. My fortnightly visits to Middlesbrough also ceased when in the 1960s Dr Michael Saunders was appointed as a consultant neurologist to Teesside. Later the Regional Hospital Board produced additional sessions at Sunderland, allowing Jack Foster to give up his responsibilities there. Peter Hudgson was appointed as a four-session consultant neurologist in Sunderland with two sessions in clinical neurology at the NGH and five as a principal research associate paid for from my research funds to enable him to continue his work in experimental neuropathology in our laboratories.

Meanwhile, some unforeseen changes occurring in the University were to have unexpected effects upon my subsequent career. In 1960 Henry Miller was awarded a personal honorary readership and I was made honorary lecturer in neurology. Two or three years later Henry was given a personal chair. The University had decided to establish a sub-department of Speech Studies in the Department of Education so as to offer an honours degree course in speech studies which would be coupled with registration with the College of Speech Therapists. The course was to be directed by the indefatigable Miss Muriel Morley whose work in the Department of Child Health on speech disorders in childhood and whose book on the topic had been widely acclaimed, both nationally and internationally. That course would clearly require substantial teaching in neurology and neuroscience and Miss Morley invited me to undertake the task. I had to say that my massive clinical commitments in Newcastle and throughout the region would make such a commitment impossible. The University soon recognized that it would be necessary to create a whole-time neurological post in order to provide the teaching required. A senior lecturer post was therefore established and David Shaw, lecturer in neurology at Queen Square and newly returned from the Mayo Clinic, where he had done some excellent work on cerebral vascular disease, was appointed and was given clinical facilities with Henry at the RVI.

Not long after Henry's personal chair was approved, Andrew Lowdon, Professor of Surgery and Dean of Medicine for over seven years, whose contributions to the Medical School had been outstanding, died unexpectedly and prematurely. After the usual consultations Henry was invited to become Dean and, on accepting the appointment, relinquished his extensive private practice so that the load of private work coming to me and Jack Foster quickly escalated. In 1967, as the Vice-Chancellor, Dr Charles Bosanquet was due to retire in 1968, the University established the usual committee to appoint his successor; Henry, as Dean of Medicine, was an *ex officio* member. After innumerable interviews and consultations, the post was offered to Professor Holder, Professor of Engineering at Oxford, who after careful consideration, turned it down. In the end the committee concluded that they should offer the appointment to Henry himself. While he accepted with some reluctance in view of his continuing commitment to neurology, he nevertheless took up the appointment in October 1968. Once again the University Council and Faculty of Medicine went through the lengthy process of selecting a Dean and eventually chose George Smart, Professor of Medicine. In the meantime, unknown to me Henry and George had jointly decided to recommend me for promotion to a personal chair in neurology and that appointment, too, was approved by the University Senate and Council in 1968. Increasingly, I had found the stress and load of work involved in part-time private practice oppressive, though I would never have wished to be without that very fruitful experience. Hence while my entire salary was provided by the NHS and not by the University, I decided that this was a convenient moment to relinquish my part-time contract and private practice in order to concentrate more fully on clinical work, teaching and research. But then, after fewer than three years in the appointment, George Smart decided to accept the Directorship of the British Postgraduate Medical Federation in London, so once again the Deanship was vacant.

Under the statutes of the University of Newcastle (taken over almost without modification from the University of Durham when Newcastle became independent in 1963) the Dean of Medicine holds an exceptionally powerful position, no doubt because the Faculty of Medicine was one of the oldest parts of Durham University, having been established in 1834 just two years after Durham University itself was founded (see Chapter 15). Unlike all other deans in the University who were elected by their respective faculties, the Dean of Medicine was, and indeed still is, appointed by a joint committee of Senate and Council which is required to consult opinion generally in the Medical Faculty and University before recommending an appointment. Hence the office is not an elected one and, again unlike other deanships in the University, it is for five years in the first instance and renewable.

This then was the process which began in late 1970 when George Smart had intimated that he would be leaving in 1971.

David Kerr, who had followed him in the chair of medicine, was nominated by the joint committee of Senate and Council to sound opinion in the Faculty. When, in early 1971, he came to see me at the General Hospital on a confidential matter, I was astounded to learn that there was a strong majority view in the Faculty that I should be invited to accept that office. The fact that this would mean that the University would have a Vice-Chancellor and a Dean who were both neurologists did not seem to concern my colleagues. Until a week or two earlier this possibility had not crossed my mind as I had hoped to be able to continue as a whole-time professor developing my teaching and research skills as well as my clinical work up to the time of retirement. Nevertheless the warmth of the invitation and the clear evidence of widespread support throughout the Medical Faculty and University was so strong that I felt I had no alternative but to accept and to consider how best to reorientate my life in view of the many new pressures which the appointment would invariably impose. I knew, for example, that quite apart from *ex officio* membership of Senate and Council, Senate Development Committee and many other major committees of the University and Medical Faculty, the Dean would also be the University's representative on the General Medical Council. I could not but feel concerned as to how I would interrelate these many commitments, especially since I had been appointed a year or two earlier as a member of a Medical Research Council Grants Committee and later of the Clinical Research Board on assuming the chairmanship of that committee.

I therefore looked forward to my new life with keen anticipation but also with some apprehension. Plainly a first essential was that I must be given a formal university appointment as Senate and Council were agreed that they could not have as Dean of Medicine a whole-time NHS employee. It was also clear that I must have some additional support in neurology because of my clinical, teaching and research commitments. By this time the research being done by Walter Bradley as Wellcome Senior Research Fellow in Clinical Science had been highly commended and he had also continued to develop his clinical expertise. His work on the pathology of peripheral nerve, on periodic paralysis, on myotonia and on the dystrophic mouse had won for him national acclaim and he was beginning to acquire an international reputation. I therefore negotiated with Henry Miller an arrangement whereby I would become Professor of Neurology and Dean of Medicine in the University, being paid for six sessions on the clinical professorial scale, while retaining five NHS sessions at the NGH. The University agreed to establish a mirror image A + B appointment for a senior lecturer in neurology who would have five university sessions and the six in the NHS which I was relinquishing. Eventually Walter Bradley was appointed to that post as joint senior lecturer/consultant. Arrangements were also made to establish a second NHS consultant post in clinical neurophysiology at the NGH in view of the increasing demand upon David Barwick's services, and Peter Fawcett, who had followed David as senior registrar, was appointed. At much the same time the University, in the phase of post-Robbins expansion, had decided to establish taught MSc courses in clinical psychology and in educational psychology, each requiring neurological input. The demand for neurological consultative services throughout the region continued to increase; requests had come from Ashington, Carlisle and West Cumberland for such consultative sessions. Hence further A + B (joint university/NHS) consultant appointments were established at the RVI. Dr Niall Cartlidge was appointed to the first of these and took over Jack Foster's Dryburn and Chester-le-Street commitments. Eventually Dr David Bates was appointed to a second post, also to work at the RVI but to help with teaching in the MSc courses in which Dr Cartlidge had been involved from the beginning, while also giving clinical services to Carlisle and West Cumberland.

As our research programme continued to expand, David Gardner-Medwin was appointed as the first consultant paediatric neurologist in Newcastle but continued to contribute effectively to clinical and genetic research and to supervise our children's neuromuscular clinic, while Peter Hudgson shared with Walter Bradley supervision of our adult neuromuscular clinic and continued to work on the histology, histochemistry and electron microscopy of muscle with Margaret Johnson and Mike Cullen. A most able overseas visitor who joined us for two years was Dr Frank Mastaglia from Perth in Western Australia, a well trained and industrious clinical neurologist who demonstrated a flair for laboratory research comparable to that displayed by Walter Bradley and Peter Hudgson. Malcolm Campbell had now been appointed as a Wellcome Senior Research Fellow. Later, when Malcolm became a consultant neurologist in Bristol, we obtained yet another such fellowship for Dr Russell Lane, a first class honours graduate in medicine in Newcastle who, after working with Allen Roses in Durham, North Carolina, USA, did some outstanding work with Ron Pennington on creatine kinase binding to the muscle fibre membrane in health and disease. Ultimately (after I left Newcastle) he was appointed to a consultant post in neurology at Charing Cross Hospital in London where he continues to work on neuromuscular disease and has a particular interest in motor neurone disease. Yet another important recruit to our research staff was Dr Clarke Slater who had done a PhD with Sir Bernard

Katz at University College in London and who later had worked with Dr Sid Brenner at the Laboratory for Molecular Biology in Cambridge. A first-rate experimental neurophysiologist, Clarke Slater's expertise, working in harness with John Harris, helped to maintain the viability and originality of our experimental neurophysiology section after Alan McComas left for McMaster. Later too, after Keith Ross had left in 1973 to become Senior Lecturer in Anatomy at the University of Aberdeen, he was succeeded first by Dr Roger Parsons and then in 1979 by Dr Marion Ecob (later Ecob-Prince) whose special expertise in tissue culture and in combined cultures of nerve and muscle added a new dimension to the work of the department.

In the mid-1970s the Muscular Dystrophy Association of America had at last concluded that with the increasing success of the Muscular Dystrophy Group of Great Britain in fund-raising and in supporting research, it must reluctantly discontinue our grant. However, by now our centre grant from the MDG had increased to almost £200,000 a year and, with our programme grant from the MRC and project grants obtained by various members of the department from the MRC, Wellcome Trust or other bodies, the research income of the Department of Neurology for work on neuromuscular disease alone was over £330,000 per annum. Additional were the grants which David Shaw, Niall Cartlidge and David Bates were obtaining for work at the RVI on cerebral vascular disease, head injury and other topics. In the mid-1970s, therefore, when neurology was still a part of the University Department of Medicine but when its research grant income exceeded that of the remainder of the department, the University agreed that neurology should become an independent department with its own modest departmental and departmental equipment grants. Despite the fact that I was then Dean, my colleagues insisted that I should assume the headship. This did result in my having once, as Dean, to write to myself as head of the Department of Neurology to point out that my departmental grant was overspent; I did so with tongue in cheek when writing to other heads of departments who were in a similar situation!

Two other unexpected events were to transform our academic prospects. In 1973 an advertisement appeared in the national medical and scientific press to the effect that the National Fund for Research into Crippling Disease (formerly the Polio Research Fund) wished to endow two research chairs in UK universities in order to allow them to appoint individuals who would promote research into crippling disease in childhood. This seemed too good an opportunity to miss; after some speedy consultations with the University and with my neurological colleagues (who were anxious about the potential pressure which might be imposed upon our clinical facilities and accommodation if someone from outside Newcastle were to be appointed to such a chair) I submitted a detailed application and eventually learned from Duncan Guthrie of the National Fund that 39 applications had been received. In my application I summarized work previously done and our current and proposed future programme of research in the Muscular Dystrophy Laboratories, suggesting that subject to the agreement of the Fund but more particularly of the University, Walter Bradley would be an outstanding candidate for such a chair. I also pointed out that the sum of £200,000 would allow the University to endow through its Development Trust not only a chair but also a non-medical senior lecturership and a secretarial post. Eventually, I was delighted to learn that our application was the first choice of the assessors, who included the Presidents of almost all the Royal Colleges. The second chair was offered to the University of Nottingham to establish a chair in experimental orthopaedics.

Henry Miller, as Vice-Chancellor, was delighted to learn of our success, but the Registrar, Ernest Bettenson, a man for whom I had the highest regard and whose judgement I always respected, was not best pleased because I had nominated in the application potential holders of the two university posts to be endowed if our application succeeded. This, in his view, ran contrary to the University's firm policy relating to the establishment and filling of chairs and senior lecturerships. Nevertheless, after much discussion and negotiation, the University agreed to establish a Chair of Experimental Neurology and a non-medical senior lecturership and to establish committees to interview known candidates. Walter Bradley was eventually appointed to the chair and John Harris to the senior lecturership; for the first time we were able to establish a university secretarial post in the department, alongside the appointment in the Muscular Dystrophy Laboratories supported by our MRC programme grant.

My own secretarial support had been provided by Rosemary Allan who came to the Medical School in April 1960 as assistant secretary to Shirley Whillis in order to work for David Barwick, Geoffrey Pearce and Ron Pennington. She subsequently moved to the RVI in August that year to work for me after Shirley resigned following her marriage to Rob Uldhall. Joining the department when she was only 19 years of age, Rosemary became a consummately efficient secretary who cheerfully and readily shouldered an enormous burden of work and who regularly turned out typed manuscripts of outstanding quality more rapidly than any other secretary I have known. Not only was she very efficient in that regard but she also assumed much of the burden of departmental administration. As my literary work increased, I came to rely upon her more and more, as in preparing a chapter or scientific paper she was much more efficient in listing and checking the references than I had ever been. She continued to work for me on our MDG grant in Newcastle until we left together in 1983 to move to Green College and she is still working with me in my retirement in Norham Gardens, Oxford. After more than 30 years of working together, I owe her a debt which is impossible to overstate.

Having now been able at last to establish two university posts in our research laboratories, we could redeploy the appointment vacated by Walter Bradley. Two of his university sessions contributed to the new A + B appointments at the RVI held by Niall Cartlidge and David Bates, but four went to Peter Hudgson so that he became an established senior lecturer in the department while continuing to hold NHS sessions relating to his clinical work in Newcastle and Sunderland. Since then another consultant has been appointed in Sunderland and Peter has contracted back into the NGH while continuing to hold an A + B appointment.

Another important development was that I had come to know Mr William Leech, the noted Newcastle builder who, beginning in a very modest way before the 1939–45 war, had gradually built up a very large building empire. Most of the houses that he had built for rent before the war, and those which he later sold, had been sold leasehold. Income from the ground rents all went into a charitable trust which had increased enormously in value through wise investment. As a dedicated Christian, William's first charitable benefactions went to five Christian charities, including the Church Missionary Society and the Methodist Missionary Society. In the end it is estimated that between £20 and £30 million were devoted by him to these good causes. After he consulted me as a patient, however, we became friendly and I raised with him the possibility that he might consider supporting medicine and the University, a suggestion which he willingly accepted. His first such act was to provide an annual grant of £3,000 as a neurological research and travelling fund under my administration; this was an invaluable addition to our departmental funding as it allowed us to invite academic visitors from the UK and from overseas to come to Newcastle to address our research discussion group. It also helped to defray the travelling expenses of members of the department who were invited speakers at various symposia in the UK and overseas at a time when NHS and university travel funds were becoming increasingly scarce. As time went by William's contributions to the University increased steadily. As Dean I pointed out to him several important gaps in university funding, specifically in relation to the academic acknowledgement of emerging medical and surgical specialties. I also stressed the difficulty we all had in finding secure career posts for scientists wishing to work in clinical departments. Hence William and his fellow trustees agreed to establish by endowment several new readerships and lecturerships in the University in subjects such as neurosurgery, rheumatology, transplantation surgery, renal medicine, etc. Of especial importance to our department was his agreement to establish three lecturerships in clinical science to be held by scientists without medical qualifications. These were advertised to be filled by open competition within the University; I was not unnaturally delighted when two of the posts were filled by members of the Department of Neurology, Clarke Slater and Margaret Johnson, each of whom was holding an appointment funded on 'soft' money.

In the latter years of my Deanship I became a trustee of the William Leech Property Trust and we made an agreement through which a designated percentage (25%) of the income of that Trust went to the Development Trust to be deployed as the University saw fit, but largely to establish appointments in the Medical Faculty. I was very pleased to learn after I left Newcastle in 1983 that my successor as Dean (David Shaw, who had become my Associate Dean and who succeeded me when I decided not to consider reappointment in 1981) had persuaded the Faculty to agree (with acclamation) that one of the major blocks of the new Medical School, opened in 1985, should be called 'The Leech Building'.

William Leech, who had followed his father into window cleaning in his youth, was a man of simple tastes but a very astute businessman and a kindly person whom I became proud to call a friend. The contributions that he made to innumerable charitable causes in his beloved North East are beyond praise. Betty and I were delighted to have been able to attend his 90th birthday party in his beautiful home near Morpeth in July 1990. For several years I and other admirers had striven to obtain for him a national honour. We were pleased when he received the CBE in the 1970s but felt that he deserved more. It was therefore a particular delight that he received a knighthood in the 1991 New Year's Honours List, though sadly this was conferred eight days after he died at the age of 90. At least his widow, Dot, was able to go to Buckingham Palace to receive the insignia and to enjoy the privilege of becoming a Lady. Long before these national honours were conferred the University, on my nomination, awarded William an honorary Doctorate of Civil Law in 1975. This was a distinction of which he was exceptionally proud, just as I was proud to deliver an address at his memorial service in St Nicholas' Cathedral in March 1991.

To William Leech and to innumerable other benefactors in the North East, not least Ruth Jacobson who continued to support the department after her husband Lionel had died, and to the many other local trusts and foundations who supported us, the department owed a very great debt.

We were, however, disappointed when in 1977 Walter Bradley, who had been a trifle unsettled, decided to leave for the United States. While he had continued to contribute very effectively to our departmental research programme, I believe he felt the tenure of a research chair to be a little restrictive; while he wished to continue in research, he also sought a wider role in teaching, clinical work and administration. Thus he accepted a professorship of neurology at Tufts University Medical

School in Boston, before later moving to Burlington, Vermont, and later still to the headship of the Department of Neurology at the University of Miami. Hence the chair of experimental neurology fell vacant. We were fortunate in being able to attract from Australia Frank Mastaglia who had been such an effective visiting research worker in the department a few years earlier. He in turn continued to develop and expand our research programme but after three years in Newcastle decided that he must return to Australia where he has continued to contribute effectively to neuromuscular research, not least in relation to the drug-induced myopathies; he now holds a chair of neurology in Perth. Yet again, therefore, we went through the appointing process. In view of his growing maturity of approach, continuing originality and powers of leadership, John Harris, the non-medical senior lecturer, was appointed to the chair; he has been a great success; since then he has been appointed head of the newly-developed School of Neuroscience in the University of Newcastle. His accession to the chair allowed us to appoint a clinical lecturer; Douglas Turnbull, who was developing an outstanding programme of research into mitochondrial disease, was appointed. Since then he has become nationally and internationally recognized as an authority on this topic. These research contributions, in addition to his personal qualities, fully justified his appointment to the chair of neurology in Newcastle in early 1990, following the retirement of David Shaw who, before becoming Dean, had been promoted from senior lecturer to personal professor; after his retirement the University agreed for the first time to convert his post into an established chair of clinical neurology.

A highlight of these exciting and fruitful years was the International Congress on Neuromuscular Diseases which we organized in Newcastle in September 1974. This was the third such congress, the two previous meetings having been held in Milan in 1969 and in Perth, Western Australia in 1971. It proved to be an exceptionally memorable event. The entire organization was undertaken by ourselves with the aid of our departmental staff including not only the doctors and scientists but also the secretaries and technicians. Betty assembled a formidable and effective ladies' committee of departmental wives and Rosemary Allan played a key and crucial administrative role. His Royal Highness, the Duke of Edinburgh, as Patron of the Muscular Dystrophy Group graciously agreed to be Patron. Fred Nattrass was appointed Honorary President; the Duke of Northumberland, Richard Attenborough, William Leech and many local and national notables became Vice-Patrons; I was Chairman and Walter Bradley Organizing Secretary. Funds came not only through sponsorship from the University and the Health Authorities and from various drug companies, but also from a number of trusts and foundations and from the Muscular Dystrophy Group and other muscular dystrophy associations throughout the world. As we did it all ourselves, administrative costs were exceptionally low and we even made a small profit for our departmental research funds. The effects which inflation has had upon the economy since that time can be judged from the fact that we charged a £20 registration fee and the excellent banquet in the elegant hall of the Civic Centre cost £5 inclusive of wine; we thought at the time that it was pretty expensive! Our overseas guests, however, were astonished at the cheapness of the meals and social events. I was able to persuade the University to hold an honorary degree congregation at the opening of the Congress when the Chancellor, the Duke of Northumberland, conferred honorary Doctorates of Civil Law (DCL) on Fred Nattrass and Richard Attenborough and an honorary DSc on Raymond Adams. That congregation was followed by a piano recital by our noted Professor of Music, Denis Matthews (formerly a concert pianist of great repute) who performed superbly despite momentarily losing his way while playing Beethoven's Pathetique Sonata. He and his wife, the Duke and Duchess, the honorary graduates, senior University officers and some of our principal overseas guests joined us for a champagne party at Beechfield Road afterwards, before a splendid dinner at the Airport Hotel.

Fortunately the weather was kind; although this was mid-September, the ambient temperature was warm and the sun shone from a cloudless sky, so that the ladies' trips to Bamburgh, to the Roman Wall, to Wallington and to many other famous and popular sights of Northumberland were hugely successful. So, too, were the forays of most of the participants and their spouses to mediaeval banquets at Lumley Castle and at Seaton Delaval Hall where the master of ceremonies, Bill Midgley, and his acolytes sang superbly and where Betty and I were 'Baron and Baroness'. That event brought back memories of an earlier outing to Seaton Delaval to which we had invited several overseas visitors as our guests. On that occasion we were again Baron and Baroness; Bill Midgley said that he hoped that in my little speech after dinner I would mention the places from which our visitors had come. I therefore said that as Baron it was my privilege to welcome guests from Los Angeles, Rio de Janeiro, Buenos Aires, Beirut, New Delhi and Perth (Western Australia), to which a Geordie voice from the end of the table loudly proclaimed 'I'm from Cullercoats meself'. The social events of the congress were also enlivened by a superb performance of 'Joseph and his Amazing Technicolour Dreamcoat' at the University Theatre. This was the first time that some of our overseas guests had been exposed to the music of Andrew Lloyd Webber; the performance left a lasting impression.

Many of our visitors, even including some from the UK who had never before ventured to the North East, were greatly impressed by the architecture, friendliness and even by the restaurants of Newcastle, as well as by the beauties of the surrounding countryside which came as a revelation. One other tale is worth recounting. Peter Hudgson had been put in charge of transport arrangements, ordering buses to take participants to and from the hotels and halls of residence to the locations where the scientific sessions and social events were being held. A few weeks earlier Gianni Meola from Milan had come to work with us and was just beginning to improve his English. On the first morning of scientific sessions Gianni was greatly impressed not only by the weather but also by the quality of the science. Bubbling with enthusiasm, he came into the University Refectory for lunch where he met Jack Foster's sister who was there as a guest. Turning to her he said 'What a f...ing lovely day!', which he quickly followed up by saying 'We've heard some f...ing good papers this morning'. Jack's sister Eleanor quickly suppressed a smile; however, she collared Jack and said 'For heaven's sake get hold of Gianni and tell him that that's not polite English terminology'. When Jack explained the position, Gianni was mortified but said that having heard Dr Hudgson talking on the telephone to the bus company about transport a few days earlier, he had thought that the word was a part of everyday English parlance as Dr Hudgson used it all the time!

Of the scientific sessions little needs to be said except that the planning and organization went like clockwork. All of my colleagues, and especially David Gardner-Medwin and Walter Bradley, deserve enormous credit for their hard work and efficient administration. I also remember well Henry Miller's speech at the banquet in which he said that it had always been known that John Walton was a muscle man, whereas he was a brain man himself! At the end of the week Mel Moss, along with many others who attended from the Muscular Dystrophy Association of America, told us that this was the best organized congress they had ever attended and that it was the congress to end all such events! Not unnaturally, such comments filled us all with pride, having coped with all of the needs, requirements and even the demands of 700 active scientific participants and over 350 accompanying persons. Betty decided, even at the end of an exhausting week, to have all the departmental workers round to our house on the Saturday after our visitors had departed for a 'thank-you party' before the glow of achievement faded. Since then of course, these international congresses have grown steadily and the last one in Munich in 1990 attracted well over 2,000 participants.

At other times, too, the social activities of the department were not neglected. There were innumerable departmental parties, both large and small, lunches in the conference room of the Regional Centre when we entertained overseas guests or dinners for visiting lecturers in the Alnwick Room at the University Refectory; during one such event Henry Miller and Macdonald Critchley had a tremendous verbal battle in which honours were eventually even. On another occasion when the paediatricians were dining in a private room next door and emerged with girlish giggles into the corridor as we sat over our brandy and coffee, Jack Foster said 'Ha, ha—play time!'. I hope and believe that the department developed an exceptional reputation for hospitality and for entertaining visitors from both the UK and overseas which we were all determined to maintain. Betty and I invited senior members of the department and overseas visitors each year to join us in July or August for a day at Ivy Cottage. Weather and tide permitting, we would visit Holy Island in the morning with lunch at the Seafield Restaurant in Seahouses and a visit to the Chillingham wild cattle in the afternoon, followed (if time allowed) by a sharp climb up the steep incline of Ros Hill, from which one can see one of the finest views in Northumberland. From the top of the hill one looks down over the castles on Holy Island and Bamburgh and all the Farne Islands are visible. On a clear day Dunstanburgh Castle, Norham Castle, Coquet Island and Alnwick can also be seen. There is a plaque at the summit which says that Earl Grey, when Foreign Secretary, loved to sit at that point to contemplate the beauties around him. Only after we had continued this programme for a few years (often finishing with a game of cricket in the garden at Ivy Cottage) did I once overhear a registrar (not Peter Hudgson this time) asking an overseas visitor whether he had received 'the Ros Hill medal' yet.

Parties at Christmas time were also the order of the day. Henry normally held a very large cocktail party at Akenside Terrace on his birthday on 15th December, while Betty and I customarily arranged our departmental Christmas party at Beechfield Road on the first Saturday in January. Invariably we served cocktail sundries and a punch which some called delightful but lethal! It was based on Merrydown vintage cider with the addition of dry and sweet white wine and varying amounts of brandy and soda water, with fruit floating on the top. This palatable but powerful beverage often meant that long after the normal cocktail hour had passed, members of the department hung around until late in the evening consuming what was left of our sausage rolls and other titbits and ending up with a sing-song around the grand piano. Having given up smoking cigarettes in view of medical evidence in the 1950s, I then turned to a pipe but that too went in the early 1970s when as Dean I felt I should show an example, especially after a departmental dinner at which I was the only smoker. Our parties steadily grew over the 15 years or so that we held them, until finally in the mid 1970s when departmental commitments began to conflict with some of my entertaining responsibilities as Dean, we were reluctantly compelled to call it a day. I am sure that our decision to give up was not precipitated by the occasion when I saw a senior colleague leering suggestively at 15-year-old Judy on the stairs nor by Ann's offhand comment (at 18) that she was weary of life and thought it was about time that she had an affair with an old man like Alan J..... or Peter H.....! The last such party attracted some 120 people and Beechfield Road was bursting at the seams.

Such events, like other sightseeing trips we arranged for visitors, including departmental trips to the Farne Islands and to the Roman Wall, live in the memory as part of the ethos of the Newcastle Department of Neurology. While my increasing responsibilities when I became Dean, as well as the overseas visits in which I was inevitably involved, along with my growing national responsibilities with the BMA, GMC and RSM, all eroded the amount of time I was able to spend in the department, these years of immersion in neurology were among the happiest of my life.

As time went by our children matured steadily. All were average performers academically at school and continued to be very different in personality. Ann, the eldest, was generally cheerful and outgoing though her outward calmness and laissez-faire attitude often concealed a good deal of suppressed anxiety. Judy was also pretty cheerful but was also subject to occasional outbursts of acute anxiety tinged with anger which probably replaced the temper tantrums of her early childhood. Ann's attitude towards work was generally cavalier; she enjoyed life to the full and only did, under pressure, a sufficient amount of school work to enable her to achieve the minimum results required to undertake any objective upon which she had set her heart. Judy, by contrast, was more conscientious and hard-working but often became anxious about her school work and seemed to have a particular antipathy towards biology, a subject which caused her great concern. Ann's teenage years were much more traumatic, at least so far as we were concerned, than Judy's, though both girls at times demonstrated features of adolescent rebellion. Ann, however, went through the phase of peroxiding her hair or alternatively back-combing it to such an extent that it looked like a tangled beehive. She it was who terrified us by going off when 13 as a pillion passenger with an 18-year-old boyfriend on a motor scooter, and she all too often defied the rules we attempted to impose by returning home later at night from parties than we had prescribed, little realizing the many hours that Betty and I spent in Dilston Terrace standing in my darkened study to gaze out of the window awaiting her return.

Academically there was a major hiccup so far as she was concerned when the time came for her to transfer from the Newcastle Central High School junior department to the senior school. Girls who performed exceptionally well in the senior school entrance examination were invited to attend for interview to see whether they might be considered for a free place. We always knew that she had a flair for English and many of the essays and poems which she wrote as a 10-year-old seemed to us of exceptional quality. We were delighted (and not a little surprised) when she was called for interview as we had never anticipated that she was good enough to be considered for a free place. That surprise soon turned, however, to anger when I was summoned to see the headmistress, the formidable Miss Belton, who began by saying that we must have concluded that Ann had done very well in the examination. She went on to say that she had in fact submitted exceptionally good English papers; however, at the time the interviews were arranged the mathematics papers had not all been marked and in those she had failed badly. In the light of that performance, Miss Belton proposed that she should stay down in the junior school for an extra year. Not unnaturally I challenged vigorously what seemed to me to be an extraordinary decision; after a rather contentious discussion she eventually agreed that Ann would be given a further maths examination two months later and that if she succeeded in passing that, she would after all join her friends in the senior school. There followed a few weeks of hectic revision with a little private coaching, after which she passed her test and moved on to the senior school with her friends.

Later she went on to pass a sufficient number of 'O' and 'A' level examinations to achieve her objective of being accepted for Dorset House College of Occupational Therapy in Oxford, along with her closest friend, Gillian Lough. From early in her senior school career she had decided that she wanted to work in a hospital and did some part-time work as an orderly over one Christmas period at the RVI. However, she felt that even if she was good enough academically to become a doctor (which she doubted) the course was far too long for her as she felt sure that she would wish to get married long before it ended. Nursing she thought was too much like hard work and physiotherapy too much 'jolly hockey sticks'; hence occupational therapy seemed the perfect choice. She enjoyed her course in Oxford immensely (and especially her social life with forays into many of the colleges) and apparently performed competently, qualifying after the standard three-year course. Betty and I were pretty shocked by seeing the comparative squalor of the basement flat in which she and three others lived in Warnborough Road, though I must confess that when, many years later, we ourselves moved to Oxford and saw some of the private student accommodation available for rent in the city, we realized that hers was not too bad after all.

Ann inevitably had a succession of boyfriends during her adolescent phase and both she and Judy enjoyed several overseas holidays with the Children's International Summer Village organization; reciprocal arrangements with that organization meant that we from time to time accommodated for two or three weeks German, Norwegian, Swedish and French girls in our home, an arrangement which certainly added a component of liveliness to our domestic life.

Teenage parties, too, presented a real challenge and the studio room on the top floor at Beechfield Road could not possibly have been more ideal for that purpose. After the first of these which Ann had organized when some 60 or 70 youngsters foregathered in our house at a weekend, we learned a salutary lesson. We had provided beer, cider and soft drinks, as well as eats, but when we came to clear up the ravages next morning we found empty half bottles of whisky, vodka and gin strewn around and it was clear that many of the party-goers had brought their own refreshment. Subsequently it was our rule that whenever Ann or Judy held such a party, some of the bigger boys were pressganged as doorkeepers, first to repel gatecrashers and secondly to search the youngsters coming in and to remove bottles of hard liquor which they were able to retrieve on leaving. Fortunately the succession of parties, organized first by Ann and later by Judy (though less often by Christopher, who was away at school for much of the time) resulted in very little damage or disruption and in no untoward incidents. The girls went through a phase when, according to them, they 'lost face' if it was known that a parent was in the house. On one notable occasion when Betty, Judy and Chris were at Detchant, Ann locked me into my consulting room throughout the evening, saying 'Daddy, I don't want anybody to know you're in the house, but I'll be glad to know you're there, just in case there's trouble'. She provided me with chicken and salad and a bottle of wine on a tray so that I could be suitably refreshed throughout the evening while the party continued. She even had the foresight to lock the doors of all the bedrooms and to present me with the keys for safe-keeping until the party was over. There was even one less traumatic occasion when, in accordance with an ephemeral craze, a party was actually held in the garage. Our top floor studio was a godsend and a year or two later one of Judy's boyfriends painted a remarkable mural covering one of the walls, an unusual piece of art which was widely admired. Even excluding party nights, the room was, so the girls told me, invaluable for courting purposes, though there was a stage when each of the girls entertaining their boyfriends there were regularly interrupted by Christopher who extorted significant financial contributions as a reward for refraining from spying on their amorous activities.

While my busy professional life meant, as I mentioned earlier, that none of the children felt themselves as close to me as perhaps they might have wished, they each in their different ways confided regularly in Betty and found her support and counsel invaluable. I nevertheless remember one occasion when Ann, determined to shock when about 18, came down to breakfast one morning saying 'I felt awful when I woke up this morning; I felt quite sick; for one awful moment I thought I might be pregnant'. The appropriate riposte was, of course, to say, as I did 'Oh yes, dear' and to take another spoonful of cornflakes. I thought, and she knew, that she was not intending her remark to be taken at all seriously, and happily there were other occasions when we could enjoy that kind of friendly banter.

The quality of the education which both Ann and Judy received at the Newcastle Central High School was, I believe, excellent. Inevitably, however, even in their early years of comparative innocence, despite our faltering attempts to offer education about 'the facts of life', they were each exposed even in that school to some of those crudities which constantly surface at times in every educational system. Ann at about eight told us that one of the girls had passed on to her a poem about Davy Crockett who milked a cow when he was only three; he pulled on the tail instead of the tit and all he got was a bucket of s..t. As she related this to us at supper table, we each had the greatest of difficulty in keeping a straight face before explaining to her the indelicacy of her comments. And Judy at 11 (or perhaps 12) was discovered with, in her school satchel, a copy of *Lady Chatterley's Lover* in a cover of *What Katy Did* at 6d. a fortnight. That reminded me irresistibly of the review published in *Field and Stream* which said that that book did not give a typical pen-portrait of the life of the usual British gamekeeper. Some wag said that the question was not so much whether one would give the book to one's daughters but whether one would give it to one's gamekeeper.

One day in November (I think in 1965) I had to fly to the United States to lecture and teach and Betty drove me to RAF Ouston which was serving as a temporary airport while Newcastle Airport was being developed and extended. On the way back a heavy snow storm (very unusual for November) developed but Betty got safely home and put her car in the garage. Almost immediately she was approached by Ann, who a month or so earlier had proudly passed her driving test and who asked whether she might possibly borrow the car to go to Fenham to see her friend, Gillian. With some reluctance in view of the weather conditions, Betty agreed. Unfortunately the snow continued to fall and on the way back, coming along Grandstand Road across the Town Moor, Ann braked, skidded and the car ran off the road, fortunately between two trees, breaking through a fence on to the Moor. There, in the snow, a young man (Ian McNeil) was practising golf, a circumstance which has always struck us as a little odd. Nevertheless, he came to her assistance and although the radiator of the car was punctured, they were able to drive the mile or so back to Beechfield Road where he, standing behind her, clearly had a major effect in assuaging Betty's wrath. Subsequently a friendship beginning in these rather inauspicious circumstances flowered; and eventually Ann and Ian became engaged and were married on 4 January 1969. Sadly my father had died a few months earlier and was not able to see the marriage of his eldest grandchild, but my mother had recovered sufficiently from the stroke she suffered the day after his funeral to be there. Ian, the son of a police inspector from Cumberland, had taken a degree in economics in Newcastle before becoming a chartered accountant with Price Waterhouse in the Newcastle office. Subsequently they moved after the wedding to London, first to a tiny flat in Islington, later to a series of maisonettes in Barnet and ultimately to an attractive detached house in Brookmans Park, while Ian worked first as a management consultant for Price Waterhouse at the London office and later for the merchant bank Keyser Ullman, before being head-hunted by Chase Manhattan and moving to their bank in the City.

Their wedding in January 1969 was a splendid occasion. We had arranged originally that they would be married at the Church of the Holy Name in Jesmond (Ian had been brought up as a devout Roman Catholic) and had had the invitations and orders of service printed. But the wedding had been arranged initially by a young priest and when the senior priest (who had been ill) returned, he refused to allow the marriage to proceed since Ann was a Methodist. Fortunately, through the good offices of our friend Dr Merlin Marshall (himself a Catholic) we were able quickly to rearrange the event (with new invitations printed at short notice) at St Mary's Roman Catholic Cathedral, where Canon Murray even invited our Methodist minister to participate in the service. The only minor snag on a splendid day was that the introit chosen by Ann and Ian, namely the well-known Widor Toccata which Betty had often played, was quite beyond the capabilities of the Cathedral organist who played it at a funereal pace. Fortunately the weather was brilliantly sunny, if cold (our good friend Austin Laws took a cine-film of the occasion) and at the reception afterwards at the University Refectory we were able to entertain many family members and friends, professional colleagues and their spouses. All our neighbours in Beechfield Road who had regularly entertained us, as we had entertained them in biannual Sunday morning cocktail parties (so called 'street' parties) which we had each held regularly, were also invited. The champagne for about 150 guests cost £250 and the actual reception itself just over £500 (how subsequent inflation has eroded the value of the pound!).

Betty and I enjoyed innumerable brief visits to Ann and Ian's homes in London where they benefitted from the subsequent inflationary spiral, particularly in the housing market, by selling each of their successive homes for a large profit so that they were able to move progressively up market every year or two. I recall with especial pleasure the rounds of golf which I enjoyed with Ian at Brookmans Park Golf Club where he was beginning to take the game seriously and was working hard on his handicap.

We were immensely proud when our first grandchild, Drew, was born in 1971. Ann was admitted to hospital in Barnet for the delivery and on that very day I was attending a meeting of the Council of the Association of British Neurologists in London. Happily I was able to slip up to Barnet to see Ann and Drew before catching the sleeper to Newcastle. About 20 months later Victoria was born; this time we arranged for Ann to have the baby in the Newcastle General Hospital so that Betty could look after Drew for a while before she went with Ann and both children to London to help out for a couple of weeks.

Unexpectedly, in 1977 Ian was sent by Chase Manhattan to Geneva for three months in order to revise the financial procedures of the Chase branch there. Naturally they decided to go as a family and rented accommodation while letting their own house furnished in Brookmans Park. Ian's stay was repeatedly extended on a short-term basis until it became apparent that they were likely to be there permanently and so the house in Brookmans Park was sold. Difficulties arose over the very rigid Swiss requirements for a work permit. On one occasion while Ian was on a professional visit to Milan and while Betty was staying with Ann and the children in their rented house near Geneva, the Swiss police arrived to say that Ian's permit to stay in Switzerland had expired and that they had come to escort the entire family to the frontier. When Ann explained in her French, which by this time had improved, that her husband was away in Italy, they relented. Soon afterwards, to their great relief, Ian received the appropriate permit to allow him permanent residence. In fact Ann and Ian have remained in Geneva ever since and later built a beautiful home in Founex. Their two children, Drew and Victoria, who are totally bilingual and who attended the international school there, taking the international baccalaureate, are now students in Durham University, Drew reading physics and Victoria reading social sciences. Drew is not only an outstanding golfer and a regular member of the successful Durham University team, and a fine skier, but he is also a tall, charming and thoroughly delightful young man who gives little away about his personal life. Victoria by contrast, now a stunningly lovely young lady and also a fine sportswoman, is a bubbly, talkative and vivacious creature destined, we are sure, to break many hearts. Now that the children are away in university, Ann has returned whole-time to her profession of occupational therapy and with a colleague is running a private service in Switzerland.

Judy, too, has had an interesting and varied life. Though the traumas of her teenage period were, at least for us, less severe than those we experienced with Ann, she too had a succession of boyfriends while at school, several from the Royal Grammar School whose main gate was directly opposite that of the Central High School. As her school career progressed, it became clear that she was very enthusiastic about becoming a nurse. After one year in the sixth form, and having completed her 'O' level examinations, we arranged with some Swiss friends (long before Ann and Ian went there) for Judy to go to work at the Clinique Beaulieu as an aide-infirmière (nurses' aid) for a six-month period. It must have been alarming for her at 17 to go off alone to work in a country where her knowledge of the language was so limited, but she took it cheerfully and in her stride, thoroughly enjoyed the time that she spent there and became fluent in French. Betty and I managed a memorable holiday in Geneva while she worked there; this gave us the opportunity of visiting many of the finest tourist sights including the Jungfrau, the Eiger and the Matterhorn. On her return from Switzerland Judy took a six-month secretarial course and applied for admission to three London hospitals for nurse training, feeling that she did not wish to work in Newcastle where Daddy was on the staff. She was interviewed at Guy's, the Middlesex and St Thomas's. At Guy's and also at the Middlesex she was interviewed by two assistant matrons who were stiff and formal but efficient. Each ultimately offered her a place, though one did so only on condition that she took a correspondence course in history because of her rather poor performance in history in her 'O' level examinations. At St Thomas's, however, she was interviewed alone by the Matron, Miss Adamson, who said to her secretary 'Judy's come a long way, Miss So-and-so—please get her a cup of coffee. Come in, Judy, and have a seat'. A friendly discussion ensued and, as Judy said at the end of the day 'After that kind of experience, which one would you have accepted?'. Hence a Nightingale at St Thomas's she became and made several lasting friendships with girls with whom she shared a flat in Clapham, which was significantly more salubrious than the accommodation that Ann had survived in Oxford.

Not unexpectedly, as time went by Judy became friendly with a medical student and he asked if he could see me. I arranged to give Andrew Brown dinner in my club, the Royal Societies Club, of which I was then a member and which shared premises with the Public Schools Club at 100 Piccadilly. We had an interesting evening and I was greatly taken by his forceful personality but even more by the fact that he opened the bowling for St Thomas's and was also a reasonable bat. In a rather old-fashioned way, he had really come formally to ask for my daughter's hand in marriage; of course we were delighted to agree to their engagement. When Judy eventually qualified as an SRN, she took a job as a staff nurse in theatre in St Thomas's while awaiting Andrew's eventual qualification. They married on a brilliantly hot and sunny day in July 1972, this time at our own church, West Avenue Methodist Church (Andrew had been brought up a Methodist and had attended The Leys School in Cambridge before going to medical school). My brother-in-law, the Revd Sidney Groves (Mary's husband) gave a splendidly moving address. Again we had a large number of guests for an excellent reception, presided over by the indefatigable George Elliott, the University Catering Officer, at the University Refectory. Many of us went back to Beechfield Road for a party in the house and garden where many of the men sneaked into the drawing room during the party to watch the last stages of the British Open Golf Championship on television.

Andy and Judy acquired a small flat in London while Andy completed his course and they later moved to Colchester and Scarborough where he did his house jobs. He had always intended to travel the world and no sooner had he completed two house officer appointments than they went off together to South Africa where he worked as a medical registrar with Professor Adams at the Addington Hospital in Durban. There they spent a delightful 18 months, living in married accommodation close to the hospital and next door to J.P.R. (the famous Welsh rugby full-back) and Cilla Williams who were also working there at the time. They became close friends with the Williams; in later years whenever I visited Wales and mentioned that I had a daughter and son-in-law who were close friends of J.P.R. and his wife, this gave me a very special status, far more than any professional attainments of my own. From South Africa, Andrew returned to be a senior house officer (SHO) in neurology with our good friend Michael Saunders in Middlesbrough and soon acquired an MRCP. From Middlesbrough he went to Otley as medical registrar with Dr Patricia Kendall-Taylor (subsequently Professor Kendall-Taylor of Newcastle). Later he returned to Newcastle to do three SHO appointments in succession, one in obstetrics, one in anaesthesia and one (which was actually a house officer appointment rather than an SHO) in paediatrics. These appointments were interspersed with short periods of working as a locum for an old St Thomas's friend in Lafleche in Saskatchewan (Canada), when Judy accompanied him. He also managed to fit in a period of general practice as a locum in Throckley for Ian Telfer and a full month in Belford working as a summer locum for our friend Denis Byers, during which time Judy and Andy and their children lived in Ivy Cottage, even though they had bought a house in Ivy Road, Gosforth. While working in Newcastle Andrew acquired the DRCOG and the Diploma in Anaesthesia (DA) and began to feel that he might wish to make a career in intensive care medicine. Nevertheless, the call of general practice seemed strong and this, combined with his 'itchy feet', eventually led him to apply for an appointment in a small general practice in Australia. By this time they had two children, Nicholas and Lucy, born within a year of one another in Newcastle. Eventually off they all went to Omeo in northern Victoria where for the next 18 months Andrew worked in single-handed general practice with his own 14-bedded hospital. When Betty and I went to spend Christmas with them in 1980 (we combined this with a couple of lectures in Perth and in Melbourne and a trans-Australian train journey across the Nullarbor Plain since the Australian air traffic controllers were on strike) we were very impressed by the quality of the practice in which Andrew was engaged. They had a comfortable home and colourful garden in the friendly little village of Omeo, not far from Mount Hotham where winter skiing was available. It seemed extraordinary to be eating an English-style Christmas dinner when we were enjoying temperatures of more than 100°F; nevertheless the dry heat was such that we were not too uncomfortable.

When we said a sad farewell to them and flew back to the UK, we thought that it would be a long time before we met again as Andrew had signed a three-year contract to work in the practice. However, a month or two after we returned to the UK Judy rang us in considerable excitement to say that another of Andy's student friends, Oliver Sharpley, had telephoned him from Burford in the Cotswolds inviting him to join the practice in which he, Oliver, had joined his father. The senior partner, Dr Eager, had decided to retire and Dr Sharpley senior planned to do so before long. Andrew jumped at this opportunity. There was only one important snag; he had not held a traineeship in general practice in the UK and despite his very broad experience and multiple qualifications it was uncertain as to whether he would be accepted by the Joint Committee for Postgraduate Training in General Practice as being qualified to become a partner. Fortunately, through the good offices of my friend and colleague Dr Donald Irvine, then Chairman of Council of the Royal College of General Practitioners, the committee was persuaded that the experience which Andrew had had in Denis Byers' training practice in Northumberland and his short period as a locum in Throckley was sufficient, when combined with his other experience, for him to be accepted as being vocationally trained. Naturally we were delighted that Judy, Andy and the children were to return to the UK. When we ourselves moved to Oxford in October 1983, the knowledge that Judy and the family were close by was an additional incentive in encouraging me to accept the Wardenship of Green College. Since then, the Brown family have settled happily in Burford. They first bought a modern house in Milton-under-Wychwood, from which after two years they moved to a larger and commodious home, beautifully situated in Swan Lane in Burford, where we see them regularly. Andrew and his partners have built a superb new surgery; Judy now works in the casualty department of the Burford Cottage Hospital which, almost single-handedly, she runs each morning, while the third partner, Dr Peter Wragg, FRCS, does some minor surgery (including hernias under local anaesthesia) while Judy assists in the theatre. Nicholas and Lucy have both moved into the excellent senior school in Burford; Nicholas is a very capable trumpeter and a thoughtful, reflective teenager of practical bent who has just, with a friend, submitted a successful tender for grass cutting and general maintenance at his father's surgery. Lucy is an excellent dancer (she has won many trophies) but is also a lovely and lively young lady of decided views who claims (at 13) to be writing a novel.

Christopher, our son, was born in February 1956, after we returned to Newcastle from London; being five years younger than Judy, he was rather less of a companion to the girls than might have been the case if the gap had been shorter. As we told our friends, we simply could not afford to have a third child while in the United States. Chris attended Ascham House School in Gosforth, close to our home. We considered the possibility of trying to arrange for him to go to the Newcastle Royal Grammar School, but as most of his friends were going away to school, we eventually decided that we would like him to attend a public boarding school at 13, perhaps because this was still regarded as a privilege and was one which I had never myself experienced. Possibly my ideas of public school life acquired from my childhood reading were slightly glamourized. Betty and I inspected a number of public schools on a car tour which we combined with visits to a number of well-known hostelries listed in the Good Food Guide. We saw Shrewsbury, Harrow, The Leys and later Fettes in Edinburgh, before ultimately deciding to send Christopher to Sedbergh where the headmaster, Mr Thornley, had impressed us greatly. We entered his name for Sedgwick House where the housemaster, Mr Inglis, was a delightful man whose principal subject was art. During Christopher's stay there he retired to be replaced by John Challenor, who was efficient and enthusiastic but who seemed to us at times to be a little less tolerant of adolescent foibles than we might have wished. Ascham House, under the lively and witty Mark Aldridge, was an excellent environment from which Christopher passed the common entrance examination without difficulty, though we recognized that he was not academically in the very top flight. He became a more than competent tennis player, performed reasonably well on the rugby field, and also learned to play the violin sufficiently well to be one of the first violins in the excellent school orchestra. Soon at Sedbergh he became a regular member of the school tennis team.

However, he was a deliberate and methodical but invariably conscientious worker, who needed time to complete his studies so that in retrospect Sedbergh may not have been the perfect environment for him academically. After performing reasonably well in his 'O' levels he found that in his 'A' level term at Sedbergh he was playing four hours of tennis every day and simply did not have the time to work as hard and as long as he would have wished for the examinations. His was a case in which the old adage *mens sana in corpore sano*, if too strictly interpreted, was clearly inappropriate. I believe that the school should have recognized that he needed more time for private study than circumstances allowed. Having decided that he might wish to follow me into medicine and having had an offer after interview for King's College Medical School in London, his results in the 'A' levels were insufficient and the offer lapsed. After he left school there followed a year of part-time study at the Tyneside College of Further Education, and then retaking the 'A' levels. After the examinations he enjoyed a superb holiday in Canada that summer, through the good offices of our friends the Barnetts from London, Ontario. They arranged for him to share the driving with Charlie Bolton, another neurologist, on a journey to Saskatchewan. Christopher then went on by himself to the Yukon and greatly enjoyed a few weeks of work in a gold mine before returning home.

With his improved 'A' level results, Newcastle University accepted him to read general science; after spending the first term living at home, he then moved into the Ethel Williams Hall, worked very hard and performed very creditably at the end of his first year. Indeed we were told that in physiology, one of his three subjects, he did well enough to be considered for a possible transfer to medicine, which by this time he no longer wished to consider. He therefore read joint honours in zoology and psychology and graduated two years later. He achieved a very good II(1) performance in zoology and might well have been invited to do a PhD in that subject because of his research ability. Apparently he did two very good research projects, one on the zebra finch (we housed some of these birds for a time in our top floor studio room) and the other on small mammals. However, by this time he had become very interested in ecology, in wildlife and in farming and had spent two vacations working with our friend Jim Scott on his farm at Buckton, close to Detchant. He was therefore determined to farm, even though I told him that I did not happen to have a million pounds to buy one! Nevertheless, after taking advice we arranged for him to go to the Royal Agricultural College at Cirencester where he much enjoyed a one-year practical farming course in the same class as Captain Mark Phillips and emerged with a creditable performance. Jim Scott then kindly took him on for a year as a trainee farm manager at Buckton. By this time Betty and I had moved into 'The Old Piggery' at Detchant and Christopher therefore lived alone for a year in Ivy Cottage (which we continued to rent). He worked happily with the Scotts, acquiring much practical farming experience, though not unnaturally, being of gregarious disposition, he occasionally felt a little lonely because of his comparative isolation.

But he was determined to acquire yet further experience and so we agreed to support him during a further year at Wye College in Kent where he read for an MSc in Agricultural Economics. Again that year proved to be fruitful academically and enjoyable socially as he lived close to Wye with other students in a house at Brabourne owned by the Romsey family, relatives of the Mountbattens. At Wye he met and became engaged to Denise Daly, an attractive, cheerful and effervescent Irish lass, who had a BSc in Horticulture from London and who was reading for an MSc in Landscape Ecology, Design and Maintenance. In October 1982 they were married in a Roman Catholic church in Church Road in Gosforth and the reception was held in a large marquee installed on the lawn in our garden. This was another exceptionally happy family occasion and afterwards Chris and Denise returned to the South to live in a small bungalow in Compton Abdale, close to Cheltenham, where he had found a post as a trainee agricultural consultant. After a year of valuable experience he resigned, having been invited to return to Northumberland where he worked as a farm foreman with Bill Nesbit at East Ancroft Farm, about six miles from Detchant. Four happy years were spent there but eventually Chris decided that to be a really effective agricultural consultant he also needed accountancy experience and so he became articled to Greaves, West and Ayre in Berwick-upon-Tweed. Although Denise soon acquired a substantial practice in landscape architecture and design, both in private work for various clients in Northumberland and in ecological and landscape assessment before and after open cast mining for British Coal, they were not at first able to buy a home of their own, but lived, while Chris worked for the Nesbits, in a cottage on the farm in East Ancroft. However, their luck seemed to have changed at last when a friend, Sonia ffrench, told them that her family estates, which had been broken up at the end of the First World War so as to provide a series of smallholdings for returned servicemen, were being repurchased from the Scottish Ministry of Agriculture and were being sold off individually. Among these was one at Mordington Hill on which there was a solid but neglected house with three bedrooms, two good reception rooms and a large range of outbuildings, along with 20 acres including 15 acres of pasture and five of woodland. This was on the market at a very reasonable price; after much negotiation and delay on the part of the Ministry because of complex legal negotiations, Chris and Denise bought the house and land. A great deal had to be spent upon installing central heating, improving the plumbing, the electrical wiring and the like. Eventually they moved in in January 1990, having at last achieved their principal long-term objective of having a smallholding of their own in which they could both indulge their love of farming and country life.

Their son, Angus, was born in 1984 while they were at East Ancroft. The delivery had been arranged at Berwick Cottage Hospital and all appeared to go well until after an hour or two in labour signs of fetal distress appeared and Denise was taken by ambulance from Berwick to Ashington Hospital where a Caesarean section was performed and it was found that the baby had the cord around his neck. Fortunately there were no other complications and Angus is now a vigorous, twinkling and mischievous seven-year-old with a lively imagination; he is attending a primary school in Foulden, near Berwick-upon-Tweed, where he has acquired a north Northumbrian accent and is a great delight to us all.

In the meantime, seeking professional advancement, Christopher moved from Greaves, West and Ayre as an agricultural consultant to Grant Thornton in Edinburgh. However, the problems associated with regular commuting to and from Edinburgh, combined with work on the farm, meant that life has not been as settled as he and Denise would wish, the more so because having passed his first and second accountancy examinations, he has yet to complete his final examination in order to become a chartered accountant. However, they have entered into a very beneficial partnership with Sonia ffrench's sister, Amanda Caley, who owns the adjacent farm of over 180 acres. Chris and Denise are managing this with her, so that in all they have over 200 acres (and a large number of animals) to look after. That, combined with work on the house and outbuildings, which still require attention, and regular commuting to and from Edinburgh, while also preparing for the final examination, created some problems for Chris, Denise and Angus, but we are in no doubt that these will be overcome. It is always a joy to get together with them when we are in the north.

To conclude, I have been exceptionally fortunate in being presented with new and different challenges every few years. When in 1981 I had decided not to seek reappointment as Dean because of additional GMC responsibilities which were then looming, I was approached by Trevor Hughes at the World Congress of Neurology in Kyoto about the possibility that I might agree to be considered for the Wardenship of Green College in Oxford when Richard Doll retired in 1983, this seemed to me to offer a challenge well worth considering, even though I had always felt that I would wish to stay in the North East for the rest of my professional life. Betty and I will never forget the magnificent departmental party which was organized in our honour when I received my knighthood in January 1979, or the dinner of senior colleagues superbly organized by Jack Foster at Gosforth Park Hotel at the same time. Just as moving and incredibly nostalgic as we look back was the farewell symposium and dinner in September 1983 splendidly planned and executed by David Gardner-Medwin and the wonderful garden party on a blazing hot day in Mike Cullen's garden at Ponteland where his wife Anne had produced a sumptuous repast and at which Betty was presented with a pair of bird-watching binoculars which she treasures and I with a set of Bewick prints of Northumbrian interest which hang proudly on the wall behind me as I write.

Appendix

Among the many other young neurologists who passed through the research registrar posts established first on MDA and MDAC funds and later on funding from the MRC were not only Drs Hudgson, Gardner-Medwin and Bradley but also Dr Simon Currie (now consultant neurologist at St James' Hospital, Leeds), Dr Rod Hughes (consultant neurologist in Wolverhampton), Dr Malcolm Campbell (consultant neurologist at Frenchay Hospital, Bristol), Dr Chris Davis (consultant neurologist at the Radcliffe Infirmary, Oxford), Dr Michael O'Brien (consultant neurologist, Guy's Hospital, London) Dr Graeme Boddie (consultant neurologist, North Staffordshire Royal Infirmary), Dr Ram Ayyar (associate professor of neurology in Miami, USA), Dr Max Williams (consultant neurologist, Royal North Shore Hospital, Sydney, Australia), Dr Ron DeVere (consultant neurologist, Methodist Hospital, Houston, Texas, USA), Dr Sonny Gubbay (consultant neurologist, Perth, Western Australia), Dr Arthur Rose (paediatric neurologist, Albert Einstein Medical College, New York), Dr Peter Payan (now a consultant neurophysiologist in London), Dr Adrian Upton (later consultant clinical neurophysiologist with Alan McComas at McMaster University, Hamilton, Ontario), Dr John Polgar (consultant neurologist, University of New South Wales, Australia), Dr Ken Cumming (consultant neurologist, Withington Hospital, Manchester), Dr Akira Enomoto (consultant neurologist, Tokyo, Japan), Dr Peter Fawcett (now consultant in clinical neurophysiology at the NGH), Dr Garth Nicholson (consultant neurologist, Repatriation Hospital, Sydney, Australia), Dr Ian Livingstone (later a consultant neurologist in the USA), Dr Toshi Murakami (consultant neuropathologist, University of Tokyo, Japan), Dr Grant Walker (consultant neurologist, Royal North Shore Hospital, Sydney, Australia), Dr David Serisier (consultant neurologist, Adelaide, Australia) Dr Tim Walls (now consultant neurologist, NGH) and Dr Douglas Turnbull (now professor of neurology, University of Newcastle upon Tyne).

Among the visiting workers from overseas spending between three and twelve months (and occasionally longer) in Newcastle over the years were Dr Frans Jennekens (now professor of neurology in Utrecht), Dr Paul Larson (George Meany fellow of the MDA and later professor of neurology and Dean at the Medical School of the University of Louisiana, New Orleans), Dr Roberto Sica (now professor of neurology in Buenos Aires), Dr Albert Aguayo (Head of Neurology, Montreal General Hospital), Dr Ted Munsat (professor of neurology, Tufts Medical School, Boston, and Past-President, American Academy of Neurology), Dr George Ristow (Detroit, USA), Dr Alvaro Villegas (Caracas, Venezuela), Dr Nestor Bravo (Caracas, Venezuela), Dr M. Gourie-Devi (Delhi, India), Dr A. K. Susheela (Delhi, India), Dr John Fewings (Adelaide, Australia), Dr Ted Stewart-Wynne (Johannesburg, South Africa), Dr John Pearn (Brisbane, Australia—now professor of paediatrics there), Dr Frans Verster (Johannesburg, South Africa), Dr M. Aziz (Khartoum, Sudan), Dr Lawrence Zrinzo (Malta), Dr Gianni Meola (Milan, Italy), Dr Frank Petito (New York), Dr I. Diaz-Torres (Madrid, Spain), Dr Paul Verheecke (Liege, Belgium), Dr George Cremier (Marseille, France), Dr Roland Eastman (Cape Town, South Africa), Dr Hyam Dubo (Detroit, Michigan), Dr E. M. Sundaram (Madras, India), Dr Adel Al-Jishi (Bahrain), Dr Joe Scopa (Perth, Western Australia), Dr Fahmy Ragab (Cairo, Egypt), Dr Sotiria Harmoussi (Athens, Greece), Dr Tania Terenty (Sydney, Australia), Dr P. Q. R. Siddiqui (Karachi, Pakistan), Dr J. M. Nobrega (Sao Paulo, Brazil), Dr Guiseppe Cazzato (professor of neurology in Trieste, Italy), Dr Jean Rebeiz (American University, Beirut), Dr Theo Papapetropoulos (now professor of neurology, Patras University, Greece), Dr Roberto Cotrufo (professor of neurology, Naples), Dr Mario Medici (Montevideo, Uruguay), Dr Anil Desai (Bombay, India), Dr Manuel Martinez-Lage (now professor of neurology, Pamplona, Spain and former Vice-President, World Federation of Neurology), Dr David Pleasure (Philadelphia, USA), Dr Zohar Argov (Jerusalem, Israel),

Dr Lukas Fierz (Berne, Switzerland), Dr Santiago Fontiveros (Oriente, Venezuela), Dr Colin Hall (Chapel Hill, North Carolina, USA), Dr Heather Johnston (Sydney, Australia), Dr Margaret Jones (Michigan State University, USA), Dr Ugur Karagol (Ankara, Turkey), Dr Jesus Llabres Olmo (Tenerife, Canary Islands), Dr Ferenc Mechler (Debrecen, Hungary), Dr Surendra Misra (Varanasi, India), Dr Isaac Mosquera (Caracas, Venezuela), Dr Jean-Marie Mussini (Nantes, France), Dr Mark Nameroff (Seattle, USA), Dr Mirko Serena (Venice, Italy), Dr S. Shoji (Tokyo, Japan), Dr Slobodanka Todorovic (Belgrade, Yugoslavia), Dr Giuseppe Vita (Naples, Italy), Dr Martin Nogues (Buenos Aires, Argentina), Dr Ramon Leiguarda (Buenos Aires), Dr Konstanty Mrozek (Warsaw, Poland), Dr Shobha Goyle (New Delhi, India), Dr Joao Kouyoumdjian (Sao Paulo, Brazil), Dr Juan Idiaquez (Valparaiso, Chile), Dr Phiroze Hansotia (Marshfield, Wisconsin, USA), Dr Dora Kucukyalcin (Istanbul, Turkey), Dr E. Natale (Palermo, Italy), Dr G. Savettieri (Palermo, Italy), Dr J. R. Slack (Auckland, New Zealand) and Dr Keitchi Takahashi (Kobe, Japan). Each in their innumerable ways made major contributions to the life and research work of the department. Many, depending on their seniority and experience, made major research contributions (notably, for example, Dr Paul Larson, Dr Ted Munsat, Dr Frans Jennekens, Dr Albert Aguayo, Dr John Pearn, Dr Zohar Argov, Dr Colin Hall, Dr David Pleasure and Dr Roberto Sica) but many others received training in the diagnosis and management of neuromuscular disease and virtually all completed some form of research project during the time they spent in the department.

CHAPTER 13

The Territorial Army

While, as I said in an earlier chapter, my principal motive in accepting Robert Mowbray's invitation to join his Territorial Army (TA) unit was my need to earn some additional money to eke out the failing family finances, I had enjoyed my Army service. I often said that if I had had to choose an alternative career (while accepting that medicine would always have been my first love) my second choice would have been to become a barrister and my third to be a regular Army officer. In the Army, while my medical skills were in danger of decaying, I much enjoyed the comradeship with other officers and with the men. I was also attracted by the precision of military training and administrative procedures and appreciated the opportunities which the Army afforded for travel, both in the UK and abroad. The TA seemed to me to combine some advantages of regular Army service with an opportunity to enjoy a totally different part-time activity which offered refreshment from the at times oppressively demanding professional life in which I became increasingly embroiled.

The No. 1 Northern General Hospital was the oldest general hospital in the TA, having been created as part of the original Territorial Force in 1912. During the 1914–18 war, the unit occupied for a time the Armstrong Building of what later became King's College (subsequently Newcastle University). In the 1950s when I used to visit Ursula Philip in the Department of Zoology in that building to discuss my genetic research into muscular dystrophy, a notice was still affixed to the wall of the elderly lift saying 'This lift is for stretcher cases only—No. 1 Northern General Hospital, Territorial Force, 1914'. The fact that we in the North East had the No. 1 TA hospital was always looked upon with some envy by units such as, for example, the 10th and 17th London General Hospitals, some of whose officers we came to know well.

Joining the unit as a medical registrar in a teaching hospital made it possible for me to be graded immediately as a physician. When I obtained my MRCP, Robert Mowbray recommended that I be upgraded to full specialist status; this was rapidly approved so that I was soon restored to the rank of Major which I had held on leaving the Army. TA service meant that one would, whenever possible, attend for training on Tuesday evenings. One was also expected to attend two weeks of annual camp per year (of which one week had to be taken as part of annual leave while the other was extra leave, under the NHS terms and conditions of service). In addition, the unit normally held three or four weekend exercises each year, some in barracks but others in various field locations. When I joined, the headquarters was in a hutted militia camp in Barrack Road, Fenham, opposite the main entrance of the gaunt and forbidding Victorian pile of Fenham Barracks. Shortly afterwards we moved to a more convenient and better appointed drill-hall in Northumberland Road in the centre of the city, premises which we shared with a TA artillery unit. Later still we moved yet again on to the Fenham Barracks site, into an old Victorian building which was completely refurbished for our sole occupancy. Here we had attractive training accommodation for drills, stretcher and other exercises, access to a parade ground and well-appointed officers' and sergeants' messes, each with their own bars, dining areas and facilities for billiards, snooker and darts. We remained there for several happy years and throughout my period of command. Subsequently, when it became clear that many buildings on the Barracks site had outlived their useful life, the most modern building (the 1940 Sandhurst block) which had been vacant and unused for several years was completely refurbished and now houses the 201 Northern General Hospital (T & AVR) (which succeeded the No. 1) as well as many other TA units. Much of the rest of the site was cleared and the BBC's new North Eastern Radio and Television Centre now occupies the area where our accommodation once stood.

The unit was singularly fortunate in its commanding officers. When I joined in 1950, the CO was Col. Robert Mowbray, senior physician at the Durham Group of Hospitals and a most likeable and able man. The OC Surgical Division was Lt Col J. V. Todd, a skilful orthopaedic surgeon whose life was divided between his love of orthopaedics on the one hand and that of golf on the other. In five successive seasons before the Second World War he had been Durham County golf champion and at one stage played off a handicap of plus 2, even appearing as an amateur in the Swiss Open and in a number of other important tournaments. John Todd succeeded Robert Mowbray as CO and, exceptionally, held the appointment for almost six years; the normal term of office of a commanding officer was three or at the most four. He was followed as OC Surgical Div. by Lt Col Robin Sykes, an anaesthetist in the Regional Cardiothoracic Unit at Shotley Bridge. Robin was an old Etonian whose family had estates in Shropshire; his slightly off-hand and at times ethereal and unworldly manner concealed a keen intellect and a thorough knowledge of military life and procedures. He later commanded the unit after John Todd, while in the interim I had become a lieutenant colonel and OC Medical Division of the hospital, before in my turn I followed Robin as CO from 1963 to 1966. For most of the 16 years that I served we were up to strength with medical and dental officers and also had an excellent complement of nursing officers, of whom Lt Col 'Queenie' Prout was Matron when I first joined, being followed by, among others, the redoubtable Nancy McQueen and Nancy Wilson, each of them nursing sisters in hospitals in the Newcastle and Sunderland area. We were also exeptionally well served by two permanent staff officers, the first Major C. E. 'Cora' Ball and later Capt. Bob Campbell. Both were long-serving non-medical officers who had risen from the ranks (Bob Campbell had joined the Army as a boy); each was totally dedicated to the RAMC. When we asked Cora how he acquired his nickname, he said that when he was serving in the Middle East he was wakened one morning after an excellent mess dinner to find himself being shaken vigorously by an orderly who was calling out 'cora, cora, cora'. It seems that 'cora' was the word for 'ball' in the orderly's native language; the nickname stuck throughout his military career.

No military unit can function effectively through its officers alone and we were exceptionally well served by many able NCOs. They included miners, carpet salesmen, labourers and men employed in many other diverse occupations, including a few nursing orderlies or laboratory technicians in local hospitals. Some had seen regular army service, some had served during the war and a few joined us after completing national service. Indeed before national service ended in the late 1950s, all conscripts were required to spend some two years after leaving the Army undergoing part-time training as members of a TA unit. That regulation gave us for a few years a unit which was almost totally up to strength with more than 20 medical and dental officers, a similar number of nursing officers and about 150 other ranks. When our national service personnel left us (they included a few notable doctors and dentists) our numbers of other ranks declined sharply so that at one stage we had more NCOs than private soldiers. That situation was partially corrected, however, when we became able to recruit female other ranks into the Queen Alexandra's Royal Army Nursing Corps. They came forward in considerable numbers so that we sometimes had about 40 or 50 male other ranks and between 25 and 30 females, local Geordie lasses who were mostly very keen and enthusiastic. They would willingly undertake any number of tasks, including tent erecting, cooking in the field, even stretcher bearing and other physically demanding activities, while also receiving training in first aid and simple nursing methods. At one stage the unit strength was also boosted when we had posted to us several medical and nursing officers who were members of a TA casualty clearing station based in Leeds which was closed down; they made a major contribution to our work.

On Tuesday evenings all of the officers in turn took part in training the other ranks while the officers themselves were also instructed in such matters as staff duties in the field, military regulations and procedures, anti-gas, nuclear warfare and civil defence precautions, first aid and the like. But there was always time for socializing in the well-appointed bar and mess and some of us, after training was over, could hone our declining skills on the snooker table or dart board. Our weekend exercises took us to many different locations around the north of England, usually beginning on Friday evening and ending on Sunday evening. And every December we hosted the Assistant Director of Medical Services (ADMS) Northern Command medical exercise which was attended at our headquarters by large numbers of TA medical and dental officers from throughout the North East. Lectures, demonstrations (including tactical exercises without troops (TEWTS)) and other training were offered, interrupted only on the Saturday night by the annual RAMC dinner for past and present RAMC officers, usually held in a convenient Newcastle hotel, after which we returned to the mess. Sometimes we were privileged to have the Director-General of the Army Medical Services (DGAMS) as our guest, and invariably many senior serving officers joined us for the weekend. An indefatigable attender was our honorary colonel, Col J. B. S. Guy, OBE, a general practitioner from Loftus in North Yorkshire who had had a distinguished war career. His OBE was conferred after he had been in a ship off the Italian coast during that campaign when it was sunk by German aerial action. The citation said that having been thrown into the water, Col Guy swam about a mile to the shore, pulling with him in accepted life-saving style a young soldier who was a poor swimmer and who would certainly have drowned if the redoubtable John had not come to his aid. The one disadvantage of having John Guy as honorary colonel, particularly when John Todd, of like mind, was CO, was that at training weekends neither seemed to wish to go to bed. On more than one occasion we had the greatest difficulty in ejecting them from our home between 2.00 and 3.00 in the morning. My friend Major Rex Belas, then serving in the TA as medical officer to the Green Howards in Middlesbrough, regularly stayed with us for the December training weekends and more than once he and I hid in the mess toilets to avoid being embroiled with the two Johns late at night after an RAMC dinner.

Another regular annual event was an Easter-time exercise laid on by the Deputy DMS Northern Command at York which we regularly attended in Fulford Barracks. Sometimes too, as one became more senior, one was invited in March to attend yet another weekend of training based at the Grand Hotel in Scarborough and led by the General Officer Commanding (GOC) Northern Command. This gave us RAMC officers the opportunity of meeting senior officers in other army units, including the infantry, the tank corps, the artillery, the service corps, etc. I shall never forget a magnificent lecture on leadership being delivered at one such weekend by Sam Watson, the Durham miners' leader, who held a large audience of several generals, brigadiers and innumerable colonels enthralled by the quality of his delivery, by his humour and his cogent advice. One memorable incident of a Scarborough weekend was the occasion when several distinguished and highly decorated senior officers were seen competing to determine who could be quickest at descending the hotel grand staircase after dinner using a large tin tray as a sledge. One GOC Northern Command I remember with particular affection was General Tony Reid, an exceptionally friendly, urbane but incisive senior officer who once came as our guest to a mess dinner in Fenham Barracks. After dinner the less than polished Major 'Skem' Hutchinson of the Amble general practice (see Chapter 11) went up to the General and slapped him on the back, saying in his broad Geordie accent 'General, you're a reet canny bugger'. We waited in fearful anticipation of the explosion which we expected to follow, but Tony Reid was greatly touched; as he pointed out, that was the greatest compliment that a Geordie could pay.

Inevitably memories crowd in of the friendships and comradeship which TA service engendered. Among the many medical officers with whom I served was the late Roland Goodhead, a GP in the west end of Newcastle who was also a member of the musicians' union. Having written several rag revues when a student, he later wrote innumerable summer shows which were performed in various coastal resorts. He was tireless, irrepressible and at annual camp seemed to be capable of existing virtually without sleep. Nevertheless he was an efficient officer and dedicated to the TA. Not only did he play the piano with effortless ease, covering a vast repertoire when we had our sing-songs in the mess after dinner, but he was an outstanding organizer of map-reading exercises. Some such were arranged at weekends but the most complex was our annual officers' map-reading exercise at annual camp. This took the form of a well-organized motor rally but had the secondary consequence of teaching our officers, including the nursing officers (who usually navigated when the male officers drove) a great deal about map-reading and navigation. Among the many other officers with whom I served were Bill Ross (who later became President of the Royal College of Radiologists), a member of my own year who as a consultant radiotherapist with an FRCS became OC Surgical Division during my period in command and who succeeded me as Commanding Officer; Alan Horler, consultant physician at the RVI (now President of the Medical Defence Union) became OC Medical Division; Tom Bird, a senior pathologist at the Newcastle General Hospital and a keen Victorians cricketer, was our pathologist; and John Inkster, a distinguished paediatric anaesthetist, was yet another long-serving member. Notable, too, was Col Hugh Brown, an outstanding plastic surgeon, who succeeded Bill Ross first as OC Surgical Division and later as CO. He, during Robin Sykes' command, led our team in the annual Territorial Army Shield competition; they won by a considerable margin after putting up an outstanding and sparkling performance under the scrutiny of a posse of critical senior officers at Mytchett. Among the many general duty medical officers who were the unit's GPs and who came and went, Major J. F. S. T. McClory, Major Donald Golightly of Prudhoe and Major Brian Wolstenholme (John Guy's partner from Loftus) were some of those who served for long periods. And we also had several remarkable dental officers, beginning with Major Alan Morton who later became Secretary of the Dental Estimates Board; Major Geoffrey Howe, who had served with me in the Hospital Ship 'Oxfordshire' joined us on detachment from the 17th London General Hospital when he came to Newcastle as professor of oral surgery. Later, when he left Newcastle to become Dean of the Eastman Dental School in London, he rejoined his parent unit and, being both medically and dentally qualified, eventually succeeded to command. A number of padres of all denominations also came and went, but among these was the long-serving Major Robin Macey who often conducted moving church services at annual camp, including some in the field during exercises.

Time and space would not allow me to recount all of the memorable events which occurred during our weekend exercises or annual camps, but a few outstanding recollections seem worth mentioning. In the early years we had more than one weekend exercise at a training camp in Marske in North Yorkshire which included map-reading jaunts around that notable landmark, Rosebery Topping. In one late November we set up a tented camp and small casualty reception station in the Northumbrian hills of Redesdale, close to Alwinton, where despite sleeping bags and heavy clothing we virtually froze in the late autumn frosts. Perhaps, however, one of the most memorable weekends was our exercise in air/sea evacuation carried out in collaboration with RAF Boulmer and the Amble life-boat when the unit took part in an exercise involving lifting casualties by helicopter from the life-boat and carrying them to a small tented casualty reception station on the shore. At the time I was in command; soon afterwards I received a formal letter from a Corporal Jones which read: 'Sir, I have the honour to report that during Exercise "Wet Blanket" off the Northumbrian coast I was stationed in the Amble life-boat and the weather was rough. I regret to say, Sir, that I became seasick and I vomited my dentures over the side. Sir, I claim compensation. Sir, I have the honour to be, Jones, J., Cpl.'. Needless to say, we found some way from a contingency fund (or it may have been my CO's entertainment allowance) to see that the lost articles were rapidly replaced.

As for the annual camps, these were all enjoyable in many different ways. During my service a three-year cycle was established. One camp was spent in a hutted training camp somewhere in the country from which field exercises of various kinds could be carried out. The unit would move out into an appropriate training area to set up a tented hospital and then to receive and treat mock casualties, usually supplied by arrangement with a combatant unit training nearby. In the second year of the cycle we went to an appropriate military hospital such as the Cambridge Hospital at Aldershot, Colchester, Catterick or in the earlier years Chester (before it closed) so that medical and nursing officers could work on the wards in order to learn or to revive their experience of military medicine and the relevant administrative procedures. The other ranks were able to obtain hands-on nursing experience. As the unit's war role became precisely defined and it was decided that on mobilization it would move immediately to BAOR to reinforce hospital facilities there, we were given the opportunity every third year of going to camp in Germany. I attended two such, one when Robin Sykes was CO and the second during my own period of command; each time we went to Sennelager near Paderborn. But even when we were attached to a military hospital, we always managed to fit into the fortnight a two or three-day field exercise and our usual officers' map-reading exercise. In the mid-1950s we went twice to Chester Military Hospital where two memorable exercises took us through the mountains and valleys of North Wales and included an exploration of the charming northern coastline, of a part of Snowdonia, of the valleys around Llangollen, the Horseshoe Pass and the like.

Two Chester memories stand out particularly. In those days I did not take my car to camp as Betty needed the Ford Prefect at home. Hence I shared the driving with Robin Sykes in his very beautiful 1954 Silver Dawn Rolls Royce. I was rather shocked the first time he drove up to a filling station and filled the car with 'pool' petrol rather than premium (only later did I discover that the Rolls had a very low compression engine which required the cheaper petrol). He would also, by choice, drive into the most run-down and scruffy-looking transport café where he parked his gleaming and beautiful machine among a miscellany of lorries and would then walk in and haughtily order a bacon butty and a cup of coffee. Most memorable of all, however, was when we drove up in this lovely conveyance, wearing civilian clothes, to the gates of Chester Military Hospital and a young RAMC private guarding the gate came smartly to attention, gave us a spanking salute and opened it for us to drive through. Robin turned to me quietly and said 'I wonder how he knew we were officers?'.

The CO of Chester Military Hospital then was Col Ned Curran, a friendly and cheerful Irishman who loved the TA and liked nothing better than a party. As was always our policy, we invited him and the other officers of the hospital to our annual cocktail party in the first week of camp; the invitation invariably said '6.30–8.30' but, as many of our officers quipped, this really meant 6.30 p.m.–8.30 a.m.! Ned and some colleagues enjoyed themselves and stayed late; he did so again after our mess dinner next week, when regrettably things got a little out of hand and there was some damage to the mess and to some of the officers' quarters. The tireless Roland Goodhead spent some time in the early morning hours moving from one officer's room to another squirting the sleeping individuals with a soda water syphon. When this had happened to him for the third time, Major Harold Lake (later a consultant ophthalmologist in Sunderland) wakened in a rage and picked up the nearest object to hand, which happened to be a golf club (a no. 3 wood) with which he smote Roland sharply on the scalp, regrettably producing a laceration which later that night required a few stitches. Next morning Harold presented himself before the CO at an early hour and confessed that he had committed a heinous military crime by striking a fellow officer. John Todd, golfer that he was, listened carefully and at the end of the tale said 'Young man, you made a serious mistake; you should have taken an iron'. Later that morning, however, John Todd called his officers before him and delivered what in military terms was known as a 'rocket imperial'. He castigated them for their behaviour the night before, which he regarded as being unbecoming to officers and gentlemen. Perhaps he did so with tongue in cheek, having been seen himself to be removing divots from the mess carpet with a nine iron at 3 a.m.

A few years later, when we were in camp at Mytchett and were comfortably accommodated in the RAMC Mess there while working at the Cambridge Military Hospital, Ned Curran, who in the interim had become ADMS Aldershot District, again joined us for dinner. Again he over-indulged and while cavorting all alone on the polished floor of the mess, slipped and fell heavily, only to rise looking very pale and saying to John Todd that he believed he had fractured his wrist. John's immediate reaction was dismissive until he saw the typical deformity of a Colles' fracture. I was then recruited to drive John and the ADMS to the casualty department of the Cambridge Military Hospital where the young RAMC doctor on duty expressed concern that Col Curran hardly seemed fit for an anaesthetic, to which John Todd's riposte was that in his view this would be unnecessary. John himself set the fracture very skilfully under local anaesthesia and we then took Ned home. His wife, though far from surprised, was also far from pleased, more particularly because Ned, an outstanding golfer, had been due to play in the Army golf championship a couple of days later. The ways of the Army still at times seemed mysterious as later still, by which time Ned had become DDMS Northern Command, he joined us once more as a guest at the annual RAMC dinner in Newcastle. This time we had with us as principal guest the DGAMS, the great Lt Gen. Sir Alexander (Alec) Drummond, an outstanding DG but on occasion a prickly and even irascible man. After dinner, when we were enjoying a nightcap in my home, Ned and Alec got into a furious argument about a topic which I cannot now recall. It seemed so violent that it must surely have put paid to any hope Ned might have had of further professional advancement in the Corps. To our surprise, a few weeks later he was promoted brigadier and continued to hold that rank until retirement. After he retired, I acquired his mess kit uniform and on some dining nights I had to resist firmly its pressure to lead me astray.

Mention of Alec Drummond reminds me that during my TA service I came to know well many senior serving officers for whom I came to have, in different ways, a very high regard. Drummond himself was exceptional; he was tireless in his support of the medical services and introduced numerous important innovations. Later came two other notable DGs in Lt Gen. Sir James Baird, a reflective, thoughtful and able physician, and Sir Robert Drew, a cheerful, ebullient Australian and a great friend of the TA.

In the early days one who impressed me rather less was Major-Gen. Charles Greenaway, a rather humourless little man whose nickname (because of his stature, his voice and his toothbrush moustache) was Robertson Hare. I well remember an exercise which he watched at Chester where one of our best teams of NCOs and men was carrying out a casualty collection exercise over an assault course under simulated battle conditions with thunder-flashes and blank ammunition going off all around them. As he saw them surmounting a series of obstacles with a stretcher, he remarked 'Well, of course, they would never be able to do that with a man on the stretcher', to which our reply was 'Well, sir, there *is* a man on the stretcher'. Among the many good friends of our unit were General Frank Richardson (an outstanding scholar of military medical history, who wrote and spoke beautifully), the cheerfully rotund Ambrose Meneces, the two likeable Aherns (Donal and Tim), the gregarious and hospitable John Douglas, and many others with whom in my time we achieved friendly and fruitful working relationships, including Jimmy Barnetson, Bobby Franklin, Jimmy Miller and Paddy Palmer.

The events of many of our later annual camps, usually taking place in late May or in June, could fill innumerable chapters so I must be selective. There was, for example, the camp at Mytchett where we found ourselves one of a gaggle of military units. One such was an army emergency reserve (AER) field ambulance commanded by Col Graeme Warrack, OBE, a notable Edinburgh dentist who was both medically and dentally qualified and who had had an outstanding war career. His book *Travel by Dark after Arnhem* described his remarkable adventures in escaping from the Germans and in crossing the enemy lines, aided by several redoubtable Dutch civilians. Graeme, whom we later came to know well, eventually became a brigadier and the DG's adviser on the medical services of the TA. The other unit camped close by was the 17th London General Hospital, our old rivals. I knew many of their officers well since when I worked at Queen Square from 1954–55 I trained part-time with them (when they were commanded by Col Bill Tucker) at the Duke of York's Barracks in Chelsea. The administrative and transport facilities and equipment of the RAMC training wing at Mytchett must then have been extensive as we and the 17th London both set out on three-day field exercises simultaneously, each being required to establish 200-bedded tented hospitals out in the country where we were required to be prepared to admit casualties. We worked, I must say, exceptionally hard. John Todd as CO stayed behind at Mytchett and Robin Sykes and I were required jointly to take charge of the detachment which established our tented hospital. Finally, all the tents were up, the beds were made and the wards equipped by about 1.00 in the morning, at which time we were all exhausted. Nevertheless some of our officers and men found both the time and energy to carry out a night raid on the encampment of the 17th London to test (as they said) their security arrangements. Their defences were easily breached. Some of us were not particularly pleased to be visited in our temporary and very inadequate mess by the commanding officer and the honorary colonel at 1.30 a.m., demanding refreshment. They stayed on and on when all of us wanted nothing more than to climb into our safari beds. Eventually we felt that we could take no more, so I crept out of the mess tent and turned off the generator which was producing the electricity for the entire camp. This at last encouraged the CO and honorary colonel to return to Mytchett, but before departing John Todd pointed out that he would see me reduced to lance corporal next morning!

There was yet another amusing incident during this exercise. We were encamped below the Hog's back near Puttenham and were awakened early one morning by a noisy infantry exercise involving Sandhurst cadets in an area which we could overlook. A gleaming staff car full of immaculate senior officers drove imperiously into our camp, ignoring our sentries, in order to look down on the exercise. 'Skem' Hutchinson, unshaven, dishevelled in undershirt, braces and trousers stormed out of his tent roaring 'What the bloody hell are you lot doing here?'. I dressed quickly and sought an explanation (and an apology, speedily given) but one of the inspecting colonels said 'I say, old boy, your Sergeant-Major seems very upset with us!'.

Another enjoyable camp was at Netley, near Southampton, where we occupied a small part of one wing of that magnificent old edifice which had been built at the time of the Crimean War and which used to be such a striking feature of the shore-line of Southampton Water before it was demolished a few years ago. It was a huge building containing large wards with high ceilings, protected on the seaward side by a very wide corridor which stretched almost the entire length of its frontage. Legend suggests that the hospital was so designed as to withstand the heat of an Indian summer and that the plans were mixed up, so that in error it was built in England rather than India. I believe that the story is apocryphal but nevertheless the architectural style of Netley suggested that it was at least possible. That camp, like the later one in uncomfortable and equally inconvenient Victorian blocks at Colchester Military Hospital, was not particularly memorable for any specific incident. However, from my own point of view it was pleasant to return to Southampton where I had enjoyed part of my Army service and where again we saw some of the gracious transatlantic liners still in service gliding imperiously up and down Southampton Water.

More memorable, however, was our camp at Garelochhead in western Scotland, where we were accommodated in a weekend training camp, a hutted establishment close to the nuclear submarine base at Faslane and near the town of Helensburgh where in our spare time we enjoyed a game of golf. Several memories stand out. The first was that, as usual, we planned a three-day exercise to establish a tented hospital out in the country. The site chosen, by permission of His Grace the Duke of Argyll, was in the Buschang Field near his castle at Inveraray. This involved a long drive with all our trucks and equipment up that famous incline 'Rest and be Thankful', through some of the loveliest scenery in Scotland. Fortunately during the drive the weather was superb, but as we arrived at the Buschang Field the heavens opened and we were compelled to erect our tents in appalling weather. The sight of colleagues seated behind canvas screens in the pouring rain on the usual wooden structures covering deep trench latrines was hilarious but nevertheless induced in some members of the unit a state of constipation which lasted until the exercise was over. Despite the weather, the Duke kindly sent his piper to entertain us as we struggled to erect our tents and to prepare our accommodation. Fortunately we came to an arrangement with a cooperative hotelier in the village of Inveraray so that warm showers and hot drinks were available on the first day before we were able to provide our own facilities.

During the exercise the Duke was kind enough to invite a few officers to the Castle for a drink. He was charming and hospitable but we were all slightly shaken to find that as we seated ourselves in comfort in a huge drawing room, a servant placed a tumbler and a decanter by each place and proceeded to pour out almost a full tumbler of amber liquid. On seeing our looks of concern, the Duke's response was direct; he said 'Oh, don't be put off—that's pure malt whisky, it'll do you no harm'! Fortunately we had military transport with a cheerfully sober driver who was able to return us to our tented accommodation. The Buschang Field was so called because Mary Queen of Scots had reviewed her own troops there. It was beautifully situated and ringed by hills; speaking almost no English but being fluent in French, she said 'Quel beau champ' and so the name was acquired. Sadly, the weather improved very little during our three days in what would otherwise have been a magnificent location, but nevertheless the exercise went quite well. When we returned to our spartan but nevertheless watertight hutted accommodation at

Garelochhead, our first thought was to have another shower and to get warm. We were, however, dismayed on returning to camp to find that our cars, all parked in a designated car park, had been damaged. With the exception of 'Skem' Hutchinson's car which had seen better days, all of them had a series of dents and linear marks along either side, seriously scarring the paintwork. There was much talk of vandalism and the like. But next night after dinner, when one of our officers who shall be nameless was returning to his billet on his hands and knees and met a horned highland sheep face to face, the penny dropped. These horned sheep, which were able to roam freely around the camp, had been butting their own reflections in the polished bodywork of the cars. Repairing the damage certainly eroded the profit (based upon our Army pay) which all of us had hoped to make from that particular camp. In all the time I served in the TA, there was only one officer (the redoubtable 'Spike' Leaming, then a senior registrar in surgery and subsequently a senior lecturer in surgery in Brisbane, Australia, where he also served for a time as a flying doctor) who ever succeeded in having a mess bill during camp which was greater than his fortnight's pay. Indeed it was said that he had been in the TA for four or five years before his wife actually discovered that he was paid for going to camp.

Innumerable other tales could be told of my 16 years of service but, looking back, it was an experience which I always found enjoyable, if at times demanding and very occasionally frustrating. Rarely, if ever, did it interfere significantly with my professional work. Many friendships established then have lasted, and when I was honoured by being awarded a life peerage in 1989, my former colleagues in Newcastle from the RVI and NGH, from the University and from the TA planned a magnificent dinner for Betty and me which revived many poignant memories, not least of the social life we had so thoroughly enjoyed as a part of my TA experience. Unforgettable, for example, was Robin Sykes' dining out when, after dinner at Fenham Barracks, the PMC, Alan Horler, was banging for attention with his gavel and Robin quietly passed a glass of port directly under it at just the wrong moment, only to see it shatter with port flying in all directions. Another memorable remark was uttered by a nursing sister who had over-indulged and complained next day that the curry tasted just as hot coming up as it did going down.

The camps in Sennelager were a very special experience, particularly for those officers and men who had never served overseas, We flew from Newcastle Airport to RAF Gutersloh and were then transported by trucks to Sennelager, where our host unit was an RAMC field ambulance commanded on our first visit by the redoubtable Lt Col Paddy Irwin, on our second by Lt Col Paddy O'Dwyer. We were housed in splendid hutted accommodation with a magnificent mess which had been a headquarters mess of the Wehrmacht during the second world war. Close by were tank ranges and heather moorland, excellent for military exercises, and we were within relatively easy reach of the British Military Hospital at Rinteln, though this was best reached by helicopter, crossing a range of hills upon which stood the magnificent monument of Hermanns Denkmal, a landmark which could be seen for miles around. More than once, however, we travelled to and from Rinteln by road, calling on the way to see a remarkable collection of eagles which had been held in captivity in the hills for many years. News came one day that a baby had been born at Rinteln without a diaphragm, i.e. with a total hernia of abdominal contents into the chest so that the neonate was almost incapable of breathing. Fortunately we had in our unit at that time Major Hedley Brown, a well-trained thoracic surgeon, and John Inkster, a superb paediatric anaesthetist. They flew to Rinteln where they fashioned an artificial diaphragm from a sterilized portion of a sister's nylon slip; the operation was totally successful. Inevitably the news leaked out, so that for a few days the No. 1 Northern General Hospital received some favourable publicity in the national newspapers.

During our first camp, Paddy Irwin learned that there were some patients in the Berlin Military Hospital where a second medical opinion was needed and he quickly arranged for four of us (myself, Robin Sykes, Alan Morton and 'Queenie' Prout) to travel by the military train from Hannover to Berlin for the weekend, where I could perhaps help by offering my professional opinion. In those days one had to have a military identity card in which every single dot, full stop and comma had to be exactly the same as on one's travel documents. East German guards at the border could not read English but simply examined the travel documents and identity cards and turned back anyone where these did not correspond exactly. All went well, even though at movement control in Hannover as we were about to board the train the major turned to Robin (resplendent in full uniform with his red-banded hat and red tabs) and asked him 'What is the purpose of your journey, Sir?', to which Robin replied 'A swan'. With just the ghost of a smile, the officer in question wrote down 'Duty'. In Berlin my professional duties were quickly fulfilled and we were able to roam the streets of the West to see the beautiful garden which the British government gave to the people of Berlin after the war, Spandau Prison where Rudolf Hess was still imprisoned, and the magnificent concert hall, donated by the Americans, which was slightly reminiscent in style of the Sydney Opera House (built many years later). Locally it was called, because of its architectural style, 'the pregnant oyster'. Everyone wondered how it was that its roof stayed up; these anxieties were justified as some years later the roof collapsed partially and a massive programme of rebuilding was necessary.

We were also able during our stay to fit in a brief visit, through 'checkpoint Charlie', to East Berlin and were at once struck by the remarkable contrast between the bustle, prosperity, heavy traffic and cheerful attitude of the West Berliners when contrasted with the gloomy, grim, semi-deserted streets and barrack-like buildings of the East. Even the famous old Adlon Hotel on the other side of the Wall in the Unter den Linden, such a famous and prosperous street before the war, looked very run-down. And the view from the Wall of the fire-damaged Reichstag building was one to which in later years we all became accustomed through television. According to our hosts the weekend would not be complete without a trip to a night club. I cannot now recall the name of the establishment but it was famous for the fact that on every table there was a telephone which allowed one to ring up people sitting at other tables. We had gone there by bus and were in uniform as British army personnel were then required to wear uniform at all times in Berlin. We were sitting enjoying the floor show and a quiet drink when to our astonishment our telephone rang; when, with some trepidation, we answered it, an invitation in English with what seemed a strong German accent was offered. Somehow we dealt politely with the situation (Queenie's presence was a help); only later on the bus returning to the hospital did we discover that two American physiotherapists who had also been on the bus were responsible for the hoax call.

During our second camp at Sennelager when I was in command we had our usual three-day exercise. The location to which we sent a detachment with hospital beds and other facilities was not a tented one as there were on the Sennelager ranges a number of deserted buildings which could effectively be used for many military purposes. There was one which seemed to be admirable as a casualty reception station. Hugh Brown was in charge of the detachment with several medical officers and a good many male and female other ranks. After dinner in the mess, it turned out in discussion with some Guards officers who were also staying there that they planned a night exercise with troops in the area where our hospital detachment had become established. I am not sure how a suggestion of involving them arose, though I suspect that it probably came from Roland Goodhead. Things then moved apace and our unfortunate colleagues found themselves surrounded by an attacking group of Guards in the middle of the night. Although our detachment had posted sentries, they could not deter the combatant unit. While this attack, with the expenditure of much blank ammunition and a great deal of noise, clearly added realism to the exercise, our weary colleagues in the detachment, and not least Hugh Brown himself, were far from pleased at having their sleep interrupted by this fearsome invasion.

One great advantage of training in Germany was that the range of equipment available was excellent so that all members of the unit were able to obtain experience of medical activity under active service conditions, while some took turns in helping out Paddy's under-staffed field ambulance by assisting in his MI room and medical reception station. Troop carriers, tanks and many other vehicles were available so that casualty treatment and evacuation from a variety of war-like situations could be practised. Hard though we worked, leisure and social activities were not forgotten. There was a pleasant nine-hole golf course close by (Paddy O'Dwyer was an outstanding golfer who played regularly for the Army with a handicap of three; he arranged later for the course to be extended to 18 holes). Our parties were as lively as ever with the invariable sing-songs afterwards with Roland Goodhead, as always, on piano. We were visited for several days by a reporter from the Northern Echo and I look back with some amusement on the long article which he headed 'The Blaydon Races—from the Officers' Mess!'. Having been able since my youth to remember all the verses of 'The Blaydon Races', 'The Lambton Worm' and 'Keep Yor Feet Still, Geordie Hinny', as well as various other songs, everyone seemed to be amused to find the CO leading the community singing of Tyneside songs. Alan Horler almost always followed with 'Cushie Butterfield' and Tom Bird with 'The Rhesus Factor', a song cleverly written by him and Willie Walker of Newcastle to explain rhesus incompatibility and its treatment.

While, as I have said, I greatly enjoyed my TA service, by the time I was due to retire in 1966 after three years in command my professional commitments had increased to such an extent that I would have found it difficult, if not impossible, to continue to serve. My own dining out at Fenham Barracks was thoroughly memorable and I still treasure the clock with which I was presented by my fellow officers and the silver-gilt dish which I received from the sergeants' mess. To return to the unit as Honorary Colonel for five years from 1968–1973 was also a delight, though the commitment was not heavy. I attended many social events and tried whenever I could to join the unit for a day or two at annual camp. By the time I was Honorary Colonel the unit was no longer the No. 1 but had become the No. 201 Northern General Hospital (T & AVR). Bill Ross, having succeeded me as Commanding Officer, later followed me as Honorary Colonel, and he in turn was followed by Hugh Brown. Hugh had the privilege of marching the unit past the Queen Mother in 1984 when she opened the new Medical School and when the unit was awarded the freedom of the City of Newcastle upon Tyne. I regard it as a great privilege to have been able to serve with and to command that unit and to have been its Honorary Colonel. As I write, members of the unit of all ranks have recently served with distinction in the Persian Gulf and made an outstanding contribution to the care of British sick and wounded, who, fortunately, proved to be far fewer than anticipated.

CHAPTER 14

International Travel

Little did I imagine in my schooldays or even in medical school that my profession would give me the many interesting and even exciting opportunities for foreign travel which later emerged. Apart from my brief visit to Paris with other members of the school in 1939 and our memorable honeymoon in Norway, I had seen nothing of Europe. When in 1951 the opportunity arose of presenting a paper on the EEG sequelae of sub-arachnoid haemorrhage to a joint meeting of the British and Belgian EEG Societies in Brussels, this seemed an opportunity too good to miss, especially as Professor Nattrass indicated that the University would give me a travel grant if my paper were accepted. Once I heard that it was, I prepared my manuscript and slides with great care; although I learned that the languages of the meeting were French and English, it seemed to me that although my schoolboy French had never been refreshed since school, it might be taken as a compliment to our hosts if I were to present my paper in that language. I therefore asked our university medical librarian, Dr Joan Emmerson, whom I knew to be a linguist, if she would translate the text for me. She generously agreed and even spared the time to listen to me reading it so as to correct some more obvious infelicities of pronunciation. The prospect of travel by air never occurred to me, if only on the grounds of expense. I therefore set off by train and Channel ferry and found myself housed in the plain but comfortable Palace Hotel in the Place Rogier in the centre of Brussels, close to the Gare du Nord. There I met for the first time Dr Harold Millar of Belfast (later a good friend) who had also had a paper accepted. The meeting was interesting though some of the papers in French were very difficult to follow and one presented by a Finn seemed totally obscure, even though, after a few minutes, we realized that the language in which he was speaking was supposed to be English. My own paper went down surprisingly well and I was much complimented on the quality of my French (I suppose that my gift for mimicry stood me in good stead); fortunately at the end I added a phrase to the effect that I would be unable to answer questions in French. Even so, the voluble Henri Gastaut from Marseille, who was interested in my results, fired off several questions. However, Dr Grey Walter of the Burdon Neurological Institute in Bristol rapidly translated these so that I could answer appropriately.

There were surprisingly few British participants, which made it possible for the famous Professor Bremer to invite those of us from the UK to his splendid home for a meal. Harold Millar and I, in view our relative impoverishment and British exchange regulations which prevented one from taking much currency overseas, decided not to go to the Bremer residence by taxi but to try to get there by bus and tram. When I sought help from a bearded and heavily moustachioed Belgian of stately mien, the reception was frosty. 'Vous êtes Allemand?' he said coldly. When I responded 'Non, je suis Anglais' his attitude changed at once. 'Ah, Anglais!' he said with a broad smile and then insisted on conducting us to the appropriate stop and on giving us careful and explicit directions as to how to get to the address we sought. The meal itself was sumptuous and the first I had attended at which, in a huge dining-room seating about 40 people around a single long table, there were no fewer than five glasses by each place. The food was served on elegant Sèvres china, the wines in superb antique crystal glasses among a profusion of silver dishes and candelabra which decorated the table. I was confident that such a lifestyle could not have been achieved simply by work in electroencephalography. I later learned that Professor Bremer's wife came from an extremely wealthy Belgian family. Their house was a former chateau situated in a beautiful botanic garden and arboretum which had been laid out in the 15th century. The top two floors of this magnificent home were still being used by the professor as a psychiatric nursing home, though the secluded private quarters were carefully insulated from all evidence of professional activity.

Our return journey to the hotel after being superbly wined and dined was also eventful. As Harold and I crossed the Place Rogier we were accosted by two ladies of the night from whom in some embarrassment I escaped quickly while Harold engaged them in conversation. What they made of his Northern Irish French before he finally disengaged himself is a matter of conjecture. During the meeting we took the opportunity of visiting a few of the sights of Brussels, including the stately, illuminated magnificence of the Grand Place and, of course, the Manikin Pis. And on my return train journey to Ostend I had a few spare hours in Bruges. My memory of what I saw has faded over the last 40 years but I remember the quaintness of the architecture, the charm of the tranquil and leafy canals and the beauty of the main square which one could overlook from the heights of a church tower.

Two years later Betty and I and the girls embarked on our American adventure (Chapter 8). When we returned to Newcastle I was fully occupied in building up my career and my research team and had no opportunity for overseas travel. In 1958, however, shortly after being appointed as a consultant, I was thrilled to be invited by the Association for Research in Nervous and Mental Disease of New York to join in

December that year its commission which would examine neuromuscular disease. As the Association offered to cover my travel expenses and accommodation in the Roosevelt Hotel in New York City where the meeting was to be held, I jumped at the chance. On the way I paid a brief return visit to Boston to see old friends before going on to the three-day meeting in New York. I was astonished to be bearded in the hotel by a US photographic agency which insisted on taking numerous photographs of me for public use while also persuading me, before I could think too clearly, to buy some for myself and the family. The flattery of such an approach quickly palled in the light of many similar experiences in later years. New York that December was bitterly cold but brilliantly sunny and crystal clear and it was still possible then to walk freely and comfortably around Times Square, in Central Park and even in Harlem without any sense of apprehension. Yet again I saw the superb Christmas decorations on Fifth Avenue, the illuminated reindeers and outdoor skating rink at Rockefeller Center and did some Christmas shopping for Betty and the children at Macy's. More importantly, however, I renewed my acquaintance with the officers of the Muscular Dystrophy Association of America and met for the first time several American neurologists working in neuromuscular disease who subsequently became good friends and associates. I was flattered to be told by Gunnar Wohlfart of Sweden, after I had given my paper on classification, that he had enjoyed the content but more particularly wished to say that when listening to me he realized for the first time that English was a beautiful language. This for a Geordie lad was a very precious compliment.

Over the next two years no invitations or opportunities for travel overseas arose. Out of the blue, however, in 1961 there came a letter from a family in Durban, South Africa, supported by one from their general practitioner, Dr Lionel Savage, asking if I would travel to Durban to examine a 14-year-old boy in whose case a diagnostic dispute had arisen. One paediatrician and one neurologist were convinced that he was suffering from Duchenne muscular dystrophy, whereas two other equally senior and distinguished colleagues had concluded on the basis of histological appearances in muscle biopsy sections that the diagnosis was one of polymyositis and were wishing to give long-term treatment with steroids. I was invited to be the arbiter and the patient's grandparents, both born in England, agreed to cover my travel expenses and a modest fee if I would make the journey. I therefore arranged with colleagues to pay a brief call in Johannesburg and to lecture there before going on to Durban and later to Cape Town. On arriving I found that it was first necessary to register with the South African Medical Association in order to be able to see a patient. I was told that a senior British neurologist who had flown out the year before to see a wealthy diamond merchant had omitted to take that precaution and having charged a substantial fee, then found that he was compelled to donate it to the South African Medical Benevolent Fund. For reasons which now seem obscure, as he was not a registered practitioner he was prevented from taking the money out of the country. My documentation via Pretoria was quickly secured and my stay in Johannesburg was brief. It was nevertheless long enough for me to be shocked by the extraordinary contrast between white, black and coloured housing and by the transport and other facilities available for each of the racial groups. Those discrepancies were much less overt in Durban, a beautiful city where the black townships seemed far removed but where nevertheless public facilities for the various racial groups showed the same striking contrasts. I was also shattered to find that Lionel Savage, whose patient I was to see, had three waiting rooms at his consulting rooms—one for black, one for white and one for coloured. His beautiful home where I stayed was surrounded by a lovely garden but heavily fenced and guarded. He had eight black servants, all living in spartan accommodation in what might have been regarded more than a century earlier in America as the slave house. The inequity of the situation was brought home even more powerfully when I learned that several of the servants, both male and female, had families in one of the native townships whom they saw for only two or three weeks at the most each year.

The Anderson family, whose son I was to see, lived in a charming detached bungalow with a splendid swimming pool in the garden. It was quickly evident to me that their son was a typical case of muscular dystrophy of the Duchenne type and that the alternative diagnosis of polymyositis had been based upon misinterpretation of the muscle biopsy findings. While the family and the delightful grandparents appreciated that I could not in consequence offer any hope of effective treatment, they nevertheless felt satisfied that the diagnostic dispute had been resolved. I also saw several other patients for Lionel Savage and met my old Queen Square friend, Dick Cheetham, professor of psychiatry in Durban (whose brother Jack had been captain of the South African cricket team) and David Chapman, formerly of Newcastle, then professor of surgery at the black medical school of the University of Natal.

I then moved on for a few days to Cape Town to be met by Louis Vogelpoel, the cardiologist, another old friend from Queen Square, with whom I viewed that unbelievably beautiful city from several perspectives. It may be trite to say that the view from the top of Table Mountain, approached by cable car, is breathtaking, but no other word suffices, particularly when one looks down over the city or over the Hottentot Hollands range of mountains to the right, or over Pike's Peak to the left. And the Newlands cricket ground close to where the Vogelpoels lived must surely be one of the loveliest in the world. I could not but feel deeply saddened that this fascinating and beautiful country had built its prosperity upon a political philosophy of racial separation which I found frankly nauseating. While most of the medical colleagues whom I met were members of the Progressive Party, even their condemnation of apartheid in the comfortable and privileged living environment which they enjoyed occasionally seemed half-hearted. There were even some, like the Andersons, who expressed incredulity when I suggested, however, tentatively, that the way in which they treated their fellow black South Africans would inevitably bring increasing opprobrium upon them from the rest of the world. Fortunately, as I write, Mr de Klerk seems at last to be taking steps to bring his sad but beautiful country if not 'into the 20th century' at least, one hopes into the 21st with a more equitable system of government.

From 1958, when I became a member, I regularly attended the biannual meetings of the Association of British Neurologists (ABN), one being held in London each autumn, while the spring meeting rotated around provincial centres. Attending these meetings enabled one to meet neurological colleagues from many parts of the UK, with many of whom lasting friendships developed. It was through conversation with some of them that I concluded that I might offer a paper for the International Congress of Neurology due to be held in Rome in September 1961. As Betty and I discussed this, it seemed that this would provide an excellent opportunity for us to combine attendance at the congress with an overseas family holiday which we felt, at last, that we could afford. Christopher, then just 5 years of age, was too young to take and so we arranged for him to stay with the family of a school friend. I then planned a car journey around Italy with Betty and the girls. This was a time when I was still driving between 20 and 25,000 miles a year in the northern region. I had worked out a system with my bank whereby I opened a loan account which provided a capital sum sufficient to enable me to change my car every two years. I had a regular standing order through which a monthly payment helped gradually to pay off the loan. By this means we bought three successive Ford Consuls and in 1961 we had one which was almost new and seemed very suitable for our overseas adventure. We drove to Dover, spending one night in a Canterbury hotel; after leaving the ferry at Boulogne we drove on to Paris where we loaded our car aboard the night sleeper. We woke up just in time to see some mountain scenery of Switzerland and northern Italy before disembarking next morning in Milan to begin our tour proper.

From Milan we drove to Como, spending one night in a pleasant hotel overlooking the lake where Ann, aged 14, flirted outrageously with the handsome Italian waiters while Judy looked on, clearly picking up some tips. Next day we drove east into the Dolomites along the Via della Dolomiti, negotiating more hairpin bends in the course of a single day than I can ever remember before or since, yet also feeling stunned by the incredible pink grandeur of the mountain scenery which unfolded before us. Another night was spent in a delightful mountain hotel in Carezza, a village with a beautiful small blue lake where we had time to take a chairlift to a plateau half way up one of the most majestic groups of peaks. From that vantage point the vista of that splendid mountain range held us spellbound. Next day we drove on via Cortina d'Ampezzo to Venice, sharing the experience of millions of others by unloading our car in the huge garage and taking a motor boat to our hotel on the Grand Canal. This was the Hotel Monaco e Gran Canale, a splendid establishment which then seemed reasonably priced but which is now, I understand from friends to whom I have recommended it, horrendously expensive. To our astonishment, at dinner on the first night, we recognized at once a strident female voice echoing across the room as being that of Kathleen Black who, with her husband, Munro, the Newcastle ENT surgeon, was in Venice on holiday. Travel has taught us that friends and acquaintances often turn up in the most unexpected parts of the world. In the next three days we feasted on the sights of the city, its canals and splendid buildings including, of course, those surrounding St Mark's Square and the Bridge of Sighs. To keep the girls happy we took a trip on a gondola to the glassworks at Murano and another to the Lido de Jesolo for a few hours' swimming and sunbathing.

The route I had mapped out for travelling on to Rome took us down the Adriatic coast; I knew that Rimini was a huge tourist resort and had told our travel agent to choose a hotel somewhere nearby in a small, quiet and peaceful resort. It turned out that he had selected one in Cattolica, a slightly smaller replica of Rimini with a good beach but with a gaggle of hotels closely opposed along the seafront all boasting bars, and amusement parlours, and some with fish and chip shops and many of the other 'amenities' so beloved of some of our compatriots; it was as if Morecambe had been transposed to the Adriatic. Fortunately, one night was tolerable; the swimming was good and the food and wine excellent, so that we were not too distressed and left early the next day to drive into the Appennines with a brief glance at San Marino on the way. The splendour of Perugia, that lovely old mediaeval town, is legendary, with its stately basilica and palace and its panoramic views over the surrounding plains. We could happily have stayed longer but nevertheless pressed on to Assisi, which we enjoyed even more not just because of its architecture and stunning views, but also because despite the swarming tourists it had a pervasive aura of peace and piety, inevitably conveying something of the spirit and ideals of St Francis.

And so on we went to Rome where despite the hair-raising habits of the local drivers we found our hotel, the Hotel Helvetia, without difficulty. To our astonishment, during the week we stayed there we had no difficulty in parking our car on the street almost directly outside the hotel front door. It was situated close to that extraordinary monument to King Victor Emmanuel, a hugely ostentatious and gleaming white pile often compared to a huge cake lavishly coated in icing sugar. It has a certain vulgar grandeur and is a sight which no one visiting Rome can avoid seeing from many vantage points. The hotel was comfortable but unfortunately the room in which we all slept had a window opening on to the street near a sharp corner where the noise of grinding gears and squealing tyres threatened to keep us awake. This was when Betty discovered the crucial importance of having ear-plugs when travelling at home or abroad; she and they have been inseparable ever since and fortunately the children seemed each night to be so sleepy that they were little disturbed.

The congress, held on an avenue leading to St Peter's Square, was well organized and scientifically enjoyable. My paper on the muscular dystrophies (naturally) in one of the main sessions seemed to go well, but I remember little more about the meeting. Much clearer in my memory are the visits that we made as a family (and always in our car) to places like the Forum, the Colosseum, the Baths of Caracalla, the Janiculum Terrace, St Peter's, the Sistine Chapel, the Spanish Steps, the Fountain of Trevi and even to the Olympic swimming pool where we spent one leisurely afternoon. Henry Miller (irreverently called by Laurie 'the stranded whale'), Hugh Garland, Laurie Liversedge, Harold Millar and others were also there. I also remember how shocked I felt when I noted Hugh's lascivious glances at 14-year-old Ann in her swimming costume.

But even when the meeting ended, our holiday was not yet over as we had time to drive on to Florence where we spent one night overlooking the banks of the Arno and the Ponte Vecchio. We also saw Michelangelo's 'David', the basilica, the campanile and the Uffizi Gallery before moving on next day to Pisa. The remarkable architecture of the leaning tower and the nearby basilica fascinated us all. Our last night before returning by car sleeper from Genoa to Paris was spent at Rapallo, which after our experience of Cattolica we approached with some apprehension. Happily it was a more charming and relatively peaceful seaside town where most of the horrors of the massive development we had seen on the Adriatic had been resisted.

An obvious danger of trying to record the pleasures derived from travel experiences is that such an account could develop into an interminable travelogue. I have set down some details of our Italian tour if only because this was the first and indeed the only such lengthy overseas adventure upon which we embarked as a family (though Christopher, had been excluded, solely on grounds of age). My comments upon later travel will be much more selective, in the hope of describing some experiences of general interest.

1963 saw a short lecture tour in May with brief visits to Boston and Rochester (NY) and a formal lecture on muscle disease in Detroit where my hosts were John Meyer and Max Newman. In June I gave an invited talk at a congress on electromyography in Copenhagen splendidly organized by Fritz Buchthal and stayed in the Egremont Hotel, notable because it doubled as a student hall of residence in autumn and winter but became a public hotel mainly staffed by striking beautiful Danish girl students in the summer.

In 1964 I was invited by my friend George Monckton to participate in a major muscle congress funded by the Muscular Dystrophy Association of Canada in Edmonton, Alberta. After brief stop-overs to lecture in Toronto and in Winnipeg, I flew on to Edmonton where I found that Harry Links (formerly the 'El Nil' surgeon who organized the neon fish 'racket'—see Chapter 5) was now head of a large and prosperous surgical clinic. Edmonton itself was not a particularly attractive city, being surrounded by almost endless plains and prairies. This vista was broken only by a defile running through the city centre which added character and there were some reasonable public buildings, though none of particular merit. The university occupied a huge campus on the outskirts where I had a splendid room high up in a tower block of student accommodation. George Monckton had organized a comprehensive meeting dealing with the basic structure, development and biochemistry of muscle as well as with its diseases. The meeting attracted many internationally known participants and was scientifically very fruitful, leading to a valuable two-volume publication. Afterwards I was able to pay a short visit to Vancouver and to meet again Dr Bill Gibson, medical historian, neurophysiologist, neurologist and polymath, later much involved in founding Green College (Chapter 17) who had been chairman of the Scientific Advisory Committee of the Muscular Dystrophy Association of America from whom I received my first research grant. Fortunately time allowed me to travel from Edmonton to Vancouver by train on the Canadian National Railway via Jasper. Certainly this is one of the great train journeys of the world. On a single-track line the train meanders gently through the plains and foothills. Standing at the rear to watch from the observation window the mountains, conifers, streams and rivers and the silent rail tracks fading into the distance is memorable enough, but is totally over-shadowed, as one turns a corner, by the towering grandeur of Mount Robson, the tallest mountain in the Canadian Rockies—snow-covered yet gaunt and forbidding and glowering over the forests and rivers below. Even that view, however, had not prepared me for the scenic magnificence of the countryside around Vancouver. The city itself is spacious and pleasantly laid out, but the view from the campus of the University of British Columbia and particularly from the Faculty Club is breathtaking. As we made our way by car northwards along the coast in the few hours that we had to spare between professional engagements, sights such as Vancouver Island and Horseshoe Bay, whence the boats go out to Victoria Island, were spellbinding. I look forward to renewing these memories at the next World Congress of Neurology in Vancouver in 1993.

In September 1964 Betty and I attended a joint Anglo-Polish neurological meeting in the beautiful mediaeval city of Cracow, with a visit to Warsaw on the way. On arriving there we were met by the formidable Professor Irena Hausmanowa-Petrusewicz, herself a major contributor to research in neuro-muscular disease. She greeted us in stentorian if kindly tones. Her English was then rather fractured but later became very fluent, almost as good as her excellent French. She had 24 neurologists in her department of whom 21 were women; of the three men, one was Konstanty Mrozek who later worked with us in Newcastle. As we talked in her room, she said in halting English 'Will you please sit down?', but as we chatted on she suddenly said 'Sit down!', which we did promptly. Then she said 'Dr Walton, I have lots of patients for you to see and examine. Mrs Walton, Dr Mrozek will show you Warsaw. Goodbye', and off they went. My clinical activities were not particularly memorable apart from a fierce dispute that I had with Sam Nevin from London (also visiting) about the interpretation of a muscle biopsy. Later, however, we saw the old city of Warsaw which had been painstakingly rebuilt from photographs and old drawings in virtually the same style as before it had been destroyed by German military action. Attractive though the rebuilt city was, it was eerie to see on each building the twin dates of the original and of the later copy, e.g. 1616 and 1960. Professor Hausmanowa also invited us to join her with some colleagues from her department for dinner in the basement of the Polish Academy of Sciences, a splendid chateau once owned by a Polish count who was an ally of Napoleon. The vaulted crypt and the general ambience were delightful. A colleague from London, Ronald Henson, arrived late. As he sat down at the table the head waiter, hovering in the background, switched on a radio. We had anticipated that there might be some background music, perhaps by Chopin, but to our astonishment heard the Beatles singing 'A Hard Day's Night'. When we roared with laughter and turned to Ronnie Henson expressing surprise, he, no doubt genuinely, disclaimed all knowledge of the Beatles, pointing out that his major musical interest was in Bach.

On we went to Cracow where the magnificent central square and market were dominated by the asymmetrical twin towers of St. Mary's Cathedral on which each day the trumpeter's call is terminated in mid-note to recall the invasion many centuries earlier when another trumpeter had been killed by an arrow. The ancient Royal Palace, too, with its towering walls, seeming almost as awesome as the north face of the Eiger, was fascinating. Nevertheless our most moving, if chilling, experience was a bus trip which we took to Auschwitz, where the magnitude and unspeakable horror of the holocaust was savagely highlighted. The appalling dormitories, with their bare and cramped wooden benches, the gas chambers and the appliances such as crutches, artificial limbs and other items taken from the victims, as well as the bills of lading documenting the amount of gold, for example, obtained from their teeth, all catalogued with remarkable Teutonic efficiency, had a totally numbing effect. Everyone remained silent and contemplative on the coach returning to Cracow, horrified by this concrete evidence of man's inhumanity to man.

Our visit to Poland must be qualified by one memorable aside. As I was then in command of the No. 1 Northern General Hospital (TA), I was informed that as a serving officer who had been positively vetted, I had to consult military intelligence before visiting an Iron Curtain country. I therefore made a special journey to Edinburgh to be briefed, being warned especially about the avoidance of sexual misdemeanours which might lead to subsequent blackmail. I was told that Polish intelligence was among the most effective and ubiquitous of all such Eastern European organizations. I was also warned to be careful about conversation in public places and hotel rooms. In both Warsaw and Cracow we searched our room assiduously but could find nothing, though Edwin Bickerstaff swears that he found a 'bug' in a table lamp beside his bed. However, in this, our first visit to an Iron Curtain country, though we found the documentation irritating and the ever-present attentions of our tourist guide a little oppressive, we were never aware of being under surveillance. Some of our hosts even talked openly (when out of doors) about the less attractive features of the Polish Communist regime. Konstanty Mrozek even told us about a Warsaw congress at which representatives of many countries were arriving; out of the first car stepped the French Prime Minister and his girl-friend, out of the second the British Prime Minister and his wife, out of the third car the US Secretary of State and his secretary, and out of the fourth car came Kruschev and Bulganin! Such healthy irreverence induced much mirth but we were nevertheless conscious of the problems which even our medical colleagues and other professionals encountered. The preponderance of women amongst neurologists and indeed among the medical profession generally was largely related to the fact that the profession was insufficiently well paid to attract many men. Doctors could be reasonably assured of having two rooms in which to live (one living room and one bedroom) but in many parts of the city manual workers, for example, were housed four to a room and not more than 50% of the doctors had a car. Konstanty told us that it was unlikely that he would be able to afford to run a car for about 10 years, even though he had graduated eight years earlier.

In autumn 1965, having again made arrangements for the girls and Christopher to be looked after, Betty and I decided upon another extensive foray by car into Europe so that I could present some of my work on

muscle pathology at the International Congress of Neuropathology in
Zurich before going on to the International Congress of Neurology in
Vienna where I had been invited to give a talk in a plenary session on
polymyositis. This time we went by ship from Hull to Ostend, thus
avoiding the long haul to the south coast, before driving on through
Belgium to Zurich with an overnight stay in Rastatt in Germany. Zurich
was memorable first because of the outstanding hotel (the Carlton Elite)
where we stayed at reasonable cost, and secondly because we teamed
up for part of the time with Ray Adams. We also explored some of the
scenic beauty of Switzerland one afternoon but made the mistake of
choosing what looked on the map to be a short cut back to Zurich, to
find ourselves negotiating the formidable Susten pass where we ran into
cloud at about 2000 feet and did not emerge again until one and a half
hours later. As we sighed with relief on completing this horrendous and
tortuous drive in thick fog we saw, to our astonishment, a British car
towing a caravan beginning the ascent. We also spent some time with
Bernard and Betty Tomlinson, including a hilarious evening at a frightful
night club (from which we eventually escaped via the emergency exit,
wending our way between naked ladies awaiting their turn on stage)
before joining them and Professor and Mrs Ganadò from Malta at the
bibulous congress banquet in a splendid castle not far from the city where
several oxen were roasted on spits. Bernard was in sparkling (if somewhat
indiscreet) form and the roasted meat was excellent; sadly some
contaminant or toxin must have been about as the following day we were
all laid low with gastroenteritis. Fortunately we recovered in time to set
out for Vienna.

We drove through the lovely mountainous scenery of Liechtenstein,
spent a night in a delightful alpine hostelry in Kitzbuhel and even had
a little time to explore Salzburg before driving on in our Austin 3-litre
Princess to Vienna where we were housed in the Hotel Erzerhog Rainer.
This was a comfortable hotel in which many other neurological colleagues,
including Laurie and Peggy Liversedge, were staying. One disadvantage
was that our rooms overlooked a busy street and the early morning trams
rumbling by often disturbed our slumbers. Another was the extraordinary
system employed in the dining room where the routine use of a serving
table placed alongside each 'eating' table and the manipulation of multiple
plates regularly involved an almost interminable wait which was
thoroughly irritating. As the meetings were held in the Hofburg Palace,
the sheer baroque magnificence of the architecture, decoration and
massive chandeliers tended to divert one's attention from the scientific
content of the presentations. Of course we found time to visit the
Schonbrunn and Beaulieu Palaces and an evening at the Vienna opera to
see 'Don Giovanni' lives in the memory. I well remember, too, my first
encounter with a charming Russian neurologist, Professor Graschenkov,

who spoke excellent English and who even in those days of the continuing Stalinist era ostentatiously sat in the front row at various meetings reading English newspapers and/or the New York Herald Tribune. Inevitably, too, we took a bus trip en masse to Grinzing in the Vienna woods in order to sample the new wine, sitting out in an illuminated garden under the stars. That wine was so unexpectedly powerful that Derek Denny-Brown was seen to be having difficulty in remounting his bus and required help. In our group were such stalwarts as Liversedge, Matthews and Michael Ashby, each of us with our respective wives. We each enjoyed a half pint beer mug filled to the brim with white wine. When each received a second such glass, the wives, as one, passed them over to their respective husbands, each of whom therefore had three. On the return bus journey to our hotels, the men indulged in riotous singing but it was soon noted that several wives were not speaking to several husbands.

1965 was also enlivened by a week teaching at Queen Square on an exchange arrangement with Chris Earl who later stayed with us while teaching in Newcastle, and by a brief visit in November to the New York Academy of Sciences followed by a day at the National Institutes of Health at Bethesda with King Engel. Later that month I was able to relish the architecture and oenological delights of Heidelberg with its magnificent university on the banks of the Necker, while speaking in a symposium to honour the seminal contributions to muscle disease made by Wilhelm Erb.

In early 1966, after a brief visit to Holland to address the Amsterdam Neurological Society, an unexpected invitation came from Labe Scheinberg and Bob Katzman, the two professors of neurology at the Albert Einstein College of Medicine in the Bronx, New York, inviting me to spend a month there in September and October in order to teach both under-graduates and postgraduates. After consulting my colleagues and the Regional Board about leave of absence, this was an invitation which I gladly accepted. I was able to take six weeks' leave in all, so that Betty and 10-year-old Christopher could join me on a long-awaited visit to the Western USA before going to New York. We spent two happy days with Elinor Adams in Boston and then flew to Denver to visit Jimmie Stevens, Queen Square trained, head of department there, who was immensely hospitable despite the fact that he knew, as did his family and friends, that he was dying of cancer. On we went to Los Angeles where our host was Carl Pearson who, in between my professional commitments, arranged with his friends the Merrills (Howard Merrill was producer of the Dick van Dyke television show), who had a son with muscular dystrophy, to take us to Disneyland where Christopher was in his element, though Betty and I found the descent of the 'Matterhorn' on a roller coaster quite terrifying. From LA we flew to Grand Canyon where we were astonished to find that the airport 'lobby' was a caravan and the public toilets were earth closets (old fashioned 'privies'). We stayed in a log cabin at Bright Angel Lodge and spent two glorious days being driven around the rim of the Canyon. No-one who has seen this magnificent natural phenomenon can fail to be impressed by its sheer magnificence and grandeur and by the changing colours of the rock formations as the sun rises, reaches its peak and eventually sets. We then moved on to New York where the rain streamed down from leaden skies, the streets and pavements were awash and I saw Betty and Chris off at the airport before starting my Einstein commitment.

The only disadvantage was that while I was housed in a comfortable hotel and in a small and (relatively) inexpensive room on 54th Street in New York, I had to get out to 'Einstein' each morning by a subway, a streetcar and a bus, a journey which took well over an hour and a quarter. When one was invited, as I was within my first few days, to take the weekly neuromuscular conference at 7.30 a.m., this meant getting up at 5.30, so that the days became rather long. Nevertheless the month that I spent teaching in the College Hospital, the Jacobi City Hospital and at Montefiore, where Irving Cooper was then doing much of his surgical work on the treatment of parkinsonism, was both enjoyable and memorable. I saw innumerable patients and further developed the technique which I had introduced in my weekly conferences in Newcastle of having patients presented to me with the history alone, after which I would examine them personally and would then discuss the clinical differential diagnosis before asking for information about any tests which might have been done. This type of teaching was relatively new to many American students and postgraduates and seemed to be appreciated. Before I left, the class of students with whom I had been most closely involved gave me a splendid lunch and presented me with an autographed copy of *Playboy* to take home! Not for the first time nor the last time was I struck by the remarkable contrast between the quality of accommodation and facilities seen in the private College Hospital on the one hand compared with the much more spartan provision in the public Jacobi Hospital (funded by the city) on the other. That month certainly brought home to me more strongly than ever before the problems encountered in American medicine because of: (a) the profit motive, which meant that some investigations were performed because they brought income to the performer even if they were not all strictly necessary on medical grounds; (b) the fact that despite a well-developed insurance system, some families were still impoverished by the effects of illness if they sought private medical care; and (c) the evidence that while the best of American medicine was as good, if not better than any in the world, the poorest was certainly below the standard I had come to expect in the UK National Health Service.

Three clinical demonstrations stand out particularly in my memory. After one, in which I had examined a man who proved to have an obscure neuromuscular disorder about which I believe I was able to offer helpful advice, he was being taken out from the lecture theatre in a wheelchair in front of a huge audience when I heard him say in a florid Bronx accent 'Gee, who is dat guy? He talks just like Richard Burton'! On another occasion I discussed a young woman who had developed a curious posture of the affected hand following a stroke which had probably resulted from her use of a contraceptive pill which contained a high concentration of oestrogen. Her recovery from the stroke was excellent until this bizarre contracture developed; Irving Cooper proposed to operate upon her as he felt that this was a dystonic phenomenon. I was entirely convinced that the phenomenon was hysterical and was glad to discover after I reached that conclusion that my host, Labe Scheinberg, a skilful clinical neurologist, who was sitting in the front row, agreed entirely. Neither of us, however, could dissuade Irving from operating; we were not surprised to learn that the operation was unsuccessful. On another day I held a neuromuscular conference in an unusual room in the College Hospital and said my piece from what looked very like a pulpit. There was a long window, curtained on its other side, which stretched down the entire length of one side of the room. It was only later that I discovered that the conference was being held in what was normally used as the ritual circumcision room.

Four weeks in New York gave me a considerable affection for the city, though I would never wish to live there permanently. I strolled in Central Park, visited several museums and a few of the less expensive restaurants when work was done, and was also able, through the good offices of Richard Deffendini, a neurologist at the Presbyterian Hospital who was a subscriber, to go occasionally to 'the Met' to hear grand opera, or to attend under my own steam the New York City Opera or symphony concerts at the splendid Lincoln Centre which had opened a few years earlier. While the new 'Met' lacked the charm of the old building where I had seen opera once before, the stage, decor and quality of the productions, as well as the acoustics, were outstanding; I recall with particular pleasure hearing that ageing but distinguished baritone, Lawrence Tibbett. As my Einstein commitments occupied only Monday to Friday, I managed to fit in three weekend visits to friends in Boston, Philadelphia and Cleveland with more Saturday morning talks and clinical demonstrations. Cleveland was especially notable, not least because I saw there my old friends Joe Foley, Maurice Victor, Betty Banker and Dick Johnson, but also because of the phenomenal contrast between the blight and decay of the downtown area and the spacious and beautiful homes in which my colleagues lived by the lakeside or in Shaker or Cleveland Heights. I even managed to crew a Sunday morning yacht race in a

'Highlander' on Lake Michigan and to visit the superb Metropolitan Museum in the afternoon.

In early 1967 a pattern developed which eventually led my colleagues to ask tentatively where I was planning to go next for a professional visit overseas so that they could avoid that area. Practically everywhere that Betty and I went we ran into some kind of political or natural catastrophe. In April an Anglo-Greek neurological meeting was planned in Athens and, as we had never visited Greece, we felt that we must go. The scientific sessions in Athens were good and, of course, we visited the principal historical sights of the city, not least the magnificent Acropolis, Parthenon, Temple of Winged Victory, the Forum and the Tower of the Winds below, and many more. One splendid evening meal sitting out under the stars on the Plaka with some colleagues, including Paddy Fullerton, stands out. Temporarily we even acquired a taste for retsina, that powerful resinated Greek wine which seemed a proper accompaniment for the many varieties of mousaka which were regularly and attractively served. Fortunately our package deal, which had been negotiated on behalf of the UK neurologists, included a couple of days in Delphi, which we reached by bus, noting as we approached, the magnificent towering grandeur of Mount Parnassus. Two delightful nights were spent there and, like thousands before and after us, we revelled in the archeological glories, including my favourite, the stadium on the heights of the mountain. Our visit was only slightly marred by the fact that in our hotel Betty (despite her ear plugs) was awakened by snoring and pushed me over, a technique which she claimed had invariably worked in the past but on this occasion did not do so. It was only when she became wide awake that she realized that the sound was coming from the next room. Discreet enquiries next morning revealed that it was occupied by our friends the Millars from Northern Ireland. We just had time to buy a sheepskin in the village before returning to Athens for one night in our hotel near the main square, where the traditionally garbed Evzones guarded the parliament building. Next morning when we came down for breakfast, prepared to fly home in the afternoon, we were met by a skeleton staff with long faces, telling us that overnight there had been a military coup, that troops and tanks were on the streets, that the government had been deposed, there was no telephone service, the airport was closed and all public transport was suspended. Nevertheless, the few staff resident in the hotel coped manfully and produced a simple but adequate breakfast. Ample supplies of Metaxas brandy, which soon began to flow freely despite the early hour, were also made available (on the house) to encourage the faint-hearted. To venture out on the streets was to be met by grim-faced soldiers who persuaded everyone to return into the hotel. Nevertheless from our balcony, looking down over the street, I took some cine pictures of tanks and troops which I thought would make an interesting record.

To our surprise, in the middle of the morning there appeared at our hotel a Greek neurosurgeon, Dr Kapsilakis, whom I had known at Queen Square and who had become very friendly with James Bull, the senior neuroradiologist, and his wife Edith. As a neurosurgeon, he had a special permit to be able to drive around the city. He pressed us and the Bulls to join him and his wife for lunch at his home three or four miles from the hotel, in the suburbs. Not unnaturally, we felt some apprehension about leaving our belongings in the hotel and were also concerned that neither through the British Embassy nor through any other avenue could we communicate with our family to explain why we would be unable to return home that day as planned. Reluctantly, in the end we agreed to go, though our apprehension was enhanced when we discovered that his delightful home and garden were just a few doors away from that occupied by the deposed Greek Prime Minister, Mr Papandreou, which was ringed with troops. Nevertheless, in unbroken sunshine in the garden we enjoyed an excellent buffet lunch and accompanying liquid refreshment, prepared with great aplomb by Mrs Kapsilakis. Throughout the day martial music was played on a portable radio, interspersed with stern announcements. Hesitantly we enquired as to what these conveyed, to which our colleague responded casually that a curfew had been imposed and that anyone out on the streets after dark would be arrested or shot. This added not a little to our sense of inquietude, and as the afternoon wore on, our edginess increased. Eventually we persuaded our friend that it was time to return to the hotel. He took the precaution of visiting the home of the local mayor (who knew him well) who gave him yet another transit permit so we felt sure that all would be well. However, at the first military checkpoint, a fierce-looking soldier took one look at us, waved the permit aside and told us to go back the way we had come. Fortunately, Dr Kapsilakis knew of another more circuitous route back to the city centre which we followed without serious difficulty. At each subsequent checkpoint, manned by soldiers with automatic weapons, we were allowed through and reached our hotel without further incident. Next day the airport reopened and we flew home.

As we were on the first plane out of Athens into Heathrow, we were besieged by reporters seeking comments. Betty and I were pursued by correspondents from the BBC and ITV as we endeavoured to push our luggage through the hordes to see if we could make a flight connection to Newcastle. Eventually we each gave brief radio interviews. Perhaps more foolishly I surrendered my cine film, including shots of the tanks and the troops on the streets taken from our hotel. I say foolishly since although a brief snippet of my film was shown on ITV news, my colour film had been rapidly developed in black and white, so that some of our most attractive pictures of Delphi were less glorious than they would otherwise have been. ITN eventually returned my film with a cheque for

£10.00, which struck me at the time as being a little ungenerous. And unfortunately, having missed our connection, all flights to Newcastle were fully booked so that we had to take the train. As luck would have it, the carriage in which we travelled developed a mechanical defect but not one which would, it seemed, cause any hazard, even though the noise of loud continual clanking beneath us did not make our return journey as tranquil as we would have wished. When the train actually stuck for 30 minutes on the bridge over the Tyne, just outside Newcastle station where the family were waiting to meet us (after a hurried telephone call from Kings Cross) we really felt that the fates were against us.

May 1967 was also notable because of the few days that I spent as visiting lecturer at the University of Groningen, with which Newcastle had an exchange arrangement. My charming host was Professor Drooglever Fortuyn, professor of neurology and a distinguished neuroanatomist, but I also spent some time with Heinz Prechtl, famous for his work on cerebral palsy and child development. While northern Holland is incredibly flat, the virtually unending expanse of the Zuider Zee has its own stark beauty. On the day we went there, the streets were bedecked with flags, parades and bands were marching by and people thronged the streets in festive mood. When I asked my host what they were celebrating, he looked at me incredulously and said 'Don't you know? It's VE Day!'. As we had never celebrated that day, at least to such an extent, in Britain, I was at first taken aback but then, of course, appreciated that its significance must be much greater for those who suffered under German occupation during the Second World War. Brief visits to Utrecht (Professor Kemp) and Amsterdam (Prof. den Hartog Jager) followed. In all three centres I was greatly impressed by the command of English displayed by the Dutch students. They all seemed to understand my lectures in English, even laughing appropriately at my few weak jokes. Nevertheless something of the Germanic tradition, which dominated prewar Dutch medicine, persisted; at the end of each lecture even senior members of the audience had to ask the professor's permission to pose a question to the visitor.

In the autumn of 1967 I was invited to the University of Miami as a visiting professor; my host was the genial Peritz Scheinberg whom I had known and admired when we worked together in Ray Adams' department in Boston in the 1950s. A prominent member of his department was the ebullient and extraverted Nobbie David with his superb southern accent, a fine neurologist and an excellent lieutenant (later he was joined by Ram Ayyar, my former registrar from Newcastle, and in 1990 when Peritz retired, my Newcastle colleague Walter Bradley moved from Burlington, Vermont, to head the department). Working there, too, was Harry Webster, again from the Boston stable, who by that time was making his name as an expert on electron microscopy of the nervous system. The work I did was fascinating and demanding, not least in the usual clinical demonstrations, in one of which I saw a young woman who had had three laminectomies for presumed cervical disc disease but whom I found to have a thoracic outlet syndrome, quickly relieved by surgery. It was also enjoyable to go on a ward round with the legendary neuro-ophthalmologist, Dr Lawton Smith, who was not only technically brilliant but also a rabidly evangelical born-again Baptist who prefaced all his talks and clinical demonstrations by praising the Lord in a few sentences with the kind of religious fervour I remembered from my early Methodist childhood. Those visiting Miami are, of course, always allowed some brief relief from the strenuous professional programme arranged by one's hosts. At least I saw the Seaquarium with the famous dolphin, Flipper, and some other sights which, though specifically targeted at the tourist industry, nevertheless had considerable charm. I also glimpsed the margins of the Everglades, a sight which whetted my appetite for the lengthier visits which Betty and I enjoyed in later years when we had more free time to feast upon the scenery, but above all to view the abundant wildlife.

From Miami, I flew to Montreal to participate, again by invitation, in a major congress on neurogenetics. Expo was running at the time and I was much impressed by the splendid British pavilion, even though, by general assent, among the many and varied national displays, that of Czechoslovakia with its superb display of glass stood out as pre-eminent. During one lunch break I wandered into an antique shop close to the hotel and spotted an old cricket bat, marked at 15 dollars, hanging on the wall. The proprietor told me that he had bought it in a 'lot' many years earlier. When I expressed interest, he reduced the price to 10 dollars and I clinched the deal, having noted that it was signed by W. G. Grace. He then said 'It only goes to show that if you keep sumpin' long enough, some nut'll come in and buy it'. When Betty met me at Newcastle airport she expressed interest in the curious parcel she had seen under my arm as I disembarked from the plane. 'For one moment', she said, 'I thought it was a cricket bat!'. Later I discovered in correspondence with E. W. Swanton that the bat had been presented by WG to the captain of the Canadian national team during a tour in 1878. It is still one of my prized possessions.

May 1968 was a month which will always be vivid in our memories since we had both been invited to go first to Barcelona and then to Marseille. I was to participate in a major symposium on neuromuscular disease being organized by Dr Espadaler in Barcelona, while in Marseille I was to take part in the first of a series of biennial meetings on neuromuscular pathology. These were planned with consummate skill by Georges Serratrice, then a rheumatologist, who subsequently, because of his dedication to the neuromuscular field, moved progressively into neurology, eventually becoming President of the Société Française de

Neurologie. He also acquired many new and arduous responsibilities (which he always saw as being peripheral to his scientific and neurological interests) first as Premier Assesseur of the University of Aix Marseille and subsequently as its President or Vice-Chancellor.

This, our first visit to Barcelona, was delightful, not least because we were housed in a charming old hotel on the slopes of the Tibidabo, that splendid hill ruined, I fear, beyond repair by the huge and ugly television mast which overshadows the otherwise stately basilica at its summit. The meeting was good, with simultaneous translation, and the hospitality superb, though the Spanish concept of time came as a considerable shock to us both. We began to recognize what to expect when on the evening of our arrival we were invited by Dr Subirana and other senior Spanish neurologists to join them and their wives for dinner at the boat club, superbly situated in the harbour area. Dinner was officially to be served at 9.00, but in fact after several rounds of drinks we eventually sat down at about 11.00 p.m. and were returned to our hotel at 1.00 in the morning. Recognizing that the meetings the following day did not begin until 10.00 (my guest lecture was due at noon), we hoped nevertheless to catch up on a little sleep. Dr Espadaler called for us at the hotel shortly before 10.00 and took us to the hospital, where his wife swept Betty away to see some sights. On entering the lecture theatre a few moments after 10.00, I was astonished, but Manuel Espadaler was not, to see a totally deserted theatre. By about 11.15 the audience began to drift in in a desultory way and eventually the first papers were delivered just before noon. My lecture, due at 12.00, was eventually given, with simultaneous translation, at about 1.45. Immediately afterwards we were ushered out into a beautiful courtyard in the hospital grounds, under the unremitting Barcelona sun, to see drinks set out and a vast range of canapés with selections of cold meat, cheeses and fruit, etc., all on display. Betty and Senora Espadaler had now returned to join us, as she and I thought for lunch, and we enjoyed ourselves by sampling many of the delicacies. After about an hour, to our horror our hosts said 'Now we go for lunch'. We were then taken to a huge and spacious restaurant and were plied with sangria, which we were each invited to drink from a typical Catalan container which had to be held above the head so that a stream of delicious fluid emerged from its spout. The only problem was being able so to position the container that the stream of fluid hit one's mouth rather than one's clothing. There followed several courses, including the inevitable paella; lunch eventually concluded by about 4.30 p.m., by which time we were more than replete and ready for a siesta before dinner, which we now recognized would be served very late.

The next two days passed in a blur of activity, but as news emerged from France our concern about our subsequent Marseille commitment began to grow. We learned that the students were rioting on the streets of Paris and other major cities and that a strike of all transport facilities had been called through the activities of Tariq Ali and his revolutionary colleagues. We telephoned the British Consul in Barcelona, recognizing that we would surely face transport difficulties as the flight we had intended to take from Barcelona to Marseille had been cancelled. With typical sangfroid, he said we must certainly go, that he was confident that we would be perfectly safe and would not be troubled by 'these little local difficulties'. However, we also consulted Michel Fardeau from Paris who was himself anxious and made it clear that although he was due to speak in Marseille, he would not be going there as his first priority was to get home from Barcelona to his wife and family in Paris. He telephoned our hosts in Marseille and Dr Hubert Roux, who was helping Georges Serratrice with the organization, was adamant that if Dr Walton did not attend, the symposium would be cancelled. After much heart-searching, and after taking advice from the extraordinary Pierre Salisachs of the fluent Castilian Spanish and equally fluent English and French, we eventually decided that we must go ahead and so hired a Morris Mini in order to drive to Marseille with an overnight stop at Perpignan.

The drive proved uneventful and we enjoyed a brief stop in Montpellier to see the ancient medical school, and arrived in Marseille without any difficulties. Outwardly the city seemed calm, but knots of students and others were gathered in earnest conversation on many street corners, no public transport was running and even some petrol filling stations were closed because of the general strike, as were many shops. Many hotels were also affected and we were therefore housed in a charming villa, the Villa Gaby, situated high above the Corniche with views across the Mediterranean to the Chateau d'Assy (of Count of Monte Cristo fame) on an island in the bay. Fortunately this villa (the university guest house) was tranquil and the staff there were working normally, so that we were comfortably housed. My lecture and the other presentations of the international symposium were delivered in the splendid old lecture theatres of the Palais de Pharo, overlooking the magnificent harbour which sparkled in the sunlight. It would all have been idyllic were it not for the social and commercial disruption around us. Our hosts tried manfully to be cheerful and on the first evening we were entertained to a magnificent cocktail party in the home of Georges and Janine Serratrice in the Rue Daumier. Their home, with a spacious garden, was striking in its elegant simplicity but also in the quality of the furnishings and pictures; many of these must surely have been heirlooms as the display challenged many a museum in the range and variety of the paintings and objets d'art which graced every room.

Not surprisingly, the programme of the two-and-a-half day scientific symposium was somewhat truncated, if only because none of the French participants from outside Marseille arrived, even those from Bordeaux and Lyon. Indeed the only speakers from elsewhere were myself and Fritz Buchthal from Copenhagen who had flown to Genoa and who, like ourselves, had hired a car to drive to Marseille. Despite the kindness of our hosts, we began to feel increasingly uncomfortable in a political situation which deteriorated hourly and were not reassured when Henri Gastaut, Dean of the Faculty of Medicine, said to us at dinner on the second evening 'I would get out if I were you. It's not safe'! While we would probably have been willing to retain the car in which we had driven from Spain, our hosts felt that we should not take that risk because of the uncertainty of obtaining supplies of fuel. Hence Hubert Roux and his wife loaded up their large Citroen with cans of petrol and drove us to Nice where arrangements were made for us to hire yet another car. The drive along the Riviera was fascinating, particularly since we took the scenic coastal route. We had never before realized that such a variety of hills, forests, coves, bays and elegant resorts existed in that area, so that despite our anxiety we enjoyed the journey. We arrived in Nice in the late afternoon, picked up a hired Fiat and then drove north-east through the Alpes Maritimes over the Italian border, arriving fairly late at night at Limone, a ski resort in the mountains where we found, out of season, a comfortable hotel and dined in state virtually alone in the dining-room. At last we had escaped from the disruption in France which went on for several more weeks before being resolved. Later I often said to our friends that we had been caught up in the second French Revolution.

Our purpose in driving north-east was that having cut short our visit, which had been intended to last several days more, we felt it would be pleasant to call at Geneva to see Judy who was working there in the Clinique Beaulieu. Next morning, suitably reassured and refreshed, we drove through Turin, over the St Bernard Pass and arrived in Geneva in time to check into the Hotel Richemond (then surprisingly inexpensive but now well out of our price range) before contacting our astonished daughter. We had a delightful dinner with her and a few hours of relaxation before flying home. None of our subsequent visits to Marseille or to Barcelona were as exciting or memorable, though each time we were able to renew old friendships and to undertake leisurely if comparatively brief visits to places of interest. Slowly, too, my French improved sufficiently for me to be able to lecture with greater assurance in that language and even on occasions to make an occasional brief and reasonably spontaneous after-dinner speech.

My halting French came in handy again in 1971 when I was invited to deliver the annual Osler Lecture to the Canadian Medical Association meeting in Halifax, Nova Scotia. Halifax is a charming, if rather gaunt and exposed seaport, somewhat lacking in greenery but surrounded by bleak and compelling countryside with rocky coves and bays and moorland-type scenery, very reminiscent of parts of north-west Scotland.

Its early colonial origins are clearly evident in its wooden houses and churches, and in the nearby Peggy's Cove, a little fishing village, where the variegated frame houses and other buildings have been so well preserved and restored as to make an exceptionally attractive sight. I say that my French came in handy because I was able to begin my lecture with a paragraph or two in French before saying that having demonstrated that I was bilingual, I would continue in English!

In 1968 another unexpected opportunity arose, this time of a visit in September to South America organized by Dr Gustavo Poch, who was himself working on neuromuscular disease and wished me to give some lectures and clinical demonstrations to his junior staff. Buenos Aires seemed to be in some ways a remarkably Anglicized city with its English tower and London pubs. Several other establishments dated back to the days when Britain was largely responsible for controlling much of Argentina's development and economy, including the building of its railways and of many of its finest hotels. Even the sumptuous premises of the Buenos Aires Jockey Club, where I had the privilege one day of playing golf with three Argentinian doctors, were provided with British capital. Never before had I seen a golf clubhouse of quite such size and splendour (Chapter 10). While in later years I saw some similar results of British colonial development in parts of the old Commonwealth such as India, I had never before realized that Britain's influence in Argentina had been quite so great. The premises of the Jockey Club, for example, were quite as good as many that I was to see later in wealthy US cities.

By contrast, the principal hospitals which I visited, including the English hospital, were not as luxurious though they were reasonably clean; most of the medical staff spoke good English and were well-informed. Nevertheless, when I went as a guest to a meeting of the Argentine Neurological Society in another splendid (British-built) country hotel outside Cordoba, there was no simultaneous translation and I had to deliver my lecture paragraph by paragraph while each was translated more or less verbatim by an Argentinian colleague. This certainly interrupted the flow.

In Cordoba itself I was especially surprised to find a rather scruffy-looking car park attendant at the main hospital speaking what seemed impeccable public school English, almost as good as that of the young neurologist who was one of my hosts and who had been educated at the English school. However, it proved that the attendant, with whom my host had a lively conversation in English as we arrived, came from the Falklands (no-one then called them the Malvinas). Gustavo Poch, who had himself been involved in Argentinian politics with the Conservative Party but who was by this time out of favour, nevertheless had several friends in senior positions in government, some of whom we met at various parties. Argentinian beef was, as I expected, magnificent, but in a culinary sense I was also introduced to such delicacies as empanadas and parillada, the latter a phenomenal mixed grill of various components of cattle anatomy. While enjoying a large helping, there was one item which was difficult to identify; having enjoyed it, I was informed that I had just consumed part of the testis of a bull. Much Argentinian wine was also of excellent quality; indeed the time that I spent in that country offered a memorable gastronomic assault course. Dr Poch was clearly an exceptionally wealthy man with a flourishing private practice. He had a delightful flat in the centre of BA from which, being a football enthusiast, he took me one afternoon to see a game in the stadium of his favourite team, Boca Juniors. This was the first time that I had seen a football ground ringed by fearsome high fences to prevent pitch invasions. Little did I think that similar fences would eventually become necessary in the UK because of crowd violence. That evening we went to a delightful city restaurant to hear some traditional Argentinian tango music which, though interesting and enjoyable in relatively small doses, struck me after a while as becoming boringly monotonous with lack of variety.

Another curious feature of Buenos Aires was the extraordinary traffic management. The city was laid out on a strictly geometrical pattern, at least in its centre, with roads crossing the main streets at right angles; in many such crossings there were no traffic lights. Dr Poch himself did not drive; having had a serious accident some years earlier, he had never driven again. Hence we went everywhere by taxi and the typical technique seemed to be to drive up to each intersection at high speed and to ram on the brakes just as one reached it, after which it was invariably the most fearless driver who negotiated the crossing first. Those more timid often sat waiting for some time before daring to inch forward into the maelstrom.

Gustavo's wealth, I soon learned, must have derived not only from his very large private practice but also from the fact that he paid, as he told me, practically no income tax. As in the United States, Argentinians were required to file their own tax returns; it seemed that there was then no investigating machinery established by their Inland Revenue or comparable organization. His returns, indicating a very low income from professional practice, had never been queried; apparently this was an accepted custom. Not surprisingly, therefore, the country's revenue from income tax was low, so that taxes were levied on many other commodities and services to maintain the government which was a military dictatorship (though there was no obvious evidence of this in the city apart from the occasional appearance of uniformed troops in one or two areas). The Poch family income enabled him to have two other homes outside Buenos Aires, one a spacious country home or cinta with a large garden and swimming pool and a separate cottage for the devoted couple who looked after it when the family were away. There we spent a delightful weekend, marred only by the fact that Gustavo's son, aged 10, was a soccer enthusiast who persuaded me against my better judgement to play football with him even though I had not touched a soccer ball for many years. At least I was able to soothe my aching limbs in the warm waters of their pool before becoming involved in another round of eating and drinking in the evening. Next day we went on by car to see their third home, a summer retreat across the River Plate in Uruguay at the luxurious and upmarket coastal resort of Punta del Este. One of the popular sights of that town was the home (now a museum) of the famous revolutionary Che Guevara. Everywhere were the large and sumptuous but well-guarded homes of many of the South American rich. Apparently the national income of impoverished Uruguay was considerably boosted by the spending of Argentinians and others who came to Punta del Este in the summer.

From Argentina I went for two or three days to Montevideo where I was greeted by the head of neurology, Dr Deffeminis Rospide, a charming and scholarly man. I hardly dared to ask him why when he met me at the airport he was driving a motor car of splendid antiquity, a British pre-war Standard 14 saloon. Only later did he tell me that because of a 500% import duty on car imports, very few people in Uruguay could afford a new car and a major industry had developed of maintaining and repairing pre-war cars, which abounded. Many old Packards, Buicks, Chevrolets and other American makes were in evidence, but so too were innumerable British Austins, Fords, Morrises, Standards and others. The streets of Montevideo would have delighted many a veteran or vintage car enthusiast. Montevideo itself was a city with a charming curved waterfront of white (if crumbling) buildings looking down on a wide beach and attractive bay, but everywhere one looked there was evidence of genteel decay. The country was then one of the few remaining democracies in South America, even though the activities of some urban guerillas were threatening the government's viability. We visited the imposing parliament building before going on to the university, where even the medical school was daubed with revolutionary slogans and festooned with posters and banners of a fervently left wing character, declaiming opposition even to the ruling socialist government. Indeed within the few days I was there, the medical school was closed by university decree because of revolutionary activities and militant students roamed the streets imparting a sense of unrest to what had been a tranquil urban scene. Despite this disturbance, my lecture and clinical demonstration were well attended by students and doctors and my hosts could not have been more friendly. Yet again I was royally entertained in the luxurious and beautifully appointed home of the senior neurosurgeon, a man of outstanding international reputation, Professor Arana Iniguez. This was yet another country where the British influence was far stronger than I had expected. I was taken by my hosts along the banks of the incredibly wide River Plate to be shown the memorial to the British cruisers HMS Ajax and Achilles who had, together with HMS Exeter, driven the German pocket battleship Graf Spee to take refuge in Montevideo early in the Second World War. On the memorial was the anchor of HMS Ajax proudly displayed in a park-like setting and carefully maintained. In the peaceful deserted area where we saw it, it had an eerily nostalgic effect.

When I asked my hosts why the country seemed prey to such personal and corporate poverty, they explained that under their democractic socialist government the welfare state concept had run riot to such an extent that the retirement age, with entitlement to pension, had been brought down to 55. In addition, a huge range of social security benefits was being offered so that the country's exchequer had become seriously impoverished despite its flourishing meat exporting industry. Later I believe that revolutionary activities, some of which I had witnessed, brought down the government but democracy survived and later some of the worst excesses of over-provision by the state were reversed.

September 1969 saw the quadrennial World Congress of Neurology, splendidly organized in the Hilton Hotel, New York, by Houston Merritt and his colleagues. Afterwards Betty and I went to Duke University in Durham, North Carolina, where my old friend Albert Heyman was head of department and was working effectively in harness with Dr Farmer, only recently retired from the chairmanship. The Duke campus is superb and spacious, built largely from tobacco money but also with a strong Methodist tradition, boasting a huge chapel which would rival many a smaller cathedral in the UK. There is something about small-town USA, as in Durham, Chapel Hill and Winston-Salem, which confers a sense of ease and tranquillity, standing in striking contrast to the energetic and demanding bustle of major cities like New York and even Boston. We then went on to New Orleans (our first of several visits) where we were bowled over by the charm of the French-style early colonial architecture with the decorative wrought iron on the balconies of many major buildings, and where we stayed in a traditional and luxurious hotel in the Vieux Carré (the old town). Apart from the standard routine of lecturing and of clinical demonstrations where, as always, I worked pretty hard, we were encouraged to see the city sights. We listened to jazz (a jam session) in Preservation Hall, were taken to hear Pete Fountain and his orchestra in an opulent night club away from the less salubrious area of Bourbon Street with its topless bars, and of course had breakfast at Brennan's where there is only a single menu. Our hosts told us that the usual routine was to have two Bloody Marys to start, followed by oyster stew, eggs Benedict and bananas Foster. Fortunately breakfast is served from 7.00 a.m. until midnight so that we were able to enjoy this not inconsiderable repast in the evening. Perhaps the highlight was our last night when Richard Paddison, head of department, had arranged a dinner in our honour at Antoine's in a private room (the Rex Room). As we arrived (some 24 people in all, members of department and their spouses) we found an altercation going on in the hallway. Two large and aggressive gentlemen, plainly the worse for wear, were arguing with the proprietor and insisting upon having the Rex Room, while he in turn was insisting equally firmly that it had been booked by the Department of Neurology. We had no difficulty in recognizing John Wayne and Rock Hudson. Happily our booking prevailed. This was one of our few overseas trips in which we managed to wangle a few extra days of relaxation. I knew that our farewell dinner was to be on the Saturday evening and that on the following Thursday I was due in London for a meeting of a grants committee at the Medical Research Council. A line on the map from New Orleans to London passed almost directly over the Bahamas. We therefore arranged a short stop-over in Nassau at the Emerald Beach Hotel where we lay in the sun, swam and even managed two rounds of golf on the Nassau golf course. Until then we had never recognized how often brief tropical thunderstorms blew up and as quickly departed. Twice during our rounds we were soaked by torrential downpours which lasted no more than 10 or 15 minutes and quickly, as we continued to play, we dried out in the tropical sun.

In March 1970 I paid another enjoyable visit to the United States where, at Emory University in Atlanta, Georgia, I met again Dr Geoffrey Bourne, formerly reader in anatomy at the London Hospital Medical School, who by this time, after being professor of anatomy at Emory, had become director of the Yerkes Primate Center, one of the most impressive primate centres in existence anywhere in the world. His wife, Nellie Golarz, had done some interesting work on muscle and I found the out-of-town campus of Emory exceptionally well laid out and the quality of the neurology very high.

This was followed by a brief visit to St Louis with its impressive towering archway (the gateway to the West) where I spoke at a symposium on muscle pathology organized by Carl Pearson and also lectured and saw patients with William Landau and Phil Dodge. I was delighted to deliver the Bernard J. Alpers lecture at Jefferson University Medical College in Philadelphia in 1971. Dr Alpers was in the audience and I well recalled his kindness to me as a young visitor from the UK in 1954.

1970 also brought a brief and exciting visit to Paris, with a splendid evening at the Opera, and I gave a guest lecture in French to the Société Française de Neurologie, who were kind enough to make me an honorary member. In December I lectured at a course on muscle disease in Oslo, revelling briefly in the Norwegian winter landscape and renewing contact with our close friends Sigvald and Sigrid Refsum.

There followed two short visits behind the Iron Curtain, the first in March 1971 to Prague and Janske Lazne, again in order to teach on neuromuscular disease. That great neurophysiologist, Professor Gutmann, formerly head of the Neuro-sciences Institute in Prague, greeted me. He had been deposed from his senior position, not being a member of the Communist Party and having family in the West. He was confined to a single small room in the Institute which he had previously directed and had had to hand over the direction to his colleague, Professor Hnik, who also had Western connections and spoke immaculate English, having had part of his education in the UK. Professor Hnik, too, was deposed a year or two later, to be replaced by a much lesser scientist who was a faithful member of the Party. Only then did I begin to appreciate fully the oppressive nature of Communist rule in countries like Czechoslovakia. Prague, however, is a wonderful city and the view of Charles University and of its approaches was stunning in its stately grandeur. Close by was the finest and most beautifully preserved apothecary's shop which I can recall seeing anywhere. The only disturbing feature was that on the Sunday when we made our brief tour, there were swarms of arrogant Jack-booted Russian troops in full uniform also bent on touristic activities. Janske Lazne was, by contrast, a spa town in the mountains, some 50 or 60 miles from Prague. The domestic symposium on neuromuscular disease to which I had been invited was held in a hospital close to the spa where an impressive range of physiotherapy and rehabilitation facilities for the management of patients with neuromuscular diseases was available. The only disadvantage to what would otherwise have been an idyllic setting was that the hotel in which the few foreign participants were housed had to be approached by a funicular as it was near the top of one of the snow-covered mountains which overlook the town. It was spartan in its simplicity not least because water could only be supplied for one hour each morning and evening, so that the toilets were provided with multiple buckets of water, to be used as necessary.

In May 1972 I also went, with Walter Bradley and several other UK and American participants, to speak at a neuromuscular symposium being organized by the indefatigable Professor Irena Hausmanowa-Petrusewicz at Kazimierz in Poland. This again was a small, attractive town some distance from Warsaw and lying amongst wooded hills; the peaceful ambience added to the friendly and fruitful content of our deliberations. At that meeting one of the young, blond, buxom neurologists in Hausmanowa's department enquired of Walter Bradley as to how long Professor Walton had been dyeing his hair!

In 1969, the first International Congress on Neuromuscular Diseases, outstripping in importance the European and domestic symposia to which I have referred, had been held in Milan, organized splendidly by Nicola Canal and Giuseppe Scarlato, both of whom remain active in neuromuscular research. The meeting took place close enough to the centre of the city for us all to enjoy the spectacular views over the main square from the roof of the Duomo, that basilica with its immensely impressive frontage, surely one of the finest sights in Italy. The participants were so enthusiastic that it was decided that regular international congresses should be held in future, possibly at four-yearly intervals like the World Congresses of Neurology. However, Byron Kakulas of Perth in Western Australia, notable for his work on the myopathy in the Rottnest Island quokka (a small marsupial unique to the island), jumped the gun by arranging the second such meeting in Perth in October 1971 and generously invited me to be a guest lecturer. I had no idea when he approached me that my life would be changing through my appointment to the Newcastle deanship. Betty and I therefore accepted the invitation with alacrity. As we were going so far, we decided that it would be sensible to arrange a round trip over a full six-week period (for which I obtained leave of absence from the NHS and University) by calling in India, Thailand and Singapore on the way out and by accepting invitations which I had received to lecture in other principal Australian cities before finally attending the Asian and Oceanian Congress of Neurology in Bombay on our way home. We had begun to think that our ill-luck in relation to travel, after our Greek and French experiences, was behind us, but little did we realize what was to come.

Our flight to Delhi was uneventful. We arrived on a Friday morning and were comfortably housed in the guest house of the All-India Institute of Medical Sciences where my former research associate who had spent two years in Newcastle, Dr A. K. Susheela ('Su'), was a member of staff. The house was reasonably cool and airy with a plain but pleasant bedroom, private bathroom and sitting room; all of our anxieties aroused by the tales told by old India hands about such problems as 'Delhi belly' were immediately allayed. On the Saturday after we arrived, I gave my first guest lecture and saw some patients. Our hosts were kind enough to suggest that perhaps on the Sunday, a free day before more work was due, it might be exciting for us to go to Agra to see the Taj Mahal. Eagerly we agreed; when it was suggested that we might choose either to fly, to travel by first class train or by road, we immediately chose the latter as on this, our first visit to India, we thought we would see more of the country. Our enthusiasm waned a little when a senior zoologist, one of Su's colleagues, turned up with her the next morning in his car, an elderly Dodge sedan with tyres which looked suspiciously bald. Nevertheless, we set off in high spirits, though we could not help wondering why our driver and host had brought a technician along with him. We were greatly struck by the evidence of abject poverty that we saw as we drove through the city outskirts; and for anyone who has never visited India the extraordinary variety of the traffic, the driving technique, the quality of the ancient-looking Ambassador motor cars (the post-war Morris Oxford) and motorized rickshaws ('tuc-tucs') are remarkable. The cows which, with other animals, wander aimlessly across even main city streets, as well as the people who seem unaffected by vehicles which almost brush their clothing as they pass, are all a source of continuing astonishment. The tendency of drivers when overtaking to pull out completely on to the wrong wide of the road, facing on-coming traffic, and then to pull across to the left at the very last moment was alarming at first, but we soon became attuned to it. The sun shone and the temperature slowly rose towards 90°F, but we were so excited by the varied dress of the people, the teeming crowds and the flocks of animals which recurred endlessly along the road, that we took less account than we might otherwise have done of the squalor we saw all around us. We were also unimpressed by the nature of the road surface, with many loose, sharp stones as well as innumerable pot-holes which slowed our speed substantially. It was therefore no surprise when, after some 50 miles of our 120-mile journey, we developed a puncture. It was then clear why the technician had been invited as he changed the wheel and off we went again. Unfortunately after another 20 or 30 miles we had a second puncture and hence did not have a spare. Our host therefore flagged down an approaching motor cycle and our valiant technician, carrying a wheel, went off on the pillion seeking a 'puncture wallah' to repair the damage. In blazing sunshine, with a temperature in the nineties, we sat quietly by the roadside watching the passing scene for about an hour before our friend returned with the wheel and we set off again. This time we reached Agra without further ado, the puncture in the remaining wheel was quickly repaired by another 'puncture wallah' (a young boy of about 12 or 13 years of age) and we set off on foot to see the Taj.

The stunning impact of that building almost beggars description. It has elicited timeless prose, faultless poetry, banal commentary, and many a lyrical description. It is quite justifiably classed as one of the wonders of the world, not least because of its architectural style and the superb inlaid marble of which it is constructed, but also in view of its setting, dominating in suitably lordly manner the Ganges below; the approach through an archway and along a splendid avenue of pools and fountains, is the stuff of fantasy. We lingered, we drank in the scene, we bought some small marble ornaments, we watched the snake charmers and our delight and sense of awe were in no way tempered by the horrors of the public toilets nearby, as we had been warned by Su and others what to expect. Squatting over a reeking open hole soon became second nature. At last, in excellent spirits, we set off in the late afternoon on our return journey; within a mile or so, fortunately before we had left the outskirts of Agra, our host, with grave concern, reported a fault in the car dynamo as the ammeter showed that the battery was not charging. There was nothing for it but to drive up to what claimed to be a garage but seemed to us to be nothing more than a small, dark, open shed facing the road where several men handling ill-defined equipment in the gloomy interior were sitting on their haunches. Quickly another young boy in his early teens crawled underneath the car and removed the dynamo. There followed a period during which it seemed as if men in the darkened interior were beating it with hammers. What they did was unclear, but in about an hour the same young boy replaced the faulty item; glory of glories, the battery started to charge and off we went.

Sadly, night was now falling and when, after about 60 miles, we suffered yet another puncture, our hosts, like us, were becoming increasingly apprehensive. There was then a rapid consultation in the inky darkness by the side of the busy road and it was decided that as we were only some 10 miles from a town called Muttra, the right thing to do was to drive to the railway station and to get Betty and myself, with Susheela as our guide, on to a train to Delhi. Muttra turned out to be a holy town and we arrived in the middle of a pilgrimage. There were thousands of people literally lying in the streets, all clad in white dhotis, and the station platform was littered with bodies. We stepped gingerly over and between them but fortunately soon identified a train for Delhi, to find that it only carried third class passengers. The carriages contained hard wooden latticed seats, sometimes in two or three layers with individuals stretched out and trying to sleep on the upper layers. We crammed ourselves into the corner of one hard bench, surrounded by a mass of seething humanity. Lying on a seat opposite was a young Indian woman with a baby wrapped in her sari. Soon after the train left she fell asleep and rolled over; as she did so, the baby fell out of her sari on to the floor (happily without apparent injury). The train crawled along, stopping repeatedly at station after station, and we eventually reached Delhi at about 1.00 a.m. A taxi delivered us safely to the guest house at the end of a remarkable day. We were deeply touched to find that the principal servant had kept dinner waiting for us until 1.30 a.m., but by that time the idea of food had vanished from our minds and all we could think about was crawling into bed before preparing ourselves for more work on the Monday before our onward journey to Madras.

In Madras we were met at the airport by Krish Srinivas, my former registrar in Newcastle, and some of his junior staff and were festooned with garlands. He then took us to his pleasant home in the outskirts and introduced us to his family. Only then did we realize that it was customary in brahmin households such as his, and perhaps in many other similar Indian homes, for the grandparents, parents, children and grandchildren all to live together. This worked well in the Srinivas family as their home was spacious, but must have been much more difficult for those less well endowed with this world's goods. In Madras we were comfortably housed in the old Connemara Hotel, although in the absence then of air conditioning (it had been installed when we stayed there again in 1989) the huge fans (punkahs) above our bed worked overtime. We were greatly touched by the calm, almost resigned attitude of acceptance of many Indian people. A servant was on duty outside the door of our room virtually all night. He was there when we went to bed and was certainly there to announce breakfast from room service early each morning. The neurological institute in Madras was impressive, having been established by yet another brahmin, Dr Ramamurthi, a neurosurgeon who had trained with Rowbotham in Newcastle; certainly the quality of the neurological and neurosurgical work which I saw was good. Our stay was to some extent marred by the monsoon and by the endless brown rain which fell from a leaden sky, so that more than once we were up to our ankles in water when simply trying to cross the main street.

In Madras, the university was housed in a group of impressive buildings (even though it was then surrounded, even on the pavements, by primitive temporary shacks in which whole families lived in squalor). Throughout India we were continually astonished by the grandeur, scale and sheer magnificence of some of the British (especially the late Victorian) architecture used in the public buildings. It was also interesting to note some of the bureaucracy (e.g. forms completed in triplicate) which abounded; this was clearly a throw-back to 1930s-style British Civil Service red tape, much of which persisted in many parts of India even in the 1970s. Nevertheles, despite the criticism of British rule which we heard in the Red Fort during a performance of *Son et Lumière* in New Delhi, the clubs to which we were taken, all built with British capital, and many of the public buildings and utilities, reminded us incessantly of some of the benefits which the British Raj had conferred upon the country. Many Indians to whom we talked, particularly the older ones, looked back upon those days with nostalgia and affection. In the beautiful Madras Club the servants were particularly friendly (in its spacious grounds it boasted not only tennis courts and a superb swimming pool but also a nine-hole golf course). But we found in India, as in South America, that striking contrast between rich and poor which still exists in many parts of the developing world. Krish Srinivas introduced us to Mr T. S. Srinivasan, later a patient of mine, a founder of the Indian automobile industry, who lived in a phenomenally luxurious house, abounding with servants, in Madras. Years later I was honoured to be a T. S. Srinivasan Memorial Lecturer in Madras; this lectureship was endowed by his widow in his memory.

From Madras we flew on to Singapore, to be met and entertained by Gordon Ransome, professor of medicine, who insisted on taking my photograph for his collection as he said that I reminded him of one of his neurological heroes, W. J. Adie. We stayed at the charming Goodwood Park Hotel, took in the astonishing sights of the skyscraper development of that prosperous, bustling and crowded but beautifully clean city (the litter laws were strictly enforced) and the splendid Jurong bird sanctuary. I visited the principal general hospitals where, as usual, I lectured and saw patients, before travelling north to Bangkok. Our host there was another Newcastle trainee, Professor Athasit Vejjajiva, who later became Professor of Neurology and Dean of the Medical School at the Ramathibodi Hospital in Bangkok, and also physician to the Thai royal family. Once again we enjoyed legendary hospitality and, when work was done, we saw the magnificent ornate temples of Bangkok, the floating market, the Thai village and Thai boxing, while also being treated to interesting Thai food in some of the best restaurants. We soon became accustomed to sitting on the floor and to watching the beautiful, lithe, delicate and elegant Thai dancers whose every flowing gesture was enhanced by the long finger attachments which they wore.

After three thrilling days in Bangkok, we swept on to Hong Kong, yet another astounding experience. Landing at Kai Tak Airport gave us our first view of this fantastic city of skyscrapers climbing imperiously up to the peak district, with Hong Kong Island itself on one side and Kowloon on the other. Even though we had travelled economy class, we were astonished to be met by a uniformed driver and limousine ready to convey us to the Hong Kong Hotel where we had booked in advance. It is next to the Ocean Terminal and from our room we had a superb view of the harbour and of the extraordinary variety of craft, both large and small, criss-crossing the waterway. Since then, we have visited Hong Kong several times and have been much impressed by the university and its students and by the friendliness and hospitality of the local medical fraternity. Even on that first visit, young trainees who had been with us in Newcastle took us around to the peak district, Repulse Bay, Aberdeen and Port Stanley. We enjoyed a splendid meal on a floating restaurant in Aberdeen Harbour, approached by sampan, and also dined with Professor McFadzean and his wife in the old Hong Kong Club, now sadly demolished but then demonstrating the colonial grandeur and traditional British ambience which we had already experienced in India. My medical responsibilities in the city were few and quickly fulfilled. We therefore had a couple of days to spare to do much of our Christmas shopping and arranged for many items to be shipped back to the UK. Everything arrived safely in good time for Christmas at relatively low cost.

From Hong Kong we flew direct to Brisbane overnight by Air New Zealand, arriving at 7.35 a.m., to be met at the airport by our enthusiastic host, Dr John Sutherland, who took us straight to the guest flat at the Royal Brisbane Hospital. I was offered a couple of hours in which to catch up on sleep, to have a quick shower and to breakfast before undertaking my first clinical demonstration in paediatric neurology. I have never quite forgiven the professor of paediatrics, Professor Rendle Short (originally from Bristol) for producing some children with obscure neurological storage disorders and for casting slides on the screen asking me whether I felt that these were truly sea-blue histiocytes! Apart from this little contretemps and shortage of sleep, the day went well and enjoyably and John Sutherland, Mervin Eadie, Peter Landy and the other neurologists were exceptionally welcoming, as later was Spike Leaming, formerly of Newcastle (and the TA) but now reader in surgery at the University, having previously been an active member of the Flying Doctor Service in Northern Queensland.

Frankly, the next week or two in Australia passed almost in a blur in that we were wined and dined each night by warm-hearted and generous colleagues. I lectured repeatedly and saw innumerable patients and we also experienced the sights, the gastronomic delights and the oenological pleasures of Sydney, Melbourne and Adelaide after leaving Brisbane, before moving on to Perth for the muscle congress which had been our primary reason for going to Australia. Sydney Harbour Bridge was for us, as Tynesiders, simply a big brother of the Tyne Bridge in Newcastle, its prototype; the Opera House was approaching completion and had become a notable feature of the skyline. In Melbourne our old friend Arthur Schweiger was our host, but we also saw Alan and Rita Jenkins, formerly of Newcastle. The only problem about Melbourne was disturbed sleep; we were pleasantly accommodated in the guest flat at Prince Henry's Hospital; this well-appointed flat had been created on a large landing within the hospital. Unfortunately its walls were thin and the telephone calling out housemen during the night was on the other side of our bedroom wall so we were constantly disturbed. Replete with food, wine and professional activities, we moved on to Adelaide, to be greeted by Dick Rischbieth, where at least between my professional commitments (I delivered the Cairns Lecture in honour of Hugh Cairns to the neurologists and neurosurgeons in the city) I did manage a game of golf with Rick Burns, the associate professor, at the Royal Adelaide and we also had a splendid trip up into the hills overlooking the city to taste some of the excellent wines of McLaren Vale.

Perth was exceptional. It is one of the loveliest of Australian cities, intersected by the broad sweep of the Swan River with its black swans. The elegant and spacious university campus was home to the conference, which was superbly organized by Byron Kakulas with the help of his wife, Val, and his colleagues from the Departments of Neuropathology and Neurology. Betty had (for her) the unusual experience of being interviewed by a local TV station, being asked what it was like to live with me! She was forthright but reasonably discreet and I thought she came over very well. We stayed in the Parmelia Hotel but also experienced the hospitality of the Perth Club with Dr Graeme Robertson, not only a distinguished neurologist but an internationally acknowledged expert on Australian wrought iron. We even managed a little shopping, acquiring a couple of Western Australian oil paintings portraying the ambience of the West Australian desert which we saw for the first time some years later when we crossed the Nullarbor Plain from Adelaide to Perth by the trans-continental train. Robert Whelan, Vice-Chancellor of the University, who was subsequently Vice-Chancellor at Liverpool, played host at a major university reception and we later came to know him and his wife, Betty, very well.

By this time we were both beginning to flag. We have often told our friends that in the six weeks that we were away, we were wined and dined every night but two, one in Perth and the other in Adelaide where we had insisted to Dick Rischbieth that we should have just one night in the hospital guest flat so as to eat scrambled eggs by ourselves and to have an early night. He was very understanding and we caught up a little on our sleep deficit which had built up steadily throughout Australia, largely through the indefatigable energy and unfailing kindness of our hosts. The one night we had to ourselves in Perth was a delightful, peaceful interlude spent in a log cabin on Rottnest Island just off the coast. This charming and beautiful island, free of motor cars, is the home of the quokka (early Dutch sailors thought that these small marsupials were large rats, hence Rottnest). We spent an idyllic day cycling for part of the time and for part of it being shown the wildlife, including dugongs and nesting ospreys, by Tom Riggert, an American naturalist who was then producing some programmes on Australian television on natural history which had become extremely popular. Sadly, several years later when we returned to Rottnest it had become a favoured retreat of hard-drinking, drug-taking youngsters.

Our last day or two in Perth were clouded slightly by learning from the airline that whereas our flight to Singapore was confirmed, the connection from Singapore to Bombay was not as the flight was overbooked. Fortunately in the end, after an anxious wait as we sat perspiring in a fiercely hot and humid corner of Singapore airport, we were able to transfer (though at considerable cost) to first class. This got us to Bombay in time, which was just as well, because I had accepted an invitation to deliver the annual award lecture on polymyositis to the Indian Rheumatism Association in Bombay soon after our arrival. Afterwards I was presented with a delightful gold medallion, heavily embossed with the initials of the association (IRA)! In Bombay we were met by our old friend, Anil Desai, who had trained in neurology in Newcastle with Fred Nattrass and who had kindly arranged to accommodate us at his club, the West Indian Automobile Association Club, which overlooked the principal bay of the city. Our first sight of the Club and of our room was chastening after the relatively luxurious comfort of the guest flats and hotels in which we had stayed across Australia.

Grey-looking sheets and pillow cases of unbleached cotton, a bathroom with a damp stone floor and mottled stone walls stained with rust dripping from exposed water pipes did not create a favourable initial impression. Soon, however, we settled and found the accommodation quite comfortable, while the food was pleasant and incredibly inexpensive. The Asian and Oceanian Congress was very well attended in the Taj Mahal Hotel. In that hotel, at lunch one day with an international group of neurologists, Dr Mahludji, an Iranian neurologist from Shiraz who had graduated in medicine in Leeds, told a tale which I have often quoted. He was the only Iranian I have ever met who, because of his Leeds experience, spoke English with a strong Yorkshire accent. He said that Fred Trueman had been playing cricket in the Middle East and after the match went into a bar with some of his opponents (this was not one of the fundamentalist 'dry' Middle Eastern states); in the bar one of his hosts pointed out a sheikh sitting across the room and in terms of awe said 'Fred, do you see that man over there? He's a sheikh, a very wealthy man, he has 199 wives', to which Fred riposted quickly 'Does he know that if he'd had one more, he could have had a new ball?'!

As the Congress in Bombay proceeded, however, another cloud appeared on the horizon. It had been clear for some time that relations between India and Pakistan were deteriorating. On the third or fourth day of the meeting war was declared and Bombay immediately introduced a blackout. As luck would have it, that evening we were invited, through one of my former Indian medical associates, to dine at Government House in Bombay where his brother was ADC to the Governor. He was a delightful, cultured Indian who spoke English with a style and terminology reminiscent of the 1930s. Whenever I tried to tell a joke, however feeble, he would slap his thigh and roar with laughter, saying 'That was a jolly good one, sir'. However, while dinner was being served the air raid warning sounded and we were later told that a single Pakistani aircraft had been repelled from attempting to attack Bombay. Clearly, however, it seemed sensible to try to advance our departure. Eventually we managed to book an earlier flight; but we shall not easily forget being driven through the night to the airport in a taxi virtually without lights, before being flown safely home. The drive was hair-raising along unlit roads, not least because people were living in huge drainage pipes from which they sometimes emerged at the edge of the road. And so, as we later told our friends, having experienced the Greek military coup and the second French Revolution, we found ourselves only three years later involved in the India/Pakistan war.

Plainly, therefore, our jinx on overseas travel had not abated fully, though we felt that it was probably passing when in 1972 I was asked to give the Wilder Penfield Lecture to the Middle East Medical Assembly at the American University, Beirut. Flying with Betty in May that year to the Lebanon, we found a lovely, peaceful and tranquil country. Our host, Jean Rebeiz, took us to Tyre and Sidon and to Baalbek and entertained us splendidly to a meal at the casino on the coast. Little did we think that only some 12 months later the country would be torn apart by civil war, that the sumptuous hotel in which we stayed, overlooking the ocean, would subsequently be destroyed, that the splendid American University and its medical school would be rent by fear of kidnap and that, in consequence, one of the most beautiful and peaceful little democracies in the world would be in danger of disintegration.

In 1972, we began at last to feel that we could travel abroad without anxiety. However, in 1979 I was invited to contribute to a muscle symposium in Dubrovnik in Yugoslavia. When we arrived at our splendid hotel, where the conference was to be held, overlooking the old city, we learned that we had arrived just an hour or two after a serious earthquake; indeed we were ourselves troubled by after-tremors for several hours. Fortunately since then, at least up to the moment of writing, no other major catastrophes (apart from a minor contretemps in Tunisia—see below) have befallen us on our extensive travels to many parts of the world where we have been privileged to make many new friendships and to cement old ones, and to see places, people and both natural and man-made wonders which we would never have been able to visit had it not been for the invitations which stemmed from my professional work and responsibilities.

Thus in September 1972 I was invited to talk on medical education in the newly established medical school in Tromso in northern Norway. Betty and I combined that visit with a short holiday, flying from Newcastle to Bergen and then hiring a car to drive to Oystese where we enjoyed two nights in the same room of the hotel where 26 years earlier we had spent our honeymoon. We then took the boat from Bergen up the coast, calling at scenically beautiful locations like Aalesund, Trondheim (where we visited the superb Chopin Museum) and Bodo. Betty awakened me at 5 o'clock one morning to look out of the port-hole from our cabin simply to see, as we sailed past, a statue on a rock indicating that we were crossing the Arctic Circle. Eventually, after a calm and beautiful cruise, we arrived in Tromso, a charming little northern city with its splendid modern Arctic Cathedral perched on a hill overlooking the town. In that cathedral, when on a trip with the ladies who had accompanied their husbands to the educational symposium, Betty had the privilege of playing the organ. The magnificence of the northern Norwegian scenery, with the snow-covered mountains reflected in the dark and forbidding fjords below, is exceptional; this is a country for which we have always had the greatest affection. Many years later, indeed, when I was privileged to be elected an honorary member of the Norwegian Academy of Science and Letters on the nomination of my great friend Sigvald Refsum, former professor of neurology in Oslo and former President of the World Federation of Neurology, we flew together to Oslo so that the honour could be conferred upon me and a number of others from around the world by His Majesty King Olav V. At the dinner which followed, I was sitting near the king and he engaged me in conversation, discussing Newcastle (for which, like many Norwegians, he had a great affection—he had opened the Civic Centre there in 1968) and also Oxford as he had been a student at Balliol. When the meal was over, his equerry invited Betty and me to join him at his table in the ante-room where, with a twinkle in his eye, he said that he was not going to ask us what we wished to have to drink but was going to tell us that we would drink good Norwegian beer. He explained that some years before, the same Academy had elected a senior Norwegian brewer because of his contributions to the science of brewing; since then his brewery had given free beer to the Academy and His Majesty felt that this must certainly not be allowed to go to waste. That delightful experience encouraged us to attend the moving and majestic memorial service held in his honour in Westminster Abbey in March 1991.

1973 was notable for a short visit to Helsinki and Turku, including a visit to the Sibelius Museum and my first experience of a sauna—both stimulating and refreshing, though I often wondered just how often individuals, having cooked in the steaming heat of the sauna, who then plunged into the cold water of the nearby pool, developed a sufficiently sharp constriction of the coronary arteries to present a potential hazard to life. The sauna was followed by a splendid if slightly bibulous dinner, superbly hosted by my friend Professor Urpu Rinne who explained, when he called for me in a taxi next morning, that even on the morning after such an occasion sufficient alcohol might still be present in the circulation to lead to the loss of a driving licence under Finnish law. And in October that year Betty and I were privileged to attend a major muscular dystrophy congress in Carefree, Arizona, where we worked from 8.00 a.m. to 1.00 p.m. and then from 4.00 p.m. to 7.00 p.m. so that in between we could swim, play tennis or golf, view the incredible flora (mainly cacti) of the Arizona desert, go horse or bicycle riding or simply rest. The air was so dry that Betty found cycling comfortable even in a temperature of 100°F.

Of the Barcelona World Congress of Neurology in 1973 (where Henry Miller entertained us royally to celebrate my birthday), of the 1977 Congress in Amsterdam (where we were entertained by Her Majesty The Queen of the Netherlands and where Betty flew home two days before the end of the Congress on learning of the arrival of our third grandchild), of the muscle congress in Montreal in 1978 (where I was honoured to have been made President), of the next such congress in Marseille in 1982 (where I celebrated my 60th birthday), of Los Angeles for yet another muscle congress in 1986, of the World Congresses of Neurology in Kyoto (1981), Hamburg (1985) and New Delhi (1989) much more could be said. Each in its own way was exceptional scientifically and socially, though I do not think that anyone who was in Delhi in 1989 could possibly forget the sheer splendour of the procession of Indian elephants with mahouts, of open carriages, of Bengal lancers and of splendidly attired Indian troops in Victorian-style uniforms of the era of the Raj which carried some of us as officers of the WFN around from one entrance of the Taj Palace Hotel to another before the magnificent banquet.

In 1974 I went as a visiting professor to Winston-Salem, North Carolina, and played golf with Jim Toole at Tanglewood, and later that year I attended the Brazilian Congress of Neurology in the scenically beautiful city of Rio de Janeiro and also spent a day or two in the huge, oppressive, concrete metropolis of Sao Paulo.

1975 saw a brief foray in July to London, Ontario, and to McMaster University at Hamilton, Ontario, with splendid visits to the Shaw Theatre at Niagara-on-the-Lake and to the Shakespeare Theatre at Stratford, Ontario. In January that year I was honoured to be the Milton Shy Visiting Professor in Philadelphia (where I enjoyed a private visit to the incomparable Barnes collection of impressionist paintings), with short visits to New York and Washington, and in late September and early October I was the Robert Aird Visiting Professor in San Francisco and Los Angeles. Squeezed in between (in April) we managed a week in Sicily where Professor Bonavita and our friend Roberto Cotrufo had organized a two-day muscle symposium at which they had asked me to lecture. They were good enough to offer my return economy class air fare from Newcastle to Catania and, to our astonishment, we found that we could arrange, for Betty and myself, a one-week inclusive package with British Airways Sovereign Holidays at Taormina, just a few miles from Messina where the lecture was to be delivered, for less than the ordinary return air fare. We therefore enjoyed a day or two visiting the region of Mount Etna and Syracuse and some of the other archeological sights of Sicily, while exploring the delights of Taormina with its splendid amphitheatre. The only fly in the ointment was that Betty's suitcase did not arrive for three days but, if the reader will forgive yet another cliché, every cloud has a silver lining as, with Signora Cotrufo, she acquired some delightful Italian clothes on a shopping spree in Messina. Several paragraphs of my talk were translated for me by Roberto and this was the first time that I had given any part of a lecture in Italian (again I suppose my gift for mimicry helped). I was sufficiently emboldened by that experience to give a few more short talks in Italian years later in Rome and in Porto Cervo in Sardinia, where close to that lovely little village with its excellent conference facilities was the magnificent Porto Cervo golf course where we managed a round during our stay.

1976 was another exceptional year as I was invited by the UK Friends of the Hebrew University of Jerusalem to be the Henry Cohen Visiting Lecturer and spent several days lecturing and teaching in Jerusalem and in Tel Aviv. The terms of the lectureship also specified that I should be accompanied by my wife and that I should visit other parts of Israel. Professor Shaul Feldman and his wife, Aviva, were immensely hospitable and a driver and car were arranged to take us to Tel Aviv, to Caesarea and up the coast to Haifa and Acre with its ancient fort. Haifa was particularly interesting in the light of my previous experience of that beautiful port during my Army service. From Haifa we went on to Tiberius, Caperneum (deeply affecting was the quietude of the lovely temple to anyone familiar with the Sermon on the Mount), the Sea of Galilee and up to the Golan Heights, to the border of Syria, before returning via Nazareth to Jerusalem. Nazareth was disappointing because of its strong tourist orientation, after the wonders of Jerusalem with its old city, Western wall and Dome of the Rock, but the little Anglican church next door to the major temple had a quiet and impressive simplicity. Later we fitted in a short visit to the Dead Sea, past Jericho and on to Masada. There was time for a brief swim in the Dead Sea, an extraordinary experience where one lies on the water, which feels curiously thick and oily and into which it is virtually impossible to sink. The huge pile of Masada is most impressive, with the fortifications, ruined synagogue and other buildings on the summit and with the huge ramp which was built by the invading Romans to enable the fortress to be stormed. Seeing the settlements on the West Bank and on the Golan Heights and the way in which so much of the desert had been reclaimed by the immense energy and ingenuity of the settlers made one realize and understand, even if one could not totally share, the wish of these Jewish settlers to cling to the land that they had taken over from the local Arab population.

1976 also saw our first visit to Tunis where our host was the noted neurologist, Mongi Ben Hamida, and where we were greatly charmed by the Tunisian architecture and the distinctive blue colouring with which many of the buildings were decorated, especially in the picturesque little village of Sidi Bou Said. The royal cities of Hammamett, of Sousse and of Kairouan were also impressive and one could not but be stunned by the sudden vision, appearing almost out of nowhere in the centre of the desert, of a colossal amphitheatre rivalling in its architectural style and magnitude the Colosseum. Professionally I managed to cope with conversations with doctors and patients in French in each of the cities where I worked. A bonus on a later visit in 1980 was a journey to the oasis of Nefta in the Sahara Desert organized by our friend, Mongi, who had been Minister of Health and who provided a Ministry car and driver to take us there. We spent a delightful evening and night in a luxurious hotel near the oasis, where the desert sunset and sunrise were both spectacular and we saw several mirages. Next morning we set off on our return journey shortly before noon; after about 20 miles we stopped for lunch in a pleasant hotel, while our driver went off to eat elsewhere. We then continued our journey in the large Peugeot diesel estate car which the Government had provided, but after a few miles the driver went more and more slowly, eventually pulling up by the side of the road and disappearing behind some bushes. At first we thought he might be praying, but when after some minutes he failed to reappear I went out to find him vomiting and complaining bitterly of vertigo—'Vertige, vertige extraordinaire, monsieur!'. There was nothing for it but to lay him down on the back seat of the car and for me, without a Tunisian licence, to take over the driving along desert roads with more than 200 km. still to go to get back to Tunis. But first the driver insisted on finding an 'apotheque'. After making enquiries, we left the main road and found a small local hospital where, as soon as the doctors discovered that I was an English neurologist, I was invited to examine the invalid. Finding nothing seriously wrong and having concluded that he had probably had something unpleasant to eat for lunch, I searched the drug locker and eventually decided to give him an injection of an antihistamine (®Phenergan). This was given, he promptly went to sleep on the back seat of the car and I drove about 180 km. towards Tunis. Dusk was beginning to fall and we were running short of fuel. I was therefore compelled to awaken the driver as we knew that he had vouchers with him. The tank was refilled but he then insisted that he was well enough to take over the wheel, even though we both felt that he still seemed rather drowsy. The last 30 or so kilometres into Tunis were hair-raising as his driving was not of the quality he had demonstrated earlier; at last we returned to the Ben Hamidas' home shaken but unscathed after a particularly memorable journey.

No similar problems arose when we went together to Venezuela in the spring of 1977 with Alvaro Villegas as our host and the head of neurology, Professor Pedro Ponce Ducharne, in charge of my hectic professional programme. Despite the pressure of lecturing and clinical demonstrations, we managed three days over a weekend by the sea at Cumana with Alvaro and his wife and visited the caves nearby where the remarkable guacharo birds live in virtually total darkness. Unfortunately we did not manage to find time to visit the Angel Falls, which I believe are magnificent, but we did see Colonia Tovar, a fascinating village in the hills above Caracas where all the buildings have been created in a German style of architecture and most of the inhabitants still wear traditional German or Tyrolean dress. We noted yet again the extraordinary contrast between rich and poor and were shocked by the tiny shacks which abounded in the hills above the bustling, prosperous centre of the city and in which we were told that many squatters living in squalor endangered themselves and their families by tapping illegally into the electricity supply.

In June that year I made a brief return visit to Boston and then went on to Dartmouth/Hannover in New Hampshire where my host was Dr José Ochoa who showed me a patient with severe trichinosis. I happened to be in Dartmouth on commencement (graduation) day and was startled to see the swarms of alumni, wearing badges which showed that some had graduated 40–50 years before.

1978 was memorable, first because I gave the prestigious Wartenberg lecture to the American Academy of Neurology, then presided over by Bob Joynt from Rochester, and secondly because this was the year in which I made my first visit to Japan and lectured in Tokyo, Nagoya, Kyoto and Fukuoka. I was the guest of the Japanese Neurological Association and was the only foreigner invited. It was a fascinating experience to discover that that Neurological Association had over 3000 members and my guest lecture in English was delivered to an audience of well over a thousand. The extraordinary and legendary generosity of the Japanese was demonstrated by the fact that after my talk I was presented with a splendid new Nikon camera, which I still treasure, as a memento of that occasion. The President then, Professor Tsubaki, and our host in Fukuoka, the ebullient Professor Kuroiwa, are both, sadly, no longer with us but our Tokyo host, Eijiro Satoyoshi, has become a close and valued friend. One remarkable development was that as Betty was with me, our hosts decided that, unusually, they would invite the wives of the officers of the Association to the dinner which had been arranged in our honour. Only later did we discover that this was the first time that wives had attended an official Association dinner as these had been all-male affairs in the past. Mrs Satoyoshi, herself a professor of anaesthesia who had worked in the United States, was completely at home, but some other wives who had never been present at similar social occasions were at first ill at ease. Fortunately, this was the first of several similar events, which was just as well as when the World Congress of Neurology was held in Kyoto in 1981, the ladies had to form a committee to plan the social programme for the accompanying persons, a task which they undertook at first with some diffidence but ultimately with enormous success.

We have had many more delightful travels since those days, including the opportunity of going as Cecil and Ida Green Visiting Professor to the University of Texas in Galveston in 1984, after I had become Warden of Green College. We were royally entertained by Cecil and Ida and their great friend, the indefatigable Andy Suttle. It was also a privilege to lecture as the Richard Paddison Visiting Scholar at the Louisiana State Medical Center in New Orleans, with Paul Larson, formerly with us in Newcastle, as our host, and to return in February 1983 to Bombay, Madras and Bangalore, that city of superb public buildings, in order to deliver the T. S. Srinivasan Memorial Lecture in Madras, as arranged by Krish Srinivas, the H. J. Mehta Oration in Bangalore and the Bharucha Oration in Bombay. This time there was no war but on our return to the UK, Newcastle airport was closed by snow, we were diverted to Teeside and continued our journey by bus. On being deposited at Newcastle Central Station taxis were unobtainable; with our heavy baggage we struggled on to the Metro, disembarked at Regent Farm and then, in light clothing which we had needed in India, manfully dragged ourselves in ankle-deep snow back to Beechfield Road. Even with whisky and hot baths, we took some time to thaw out.

Perhaps of all our ventures overseas, one of the most outstanding was that in 1981 when, after I had completed my 10 years as Dean of the Newcastle Medical School, I was given a month's leave of absence. My first commitment was to deliver the Paul Garvey Memorial Lecture in Rochester, New York, and then to go on to Michigan to give further lectures in Lansing. There was then a gap of some 10 days before we were due to attend the meeting of the American Neurological Association in San Francisco, before I went on to the World Congress of Neurology in Kyoto. Betty and I decided that this was a welcome opportunity to see a part of the central and western United States which we had never previously visited. We were royally entertained by Bob Joynt, head of neurology in Rochester, and his charming wife and were much impressed by the surrounding countryside and by the Eastman Kodak Museum. In Lansing, with our friend George Ristow, who had worked in Newcastle, we played golf (and I had some coaching from the university's professional). We then flew to Denver, hired a car and drove north to Mount Rushmore to see that superb rock carving of the heads of the former American Presidents, before driving through the Black Hills of Dakota to Newcastle, Wyoming. We then learnt a salutary lesson on the semi-deserted roads of the western USA. We travelled almost 200 miles at one stage without finding a single petrol station open, and thereafter were assiduous in making certain that the tank was full before we set out on another long stage of the journey. Newcastle, Wyoming, was a pleasant little western town with typical wooden buildings, not even remotely resembling its namesake in the north-east of England; nevertheless during our brief stay for a sandwich lunch the locals were very hospitable when they learned where we came from. On we drove through rolling prairie-type scenery, having left the Black Hills behind us, to Cody, where naturally we visited the Buffalo Bill Museum before pressing on into Yellowstone where we had booked accommodation in advance; this was just as well as we learned on reaching the park that there was not a single bed to be had unless one had a reservation. That park is magnificent with its fossilized rock formations, its bubbling hot springs and its geysers, of which 'Old Faithful' is by far the most impressive. We did a complete circumnavigation of the park, enjoying the herds of bison and we even saw a few bears.

After two exciting days we drove on through the Grand Tetons, which must surely be among our favourites with its extraordinary mountain scenery of sparkling grandeur, overlooking tranquil lakes and forests; in our view it is probably the most fascinating of all the national parks we saw (with the exception of the almost unbelievable Grand Canyon). To our astonishment, while visiting an isolated but attractive church in Grand Teton Park, the tourists signing the register before us proved to be from Longbenton in the outskirts of Newcastle upon Tyne. Our next stop was Salt Lake City, after traversing Bryce Canyon on the way; after a relaxing night (we usually stayed in Best Western motels, which were of excellent quality) we drove alongside the expanse of the Great Salt Lake with never-ending salt flats on either side and managed without undue strain to complete 600 miles in the day so as to reach Tonopah in central Nevada for another overnight break. One striking feature of driving in the American west is that the road, virtually deserted, often goes dead straight for as much as 50 to 100 miles; in the heat of the day the horizon shimmers in the haze and the distant mountains seem much closer than they are. Indeed we saw more than one mirage, reminding us of the sights of the Sahara which we had seen from Nefta. Leaving Tonopah, we crossed the foothills of the Rockies, passing a splendid lake with fossilized bushes and trees and teeming with wildlife, before entering Yosemite, yet another superbly memorable national park where the lowering, bulky rock formations like 'El Capitan' look down on a narrow park area where we had booked our accommodation in a pleasant log cabin for two nights. We were able to see most of the sights of the park, including the huge redwood plantations, the waterfalls and woodland walks which were remarkably tranquil despite the large number of visitors who thronged the area. Here again, to our surprise, when seeking nourishment, we met Dick Evans (the Newcastle radiotherapist) and his wife. Although it was mid-September, warnings of the forthcoming winter were evident with flecks of snow on the higher peaks and we were told that the park would close in another three or four weeks as many of the entrances would become hazardous because of snow. Another fascinating but alarming sight was to see the hang-gliders launching from the highest mountain blocks and slowly floating down into the valley. The drive from Yosemite into San Francisco was simple and the meeting of the American Neurological Association proved to be stimulating and enjoyable both professionally and socially. Betty had decided not to go on to Japan with me and so I saw her off on her return flight to the UK before I went on to Kyoto for a week at the World Congress before returning home.

Among our closest overseas friends with whom we have been in touch regularly over the years are Henry (Barney) and Kay Barnett from London, Ontario, with whom we have shared many exciting professional and non-professional experiences. These have included brief sojourns in Bermuda and Florida and innumerable bird-watching expeditions from their second home in King City, near Toronto, and ours in Detchant. On Barney's invitation I have twice given the Flavelle Lecture in London and in 1987 became a member of the Board of the Robarts Research Institute which he founded. Barney was born in Newcastle upon Tyne but his family left for Canada when he was three years of age. Years later when visiting us, we discovered that the home in which he had lived in a decaying Georgian street in Elswick had allegedly become a house of ill repute. This encouraged the irrepressible Barney to tell some tall tales about his origins on returning to Canada. When the house was demolished I retrieved, at his request, a single brick which I later took to Canada, though a rather tortuous explanation became necessary when I tried to carry it through the airport security check.

As I said at the outset, my professional life has brought innumerable advantages and there have been since then many other journeys to places as diverse as Saudi Arabia, Thailand, France, Spain, Germany and Indonesia which have given me, or more often both of us, great pleasure. In May 1989 we had the privilege of going on a Swan Hellenic tour 'In the Steps of Hippocrates' when I gave some lectures and we visited Venice, Padua, Split, Dubrovnik, Corfu, Corinth, Delphi, Mycaenae, Athens, Crete, Alexandria, Cairo, Rhodes, Cos, Dikili, Pergamon and Thessaloniki. This was a splendid experience, marred only by the fact that Betty picked up giardiasis (presumably in Cairo). In April 1991, when the American Academy of Neurology honoured me with a special award at its annual meeting in Boston, we were both able to make nostalgic visits to the homes in which we had lived and to other places we had visited during our first American adventure in 1953–4. Through my Presidency of the World Federation of Neurology later in 1991 we went to Japan, Hong Kong, Hawaii, Vancouver, Uruguay, New Zealand and Australia. In Hawaii we revelled in the sights and sounds of Maui and played golf as we also did in Japan and New Zealand.

As William Evans prestige visitor to the University of Otago we were privileged in New Zealand to see Christchurch, Queenstown, Dunedin, Wellington and Auckland. Moving on to Australia gave us the opportunity, long awaited, of seeing Ayers Rock and Alice Springs and the Great Barrier Reef. In Sydney I lectured to a very well-attended symposium organized to honour the retirement of Jim Lance. He and his wife Judy were kind enough to entertain us to dinner with their close friends the Dodshons (Derek Dodshon, formerly of Spennymoor, has been mentioned in several earlier chapters). Perhaps in another few years our travelling days may be over, but for the present we can both look back upon a multitude of rewarding and pleasurable experiences and upon many friendships made and renewed in innumerable overseas locations.

CHAPTER 15

On Becoming and Being a Dean

Although my initial five-year appointment as Dean of Medicine was not due to begin until 1 October 1971, once it had been confirmed by Senate and Council it became clear that summer that I was to be involved more and more in medical school and university affairs even before assuming my new post, as George Smart planned to begin as Director of the British Postgraduate Medical Federation in September. The Dean of Medicine in Newcastle carries exceptional powers and responsibilities, as the statutes of Durham University relating to the Medical Faculty were adopted by the University of Newcastle in 1963 virtually without amendment. Whereas there were three component parts of Durham University, namely the Durham Colleges, King's College Newcastle, and the Faculty of Medicine, Newcastle University on becoming independent absorbed the medical Faculty, including the Dental School and its Sub-Faculty, within its corporate structure. Nevertheless, it retained two crucial statutes effectively ensuring that the Dean was both the planning authority and the spending authority for the Faculty of Medicine. The statutes also required that the Dean must be a registered medical practitioner. It was also agreed that the Dean of Medicine, along with the Vice-Chancellor and two Pro-Vice-Chancellors elected from all other Faculties, should be members of the informal University Cabinet which met every Monday morning at 9.30 with the Registrar, Finance Officer and Bursar in attendance. These responsibilities gave the Dean of Medicine a very special place in the University hierarchy, as all other Deans of Faculties such as Arts, Science, Law, Agriculture, etc., were elected by their respective Faculty Boards for a three-year term. No other Dean sat on the University Cabinet and, although many were appointed to Senate and Council, they were not necessarily there by virtue of their appointments, nor did they all serve on the most important university committee, namely Senate Development Committee, which was responsible for predigesting all proposals relating to academic change and development before these were presented to Senate (the academic governing body of the University). Senate later passed on its decisions and recommendations, especially those with financial implications, to Council for consideration. Council, chaired by a layman (unlike Senate, which was chaired by the

Vice-Chancellor) was the financial and administrative governing body of the University, with many lay, as well as academic, members. Newcastle also differed from many other universities in that from early in its short history it had students as voting members of Senate and Council.

As Dean, then, I found myself *ex officio* on Senate Development Committee, Senate, Council, the University Cabinet (later known as the Administrative and Planning Committee) and many other statutory bodies including the Honorary Degrees Committee, Site Development Committee, Senate Nominating Committee, Promotions Committee, Higher Degrees Committee and many others, quite apart from those committees in the Medical School of which the Dean was *ex officio* chairman. These included the Board of the Faculty of Medicine, the Curriculum Committee, the Medical School's Buildings Committee, the Staff/Student Committee, the various examinations sub-committees, and many more. The Dean was also required to represent the University's interests and those of its Medical Faculty on many Health Service bodies. Having been appointed to the Regional Hospital Board in the mid-1960s, long before I was Dean, I continued to serve on that body. I had also been a member of the Newcastle General Hospital Management Committee and of the St Nicholas Hospital Management Committee. However, in 1971 all the Health Authorities in Newcastle bravely decided to bring the management of all major hospitals in Newcastle, including the General Hospital, the Royal Victoria Infirmary (formerly controlled by its Board of Governors) and the mental hospital at St Nicholas, under the ambit of a single University Hospital Management Committee. I then became a member of that body, which subsumed all the responsibilities previously carried by the individual hospital management committees. The RVI, the principal teaching hospital, was virtually the first in the country to relinquish its independent Board of Governors status, agreeing to integrate with the other hospitals in view of the assured substantial university voice upon the new body.

Being confident that arrangements for the continuing supervision of clinical work and research at the General Hospital (NGH) were in place following Walter Bradley's appointment as a joint senior lecturer/consultant, I looked forward to my new and arduous university responsibilities with keen anticipation but also with considerable trepidation. For many years I had not been involved in university affairs and much of what I later learned about its committee structure and procedures was still unfamiliar. With the encouragement and full support of my neurological colleagues, I had also made it clear to Henry Miller, the Vice-Chancellor, that I did not propose to give up my headship of the Department of Neurology. I hoped to continue to teach, to direct the research programme in the muscular dystrophy laboratories at the NGH and to retain limited clinical practice, while relinquishing my day-to-day responsibility for the care of patients, whether admitted as emergencies or from the waiting list. Those responsibilities were taken over by Walter Bradley. This change in my life required substantial reorganization of my administrative responsibilities and secretarial support. As Dean, I now had a pleasant and well-appointed office in the Medical School where Nancy Deegan, that outstanding diplomatic organizer and secretary who had served successively R. B. Green, Andrew Lowdon, Henry Miller and George Smart before me, ran the office with consummate efficiency.

Across the corridor sat the indefatigable Norman Shott, DFC, former RAF fighter pilot, who had come into university administration after leaving the service without any prior knowledge of university structure and administration. He worked his way up the administrative ladder through sheer determination and unremitting hard work; his knowledge of the school was encyclopaedic and his command of what I called registrarial language and technique outstanding. His obsessionalism and attention to detail and his familiarity with university statutes and regulations were unrivalled. He also displayed a very tactful ability to bring back into line any Dean whom he deemed to be exceeding his responsibilities or to be trying to flout what he believed to be well-constructed and sensible university regulations. I came to rely upon him absolutely, although in the early days we occasionally had minor disagreements, especially when he thought that in my eagerness to fulfil my new responsibilities I was attempting to assume tasks which more properly fell into his sphere of responsibility than mine. Sometimes, too, his attention to detail and slavish acceptance of the rule book seemed to impose a hint of rigidity upon an ossified system which I was anxious to do what I could to circumvent. As I often said, there were few rules which could not be manipulated by a gentle 'fiddle'. Whenever I tried to get around regulations which seemed tedious or unnecessary, Norman's first horrified reaction was invariably to the effect that what I suggested could not be done. Half an hour later he would come into my office wearing a charming smile to tell me how we could do it. He slavishly protected the Faculty contingency fund, which he saw as the departmental grant of the administration, but nevertheless after friendly discussion, argument and persuasion, I could sometimes wheedle out of him sufficient funds to undertake an important new development which I could not fund through the Faculty's allocation from Council given on the recommendation of Senate. Throughout, our relationship was a splendid and friendly one and he was even foolish enough to be my partner in the de Loriol Salvers foursomes competition at the Northumberland Golf Club. When, sadly, he decided to retire a year or two before the normal age, I missed him enormously, but was delighted to be able to appoint in his place Derek Nicholson, an assistant registrar from the main university offices whom I knew well and whose work, though very different in style, was just as efficient as Norman's. Indeed he deployed his administrative skills so effectively that I was able warmly and enthusiastically to support him for the post of Registrar in the University when that appointment became vacant in 1982. I was delighted when he was appointed as he has proved to be a great success in that post which he still holds.

However, secretarial support did begin to present some problems. Nancy Deegan was a splendid organizer and diary manipulator, as obsessional in many ways as Norman Shott and superb at dealing with personal or telephoned enquiries from colleagues in the University or outside. Rapid typing of long documents, however, was never her forte; she soon found that my wish to produce reports on various aspects of medical school affairs swamped her ability to cope with such new material in addition to the regular correspondence which crossed my desk. Clearly additional help was needed. Norman, as usual, found some way of funding an additional half-time post to which Mrs Beryl Blanks was appointed. She, too, proved to be an admirable colleague so that together we soon had the Dean's office running smoothly. In the meantime my long-term right-hand woman, Rosemary Allan, continued to function whole-time in my office at the NGH, dealing with my professional and neurological correspondence and with the preparation of reports and grant applications relating to research at the NGH, as well as my various literary commitments. I had also retained, on a part-time basis for three afternoons a week, my private secretary, Mrs Betty Dodds, at Beechfield Road since although I had given up private practice on becoming a whole-time professor in 1968, I continued to see a few patients for medico-legal examination and report at home, as my contract allowed. I was therefore in the fortunate position of having excellent secretarial back-up for all aspects of my work. As I often said, I sprayed tapes around each of the offices into which I had introduced compatible recording and dictating equipment to allow transcription of the material I had dictated using the portable equipment I carried around with me.

On 15 June 1971 I first had an inkling of some of the new experiences I would inevitably encounter as Dean. My appointment had been announced and I was well known to the students, many of whom I had taught and others I had come to know well through my one-year presidency of the Students' Medical Society a few years earlier. I had also become an examiner in the final clinical qualifying examination. That exam had changed greatly from my student days when we had three-hour essay-type question papers to answer in each of the major specialties of medicine, surgery and obstetrics and gynaecology, and a detailed clinical examination with a 'long' and several 'short' cases in each, followed by vivas in each subject. When the new and partially integrated Newcastle curriculum was introduced through the combined energy of Professors

Court, Smart and others in 1962, with the warm support of the then Dean, Andrew Lowdon, the final examination was simplified and integrated. A percentage of the marks was based upon in-course assessment in Stage IV of the curriculum, and although essay-type question papers survived in Part I Finals taken 12 months before Part II, the only written component of Part II was a problem-solving three-hour multiple choice question paper. A clinical situation was described with, where necessary, accompanying clinical photographs, reproductions of X-rays, electro-cardiograms or other test results, and five questions were then posed, any or all of which could be right or wrong. The clinical examination was also integrated in that each student was required to take a history from and to examine one patient over a 55-minute period, then being examined for 25 minutes by a pair of examiners, one of whom would be an expert in the subject to which the patient's illness related, while the other would be from a completely different specialty. The patient's condition could be medical, surgical, obstetric, gynaecological, dermatological, ophthalmological, psychiatric or indeed could relate to any medical specialty. This 'long case' was followed by 30 minutes spent on physical signs where the candidate would be invited to examine several patients consecutively, each for a few minutes at a time, eliciting symptoms or signs in any one of the bodily systems. In this part the second examiner, not expert in the field from which the 'long case' was derived, was given free rein in choosing which particular patients he or she would select from a large number who had volunteered their services. The examination then concluded with a short session in a clinical laboratory, and this was followed by a *viva voce* examination before two pairs of examiners. In accordance with the British tradition, several external examiners from other medical schools took part each year, with representatives in all major and several minor specialties. During my Deanship, some experenced general practitioners were added to the examining cadre.

The clinical laboratory session then consisted largely of urine testing under the scrutiny of a single examiner. The candidate was invited to inspect, describe and subject to appropriate laboratory tests several urine samples arrayed before him or her in labelled containers. In the early years new and untried examiners taking part in the examination for the first time were allowed to 'cut their teeth' on the urine testing. Like others I did so, though after one or two such sessions I was let loose on the clinical examination proper. When, a few years earlier, the irrepressible Henry Miller was invited by Andrew Lowdon to participate, one examinee, having been asked to test urine specimen D, was looking at it held up to the light when out of the corner of his eye he saw the examiner take a long swig from the glass labelled A. The perspicacious student had already noted the bubbles rising in that glass which Henry had filled with lager, and so was not disconcerted. When the tale was relayed to the Dean, his amused reaction was predictable; nevertheless Henry was quickly moved on to the more serious clinical part of the examination. Soon afterwards the Examination Committee decided, as urine testing had become 'automated', to discard that session. Speaking of Henry as an examiner reminds me, as an aside, of the occasions when he examined in neurology candidates for the Diploma in Pychological Medicine. One senior gentleman who had taken up psychiatry on completing his service in the medical branch of the Royal Navy asked to see the Dean after his 'clinical'. He said that it was not so much failing the examination that distressed him as the fact that one of the examiners so far forgot himself as to say that he was talking 'hot cock'. When yet again Henry was confronted by Andrew Lowdon as Dean, his response was brief but compelling—'Well, he was', he said. It was also Henry who, being much involved in discussions on curricular revision in Andrew Lowdon's day, uttered the memorable obiter dictum to the effect that curriculum review was an occupational disease of deans which resulted in the same subjects being taught in a different order. Despite that trenchant view, when Henry himself became Dean he was one of the staunchest supporters of the new curriculum.

However, I digress. The reason why 15 June 1971 is firmly etched in my memory is because after the exam results had been announced, and Betty and I had joined the newly-qualified doctors at the traditional BMA/Medical Insurance Agency cocktail party at the Medical Institute, we returned home for supper, leaving the joyous young people to their carousing. After supper I settled down behind my desk to do some writing and, as I had decided to work late, Betty retired to bed just after 11 p.m. At about 11.30 I heard cars revving up and down Beechfield Road and thought to myself that this was a peculiar hour for anyone to have a party. Then the door bell rang and I realized that the people having a party were ourselves. We were invaded by large numbers of newly-qualified doctors seeking refreshment. Betty quickly dressed and joined the throng, while I raided the kitchen and pantry for drinks, both hard and soft. I then recalled that it was a hallowed custom for the newly-qualified doctors to visit the Dean on Finals night. As George Smart was abroad, they had chosen me, as Dean-elect, as the next best bet. We also discovered that they had been to see our friend David Shaw and the Professor of Dermatology, Sam Shuster, who had apparently been deposited semi-clothed in his bath before they left for Beechfield Road. Fortunately I escaped that or any similar fate and by 1.00 a.m. our invaders, in excellent spirits, had moved on elsewhere. This was, however, a foretaste of things to come; in every one of the subsequent 10 years that I was Dean, we entertained the new graduates on Finals night. Fortunately in later years we were well prepared with suitable refreshment and were visited at an earlier hour; even in the North-East, in every one of those years the sun shone and we were able to use the garden. There was only one unfortunate contretemps when, on the only occasion when Betty was away at Detchant, the garden party ended but the hard core moved indoors to sing Geordie songs around Betty's precious grand piano. That notable year included such charismatic figures as Maurice Scanlon (former President of the Medical Students' Sub-Council and now Professor of Endocrinology in the University of Wales), Geoffrey Gill (now a consultant at the Liverpool School of Hygiene and Tropical Medicine) and Russell Lane (who came at the head of his year and who is now consultant neurologist at Charing Cross Hospital in London, having worked for several years in my department in Newcastle). Fortunately beer damage to the piano was trivial, though Betty did point out later that despite my ministrations (assisted by the new graduates who, despite their revelry, demonstrated an unexpected sense of responsibility) the keys remained sticky for some weeks. On one other occasion when the marauding herd had unscrewed and removed my professional name plate from the gate pillar, I paid the ransom demanded and was rewarded with a bottle of gin for my pains. Brian Fleming, by contrast, found 10 pints of milk on his doorstep next morning as his order to the milkman had been quietly changed by his departing guests.

As George Smart had agreed to spend several weeks that summer in Thailand before moving to London, I found myself acting as Dean several weeks before my appointment began. I attended the Monday morning cabinet throughout August and September and quickly recognized that Henry handled that body, as indeed he did Senate, with the same kind of wickedly eccentric panache that he had employed first as consultant and head of neurology and later as Dean. George Smart, before going abroad, invited us round for dinner in order, as he put it, to discuss 'deaning', warning me privately that a major problem any Dean would face was that Henry, despite his love of the Medical Faculty, leant over backwards so as not to favour it when issues of management and resource allocation were to be discussed. I therefore recognized that some conflict was inevitable. However, Henry and I had been colleagues and friends for so long that even though we discoursed at times in scathing and even combative terms, to an extent which sometimes astonished the non-medical Pro-Vice-Chancellors, we nevertheless got along well. I was always careful, except on very rare occasions, not to overstep the mark in displaying excessive familiarity or in coming into open conflict with the Vice-Chancellor. Fortunately the immensely experienced, urbane and witty Ernest Bettenson, whose history of the Medical School and of the problems which emerged in the 1930s is still a very readable and yet dispassionate document, kept a firm hand on the tiller and never allowed contention or fierce debate to get out of hand. His relationship with Henry was also of the love/hate variety. When the Vice-Chancellor proposed to embark on some totally outrageous scheme, Ernest, looking pointedly at Henry's exceptional girth, said 'I shall find a way to get round you on this, Vice-Chancellor, even if it does take a very long time'. Bettenson's contributions to the University cannot be over-estimated. He had an encyclopaedic knowledge of its statutes, history and administration based upon his long experience first in Durham and subsequently in Newcastle. When conflict arose, he invariably took a sound and balanced view and I found his judgement impeccable. He always kept a weather eye open for attempts by Henry and myself (these eccentric medicos who, in his opinion, were always looking for a 'fiddle') to break or bend the rules. At times this engendered what seemed to be irritating inflexibility. However, as with Normal Shott, if Henry or I were determined to pursue some specific objective which seemed at first sight to flout established convention but nevertheless, on reflection, appeared desirable, Ernest would be the first to help one to achieve the appropriate goal.

The University was also exceptionally well served by its other officers. Ken Smith, the Finance Officer, was particularly skilled in husbanding the University's financial resources and, in collaboration with the Honorary Treasurer, in handling its investments. Even though Hambros, the merchant bank, were retained as advisers, Ken Smith had an enviable aptitude for manipulating the University's financial reserves in such a way as to achieve maximum returns on investment. At one stage we feared that he might be spirited away to become the Keeper of the University Chest in Oxford, but he resisted this temptation in the light of his love of the North-East. Sadly (he was a very heavy cigarette and cigar smoker) he suffered a stroke at a relatively early age and was left moderately disabled; eventually he took early retirement and was succeeded by his able deputy, Eric Bell, who followed competently in the Smith tradition. Hugh Scott, the Bursar, was also a man of urbanity who supervised the University's estates very skilfully and managed diminishing resources effectively in ensuring that new buildings were, as far as possible, kept within budget and that older ones were properly maintained. He also achieved considerable success in controlling the University's energy costs at the time of the international oil crisis, though he was not always popular with members of staff who found themselves shivering in cooler than normal rooms and laboratories, especially during vacations. I also joined in the University Cabinet with a series of able Pro-Vice-Chancellors elected from other Faculties. One, elected under Statute 11(2), represented and was elected by Senate, while the other (the senior), appointed under Statute 11(1), was effectively Council's nominee. Chairmanship of many university committees not chaired by the Vice-Chancellor was divided between the two of them, and 11(1), as he was regularly called, had to deal with some of the most difficult bodies such as Staff Wages Committee and Catering Committee. Thus he was much involved in negotiations with technical, secretarial and other members of staff on issues relating to pay and conditions of service. When public service unions were becoming increasingly militant, this was not easy and it was equally difficult to keep the University's catering deficit within reasonable bounds. Any organization feeding large numbers of staff throughout the year inevitably finds it difficult to cope with a situation where many of its customers are students who are likely to use the facilities for only about 30 weeks out of the 52. Nevertheless, I much admired George Elliott, the Catering Officer, who was invariably cheerful, willing and cooperative and produced excellent food, either simple or sumptuous as occasion demanded, with smooth efficiency. George recruited and retained many splendid Geordie waitresses, some of whom continued to work long after the normal retirement age. Their loyal, cheerful (and even at times mildly disrespectful) service to the University was beyond praise. Betty and I enjoyed meeting them at the innumerable lunches, dinners or other social events to which we were invited or which we ourselves organized in the University Refectory over the years. It was always a pleasure, even after we left, to be greeted on returning to Newcastle by some of them as long-lost friends.

Of the many Pro-Vice-Chancellors with whom I worked several stand out in the memory. 'Mac' Cooper, Professor of Agriculture, a distinguished New Zealander, left soon after I became Dean to take on a major agricultural responsibility in Spain. Professor Bill Elliott, Professor of law, was remarkably successful as PVC under Statute 11(1); with his clear, deliberate but judicial reasoning, he had an unusual ability to achieve rapport with the unions and to achieve consensus in potentially difficult or even inflammatory situations. Ewan Page, Professor of Computing, had a very different personality but also proved to be an exceptionally dedicated, hard-working and efficient PVC, first under Statute 11(2) before he succeeded Bill Elliott in the more senior post. He was notable for his clarity of thought, his decisiveness and his ability to pursue argument and desirable objectives to a logical and satisfactory conclusion, even in the face of spirited opposition. Admittedly, as he recognized, he did at times have a rather short fuse and was thought by some to wage war on some sections of the University where he perceived evidence of less than the highest standards of academic excellence or less than total dedication to the University's interests. Nevertheless, he was much respected and admired. After Henry's untimely death Ewan took over as Acting Vice-Chancellor and saw to it that both academically and financially the institution was kept in good heart and on an even keel until Henry's successor was eventually in post. We were not therefore surprised when Ewan was invited to become Vice-Chancellor of Reading University, an appointment in which I understand that he has proved to be a great success. Much less vigorous, forthright and outspoken was a notable Pro-Vice-Chancellor from the Arts Faculty, Professor David West (Professor of Latin). But he was quietly and firmly effective; studiously reflective, he had charm, persuasiveness and an ability to sustain argument by force of logic and persuasion but without the directly combative tactics which Ewan Page was sometimes compelled to employ. He was not as well suited to the hurly-burly of union negotiations as Ewan and Bill Elliott had been, but served with distinction in the Statute 11(2) position. Later during my Deanship came Professor Jim O'Callaghan, Professor of Agricultural Engineering and Dean of Agriculture, who having first been elected to the 11(2) appointment, then moved on into the senior post and demonstrated a degree of commitment and dedication to the University's interests which was exceptional. However, he assumed that appointment at a time of increasing financial constraint and this may have caused his popularity to decline slightly in the latter years of his distinguished service. He was impatient of inefficiency and always ready to criticize or even to castigate those whose academic and administrative standards were lower than his own. After Professor Laurence Martin had arrived as the new Vice-Chancellor, there were times when the Monday morning cabinet meeting was not only lengthy but also (occasionally) embarrassingly contentious when Jim felt it right to criticize the performance of some of the University's officers. But this was always done with the best of intentions and with the interests of the University at heart. Even I, throughout this period one of his strongest advocates and supporters, came into conflict with him occasionally when I felt that he was being a little inflexible and rule-driven in some of his attitudes and recommendations, particularly when the freezing of posts falling vacant in various departments and faculties was necessary. Nevertheless, Jim served the University well and with total dedication; I have always regarded him as a good friend. Even after his many years of service as Pro-Vice-Chancellor ended, his colleagues in the Faculty of Agriculture re-elected him as Dean. The lay Chairman of Council, the late Col Osmond Alexander of Procter & Gamble once commented thoughtfully that Ewan Page, who began as Pro-Vice-Chancellor with striking irascibility, seemed to mellow as he became more senior, whereas Jim O'Callaghan, who began in a more quiet and dispassionate manner, perhaps gained a little in combativeness as the years went by. During Jim's period of service David Whiffen, a distinguished Professor of Physical Chemistry, with his quieter and more studied approach, acted as an effective counter-balance and also served the institution well, even though he may have lacked some of Jim's incisive clarity of insight and determination.

Henry's style as Vice-Chancellor was often extraordinary but it was no more than a reflection of his unusual and distinctive personality. That same mordant wit which I had experienced when I worked with him in neurology regularly came to the fore. On many occasions some exceptionally clever remark of his provoked gales of laughter in Senate or Council while he was quietly slipping through some unusual or even unpopular policy which had initially been strenuously opposed, if only by a small group. Unquestionably, some of his wickedly clever remarks had a distinct cutting edge which wounded those who knew him less well and especially those who were not willing or able to respond in like vein. He enjoyed nothing better than a strenuous verbal battle of wits and even an exchange of insults. Most people, like myself, recognized the danger of attempting to respond with comments which one intended to be similarly amusing but which inadvertently seemed insulting and not at all funny. Occasionally, too, there were times when Henry went way 'over the top' in a desire to shock and succeeded in causing deep offence, as on the occasion when he gave a splendidly racy and characteristic speech at the bankers' dinner in Newcastle, with many wives present, but foolishly introduced a four-letter word into his final story and sat down in almost total silence. And on more than one occasion in committee I cringed at some of his more outrageous comments, as when in Promotions Committee a particular individual had received strong support for advancement to a personal chair, to which Henry responded 'I will not have that bloody man as a personal professor in my university under any circumstances—he smells!'. And he also offended a senior and distinguished gastroenterologist from elsewhere when he (Henry) was President of the Association of Physicians of Great Britain and Ireland during its Newcastle meeting. A young associate introduced by the gastroenterologist gave a paper which left Henry (and some others) unimpressed and unconvinced. When discussion opened, Henry asked the senior author whether he had anything to add. When the gentleman concerned asked what the President had in mind, Henry responded 'Well, do you believe it?'. Despite some such drawbacks due to his 'larger-than-life' personality, Henry was a fine Vice-Chancellor with an innate ability quickly to get to the root of a problem and to foresee snags which others might have overlooked. He always delegated authority to those whom he felt were capable of accepting and justifying it, and controlled Senate and Senate Development Committee, as well as the other committees which he chaired, with a firm but judicious hand, with humour, patience and wisdom. His relationship with the student body was generally excellent. In the late 1960s at a time of national and international student unrest, some militant students demanded to see the files which they were sure the University kept about individual trouble-makers. Henry offered them the freedom of all of the filing cabinets in his office and department. After they had searched for hours without success, they departed with tails between their legs, recognizing that there were no secret documents recording their peccadilloes and political activities. And when somebody attached a notice to the Vice-Chancellor's door which read 'Fat Fascist Bastard' Henry's response was simple; he pointed out that the noun was a matter for his parents and not for himself, that the first adjective was one which he could not possibly deny, but that he indignantly refuted the second, having once been a card-carrying member of the Communist Party and being still an ardent Labour supporter.

Sadly, the last year or two of Henry's reign were blighted by illness. Rather too late, he recognized that his life of self-indulgence had seriously damaged his health and eventually went on to a strict reducing diet which he wickedly described as being a diet of meat and alcohol! There were indeed times when, if one went to see the Vice-Chancellor in an afternoon, he would say 'Tea time' and would stretch out a hand to the small refrigerator which sat on his desk, extracting a couple of glasses and the gin bottle. Unfortunately, too, there were a few public occasions when he was evidently weary and was no longer his incisive, witty and ebullient self. Despite substantial loss of weight, he soon began to develop the cardiac symptoms which blighted his last few years. He often quoted with approbation the comment of his friend Henry Cohen (Lord Cohen of Birkenhead) to the effect that the only treatment for a cardiac infarction was to stay at home in bed with a bottle of Scotch on a table by one's side. When Henry himself had such an infarct and was admitted to intensive care at the NGH, he was found a few hours later walking to the toilet, trailing broken wires! When, sadly, he died at the age of 62, just a few weeks after learning that he was to be offered an honorary degree at the University of Hull, those of us who admired and indeed loved him felt totally bereft as we knew that we would never see his like again. His sterling qualities as a doctor, teacher and Vice-Chancellor, his love of life, his talent for friendship, his never-failing support of friends and colleagues whom he thought deserving of approbation, his dislike of the second rate and his undivided loyalty to his profession, his subject, his medical school and his university made him one of the greatest figures that Newcastle has known or will ever know. We who mourned him were happy to contribute to the book *Remembering Henry*, edited by Stephen Lock and Heather Windle and published by the *British Medical Journal* a few months after his death.

To return to my own decanal responsibilities, my first term was somewhat disrupted by the long-awaited professional visit to India, the Far East and Australia which had been planned long before I was aware that I might be moving into university affairs. Once that tour was over and I had waded through the massive accumulation of mail which awaited my return, we established a routine whereby invariably I would go to the General Hospital at 8.15 or 8.30 in the morning to deal with some of my hospital and professional correspondence with Rosemary before going down to the Medical School and/or University. Monthly Council meetings fell on Monday afternoons. Senate met monthly on a Tuesday afternoon, two weeks after Senate Development Committee, also on Tuesday afternoon, had predigested the agenda. Twice a term there was the Board of the Faculty of Medicine on a Thursday afternoon, three times a term the Joint Project Management Committee to plan the new medical school and ward block behind the RVI. Fortunately the many other committees upon which I sat were all planned well before the beginning of each term, so that I was able to interdigitate these university commitments with my professional responsibilities to the department at the General Hospital, with closed out-patient clinics also at the NGH and with the increasing number of meetings I was required to attend in London at the Medical Research Council or General Medical Council. To interrelate these innumerable responsibilities (Nancy Deegan once worked out that I was a member of 146 committees locally, nationally and internationally, but fortunately some met very rarely, while there were others, like the Sub-Faculty Board of Dental Surgery, which it was thought inappropriate for me to attend save by special invitation) we worked out between us a suitable modus vivendi. This did involve a tremendous amount of to-and-froing between the NGH, the Medical School, the RVI, the Regional Hospital Board and other locations in Newcastle, as well as innumerable nights on the London sleeper. My record was four consecutive nights on the train, going down one night for a meeting in London, back the next night for meetings in Newcastle, down again the next night to London and then back again the next. Fortunately Rosemary, Nancy and Betty Dodds achieved an excellent rapport and each kept a separate diary, regularly updated, just as I tried to keep my own pocket diary in line with theirs (to lose it would have been disastrous). At times the work-load became horrendous, if not intolerable, especially when, in the evenings or at weekends, I also tried to revise and update various books and to fulfil my continuing responsibility as editor-in-chief of the Journal of the Neurological Sciences. Nevertheless, these were happy and fruitful days and the relief of no longer being on emergency call for the clinical care of patients meant that I could usually go with Betty and the family to Detchant at the weekends with an easy mind (often taking a load of paper with me, but nevertheless being able to spend at least a few hours walking the hills with them or playing golf at Bamburgh).

So the unending stream of meetings began slowly but surely to dominate my life. Not only did I have the recurring committees but there were innumerable ad hoc meetings called intermittently on such topics as student projects, the Bachelor of Medical Science degree, the administration of the Medical Care Research Unit and of various other major research projects. Each term I also held a meeting of heads of departments to consider Medical School policy and also met with representatives of the student body in the Staff/Student Committee to discuss student affairs. There were also regular meetings of the Medical School Building Committee and of the Joint Project Management Committee jointly established between the University, the Regional Hospital Board and the University Hospital Management Committee to look at projected developments on the RVI site and especially the planning and building of the new School, and of course many other university and NHS committees regularly intervened. The Dean was also expected to chair inaugural lectures given by newly-appointed professors as well as examiners' meetings relating to the Final Examination in Medicine. Postgraduate and vocational training in medicine was not overlooked either, as although the Postgraduate Committee was chaired by the Postgraduate Dean, the Dean of Medicine was expected to attend and was also regularly involved in committees examining the distribution, content and approval of pre-registration appointments for newly-qualified doctors in the northern region.

Interrelationships with the NHS also brought many commitments. After the disastrous McKinsey-designed 1974 reorganization of the NHS which created additional tiers in an already cumbersome NHS administrative structure, I relinquished my membership of the Regional Hospital Board (RHB) (which then became the Regional Health Authority (RHA)) to serve on the Area Health Authority (Teaching) (AHA(T)) for the remaining duration of my decanal appointment. Nevertheless I continued as Chairman of the RHA's Research Committee which assessed locally-funded research proposals and which met quarterly on a Saturday morning not only to assess and grade applications and to award grants but often also to interview the applicants. It had also become the convention that when the northern region Fellows of the Royal College of Physicians met once a year to consider which of their colleagues they would wish to propose for election to the Fellowship, the Dean took the chair (and provided sherry). A similar arrangement also existed relating to the nomination from Newcastle of those physicians whom we wished to see elected to the Association of Physicians of Great Britain and Ireland. These, like many of the Health Service meetings and especially the medical advisory bodies which gave professional advice to the AHA(T) always met in the early evening, so that on at least two or three evenings each week I was unlikely to be home before 7.30 or 8.00 p.m. Finally, the Dean or his nominee was also expected to chair committees established by the University to appoint readers or lecturers within the Faculty of Medicine; in the case of appointments to chairs, the Dean was always a member of the committee but the Vice-Chancellor or a Pro-Vice-Chancellor took the chair.

Two other major commitments also loomed large, one related to student affairs and the other to the organization and content of the medical curriculum. On being appointed I decided to try to meet all of the fresher students as soon as possible after they arrived. I therefore invited them all to sherry parties in our splendid Howden Room (see Chapter 3). That venue was spacious enough for me to be able to meet them in a series of four sherry parties held early during the Michaelmas Term. I told them, as I did students in Green College when we moved there in 1983 (Chapter 17) and held similar parties in the Warden's lodgings, that I could rarely remember the name of a student after one interview or even perhaps after two, but was very disappointed if I could not do so after three meetings. In 1971 we admitted 100 new students; however it was agreed between the Department of Health and the University Grants Committee (UGC) that in the light of the planned target for UK medical school admissions in the late 1970s of 4080, Newcastle would be required to take 200 students annually after the new medical school (planned to open in the 1970s) had been built. I was therefore anxious, if possible, to increase our student numbers on an interim basis as I knew that this would be the only means through which we would have a claim on additional funding from the UGC, via the University, in order to introduce much-needed developments in the Faculty and to obtain the new recurrent funds needed to appoint additional staff members. At first I met considerable resistance, not least from some preclinical colleagues who claimed that the available facilities and space were insufficient. Nevertheless, they were first persuaded that a modest increase in our annual quota to 108 was feasible; when this was agreed by the Faculty and by Senate and Council, we were able to obtain modest additional funding, sufficient to enable us to appoint three or four additional lecturers to fill much-needed gaps in staffing. In fact we often exceeded even this quota as each year we normally took between six and 10 students from Oxford or Cambridge who had completed their preclinical training in one or other of those universities but wished to come to Newcastle for the clinical course. A few years later, even when it became clear that the opening of the new medical school was to be substantially delayed (see below) we pushed up our annual intake yet again to 140 students, including those from Oxbridge, and so were able, before clouds of financial restraint began to loom large over the universities, further to increase our staffing in under-privileged areas.

My contacts with the student body were among the most rewarding features of the 10 years that I spent as Dean (my appointment was speedily reconfirmed for a second five-year term in 1976). I attempted to preserve as inviolate the Wednesday morning clinical demonstrations which I gave for undergraduate and postgraduate students alike at the NGH and which were attended by the clinical students who were attached to neurology for a three-week period as part of their clinical training. Even more fruitful and refreshing was the relationship I established with innumerable consecutive student officers, including the President and Secretary of the Medical Students' Representative Council and the officers of the Medical

Society. Among those who stand out in my memory are, in particular, Cynthia Brook, who became President of the British Medical Students' Association (BMSA). She was delightful and effective, though I have never quite forgiven her for her decision, admittedly taken along with her colleagues, to disband that organization and to merge it with the Health Students' Group of the National Union of Students. Of course many thought that the BMSA was elitist, and in the light of the sociological trends of the mid-1970s, they concluded that to merge their organization with that representing all health students would be sensible. In consequence, however, the medical student voice became much less effective in national student affairs. As I write, I have been rather saddened, as a former officer of the BMSA, to note that there are now two competing organizations representing medical students, first the Associate Members Group of the BMA, and secondly the newly-formed National Association of Medical Students, in which Oxford students, including some whom I knew well in Green College, have been much involved. I hope that a merger will eventually be possible so as to establish a single cohesive voice expressing the national medical student view, as if the old BMSA were re-emerging like the phoenix from the ashes. Another outstanding student officer was the redoubtable Maurice Scanlon, now Professor of Endocrinology in the University of Wales School of Medicine in Cardiff. A man of boundless energy, bubbling with ideas and initiatives, he embarked upon two outstanding questionnaire exercises inviting comment from the student body about various aspects of medical school administration and teaching (which reminded me very much, though I did not tell him so, of similar exercises I had undertaken when I was Secretary and later President of the Medical Sub-Council of the SRC in my student days). One such investigation gave us invaluable feedback about the quality of clinical teaching in the various attachments to clinical firms throughout Newcastle which students had held during the preceding year. The frank and invaluable information derived from that exercise helped us to restructure clinical teaching, or at least to bring major deficiencies to the attention of certain teachers. It was chastening to discover that some of the less effective teaching seemed to be offered in some prestigious academic units.

Contact with students brought innumerable rewards and benefits, much amusement and occasional irritation, though I believe I can claim that our relationship was usually friendly and fruitful. I have often quoted the somewhat apocryphal story of the newly-installed hot air hand driers in the basement toilets in the Medical School, next to one of which a wag attached a notice saying 'For a short message from the Dean, press the red button'. I also much enjoyed the occasion when an exceptionally attractive young female student who, in accordance with the usual practice, was enticingly attired and had had a special 'hair-do' before the final viva in her Final Examination in Medicine, was being questioned by a relatively young and no doubt highly eligible bachelor professor of surgery who, at the end of an excellent viva in which she had performed superbly, thought he would take an interest in her future career. He therefore enquired 'Well, my dear, what were you thinking of doing after this?'. To which she replied 'Well, I *was* thinking of going straight home'. We soon recognized that the annual invasion of our home after the results of the examination were announced was inevitable and it was our custom invariably to go to the annual graduation ball a few days after that exam. I was deeply touched, in my last year as Dean, to be presented at that event by the redoubtable John Dowden with the Lindisfarne trophy awarded annually to the outstanding teacher/personality of the year. Betty and I also attended, whenever we could, the annual Medical Society dinner. Until the 1960s that had been a strictly all-male preserve at which members of staff were regularly invited after the meal to stand up on their chairs and to regale the audience with risqué stories or Rabelaisian recollections. During my year as staff president of the Society, a few years before I became Dean, the dinner was invaded by two redoubtable female students dressed in dinner jackets. They were lifted up bodily and borne out of the room three times before eventually being allowed to join the company. That was the breach in the dyke; as the proportion of female students steadily increased to the 50% or more which it is today, ladies have regularly been admitted to that annual occasion (and have contributed some of the more hair-raising stories).

Another outstanding event of the student year was the annual revue, usually held in March in the Gulbenkian Studio Theatre, part of the University Theatre. Occasionally the crudity of the humour repelled, but throughout my 10 years as Dean I was increasingly impressed not only by the range of musical and choreographic talent, as well as by the sparkling libretto and repartee of these highly professional performances, but by the skill demonstrated by the organizers and the performers in mimicking the mannerisms of their teachers. It was a grave disappointment to some teachers if they did not receive a mention and I was vigorously lampooned on many successive occasions. In those days in the winter I usually wore suits with waistcoats and kept a selection of pens and propelling pencils in one waistcoat pocket. As soon as a young man appeared on stage in a suit with a waistcoat, with about 20 pens and pencils in his waistcoat pockets, I recognized whom he was intended to be. When I received my knighthood in early 1979, I (and Betty too) came in for special attention (the title of the revue was 'Once a Knight is enough'). Perhaps another highlight was when in early 1982, after I had resigned from the Deanship, my sister Mary's son, Peter Groves, an outstanding medical student, produced a virtuoso performance in several sketches, impersonating first Jomo Kenyatta and then, as my colleagues told me, 'doing' me with great skill and effect. And I also remember well March 1981 when it was generally known that I was relinquishing the post at the end of September that year. At the end of the revue I was invited, with Betty at the piano, to perform some Geordie songs. I gave them 'The Blaydon Races' and 'The Lambton Worm', the verses of which I have remembered since my childhood, just as Betty has always remembered the music; the genuine warmth of our reception brought tears to our eyes. The news of that episode must have leaked out, as a week or two later, in the annual party at the Senior Common Room in the University, in the inter-faculty competition for 'music hall turns', Betty and I performed again, this time interspersing the musical items with a few Geordie anecdotes; to our astonishment and delight we carried off the prize on behalf of the Medical Faculty. Certainly it was the prospect of continuing contact with students which was a major attraction to us both in deciding that we would accept the move to Green College in 1983.

An important matter which exercised me greatly was that of student admissions. Regularly, through the Universities' Central Council on Admissions (UCCA), we received each year about 2600 or more applications for the available places in our medical school. Even though each student could nominate five choices on the form, the chance that any individual would be accepted by us was less than one in five. My predecessor as Dean, George Smart, was convinced that the interview was a poor method of selecting students and had introduced a policy whereby offers, provisional upon achieving specified 'A' level grades, were based almost wholly upon the information given by the student himself or herself and by the schoolmaster or mistress on the UCCA form. In the 1960s the minimum standard for admission was three passes at grade C at 'A' level, but when I became Dean it was clear that if that standard were maintained we would be seriously overcommitted and would far exceed our quota. Because of increasing competition, therefore, we increased the entry standard first to a B and two Cs, later to two Bs and a C, and within three years of my becoming Dean it had risen to BBB or better. I was greatly concerned about the policy over interviews. Admittedly George and his colleagues had based their decision upon the fact that a few years earlier all candidates had been interviewed in a massive exercise where as many as a dozen interviewing panels of three had been appointed and individual applicants were randomly allocated to any one panel. That method was unsatisfactory, if only because some of the consultants or other staff members involved had had little experience of interviewing and tended inadvertently to grade some candidates more highly on the grounds of appearance and personality rather than of intellectual attainment and potential achievement. This resulted in the admission of some students who fell so far below the minimum academic standard required to cope with the medical curriculum that they then fell by the wayside. It then became customary only to interview a few candidates, including graduates and other mature applicants worthy of consideration, along with others who had problems relating, for example, to health or other factors which might impair their ability to complete or cope with the medical course.

While I recognized that many other schools had adopted a similar policy, I felt that it was at least possible that we might admit some highly intelligent individuals with personality defects which could well impair their ability to practise medicine. I therefore introduced a system of grading all applications. Those who were clearly of outstanding intellectual ability, with nine or ten passes at grade A in 'O' levels and a prediction of similar achievement at 'A' level, and in whose cases the sporting or cultural information, together with the school report, indicated an outstanding level of all-round achievement, were graded A+ and were given an offer of a place without interview. Many of these were also Oxbridge candidates but we sent out our offers early in the hope that some would decide to come to Newcastle, and many chose to do so. There were then very many applications graded A, clearly from individuals of well above average ability and achievement who were nevertheless not quite in the top grade. We arranged to interview many of these, particularly if we saw any potential discrepancy between past academic achievement, predicted 'A' level results and comments in the headmaster's or headmistress' report relating to personality, dedication, initiative and the like. Gradually we began to interview more and more such candidates, but invariably saw to it that at least one experienced interviewer was a member of each panel and that the panel members were carefully chosen for their experience and judgement. I believe that this policy made our admissions arrangements more fair and effective. Of course, there is room within the medical profession for people with many different personality traits. We need the bright, innovative and perhaps prickly or aggressive scientist to work in medical research, just as we need the compassionate, kindly and caring individual with good communication skills who is likely to excel clinically, whether in a hospital specialty or in general practice. Nevertheless, I think that our interviewing policy helped us reject some of those who were unsuited to a career in any branch of medicine. We were also able, after many discussions in our students' admission review group, so to structure the interviewing process as to make it more effective as a discriminator. George Smart and his colleagues had carried out some studies, and reviewed others, which strongly suggested that success or failure in the medical course was to some extent correlated with 'O' level examination results, but by far the most accurate discriminator of subsequent performance was the grade of 'A' level pass achieved. They found no correlation with graded interview performance. Subsequent work, however, done by Peter Richards and others in London has shown that a carefully structured interview, carried out by experienced interviewers, does correlate positively with later achievement in medicine. I understand that since I left Newcastle the number of interviews has increased steadily and that all now being considered for admission meet a panel of experienced staff members before an offer is made.

Another matter which concerned me was the curriculum. The revised version introduced in 1962 through the energetic intervention of George Smart, Donald Court and Fred Harper, and acquiesced in, if not wholly supported initially by Henry Miller, had proved both successful and innovative. Nevertheless, it seemed to me and others to preserve to an unacceptable degree some components of the pre-existing barrier between the preclinical and clinical phases of the course. Admittedly some limited clinical exposure and a reasonable amount of social and behavioural science had been introduced into Stage I, but Stage II, offering formal courses in pathology, clinical chemistry, microbiology and pharmacology still stood apart from Stage I of the basic natural sciences on the one hand and Stage III of clinical training on the other. Hence I decided, with the support of the Faculty, to establish and to chair a Curriculum Review Committee which met at first fortnightly and later monthly on Tuesday evenings in the Howden Room to examine how best we could further revise our curriculum and integrate it more fully. These were heady days; I chose colleagues who seemed sufficiently young but also clear-thinking and far-sighted to join me in that committee (along with two student officers). Norman Shott even bored a hole in the centre of the magnificent long oak table in the Howden Room through which the lead to a microphone could be passed so that the proceedings of the committee could be recorded on tape. Fortunately the hole was in the centre of a carved rose and the plug which was regularly removed when the microphone was in use could be re-inserted so that no evidence of damage could be detected by the casual observer. It soon emerged that a major element obstructing further change was the structure of the then Curriculum Committee which consisted solely of heads of all medical school departments. I, like many others before and since, was well aware that defence of territory by a few departmental heads who refused to relinquish their hold on any part of the curriculum was a major obstacle to innovation and review. One of the first recommendations, therefore, of the Review Committee was that the Curriculum Committee itself should be restructured so as to consist of the Faculty officers with no more than 12 independent members, chosen for their own personal merits and specific talents and not on the basis of any departmental affiliation. It was also agreed that there should be four students on the Committee, nominated by the Students' Representative Council. We also concluded that the barrier between Stages I and II should be abolished and that core courses in the medical laboratory disciplines such as pathology, microbiology, clinical chemistry and pharmacology should be fully integrated with teaching of the basic sciences on a system-based principle. And we accepted that the amount of clinical exposure in Stage I should be increased. Many meetings were held before our ideas finally crystallized and were put to the Board of the Faculty of Medicine in 1973, before being finally approved by Senate and Council later that year. Because of inevitable problems relating to the staffing implications of having two curricula running side by side, the new curriculum and newly structured Curriculum Committee did not come into operation until 1976. Since that time it has been generally agreed that the innovation was immensely successful.

Briefly, the principles underlying the 1976 curriculum which, with minor amendment, continues are, first, that students are introduced to patients on the first day they arrive in the Medical School. A clinical demonstration with a volunteer patient is arranged to highlight the importance of basic science knowledge in anatomy and physiology which students will be acquiring, with a pathophysiological analysis and a discussion of management. Secondly, every student within the first week is introduced to a general practitioner who then, in turn, introduces him or her to a family in the community which the student is expected to follow through to the end of the course, taking an interest at first in them as individuals in their specific social environment, but increasingly becoming more and more interested, as the student's knowledge increases, in the medical problems which they encounter. Fortnightly visits continue throughout the course, and after two years the students write an interim report on their experiences. Thirdly, under the auspices of the Curriculum Committee, there are 18 system and topic sub-committees, each containing basic scientists (physiologists, anatomists, biochemists), pathologists, microbiologists, clinical chemists and clinicians, and also two student members. These committees are responsible for designing an integrated course on their specific system or topic throughout the curriculum, beginning with the basic sciences, weaving into teaching issues relating to pathological changes in function caused by disease (pathophysiology), and later concentrating upon the clinical phenomena of disease and its management. There are system and topic sub-committees dealing, for example, with the cardiovascular system, the nervous system, etc., but also with other topics which do not fall readily into any single bodily system, such as blood, immunology, oncology, etc.

Within Stage I, therefore, the student concentrates on anatomy, physiology and biochemistry, but teaching (and programmed self-learning) is arranged on a system-orientated basis with regular clinical demonstrations relevant to the particular system being taught. Throughout this stage there is also regular teaching on human development, behaviour and ageing, involving much work in psychology, sociology, behavioural science, biostatistics and epidemiology. In the second year of Stage I there are core courses on the principles of the medical laboratory disciplines of pathology, pharmacology, microbiology and clinical chemistry, while throughout this stage students are taken one afternoon a week by a clinical teacher in small groups and are taught the approach to the patient, communication skills and the principles of history taking and examination. Hence by the time they enter Stage II, the beginning of the clinical curriculum proper, they have learned not only much basic medical science but also about man in society, epidemiology and the ability to communicate. Despite the additional subjects included in Stage I, the reports of external examiners suggest that the knowledge and performance of Newcastle students in the basic science subjects of anatomy, physiology and biochemistry have not suffered. Partly this seems to be because the number of contact hours has been reduced and more time has been provided for students to engage in self-education. Nevertheless, some traditional methods of teaching on prosected anatomical specimens and a limited amount of dissection have been retained.

Stage II of the curriculum consists of a series of rotating clinical appointments in the mornings, mainly in the Newcastle hospitals or in others close by, in disciplines such as medicine, surgery, psychiatry, paediatrics and obstetrics. There is a compulsory four-week attachment to general practice within this stage, so that all students have some experience of medical work in the community. Some brief attachments are included in the super-specialties like radiotherapy and oncology, plastic surgery and others, as well as longer attachments in ear, nose and throat surgery and ophthalmology, so that each student receives some clinical experience in almost every medical specialty throughout this phase. The afternoons consist of integrated courses organized and planned in rotation by the individual system and topic sub-committees. Thus, for example, neurology has a three-week afternoon lecture and demonstration course, including a number of seminars. In these sessions students are taught not only clinical neurology and the management of patients with such problems, but also the principles of the pathological disciplines and clinical pharmacology insofar as these are important in relation to diseases of the nervous system. Structured reading lists are provided, with hand-outs summarizing the content of the teaching programme and giving advice upon topics which students must learn for themselves. At the end of Stage II comes the Final Examination Part I, consisting of a series of essay-type question papers, one multiple choice question paper of three hours with 60 questions, and two viva examinations each with a pair of examiners. Half-way through the two-year Stage III course there is a three-month summer elective during which students can undertake elective study either in general practice, in a hospital in another part of the UK, in a research laboratory or in a variety of locations overseas, working either, for example, in a hospital in the United States or in a rural health centre in the third world. These elective periods have proved very successful in broadening the students' experience.

The most popular component of the Newcastle curriculum is Stage III (the final year) in which all formal lecturing and didactic teaching has ceased and in which students are attached in groups of no more than two to hospital units, either in Newcastle or elsewhere throughout the northern region, where they function as assistant house physicians and surgeons and are thus able to expand greatly their clinical experience and expertise. Many specialties are included in addition to medicine, surgery, psychiatry, obstetrics and gynaecology and paediatrics, but there are also elective periods which allow students to undertake further attachments in subjects in which they feel that they require additional experience. At the end of the final year, the Final Examination Part II, as described earlier, is taken, with detailed grades and assessments awarded to the individual students by their clinical supervisors in Stage III providing a significant component of the marks. While the integrated final examination has proved very successful, I recall more than one occasion when some older members of staff present at the final examiners' meeting thought that we were allowing our students to pass much too easily and were not failing a sufficient number. Subsequently, therefore, I mounted an investigation in which we invited consultants who had supervised the work of our graduates in their pre-registration appointments over a four-year period to grade them independently on a five-point scale. Simultaneously we asked the registrar or senior registrar on the same clinical firm to give an independent grading. While the junior hospital doctors tended to mark the newly-qualified doctors rather more strictly than did the consultants, the results were reasonably consistent. They showed that even some students who had been classed as marginal pass/fail in the Final Examination and whom some of our more traditional colleagues would have wished to see fail had performed as effectively in their subsequent clinical appointments as had some who had passed the examination with flying colours.

In my view this Newcastle model of an integrated curriculum with defined goals and objectives (many adopted by other schools) relating to knowledge, skills and attitudes set a standard against which many other curricula in the UK and in other parts of the world have had to be judged. It has not been as radical or innovative as those introduced, for example, in McMaster University in Canada or in Newcastle, New South Wales, where much of the teaching has been organized on a problem-solving basis, but it has proved popular with both students and staff. I left the Medical School in 1981 feeling that its introduction had been well worthwhile. The new Curriculum Committee had also effectively eroded the power of potential 'robber baron' heads of departments who had so often been opposed to curriculum review. Having made this point, I must at once say that the heads of the departments of anatomy and physiology like Raymond Scothorne, Fred Harper and later Eric Blair were among those who were most helpful in the review exercise. While there were obviously some who, for what they felt to be good reasons, opposed our reforms, most of my colleagues supported them whole-heartedly, even when their views, often expressed forcibly in committee, were rejected. While some significant further changes have been introduced since I left Newcastle in 1983, the basic structure of the 1976 curriculum remains more or less unchanged and continues, I believe, to be the envy of many other schools.

Time and space will not allow me to go into detail about other innovations we introduced. The Bachelor of Medical Science examination (Honours) which replaced in the Medical Faculty the Honours BSc previously available only to students in anatomy, physiology, pharmacology and microbiology also proved successful. This allows students to take an intercalated year, either between Stage I and Stage II or between Stages II and III of the medical curriculum, and to study a topic in depth, producing a dissertation but also receiving instruction in a core course on such topics as medical laboratory science, statistics and epidemiology. The degree can be awarded for options which are either physical science-based, as, for instance, in anatomy, physiology, pharmacology, immunology, biochemistry, pathology, microbiology or clinical chemistry, or social science-based, as in community medicine, general practice, geriatrics, etc. The student project scheme in which all students entering stage II of the curriculum are invited, in association with a supervisor in the Medical School, to undertake a research project in their spare time has also been invaluable. In my day, about 50% of the students embarked upon a project and about half of these completed it. The first phase inevitably involves a literature search relating to the chosen topic, after which a preliminary dissertation is prepared before experimental work or other investigative studies relating to the project proper begin. Before I left Newcastle I was glad to be able to endow a prize in my name for the best such dissertation submitted annually. I have been much impressed on reading the entries which have been chosen for that prize year by year; many of them, and many student project reports which were completed during my time as Dean, would challenge in their scope and quality submissions I have seen presented for higher degrees in the medical and other faculties.

Social activities and responsibilities were not, of course, forgotten. We entertained regularly at home. I spoke at innumerable dinners, we wooed potential benefactors at University lunches and dinners and entertained visiting medical dignitaries of great distinction (including Francis Moore from Harvard, Professor Ramalingaswamy from Delhi, David Sabiston from Duke, and many more). The latter three came as Jacobson lecturers under a programme generously endowed by Henry's friend and mine, Lionel Jacobson, managing director of Burton the Tailor, and his charming wife Ruth. This enabled us to invite each year a distinguished academic visitor to spend a week lecturing and teaching in Newcastle. The invitation to such guests rotated around the medical school departments (when it was neurology's turn we asked Ray Adams). Entertaining the Jacobson lecturer allowed Betty and me at the Dean's buffet supper to entertain many other guests as well as the Jacobsons. Subsequent distinguished visitors to the Department of Neurology, also made possible through a Jacobson donation to Jack Foster, included Fred Plum, Bob Fishman and our old friend Henry Barnett (Barney) from Canada who wickedly introduced himself at a social event (he was another man of mordant wit) as the President of the Western Ontario Wife Exchange Society.

As my responsibilities as Dean continued to grow, I soon realized that if I were to discharge my major national commitments while also maintaining a clinical presence at the NGH and fulfilling my responsibilities to the University, I simply could not manage to cope with all the new tasks which were continually arising. My increasing involvement with the Medical Research Council and General Medical Council (Chapter 16) meant that I was being required more and more often to travel to London or elsewhere, and despite skilful manipulation of my diary, orchestrated by Nancy Deegan and Rosemary Allan, I often found that I was supposed to be in two places at once. But when it turned out that I was sometimes supposed to be in three or four places at once, I realized that action was needed, even if I was becoming adept (I hope) at choosing between different competing priorities. I also found my major responsibilities as spending and planning authority for the Faculty of Medicine increasingly burdensome and demanding. As student numbers increased, it was my sole responsibility, for example, to decide between competing demands in the medical faculty, as to where limited new funds coming to us from Council, after predigestion of our claims by Senate Development Committee and Senate, should be deployed. Which among the many departmental heads in medicine who sought new posts should be successful? In the early years I made these decisions after consultation and consideration of all competing claims and was also alone responsible for allocating departmental grants and departmental equipment grants, in consultation with Norman Shott, to the different departments. Few complained and only rarely did I have to change my mind. Nevertheless, it seemed to me that there was an increasing need to develop a committee structure which would allow me to delegate or at least share the authority for some of these arduous and potentially controversial responsibilities. I therefore proposed, and the Board of Faculty agreed, that I should establish a Dean's Advisory

Committee to advise me on my responsibilities in relation to spending and planning. I also proposed that the University should establish an appointment of an Associate (Deputy) Dean to complement the posts of Academic Sub-Dean and Clinical Sub-Dean which already existed.

My neurological colleague, David Shaw, had been Clinical Sub-Dean and had dealt skilfully with the innumerable problems relating to the allocation and dispersal of clinical medical students to different units in the Newcastle hospitals and around the region. John Anderson, senior lecturer in medicine, whose statistical expertise and knowledge of examination techniques was outstanding (he had been an adviser to the Royal College of Physicians of London on their multiple choice question papers), was Academic Sub-Dean. I was able increasingly to delegate to him responsibility for planning examinations, completing the statistical analysis of results and other related matters. He also served as the invaluable secretary, alongside Norman Shott, of the Curriculum and Curriculum Review Committees and gradually assumed more responsibility relating to admissions as well as examinations. But even their invaluable support was not enough; Senate and Council agreed that we should have an Associate Dean who could act as my deputy and who could also chair some of the advisory appointments committees relating to readerships and lecturerships, etc. After establishing a mechanism similar to that required to appoint a Dean, David Shaw was unanimously chosen as Associate Dean. When he relinquished the post of Clinical Sub-Dean, Brian Fleming, a surgeon in the RVI, succeeded him. These three, along with one independent member, Professor Eric Blair (head of the Department of Physiology) constituted my Advisory Committee, upon which I relied greatly in the remaining years of my appointment.

I had always hoped that the long-awaited new medical school in Newcastle would be open and occupied in my time. Unfortunately, the inevitable delays and disagreements which regularly beset university and hospital building programmes in the UK meant that this dream was not realized. The school had been designed in outline long before I took up my post, and the final agreement with the UGC had been signed during George Smart's reign. This had meant that the departmental structure of the school was based upon the departments in existence in his day and no particular account, it seemed, had been taken by the UGC of the possibility that new departments in the Faculty of Medicine might subsequently emerge before the school was built. It had also been decided that the school would have multidisciplinary laboratories for each phase of the curriculum (i.e. Stages I, II and III) and that a manager of professorial status of these multidisciplinary laboratories would be appointed to manage their administration. The principle was a worthy one which in other times and circumstances and with unlimited funding would have been potentialy superb. These laboratories were designed on a modular system, with each student having a personal desk and place available not only for reading but also for microscopic, laboratory and other similar work, where appropriate. Alongside this personal bench area, each student would have drawers and storage space for books and other belongings. The fundamental principle required that the student would remain static and that teachers would come to the students, bringing with them the necessary materials for all laboratory classes, etc. Students would then be taught in groups of eight in each module. As planning proceeded we became increasingly alarmed about the financial consequences and staffing implications of this arrangement, but it was made plain that to revamp the scheme at this late stage would produce further serious delay.

Of the many other problems we encountered in the planning process, I can mention only a few. The new medical school itself was intended to be phase one of a major new development, with phase two being a very large new ward block behind the RVI, adjacent to, and having several cross-connections with, the medical school component. In this joint scheme, the officers of both the UGC and the RHA (and its predecessor, the RHB) as well as the Department of Health were involved; but the UGC and the DHSS worked on different cost limits with different planning guidelines. The plans required that about 10–15% of the medical school would be health service accommodation for subjects like microbiology and clinical chemistry, while about 20% of the new ward block, because of similar interrelationships, was due to be accommodation for the university components of laboratory medicine departments such as pathology. It was therefore necessary to work out a complex costing arrangement whereby the capital costs of each development would be shared between the two authorities on the basis of an agreed formula. During my time a major crisis arose when it was discovered, for example, that one of the two authorities measured floor area as between the interior walls of a room or department, whereas the other measured from the centre of each dividing wall. Hence when one authority measured the total floor area of the new medical school, as planned, it turned out to be something like 3–4% over that agreed. Substantial cost reduction therefore became essential, despite our protests, and many plans had to be redrawn.

Another fight ensued when we discovered that the lecture theatres which were to be built to serve the needs of both the Medical School and the new Dental School (then under construction) did not include one which would be capable of taking an audience of about 400. The largest lecture theatre in the new building would have a maximum capacity of 210. This seemed reasonable at first sight as our maximum projected annual student intake in medicine was to be 210. Nevertheless, we all recognized that there were times when national and international bodies might wish to meet in Newcastle and that many of these required a much larger auditorium. We also felt that there might be occasions when two cohorts of students would be required to attend a single lecture. We were determined to have a theatre with 400 seats and could only achieve this in the end through having a movable screen which would divide the very large 400-seat lecture theatre (subsequently named after my teacher and mentor, R.B. Green) into two 200-seat theatres. Fortunately that central divider proved effective and sound-proof and the arrangement, after much hassle, worked well.

Yet other major problems emerged when it turned out that under the Health and Safety Act of 1974, university and hospital buildings fell for the first time under the eagle eye of the Health and Safety Executive (HSE). As soon as they saw the plans for the new Medical and Dental Schools, several changes were forced upon us as the piping systems for hot water, gas supplies and cabling for electricity had to be separately ducted. This caused an abrupt halt on the construction of the new Dental School and a total re-think of the planning of the Medical School. An even greater problem was the fact that the architects had cleverly planned an arrangement whereby in the Dental School and new Medical School each window would be surmounted by a horizontal stone or concrete 'eyebrow'. It was thought that for window cleaning purposes it would be reasonable for the cleaner to climb out of each window, to stand on the 'eyebrow' above the window below. This, however, did not satisfy the HSE who required that at each level around the Dental School and new Medical School a metal rail should be installed at a cost of several hundred thousand pounds, so that each window cleaner could wear a harness attached to the rail for safety reasons. Yet again, therefore, another major delay was introduced into the programme. Whether or not the window cleaners now use the harness or whether they step out on to the 'eyebrows' as originally intended is a matter over which I draw a veil.

There was another 'hiccup' when it emerged that the carefully chosen, white, self-cleansing brick which the Joint Project Management Committee had chosen for the new Dental School proved no longer to be in production and was not therefore available for the Medical School, which we hoped would be built in the same style and in the same materials. Eventually, after much delay, another brick was chosen but was, of course, quite different in appearance and cost. Of the inevitable further delays which arose when, for example, we chose a comfortable type of lecture theatre seating only to discover that its cost was far above the limits set down by the UGC and Department of Health, and of the many other vicissitudes which beset the planning programme, I could say much more. Perhaps these experiences alone will suffice to indicate why it was that year by year the start on site slipped back even further. Another major setback arose after a visit by Dr Gerard Vaughan, Minister of Health in the first Thatcher government, when he discussed the new ward block. He refused to accept that the Government would be able to find any additional revenue to run the clinical facilities in that block and also cast

The Medical Research Council, 1978.
Standing, from left
Dr K. P. Duncan, Prof J. N. Walton,
Prof A. R. Currie, Sir Henry Yellowlees KCB,
Sir Arnold Burgen FRS, Prof A. J. Buller,
Prof W. J. H. Butterfield OBE
Seated, from left
Dr H. Kay, Dr Cicely M. S. Saunders OBE,
Sir Douglas Black, Sir John Gray FRS,
His Grace the Duke of Northumberland KG PC FRS,
Dr Helen Muir FRS,
The Rt Hon, The Earl of Halsbury FRS,
Prof A. C. Dornhorst CBE, Prof A. P. M. Forrest
Members not present
Sir John Brotherston, Bryan Davies MP,
Prof I. M. Glynn FRS, Prof D. C. Phillips FRS

(above)
With Betty after my installation as BMA President, Newcastle, 1980.

(left)
Handing over the Presidential badge of office of the BMA to HRH Prince Charles, July 1982.

(opposite)
As President of the Royal Society of Medicine, greeting Her Majesty the Queen when she came to open the new building, July 1986.

13 Norham Gardens
('The Open Arms').

(top opposite)
With Dr Cecil Green and a
representative of Sir Robert
McAlpine and Sons, at the
foundation stone-laying ceremony
for the new buildings of Green
College, March 1988.

(bottom opposite)
With Sir Richard Doll, founding
Warden (L) and Sir Crispin
Tickell, my successor, at the
Tenth Anniversary Celebrations,
Green College, June 1989.

With Judy and Betty at Buckingham Palace Garden Party, a few days before Judy's wedding, July 1972.

At a party to celebrate my knighthood, in Newcastle United colours, Regional Neurological Centre, January 1979.

With Ann, Betty and Christopher outside Buckingham Palace after my investiture, March 1979.

At my introduction into the House of Lords,
with Lord Porritt (left) and Lord Richardson, 1989.

doubts upon whether it would be possible to include within it university accommodation for the departments of pathology and microbiology. These had been excluded from the Medical School solely on the grounds that they were to be contiguous with clinical facilities in the new ward block. Our argument to the effect that this was a joint project and that there were already Department of Health facilities being provided in the Medical School, then under construction, and that this was an arrangement agreed between the Department of Health and the UGC seemed at first to fall upon deaf ears. However, after much contentious argument it seems that he was ultimately persuaded of this aspect of our case. Even so, his intervention resulted in yet a further delay in the planning of the ward block, the content of which had subsequently to be greatly revised. Construction of that particular component of the scheme finally got under way in 1990, and the building, very different from the one we planned more than 10 years earlier, is now complete and in use.

At last, after all these vicissitudes, the great day dawned when our final plans for the new Medical School were jointly approved by the UGC and the RHA and the capital allocation necessary to start on site was finally agreed by both authorities. On a snowy morning in March 1979, I, together with Michael (later Sir Michael) Straker (Chairman of the AHA(T)) and the Chairman of the RHA went to a location just behind the RVI and turned the first sod so that construction could begin. Later in 1981 I had the privilege, with the then lady Chairman of the Medical Students' Council and with Arthur Taylor, now Chairman of the AHA(T), of conducting the topping out performance of the School and of seeing the outline of the building beginning to emerge as the roof was completed. And after we had left Newcastle we were delighted in 1984 to be present when Her Majesty Queen Elizabeth the Queen Mother performed the formal opening ceremony of the new School on the same day that she reviewed a march past when the Freedom of the City was conferred upon my former unit, the 201 Northern General Hospital (TA).

In the meantime one other irritating episode deserves mention. We were greatly exercised about the nature of the fuel that should be used to fire the furnaces in the boiler house which would supply heat both to the Dental and Medical Schools and to the new ward block, and which would replace some ageing boilers providing heating for the existing RVI. We all wished to use natural gas, which would be the cleanest and probably the cheapest fuel, but unfortunately, despite repeated overtures, Northern Gas could not be persuaded to provide an adequate supply on site. Our second choice would perhaps have been liquid petroleum gas, though we were concerned about the size of the containers that would be needed and in any event the authorities made it clear that this would not be acceptable. We therefore plumped for light fuel oil, taking the view that this would produce less environmental pollution than would heavy fuel oil, which we knew was the preferred option of the Department of Health. In the end, after argument after argument and battle after battle, the Department insisted that we must use heavy fuel oil as the cheaper alternative (this was before the major oil crisis of the late 1970s had changed everyone's perception of relative fuel costs). However, in order to deal with the environmental aspects, the Department insisted that there should be a single chimney, 110 metres high, which would carry the effluent from the boilers across the North Sea and would not, therefore, contaminate the surrounding countryside. Whether they took any account of the wishes of our neighbours in Scandinavia was not mentioned. We were therefore compelled to construct an enormous chimney which Michael Straker and I and others climbed shortly before the building scheme was completed, on a beautiful sunny day. The view of Tyneside down to the coast and the surrounding countryside was breathtaking and I shall always regret that having ascended, as we did, in a rather rickety lift on to a platform at the top surrounded by not very substantial railings (Michael looked quite pale) I did not have my camera with me. That experience reinforced my long-held view, coupled with my personal horror of heights, that anyone who decides to become a steeplejack must be an individual of outstanding grit and courage.

There were many other notable planning battles with central bureaucracy. Henry Miller before me, and I myself with the support of the late Dr George Richardson of the NGH and many others, were bitterly opposed to the construction of the new Freeman Hospital in Newcastle, feeling that the concept of one teaching hospital on three sites, which was introduced early in the day, was misguided. Many of us felt that it would be preferable to expand the NGH and the RVI each to about 1500 beds instead of having a third major general hospital in the city. This resulted in fiercely fought press campaigns and in spirited arguments in the AHA(T) and RHA; eventually we were visited by the then Minister of Health, Richard Crossman. With the judgement of Solomon, he agreed with the views fiercely expressed by me and by my fellow consultants that there should ultimately be only two major general hospitals in Newcastle. However, he concluded that one should be the Freeman Hospital, into which the major regional and other specialties from the NGH should ultimately be decanted. Our principal concerns related to the cost of providing all the expensive supporting laboratory and other services for three hospitals rather than two and to the problems that would inevitably emerge in relation to the management of casualties if orthopaedic surgery and thoracic surgery were on one site and neuro-surgery on another several miles away. Three hospitals involved a multitude of other interrelational problems which we saw as being likely in the longer term to impair medical care in Newcastle. Despite the Crossman edict, Newcastle now has three major general hospitals in spite of our strictures, and Freeman Hospital has become one of the first of the self-governing trusts in the reformed NHS. It seems to be very successfully managed and to be providing an outstanding range of services, not least in cardiothoracic surgery, with one of the country's major heart transplant programmes. Perhaps our predictions of woe were unjustified, but nevertheless I would still prefer to see two large hospitals rather than three serving the city of Newcastle upon Tyne. That dream will never become a reality, I believe, in times of financial constraint upon both capital and revenue in the NHS.

Being a Dean carried certain national as well as local responsibilities, not just in relation to the GMC. I represented the University on the Medical Sub-Committee of the Committee of Vice-Chancellors and Principals and even on rare occasions deputized for Henry on the main body. I also attended regularly the Committee of Provincial Deans, which often met in London in association with meetings of the London deans in order to discuss matters of mutual concern. On two occasions I joined the European deans so as to consider matters of mutual interest, such as medical education. I also attended regularly meetings of the Association for the Study of Medical Education (ASME), of which I now have the honour to be President. That body has striven manfully over the years to promote and develop programmes of research into medical education but has never received the degree and range of support from its constituent bodies for which it had hoped. Nevertheless, having been started by enthusiasts like Professor (later Sir John) Ellis, Dean of the London Hospital Medical School, and George Smart, with the subsequent able and energetic support of my Newcastle colleague, John Anderson, its activities have steadily expanded; students regularly attend its annual meetings and contribute effectively to its debates. I believe the quality of research in medical education has improved greatly over the last 10–15 years, even though it has proved impossible to identify a single agency which is willing to give priority to funding such studies. Nevertheless, under the inspired leadership of Sir Peter Froggatt, former Vice-Chancellor of Queen's University, Belfast, who followed the energetic Professor Stuart Kilpatrick as its Chairman of Council, it continues to strive to improve and influence patterns of medical education in the UK. Apart from John Anderson, among its most ardent supporters are Professor Ronald Harden from the Centre for Medical Education in Dundee and Dr Janet Gale, whose dedication to its interests and whose invaluable reviews of its activities, carried out in collaboration with her husband, have been such a striking feature of its programme within the past few years.

I cannot end this commentary upon my exciting 10 years as Dean without mentioning some other innovations that I tried to introduce. I was particularly concerned to try to develop some academic recognition of the so-called minor medical specialties. Just as I tried to establish chairs in subjects such as geriatrics by arrangement with the RHB (and later the RHA), I also endeavoured to create, either through public but more often through private funding, readerships and lecturerships or first assistantships in specialties as diverse as neurosurgery, plastic surgery, urology, immunology and rheumatology, to name but a few. Having arranged an NHS appointment with a simultaneous personal chair for Grimley Evans in geriatrics, we achieved a similar aim in medical physics on appointing Professor Keith Boddy. We also created many more A + B appointments by splitting NHS consultant posts and university senior lectureships in such a way that many more NHS consultants could have two senior lecturer session in the University to acknowledge their academic contributions. Admittedly this was not invariably necessary as I also introduced a policy at the beginning of my Deanship of inviting to all departmental and other appropriate Faculty meetings NHS consultants with honorary university clinical lectureships who were involved in our teaching programme. I also persuaded heads of academic departments to do the same, on the grounds that those involved in teaching medical students, even if employed by the NHS, were as much entitled to influence university policy as were those individuals holding academic appointments paid by the University. This policy paid dividends, not least in pathology where, after much discussion, a much closer degree of integration was achieved between the RVI department, staffed by the University (although the health authority refunded 50% of the cost in acknowledgement of the clinical services it provided) and that so skilfully led by Bernard Tomlinson at the NGH, where at first there were no university appointments at all. Before long, in view of his outstanding contributions to research in neuropathology, I was able successfully to nominate him for a personal chair.

This policy of obtaining personal chairs for NHS consultants of outstanding academic achievement was one which I tried to pursue vigorously. My hope was that if one injected modest university resources into subspecialties with good research records, this might encourage those disciplines to expand their academic activities, to bring in soft money by research grants from outside, to raise sums to endow further university appointments, and eventually to become strong enough to achieve independent university status for themselves. Certainly this happened in cardiology, where the British Heart Foundation endowed a chair and other supporting appointments and where Desmond Julian, as the first appointee, was a great success. Dermatology, first under John Ingram and later under Sam Shuster, flowered similarly, and my own department of neurology eventually became so large, with university posts, NHS appointments and newly-endowed appointments provided by charities or other benefactors, that it too became independent in 1976. In some other specialties, particularly in some branches of surgery, that hope of growing academic stature was not realized as fully as I would have wished, but nevertheless the policy seemed to be successful. I shall always be grateful to the late Sir William Leech, to his Trustees and to his Foundation for the tremendous impetus that they gave to the establishment of new posts to acknowledge the emergence of medical academic excellence. Similarly, through my membership of the University Development Trust I was able to initiate many fund-raising projects, including that which helped us, with the support of north-eastern industry, to re-establish the chair of industrial health (later of occupational health), one of the first posts to be lost when the academic freeze afflicted the University. That freeze with progressive reduction in university funding was something which was only just beginning to emerge in my latter years as Dean. After Henry Miller's premature death, I became very closely associated with the redoubtable Ewan Page who functioned as Acting Vice-Chancellor for well over a year. He and I were much involved in the work of the committee established to appoint Henry's successor. I have often said that that responsibility took almost a year out of my life with 23 meetings, 11 interviews, 9 dinners and 10 lunches before we eventually persuaded Professor Laurence Martin to join us. As I write, he has just left after 12 very successful years as Vice-Chancellor. He and his wife, Betty, had a tremendous impact on the life of the University and indeed on the life of Newcastle; I believe that he was an inspired choice.

Laurie came to Newcastle in exceptionally difficult times and was soon faced with the first signs of financial constraint and the end of that era of expansion from which many of us and our faculties had benefitted. His difficulties were to some extent enhanced for a while when, after Ernest Bettenson's retirement, we appointed as Registrar Roy Butler from Lancashire; he interviewed superbly and his ideas greatly appealed to most members of the committee. Roy proved to be a most unusual figure with remarkable managerial expertise who possessed a degree of organizational skill and a demand for precision in a university setting which did not totally fit with the Newcastle ethos. His desire to impose a rigid planning sequence and timetable caused us all serious difficulties, especially since the timetables of Faculty meetings did not fit easily with his proposals. Though we admired many of his qualities, we did not find him quite so easy to work with as many of us had hoped and we were not therefore too distressed when he was spirited away to Oxford as Secretary to the Faculties. He was replaced by the quietly urbane and effective, if not electrifying, Bill Andrew, then Deputy Registrar. He held the appointment for only about three years before retiring, when he was replaced by my good friend and colleague Derek Nicholson, Senior Assistant Registrar in the Medical School, whom I recommended warmly for the post and who has, I believe, been very successful during the last 10 years.

While Laurie Martin and Jim O'Callaghan did not invariably see eye to eye, and while there were times during my period of office when in 'Cabinet' I felt some discomfort over the contention which occasionally arose over policy issues, I came to have an increasingly high regard for Laurie as an exceptionally capable, well-organized, thoughtful administrator and leader. Later, he had to deal with many urgent and some insoluble problems but was assisted by several able Pro-Vice-Chancellors including my erstwhile cricketing colleague, Duncan Murchison, who became Acting Vice-Chancellor after his departure. When Laurie left at the end of 1990 to become Director of the Royal Institute of International Affairs at Chatham House in London, everyone in Newcastle was saddened by his departure but wished him well in his new and challenging appointment. We were all delighted when in May 1991 he received the richly deserved honorary degree of DCL of the University. Mr James Wright from Cambridge, who has succeeded him, will appreciate that Laurie left the University in exceptionally good heart and in a better financial state than many other comparable institutions in the UK. I was delighted to read that in the recent Universities Funding Council (UFC) assessment of the research capability of different departments in universities throughout the UK, Newcastle was the only undergraduate medical school outside Oxford and Cambridge to have received a grade 4 assessment for its clinical school, and many other departments of the university also received high gradings.

In the late 1970s I realized that with my escalating national commitments it would be unwise and indeed improper to seek re-election as Dean for a third five-year term. I was approaching 60 years of age, I had become Chairman of the Education Committee of the GMC and was just beginning to recognize that there was a possibility, even if remote, that I might be ultimately elected as its President. I had been invited to become President-elect of the BMA in 1980 (Chapter 16) and was beginning to be slightly battle-weary in the never-ending round of committee meetings in which, as a result of financial constraint in both the NHS and the university, more and more contentious argument was continually arising. After earnest consideration I reported to the Faculty in the autumn of 1980 that I would not be seeking re-election as Dean in 1981. As I did so I could barely suppress the tears, not least because I had enjoyed the privilege of leading the Faculty through many exciting years and because I had found the appointment immensely rewarding if increasingly demanding. Slowly the University's mechanisms ground into action and the usual joint committee of Senate and Council was established to recommend the appointment of my successor. I was very pleased when it was decided that my Associate Dean, David Shaw, would succeed me.

I was also glad to learn that the Dean of Dentistry, Roy Storer, also a close friend, was becoming more deeply involved in university affairs and was appointed to Senate Development Committee. With him and with his predecessor, Maurice Hallett, who is still hale and hearty and regularly attends university events, I had, I believe, achieved a mutually fruitful understanding. Only once during my Deanship did I attend, by invitation, a Sub-Faculty Board of Dental Surgery, but found that an illuminating experience and was delighted to help Roy as best I could with the major problems that arose in completing and commissioning his new Dental School. That School was opened elegantly by the Chancellor of the University, the Duke of Northumberland, in the mid-1970s. Apart from some problems relating to noisy air conditioning on the upper floors, it has proved to be an excellent building with splendid teaching facilities in which students of increasingly high quality are now being taught. The School has rightly continued to achieve high national ratings and I was pleased to learn that Roy Storer was elected President of the EEC's Advisory Committee on Dental Training, a well-deserved accolade in the light of his many contributions and devotion to his subject.

In my last year as Dean I was thrilled to be invited to deliver (in January 1983) the annual John H. Holmes series of three lectures to schoolchildren. I found this an exceptionally exciting experience in trying to demonstrate principles relating to the function of the nervous system and the muscles, using numerous practical and audio-visual displays, with audience participation. It was quite inspiring to find that whereas in my first lecture members of the audience were very reluctant to volunteer as subjects to participate in some of the neurological tricks I was demonstrating, in the second and third they were queuing up to take part.

And so, at the end of September 1981, I cleared out my books, pictures and papers from the Dean's office in the old Medical School on Queen Victoria Road and carried them back, after saying a fond farewell to Nancy Deegan, to my already over-full office at the NGH, with a wistful glance at the two-thirds completed new medical School as I drove up Richardson Road. It was a curious sensation to leave behind those major administrative responsibilities, including my membership of the AHA(T) and of innumerable other committees, and yet again to immerse myself, if only temporarily, in neurology and in neuromuscular disease. I did so knowing that under David Shaw the Medical School would prosper, and so it has proved. The major reconstruction that was carried out under his inspired leadership in creating schools, for example, of basic and clinical neuroscience, and of bringing into the Medical School basic science departments from the Science Faculty, including biochemistry and genetics, has been of great benefit to the Faculty in the difficult days of financial constraint and planning blight which escalated after my retirement from the Deanship. Henry Miller often said that he was never happier than in the few years that he was Dean. I too can say truthfully that whereas in 1981 when I relinquished that appointment I had no inkling of many of the things that were to come, that decade was one of the most enjoyable and fruitful of my professional career.

Following my cherished principle of not looking over the shoulder of my successor, I kept away from the Board of the Faculty of Medicine for over a year. When at last I went back, I made a point of sitting in the back row and of not intervening in debate unless asked. It was nevertheless a curious feeling when many colleagues asked me what was happening about this or that aspect of university activity and I had to say truthfully that I had no idea. When one relinquishes office, the flow of information ceases abruptly; this is something which I have experienced in several other situations. Nevertheless, the next 18 months or so gave me the opportunity, which I much appreciated, of returning to many neurological professional activities (though never to day-to-day control of ward work or emergency responsibility) and of helping John Harris and others to reorganize some of the research programme in the muscular Dystrophy Research Laboratories, while also being able again to attend professional and other meetings in Britain and overseas, some of which I had had to deny myself during the time that I was Dean.

CHAPTER 16

National Responsibilities

Just as my administrative responsibilities in the Newcastle district and region increased in the 1960s and 1970s, so I found that my national responsibilities escalated. In the early 1960s I served for three years on the Council of the EEG Society, a body which had extended its field of interest in order to embrace other branches of clinical neurophysiology including electromyography, nerve conduction velocity measurement and evoked potential recording. It may have been influenced by the acidulous comment of Sir Francis Walshe who commented that the journal which that society and other similar bodies throughout the world had sponsored, the *Journal of Electroencephalography and Clinical Neurophysiology* was the only one he knew in which, in its title, a technique took precedence over a science. The EEG Society, started through the energy and initiative of W. Grey Walter of Bristol and other pioneers, served the useful purpose of bringing together doctors and scientists interested in clinical neurophysiology on the one hand and technicians who built and serviced their equipment as well as EEG recordists on the other. The leadership of the Society soon led to the establishment of the Electrophysiological Technologists Association (EPTA) which laid down training standards and developed an examination structure, to the ultimate benefit of the profession. And it ultimately spawned a Society for Clinical Neurophysiology in which at last the science took precedence and the quality and range of scientific presentations steadily increased.

The Medical Research Council

In 1966, out of the blue, I received a letter from Dr (later Sir) John Gray, Secretary of the Medical Research Council (MRC) inviting me to join a grants committee established under the Clinical Research Board (CRB Grants Committee II); this was charged with the responsibility of assessing and awarding grants in clinical neuroscience and related disciplines. In accepting what I saw as a singular honour, I little realized that this foreshadowed 12 fruitful, if demanding, years of intimate involvement in the work of the Council. The discipline of reading and of assessing carefully grant applications proved to be an arduous but rewarding task

417

and served as a splendid postgraduate course, inevitably bringing me up to date with developments in areas of basic and clinical neuroscience with which I had not become familiar through my reading. The Chairman of CRB II when I joined it was Martin Roth from Newcastle, our outstanding Professor of Psychological Medicine, a man of fluent speech, brimming over with original ideas but also at times enamoured of extravagant phraseology. Martin had proved to be an excellent head of department, capitalizing upon the major developments which Alexander Kennedy had introduced before he departed for Edinburgh. He initiated many high-quality research projects in psychiatry and recruited some outstanding members to his consultant team. Perhaps his major problem was his lack of time sense, combined with a degree of personal distractibility and absent-mindedness which sometimes led to an amusing degree of personal disorganization. It was well known in the university that almost invariably he turned up late for meetings and even occasionally on the wrong day, so that he was affectionately known locally as 'the late Professor Roth'.

At the MRC, however, Martin's chairmanship was precise, judicious and well-organized and I learned much from him; no doubt the careful briefing and firm administrative control exercised by several outstanding scientific and administrative officers of the Council ensured that he was kept firmly on the rails. Nevertheless, it was well known among taxi drivers of the Newcastle firm which he and I both used that they always called for him early to take him to the station or airport; often he would have to be taken back home to collect his passport, overcoat or some other important item. On one occasion at the MRC when he and I were due, with others, to go on a site visit to an MRC unit, we gathered for our preliminary briefing at 20 Park Crescent and were then given all the necessary documentation, including our rail tickets. We all embarked on a minibus to be driven to Waterloo. On reaching the station barrier, Martin had lost his ticket. How he succeeded in doing so and where it went to remains a mystery; eventually another was acquired and we got there without further incident.

The scientific assessment of grant applications was always fascinating and while I served on CRB II a method was introduced which, so far as I am aware, continues to this day. Each member of the committee was invited to read and to make notes about each of the 20–30 applications under consideration at a single meeting, without cognisance of the views expressed by independent referees. For each such application the office staff, after taking advice, invited two, or occasionally more, committee members to open the discussion because of their particular knowledge or expertise in the field of research concerned. Any other committee member was then free to comment, before an officer of the Council read extracts from reports submitted by two or three referees. We each then scored the application independently on a 7-point scale, with 6 being awarded for an application of 'Nobel Prize standard' and 0 for one 'beyond the pale'. In the 12 years I served on various MRC bodies, I cannot recall any application being graded 6. A 5 meant excellent, 4 very good, 3 good, 2 moderate, 1 poor and 0 very poor. At the end of the meeting the marks awarded by the members of the committee were read out and averaged to provide a single mark for each application. Those scoring above a certain cut-off point were automatically awarded and those below were rejected. The cut-off point varied from one meeting to another but usually depended upon the assessment by the office of the amount of money available to be awarded for project grants at each such meeting. Occasionally a loading of 0.1–0.2 marks was allowed in applications in a priority or relatively under-privileged area, and in some instances applications marking just below the cut-off point were referred to the Clinical Research Board as a whole for a final decision. In this fascinating exercise we learned a great deal of science but also learned much about our colleagues who acted as referees. Soon we recognized that some were excessively kindly and some excessively tough; often, therefore, we applied a correction factor, dependent upon our knowledge of how each referee had performed in the past.

After I had been on the committee for a year, Martin retired and was replaced by Professor (later Sir) Gordon Robson, Professor of Anaesthetics at the Royal Postgraduate Medical School. The ending of Martin's term of office was timely as soon afterwards he was elected as Foundation President of the newly-established Royal College of Psychiatrists and quickly received his well-deserved knighthood in acknowledgement of his manifold contributions to his profession. Later still, we were sad to lose him from Newcastle when he became Foundation Professor of Psychiatry at the University of Cambridge where he gave distinguished service up to the statutory retiring age and continues to be a dedicated Fellow of Trinity College. Gordon Robson, whom I came to know well and who had previously worked as first assistant in the Department of Anaesthesia in Newcastle with Edgar Pask, was very different in style as a chairman, but equally effective. He was quietly reflective in his approach but deployed an encyclopaedic knowledge of neurophysiology which occasionally electrified the committee. On one occasion when we were trying to assess a grant application dealing with a proposed method of recording electrical activity in the auditory nerve, after a prolonged discussion Gordon pointed out that the technique proposed would only be capable of recording a cochlear microphonic and not the nerve impulse; hence the application failed. Gordon also moved on after two years; to my delight, I was invited by Sir John Gray to succeed him. The chairmanship of the Grants Committee carried automatic membership of the Clinical Research Board where one was involved not only in determining the decisions to be made on marginal applications referred by each of the Grants Committees but also in policy issues relating to clinical research in general. We also assessed applications for programme grants for the longer-term support of research (a minimum of five years in the first instance) as distinct from the three-year project grants with which the Grants Committees normally dealt. This now involved monthly meetings at the Council in London and also resulted in my being invited to join various visiting sub-committees to MRC units including sections of the National Institute for Medical Research (NIMR) at Mill Hill and the Clinical Research Centre (CRC) at Northwick Park, as well as free-standing units in different parts of the UK. I was invariably impressed by the quality of the paperwork provided not only by applicants for grants and the unit directors, but also by the supporting documentation which was carefully marshalled and prepared by the Council's staff. Their organization of travel schedules and sub-committee programmes was impeccable.

The deep sense of awe, combined with the apprehension which one felt on first entering the portals of 20 Park Crescent soon evaporated, to be replaced by affection and respect. In particular I came to know, like and admire John Gray, who had been Deputy Secretary to Sir Harold Himsworth, a man of outstanding flair and vision. Of John's dedication to the Council there could be no doubt; he was immensely dedicated and hard-working, though there were times when his zest for organization and structure may have led him into administrative decisions which made for complexity rather than simplicity. However, his reorganization of the MRC Board structure in the late 1960s was long overdue and has subsequently stood the test of time. He took the view that the division then existing between basic research on the one hand and clinical research on the other was inappropriate. He therefore proposed a new structure in which the division of responsibility between Boards would not occur at the science/clinical interface but would be related to the kind of system- and topic-based structure which we, for example, had used in the Newcastle undergraduate curriculum. Hence three new Boards were created, namely the Cell Board (dealing, for example, with cell and molecular biology, general pathology, microbiology, virology, oncology and many more related topics), the Neurosciences Board (which would embrace neurophysiology, neurochemistry, psychology, psychiatry, neurology and all other related disciplines), and the Physiological Systems and Disorders Board (which would embrace research relating to all other bodily systems). Each Board would have its own grants committees concerned with the assessment of project grants, as before. While the system took time to shake down, and whereas the lines of demarcation between the responsibilities of the different Boards later required modification, it is my understanding that this structure, which worked well in my time, has continued to do so.

Chairman of the Council at that time was the Duke of Northumberland, also Chancellor of Newcastle University, who had previously chaired the Agricultural Research Council and for whom I came to have an increasing respect as the years went by. A man of urbane manner and incisive intelligence, he rarely intervened in debate but pushed through hard decisions whenever he felt that these were needed. I was also delighted when my old friend S. G. (Griff) Owen, formerly physician and Clinical Sub-Dean in Newcastle, was recruited to be Deputy Secretary to John Gray, with whom he worked closely and effectively, so that the team seemed a very harmonious one. Also prominent in the Council's affairs was Dr Joan Faulkner (Lady Doll) whose consummate administrative efficiency was so evident in all she handled, even if her vigorous and forthright manner was occasionally a trifle forbidding. I confess that as a new chairman of a grants committee in my relatively early Council days there were even times when I felt a little frightened of her, but her views invariably commanded respect. Her associate, Dr Katherine Levy, who headed the division dealing with basic and clinical neuroscience, was someone with whom I established a close and friendly working relationship.

As the working life of the Clinical Research Board drew to a close, I transferred briefly to membership of the Neurosciences Board before receiving from the Secretary of State an invitation to join the Council itself for a four-year period from 1974–1978 during which time I became Council observer on the Systems Board. Membership of the Council proved interesting and demanding in a very different way, as one was now concerned with major policy issues and the definition of priorities in medical research. Council was also required at times to adjudicate on disputes that might arise between the different Boards and about the future of its major establishments at Mill Hill and Northwick Park and of its units. One was at least spared the enormous burden of reading to which over many years I had become accustomed through having to assess applications for project and programme grants. Soon after joining Council John Gray invited me to chair a committee examining the administrative structure and interrelationship between NIMR and CRC, but as that committee had no administrative or scientific teeth, it proved after a few meetings to be somewhat ineffectual and was disbanded. These were the years when the first evidence of Government restraint on MRC expenditure began to emerge. On one occasion we were addressed by the redoubtable Shirley Williams, then Secretary of State for Education, who was listened to so politely that afterwards she told John Gray that she did not think much of his Council as our questioning of Government policy in respect of science was expressed with rather less vigour than she had anticipated. This was the era, too, when the Rothschild Report fell like a bombshell on the scientific community. That report proposed

422   The Spice of Life

that the support of medical research should be based on the customer/ contractor principle; in clinical research it was suggested that the customers should be the Health Departments which ought to be responsible for defining priorities and allocating funds, rather than the MRC. Rothschild therefore recommended that a substantial part of the funds allocated by the Department of Education and Science (DES) for the support of medical research should be transferred to the Health Departments. This view was vigorously supported by Sir Henry Yellowlees who, as Chief Medical Officer to the Department of Health and Social Security, then sat on Council. The Chief Scientist, Sir Douglas Black, seemed rather less enamoured of the proposal, but nevertheless it was accepted by the Government. There followed a series of complex administrative adjustments by means of which clinical research projects and programmes then being undertaken with MRC support were technically transferred to Health Department control, even though the funds were still administered by the MRC. It later became apparent to many that the Department of Health had neither the scientific structure nor in some fields the expertise needed to handle effectively the transferred funds in the interest of future research in clinical disciplines. Arthur Buller, former professor of physiology in Bristol, who later became Chief Scientist, was a leading advocate of the view that the Rothschild decision should be overturned. Eventually, after much contentious argument, that view prevailed and the transferred funds were returned to the MRC, from which, in my opinion, they should never have been removed in the first place. In consequence, the relationship between Henry Yellowlees and Arthur Buller became rather less than friendly.

One major crisis involving Newcastle and the MRC arose at about this time. Professor E.J. Field, the first director of the MRC Demyelinating Diseases Unit in that city and Professor of Experimental Pathology, had worked closely with us in neurology and had done some good quality research on multiple sclerosis (MS) and related diseases. However, he became convinced that a method of measuring macrophage migration inhibition could be the basis of a specific diagnostic test for MS and could even detect in childhood those individuals who would develop the disease later. He believed that to offer those children a diet high in polyunsaturated fats would prevent them from developing the condition. We, his clinical neurological colleagues, were satisfied after careful investigation and after submitting to him blood samples from ourselves and our patients that these views were unfounded. Eventually after much arduous and contentious negotiation his directorship of the MRC unit was terminated. We were fortunate in being able eventually to recruit as his successor Dr Henryk Wisniewski from New York, an able scientist whose research record was outstanding. Unfortunately, however, for a variety of reasons we were unable to create a consultant paediatric neurologist appointment for his vigorous wife, Krystyna, and after little more than two years Henryk returned to New York. Later, the unit changed its remit and now functions very effectively in the grounds of the NGH in neurochemical pharmacology under the able direction of Professor Jim Edwardson.

These were also times of change for other reasons. First, John Gray, having seen through his revised Board structure and several other administrative reforms, eventually decided to take early retirement in order to return to physiological research, which had been his first love. Council was therefore faced with the necessity of having to appoint a successor and also had to decide whom to appoint as Director of the CRC to succeed Sir Graham Bull. I was approached by several members of Council and some of the staff asking whether I would allow my name to be considered for the appointment of Secretary and was not therefore invited to serve on the Council sub-committee appointed to choose John Gray's successor. However, after much thought I made it clear first that I was unwilling to leave Newcastle to move to London; secondly, I did not wish to give up clinical neurology and my deanship to undertake an administrative appointment which, despite its great national importance, would take me away from my major interests in teaching, research and administration as Professor of Neurology and Dean. It would also be difficult for me to continue writing and editing books on neurology and neuromuscular disease. I therefore declined to be considered and was delighted when the committee unanimously recommended Professor Jim Gowans as the new Secretary. From my knowledge of him on the Systems Board, he seemed to me to have all the right scientific, personal and administrative attributes to become an outstanding Secretary. I was, however, appointed to the sub-committee to choose a new CRC Director. After considering many names, we narrowed down the choice to two close friends and colleagues from Hammersmith, namely Professor Colin Dollery and Professor Christopher Booth. After almost interminable discussion, as it proved virtually impossible to choose between the two on personal and scientific grounds, Colin Dollery eventually decided that he did not wish to be further considered and Christopher was appointed. Colin has enjoyed an outstandingly successful career since then, not least in the Chair of Medicine at Hammersmith in which he succeeded Chris Booth, but also as Chairman of the Medical Sub-Committee of the University Grants Committee; now, as Sir Colin, he has become Dean at Hammermith in succession to my old friend, formerly from Newcastle, David Kerr. Chris (now Sir Christopher) Booth has recently retired from the CRC, being saddened as he did so to learn that the Council had decided for a variety of reasons to disperse the scientific activities of that centre to many different locations throughout the country. Sir Christopher has now returned to one of his earlier loves, medical history, as Harveian Librarian of the Royal College of Physicians and as Chairman of a

Wellcome Trust Research Group on the History of Medicine. I was pleased when he succeeded Gordon Robson, who in turn had followed me as President of the Royal Society of Medicine when my term of office came to an end in 1986 (see below).

These, then, were heady and fruitful years. A few more memories stand out. One was the 'long weekend' when we met as a Council all day on Friday, Saturday and Sunday at 20 Park Crescent, being regularly regaled with refreshment throughout, in order to hold oral hearings of those who had been refused tenured appointments. I am sure we were right to go through with that time-consuming exercise, even though in the end, for many scientific and personal reasons, few, if any, of the appeals were successful. And in the days of the CRB I recall the agonies experienced by some members of the Board and Council in giving up smoking after a succession of reports from the Royal College of Physicians had amply confirmed the views of Richard Doll and Austin Bradford Hill about the serious effects this habit had upon health. When one such report suggested that cigars and pipes were much less harmful than cigarettes, several distinguished doctors turned to cigars with relief. Indeed for a time Martin Roth, formerly a non-smoker, was converted through his MRC membership to being a chain-smoker of small cigars! An even more amusing incident arose when an annual photograph was taken in the Council Chamber for publication in the annual report. Someone suddenly noticed the ashtrays on the table. These were hurriedly removed to the floor beneath. Unfortunately, the photograph (subsequently discarded and replaced by another) clearly showed the table, the Council members and the ashtrays on the floor!

One great advantage of MRC service was the friendships one made with people working in many different fields of medicine and science. For example I came to know well and to admire as scientists and as individuals Sir Arnold Burgen, the Director of the National Institute for Medical Research, a distinguished pharmacologist who subsequently became Master of Darwin College in Cambridge, and Sir David Phillips, that outstanding Oxford biophysicist who was later an outstanding Chairman of the Advisory Board for the Research Councils. Alastair Currie, too, notable for his seminal contributions to pathology from his academic base in Edinburgh, was an exceptional Chairman of the Cell Board and Council. I also saw a great deal of my old friend and fellow Medical Pilgrim (see below), Sir John (later Lord) Butterfield, formerly of Guy's Hospital, subsequently Regius Professor of Physic in Cambridge, Master of Downing College and Vice-Chancellor. Two notable ladies also made important contributions to the MRC during my service, namely Helen Muir of the Kennedy Institute for Rheumatology, initiator and executor of much important research in that subject, and Dame Cicely Saunders, distinguished founder of the hospice movement, whose common sense approach and practical advice always commanded attention.

While I was on Council the term of office of the Duke of Northumberland (Hughie to his friends) as Chairman came to an end; he delighted us all by inviting us to join him for a farewell dinner at Syon House, his London home. Having been, as a Northumbrian, greatly impressed by the decor, furnishings and art collection in the Duke's northern home at Alnwick Castle, I expected something exceptional but was nevertheless stunned by the sheer magnificence of all of the appurtenances of that dwelling. We had drinks in a superbly appointed anteroom and dined in incredible splendour on a long dining table in a sumptuous gallery. The plates may have been silver gilt, but the general impression they gave was of pure gold. Only then did we begin to appreciate to the full the extent of the wealth of the Percy family. The Duke was a magnificent host; he spoke eloquently of his experiences on the MRC and of his affection for the organization. Some of us moved on after dinner into the family quarters for more coffee and I believe that Harry Kay, Vice-Chancellor of Exeter, and I were among the last to leave.

We all missed the Duke when he retired but I continued to see him often as Chancellor of Newcastle University which he served with distinction until his untimely death in 1988. I shall never forget his memorial service in Westminster Abbey and the emotional impact made by the formal procession led by the Duke's piper, Kathryn Tickell, playing Northumbrian airs on those superbly plaintive but melodious Northumbrian pipes. The dinner at Syon House was also memorable for me as Henry Yellowlees, then serving on the MRC as CMO to the Department of Health, approached me to ask whether I might be prepared to become Chief Scientist to the Department of Health, following Douglas Black. My response was immediate. As I told Henry, while I was honoured to have been considered, this was not an appointment in which I was interested. I knew that the post, as then defined, was interesting and important but nevertheless involved some in-built frustrations; I also explained that I hoped to go on practising neurology and to continue as Dean in Newcastle for many years; above all, I did not wish to move to London for all of the personal reasons that I had discussed when asked to consider the possibility of becoming Secretary to the MRC. It has always been difficult for my London colleagues to accept and understand my view that the quality of life in Newcastle and its environs is so much better than that in the metropolis. They clearly thought that my north-eastern roots had made me biased; but many of those who have moved to medical or university appointments in Newcastle or Durham from the south have recognized the justice of that opinion, one to which I adhere just as strongly today.

The Duke was succeeded by Lord Shepherd, a hereditary peer and long-term member of the Labour Party (at the time we had a Labour government, with Barbara Castle as Secretary of State for Health). His style as Chairman was less avuncular and more direct but I found him effective, capable and likeable. However, as time went by it became clear that he and Jim Gowans were not invariably on the same wavelength. Jim, himself an outstanding scientist, was someone who always espoused the highest scientific standards. A hint of aloofness concealed a sharp, analytical brain; my contacts with him were invariably fruitful and beneath the surface he deployed much human warmth and understanding. His knighthood did no more than to acknowledge his outstanding leadership and dedication to the Council's interests. It was easy to see how Malcolm Shepherd's blunt directness sometimes conflicted with Jim's more detached scientific approach. Griff Owen as Deputy Secretary, who could sometimes be outspoken in accord with his north-eastern origins, found himself acting at times as a kind of arbiter. Some years after I had left the Council his friendship with the Chairman, as I understand it, made his relationship with Jim occasionally a trifle uncomfortable. Eventually Griff developed a serious illness from which after some time he made an excellent recovery. Nevertheless this seemed to be the right moment for him to take early retirement from his MRC appointment. I and all his friends were delighted when, in the light of all of the hard work and dedication which he had shown during his long years of service to the Council, he received a CBE shortly after retiring.

The General Medical Council

Another organization with which I became increasingly involved was the General Medical Council (GMC) to which I was appointed on becoming Dean in 1971. The long-serving President then was Lord Cohen of Birkenhead, former Professor of Medicine in Liverpool and a physician of great distinction. I had come to know him slightly because he had often visited Newcastle to lecture and was friendly with Henry Miller, whose ebullient and Rabelaisian life-style had always attracted the other Henry, even though they were very different in personality. Henry Cohen was a brilliant lecturer who almost always spoke without a note, whether he was discussing hypoglycaemia or old silver (of which he was an acknowledged expert collector), as he did when addressing the Newcastle upon Tyne and Northern Counties Medical Society. He also spoke after dinner with charm, wit and relentless fluency. Invariably his delivery suggested total spontaneity but those who knew him well explained that he prepared his talks with infinite care and, being gifted with a photographic memory, learned them by heart in advance. A man of prodigious energy and razor-sharp intellect, he was an acknowledged leader of the profession and a much-admired consultant. Indeed it was said, perhaps aprocryphally, that because his opinion was so widely respected, no wealthy member of the Jewish faith in the UK was allowed to meet his maker without having had Henry's medical attention. A man of humble upbringing in Birkenhead, he never married and lived for many years with his elderly mother in Rodney Street (the Liverpool equivalent of Harley Street) from which he conducted his extensive practice. While he did much for medicine in Liverpool, he had a blind spot insofar as the specialties were concerned. He was interested in neurology but was so totally convinced that general medicine should continue to embrace all of its sub-specialties that he resisted for many years during his reign the appointment of specialists. Thus the development of neurology in Liverpool lagged behind that in the rest of the country, largely because of his influence.

I first met him personally when acting as local organizing secretary for the BMA Annual Meeting in Newcastle in 1957. I quickly recognized, as did everyone, that he was a man of remarkable ability and stature whose patrician, even regal, air and elegant dress and diction belied his humble origins. Later, when I came to know him better during my membership of the GMC, we became close friends. If one walked into the drawing room or dining room at the Athenaeum and Henry was there alone, his eyes would light up and we would always eat or enjoy a drink or two together while with his usual clarity, force and insight he expounded his views on medicine and the world in general. Nevertheless, when I joined the GMC, Henry had been President for about 10 years; despite the respect in which he was held, it was then clear that his leadership was becoming tinged with more than a hint of unacceptable autocracy and rigidity. He displayed a powerful aura of 'father knows best', an attitude which tended to brook no dissent and a style of chairmanship which often stifled legitimate debate. At my very first meeting of the Council in November 1971, when I knew that I could not be present for the afternoon debate because of a competing MRC commitment, the fateful decision was made, on the report of the Registration Committee, that those doctors failing to pay the newly-introduced annual registration fee to the Council should be erased from the Medical Register. Many members of the Council expostulated in vain, but I, having been introduced only that morning and having, like all new members, shaken the President's hand on taking my seat in order to listen to the introductory eulogy which he always prepared about new members, felt so over-awed by the proceedings that I did not contribute to the discussions. Perhaps this was not entirely due to unfamiliarity and apprehension but also to the fact that the debate would clearly continue until after I had had to leave for Park Crescent. Many other notable members of Council to whom I spoke, including the late Sir Denis Hill, Professor of Psychiatry at the Maudsley, whose subsequent service to the Council was in every respect exemplary, shared my own belief that a further period of discussion and negotiation with the profession was necessary before the final decision was taken. Henry, however, would have none of it, the recommendation was put to the vote and the matter was decided.

That decision led to a massive professional outcry, orchestrated by the several hundred doctors whose names were erased from the Register. The cry was regularly heard of 'no taxation without representation'. The profession, recognizing that the Council's membership was then dominated by the appointed members representing the universities with medical schools and the Royal Colleges and that the 12 elected members were very much in a minority, made a very persuasive case for reform. Soon, therefore, the Government decided to establish the Merrison Royal Commission on the regulation of the medical profession. This recommended a complete restructuring of the GMC to ensure that it should include a majority of members elected from the entire UK profession. That experience taught me and, I believe, the Council a salutary lesson. I believe that it is an important rule of life that leaders, however notable, distinguished and capable, should not continue indefinitely in office. Some years later, the Council very properly passed a resolution that no future President should serve more than seven years. A five-year maximum they thought was too short, while 10 years was too long. I myself was affected by that decision, as on subsequently being elected President on 17 February 1982, I had to retire on 16 February 1989, a date which was in some respects inconvenient not so much for myself but perhaps for the Council as a national election was pending. I confess that I should have been happy to continue for a few months longer, but recognized the good sense and validity of the decision. It is one which many other organizations could usefully adopt in principle. I had an enormous respect for the personal and leadership qualities of Mrs Margaret Thatcher who will surely go down in history as one of the outstanding leaders of British government in the 20th century. She gave the country back its pride, she tamed the trade unions, she achieved a turn-round of efficiency and prosperity in British industry for which she will long be remembered. She was someone for whom I had the highest admiration depite her obsession with reduced public expenditure which did so much harm to science, technology, medical research, education and the health services. But I wish that after two successful terms as Prime Minister she had stood down voluntarily half-way through her third term at the height of her powers, without having to be deposed by an electoral contest in the Conservative Party. Regrettably, it had become all too evident, even to some close associates, that she was beginning to display manifestations of rigidity, inflexibility and autocracy similar to those shown by Henry Cohen in the latter years of his GMC Presidency; it was therefore inevitable that she would be supplanted. Perhaps one day the major political parties in the UK will decide that no Prime Minister can be in office for more than two full Parliamentary terms. I am in no doubt that this would be a sensible decision.

Despite Henry Cohen's burgeoning autocracy, his skilful use of language and his experienced deployment of the art of chairmanship enabled him to handle effectively those mavericks who served on the Council in his day. Both in the old Council of those days and in the one reconstituted with a majority of elected members in 1979, there have always been a few members displaying varying degrees of eccentricity or anti-establishmentism who have succeeded in being something of a thorn in a President's flesh. One such was Myre Sim, an elected member and distinguished psychiatrist who subsequently continued his notable career on the other side of the Atlantic and who also became a major benefactor of the Royal College of Physicians of Edinburgh, of which he was so proud to be a Fellow. Dr Sim often took a view of a controversial situation which was opposed to that of the President and proved to be a regular and consistent debater; sometimes, though rarely, his view prevailed, but usually the President won the verbal contest. Henry also came into conflict regularly with Dr Francis Pigott, a spirited spokesman of the junior hospital doctors who later became an Assistant Secretary at the BMA. His proselytizing on behalf of the younger members of the profession and his slavish adherence to the BMA political line did not always commend itself to Henry but he certainly enlivened our debates. Less effective in debate but equally persistent was Mr Paul Vickers, an accident surgeon from the North-East, another elected member whose views were regularly anti-establishment in tone; a few years later Mr Vickers was convicted in the High Court on a charge of murdering his wife and his name was erased from the Medical Register. Among the elected members there were also many senior and distinguished members of the profession including, for example, Mr Walpole Lewin, the distinguished Cambridge neurosurgeon, then Chairman of the BMA Council. He, like myself, was not totally popular with Henry Cohen when, at Council, elections to committees were taking place, and Henry made an impassioned speech stressing how important it was that all members of Council should accept election to any committee for which they were regarded as being suitable by their peers. Walpole, because of his chairmanship of BMA Council, and I, because of my membership of the MRC, each asked to be excused from being elected to the then Disciplinary Committee, solely because of constraints of time and other responsibilities. This request was grudgingly agreed to by the President who gently indicated his disapproval.

A striking feature of the GMC throughout my 18 years of membership was the outstanding contribution made to its affairs by the lay members appointed by the Privy Council. When I first joined, these were only four in number, but after Merrison they were increased to seven. During my

Presidency as I was much impressed by the quality of their contribution and because it became increasingly clear that the pressure of responsibility imposed upon each of them was so great, we invited the Privy Council to increase their number first to nine and then later to 11. I understand that yet a further increase is now under consideration. One notable lay member in the early days was Sir Brynmor Jones, Vice-Chancellor of Hull University, an able scientist who chaired a working party of Council which examined its constitution. That working party recommended a doubling of the number of elected medical members. However that recommendation, approved by Council, failed to satisfy the professional activists. Despite the large increase in membership which would be necessary (with an inevitable increase in costs and in the annual retention fee which provoked the row in the first place) the Merrison Committee firmly recommended that there must be a majority of elected medical members over all other members of Council, including those appointed by the universities, Royal Colleges and Faculties and the Privy Council. That splendid report, produced by a most able committee chaired with great skill by Sir Alec Merrison, Vice-Chancellor of Bristol University, contained many other imaginative proposals. A spirited debate followed during the consultation period during which the views of the profession and of the public were sought. One obvious but tentative proposal was that in order to restrict the size of the Council, it might be reasonable to reduce the number of members appointed by the universities and the Royal Colleges and their Faculties. However, when it was suggested that two universities should agree to appoint one member to represent them both, the idea was summarily rejected and, not surprisingly, the Royal Colleges in both England and Scotland took a similar view. However, the profession and others consulted mostly supported the proposal that the Education Committee should have statutory independence with the right to make decisions on educational issues without having to seek the formal approval of Council. It was also agreed that there should be a majority of appointed members on the Education Committee, and while that proposal did not receive quite as much professional support, the view of the universities and colleges prevailed. One other proposal tentatively floated by Merrison which was ultimately rejected was that there should be a Chairman of Council in addition to the President; it was felt that such a suggestion would erode the President's status and restrict his or her executive powers. Nevertheless, it was agreed that the President must choose whether or not he wished personally to screen all complaints against doctors. If so, he would chair the Preliminary Proceedings Committee which had to determine whether the case should be dismissed, the doctor should receive a warning letter, or the case should be referred for formal enquiry. If he chose this option, the President would not, however, be able to chair, or even to sit as a member of the Professional Conduct

Committee, which was created to succeed the former Disciplinary Committee. Lord Cohen had undertaken the preliminary screening and had chaired the Disciplinary Committee. However, it was now agreed that the individual determining in the first instance, with the help of a committee, whether or not there was a case to answer, should not subsequently sit in judgement if the case proceeded to a more formal hearing. That eminently sensible provision certainly worked well during my Presidency.

Yet another crucial innovation for which Sir Denis Hill had campaigned tirelessly was that a separate health procedure should be established to deal with doctors who were sick rather than being accused of serious professional misconduct. All too often he had been struck, as I had been, by the fact that many doctors coming before the Council's disciplinary procedures, and often referred to a formal hearing before the Disciplinary Committee, were not so much wicked as ill; this applied particularly to many addicted to drugs, including alcohol. It was therefore proposed under Merrison that the Council should establish a Health Committee to deal with these doctors, while recognizing that this would inevitably involve the introduction of a preliminary screening procedure for health as well as for discipline.

Generally the profession, the public and the members of the judiciary who were consulted, as well as the Privy Council, commended and accepted most of Merrison's proposals. There remained the problems of bringing them to fruition. Martin Draper of the dedicated, determined, precise and orderly administrative mind, along with the new President, Sir John Richardson, who was elected to succeed Lord Cohen in 1974 (see below), regularly lobbied Government and the Privy Council once the consultative process had been completed. They were eventually told that because of pressure of Government business and shortage of legislative time it would not be possible to introduce more than a simple enabling act in order to allow a new GMC to be established with a majority of elected members. A short enabling bill was therefore introduced into the House of Lords. It is to the everlasting credit of the late Lord Hunt of Fawley (formerly Sir John Hunt, a distinguished early President of the Royal College of General Practitioners) that he, continually advised and briefed by Sir John and by Martin, was able to introduce a series of amendments when the Bill was debated in the Lords. These received Government support and the Medical Act of 1978 was eventually passed, much expanded from the original Bill and embodying virtually all the reforms which the profession had sought. The new Council with 50 elected and 45 appointed members first met in November 1979. Since then a national election in each of the constituencies of Northern Ireland, Scotland, Wales and England and designed according to an electoral scheme approved by the Privy Council has been held every five years, the last such in 1989.

But to return to earlier days, I was delighted in my first year on Council to be elected to its Education Committee, not least because of my recently refuelled interest in medical education resulting from my appointment as Dean. The chairman of the Committee then was Sir John Brotherston, Chief Medical Officer to the Scottish Home and Health Department and former Professor of Public Health in the University of Edinburgh. John Brotherston, if perhaps a trifle conventional in orientation, had a deep interest in, and experience of, medical education. At first sight a quiet and somewhat reflective man, he could nevertheless be a vigorous and decisive advocate when the need arose. I found him to be someone of vision and authority who, despite having been steeped in the traditional Edinburgh educational system, recognized that substantial changes were needed. The 1967 recommendations on basic medical education in which he and Denis Hill were much involved were then regarded as being very radical in no longer defining by numbers of hours the time which should be devoted to individual subjects in the medical curriculum. They also permitted, for the first time, some welcome flexibility in defining how the licensing bodies could teach medical students. One major task upon which Sir John and his committee embarked soon after I joined it was to initiate a survey of basic medical education in order to determine the extent to which these 1967 recommendations had resulted in change and innovation in the medical schools of the UK and Ireland (see below). As a first step, Sir Douglas Hubble, a member of the committee and latterly Professor of Paediatrics in Birmingham, was asked to design a preliminary questionnaire. It soon emerged that such an exercise would require careful organization and planning and full-time professional help.

After obtaining Finance Committee approval of the substantial expenditure involved, we recruited Mr Richard Wakeford, a graduate in psychology, with a small team of workers who produced a much more detailed and complex set of questionnaires which, after being piloted in a few schools, were extensively modified and then applied nationwide. The Deans were very cooperative in nominating GMC correspondents in each school to be responsible for arranging visits by members of the team and for arranging such interviews as the survey demanded. The Nuffield Provincial Hospitals Trust happily agreed to publish the results of the survey which, after much expenditure of time and effort, appeared in two volumes in 1977. No doubt Lord Cohen's trusteeship of that Trust and his membership of its editorial committee had a major influence in arranging publication. This notable work represents an impressive factual survey, including detailed profiles of the individual schools and a full analysis of the teaching of individual subjects, in the mid-1970s. The survey embraced the medical schools of the Republic of Ireland which were still subject to the authority of the GMC. Until the Medical Act of 1978 became law we still had Irish members representing the National University with its three medical schools, and Trinity College, Dublin, with its single school, as well as others representing the Royal College of Physicians and the Royal College of Surgeons in Ireland. Among these notable Irish members were Tom Murphy (subsequently Principal of the National University) and Paddy Meenan (Professor of Microbiology at the National University, later Dean, and many years later, when the independent Irish Medical Council was established, its second President).

In 1974 Henry Cohen, on the grounds of health, decided at last that he must reduce his professional responsibilities and intimated that he wished to resign the Presidency; hence a presidential election was upon us. The election took place when Henry was still convalescing, and so John Brotherston, as Chairman of the Education Committee, took the chair. All members of Council were invited to intimate if they did not wish to be considered for election; I pointed out, as a member of Council of only some three years' standing, that it would seem presumptuous for some of us even to intimate that we did not wish to stand. The matter was, however, quickly resolved as only four members of Council wished their names to go forward; these were Sir John Richardson, Sir John Peel (former President of the Royal College of Obstetricians & Gynaecologists and former obstetrician to the Royal Family), Sir John Henry Biggart (former Dean of Medicine and Professor of Pathology in Queen's University, Belfast) and Mr Robert Wright (a noted Glasgow surgeon who chaired the Council's Overseas Committee). John Richardson, a noted physician on the staff of St Thomas' Hospital, had been narrowly defeated in two successive contests for the Presidency of the Royal College of Physicians of London. Many of us who admired him and who had come to have a high regard for the quality of his interventions in Council debates felt that he was the ideal candidate. While we also admired the other three contenders, each with his own distinctive personality, Sir John was elected. He was President for the next six years until his term of office on Council as the member appointed by the Royal College of Physicians of London expired in 1980. He was then in any event approaching the statutory retirement age laid down by the 1978 Medical Act which required that no-one could continue as a member beyond his or her 70th birthday.

Under John Richardson's expert tutelage and with his warm and constant encouragement I became more and more involved in Education Committee affairs. In 1975, after completion of the survey on basic medical education, when John Brotherston felt it was time to relinquish the chairmanship, I was elected as his successor. We then embarked upon several initiatives, including efforts to reform and improve the pre-registration year. Lord Cohen, in the latter days of his presidency, had raised money from trusts and foundations to enable the Council, at no expense to itself, to hold annual educational conferences to which deans, other medical educators, representatives of the profession, of medical students and of the public were invited. It became increasingly clear to us that the Education Committee, which had formerly left the regulation of postgraduate and vocational education in medicine to the Royal Colleges and their Faculties, would need to have a more pro-active role in this regard. We also recognized that the recommendations on basic medical education required updating and innovation. We therefore established several sub-committees to undertake specific tasks, including one to try to define the objectives of basic medical education. Throughout this period, too, we arranged regular visits by groups of inspectors to the new medical schools (Southampton, Nottingham and Leicester) so as to be able to recommend to the Privy Council that their degrees, when conferred, should become registrable under the Medical Acts. The enthusiasm of the teachers in these new schools and the quality of the education they each offered in very different ways were so impressive that the Council had no reservations about recommending recognition. This contrasted with the decision which the Council had been compelled to make earlier to recommend to the Privy Council that recognition of the qualification conferred by the Apothecaries Hall of Dublin should be withdrawn as we received evidence to suggest that it was not of appropriate quality. Sadly, too, because of political upheaval in Malta, recognition of the degree conferred by the medical school in that island for full registration, and indeed for all forms of registration, had to be withdrawn on the advice of the Council's Overseas Committee. Regrettably similar action became necessary in respect of degrees being conferred by medical schools in Bangladesh (then accepted for limited registration) because of clear and irrefutable evidence that the standard of medical education had fallen below an acceptable level.

During this period Sir John Richardson, having previously sat on the Professional Conduct Committee, decided that he would undertake the preliminary screening of complaints relating to conduct and appointed Dr John Fry, Treasurer of the Council and a distinguished general practitioner, to help him in that task, while inviting Professor Philip Connell, a noted psychiatrist, to assist Sir Denis Hill as preliminary screener for health. Sir Gordon Wolstenholme, then Director of the Ciba Foundation, chaired one panel of the Disciplinary Committee and Sir Robert Wright the other, in addition to his chairmanship of the Overseas Committee. An elected medical member who came into prominence (and received most votes in the elections) was the medical journalist, a man of sparkling wit and literary expertise, Dr Michael O'Donnell, then editor of *World Medicine*, whose contributions were always erudite and to the point. As he often said, Sir John chaired the Council with grace and distinction and removed something of the rigid formality and autocratic air which characterized the last year or two of Lord Cohen's otherwise distinguished presidency.

Martin Draper, the outstanding Registrar, was aided by two remarkable Deputy Registrars, Robert Gray who had previously worked in university administration, and Robert Beers. Robert Gray was intense, immensely conscientious and hard-working; his advice was invariably cogent, particularly on the Conduct Committee where his drafting of judgements was impeccable. Just occasionally, however he did indulge in circumlocution, always preceded by that characteristic cough with clearing of the throat which was his trademark. Robert Beers, who specialized in overseas affairs, was also capable and efficient; he had a much more suave approach with an occasional hint of addiction to the rule book; at times this seemed potentially to obstruct a route which to me and to some other members of the Council appeared to offer a useful way out of an unfortunate impasse. The Council was also fortunate in the quality of its staff at Assistant Registrar and comparable levels. David Eldred, the Finance Officer was an impeccable and dedicated servant. Wendy Cogger, Heather Brown and Eleanor Lord, each of whom rotated around the various divisions in order to gain experience, were invariably cooperative and totally reliable. Among the recruits who came in at lower levels and who have steadily risen, as Wendy and Heather have done, in the Council's ranks over the years were people like Alan Howes, Alan Kershaw, Kate Horne and many others whose services, advice and hard work I remember with deep affection. Martin Draper will always have a very special place in my memories. Having been steeped in what one might call the Cohen tradition, he was at times a little suspicious of innovation, but as he sat in his chair and gazed out of the window screwing up his eyes when deep in thought, he invariably delivered, after a period of cogitation, wise advice which any senior committee chairman or President would have been very unwise to ignore. With his cheerful, rubicund face and mop of curly white hair, Martin was an impressive figure as he bestrode the Council's affairs. When he retired to the Cheviot area to which he and his wife had become greatly attached during various holidays, we missed him greatly. However, we were exceptionally fortunate in recruiting to succeed him a man of comparable judgement and efficiency, more quietly reflective but nevertheless incisive when the need arose. Peter Towers came from the higher echelons of the Civil Service, having been much involved in the work of the Cabinet Office. When we interviewed him and other members of the short-list drawn from an exceptionally able group of applicants, including a senior officer of the Medical Research Council, I remember Michael O'Donnell's enthusiasm in supporting Peter's candidature, shared by myself; our confidence was not misplaced.

During these years we all much enjoyed the quality of the Council's catering provided by a private catering company (Annie Fryer). They used the same delightful group of waitresses led by the tiny, bustling, white-haired figure of Faye Bishop, for whom we came to have a deep affection. Many of us felt mildly uncomfortable in Henry Cohen's day when at lunch we were offered a wide range of pre-lunch drinks, followed by a choice of red or white wine; afterwards a bottle of whisky circulated freely around the table. Relatively few people sampled it, but I often wondered whether the judgement of those who did was as acute in the afternoon sessions as in the mornings. When Henry Miller realized that I would automatically assume the seat on the GMC which George Smart had held before me and Henry for three years before that, his sole comment was that I would enjoy the excellent lunches! One of John Richardson's first acts on becoming President was to dispense with the whisky and to curtail the sumptuous lunch which he thought, I am sure correctly, carried the risk of inducing post-prandial somnolence; this could not be contemplated either in the Council's meetings or more especially during hearings of the Conduct Committee. Dinner, however, during Council week, which followed upon meetings of the Overseas, Education Executive and other Committees and was held on the night before the meeting of the full Council, was a much more lavish affair (and excellent value), impeccably served in the Council's dining room by the same team with an even more extensive range of liquid refreshment, ending with excellent port from the Council's cellars. It was regularly said that only the General Dental Council as a statutory body could compete and at times out-do the quality of the food provided at the GMC.

When the new Council with a majority of elected members came into being, we could no longer dine in the Council's premises as the room was too small and we had to occupy two rooms for our buffet lunches. The routine of dining at the Apothecaries Hall then began and continues today. That impressive old hall is one of the finest dining locations in London and the quality of the food was no less good than before. The long-established system of having named places only at the top table but of allocating numbered places to other Council members as they enter the dining room at random means that all of the members gradually come to know everyone else. Hence there is never any question of clustering into small cliques of those members who believe that over dinner they might discuss medico-political issues. It was Council policy, even throughout John Richardson's more relaxed term of Presidency, that spouses were never invited to set foot in the premises. When I broached this matter tentatively with Martin Draper, he said a little sternly 'I would, I think, counsel caution'. However, it was customary for the President always to speak after dinner and often to invite a guest who might, for example, be a Cabinet minister, a President of a Royal College, the Clerk of the Privy Council or someone else who might have something interesting to say. When I became President, we gradually eroded the 'no spouse' rule and I regularly brought Betty to the Council dinner and also invited the wife or husband of our principal guest whenever this seemed appropriate. Later, too, I introduced an annual spouses' night so that Council members and their guests could have an evening party in the Council's premises with drinks in the Council chamber and a buffet supper in the committee rooms and dining room; I believe that these events proved popular and successful.

A highlight of John Richardson's presidency was the major conference held at the Royal Institute of British Architects in Portland Place to discuss the Merrison report with representatives of all branches of the profession, of the universities and of many other organizations. Characteristically, Henry Miller, who came as a Vice-Chancellor, intervened to say that this was one of the most boring conferences he had ever attended and that he would advise Sir Alec (who was present) to chair yet another commission in order to investigate the Vatican as he felt sure that that endeavour would be crowned with equal success. This was a typical tongue-in-cheek Henry remark but was perhaps related to the fact that several vested interests, not least the Royal Colleges, seemed to be convinced that they must retain unfettered control of postgraduate education. Clearly, they did not wish the independent Education Committee of the reshaped GMC to interfere in what they thought was their domain. Nevertheless, as already mentioned, through the advocacy and hard work of John Richardson, Martin Draper and Lord Hunt, the Medical Act of 1978 included a provision that the Education Committee of the GMC would have the authority, and indeed the responsibility, of co-ordinating all stages of medical education, so that that battle was won. In 1979, John Richardson presided therefore over the first meeting of the newly-constituted GMC. The newly elected membership, now the dominant voice in the Council, gave him a slightly uncomfortable time. So, too, did some of the new lay members, including the indefatigable Mrs Jean Robinson, Chairman of the Patients' Association, and Professor Margaret Stacey, Professor of Sociology from the University of Warwick. She, like Jean Robinson, was determined that the voice of the patient and of the public should be more strongly heard and should have a greater influence upon future Council decisions. John Richardson coped with his customary smooth dignity and soon, despite the numerous shades of opinion and dissenting views regularly expressed, the Council began to shake down into a cohesive entity. This was so despite the fact that there were some Council members who felt themselves on a limb by virtue of the fact that they were not in the first round elected to any committees. Strenuous attempts were subsequently made to broaden the responsibility and experience of all Council members, particularly when new working parties were established to deal with specific tasks. Council members not otherwise involved in committee work were regularly appointed to such sub-committees.

As John Richardson's presidency drew to a close in 1980, lobbying relating to the election of his successor began. I had begun to recognize that I might possibly be a candidate. Hence when I retired from the MRC in 1978 I accepted election to the Professional Conduct Committee and had served on that committee for almost two years as the election loomed. From what I heard, it seemed likely to be a straight contest between myself as Chairman of the Education Committee and Sir Robert Wright, who had continued to chair the Overseas Committee and a panel of the Conduct Committee and who was several years older and more senior than myself. We knew that the presidential election would be almost the first item of business during the Council meeting on 22 May 1980 as Sir John's term of office ended on 16 June. Many Council members encouraged me in the belief that I might be elected, though I knew that in Scotland, and among many Scots representing various English universities, there was strong support for Sir Robert. I also realized that if I were elected, I would have difficulty in interrelating my presidential responsibilities with my continuing duties as Dean in Newcastle, even though I had already decided that I would not seek to be reappointed Dean when my term of office ended in September 1981. For several weeks before Council met, I was in a state of some anxiety which clearly communicated itself to Betty, so that neither of us slept well that spring. Indeed I found myself waking daily at about 4.30–5.00 a.m. Betty had quietly decided that she would come to London with me as we had agreed to have a celebratory dinner if I were elected. Since I was then chairing a working party of the Nuffield Provincial Hospitals Trust on communication between doctors and patients and between doctors and the other caring professions, we were able to stay at the comfortable premises of the Trust in Prince Albert Road, off Regent's Park, through the good offices of the Secretary, Gordon McLachlan.

On the day of the election the sun shone from a cloudless sky and we took a long walk around Regent's Park before I walked on to 44 Hallam Street and Betty returned to Prince Albert Road to await a lunch-time telephone call. In the event, Sir Robert Wright was elected (I am told by a relatively narrow margin, though Martin Draper, ever tactful, was never willing to disclose the numbers of votes cast in any election). Of course I was disappointed but was pleased for Sir Robert, who had been knighted a few years earlier in the light of his outstanding contributions to surgery and to the Council. Betty shared my disappointment on learning the news when I slipped away to a phone at the end of the morning session, but we decided to have our dinner that evening after all. After swallowing the initial shock of disappointment when the result was announced, I was able to follow Sir Robert in paying a tribute to Sir John and in expressing not only the thanks of the entire Council but also my personal thanks for the guidance and support he had given me during his outstanding years of office. Just as Fred Nattrass, Ray Adams and Henry Miller had helped to mould my neurological career, John Richardson's wise guidance and impeccable judgement had a profound influence upon my work as Chairman of the Education Committee and upon my subsequent work in the GMC. After I presented the report of the Education Committee later in the meeting, many friends who had supported me were kind enough to say that they had admired the way in which I had concealed my disappointment by participating fully in subsequent debates. I recognized, too, how appropriate it was that Sir Robert was able to serve as President an organization of which he had been such a faithful member and to which he had devoted so much unstinting effort over many years. And I soon became aware of the almost impossible task I would have faced if I had been elected at a time when I was still carrying a heavy load as Dean, while also being about to assume new responsibilities as BMA President (see below).

Sir Robert was a remarkable man. He was a skilful surgeon, a much admired consultant colleague and an able teacher of medical students and postgraduates. He had had a distinguished war record in the RAMC, being awarded the Distinguished Service Order. He was also a rather private man, a total abstainer and abstemious in many other respects with somewhat spartan and Calvinistic views on life. He was a devoted father, a committed Christian and an elder of his church in Glasgow; but there seemed to be a veneer of reserve which made it difficult for one to get beneath the surface and to get to know him really well. As a keen cricket supporter myself, I was unaware until after he died that cricket was one of his life-long passions and that he would slip away to Lords whenever he had time to spare when in London. A dedicated Scot, he regularly stayed at the Caledonian Club, but his tastes were so simple that soon after he was elected he installed a shaver point and wash-basin in the President's small office. It is alleged (though I have no proof of this) that just occasionally he slept on the couch. Much more often, I imagine, he came off the sleeper from Glasgow and repaired at once to his office to freshen up before the morning's activities. As President, he was calm, precise and sound if not inspired in debate, and all of his comments and decisions were characterized by scrupulous honesty and total integrity. While everyone who knew him in Glasgow, including some of his close friends, spoke admiringly of him, not just in his professional capacity but also as a devoted husband and father, his occasionally secretive nature was well characterized by the fact that a day or two after he had been elected I was told that he was attending a social event in Glasgow with his wife, Helen, when a colleague came up and congratulated him warmly on his new appointment. Helen turned to him in mystification and asked to be told. She knew all about his work with the GMC but he had not troubled to tell her that he had just been elected President. Bob's

Calvinistic views were also well exemplified by the fact that when he was knighted, he felt it quite unnecessary to go to the College of Arms to sign the Knights' Roll. When approached by Lord Lyon, King of Arms (head of the College of Arms in Scotland) who invited him to have his own personal armorial bearings (coat of arms) prepared, he did not even consult his family. In discussion later when I had been similarly honoured, I told him that my first reaction on being approached by Garter King of Arms (the comparable officer in England) was to decline. But when I consulted my family they insisted that we should accept and hang the cost (then £750 in England, but £500 in Scotland!). Bob's reaction was that he was not interested in that kind of nonsense. This later caused the GMC considerable difficulty as it had been the custom to display the coat of arms of each successive President on the stained glass window in the Council chamber. On this issue Martin Draper and Bob engaged in a kind of running battle over many months. When eventually Sir Robert died in office, we had to obtain the special permission of Lord Lyon to use the arms of the Royal College of Physicians and Surgeons of Glasgow, of which Bob was a former President. Similarly, when it came to having his portrait painted posthumously in order to hang it in the Council chamber, we borrowed a photograph from his College and arranged for Mr Halliday, an Edinburgh artist, to produce an oil painting based upon it. Fortunately that proved successful. Yet another interesting facet of Bob's personality was that when he was elected, Martin Draper asked him how soon he would wish to take over the flat in Hallam Street which John and Sybil Richardson had now vacated. Bob remarked trenchantly that he was not interested, whereupon the Council disposed of it on the open market. Martin did ask me, as Chairman of Education, whether Betty and I wished to take it over, but that seemed singularly inappropriate and I refused, as it seemed likely that Bob, who was about 64 on being elected, would serve for at least six years. However, some months after Bob's death, when I was elected to succeed him (see below) by which time Betty and I, with the help of Martin Draper and David Eldred, had identified another appropriate presidential flat in Hallam Street, we invited Bob's widow, Helen, and members of the family to come down to the Council for the formal unveiling of his portrait; Betty invited them to tea in our flat before the ceremony. Helen looked around a little wistfully and said 'Oh, what a nice flat. How I wish the Council had had a flat like this in London when Bob was President'.

Of Bob's many contributions to the work of the Council during his long service and all-too-short presidency much more could be said. He was a fair and judicious chairman of one panel of the Conduct Committee, while Gordon Wolstenholme continued to chair the other. He made innumerable contributions to issues relating to the registration of overseas doctors, not least the introduction of the TRAB test (subsequently the

PLAB test—Professional and Linguistic Assessment Board) in order to be certain that the linguistic and professional capabilities of doctors seeking temporary (and later, under the new Medical Act, limited) registration with the GMC were adequate for them to practise safely in the United Kingdom. He also persuaded the Royal Colleges and their training committees to agree that overseas doctors coming to the UK for training could only hold appointments under limited registration which were approved for training purposes by those bodies. These initiatives alone assure for Bob Wright a permanent and unassailable place in the annals of the Council. One of his most striking personal characteristics which, like his integrity, shone through all that he did was his courage; and this was never better exemplified than in his terminal illness. After the new Council had met in 1979, we in the Education Committee and in Council began to take our first tentative steps towards defining more clearly the Council's role in the oversight of postgraduate and continuing education. Just as John Richardson had held a major conference to discuss the implementation of the Merrison report, we decided that in February 1982 we should hold another with the Royal Colleges, and the BMA, the junior doctors and other professional organizations to discuss the Council's new responsibilities in this field of education. In November 1981, during the regular meeting of Council, Bob and I, with members of staff, went round to the Royal Institute of British Architects late one afternoon to look at the facilities. We also drew up a provisional programme; it was agreed that Bob would take the chair but that I, as Chairman of the Education Committee, would clearly play an important part. Bob presided over the Council with his customary expertise and at dinner on the Wednesday evening spoke movingly and amusingly about the Council's role. On the Thursday evening, when the Council meeting was over, I had arranged in my new capacity as BMA President a dinner in the Prince's Room at BMA House to which many senior members of the profession, including Presidents of Royal Colleges, were invited. Bob as GMC President was on the guest list and he readily accepted. He had to leave the dinner early to catch the sleeper back to Glasgow but nevertheless seemed on excellent form. On my return to Newcastle next day, I was stunned to receive a call from Martin Draper telling me that the President had telephoned him from Glasgow resigning his office because of a serious and incurable illness. We were quite unaware that Bob had seen a professional colleague in Glasgow earlier that week and had had several investigations because of some recent symptoms. When he returned to Glasgow on the Friday his colleague sadly told him that he was suffering from an illness which would progress inexorably to a fatal conclusion. We shall always remember with affection and gratitude his courageous chairmanship of his last meeting as President. Subsequently we were told that he insisted upon being admitted to the hospital which he had long served with distinction, in order to relieve his wife of the burden of looking after someone who was terminally ill. For a time he welcomed visits from close friends and professional associates, but then decided that he would see only his wife and family. Having had one major blood transfusion, he indicated that if a further incident requiring transfusion were to occur, he would refuse further treatment, and so it proved. He slipped quietly away, happily without severe terminal suffering; I and many of his friends and admirers paid a final tribute to him at a moving funeral service in his own church at Bearsden in Glasgow in early 1982. So passed a great and memorable man.

The death of a serving President presented the GMC with several problems. In retrospect, John Richardson told me later how much he regretted having mentioned, half jokingly, when Sir Robert was elected that he should look to his laurels since the only surgeons previously elected to the Presidency had died prematurely while in office. Fortunately Sir Denis Hill, the father of the GMC's health reforms, was a senior figure and was nominated by unanimous agreement as Acting President. To have called a special meeting of Council simply in order to elect a President would, in the Registrar's view (and we agreed with him) have involved the Council in major and unacceptable expense. However, since all members of the Council had been invited to the conference on post-graduate education at the RIBA on 18 February 1982, it was agreed to hold a special meeting of Council on the previous day in order to elect Sir Robert's successor. Sadly, even during the short time that he was Acting President, Sir Denis developed some symptoms for which several of us urged him to seek professional advice. Eventually he was persuaded and some investigations were arranged, but these were postponed at his request because of pressure of professional work. We were all deeply saddened to learn that before the rearranged investigations could be performed, he died suddenly in May, still at the height of his powers and with so much yet to give. The Council thereby lost two of its outstanding figures within the short period of a few months.

The presidential election took place on 17 February and I was elected; though I never knew the exact voting figures which the Registrar, as always, kept to himself, I nevertheless felt that I held the confidence of Council. My first presidential act was to chair the major conference next day, and although much contention arose, it seemed to go reasonably well. We came away from it with a reasonable degree of support for the proposal that the Council should take a more definitive oversight of postgraduate medical education, though it was clear that several Colleges and Faculties still had reservations. Once elected, I decided that I must relinquish my chairmanship of the Education Committee, particularly in the light of its statutory independence. Here again there was an interregnum during which I continued as chairman until a formal election took place during Council week in May. Arthur Crisp, Professor of Psychiatry at St George's Hospital, was elected to succeed me. He had built up an excellent department with a fine reputation for postgraduate teaching and research, and his own work on anorexia nervosa had won for him an international reputation. While some thought him to be a trifle prolix and not everyone shared the totality of his views on educational principles in both undergraduate and postgraduate medical training, he was a faithful servant of the Council and an exceptionally loyal colleague upon whose support I could invariably rely. His staunch advocacy of the Council's status and of the statutory independence of its Education Committee occasionally brought him into conflict with some College presidents. There were also times when some members felt that the work of the Education Committee could have been disposed of more rapidly, but he was careful, precise, just sufficiently dogmatic and no more. He persuaded his committee to embark upon several important initiatives in drafting and eventually publishing reports on basic specialist training (which the Colleges insisted on continuing to call general professional training) and later on higher specialist training. The committee also revised its recommendations on general clinical training in the pre-registration year and began for the first time to look carefully at continuing medical education for all doctors.

Arthur pursued these and other objectives upon which he had set his heart with dogged persistence. He and I also agreed that in the light of comments made by the Presidents of the Royal Colleges of Physicians about the standard of clinical competence of candidates presenting themselves for the MRCP (UK) examination, it would be wise to embark upon a new programme of inspection of the final clinical examinations in medicine of all the UK medical schools. That programme went ahead smoothly, with different inspecting teams being chosen to visit and report upon up to three medical schools a year; I understand that the programme has now been virtually completed. These inspections confirmed that the standard of clinical competence of UK graduates at the time of the final examination was generally satisfactory, but a number of problems which were identified in many schools were speedily corrected. Similarly, it seemed that the final qualifying examinations of the non-university licensing bodies (the Conjoint Board of the Royal Colleges in England, the Society of Apothecaries and the Board of the so-called Scottish Triple qualification) had not been updated as much as the committee would have wished. Numerous consultations then ensued with the result that the examinations offered by these bodies were substantially modified. Many voices were raised from time to time suggesting that these routes to qualification in medicine might be closed by requiring all intending doctors to obtain a university degree. However, the knowledge that these examinations provided a mechanism through which refugee medical students and doctors from overseas countries could qualify in order to practise in the UK helped them to survive. Among Arthur's many other initiatives was the establishment of a working party on the teaching of behavioural sciences and communication skills in medicine; this too resulted in the publication of a valuable report on the importance of teaching all medical students the principles of sociology, psychology and skill in communication. Shortly after Arthur had to relinquish his chairmanship of the Education Committee after the maximum five-year term which the Council had imposed upon holders of that office, the University of London, which he had represented as one of its three appointed members, replaced him with another medical colleague so that the Council lost his skill and expertise which had proved so invaluable. I was delighted when the committee elected Sir Robert Kilpatrick of Leicester as his successor. When he succeeded me as President, I learned with pleasure that the committee then chose my old friend and former colleague Professor David Shaw, who had succeeded me as Dean and as head of academic neurology in Newcastle and who is still serving as Chairman. I understand that the committee is making good progress in revising the recommendations on basic medical education, last published in 1980, which I had drafted personally but which had then been extensively revised by a small sub-committee and by the Education Committee before being published. The intention now, I believe, is that all of the Council's reports will eventually be put together in a book of recommendations covering medical education from entry to medical school to eventual retirement.

One of the most interesting and welcome, if arduous, responsibilities I had acquired as Chairman of the Education Committee had been to represent the GMC on the Advisory Committee on Medical Education in Europe. This had been established under the auspices of the EEC after promulgation of the medical directives which were designed to allow free movement of doctors between the member countries and to establish comparable standards of undergraduate, postgraduate and vocational training in medicine throughout the Community. Each country was allowed three representatives and three alternates. The practising profession was represented by a general practitioner, Sir James Cameron, and a hospital consultant, Mr Roger Brearley, both nominated by the BMA; the universities and postgraduate teaching authorities were represented by a nominee of the Committee of Vice-Chancellors and Principals (at first Professor Robert Whelan from Liverpool) and one from the Royal Colleges (Sir Stanley Clayton, former President of the Royal College of Obstetricians and Gynaecologists); the two from the regulatory authorities were myself (representing the GMC as Chairman of its Education Committee) and Sir John Brotherston (Chief Medical Officer to the Scottish Home and Health Department, representing the

Government medical service). We met twice a year in Brussels to discuss the promulgation of ideas and the preparation of formal reports on medical education. We quickly learned about the very different standards then existing throughout the Community and about the very different means by which the medical profession was regulated and education provided. We had known that there was no *numerus clausus* in Italy, for example, or in Belgium and some other countries, so that there was unrestricted entry of huge numbers of young people graduating from high school into medical training. We also knew, to quote but one example, that the regulation of the medical profession in Germany was not in the hands of doctors but of lawyers. For a time, therefore, we found it difficult to achieve a rapport with some of our European colleagues. Simultaneous translation into five (later seven) languages did not help, but slowly after 18 months to two years the committee began to develop a cohesive corporate identity. Many European colleagues were anxious that we and the Irish should do what we could to try to apply pressure to their respective governments to introduce *numerus clausus* so as to restrict entry to their medical schools, and after a few years it began to seem that this objective was slowly being achieved. It was horrifying to learn from the medical Vice-Chancellor of a Belgian university that he was being required by law (as in Italy, any student leaving high school was entitled to embark upon university training in any subject of his or her choice) to admit some 1200 students to his medical school each year. About 50% were dismissed at the end of the first year on academic grounds, another 200 at the end of the second, another 200 at the end of the third, and so on. The class eventually reached manageable proportions towards the end of the students' clinical training. Italy seemed less successful in achieving such a reduction, so that many Italian medical students, even in their senior years, had great difficulty in finding an opportunity personally of examining patients.

Slowly but surely, the committee established working groups which drafted a series of reports, each being amended later in the committee as a whole. I produced the first draft of the report on the clinical training of medical students, while Roger Brearley was a leading light in producing several reports on the training of specialists. These and many other reports accepted by the committee were eventually accepted by the European Commission and passed to the governments of the member states for implementation. They seemed to have little immediate effect but later evidence emerged to suggest that their influence had been significant and that much more uniformity of standards was slowly being achieved. Two days in Brussels, of course, allowed one the opportunity of sampling some of the gastronomic and oenological delights of that city, and many a delightful evening was spent in company with our other UK colleagues, and sometimes with Irish or other European friends, in various restaurants near the Grand Place. The Palace Hotel in the Place Rogier, near the Gare du Nord, was our usual haunt until it closed and we had to find another reasonably priced hotel, not an easy task in that centre of European bureaucracy. On one occasion all the airports in the south of England and in northern Europe were closed by thick fog and we had to wend our way home by train to Ostende and by ferry, arriving home much later than we had hoped and anticipated, while losing a night's sleep to boot. Nevertheless, as we dined (very well) in Ostende, Stanley Clayton's almost childish delight was infectious as he regarded this as being an adventure. When I became GMC President I had to give up my position on the EEC Committee and Arthur Crisp succeeded me. We were pleased when, some two years later, he was elected chairman when it was the turn of the UK regulatory authority to occupy that position; I understand that he performed with exceptional diplomacy and skill.

As I relinquished my membership of that body, another European responsibility emerged, namely membership of the Conference des Ordres, an organization representing most of the regulatory medical authorities in Europe; this met twice a year in Paris, hosted by our French colleagues. Gordon Wolstenholme had represented us on that body for several years but his membership of the Council had ended and I decided that it was my duty to succeed him. However, I did not find the Conference very effective, if only because of the continual bickering on issues of minor principle which seemed so often to dominate its discussions. It was not concerned with medical education; its role was much more related to administrative procedures, and especially with attempts to establish relative uniformity of European ethical codes and standards of medical practice. The proceedings were largely conducted in French (only the British, Irish and the Danes used English); simultaneous translation was not always satisfactory so that when the President from France, who took the chair, broke into voluble French I was very grateful to have with me Mrs Heather Brown, GMC Assistant Registrar, whose French was fluent and who was a tremendous help. These one-day meetings (I travelled to Paris the night before and flew home on the evening after the meeting) were punctuated by a typically lavish (if unhealthy) French lunch with superb wines, after which I felt that the afternoon deliberations were always less precise and laboured than those of the morning. Perhaps it was an illusion, but it also seemed that difficult decisions were more readily resolved in the afternoon. My very first meeting of the Conference des Ordres in October 1983, just after I had become Warden of Green College, was in one respect disastrous. Having obtained a new and comprehensive key holder which could hold up to 24 keys, including those to our London GMC flat, to various rooms in Green College and doors in the Warden's residence at 1A Observatory

Street as well as others for the GMC premises themselves, I carried this in my right trouser pocket. To my horror, on arriving at my Paris hotel the keys had disappeared. In retrospect, I think that I probably left them when passing through the security check at Heathrow, but this possibility did not occur to me until later. On my return to Oxford, a flurry of activity ensued in order to replace the missing keys and the Domestic Bursar, Gerald Chambers, was not overly impressed by this evidence of inefficiency on the part of the new Warden. After three or four meetings of the Conference, by which time my responsibilities as President had escalated, I decided that its meetings, though enjoyable, were not those to which I could give highest priority. I therefore resigned and arranged for the Council to be represented by Professor Tony Glenister from Charing Cross, a fluent French speaker.

It was fortunate that I did not become President until early 1982, a few months after I had relinquished my Deanship, so that I was able to organize my personal timetable with much greater ease than would have been possible if I had still held that office. And as I knew that I would be moving to Green College in September 1983, I was able well in advance to arrange my timetable for about 18 months ahead so as to interrelate my responsibilities with the College and Council, and indeed with my continuing commitments to the BMA (see below). Having been elected to the Professional Conduct Committee before becoming President, I concluded that it would be sensible for me to chair that committee for the first two years of my presidency and then to take over the preliminary screening, which John Richardson had undertaken during much of his term of office. I also thought that I needed more experience of the Council's health procedures and so agreed to chair the Health Committee as well. Chairmanship of the Conduct Committee taught me many important lessons about human nature. A few notable cases were especially educational. The Conduct Committee sat in two (later three) panels, each of up to 10 members, always including one lay member (much later in my presidency it was decided that each such panel would have two such members). Invariably, too, a legal assessor (a senior and experienced Queen's Counsel) was in attendance to advise the Chairman on points of law. All hearings are held in public (save that exceptionally, in order to protect vulnerable witnesses such as children, the committee may resolve to exclude the public from part or the whole of a hearing), though the deliberations of the committee once the case has been heard take place in camera. The case against a doctor alleged to have committed serious professional misconduct or who has been convicted of a major offence is presented by the solicitor to the Council or by counsel briefed by him. The doctor, too is almost always represented by a solicitor or counsel. Evidence is heard on oath, with the press and others in the public gallery. If the doctor has been convicted of a criminal offence, it is first necessary for the committee to determine whether the conviction (in such cases) is proved (this is invariably the case) before deciding whether there should be any restriction on the doctor's registration, while in a case of alleged serious professional misconduct the committee must first decide whether the facts alleged against the doctor in the charge are proved beyond all reasonable doubt. If the facts are proved, then in a second stage of the hearing the committee is required to determine whether those facts (or the conviction), as proved, amount to serious professional misconduct and, if so, what penalty to impose. The penalty may be admonishment, postponement of decision, the attachment of conditions to the doctor's registration, suspension from the Register for a finite period, or erasure, in which latter event the doctor can only be restored to the Register and thus to medical practice after another formal hearing of the committee not less than 10 months later.

A memorable case was one in which two doctors were allegedly in partnership but the younger of the two was apparently being employed as a salaried assistant. It was suggested that he was being exploited by the older doctor in being required, in return for a very low income, to undertake much, if not all, of the emergency work and to carry more than a fair burden of the practice activity. The younger man soon tired of this arrangement, broke up the partnership and set up on his own nearby. Evidence soon emerged to suggest that the younger doctor was sending canvassing letters to patients still registered with the older, telling them that he had now opened his own surgery. The case brought by the older doctor alleging canvassing by the younger seemed solid until evidence was produced by a typewriter expert who showed that the alleged canvassing letters had been typed on a machine belonging to the older doctor.

Yet another salutary case was one in which a young female Vietnamese refugee student alleged that she had been sexually assaulted by a doctor in his surgery. She described clearly the nature of the assault but it was her word against his; our legal assessor advised us that it would be unsafe to find such allegations proved against a doctor in the absence of corroboration or similar fact evidence relating to other patients. And when the doctor's nurse gave evidence on oath claiming that she had been present in the consulting room during the entire examination and was satisfied that nothing improper took place, the case collapsed. However, as a result of the newspaper reporting of the case, several letters were received from other female patients of the same doctor describing similar sexual assaults; indeed one patient claimed to have been raped by him and to have become pregnant as a result. Hence, a further case was mounted which resulted in the doctor's name being erased from the Register. This case clearly showed why the Council still feels that it is right in the interests of justice that such cases should be heard in public.

The more I saw of the conduct procedures, the more convinced I was that they were essentially fair and well conducted by the officers of the Council, the Council's solicitor and those counsel whom he briefed, and by the defence societies acting for the doctor. Admittedly, there were times when we might have wished to take some action against a doctor whose offence fell short of the threshold of serious professional misconduct. Later during my presidency I suggested to a working party on the Council's disciplinary procedures that more effective means were needed to deal with lesser complaints against doctors which seemed to have substance but fell short of that high threshold. While for a variety of reasons we opposed the private member's bill proposed by Mr Nigel Spearing, MP, which suggested the introduction of a new threshold of offence called 'unacceptable conduct', there were many, including myself, who felt that something should be done to bring lesser offences within the Council's ambit. My understanding is that action is being taken in this respect by the Council under the wise and judicious guidance of my successor, Sir Robert Kilpatrick. One thing which always impressed me about the hearings of the Conduct Committee was the extent to which unanimity of view gradually emerged after a discussion of the pros and cons in almost every case, though there were just a few where the committee was almost evenly divided even after prolonged discussion. Another striking feature was that the doctor members, whether working in hospital-based specialties, general practice or some other discipline, almost always wished to take a more stern and admonitory view than did the lay members who generally tended more towards leniency.

The Health Committee was very different. The Council and profession will always be grateful to Sir Denis Hill for his initiative in advising Council and the Government that the method of dealing with sick doctors should be different from that designed to deal with those accused of serious professional misconduct. Doctors coming before the Health Committee were almost always suffering from short- or, more often, long-term psychiatric illness or were addicted to alcohol and/or drugs. Here again, a QC legal assessor would be present and a lay member was always on the committee. Hearings were, however, held in camera, and although the doctor could be, and often was, legally represented or accompanied by a relative or friend, the sessions were conducted with greater informality, more like the atmosphere of a consulting room than of a court of law; nevertheless, evidence often had to be given on oath. And the Health Committee had no power to erase a doctor's name from the Register but only to suspend for up to 12 months at a time in the most serious cases. Happily, the sanction of imposing conditions on registration (such as a ban on the prescribing of dangerous drugs) was used more often. Invariably sick doctors coming before that committee were required to be under the medical supervision of a consultant who would continue to monitor treatment and progress. During the time that I chaired the committee, more than 50% of the doctors coming before it were eventually rehabilitated and many, cured of their addiction to drugs or alcohol, were allowed to return to unrestricted practice. The Health Committee was in a sense the end of the road, as I recognized more fully later when I undertook the preliminary screening of both health and conduct cases and, having relinquished chairmanship of the Conduct Committee, assumed the chair of the Preliminary Proceedings Committee. That committee commonly prescribed a more informal health procedure (see below). I carried these new responsibilities for the last four years of my presidency. That change had advantages in relation to my personal programme as my responsibilities as Warden of Green College increased, in that although I continued to go to London, on average, on two or sometimes three days a week, I could nevertheless carry out many of the preliminary screening responsibilities by mail rather than by attendance at the Council's offices. Chairing a panel of the Conduct Committee often involved one in daily sittings from 9.00 in the morning until 6.00 in the evening five days a week and very occasionally on Saturday mornings as well. Each panel usually sat for six full weeks in the year. Since I relinquished the presidency, that commitment has almost doubled and has become, I believe, an almost intolerable burden for many active practising doctors. This was why we agreed to increase the number of members of Council elected to the Conduct Committee so as to empanel three, rather than two, panels, but even so the time commitment has continued to escalate. Preliminary screening was no less of a burden but one could read the extensive documents sent to one in relation to each case by Council officers in the evening hours or at weekends. I have often quoted the fact that one summer when I went to Detchant in August, I received in the first week no fewer than 53 postal packets from the GMC. This was a record; nevertheless, though the magnitude of the task fluctuated, it was unremitting.

On average, during my presidency the Council received about 1000 complaints per year against doctors from members of the public, from persons acting in a public capacity (such as an officer of a health authority) or from other doctors. About a quarter of these related to treatment under the NHS and these complainants were invariably advised by a member of the office staff to submit their complaint first to the relevant NHS authority, either in hospital or in general practice, simply because it was not the Council's policy to investigate a complaint under consideration by another authority. We also recognized that if there was a long delay before presenting such a complaint to the NHS, it might in consequence lapse. In every such case the complainant was told that if the complaint proved to be of substance and was upheld by the NHS authority, it would, if sufficiently serious, be subsequently referred to the GMC. Another large group of the complaints clearly came from individuals who were mentally disturbed or who were chronic complainers (like the barrack-room lawyers of my Army days) or those in whose complaints one could not find any material of substance. The response to these would be letters drafted by the office but approved (often after amendment) by myself indicating that the complaint was not of sufficient seriousness to warrant action by the Council. There would then be a much larger batch which clearly suggested that doctors might well have been uncaring, lacking in understanding or even positively rude, but where the evidence presented did not raise an issue of serious professional misconduct. These were the complaints which troubled me most, as often I had no alternative but to write back to say that the complaints were not sufficiently serious to warrant action by the Council. Of course I appreciate that doctors, like patients, may lose their tempers and behave badly. Some patients wrote to say that they did not wish to have the doctor 'struck off' but simply wished me to write to the doctor asking him or her to be nicer to people in future. This, however, I was unable to do because if one wrote in such terms to a doctor, his or her defence organization would inevitably be informed and the full panoply of legal procedures would follow. Sometimes we did manage to use an informal procedure allowed under Section XV of Council Standing Orders through which I consulted two members (one medical and one lay) suggesting that although I did not think that the issued raised was one of sufficient seriousness to justify a charge of serious professional misconduct, it would be reasonable to ask the doctor's observations upon the complaint and then to offer a letter of advice. The risk underlying that mechanism was that having taken such informal action, it was not possible to follow it up with more formal procedures if the complaint turned out to be more serious than anticipated or if the doctor's answer was unsatisfactory. Nevertheless, we used this approach more and more during the latter years of my presidency. As mentioned above, I am glad to learn that following upon some suggestions which I mooted tentatively to a working party on conduct, the Council is now trying to establish a mechanism of handling the lesser complaints more effectively than in the past.

There always remained a batch of complaints, perhaps as many as 150 in any one year, which at least raised the possibility that the doctor might have been guilty of serious professional misconduct and which, like all criminal convictions, I referred to the Preliminary Proceedings Committee (PPC) for formal consideration. The same action was taken in cases which suggested that the doctor's health might be sufficiently impaired to put patients' welfare at risk.

At the PPC, with two lay members present and a QC and the Council's solicitor in attendance, all convictions were considered first. A single conviction, for instance, involving driving with only a little more than the prescribed level of alcohol in the breath would invariably lead to a warning letter. However, a very high level of alcohol was usually regarded as indicative of a potential health problem and in such cases the doctor's fitness to practice was normally investigated. All convictions were considered in the light of observations made by the doctor or by a defence organization or solicitor acting on his or her behalf, and a decision was then made as to whether the doctor should receive a warning letter or whether the case was sufficiently serious to justify a formal hearing before the Professional Conduct Committee or an enquiry by the Health Committee into the doctor's fitness to practise. Similar decisions were taken in relation to complaints alleging serious professional misconduct. In any one year about 120 doctors would receive warning letters of varying severity, and some 30–40 cases would be referred to the Conduct Committee for a formal hearing. Almost always, too, there were 10–12 doctors each year whose problem was not so much one of alleged misconduct as of health. Unless the problem was manifestly serious and such as to warrant immediate referral to the Health Committee, most such cases were adjourned *sine die* and the doctor was invited to undergo examination by two independent consultants (usually psychiatrists, occasionally neurologists or other specialists). He or she would then be invited to give voluntary undertakings to abide by the recommendations made in the reports of the examining consultants. These might include, for example, total abstinence from alcohol or a requirement to take a particular form of treatment. Many such doctors also provided reports from consultants of their own choosing and were indeed freely invited to do so if they wished. The progress of these doctors towards rehabilitation was then monitored by the council in the light of regular reports submitted every three months or so by the supervising consultant. The monitoring was undertaken by an additional preliminary screener for health who, for much of my time, was Dr Philip Connell. If there was evidence that a doctor had breached the undertakings given, this would result in formal reference to the Health Committee at which conditions upon registration might, for example, be imposed with the force of law, instead of being simply based upon informal undertakings. This informal health procedure also proved very successful in rehabilitating many sick doctors.

Another important development arising out of initiatives taken by myself with Tony (later Sir Anthony) Grabham, then Chairman of the BMA Council, was to establish, by agreement with the profession, a national welfare and counselling service for sick doctors. This provided an early warning system by means of which doctors thought to be in danger of developing a health problem which could affect their competence to practise were reported in confidence to a central reference point which could then arrange appropriate management. Some 10–15 doctors a month have been referred to that service during the last few years. Its activities were skilfully and judiciously guided by Professor Kenneth Rawnsley, formerly Professor of Psychiatry in the Welsh National School of Medicine prior to his retirement in 1991 when he was succeeded by Professor Sydney Brandon. That service was clearly effective in reducing the number of doctors subsequently reported to the GMC's health procedures. All of these procedures seem to me to have made a major contribution to the GMC's principal role of protecting patients and have also been most effective in improving the profession's management of sick colleagues.

During my presidency I became increasingly aware that in the case of several doctors brought before the Conduct Committee the problem seemed not to be one of serious professional misconduct but rather one of incompetence or poor professional performance. I therefore floated the idea that the GMC should consider establishing a mechanism to deal with doctors who were practising at a level which their peers would regard as unsatisfactory. I believe that this issue of professional performance is now under careful scrutiny by the GMC. I hope that my tentative suggestions made a few years ago will be followed by formal action, with the agreement of the profession. Society must be assured that the profession will take action against those of its number who are performing less than satisfactorily. This is an inevitable corollary in my view of the principle of professsional self-regulation.

As President, I enjoyed seven exciting years. Especially memorable was the magnificent banquet we gave in 1983 at the Royal College of Physicians of London to celebrate the 125th anniversary of the establishment of the Council and at which Mr William Whitelaw (later Lord Whitelaw), then Lord President of the Council, spoke. Mr Norman (later Sir Norman) Fowler, Secretary of State for Health, and many other dignitaries were present. But perhaps my most treasured memories are of the relationship I enjoyed with so many members, both medical and lay. I cannot speak too highly of my senior colleagues and chairmen of committees, including my fellow preliminary screeners, John Fry and later Robin Steel, Philip Connell and later Neil Kessel, John Fry and Bert Duthie as the joint Treasurers, Arthur Crisp, Sir Robert Kilpatrick and David Shaw as chairmen of the Education Committee, Sir Robert who followed me as chairman of the Health Committee and Tony Allibone who succeeded him, and Sir David Innes Williams as the indefatigable chairman of the Overseas Committee. His advocacy for the principle, now approaching fruition, that we should move towards one form of registration for all overseas doctors was powerfully and successfully argued. The Committee on Professional Ethics and Standards of Practice (the 'Standards' Committee for short) was skilfully chaired latterly by Donald Irvine (see below) and the panels of the Conduct Committee were in the safe hands of Bert Duthie and David Bolt.

I mentioned earlier the crucial role played by the lay members of Council. Every one of them who served on the Council in my time made a significant contribution to our debates and to our affairs. Although Jean Robinson, that powerful advocate of the patient and of 'consumer's rights', and I often crossed swords during her frequent interventions in debate, we all recognized that her intentions were of the best. However her unrelenting efforts to be the voice of public conscience at times seemed to take her 'over the top' with what seemed to many medical members to be extravagant attacks on the medical profession and some of its most cherished principles and procedures. Nevertheless, her case was always well argued and presented with force and clarity. Quieter and more reflective were the contributions of Professor Harry Kay, a former professor of psychology and Vice-Chancellor of the University of Exeter, whom I had come to know well when we served together on the MRC. His judgement seemed to me to be impeccable and his stance entirely reasonable, as was that adopted by Arthur Taylor, a Newcastle solicitor and Chairman of the Newcastle Health Authority who had also been Chairman of the National Association of Health Authorities. Arthur was also a long-term personal friend, but I am sure that our friendship never swayed his judgement and he could be critical of the Council's stance, both from the legal standpoint and from the point of view of a lay health service administrator, if he thought that our proposals were flawed. He, like the Revd Frank Smith, a minister of religion from Scotland, proved to be invaluable and statesmanlike on the Conduct Committee. Dame Catherine Hall, a senior and distinguished nurse, was also a tower of strength whenever we were faced with having to make difficult and testing decisions. Both in Council itself and on the Preliminary Proceedings and Standards Committees we came to rely heavily upon the legal wisdom and balanced approach of Professor Ian Kennedy.

Donald Irvine, who many years earlier had been senior house officer in neurology on Ward 6 at the RVI in Newcastle, subsequently became a general practitioner in Ashington. Northumberland, and rose through the ranks of his Royal College to become its Chairman of Council. During my presidency when Donald chaired the Standards Committee, and found as I did that Alan Kershaw's drafting assistance was invaluable, we introduced innumerable modifications to the Council's 'blue book' on professional conduct and discipline. For example, we gave new advice on standards of medical care and on confidentiality to medical authors, and attempted to define good standards of medical practice, departure from which might give rise to a charge of serious professional misconduct. We also handled many pressing ethical issues, including problems relating to abortion and the offering of advice on contraception, etc., to young people under the age of 16. Here we came into conflict to some extent with the BMA and with the formidable Mrs Victoria Gillick, who had brought a case against a health authority in the hope of proving that it would be illegal to offer advice on contraception to a girl under that age. After her case had proceeded as far as the House of Lords, where ultimately the appeal went against her, the Standards Committee formulated, and the Council accepted, advice to the profession. This said that a doctor could offer advice on abortion and/or contraception to a young person under the age of 16 and would normally be expected to preserve total confidentiality with his or her patient unless, in line with the House of Lords judgement, the doctor concluded that the young person to whom advice was being given was insufficiently mature or capable of understanding all of the implications of the situation. Only in the latter event would it be proper to disclose the advice to a parent or guardian, having first notified the patient that the doctor intended to do so and having made every possible effort to persuade her or him to inform the parents. In that respect we came into conflict with the BMA who took the view that confidentiality was paramount; nevertheless the Council's advice was ultimately promulgated and still stands.

Conflict with the BMA and with the Royal Colleges also arose in relation to the advice given to the profession over testing for HIV infection where, after taking skilled legal advice, the Standards Committee and Council ultimately concluded that such testing could and should only be undertaken with the explicit consent of the patient. We realized that many tests, including those for syphilis, etc., had been done on blood samples obtained from innumerable patients without such consent. Nevertheless, there were special circumstances relating to the new problem of HIV infection and AIDS which convinced us that we must confirm the legal view that to carry out any procedure on a patient without explicit consent could be interpreted as an assault and could not therefore be condoned in the Council's ethical advice to the profession. Whereas a number of caveats and riders were added to that general advice, here again it is my understanding that the Council's advice still stands. Many more sensitive problems were examined during my term of office and we held innumerable consultations with representatives of the profession and other bodies.

We also continued with our annual educational conferences, interspersed with others where the Council itself examined its own disciplinary and other procedures; we lunched government ministers, dined presidents of Colleges and entertained medical journalists. Indeed we tried to expose the Council's affairs more openly in the public and political arenas, while also striving to preserve our independence and authority as the statutory body responsible for the regulation of the profession. Since I retired, the Council has been under further attack, even from some government ministers who feel that it remains far too aloof and detached from public opinion. If and when the Medical Act is revised, there are several changes which the Council itself would wish to see in relation to registration and health and, for example, it seems possible that the number of lay members may be increased yet further. My personal belief is, as Lord Hailsham said, that self-regulation of the professions is one of the most cherished ideals and indeed glories of a free society. Professor Ralf Dahrendorf (later, on assuming British nationality, Sir Ralf) in his Jephcott Lecture to the Royal Society of Medicine pointed out a few years ago that the alternative of regulation by the State is fearful; he spoke with authority, being then a German citizen, as in that country state regulation has created innumerable problems.

One great advantage of the presidency was the availability of our flat in the cul-de-sac at the top end of Hallam Street, a haven to which I could retreat during and after Council meetings and in which Betty and I enjoyed innumerable happy interludes. Several times each year we entertained Council members, staff and guests to drinks, usually before going on to our dinners at the Apothecaries' Hall, but sometimes on other occasions as well and invariably just before Christmas. As GMC President I was often invited, along with Betty, to attend, and all too often to speak at dinners of Royal Colleges, Faculties and other bodies; these commitments made the possession of a comfortable London flat even more of a godsend.

Perhaps one of the most notable invitations I received was to dine with the Irish Medical Council in 1985 after it had been functioning for only a few years, having broken away from the GMC under the 1978 Medical Act. I was comfortably accommodated overnight at the Shelbourne Hotel and particularly recall the sumptuous repast set before us. There were seven courses, each accompanied by suitable liquid refreshment. I cannot recall before or since having a meal which included smoked salmon, soup and another fish course, which was then followed by roast pheasant and a second main course with saddle of lamb, before we moved on to sweet, dessert and cheese. Being the guest speaker, I strove to be as abstemious as possible (at least until I had spoken), but as I walked the relatively short distance to my hotel at a pretty late hour feeling especially benign, I realized that my gait might have been construed by a neurological colleague as being not entirely normal.

These were stimulating if demanding years; I was increasingly aware, as my seven-year presidency wore on, that the demands upon my time were growing steadily. In my last two years, when the Council had established a working party to examine its future structure and procedures, I was able to calculate that despite my continuing responsibilities as Warden of Green College, which I hope and believe I was still fulfilling effectively, I was devoting not less than 40–45 hours weekly (including evenings and weekends) to Council business; in effect, the presidency had become a whole-time job. But my path was smoothed throughout by the quite extraordinary dedication and efficiency of the two successive Registrars, Martin Draper and Peter Towers, by their successive capable secretaries and by the Council's superb staff. As the time of my retirement approached, I recognized how wise the Council had been to decide that no President would serve for more than seven years (I was beginning to feel just a hint of battle-weariness). Betty and I decided to give a farewell drinks party to all of the staff at the Council's premises; we were deeply touched when they presented us with a set of delightful crystal wine glasses which we shall always treasure.

The election to choose my successor was, as always, a nail-biting affair in which Sir Robert Kilpatrick emerged as the Council's clear choice as its next President. With more than a hint of sadness, we drove up to London one weekend to remove our personal belongings from the flat so that Robert and his delightful wife, Elizabeth, could move in a few days later. We took a last nostalgic look around the Council's premises and Betty painted from the visitors' gallery a picture of the Council chamber which now hangs proudly in my study at Norham Gardens. Fortunately, having been persuaded by the family to have armorial bearings prepared, David Eldred had no problem about displaying my coat of arms on the stained glass window in the Council chamber, but there remained the question of a portrait. When we had all the problems over Bob Wright's portrait, Betty cheerfully said to me one day in Newcastle that just in case this kind of thing happened again, she intended to have my portrait painted in oils before we left Newcastle. After making innumerable enquiries, we eventually commissioned Stephen Rowe, an extraordinary young man, principal lecturer in art at the Newcastle Polytechnic, to undertake the task, which he did after several sittings and after taking innumerable photographs. We all liked the portrait but, as it was rather large, Betty suggested that we might donate it to the GMC if the Council would agree to have a smaller version painted, again by Stephen Rowe, which the family could keep. That smaller copy now hangs in Norham Gardens and although it is a good likeness, it is not, in my view or Betty's, quite as good as the original which now hangs in the Council chamber in Hallam Street. At the Council dinner in the Great Hall at St Bartholomew's Hospital in May 1989, three months after my retirement, Betty and I, along with John and Sybil Richardson, were guests. Robert Kilpatrick kindly presented John and me each with a medallion prepared as a copy of the presidential badge of office which I had had made and had presented to the Council shortly after my election, as I felt it would be useful for future Presidents to have an identifying badge to wear at formal dinners and on other appropriate occasions. I am glad to know that my distinguished successor continues to wear it, as he tells me, with pride.

The British Medical Association

My involvement with the BMA had begun when I was an officer of the BMSA as a medical student and later when I served two terms as Chairman of the Registrars' Group, representing the junior doctors. I had joined the Association immediately on qualification, and although there were times when I had found myself not totally in harmony with its policy, I believe that I have been a loyal member ever since. Perhaps the moment when I became most disenchanted was in the mid-1970s when, because of conflict with Government over issues relating to the NHS, the BMA Council had recommended that the profession embark upon a programme of industrial action in order to apply pressure. I was so incensed by this decision that I wrote a letter to *The Times* dissociating myself from the proposed action and expressing the view that no learned profession should ever contemplate taking an action which could only harm, however indirectly, those (namely our patients) whom we had been trained to serve. Predictably, the BMA response was hostile and I received a very strong letter from my old friend Clifford Astley, Chairman of the Central Consultants and Specialists Committee (or perhaps it had then become the Central Committee for Hospital Medical Services, only reverting to its former title in the 1990s) who castigated me for this expression of open defiance. He said that it was quite improper for me to write to the press and indicated that I should have written to the Chairman of Council expressing my views rather than to expose them publicly. I had not realized that my letter had had such an impact until in 1978 my good friend Stephen Lock, editor of the *British Medical Journal* for which I had been writing leading articles and annotations over the years, telephoned and asked whether I could possibly find time to visit him while I was in London for a confidential chat. When we met, Stephen said, a little hesitantly, that he wished to discuss a sensitive and confidential matter with me. He said that, as I probably knew, the BMA would be holding its annual Representative Body meeting in Newcastle in 1980. I told him that I was, of course, aware of this, even though for some years I had not been intimately involved in BMA activities, either locally or nationally, solely because of pressure of time. I had attended, whenever I could, meetings of the North of England Branch and of the Newcastle Division and had been for a time Student Secretary of that Division, but had been compelled to refuse the chairmanship of the Division more than once because of other commitments. In retrospect, one of my few significant actions in the Newcastle BMA was to nominate

Lionel Kopelowitz, a Newcastle GP whom I had come to know well, for membership of the Executive Committee. Lionel subsequently became much involved in BMA affairs, being elected to Council and later to the GMC. He serves with distinction as the President of the Board of Deputies of British Jews and often says, even publicly, that I was responsible for involving him in medical politics in the first place.

Following his opening preamble, Stephen went on to say (and the news came as quite a surprise) that there was strong local support for a proposal that when the Association met in Newcastle, I should be nominated as President. He hastened to add that there was strong central support as well, but that as I was known to be a man of strong views, the Council wished to be assured that if I were elected, I would be unlikely to come out with any powerful anti-BMA statements publicly. Clearly they remembered my letter. My reaction was one of amusement because, as I told Stephen, I would not under any circumstances, if elected to a position of authority, defy openly the organization's democratically agreed policy but would nevertheless reserve the right to express my opposition to any policy with which I disagreed in its inner counsels. Stephen and his colleagues on Council seemed to find this answer reassuring and I was therefore nominated. The presidency of the BMA is a very different office from that of the GMC. Whereas the GMC President has powerful executive powers and is the Council's chief officer, the BMA's President is more like a constitutional monarch. While he or she is a chief officer, the President is expected to stand aloof from politics. The policy-making body of the BMA is the Representative Body (the RB, the Association's parliament) which meets only once a year, and its chairman is nominally the head of the BMA's policy-making team. In effect, however, the Chairman of Council probably has greater power as the BMA Council meets monthly; its elected chairmanship has usually rotated as a matter of convention (though never laid down as formal policy) between a general practitioner and a hospital consultant or other specialist. The other chief officers are the Secretary (a whole-time employee of the Association), the Honorary Treasurer and the Editor of the *British Medical Journal*. While he or she serves as a member of this group, which meets regularly, the President's prime responsibility is to represent the Association in other fora or on social occasions such as the dinners, etc., of other organizations. Nevertheless the President is a member of Council and he or she may intervene, and indeed should intervene, in debates about important issues. Certainly there have been times when a touch on the tiller from the President may have prevented the Association from adopting policies which could have been injudicious or even conceivably harmful. However, if policies are agreed upon with which the President disagrees but are adhered to by the RB and by Council, their views invariably prevail. During my presidency, when the Association was served by such outstanding chief officers as Dr Brian Lewis and Dr John Marks as successive Chairmen of the Representative Body, Mr (later Sir) Anthony Grabham as Chairman of Council, Dr Jack Miller as Honorary Treasurer, Dr John Havard as Secretary and Dr Stephen Lock as Editor of the *BMJ*, the Association adopted a series of attitudes and policies with which I found myself in virtually complete agreement; there were no occasions I can recall when any serious differences of opinion emerged.

No sooner had my forthcoming presidency been agreed than we had to get together with colleagues in the Newcastle Division to begin planning for the great event in July 1980. Two years ahead we booked the Civic Centre as the obvious location for the meeting, arranging that the RB would meet in its magnificent stone-lined banqueting hall, while various committees would occupy offices else-where in the building. The local organizing committee was chaired by Dr J. S. (Stanley) Comaish, a noted consultant dermatologist, who recruited a most able team of members, aided by the very efficient staff of the BMA's Regional Office in Windsor Terrace. Betty realized that it would be improper for her, as President's Lady, to be chairman of the ladies' committee but was delighted when she was able to persuade Betty Tomlinson (wife of our old friend, Bernard) to accept that arduous responsibility. All of us (including the two Bettys) went, therefore, for a couple of days to Liverpool to attend the 1979 ARM so as to soak up the atmosphere and to learn something of the organizational problems we would face next year. We much enjoyed seeing Dame Josephine Barnes installed as the first female President of the Association and returned to Newcastle full of ideas about what we might arrange. As the Civic Centre banqueting hall was to be used all week as a meeting hall for the ARM, we booked the City Hall as the venue for the Adjourned Annual General Meeting on the Thursday evening, at which I would be required to deliver my presidential address and at which, in accordance with custom, new Fellows of the BMA would be presented to the President, as would visiting representatives of other associations from around the world. Sadly, the City Hall organ, which Betty had often played in earlier years, was suffering from terminal decay as the City had not been able to find the funds to refurbish it. Hence we had to hire an electronic organ to produce music with which to soothe the assembled company while awaiting the arrival of the formal procession. This was played by Dr Wright, Lecturer in Anatomy and the regular organist at St Thomas' Church.

When the BMA met for two weeks 23 years earlier in Newcastle, I, as local scientific secretary, was involved only with the scientific meeting and not with that of the RB, which then met in the City Hall. Some years later the Association decided to separate the ARM and the scientific meeting and from the late 1960s the latter had been held at a different time of year in another location (in alternate years overseas). Never having attended the whole of an ARM before I was greatly impressed by the quality of the planning and organization. The meeting itself was splendidly chaired by the ebullient Brian Lewis (almost a Henry Miller look-alike, with the same irreverence and spontaneous, if at times inappropriate, wit) with John Marks as his deputy. Motion after motion was debated, some being passed and thereby becoming Association policy, others being referred for further consideration by Council and yet others being rejected. Maiden speakers were invariably given careful and respectful attention, but old hands would often arouse loud acclamation or equally loud condemnation. The indefatigable Jane Richards bustled backwards and forwards as chairman of the Agenda Committee, skilfully manipulating the continual rearrangements of the agenda which became necessary. All in all, despite the demagoguery which was inevitably flaunted at times, I found my exposure to the doctors' parliament fascinating, even though I felt that the emotional atmosphere which often pervaded the proceedings resulted in the passage of resolutions which in a calmer atmosphere would have been unlikely to prevail. Often Council later found some simple, or perhaps more often devious, method of circumventing such unsatisfactory expressions of Association policy.

Fortunately the Newcastle weather was exceptionally kind. On Sunday evening, 6 July, after most of the BMA dignitaries, staff and delegates had arrived, Betty and I entertained 60 or 70 of our old friends and colleagues to drinks at Beechfield Road. Fortunately we could use the garden on what proved to be a balmy evening and the university staff helped with the catering in their typically efficient way. On Monday evening we all marched in procession in academic dress for the church service in St Nicholas' Cathedral where the President, Dame Josephine Barnes, read one lesson and I, as President-elect, another. The organ and choral music were superb, the Bishop of Newcastle, the Rt. Revd. Ronald Bowlby (later Bishop of Southwark) preached superbly, and indeed Newcastle did us proud. The ARM had been deftly opened that morning by the Lord Mayor, Councillor Kerrigan, and after the church service we had a splendid Civic Reception at the Laing Art Gallery with some typical Geordie entertainment. Tuesday evening saw the annual representatives' dinner dance at the Gosforth Park Hotel, marred only slightly by a somewhat over-long speech by Brian Lewis who began wittily and entertainingly, as he always did, in Henry Miller style, but then overdid his message, just as Henry himself had done on a number of occasions in the past. He regaled the assembled company with indelicate extracts from the BMA's family doctor booklet on *Getting Married*, directing his remarks to Lionel Kopelowitz, a long-term bachelor who had only recently been married for the first time. It could all have been splendid and some of it was very funny indeed, but dear Brian did unfortunately go a little 'over the top'.

As at all BMA meetings, I chaired the Christian Medical Fellowship breakfast and introduced it with the BMA's traditional grace. We had a splendid talk on medical ethics by Vice-Admiral Sir James Watt, a Newcastle graduate and former Director-General of the Naval Medical Services. I also opened the trade exhibition in the basement of the Civic Centre at which innumerable drug companies, medical instrument and equipment manufacturers, booksellers and others, as always on these occasions, displayed their wares. Being in the same building as the ARM and dispensing a regular quota of coffee and other refreshment, the trade exhibition was very well patronized by the representatives during breaks from the formal business. On the Wednesday afternoon I chaired a scientific symposium on 'Doctors in Society', while some more intent on exercise played in the annual BMA golf competition at Gosforth Park, organized (inevitably) by Jack Foster. On Wednesday evening, representatives were offered a choice of chamber music in King's Hall or a mediaeval banquet at Seaton Delaval; it says a good deal for the catholic tastes of the BMA representatives that both were over-subscribed. Betty and I went to the concert.

Thursday evening saw us all resplendent in dinner jackets with decorations and full academic dress at the City Hall. Happily, I had been able to persuade the University that it would be appropriate to begin that evening's events with an honorary degree congregation at which an honorary Doctorate of Civil Law was conferred by the Chancellor, the Duke of Northumberland, upon my old friend and mentor, Sir John Richardson, former President of the BMA and only recently retired from the GMC presidency; an honorary Doctorate of Surgery was conferred upon another past President, Sir John Peel, and an honorary Doctorate of Medicine upon the Association's former Secretary, Dr Elston Grey-Turner, whose father, Professor George Grey-Turner, had been professor of surgery in Newcastle before moving to Hammersmith. Elston had spent his childhood in the city and had been educated at the Royal Grammar School before studying medicine in Cambridge and London. The Adjourned Annual General Meeting followed at which I was invested with the President's badge of office by Jo Barnes and Betty received the President's Lady's badge from her daughter in front of a very large audience of University staff as well as members of the BMA. I then, in a state of acute anxiety, delivered my presidential address, to which even the Duke seemed to listen attentively. I reviewed some of my work on neuromuscular disease and also commented upon certain problems that I had encountered in the University world and NHS, while presenting what I felt were reasonable hopes for the future. We then walked in warm twilight to the University Refectory for the Presidential Reception, at which the standard fare is normally sparkling white wine and strawberries and cream. However, we had previously decided that as no-one would have had time to eat before the ceremonies, we should provide an extensive cold buffet in addition to the traditional items. As my presidential party with the honorary graduates and university dignitaries, including the Chancellor, were the last to leave the City Hall, we were virtually the only people attending the reception who could not find seats in the Refectory. Fortunately, with the aid of George Elliott, we quickly opened up the private dining room (the Alnwick Room) where I had enjoyed so many festive occasions, so that all was well. Next day we were all warmly thanked for providing such an unusual ARM reception which Brian Lewis referred to as 'sitting down hospitality'.

The publicity which surrounded this Newcastle meeting had a considerable impact locally and I was deeply touched to find that next day the *Newcastle Journal* published a leading article inviting me to 'take a bow', not just because of the content of my address but also because of what it regarded as the professional leadership I had given in the city and region. That cutting is now a treasured possession.

As President I was invited to speak at innumerable dinners or to lecture to many Divisions across the country. In February 1983 I was due to address the Halifax, Rotherham and Bradford Divisions on successive nights. The railway drivers were on strike and the country was covered in snow and ice, with temperatures down to $-15\,^{\circ}\text{C}$. We had no alternative but to travel by car; on the morning of our departure two radiators in Beechfield Road were stone cold and a pipe beneath the floor was plainly frozen. Betty, bless her, being much slimmer than me crawled between the joists and with an electric hair-dryer unfroze the offending length of pipe (next to an air-brick) just in time for us to leave together.

The BMA presidency is normally a one-year appointment and it had been anticipated that in 1981, when the ARM was to be held in Brighton, I would be succeeded by Lord Smith of Marlow, latterly Sir Rodney Smith and former President of the Royal College of Surgeons. He in turn was due to hand over the presidency to His Royal Highness the Prince of Wales in 1982, the BMA's 150th anniversary year. My year seemed to be passing by all too quickly, with a symposium in Birmingham, attendance at the meeting of the Junior Members Forum in Worcester, regular attendances whenever I could at meetings of chief officers and of Council in London, and the inevitable round of dinners. One highlight was a dinner of the Medical Society of London, chaired by Sir James Watt, its President, in the Great Hall at St Bartholomew's Hospital, at which we were invited before dinner to join with other principal guests and to meet His Royal Highness the Duke of Edinburgh who was guest of honour. He glanced at the chain of office around my neck and inquired what it was. When I told him that it was the BMA presidential badge which he himself had worn some 20 years earlier, he remembered it at once. He then asked Betty about the badge that she was wearing, to which she responded that it was the President's Lady's. Possibly with a suppressed twinkle in the eye, he said 'Ah, they didn't have that in my day'; of course they had, but its existence was quietly concealed as it would clearly have been inappropriate to invite Her Majesty to wear the lesser insignia! Later, through the good offices of Sir Ronald Gardner-Thorpe, Lord Mayor of London, whose son Christopher had been my senior registrar in Newcastle, we were able to attend in November the annual Lord Mayor's Banquet at the London Guildhall. This was a glittering occasion only slightly marred by the fact that having arrived early and having found our seats in the reception area, Betty saw to her horror the wife of another guest wearing the identical dress. Fortunately the two ladies were seated a long distance apart and did not subsequently see each other identically attired. The evening was graced by splendid speeches from Robert Runcie, Archbishop of Canterbury, and by the Prime Minister, Margaret Thatcher, who gave her customary compelling 'state of the nation' address. We coped reasonably with the loving cup and were fortunate in sitting next to Sir Nicholas and Lady Goodison whom we had previously met when we had both been guests at a bankers' dinner in Newcastle. Sir Nicholas was then the youngest ever Chairman of the Stock Exchange; he and his wife proved to be exceptionally agreeable company.

As the year wore on, we learned the disturbing news that the President-elect, Rodney Smith, had unfortunately suffered an illness which had severely affected his speech. After much thought and consultation, he and the BMA chief officers decided that it would not be possible for him to assume the presidency, to which he was much looking forward. There followed a round of tortuous consultations of which I was not fully aware, though I had told Tony Grabham and others that if the Association so wished, I would gladly do a second year; Betty willingly concurred as she was greatly enjoying her BMA responsibilities. Eventually the Association decided to invite me to continue, and so in the summer of 1981 we attended our second ARM in Brighton and enjoyed yet another series of delightful events. We were also thrilled to learn that the Association had planned a clinical meeting in San Diego, California, in October of that year, to be jointly hosted by the BMA and by the San Diego Medical Society. Clearly we would now be required to attend and I was also invited to talk at an Anglo-American symposium on illness in doctors and their families. This involved me in a good deal of research but in the end I was glad of it, even during the last few months of my deanship, as the information I gleaned formed the basis of innumerable subsequent lectures which I gave to various medical societies and upon which I eventually based my Harben Lecture to the Royal Institute of Public Health and Hygiene in the late 1980s.

The San Diego meeting was in every sense a delight. The Californian climate was benign, the scientific contributions by British and American participants alike were outstanding and the splendid Town and Country Hotel at which we all stayed in comfort was ideal with a fine range of lecture theatres and seminar rooms. Next door was the Stardust Country Club of which we had honorary membership during the week and where Betty and I enjoyed two excellent rounds of golf. As this was a time when the pound was standing at over two dollars, everything seemed remarkably inexpensive and I even bought a new set of Cobra golf clubs which I still use, paying about $300 (£150) for three woods and a full range of irons. Socially, too, the occasion was memorable; the keynote speaker at our opening ceremony was the great Alistair Cooke who not only gave us a splendid address but who, over dinner that evening, regaled us amusingly with a range of anecdotes and personal experiences which kept the company enthralled. We entertained him, past and present BMA chief officers and some of our American hosts to drinks beforehand in our suite and on its balcony which looked down over one of the several attractive swimming pools in the hotel grounds and where we were bathed in almost ethereal Californian evening sunlight. The only problem about our distinguished guest was that as the evening wore on, it became increasingly clear that he had no intention of going to bed as the wine and conversation flowed. Eventually we succeeded in getting him to his room, still talking enchantingly, at about 2.00 a.m. In our spare time we managed to visit the San Diego Zoo, to look down over the magnificent harbour and even to enjoy a brief foray across the Mexican border to Tijuana. The anti-British activities of a local Irish-American association which attempted to condemn us for our Northern Ireland policy cast only a minor shadow; I was interviewed for local radio along with one of its more outspoken supporters and I believe that in the end honours were even. One exceptional evening foray was to Sea World where we saw a fascinating display by aquatic animals and where Betty, as President's Lady, was pulled out to the front in order to be kissed by the killer whale, Shamu. As she said, the gentle touch upon her cheek was so affectionate that she felt that she would not wish to wash that cheek for several days afterwards. As I mentioned at the following night's dinner, that whale had completely alienated my wife's affections! And as we breakfasted in our room next morning we heard the American commentator on local radio say that the previous night the British Medical Association, some 750 doctors and 350 accompanying persons, went to Sea World and that the killer whale, Shamu, had kissed Lady Walton; that, he said with awe in his voice, was the first time that Shamu had kissed royalty!

The next major event to which we all looked forward was the ARM, adjourned AGM and Presidential Address in 1982 at which, in the Royal Festival Hall, along with the many other celebrations of the BMA's 150th anniversary, I was to hand over the badge of office to His Royal Highness Prince Charles, and Betty, she had hoped, would hand over hers to Princess Diana. However, the news came that Princess Diana would be unable to attend because of her pregnancy, and Prince William was born only a week or so before the ARM. In the meantime, we enjoyed a brief foray to Worcester where Dr Charles Hastings had founded the Association in 1832. An actor, suitably dressed, re-enacted in the Board Room of the Royal Infirmary the establishment of the Provincial Medical and Surgical Society by a group of provincial doctors in opposition to the several medical societies then in existence in the metropolis. That Provincial Society eventually prevailed and out of it grew the national body. Of course we faced the major London event in July with mixed pleasure and apprehension. We had a comfortable suite in the Russell Hotel, where our stay was marred only by the fact that the wife of our friend and long-term BMA activist, Gyels Riddle from Gateshead, had opened her hotel door unsuspectingly in answer to a ring, only to be mugged by an intruder. Fortunately, though bruised, she was not seriously hurt but security was then greatly tightened. We were delighted that all our family, with the exception of our son-in-law, Ian, who was obliged to stay in Geneva for professional reasons, were able to be with us. Ann, Drew and Victoria, Judy, Andrew, Nicholas and Lucy, and Chris and Denise all foregathered in our suite before going on to the Royal Festival Hall for the ceremony. They were given the Royal Box from which they had a splendid view of the academic procession in which I accompanied the Prince of Wales, suitably attired in the gown of the Royal College of Surgeons of England, of which he was an honorary Fellow. The evening went like clockwork; the Prince was charming and shook hands with our entire family as they lined up outside the Royal Box before we processed. My hand-over of the chain of office went smoothly, and Betty, to her everlasting credit, made a charming little speech when she handed over the President's Lady's badge to His Royal Highness, congratulating him upon the birth of his son and hoping that Her Royal Highness would soon be in a position to wear the badge. During the ceremony I also presented the Association with a silver Lindisfarne quaich (traditional drinking vessel) as a token of Northumbrian gratitude for two exceptionally happy presidential years. His Royal Highness gave an excellent and memorable address, notable not least because of his advocacy of complementary medicine, a contribution which certainly resulted in the establishment of a working party by the BMA's Board of Education and Science in order to investigate the place of complementary methods in medical practice. Afterwards we enjoyed a splendid reception in the Festival Hall, marred only by the fact that the rush for refreshment was such as to prevent the waitresses from entering the main reception area with additional items. Unfortunately, in consequence, some of the less rampant members and guests fared rather poorly in the food and drink stakes. We, however, the Prince, chief officers and a few others, ate in an ante-room before joining the throng outside where His Royal Highness was exceptionally gracious in seeking to talk to as many members of the assembled company as he could conceivably manage in the time available. So ended a thoroughly memorable day, of which happily we have a record on videotape which we watch from time to time to remind ourselves of an historic occasion.

Almost as historic was the reception at the Headquarters Officers Mess of the Royal Army Medical Corps at Millbank the next evening, to which the Prince, as President, came, if only briefly. Mrs Grey-Turner presented him with a token of gratitude from the BMA, expressing the hope that the item would be useful to his baby son. When he opened the presentation box and saw inside a silver spoon, suitably engraved, he said 'How splendid. Just what he needed, because he wasn't born with one in his mouth'!

As we now had a royal President, I as immediate past-President enjoyed in some respects a third presidential year, if only because the Prince, in the light of his many other responsibilities, was unable to attend many BMA events in the next 12 months and hence I often deputized for him. Nevertheless, he was assiduous in his attention to such responsibilities as he could fulfil and attended several social occasions, while also arranging a splendid reception for BMA officers and members at Kensington Palace. But as a stand-in I still went to Council whenever I could, despite having now assumed my GMC presidency, and Betty and I attended yet another ARM in Dundee in 1983. There we handed over the presidential insignia to our good friend Ronnie Robertson and his wife, Dorothy, two people whom we admired enormously and whose respective deaths in the last few years have saddened us all. Since then our affection for the BMA and its many officers whom we have admired has led us to attend, whenever we were able, the adjourned AGM and installation of subsequent Presidents. Indeed we greatly enjoyed seeing Professor Arthur Kennedy of Glasgow installed in Inverness in July 1991. One of my most prized possessions is a beautiful crystal decanter upon which has been engraved the BMA crest with an inscription to the effect that it was presented to me at the end of my two-year term of office by my friends on Council. The skilful engraving was executed by that remarkable polymath, Dr Ralph Lawrence, a GP in the Midlands and former Chairman of the BMA's Organization Committee, a man who, with his black skin and pointed beard, as I told him, often reminded me in stature and dignity of the Emperor Haile Selassie.

The Royal Society of Medicine

The next national organization with which I became involved was the Royal Society of Medicine (RSM). I had been a Fellow, on Henry Miller's nomination, since my registrar days and often attended meetings of the Section of Neurology until pressure of other commitments and the expense of the journey from Newcastle to London made my attendance more infrequent. I did, however, continue to use regularly the facilities of the library. Without question, this is one of the most outstanding medical libraries anywhere in the world. Almost invariably when I needed to trace an obscure medical book or paper to help me in my research, the RSM was able to provide it.

Although the Medical Society of London, founded by Dr Henry Lettsom, had been established in 1773 and later acquired premises in the West End which it still occupies, a group of leading London physicians and surgeons, meeting at the Freemasons' Tavern in 1805, agreed to set up 'a society comprehending the several branches of the medical profession . . . for the purpose of conversation on professional subjects, for the reception of communications and for the formation of a library', and the Medical and Chirurgical Society was born. During the next three decades the society expanded and became so important that in 1834 it received from King William IVth a charter of incorporation as the Royal Medical and Chirurgical Society (RMCS) of London. Its object was 'the cultivation and promotion of physic and surgery and of the branches of science connected with them'. From 1834 onwards, many new societies were formed in the metropolis for the promotion of various medical special-ties and several attempts were made by the RMCS to unite these into one comprehensive body. Foremost in these negotiations was Sir William Osler, who achieved his aim and that of many others when in 1907 the merger went through (the Medical Society of London remaining, however, inde-pendent); the Society's name was changed to the Royal Society of Medicine and all the cooperating bodies, of which there were 17, were represented in the reconstituted Society as Sections, each with its own council. Five years later, in 1912, the Society moved into its new home at 1 Wimpole Street.

Over the succeeding 70 and more years, the Society grew steadily. It had some 3,000 members at the time of the amalgamation in 1907 but by 1984 it had 17,000 doctors and scientists drawn from almost every country in the world in its membership. By that time its staff had increased to 130, the 17 Sections had become 33, the 80,000 bound volumes had multiplied six-fold, over 280 Society and Section meetings were held annually and accommodation was offered for about 200 meetings of other societies which did not have their own premises. As many had said before, and as I said subsequently on several public occasions, the Society had thus become the nearest equivalent in Britain to an Academy of Medicine. Its expansion required a substantial increase in accommodation. In 1952/53 and again in 1963 extra storeys were built at Wimpole Street, and in 1964, through the foresight, energy and initiative of the then Executive Director, Richard (Dick) Hewitt, the Society purchased a long lease of Chandos House, a splendid Adam house nearby, and later acquired the head lease, providing in that building the offices of three departments, a library bookstore and the Domus Medica which offered overnight accommodation for members. The elegant public rooms in that listed building were also available for official receptions. While these developments all provided extra space for much of the Society's needs, the original building in

Wimpole Street became increasingly overcrowded and the dispersal of the Society's activities between these two buildings and additional premises leased at Dering Yard off Bond Street in 1945 proved inefficient. It also became abundantly clear that a major refurbishment of the Society's primary home was essential as even the library facilities had become progressively less convenient, the lecture rooms were becoming seriously outdated and the social facilities were also inadequate. In the 1970s there was some growing evidence of diminishing interest on the part of doctors, especially from outside London, in the Society's affairs and the Fellowship began to decline in number. Again through the initiative of Dick Hewitt, the Society, during the 1950s, had sought and finally obtained from Government an undertaking that it would be offered an option to purchase the site of the Western District Post Office immediately adjoining 1 Wimpole Street when it was no longer required for Post Office purposes. That option became available in 1977 and provided a unique opportunity of acquiring land and buildings beside the Society's long-term home in the heart of the West End. It was felt that that acquisition would enable it ultimately to concentrate its activities in one location with accommodation suitable for the needs of the late 20th and 21st centuries.

I had come to know well Sir John Stallworthy who had been President of the Society for two terms from 1973–75 and again from 1980–82 and whose services to the RSM were beyond praise. He had also been one of my predecessors as BMA President and during my term of office had served as Chairman of the BMA's Board of Education and Science. I learned with pleasure from him while attending a dinner of the Medical Society of London, of which Vice-Admiral Sir James Watt was then President, that Sir John had invited Sir James to succeed him as President of the RSM in 1982 and that Sir James had accepted. However, it came as a considerable surprise to me when Sir James then approached me to ask whether I would consider becoming President-elect in 1983, to succeed him in 1984. Having only relatively recently acquired my new and arduous responsibilities as GMC President, I was at first reluctant to consider taking on this additional responsibility. Betty felt even more concerned about the additional load of work which it would involve and about the possibility that it might interfere with my new responsibilities as Warden of Green College. Being aware, however, that we would be living in Oxford from 1983 and that I would have relinquished my major BMA responsibilities, it seemed to me that I might be able to interdigitate my GMC commitments with those of the RSM. Clearly, too, the prospect was interesting and exciting, especially when Sir James told me about the Society's plans for redevelopment of its premises and for its new building on the site of the old Post Office. Hence after several discussions, and not without misgiving, I eventually accepted and became President-elect in summer 1983. That appointment at first involved me in very little personal responsibility, though I became a member of Council and developed an increasing admiration for Sir James. He was a graduate of my own medical school and a distinguished naval surgeon, a man of total integrity, a bachelor, of firm and decisive views, with a life-long and unswerving dedication to his Christian faith. His powerful personality did occasionally convey a hint of rigidity and of reluctance to change his views about decisions which others might challenge but which he firmly believed were right. Nevertheless his uprightness and his total commitment to the responsibilities of his office, which he almost converted into a whole-time job, made him an exceptionally dedicated President.

One of Sir James' major concerns, which I myself shared as soon as I joined the Council, related to the Society's financial position. The purchase of the freehold of the Post Office site, followed by demolition of the old buildings there, had cost the Society nearly £1,500,000. As the facilities offered to Fellows by the Society were becoming inadequate and outdated, Council felt reluctant to increase subscriptions significantly. As a result, despite the profits being made by the publishing division and in some other areas, the Society was in danger of acquiring an increasing financial deficit. In particular, there was concern about continuing losses on catering and certain other activities. Yet another problem arose through the unfortunate serious and lengthy illness of Dick Hewitt's deputy, Robert (Bob) Thomson, who had taken over from him as Executive Director in October 1982. The Society was fortunate that Dick Hewitt, who had served it with great distinction for 30 years and who was continuing to work as part-time consultant to it and to the newly-established RSM Foundation, Inc., in the United States, returned as Acting Executive Director until such time as Bob Thomson was fit to resume office. Dick Hewitt's business acumen and administrative ability were characterized by quiet efficiency and, as Sir James said, by a unique blend of reticence, firmness and graciousness. He it was who initiated the necessary contract through which the Society's existing building would be totally modernized and refurbished and a major extension would be built on the old Post Office site, including two floors of office accommodation available to the developer. The total scheme was estimated to cost about £20,000,000, of which some £17,000,000 was being provided by the developers in return for the use of the site, with the agreement that that portion of the new building to be occupied by the Society would be available at a peppercorn rent.

In late 1983, therefore, after I had been confirmed as President-elect, Sir James invited me to join him in an exercise through which we would arrange to interview senior staff of the Society and would draw up a report relating to its future administration and financial management in order to be prepared for the move into the new building, due to take place in early 1986. We also agreed that in order to raise the £3,000,000 needed, the Society would have to mount a public appeal. Sir John Stallworthy, as past President, graciously agreed to be chairman, with Dick Hewitt as secretary, and an outstanding and distinguished appeal committee was appointed. We also recruited public relations assistance in order to help us and I shall always be grateful to Sir Gordon Reece, former adviser to the Prime Minister, for his invaluable advice and support. The preparation of our lengthy report on future administration and financial management took us some months, but it was presented to Council at the beginning of March 1984. Some temporary difficulties then arose, based upon several misunderstandings since, for reasons which were obscure, Sir James had mistakenly concluded from previous discussions that since on occupying the new building the Society would sell Chandos House and would withdraw from the leased premises in Dering Yard, running costs of the new establishment would be lower than those of the old. Soon it was clear that with the substantial increase in accommodation and facilities in the new and refurbished building this would be out of the question. After 'a frank exchange of views' between Sir James and Dick Hewitt all was soon resolved and an agreed report, welcomed by all, was presented to Council in March 1984. By this time Bob Thomson, fully restored to health, was firing on all cylinders as the new Executive Director, we were becoming increasingly successful in recruiting affiliate members through our contacts with overseas societies and associations (many in the United States which had been identified through the RSM Foundation, Inc.) and our concerns about the prospective financial deficit soon evaporated. We were also fortunate to appoint, through the Society's commercial arm (RSM Services Limited) an outstandingly able head of the Publications Department, Howard Croft, through whose energy the profit made on the Society's publishing activities, previously substantial through the efforts of Mr John Davis, steadily grew even greater. By the time I took over from Sir James in July 1984 the prospects were looking much brighter, though we were by no means out of the wood.

The two years that I spent as President of the RSM were among the most interesting and stimulating of my professional life, which had in any event changed dramatically through my translation to Green College, Oxford (see Chapter 17) and through my increasingly demanding responsibilities with the GMC. Fortunately I found it possible to interdigitate my GMC and RSM activities surprisingly effectively, often through some administrative sleight-of-hand carefully and effectively monitored by my secretary at Green College, Rosemary Allan, who had come with me from Newcastle, by Marion Watson, Bob Thomson's capable secretary at the RSM, and by the successive secretaries who served the Registrar of the GMC. This triumvirate seemed able to manipulate very effectively the complexities of my diary. And the availability of our GMC flat made it much easier for Betty and me to attend evening engagements in London, while the comfortable presidential offices which I occupied both at the GMC and at the RSM,

with dictating machines in each location, eased my growing administrative .
burden.

The redevelopment programme proceeded remarkably well and we were able to move into much of the new building in May 1985, in order to allow the reconstruction and refurbishment of the old building to take place. A splendid reception, attended by innumerable Fellows, past Presidents, previous officers, staff and members of the Appeal Committee was held to mark the completion of the new building in June 1985. Shortly before, when my old friend and colleague Professor Roger Gilliatt from the National Hospital, Queen Square, was President of the Section of Neurology, I invited him after a meeting of the Section to have a preview of the new building. He, like everyone who saw the magnificence of the entrance hall, of the splendid conservatory, the dining-room, cloakrooms and other facilities, was enormously impressed. He remarked in passing, as we entered the splendid new premises, that he wondered where the Society had chosen to hang the portrait of his father, the former royal obstetrician, Sir William Gilliatt, a past President of the Society. He had pondered whether his father, as a life-long teetotaller, would have been hung in the bar, and so it proved! Quickly I arranged for him to be transferred to the common room and to be replaced in the bar by the portrait of another distinguished President, Sir Terence Cawthorne, the great ear, nose and throat surgeon, who we both agreed would feel perfectly at home there. All of his friends and admirers were deeply saddened to learn of Roger's premature death in the United States in August 1991.

Speaking of Roger Gilliatt's presidency of the Section of Neurology brings to mind a personal experience which was annoying at the time but very amusing in retrospect. Roger was due to give his presidential address on the first Thursday in January 1985. As a long-term friend and colleague and as the current President of the Society I felt that I must certainly be there. This was, however, a week that we had planned to spend at Detchant. In those days whenever we went to Detchant at New Year we hired a car from a firm in Berwick-upon-Tweed in order to avoid the long drive to and from the north in wintry conditions. I had hired a white Vauxhall Cavalier from Blackburn & Price and drove it to the station at lunch-time on the Thursday to catch a train from Berwick to London. This got me there in good time for Roger's splendid address and the dinner which followed. Sleepers were still running to Berwick and I travelled back on the night sleeper which unfortunately compelled one to be disgorged on to the station platform at the uncomfortable early-morning hour of 5.30 a.m. As luck would have it, it was an exceptionally cold and frosty morning with a covering of snow. As I pulled my wits together it occurred to me at once that the locks on the car would probably be frozen and that I might have difficulty in opening it. I therefore emerged, shivering, from the station and went straight to the white car ahead of me in the car-park and found to my consternation, though not to my surprise, that I was unable to insert the key into the lock. I blew on the locks at both sides, I warmed them with my hands, I tried the key in the boot. Eventually, after about 10 minutes, in some despair I recruited the help of the owner of the station bookstall who had just taken delivery of the morning papers and who was boiling a kettle to make a cup of tea. After he had done so, I borrowed the kettle and poured hot water over the locks on both sides, again without being able to gain entry. In dismay, I went to the pay telephone nearby and rang Betty in Detchant, 12 miles away, at about 6.00 a.m. explaining why I was late as I knew that she was expecting me. As I returned to the car, the man from the bookstall came out to see if I had made progress, and when I told him that I had not, he said 'That's not a Blackburn & Price car'. To my consternation, I discovered that I had been attempting to open a white Ford Sierra, whereas my hired car, the white Vauxhall Cavalier, was standing about 50 yards away; the key slipped into the lock without difficulty and I drove away feeling very foolish.

Betty and I have many happy memories of those two presidential years, during which she was a wonderful support and regularly displayed her considerable skills as a hostess. She has always been better than I in achieving rapport with people from all echelons of society, from past Presidents and officers through staff of all grades, including Marion Watson, Miss Teague of Catering and her right-hand man, Len, with whom she developed a cheerful and friendly relationship. It was customary for the President to invite speakers to come as guests to the quarterly Council dinners. In January 1985 my old friend from Spennymoor Grammar School, Sir Percy Cradock, formerly Her Majesty's Ambassador in Peking, came with his wife and told us about the recent negotiations in which he had been involved relating to the return of Hong Kong to China. Our good friend Sir Richard Attenborough, with his wife Sheila, joined us in April and talked movingly and amusingly about making movies, with particular reference to the making of his epic Oscar-winning film on Gandhi. In January 1986 we were entertained by Sir Zelman Cowen who, with his wife Anna, we had come to know well through his Provostship of Oriel College in Oxford. He described his experiences as Governor-General of Australia. I shall always remember, too, Sir Zelman's reaction on walking into our brand-new building for the first time. Quite spontaneously, he looked around in amazement at all of its glories and said 'My first reaction on coming into this building was "Good God, I'm dead, and I've made it" '! In April of that year (when we had our longstanding friends, Henry and Kay Barnett from London, Ontario, with us as guests) Sir Cyril Clarke, former President of the Royal College of Physicians of London, addressed us about butterflies and gave us a demonstration of mating between two of them. As I said later, it was not often that a Council dinner was followed by a public pornographic display in the Society's hallowed premises.

One major annual event of the Society's year is the Stevens Lecture to the Laity, very generously endowed by Edwin and Kathleen Stevens, whom we came to know and admire. Edwin invented and marketed the first fully effective hearing aid and subsequently devoted much of his not inconsiderable fortune to supporting good causes, including the RSM (one of his favourites) and his former college, Jesus College in Oxford. Two notable Stevens Lectures were given during my presidency, both by distinguished Oxford figures, the first by Lord Franks on 'The shaping of the world we live in', in which he shared with us some of his experiences in the diplomatic service (he became Her Majesty's Ambassador in Washington before returning to Oxford to head Worcester College). The second was given by my predecessor as Warden of Green College, Sir Richard Doll, On 'Cancer: a preventable disease'. Other lectures which also stand out in the memory were the Jephcott Lecture given in 1983 on 'A defence of the British professions' by Ralf Dahrendorf, and that delivered in 1985 by Lord Robens on 'Britain's potential for wealth creation'. Also memorable was the Lloyd Roberts Lecture in December 1985 by Baroness Warnock, who shared with us her experiences of 'Another 10 years in education' and fired off some trenchant criticisms of current trends in the British educational system.

Another of Dick Hewitt's major initiatives had been the establishment in 1967, with a number of American colleagues, of the RSM Foundation, Inc., in New York. Art Mahon, an outstanding lawyer from the firm of Mudge Rose in New York had by this time kindly accepted chairmanship of its Board, to which many men and women notable in medicine and in public life in the United States were recruited, including such notable medical figures as Dr Purnell Choppin (now Director of the Howard Hughes Foundation), Dr Jerry Barondess (now President of the New York Academy of Medicine) and Professor Alick Bearn (an emigré Englishman who had been Professor of Medicine at the Rockefeller University and later became Medical Director of Merck Sharp and Dohme (USA)). The Foundation was very successful in establishing and funding visiting professor programmes for distinguished Americans to come to Britain and also for UK doctors and scientists to travel in the opposite direction. Many US pharmaceutical companies, trusts and foundations approached by our distinguished Board members helped to raise the funds to further this programme, while at the same time approaches to American medical societies throughout the country enabled us to recruit affiliates, each of whom paid a subscription to the RSM in return for access to the Society's premises when visiting the UK and the right to use the Domus Medica, the library and other facilities. These activities steadily improved the

Society's financial position. Eventually premises were found for the Foundation at 7 East 60th Street, New York, in the splendid building of the Metropolitan Club, and William O'Reilly, an emigré Australian, was appointed as its first full-time Executive Director in April 1985. It was my pleasure as President to travel twice a year to meetings of the Board with Bob Thomson and we stayed in the magnificent home of the University Club, of which Bob had become a member, and to which he introduced me as a guest. These visits enabled me to make many valuable professional contacts with US colleagues. We were particularly pleased when, in order to honour Dick Hewitt's outstanding contributions to the Society and to the Foundation, Smith Kline & French generously agreed to fund a major Richard T. Hewitt Award which would be presented every two years to an individual who had made an outstanding positive contribution to the betterment of human health. The first such award in 1984 was divided equally between Group Captain Leonard Cheshire, VC, OM (now Lord Cheshire) in acknowledgement of his work in establishing the network of Cheshire Homes in the UK, and Dr Howard Rusk, who had been an outstanding US figure in the development of rehabilitation services for the disabled. The awards were presented by me at a memorable dinner at the Helmsley Palace Hotel in New York. Then in July 1986 we held another such event at the Royal College of Obstetricians & Gynaecologists in London and presented the award to Dr D.A. Henderson, formerly from the Center for Disease Control at Atlanta, Georgia, who had played a crucial rôle in the World Health Organization programme of banishing smallpox from the world.

I was also delighted to be able to confer Honorary Fellowships of the Society upon Professor Sir Stanley Clayton, Dr Charles Drake (my old friend the neurosurgeon from London, Ontario), the Revd Gordon Dunstan (for his work in medical ethics) Dr Louis Forman, Sir Desmond Pond, Professor J. Goligher, Professor N.F. MacLagan, Professor Donald Court (my long-time friend and former professor of paediatrics from Newcastle) and Mr Harold Ridley; not least, it was a particular pleasure to confer this honour on Dick Hewitt himself. I also came to know well through the appeal Lord (Edwin) McAlpine of Moffat, whom we elected to the Society's Court of Benefactors, along with a number of other major contributors.

Several other important initiatives begun before I became President continued to mature. Thus we had felt for some time that in addition to the meetings of Sections, some of which continued to thrive while others were less well attended, there would be some justification in establishing under the auspices of the Society several Forums (the Society resisted my expression of concern over the Anglicized version and refused to accept that we should revert to the proper Latin 'fora'), involving multidisciplinary meetings on several topics. Inaugural meetings were held between 1984 and 1986 of Forums on Medical Communication, on Food and Health, on Lipids in Clinical Medicine, and on Sexual Medicine and Family Planning. One which caused some difficulty was the Forum on Maternity and the Newborn, as this was the era during which the case of Mrs Wendy Savage, who had been suspended from her consultant/ senior lecturer appointment at the London Hospital, was hitting the headlines. The Society was criticized for persuading those organizing the Forum to postpone a meeting which they had planned in order to discuss the implications of that case. I made that decision solely because the date which had been chosen for an open discussion proved to be just a few days before the start of a formal inquiry established by the District Health Authority to examine the implications of the case. The meeting was eventually held after that inquiry had been completed but before its findings were published. The Society and I as President were criticized in the medical press for what some regarded as our ambivalent or obstructive attitude towards this meeting, which was intended to facilitate open discussion of all of the implications of the case. In the end, I was compelled to write an explanatory letter to *The Lancet* on 3 May 1986; soon, however, the furore settled down and, as everyone now knows, Mrs Savage was eventually reinstated.

One other unfortunate problem cast something of a cloud upon my presidency. Dr Victor Bloom had served for several years as editor of the *Journal of the Royal Society of Medicine*, but for a variety of reasons it had become clear in 1984 and 1985 that his personal style was causing some administrative problems. After much discussion in the Scientific and Executive Committee and later in Council, and after extensive discussions with Victor himself and with the honorary officers, it was eventually decided that Dr Bloom's contract as editor would be terminated on 8 July 1985, to be effective from 9 January 1986. Unfortunately some Section Presidents and editorial representatives concluded that through executive action the editorial freedom of Dr Bloom as editor of the Society's journal was being constrained. It was even suggested that responsibility for the editorial content of Society publications was being assumed by its Executive. I was glad to write an open letter to all members of Council, Section Presidents and others in July 1985 to the effect that the editor of the Journal must have total freedom in all editorial matters, subject only to advice from the Honorary Editors and the Editorial Board. It was made plain that differences of opinion between the Society and Dr Bloom, which had become irreconcilable, were concerned solely with administrative as distinct from editorial matters. In the end, a mutually satisfactory agreement with Dr Bloom was concluded and Professor Tony Harding Rains was identified as his successor. An opportunity was then taken to restructure and redesign the format of the Journal, which has continued to prosper under its new editor. Nevertheless, 'the Dr Bloom affair' caused me and the other Honorary Officers considerable anxiety and brought us temporarily into conflict with some officers of Sections, which happily I was able to resolve after much frank discussion of all of the issues involved. We were also able to satisfy some Fellows about criticisms which had been voiced relating to editorial supervision of the International Congress and Symposium Series published by the Society. New mechanisms for the administrative and editorial control of that series were introduced which seem to have worked well. Since relinquishing my presidency and since my retirement, I have been honoured by being invited to be the Editor-in-Chief of that series on behalf of the Society and am much enjoying that responsibility.

One other minor 'hiccup' disturbed the relative peace and tranquillity of my later months at the RSM and again related to an editorial matter. After careful consideration by the Honorary Editors, who had consulted me, the Society decided to publish a frank booklet on sexual education, entitled *Growing Up*. This contained some explicit text and photographs which some, including Sir James Watt and Sir John Dacie, as past Presidents, plainly found offensive. Having read and reviewed the publication myself, I concluded that it made a positive contribution to sexual education of our youth and that, although it was explicit and profusely illustrated, it could by no stretch of the imagination be construed as being pornographic. Clearly a minority, including my distinguished colleagues, disagreed; when eventually it was published, as we decided it must be, there were a few press comments suggesting that its publication was inappropriate. Nevertheless, reviews in general were very favourable and the volume proved to be a great success. I am in no doubt that it had substantial educational virtues.

I would also like to pay a special tribute to Sir James Watt for his agreement to chair a series of colloquia on complementary therapies which he had decided to inaugurate late in his presidency, after learning of the interest in complementary medicine expressed by the Prince of Wales in his presidential address to the BMA. These colloquia, which brought together doctors and representatives of innumerable forms of complementary therapy, including osteopathy, homeopathy, naturopathy and many more, proved, even if controversial, to be fora in which views could be frankly stated and discussed. Two of them were attended by His Royal Highness the Prince of Wales, who commended the Society for its initiative. Eventually a thorough and interesting analysis of the proceedings of these meetings was published, edited efficiently by Sir James.

Among other initiatives introduced during my presidency was the Save a Life Campaign, splendidly chaired with outstanding energy and dedication by Dr Andrew Raffle, a former Honorary Officer of the Society. That campaign, through its publications and through its television programmes which were widely publicized by the BBC, recruited very many volunteer teachers and many more individuals who learned through the campaign the principles of cardiopulmonary resuscitation. We later received evidence to suggest that many lives had been saved by the application of mouth-to-mouth respiration and/or external cardiac massage by those who had learned the technique through the campaign.

Only one final anxiety persisted during the latter months of my presidency. This related to the sale of Chandos House which, being a listed building with its splendidly decorated reception rooms and its magnificent crystal chandeliers (one of which was transferred to the Society's new building) did not prove easy to sell. At one stage we thought we had achieved a sale to the Jack Nicklaus organization but that fell through. Fortunately we did eventually succeed in disposing of the building for a satisfactory capital sum, though perhaps not as large as we might have achieved had we waited a little longer in an inflationary property market. Nevertheless, that sale saw us well along the road to financial stability, as did the continuing success of Howard Croft's publishing programme and the success of our appeal, so ably chaired by Sir John Stallworthy with the continuing support of Dick Hewitt. We also decided to carry out an extensive revision of the Society's bye-laws, eventually abolishing the Scientific and Executive Committee, increasing the membership and authority of Council and electing two Vice-Presidents who could deputize for the President if for any reason he or she were not available. I had, after extensive consultation, identified as my successor Sir Gordon Robson, a distinguished anaesthetist and another old friend. His support during his year as President-elect, with his charming wife Jenny, was invaluable. It would be invidious to try to name all of those who, as Honorary Officers and Fellows, helped me during my years of presidency, but I must mention the indefatigable Dr Percy Cliffe, the long-serving Honorary Secretary who, with his wife Carice, later became a major benefactor of the Society, Professor Harold Ellis, Dr Robert Murray, the late Dr Reginald Kelly (the distinguished neurologist), Professors Ken Saunders and Paul Turner who, with Dr Hugh Baron, were invaluable. Bob Thomson as Executive Director demonstrated increasing authority and initiative and rapidly emerged from Dick Hewitt's shadow in order to display his own inimitable style. We were particularly pleased to recruit as his Executive Assistant Keith Newton who came from the MRC and whose appointment proved exceptionally successful. Mr Ian Burn, Drs Barry Hoffbrand, John Turk, John Price and Anthony Cullen, and Professor Rosalind Hurley also gave me unstinting support and I was deeply touched when my presidency ended in 1986 that they collectively presented me with a very beautiful crystal jug, superbly engraved with the signatures of all of the Honorary Officers whom I had come to know and admire.

I have deliberately left until last the final event and highlight of my two-year term, namely the formal opening of the Society's new home, including the new building and the refurbished old building, by Her Majesty The Queen and the Duke of Edinburgh on 2 July 1986. The Royal party arrived on a gloriously warm and sunny day at 3 p.m., to be met by the Lord Mayor of Westminster, myself, Betty and Bob Thomson. I then presented six past Presidents and their ladies to Her Majesty and the Duke. As we moved into the main hallway of the premises our younger granddaughter, Lucy Brown from Burford, presented Her Majesty with a bouquet, after which I gave her six glasses engraved with the Society's coat of arms to commemorate the occasion. She then unveiled the commemorative plaque before meeting Lucy's brother, Nicholas, our daughter Judy and her husband Andrew, and then Sir John Stallworthy, Dick Hewitt and the Honorary Officers and their spouses, as well as Sir Gordon and Lady Robson. We then embarked, before a huge assembled company of over 400 guests, upon a tour of the building. Her Majesty and the Duke were splendid in shaking hands with, and talking to, innumerable Honorary Fellows, Presidents of Colleges and colleagues representing medical organizations from across the world, as well as members of staff in all of the sections which they visited. It soon became clear that the tour was slipping behind schedule and Robert Fellowes, Her Majesty's Private Secretary, sidled forward and suggested that perhaps we should speed up a little, to which she said in effect that Robert should go away because she was enjoying herself. Finally we repaired to the Domus Medica for a cup of tea, where major benefactors and members of the Board of the RSM Foundation, Inc., including Art Mahon and others, were presented. When I asked whether she would have Indian or China tea, she thought for a moment before selecting China. When Len brought the cup forward, I noticed a tea-leaf on the surface and commented that there was a floating impurity; her response was to remove a glove, to lick one finger and to pick out the offending item, saying that she regarded it as a lucky omen. The only 'hiccup' of the day was that having been forewarned that when she signed the Society's commemorative book we should provide an ordinary fountain pen and not a ballpoint, Bob Thomson had deliberately arranged to have his own pen fully charged with ink. He had tried it out several times during the morning, only to find that when Her Majesty used it, it failed to write and a ballpoint had to be quickly produced in its place. Nevertheless, even that incident elicited a charming Royal smile. While the ceremony some two weeks later when I handed over the badge and robe of office to Gordon Robson was yet another splendid event, nothing can ever detract from the sheer joy of that memorable occasion.

Other organizations

As I dictate, I have become increasingly conscious of the potentially intolerable length of these commentaries describing my role in major British medical organizations. One of my BMA colleagues once referred to me, publicly, as 'Rent a President'. Nevertheless, these experiences and responsibilities have given me so much pleasure that I cannot resist the temptation to share them with a wider audience. My long-term membership of the Association of British Neurologists eventually culminated in my being elected its President in 1987. In 1981 I was honoured by being invited to become President of the Association for the Study of Medical Education, and in 1988 I was asked to follow my long-term friend, Dr Donald Irvine, as Chairman of the MSD Foundation, a charitable body funded by the drug company Merck, Sharp & Dohme, which is primarily concerned with activities designed to improve standards of training, teaching and practice in family medicine in the UK. I mentioned earlier my involvement with the Muscular Dystrophy Group of Great Britain and Northern Ireland, of which I have been proud to be Chairman for 25 years, also chairing at different times its Research Committee and now its Medical and Social Services Committee. I have also much enjoyed my membership of the 1942 Club which, as its name implies, was established in 1942 as a forum in which academics in all of the clinical specialties of medicine could meet twice a year to discuss matters of mutual concern relating to health care, education, training, medical research and any other relevant topic. It was an especial pleasure to have been able to entertain that club in Green College before I relinquished my Wardenship in 1989, even if the proceedings were slightly marred by the fact that the visit arranged for accompanying ladies to the Bodleian Library succeeded in omitting one or two especially distinguished ladies solely, I fear, because of the inadequacy of toilet accommodation for the fair sex in the college premises.

The Medical Pilgrims

There is, however, one other organization which does, I believe, deserve comment, namely the Medical Pilgrims, a medical travelling club of physicians to which I was elected in 1970. I regarded my election as a singular honour as membership was then restricted to about 24 representatives of internal medicine and all of its sub-specialties. I had been aware of the existence of the club for some time and I knew that it had been established in the 1920s by Sir Arthur Hurst, that great gastroenterologist, as both of my early teachers and mentors, Nattrass and Spence, had been members; indeed Nattrass served for many years as its secretary. It was during a meeting of the Pilgrims in 1956, when

I gave a paper to its meeting in Newcastle, that I recognized the outstanding distinction of its members. Almost without exception, Presidents of the Royal College of Physicians of London and many from Scotland were elected as members. The club visits a medical centre in the UK or abroad once a year for three or four days. It is usual for the host institution to arrange an academic programme of clinical and/or research presentations in an attempt to impress their visitors. The programmes are usually pretty intensive and generally occupy all of the mornings but are followed by an afternoon of seeing some local sights and an evening of dining. As the late Sir Derek Dunlop once put it, the guiding principle is 'mornings working, afternoons sightseeing, evenings boozing'. When I think of the many distinguished physicians whom I came to know well through meetings of the Pilgrims, I must say that although there were several notable omissions of outstanding individuals (such as Henry Miller) who were never invited to join, the membership roll read rather like a Baedecker of British internal medicine and related disciplines in the 20th century. In no particular order, I recall with admiration and affection Donald Hunter, Derek Dunlop, Fred Nattrass, Macdonald Critchley, Fergus Ferguson, Douglas Hubble, Melville Arnott, D. K. O'Donovan, J. M. Synge, Denis O'Sullivan of Cork, Dick Bomford, John Butterfield, David Pyke, John Stokes, George Smart, Clifford Hawkins, Max Rosenheim, Cyril Clarke, Bill Hoffenberg, Bryan Matthews, John Badenoch, Gordon Hamilton-Fairley (sadly, later killed by an IRA bomb in London), Alan Read, John Vallance-Owen, Ian Bouchier, John Newsom-Davis, David Marsden and so many more relatively recent recruits that one could fill several more lines of print by identifying them.

It would be impossible and indeed inappropriate to recite all of the memorable experiences of the Pilgrimages that I have enjoyed, but a few highlights may be worth recounting. In 1970 we went to Denmark, visiting both Copenhagen and Aarhus. In Copenhagen we were greatly impressed by the work of Paul Astrup, though some Pilgrims did find time to glance into the newly established sex shops during our visit, while in Aarhus we noted with amusement that Professor Lundbeck always wore his shirt open at the neck with his tie knotted six inches below and that every single member of his department copied that style. He also wore a corduroy suit which John Butterfield had copied during our stay. In 1971 we went to Birmingham, where the highlight was a dinner at Coughton Court, former home of the Guy Fawkes family, arranged by Pon d'Abreu, Professor of Surgery. As part of our liquid refreshment Clifford Hawkins had identified some ancient nectar dignified by the name of 'The Black Bastard'; 1972, largely at my urging, saw a Pilgrimage to Vienna and Budapest when my neurological colleagues in Vienna entertained us royally, including the usual evening in the Vienna Woods at Grinzing with the new wine. As we left Vienna for Budapest on the hydrofoil,

Clifford Hawkins was seen unsuccessfully attempting to change some of his Viennese money into Roumanian, not perhaps realizing that we were heading for Hungary. And on one exceptionally hot afternoon outside the Schonbrunn Palace John Butterfield claimed that when visiting the toilet he had been able to produce nothing more than a few puffs of steam.

1973 saw us in Edinburgh, but because of my relatively newly-acquired decanal responsibilities I could only attend a part of the Pilgrimage. Nevertheless, I remember that the splendid Pilgrims' dinner at the Royal College of Physicians in Edinburgh had been arranged by the redoubtable Derek Dunlop, a man of epicurean tastes who had chosen a splendid menu and magnificent accompanying wines. It was only afterwards that I discovered, as did the other chastened Pilgrims, that the choice of food and wine had resulted in our being presented with a bill for what at that time probably had been the most expensive meal of our lives, costing some £35 per head.

In 1975 I was asked to be the scribe for the Pilgrimage to Nottingham, where John Butterfield as Vice-Chancellor entertained us musically, gastronomically and intellectually, before we moved on to Oxford. Sadly this was the last sight that we had of our friend Gordon Hamilton-Fairley. And on an architectural tour around some churches in the vicinity of Oxford the professor of genetics, E. B. Ford, pointed out to us some mediaeval armour in one of them and produced a most memorable quote. He said 'I'm not sure whether you've had the same experience, but if you look at that armour and note its size, you'll understand why I found that I couldn't get into my family armour when I was more than 13 years of age'!

1976 saw us in Ireland with D. K. O'Donovan as our host in Dublin (I omitted to mention that in Budapest in 1972 at a reception at the British Embassy he had worn a badge carrying the Union Jack without complaint), and Denis O'Sullivan later entertained us in Cork. There it was that John Butterfield drove our minibus with great aplomb, even though it stuck in tramlines in the centre of the city and had to be pushed by a group of perspiring Pilgrims. From Baltimore we enjoyed a splendid boat trip out towards Fastnet Rock, during which Clifford Hawkins (a most faithful and assiduous Pilgrim who sadly died in late 1991) developed an acute urological problem, not finally resolved until we landed, when he shot off at remarkable speed to the public toilets near the jetty.

In 1978 we paid an anniversary visit to Guy's and the London Hospital to commemorate the establishment of the club by Arthur Hurst, while in 1979 George Smart returned to his native heath as leader of the Pilgrimage which I organized in Newcastle. We showed them the magnificent Macmillan collection of Chinese art in the Gulbenkian Museum at Durham and toured Durham Cathedral under the inspired direction of the late Canon Gordon Berriman, whom I had formerly known as Vicar of Spennymoor. We then moved on to Newcastle where a concentrated programme of intellectual activity was arranged by some of my most vigorous and extroverted colleagues, before finally repairing to 'The Old Piggery' where Dick Bomford played Betty's organ with skill and verve. Lunch at Bamburgh Golf Club was followed by a private visit to the Chillingham Wild Cattle. The highlight of our return trip to Newcastle was when we called at Alnwick Castle to be entertained to sherry by His Grace the Duke of Northumberland. When approached earlier, his agent, Bill Hugonin, had been uncertain as to whether His Grace would be available. It later turned out that his uncertainty was due to the fact that the evening before was the date of the annual Northumberland Hussars dinner, at which the Duke normally enjoyed himself. In fact, when we arrived, he was in excellent shape and showed us the glories of the Castle before entertaining us in his private quarters. Many of us knew him through his chairmanship of the MRC, but Melville Arnott casually mentioned in conversation that he had looked after the Duke of Northumberland in the Middle East during the war, when he found him to be suffering from scurvy due to vitamin C deficiency. He assumed that he was talking of the former Duke (the present one's elder brother) who was killed during the war. However, it turned out that the elder brother had been killed at Dunkirk and that the gentleman who had been treated by Melville was our host, who remembered the occasion (and the diagnosis) with some amusement.

In 1980 the Pilgrims were exceptionally ambitious and went to China, but I was not able to join them, though I did manage to go to Bristol in 1981 when Alan Read laid on a magnificent programme and where we had the opportunity of seeing the splendid new Jenner Museum at Berkeley in Gloucestershire. In 1982 the Pilgrims again broke a long-term rule which had been broken two years earlier for the first time (on going to China). It was decided that wives could accompany them on a Pilgrimage to Norway where I was honoured to be leader and we were entertained royally by Sigvald Refsum and his neurological colleagues and by others working in internal medicine. Apart from our intellectual refreshment, which was outstanding, we also travelled by train from Oslo to Bergen where Professor Aarli and his colleagues entertained us and where we managed to fit in a boat trip on the Hardanger fjord from Oystese (where Betty and I looked nostalgically at our honeymoon hotel) before moving on to Ulvik and some of the other magnificent sights of the surrounding country.

So much more could be said of 1983 in Dundee and St Andrews, where we looked with interest upon, but did not play, the Old Course; we were back in Birmingham in 1984 and revelled in the splendour of Leeds Castle in 1985. The Pilgrims went without me to Manchester and Llandudno in 1986, but most of us repaired to Glasgow in 1987 under the tutelage of Pilgrim Kennedy. In 1988 Bill Hoffenberg and I shared responsibility for organizing the Oxford Pilgrimage, where we divided the activities between Green College and Wolfson. We tried to show off a little in Green College by producing what seemed to us to be an excellent dinner. This followed a concert by the Green College choir, accompanied by Betty, and a performance by a college string quartet of three students and one common room member, the retired plastic surgeon, Tom Patterson, who turned out to be an old student friend of David Pyke. Our Oxford medical colleagues (Pilgrims Weatherall, Ledingham, Badenoch, Matthews and Newsom-Davis among them) all turned up trumps in producing a magnificent scientific programme and the quality of the gastronomic refreshment at Wolfson, organized splendidly by Bill, was also a triumph.

Since then, we went back to Edinburgh in 1990 and in 1991 the Pilgrims returned after a long interval to Ireland with Pilgrim Muiris FitzGerald as host. My membership of that club has invariably provided me with a pervasive sense of fellowship combined with professional nourishment and fulfillment, social enrichment and unalloyed enjoyment which would be difficult to match in any other organization.

CHAPTER 17

Green College

Despite having been born and educated in Durham County, I always regarded myself as a dedicated Northumbrian. Indeed in welcoming delegates to the BMA Conference in Newcastle in 1980, I pointed out that the ancient kingdom of Northumbria stretched from the Firth of Forth to the Tees. I derived some vicarious pleasure from reminding our Scottish colleagues that King Edwin of Northumbria sent out a detachment from his royal seat in Bamburgh Castle to establish a small settlement on the southern banks of the Firth of Forth which he called Edwin's Burgh. It was, of course, from that settlement that the city of Edinburgh later developed. Nevertheless, I now accept the conventional modern view that present-day Northumbria embraces the counties of Northumberland and Durham. Because of the strong sense of loyalty that I always felt to the north-east, I had never contemplated leaving Newcastle, though when our daughter Judy and her husband and children returned from Australia to settle in Burford, and when I speculatively raised with Betty the question as to whether anything would ever take us away from Newcastle, she tentatively enquired whether I might be interested in an Oxford college.

Perhaps, therefore, the initial approach from Dr Trevor Hughes at the World Congress in Kyoto in 1981, when he asked whether I would consider being a candidate for the Wardenship of Green College, fell upon ears more receptive than might otherwise have been the case. When I later discussed his enquiry with Betty, she felt that we should at least explore the position and I told Trevor we were interested. Everything went quiet for a month or two and I thought that probably nothing more would come of it, but I was then telephoned by Brian Bower, the Vice-Warden, asking whether I would visit Oxford when next in London to have a preliminary chat with some college fellows. The visit was relatively brief but I was immediately charmed not least by the enthusiasm with which several fellows discussed my potential candidature, but also by the superb buildings and delightful ambience of the college. Its core is formed by the magnificent Radcliffe Observatory, completed in 1794 (see below). The new office block and adjacent changing rooms for the squash and tennis courts (with two self-contained flats for married students above) as well as the three-storey block of student rooms adjacent to the Observatory, separating the beautiful college gardens from the Radcliffe Infirmary to the west, had been skilfully and tastefully designed by the University Surveyor, Jack Lankester. They blended very successfully with the original buildings, including the Observatory, the Observer's house and the stables which had been converted into a student bar with a games room above. Room had also been found in the stable block for an attractive little picture gallery which was used for exhibitions of works by local artists and also by students and staff of the college who exhibited their work once a year. While some had criticized the pseudo-Georgian style of the new buildings constructed in golden stone, most experts and lay observers alike were impressed, and the new buildings received a Civic Trust award.

During my visit I was quickly disabused of a misconception then prevalent (which still persists in some degree today) to the effect that this newly-established college, created in 1979, was purely medical. Whereas it was always intended that many of its graduate students would read clinical medicine (having previously achieved an honours degree in the natural sciences at Oxford, Cambridge or elsewhere), it was the avowed aim of the college from its inception to be a multi-faculty graduate institution. It was agreed that while it would admit students of medicine and the medical and related sciences, it would also accept those studying for higher degrees in the biological, physical, behavioural and social sciences. Having admitted 30 graduate students in 1979, student numbers when I visited in 1982 had risen to 94, of whom about half were clinical medical students, while the remainder included several reading for an MSc in Applied Social Studies, and others seeking a Master's degree or Doctorate in many branches of science, including forestry.

I was also fascinated by what I was told about the history of the Observatory and of the establishment of the college. Dr John Radcliffe, the great London physician, died in 1714 leaving £140,000 amassed through his lucrative medical practice. He left this sum to Oxford University primarily to help expand University College but also to build the great library (the Radcliffe Camera of the Bodleian Library was opened in 1749) and to found travelling medical scholarships. His trustees were enjoined to apply the residue of his estate 'to such charitable purposes as they in their discretion shall think best'. Accordingly, they next established the Radcliffe Infirmary, opened in 1770. When Dr Hornsby succeeded to the Savilian Chair of Astronomy and Natural Science in 1762, he suggested that further trust funds could help fulfil Savile's wish to establish a proper astronomical observatory. Hornsby pointed out that Christopher Wren before him and later Halley, who made his observations from a loft in New College Lane, had not been able to fulfil Savile's statute which charged the Professor of Astronomy with making and recording continuous observations; Hornsby himself had found it impossible to function properly from his rooms in Corpus Christi College.

It is now generally agreed that the Radcliffe Observatory is the finest example of a particular classic style to be seen in Oxford. An article in *Country Life* published on 10 May 1930 concluded that it is one of the most remarkable buildings in England. Whereas Nicholas Pevsner felt that it was the finest English observatory, many years later John Julius Norwich asserted that it was the finest building in Oxford; no doubt many would strenuously dispute that view though I certainly would not. After the trustees had accepted Hornsby's submission, the architect chosen was Henry Keene, surveyor to Westminster Abbey, and eight and a half acres of land adjoining the Radcliffe Infirmary were leased from the Duke of Marlborough to provide an appropriate site. Work began in 1772 but in 1773 Keene's plan was modified in the light of some elevations that James Wyatt had laid before the Radcliffe Trustees; when Keene died in 1776 Wyatt was appointed as his successor. By 1778 the lower part of the building was complete, decorated with astrological signs and other ornamentation designed by J. C. F. Rossi and created in an artificial stone, coade stone, of which the exact constitution is still unknown. Wyatt's design added a large central tower modelled upon the Tower of the Winds in Athens, decorated by superb and still well-preserved sculptures of the eight winds carved in Windrush stone by John Bacon, RA. These are thought to be among the finest, if not the finest, architectural sculptures in England. The building was completed by two Herculean figures modelled by Bacon in cast iron, holding at the peak of the tower a large copper globe. These twin Atlases are also intact. For some years, the roof of the tower was marred by an ugly superstructure required for the meteorological observations of wind velocity which were made regularly on the roof. Fortunately this was moved to the University engineering building when it was constructed in the 1950s and the tower then reverted to its original pristine glory.

However, the meteorological station in the garden, established soon after completion of the Observatory, still functions and has recorded temperature and precipitation daily since January 1815. Indeed some irregular observations are extant from as early as 1767. Until 1935, when a new Radcliffe Observatory was created in Pretoria in South Africa (see below) meteorological observations were a subsidiary task of the Radcliffe Observer and his staff. Since then, supervision has been the responsibility of the Professor of Geography. For more than three decades, until the end of 1985, the Director of the Radcliffe Meteorological Station was Mr C. G. Smith, MBE, a lecturer in the School of Geography. These observations enabled Mr Smith and his successor to analyse variations in Oxford weather for over 200 years. The records of the Radcliffe Meteorological Station are among the most important in the world, specifically in relation to secular variations of climate.

Among the most striking interior features of the Observatory are, first, its superb curving staircase with each stone step resting on the one below and each (presumably) firmly embedded in the sturdy walls of the building. Architects marvel at the fact that this staircase, functional for almost 200 years, has no external means of support. The splendid octagonal entrance hall with its ornamental ceiling and imposing south-facing doorway (now permanently closed) has created an excellent common room, while the former library and lecture room on the first floor now form the college dining room, with a private dining room (the William Gibson Room—see below) to one side and a charming fellows' room to the other. One curved ground floor wing to the west houses the college kitchen and music room, while that on the east provides a splendid college library and reading room. It is joined by a curving corridor to the Observer's house, largely now converted into student bed/sitting rooms with a television room and the former Ida Green Seminar Room, recently converted into an imposing office for the Warden. Once in each wing there were slits in the roof for smaller telescopes, but these were closed many years ago. The imposing tower room housed the major instruments. In that room are two huge sash windows with doors beneath through which telescopes were once wheeled out on to the balconies for observational purposes. The magnificent curved dome, lined by decorative plaster work now elegantly restored, has a circular walkway enclosed by wrought iron railings and approached by an interesting metal staircase. That tower room, still containing much of the Observatory's original furniture, was hallowed in a famous Ackermann print of which many copies exist; and there is another well-known print by the same artist of the dreaming spires of Oxford as viewed from tower window facing south.

This, then, was the imposing building in which many important astronomical and meteorological observations were made for almost 140 years until, sadly, the Oxford skies became too murky in the 1930s for important new information to be added and the decision was made to create a new Radcliffe Observatory in Pretoria. Some telescopes went there but others were transferred to the University's Science Museum where they are still on display. William Morris (later Sir William and eventually Lord Nuffield), Chancellor of the University, and one of its major benefactors, purchased the Observatory from the Radcliffe Trustees and donated it to the University, which decided to use it for the Nuffield Institute of Medical Research. For almost 40 years it housed laboratories and mezzanine floors were installed in the wings to provide additional space. Dr (later Professor) Geoffrey Dawes and his colleagues studied reproductive physiology there and many scientists still working in Oxford recall sheep being used in these experiments and being carried up and down the splendid central staircase. As plans for building the new John Radcliffe Hospital at Headington matured, it was agreed that the Nuffield Institute should move into purpose-built accommodation on that site and so the Observatory became vacant. In the meantime, the University had acquired the imposing residence at 1A Observatory Street, formerly St Paul's vicarage, a splendid house of which the upper floors overlooked the gardens and Observatory. For a time the house provided offices for the Clinical Medical School, first established after the Second World War. Rooms in the Observer's house and the stables provided the social club for clinical medical students of Oxford then training at the Radcliffe Infirmary. The Observer's house was renamed Osler House, acknowledging the outstanding contributions of Sir William Osler, Regius Professor of Medicine in Oxford from 1907–1919; accordingly, the students' club became Osler House Club.

Following the departure of the Nuffield Institute in 1970, the Observatory was used for several University purposes but at first no definitive long-term role emerged. The idea that it might become the core of a new graduate college was largely the brain-child of Sir Richard Doll, then Regius Professor of Medicine. The progressive expansion of the Clinical Medical School had meant that some clinical students, having completed three years in an undergraduate college while reading for a BA in the natural sciences, had suggested that a move to another college location might be beneficial. There were also many members of staff of the Clinical School employed by the University who could not find college fellowships despite the University's 'entitlement' rule to the effect that all professors, readers and lecturers were entitled to such fellowships. The University could not compel colleges, as independent foundations, to increase their number, even though some did so. Thus while no-one could become a student reading for either an undergraduate or a postgraduate degree of the University without being a member of a college, a growing cadre of disenchanted University staff felt deprived through not being elected to a college fellowship.

While there was some powerful opposition to the idea of establishing a new graduate college which might specialize in clinical medicine, the idea gradually gained ground. The original intention was to call it Radcliffe College, as the University's Hebdomadal Council had agreed that, should such a college be created, the Radcliffe Observatory, for which the University was unable to find any other role, could constitute its core. Among the major problems encountered were, first, opposition to the idea of creating a college which might become a single faculty institution in view of Oxford's general policy of encouraging a broad mix of students from different academic disciplines in all colleges; secondly, though it was clear that the principal focus of clinical teaching was moving from the Radcliffe Infirmary to the John Radcliffe Hospital, there was a concerted protest from the officers and members of the Osler House Club over the prospect that, they might lose their social facilities in Osler House; thirdly, the intense loyalty felt by many medical students and staff members to their undergraduates colleges may have been underestimated. Thus, despite the obvious need for a new graduate society, fierce opposition was encountered. Nevertheless, after innumerable discussions and debates in the Faculty of Clinical Medicine and in Council, the proposal gradually gained ground and was eventually approved in principle. Fortunately a major problem relating to the Osler House Club was to some extent overcome by an agreement that the new college would buy the old Dower House on the John Radcliffe site and would then convert it into a club for clinical students, replacing the facilities which the college would take over in the Observer's house (Osler House). It was also agreed that all clinical students would be able to use some of the facilities of the new college, including the tennis courts which had been specifically provided for their use, and also to have access to the squash court and bar. Even this agreement did not defuse the opposition expressed by a powerful group of clinical students and some members of the Clinical Faculty, but at least some major objections were overcome.

An even more difficult problem was that of finance, as a substantial capital sum would clearly be necessary to refurbish the Observatory and to build office and student accommodation. These problems were heightened when Council decided that unlike other new graduate colleges which had begun with little capital endowment, the proposed Radcliffe College, with its medical emphasis (it was thought that clinical medicine should have little difficulty in raising funds) would not be allowed access to the College Contributions Committee. That committee operated a mechanism established a few years earlier in order to redistribute funds derived from the endowments of the wealthier colleges to a number of those which were less secure financially. While the Radcliffe Trustees and the Rhodes Trust offered generous contributions, these fell far short of what was needed and the project was in danger of foundering for lack of funds, despite the strenuous and indefatigable efforts of Sir Richard and a small group of colleagues who attempted to raise the necessary finance. Sir Richard then approached Paul Beeson, former Nuffield Professor of Clinical Medicine, who had returned on retirement to his native USA, asking him to mastermind a US fund-raising exercise. It was he who suggested an approach to the Greens. Fortunately, there then came forward Dr William Gibson of Vancouver, formerly head of the Department of Neurology in the University of British Columbia (UBC) and a noted medical historian. Bill Gibson was someone I had come to know many years earlier when he was Chairman of the Scientific Advisory Committee of the Muscular Dystrophy Association of America. Bill, a former Rhodes Scholar, had a great affection for Oxford, having worked for his DPhil in the Physiological Laboratory with Sherrington. Later he was co-author with John Eccles of a splendid book of reminiscences about Sherrington and his contributions to physiology. He knew well both Cecil and Ida Green, major benefactors of UBC and of many other medical and scientific institutions in the USA and Canada. Initial approaches to them by him and Richard Doll were not encouraging, but with gentle and persistent prodding the Greens ultimately expressed tentative interest and agreed to visit Oxford to meet Sir Richard and officers of the University.

The result of that visit in April 1977 is now a matter of history. The Greens were charmed by Oxford, much impressed by the Observatory and equally so by the draft plans which, subject to the availability of funds, Jack Lankester had produced for the new buildings. He recommended that these should be built in Georgian style, of stone, so as to blend harmoniously with those existing on the site. As a result Cecil and Ida agreed to give the University one million pounds to establish the college, provided a start on site was made within a year. Oxford, I believe, has never moved so fast either before or since; within the specified period plans were finalized, planning permission was obtained and work began on refurbishing the Observatory and on creating the new buildings in what the University willingly agreed to call Green College. It was soon clear that one million pounds would be insufficient to complete the scheme and the Greens generously donated a second million to allow the grand design to be achieved. In the meantime, with untiring energy and initiative, Sir Richard, aided by many national and local supporters led by Sir Raymond Pennock, embarked upon a major fund-raising exercise in order to raise endowment funds to enable the college to survive in an extremely competitive climate.

In 1979, in the presence of Cecil and Ida Green, Richard and Joan Doll, the founding fellows and many friends and benefactors, the college was formally opened by the Chancellor of the University, Sir Harold Macmillan, who, as always, made a sparkling speech. That ceremony was held in the Lankester Quad, an attractive quadrangle enclosed by the stables and Observer's house on one side, a wall and wrought iron gate leading into the garden on another, and the new college buildings on the other two sides. In 1979 the first 30 graduate students were admitted; thereafter the college moved from strength to strength with a progressive expansion in student numbers and in the size of its fellowship each year. Without Sir Richard's energy, persistence and diplomatic negotiations the college would never have been established, and his wife Joan, whom I knew previously as Dr Joan Faulkner of the MRC, also played a crucial rôle. She was tireless in her attention to the interior decoration and general decor of the college, chose furnishings, curtains and carpets for the public rooms and student accommodation, and also planned the refurbishment of 1A Observatory Street which had been allocated by the University as the Warden's residence. The Dolls moved into that house in 1980 and thus spent only three years in the attractive home which Joan created.

Cecil and Ida Green were remarkable people. Cecil was born in 1900 in Lancashire of relatively humble parentage (his father was a maintenance electrician). He spent his first two years in Whitefield, a suburb of Manchester, at Besses o' the Barn (of the famous brass band), before his parents decided to seek a new life in Canada. Charles Green found it difficult to obtain satisfactory employment in Vancouver, where they first settled, and they later moved with Cecil, their only child, to San Francisco. Even there he did not achieve the success for which he had hoped. When Cecil was five years old his father decided to return to Vancouver to seek new employment, leaving his wife, Maggie, and son behind. Cecil still recalls being awakened by plaster falling on to his bed; the home in which they were living was virtually destroyed in the severe San Francisco earthquake of 1905. Fortunately Mrs Green had just enough money to be able to travel to Canada. They knew that Charles was in Vancouver but had no idea where he was staying or whether he had found work. Remarkably, soon after they arrived they met him walking along the main street and the family was reunited. Eventually Cecil attended UBC but did not graduate there. Being interested in physics, he transferred to the Massachusetts Institute of Technology in Cambridge, Mass., and obtained a Master's degree. There then followed a series of appointments in which he crossed and recrossed the American continent several times, having in the meantime married Ida, with whom he enjoyed 60 wonderful years of marriage. Eventually, with two associates, he established a company called Geophysical Investments in Dallas, Texas, out of which grew Texas Instruments, of which he later became chairman and eventually president. Sadly, he and Ida had no children, but as his professional work prospered (he was a pioneer in developing methods of aerial exploration for oil-bearing strata and was internationally acknowledged in the world of geophysics) and as his personal prosperity and fortune grew, he and Ida decided to devote a substantial proportion of their surplus assets to charitable giving in order to promote new developments in medicine and science. Their benefactions were legion. Innumerable objectives in the University of Texas, both in Dallas and in Galveston, were supported, as were major developments in La Jolla, California, where they established their second home. These included the Green Hospital created in association with the Scripps Clinic. And they did not forget UBC in Vancouver, where several chairs were endowed in the Green name and a new Green College is being built. They also gave substantial grants to MIT and to developments initiated by Cecil's long-term friend Harry Messel in the University of Sydney in Australia. Green College was, however, the outcome of the first major benefaction which Cecil and Ida had given to the country of Cecil's birth.

It was this new and vibrant Oxford college, therefore, which asked me to consider becoming its second Warden. Betty and I discussed the implications exhaustively, weighing up the pros and cons. I was excited by the challenge and knew full well, following election as GMC president, that to live and work in Oxford would make commuting to London much easier than from Newcastle. I was also attracted and stimulated by the prospect of working in Oxford, especially because I would again be involved with students, something which I had always enjoyed. As David Kerr, Professor of Medicine in Newcastle (subsequently Dean of the Postgraduate Medical School in Hammersmith) put it when he learned later that I had been appointed, 'What a splendid way to spend your declining years, in an Oxford college'! In 1982 at the age of 60 I knew that I would only have another five years of work in the University and NHS in Newcastle, whereas the retirement age in Oxford was 67. Knowing that if appointed I would not have to retire until two years after I would have had to do so in Newcastle was an additional attraction, quite apart from the pleasure of being nearer to our daughter Judy and her family in Burford. Eventually, therefore, we decided that the advantages and opportunities offered by the appointment outweighed the dis-advantages of leaving Newcastle, though we knew that it would be a wrench to be more than 300 miles away from our newly-refurbished and extended home (The Old Piggery) in Detchant, which we had both come to love passionately.

So in spring 1982 I was invited back to Oxford, this time with Betty, again to meet several fellows. Clearly they felt they should scrutinize the potential Warden's spouse as well as the candidate. And so, in a visit orchestrated by Brian Bower, we were interviewed in the Fellows' Room by a varied group, including the redoubtable Juliet Cheetham, Lecturer in Applied Social Studies and one of the few lady members of the fellowship. Afterwards we lunched separately, each with groups of fellows and college members, and yet again, after a pleasant visit, returned to Newcastle without any commitment having been made on either side. This time, however, the interval before the next approach was shorter and Brian telephoned to arrange a date when I could return for a third visit, this time to meet the Governing Body. We arranged this following an afternoon meeting at the GMC and just before I was due to begin my Easter break at Detchant. Brian Bower kindly met me at the station and drove me to the college, where I had sherry with several fellows whom I had not previously met. At dinner I sat at one table for the soup and fish, was moved to a second for the main course and to a third for the sweet. We then retired to the common room where I was given a central seat, with a cup of coffee and a glass of port to my left, facing a circle of seats in which sat the Governing body, some 30–35 fellows. Of course I was told that the proceedings were to be informal, but nevertheless for about an hour I was challenged with questions on innumerable topics relating to medical education, student life, planning and organization, my GMC responsibilities, so that after a while I began to feel slightly bemused. Indeed, as the discussion proceeded, I became a trifle aggressive, wondering why I should be subjected to what seemed a little like the third degree; hence my responses became, though still, I hope, friendly, rather more combative. Eventually, Brian took me, feeling a little limp, back to the station, so that I could catch a late evening train to Paddington to connect with the 1.00 a.m. sleeper to Newcastle. I had given him our Detchant telephone number as we planned as soon as I got back to Newcastle to pack up and drive straight to our country retreat. As luck would have it, when we got to Detchant our telephone was out of order; later in the day I summoned up courage to telephone Brian to learn that the Governing Body had decided unanimously to invite me to become Warden from 1 October 1983.

Inevitably our pleasure at the news was tinged with regret about the prospect of leaving my alma mater. Nevertheless, having 18 months to plan our move and our future was a great help as it gave me time to notify the University and my colleagues in the Department of Neurology and to make plans to secure the future of the department and of the Muscular Dystrophy labs more effectively than would have been the case if our departure had been precipitate. I was also delighted when my secretary, Rosemary, who had been my secretarial and administrative right hand for so many years, decided that she and her mother would move to the Oxford area so that she could work with me as Warden's secretary. That decision necessitated a good deal of negotiation with Peter Garnham, the Bursar, and Brian Bower, as the salary offered to a Warden's secretary in Oxford was substantially less than Rosemary had earned at the top of the NHS administrative grade. Fortunately I arranged supplementation of her salary from the Muscular Dystrophy Group in acknowledgement of the work which she would continue to do for that organization, so that all was well and we agreed to move to Oxford together. I was also concerned about the prospect of giving up clinical work and teaching and hence had several discussions with Rosemary Rue, the Regional Medical Officer, and Alex Gatherer, the District Medical Officer in Oxford. I also had some slightly tricky discussions with Bryan Matthews, the Professor of Neurology, a long-term friend and fellow Medical Pilgrim, who nevertheless expressed some concern about the prospect of having another professor of neurology attached to his department. However, when I made it clear that I was not seeking professorial status but purely an honorary part-time contract, he and his colleagues were very welcoming and supportive. That contract was particularly important since if I had moved to Oxford without it, I would have had to relinquish my top grade distinction award in the NHS. As it was, the one honorary session with the Regional Health Authority and the one with the District which were agreed allowed me to retain one-third of that award. Clearly the move would involve some financial sacrifice as I would have to relinquish my modest medico-legal practice and my membership of Medical Appeal Tribunals, another significant source of income. Nevertheless, the knowledge that a home would be provided (the Warden's lodgings was not a taxable emolument as we were required to occupy the house as a condition of the appointment) and that I would also receive a modest salary as President of the GMC compensated to some extent for the reduction in salary.

We looked forward to the move with keen anticipation, and soon sold our home in Beechfield Road to a colleague, David Bates. We were also much encouraged when, on a subsequent visit to Oxford, Joan and Richard Doll kindly showed us around 1A Observatory Street. That tall, three-storey house, looking like an early Georgian residence with its tall sash windows, and white shutters, was actually built in 1912. The splendid view of the college gardens and Observatory beyond our small, attractive, walled garden which had a gate at the end leading directly into the college gardens, charmed us at once. Its large basement wine cellar and storage area, utility room and delightful study where I could clearly accommodate most of my books and some of my files attracted me greatly, and Betty was thrilled with the ground-floor kitchen (it would need some modification to meet her specific needs) and with the small but pleasant dining room next door. On the first floor was a huge, L-shaped sitting room in which there was ample room for her Bluthner boudoir grand piano and her Danemann upright and much of our other furniture. This room was ideal for entertaining, and on the same floor was our own spacious bedroom and bathroom en suite. The top floor provided guest accommodation with four additional bedrooms (one of which Betty converted into a studio) and another bathroom. The only minor snag was that the garage down a lane close to the house could only accommodate one car; our second vehicle would have to be parked either on the street or in the college car park.

We were delighted to be invited in June 1983 to the Dolls' farewell dinner, hosted by Cecil and Ida Green, whom we later came to know as a charming and wonderful couple. At the dinner they announced yet another munificent gift of £400,000 in order to endow in perpetuity a Joan and Richard Doll stipendiary research fellowship to acknowledge the outstanding contributions which the Dolls had made in promoting the establishment of the college and in their stewardship during its first three years. The Governing Body, with Cecil's prompting, announced that the three-storey residential block would in future be known as the Doll Building. A splendid sculpted head of Richard by Faith Tolkein, niece of J.R.R., was also unveiled, as were two pastel portraits of Joan and Richard by Raymond Stubley which now hang in the common room.

In planning our move in September 1983, we still had the emotional months of summer to face including the magnificent farewell symposium in Newcastle organized in my honour by David Gardner-Medwin, to which many friends and former trainees came from throughout the UK and indeed from other parts of the world. I shall always treasure the bound volume of papers presented at that meeting, the copy of the two-volume work presented to Osler by his colleagues in Oxford (of which David Gardner-Medwin had obtained a copy for me) and the supplement published in the *Journal of the Neurological Sciences* to mark the occasion. There was also a wonderful farewell party given by the staff of the Muscular Dystrophy Labs on a glorious day in the Cullens' garden in Ponteland, so that the summer, even including our few weeks at Detchant, passed in something of a blur. Another major problem I encountered was the need to find laboratory space and additional storage in Oxford to take the 15,000 reprints and the large number of box files and records which I had accumulated. Fortunately, through the good offices of Trevor Hughes and with the aid of funds I had accumulated from private sources, we converted a room in the Department of Neuropathology at the Radcliffe Infirmary so as to house these items, as well as my microscope and microscopic slides; there was also bench space where I could continue my studies of muscle pathology. Throughout the summer, too, Gerald Chambers, the immensely efficient, kindly and hard-working Domestic Bursar of the college, masterminded the modifications and redecoration we had sought in 1A Observatory Street. Betty also arranged in Newcastle for some of our drawing room furniture to be re-covered in material which would match the curtains in Baker fabric in the L-shaped sitting room which was to be our principal entertaining room.

Much of September, therefore, was spent in packing up personal belongings and records in a veritable mountain of packing cases, and Hoults of Newcastle transported our belongings in two huge pan-technicons to Oxford, distributing them appropriately between 1A Observatory Street, my room at the Radcliffe Infirmary, the Warden's office and adjoining secretarial office in the college, according to plan. Never, I believe, has a move gone more smoothly but it required a massive expenditure of physical effort by us both in the week or ten days before and after the event. We moved at the beginning of the last week in September; by the end of that week 1A was looking reasonably ship-shape, with furniture properly distributed, books unpacked and ensconced on appropriate shelves, pictures hung and everything ready for me to assume my new responsibilities from 1 October. However, Betty, aware of my impractical nature (she recognized my almost total inability to handle inanimate objects and recalled occasions when I had taken a Black and Decker drill in order to drill a simple hole in a wall but had ended up with six inches of plaster around my feet) invited her brother, Cliff, who had moved a year or two earlier from Spennymoor to Wargrave-on-Thames, to help with some of the more difficult practical tasks, including the fitting of various appliances. Andy Brown, our son-in-law, also of practical bent, came over from Burford to install our hi-fi equipment, and even Doris Wilkinson, our long-serving daily help in Newcastle, came to stay with us for a week to help in cleaning our new home. Without this team and without our daughter Judy's gastronomic support, we would not have succeeded nearly as well.

Our next task, and one which for two Geordies proved in some respects easier and in some more difficult than we had envisaged, was to adjust to the Oxford scene. While I had often attended meetings in Oxford, neither of us had ever worked there and the ways of the University, it soon emerged, were very different from those to which I had become accustomed in Newcastle. This struck me most forcibly when, in my first week, I turned up at a meeting of the Conference of Colleges at Rhodes House only to see the serried ranks of heads of houses and their officers sitting in gowns. Being the only one without the appropriate attire, I beat a hasty retreat. I had obtained a Durham MA gown from Gray's in Durham before moving (like all heads of houses, I had received an Oxford MA by decree) and knew that I would have to wear this at Governing Body meetings. Nevertheless, it took me some time to work out when it was appropriate to wear a gown alone, when a gown and a hood, and when a cap was also needed. Even so, there were occasions within the first year or two when I turned up for various events improperly dressed, but was always reassured to find that there were invariably several other heads of houses who were equally bemused. As I often said, such matters of Oxford protocol were not passed down in written or verbal instructions to new heads of houses, or indeed to new members of academic staff, as it seemed to be assumed that these customs were acquired or accreted by a process of genetic transference.

In our first few weeks everything was overshadowed by the unremitting kindness we were shown by the college fellows and their spouses, with many of whom we subsequently became close friends. Brian and Christine Bower in particular were a tower of strength, as were the college officers, and the staff, too, made us feel completely at home. As a former Dean, I had little difficulty in learning the customs and procedures of the innumerable college committees, including the Fellowship Committee, the General Committee, the Buildings Committee, the Academic Committee and others which I was expected to chair, while even my first Governing Body turned out to be no more fearsome than the first Board of the Faculty of Medicine I had chaired on becoming Dean in Newcastle.

Just as Norman Shott's tutelage had helped me then, so in Oxford the guidance and briefing from the Bursar, Peter Garnham, also a Senior Assistant Registrar in the University, was invaluable; so far as I could judge I committed no solecisms. Quickly Betty and I fell into the routine of dining in college each Thursday evening, when I was required to say grace at the beginning and end of the meal but there were no other formalities (and no seating plan either, except that the Warden sat at the centre of the top table). The college food, produced by the flame-haired and portly Sam Harrison, was outstanding and the wine, often unusual (including some English white wines and some uncommon Spanish, Australian and Californian vintages) was also excellent. The potential hazard of galloping avoirdupois was further heightened by the discovery that we were expected occasionally to join the students at some of their simpler but substantial meals on Monday or Wednesday evenings. The buffet lunches provided five days a week were also excellent, posing yet another potential hazard to the waistline. That risk was further compounded by the many invitations which began to pour in from other heads of houses and colleagues in Oxford through which in our first term we 'did the rounds' by dining in innumerable colleges and occasionally lunching, while Betty found herself quickly drawn into the regular lunches for the spouses of heads of houses and into the Oxford Ladies' Luncheon Club, of which she became a regular and enthusiastic member.

Outside the college, our medical colleagues were very welcoming, not least our old friends Bryan and Margaret Matthews and John and Anne Badenoch, as well as John and Kathleen Potter whom we had come to know not just through neurology but also through GMC activities. I soon recognized the enormous breadth of scholarship and academic talent which the University possessed and also realized that proud though I had been of Newcastle medical school, its range of scientific expertise and excellence in the basic medical sciences and even in some clinical departments could not invariably challenge the supremacy of Oxford medicine. In particular, the outstanding work of David Weatherall, John Ledingham and their colleagues in the Nuffield Department of Clinical Medicine was remarkable in range and quality. I was therefore rather apprehensive in my first term on being invited to give one of the regular lectures organized by that department at the John Radcliffe Hospital. I spoke on muscle disease before a very large and no doubt critical audience but was reassured to find that the talk was well received, as was the one I subsequently gave on 'Illness in doctors and their families' to a capacity audience at a meeting of the Oxford Medical Society.

Despite the intellectual and academic brilliance which we saw all around us, I soon learned that here and there, especially in a few of the older colleges, there were pockets of rather haughty intellectual arrogance, not all of it, so far as I could judge, wholly justified. In other words, there were a few senior fellows whose brilliance in their youth had been undoubted but who had apparently rested on their laurels and had produced little original work or scholarship for many years. And Betty, too, was mildly irritated from time to time on receiving the query 'And what do you do?' in slightly haughty and stentorian tones from scme north Oxford lady. The implied suggestion that she ought perhaps to be lecturing or researching in some rarefied intellectual or academic pursuit invariably produced the response 'I'm a housewife', unadorned by any comment to the effect that, as she well knew, she had substantial musical talents and not inconsiderable skills as a painter of Northumbrian water-colour landscapes. But such experiences were rare; in general our first few weeks passed in a haze of pleasure and excitement in our new environment, heightened by the proximity of Judy and her family. Nevertheless, at first we both felt very much in the shadow of Richard and Joan Doll who had created the college and had steered it through its first four years of existence with energy and dedication. Their influence was pervasive and compelling and the fact that their long-term friend and companion, Mrs 'Steve' Sutherland, was head porter meant that despite her efficiency and tact their influence lived on. For some time we regularly wondered, in taking some new initiative, whether or not the Dolls would have done the same and, indeed, whether or not they would approve. In my case, as I had known Richard for many years through our joint membership of various MRC committees and of the medical sub-committee of the Committee of Vice-Chancellors and Principals, this feeling quickly waned. In Betty's case it faded more slowly as everywhere she turned, whether in college or in other Oxford circles, innumerable people whom she met commented upon Joan's expertise and energy. Inevitably, therefore, she found some difficulty in developing a personal identity as the Warden's lady, though we were later told by fellows and students alike that her own personality and influence upon the college flowered much more rapidly than either of us had recognized.

In such spare time as we had, we also did our best in our first year to soak up as much as we could of the inimitable Oxford atmosphere by visiting the major museums (including the superb Christ Church picture gallery), by wandering along river walks by the Thames and Cherwell and by exploring the highways and byways of Oxfordshire, not least along the canal which traversed Jericho near our home. Port Meadow, flooded in the winter and occasionally frozen firmly enough for skaters to emerge, was a memorable sight, as were Christ Church Meadow and Magdalen Bridge from which a short diversion into the Botanical Gardens was always worthwhile. We revelled in the grandeur, even magnificence, of college buildings and gardens, some austere, some, despite their antiquity, infinitely more soothing and friendly, and even the initially repelling banded Victorian pile of Keble ultimately acquired its own peculiar charm.

We went to the Playhouse, saw opera at the Apollo and sat through innumerable performances by orchestras both large and small, often with choirs, in the uncomfortable splendour of Wren's Sheldonian Theatre, having become subscribers to the Oxford Pro-Musica and Music at Oxford. Perhaps above all we enjoyed the organ and choral music which we heard regularly in the imposing grandeur of New College Chapel or Christ Church Cathedral. Soon, therefore, the sheer compulsive charm and almost addictive intellectual ambience of the city took its toll and those occasional hints of arrogant superiority which had suggested to us northerners that the world began and ended in Oxford and which had irritated us both were set aside and we began to feel a part of the local scene.

Arrogance is rarely, if ever, a quality displayed by genuine scholars of distinction and one especially notable occasion stands out in the memory. Larry Bachmann, a visiting fellow of Green College, with his charming wife, Bettina (long confined to a wheel-chair) invited us for lunch to their lovely home at the Manor House, Great Haseley. On arriving there Larry said 'You must meet the Regius Professor of Ecclesiastical History from Christ Church'; under my breath I could almost hear myself saying 'Yet another 'blue stocking'!'. However, I had not talked to Jack McManners for more than a few minutes before I said with typical northern directness 'You don't come from north of the Tyne nor from south of the Tees but probably from mid-Durham'. I based that conclusion upon a Durham intonation which was still evident. His response was affirmative and when I asked him if he knew a place called Spennymoor, he said yes, indeed, he had attended school there. When I further enquired as to whether he had gone to the Alderman Wraith Grammar School his eyes lit up and he confirmed that he had, whereupon I said that both Betty and I had studied there. His father was vicar of Ferryhill and I soon recalled that his brother Joe, now a GP in Gateshead, had been at the Newcastle Medical School at the same time as myself. This distinguished ecclesiastical scholar who subsequently became Chaplain of All Souls, had had a very similar educational background to our own.

Jack, like Larry Bachmann, was a capable and enthusiastic tennis player. Larry had formerly been an MGM film producer in Los Angeles and a friend of the Eastmans (of Kodak fame) from Rochester, New York, where Bettina lived in her youth. He was also a member of the All England Lawn Tennis Club where he at times played with some of the greats of yesteryear, including Budge, Perry and others. It was through Larry's generosity and kind influence that Betty and I in later years were able to go to Wimbledon with excellent seats either on no. 1 court or on the centre court and where we enjoyed Larry and Bettina's hospitality. On one memorable occasion we had the privilege of being entertained by 'Buzzer' Haddingham, Chairman of the All England Club, and of sitting in the Royal Box along with a number of other Oxford dignitaries, including Lord Goodman and the Vice-Chancellor, Sir Patrick Neill, with Lady Neill, just behind the royal party. Larry, too, was responsible for several important initiatives in Oxford, including private showings of films including Hitchcock's 'Rear Window' and Attenborough's 'Gandhi' and 'Cry Freedom'; he also arranged a series of very well attended sports lectures in the Examination Schools. I chaired one of these, which was addressed by Ron Pickering of athletics fame and David Miller of *The Times*, among others. Larry's indefatigable support for Oxford sport, for Green College and subsequently of the Campaign for Oxford has made him an invaluable member of the Oxford community.

One of the great joys of being Warden of Green College was that I needed to walk no more than about 200 yards from the door of my home to my office, through the delightful little garden of 1A Observatory Street which Betty soon cultivated and tended assiduously. The gate at the bottom of the garden led into the superb college gardens, lovingly cared for by Michael Pirie, our able and well-spoken college gardener, and I then passed through the Lankester Quad on the way to my office. This proximity made it easy for us to entertain friends and colleagues and, above all, our students. We established a pattern whereby within the first two or three weeks of each Michaelmas Term we had several sherry parties to which all college students, along with college officers, were invited so that we could come to know them individually. We were much impressed by the family atmosphere of the college; there was then no event in the college year to which a fellow could not invite his or her spouse, although because of the restricted dining accommodation, early booking for Thursday dinners and, above all, for the fellows' Christmas dinner, was necessary. We soon realized that we would not have been as happy, nor as comfortable, in an older and more traditional Oxford college. In some of these the wife of the head of house could only dine, at most, two or three times a year, while regular dining in was expected of the Head of House on Saturday and Sunday evenings. Over many years we developed a pattern whereby Saturday evening was set aside for leisure, even in the busiest working week, while Sunday was one of the few occasions when we regularly had a light supper and put our feet up to watch television, glass in hand. Although my commitments with the GMC took me frequently to London, I was able to interrelate my college and GMC commitments (later also including those at the RSM) in such a way that it was never necessary for me to miss a major college committee. Indeed I attended every meeting of the Governing Body during my Wardenship until my very last term when, in May, the officers kindly gave me leave of absence in order to lecture on a Swan Hellenic Mediterranean cruise, 'In the steps of Hippocrates'.

I have stressed the family atmosphere of the college as children were also catered for at lunch and many fellows with families took advantage of this arrangement. The rule relating to spouses was marginally infringed by the decision Betty and I took in our first year that we should arrange an annual fellows' dinner, before which we would entertain those attending to drinks in 1A Observatory Street, after which I would conduct the gathering across to the college while Betty cleared up the debris. A week later it was her turn to entertain the fellows' spouses to dinner and to make a little speech afterwards, as I had done to the fellows, while I repaired the ravages of the drinks party at 1A. Apart from the formal dining-in nights, we also arranged private dinners about twice a term for 12–14 in the William Gibson Room of the college so as to entertain guests such as potential benefactors or Heads of Houses or fellows from other colleges who had in their turn entertained us. Sometimes, too, Bo Simmons from Bladon eased the burden of entertaining which might otherwise have become oppressive by providing skilfully prepared meals from our own kitchen at 1A which she served and even (bless her) washed up for us afterwards. However, opportunities for providing dinners and lunches at home were more restricted as we could seat only eight in our charming but small dining room.

One major factor which eased my transition from Newcastle to Oxford was the fact that Rosemary Allan came with me to become the Warden's secretary. Her skilful and diplomatic management of my diary, the rapid acquaintanceship she acquired of college procedures and regulations, and her on-going commitment to, and involvement with, the work I was continuing to handle in the neurological field and in publishing made my task infinitely easier. She was also a great help at our sherry parties in the preparation, serving, and attending the door at 1A.

Throughout my six memorable years of Wardenship I was given unstinting support by a succession of capable college officers. Brian Bower as Vice-Warden skilfully smoothed my path in the early months and was succeeded by the unflappable Trevor Hughes. Peter Garnham's skill in drafting agendas, briefing notes and minutes was exceptional, as was his handling of the college accounts and budgets. In this he was greatly helped by David Mosely, a senior fellow who handled the college's investments with consummate skill, as he also did those of the University as a whole. The successive Deans, who handled disciplinary matters and presented students for matriculation and graduation, were John Kerr, Gerald Myatt and Clive Hahn, while the academic programme of seminars, lectures and conferences was effectively handled by David Millard, Robert Turner and Colin Blake as successive Senior Tutors and by Robert Turner, Charles Warlow and Michael Donaghy as Academic Tutors. John Sear looked after our admissions during my first two years, being followed by Jeffrey Aronson, who was himself succeeded by Neville

Osborne. Through their efforts and through recruitment drives sponsored by the college but masterminded by our student body, our numbers grew steadily so that in my last year our initial target of 150 registered students was exceeded. About two-fifths were clinical medical students, about 24 were reading for the MSc in applied social studies, and the remainder for higher degrees in many subjects in the physical, biological, behavioural and social sciences, often involving research relating directly or indirectly to medicine.

A linchpin of the college throughout was Gerald Chambers, Domestic Bursar, who looked after housing and maintenance of all college accommodation, while also being responsible, under a longstanding agreement, for external maintenance of the Osler House Club at the John Radcliffe Hospital. He also supervised the work of the chefs and the domestic and catering staff and was thus the college's general factotum upon whom I came to rely completely. We developed a friendly relationship to the extent of having a regular wager, each staking a pound on the outcome of any football match played, home or away, between Newcastle United and Oxford, as I was a life-long supporter of the former and he of the latter. When I retired I was just ahead in financial terms, but he hopes that he may yet recoup his losses. His wife, Hilary, skilfully managed the college library on a part-time basis, while Sam Harrison initially and Robert Didier subsequently (who came to us from Trinity via New College after Sam left to open a restaurant in Banbury) produced excellent meals. Indeed for many years the Green College food rated very highly in the unofficial league table of college catering. And apart from my right-hand woman, Rosemary, I found myself able to rely totally upon Penelope Bide, College Secretary when we first arrived but who retired about a year later, to be replaced by the charming and efficient Diane Price. We were sad to lose her when she successfully applied for a more senior post in Jesus College; she in turn was succeeded by Louise Butler who has continued the sound administrative tradition of the college under my successors.

Not all of the college committees were concerned with academic, administrative and financial affairs. Thus the Music Society was successively chaired by James McWhinnie and Terence Ryan, the Art Committee by Terence Ryan and Peter Garnham, the Garden Committee by Brian Bower and Mike Kettlewell, and the Wines Committee throughout by Mike Kettlewell who had a profound knowledge of his subject. In this he was ably aided and abetted by Gerald whose tasting skills had been finely honed by long experience first at St Antony's and later in Green and whose relationship with local suppliers seemed so admirable that we achieved many bargains.

Sadly, our first year was clouded by a tragic family bereavement. Betty had welcomed the prospect of moving to Oxford not only because of the nearness of Judy and her family but also because we would see more of her brother, Clifford and his family, who, as mentioned above, had moved a few years earlier to Wargrave-on-Thames. In April 1984 we had invited our Bamburgh friends the Phillips to Oxford for a weekend. We had had a pleasant afternoon together on Thursday, 5 April, and were dressing for dinner in college when Roger Harrison, Clifford's son, telephoned from Wargrave, where he too lived, with the tragic news that Clifford had died suddenly from a cardiac infarction. Betty was devastated and we had no alternative but to cut short the visit of our friends and to cancel the dinner we had planned to give them next evening at Le Manoir Aux Quat' Saisons. Ann flew over from Geneva to be with us at the funeral on the following Monday. Betty's love for Cliff made it difficult for her to conceal her grief, and I, who had admired him greatly and had cherished his friendship, found it exceptionally difficult to deliver the memorial address at that service in Wargrave Parish Church. Unfortunately this sad event triggered a sharp deterioration in a smouldering depressive illness from which Betty had plainly been suffering for some time. For several weeks, though she did her best (and usually succeeded) in concealing this from people in the college and in the outside world, her illness was so severe that I was reluctant to leave her alone unless absolutely essential. Judy was a tower of strength, as was our general practitioner, Ann McPherson, whose handling of the problem was impeccable. With appropriate treatment the condition slowly resolved, but for her this was an exceptionally distressing period which cast a blight upon the latter part of our first Oxford year. Fortunately as her illness recovered, so her confidence grew, as did her involvement in college affairs, especially in relation to music and art, along with the increasing commitments she accepted with the League of Friends of the Radcliffe Infirmary and the Sunningdale School of Art.

Perhaps above all our relationship with the students most enlivened and enriched our Green College experience. Although the successive Presidents of the Middle Common Room (Sue Fox, John O'Brien, Michael Mansfield, Caroline Wingfield, Claire Johnson and Anwar Hussein) with whom we worked differed in style, each was firmly committed to the interests of the college. Successful student study days on subjects as diverse as bereavement, addiction and child abuse were arranged, as were innumerable social events, in many of which we were guests. Parties in the bar, coffee, croissants, strawberries and cream and champagne at May Morning breakfasts in the tower when we were regaled by madrigals, morris dancers or barber's shop quartets were each memorable. But the major event of the year was the joint Green College/Osler House Club Ball, usually held on the last Saturday in May in a huge marquee on the college lawn, with additional activities being arranged in the Observatory, the bar and other parts of the college premises. While Betty and I had regularly attended medical dinner dances and student hops, as well as the Graduation Ball in Newcastle, we were not prepared for what we discovered to be the norm for an Oxford college ball. The range of entertainment and of facilities provided was exceptional; exotic cocktails of extraordinary variety, often related to the different theme chosen for each year's ball, were followed by a sumptuous repast in the marquee and then by dancing which often seemed almost an irrelevance in view of the cabaret turns from Tingewick Revue, the videos and the other delights which the assiduous organizers had arranged. We had not realized, either, that gatecrashing of Oxford balls is a way of life and that the entire college had to be surrounded with a ring of steel, defended by hearty bouncers prepared to repel all boarders. The weather varied. Two of our six balls were blessed with beautiful summer weather and two at least with unseasonable cold and rain, but the varied groups of individuals whom we invited as guests each year to make up a table of ten, often including Judy and Andy and some of their friends, invariably found these events stimulating. Unfortunately the neighbours were less impressed if, as often happened, the heavy music beat went on until 4 or 5 in the morning when breakfast was served. While I, with the student chairman, did my best to warn the neighbours by circular letter that their sleep might be disrupted, we nevertheless received a few irate telephone calls, though fortunately these did not demand the attentions of the Environmental Health Officer. Indeed I was able to divert most, if not all, in the direction of the Deans who handled the situation manfully and, unlike the sequelae of some other college balls in Oxford, nothing untoward followed.

Sport also played a major role in college life. As previously mentioned, the fellows fielded a cricket team annually against the students on the Warneford Hospital ground and invariably won until the student body became stronger and more diverse; in my last year the ageing fellows were compelled to admit defeat. Nevertheless, each February the fellows, usually led with great aplomb by Wattie Fletcher, Chairman of Common Room, and aided by the skilful performances of Jeffery Burley, Director of the Oxford Forestry Institute, regularly defeated the students at indoor games above the bar. My misspent youth usually helped me to prevail on the snooker and table tennis tables, but I invariably succumbed to the quicker reflexes of the students at bar football, while honours were fairly even at darts. Betty and I also became regular and avid supporters of Osler House boats on the river during Torpids in February and the Eights in May as Osler House crews, with many Green College students aboard, were often successful. In our early years, particularly in John O'Brien's time, the men's crew were firmly ensconced in Division 2 and on one occasion when there were four Green College students in the Osler first boat, we were presented with an oar which now hangs proudly in the bar. However, the girls were even more successful and were often at the Head of the River. Indeed when Claire Johnson was Captain of Osler House Ladies' Boat Club, her crew (with four Green College girls aboard) established a record by being Head in both the Torpids and in the Summer Eights; hence in that year two elderly boats were burned on the path outside the Observatory at the Boat Club dinner. Betty and I were guests each time and watched with interest combined with horror as we saw the girls in their flimsy dresses jumping through the flames. Fortunately there were no casualties on either occasion. So regular were we in watching them performing on the river that Dr Pete Sudbury, their coach, eventually nominated Betty as official mascot of the Osler House ladies' boat. He was rather less pleased when after the girls had rowed over at the head in the Eights, they deposited him, fully clothed, in the Thames. Relationships were temporarily somewhat soured, though his pride in their performance eventually prevailed. There were also many outstanding individual sporting achievements by Green College students during our time. Kathy Griffiths rowed in the University ladies' boat and Rupert Vessey became Captain of the Oxford Rugby XV, achieving six successive blues. In his last year Oxford defeated Cambridge resoundingly and a large Green College contingent, having travelled to Twickenham by coach, were there to cheer. In my last two years a common room member, Dr Gerald Sacks, initiated a Green College golf day at Southfield Golf Club in which I have played each year and for which I provided a trophy which I hope will be competed for annually for many years to come.

In the early years of the college's existence relationships between it and the Osler House Club were somewhat soured by the persistent view of some students in other colleges that Green College had hijacked their social accommodation in the Observer's house and adjacent stables and that the new accommodation on the John Radcliffe Hospital site had neither the same space nor the ambience. That view, which had caused many vehemently to oppose the establishment of the college, was shared by several senior members of the medical staff of the Oxford hospitals, not least the University's Medical Officer, Dr Bent Juel-Jensen, a fellow of St Cross and Senior Member of the Osler House Club. Before I arrived in Oxford the standing consultative committee which had been established between Green College and the Club was not, I am told, a very friendly gathering, though Richard Doll worked hard to repair fences and to improve the relationship. Fortunately in August 1983 Janet Morris, a Green College student, was elected president of the Club and she and I did our best to establish a more satisfactory relationship. Recognizing that the premises at the John Radcliffe required refurbishment, modification and extension, we embarked jointly upon an appeal to former Oxford graduates and to trusts, foundations and other bodies in order to raise the capital required. A parallel appeal was launched by Bent Juel-Jensen and the Oxford Medical Graduates Society, as Bent (with whom I subsequently became more friendly as we got to know each other better) did not wish to be associated with any appeal launched by Green College. With the help of a most generous contribution from the Rhodes Trustees, we eventually achieved our target of £60,000 and so the extension went ahead; it was eventually completed in early 1985, so that the club premises were much improved. Thereafter the relationship between the two bodies steadily became warmer, and Sam Kaddoura, a later president of the club, and I felt that we had achieved a modus vivendi which would be of lasting benefit to both organizations. Unfortunately in the next year (my last in the college), for reasons which are rather obscure but which related mainly to the failure of the Osler House Club to minute a previous informal agreement, there was a temporary worsening of the relationship. However, I now understand that the original objective has been achieved whereby all clinical students and members of Osler House Club are entitled to the use of some Green College facilities, including the tennis and squash courts, and are thus associate members of the college, while all non-medical students of Green College automatically become associate members of the Club and are entitled to use its facilities. I hope that the frictions and misunderstandings of earlier days are now forgotten and that the two organizations will now work in harmony. Osler House is exceptional in Oxford in being able to field crews on the river and teams in intercollege competitions without being a college. Attempts have been made to overturn this arrangement but have invariably been defeated on the grounds that clinical medical students have arduous and time-consuming responsibilities and are not therefore available to participate in sporting activities of their colleges when other students can. Thus it seems that the place of Osler House on the river is assured and that, at least in the immediate future, Green College will fulfil its sporting aspirations by encouraging its students to participate in Osler House activities.

One problem faced by every head of house in Oxford is the continuing need to raise additional funds over and above the income derived from interest on such endowments as the college may possess, along with rents derived from letting accommodation and from student fees. Gerald and his colleagues were remarkably successful at achieving a profit on the college catering account, while also providing excellent meals at surprisingly low cost. Nevertheless, as I often said, I spent much of my time in the college with my hand in other people's pockets trying to raise money so as to increase our endowment capital and expand our accommodation. From its inception, the college adopted the commendable policy of offering all fresher students a place in college rooms and of assuring the student body that each would be able to spend two out of the three years that most were to be in Oxford in such accommodation, thus being required to find lodgings in the open market for only one year of three. When we arrived there were some 60 student rooms on the principal site, in the Doll building and in the Observer's house, recently extended, along with an annex providing another 10 rooms at Bradmore Road. There was some additional married accommodation in houses in Observatory Street and in four flats at 13 Norham Gardens, the house formerly occupied by Sir William Osler when Regius Professor of Medicine. As our student numbers increased, more accommodation was clearly needed. It also became apparent that as the college's administrative and academic programme grew, more office space and rooms for academic visitors (who were beginning to come from other parts of the UK and from overseas in increasing number, would be required. Within my first year we bought No. 1 Observatory Street, next door to the Warden's home, and this enabled us to accommodate an additional married student with children. Not long afterwards the Lord Napier public house in Observatory Street came on to the market. When we looked at it, it was evident that it could readily be converted into student rooms; our offer of £100,000 was accepted. With the aid of Mr Graham Jessop, a local architect, although we encountered some problems relating to adaptation of the basement, we were able to provide an additional 10 student rooms of good quality, close to the college, at a total additional cost for conversion of £100,000. We thus obtained 10 rooms at a capital cost of £20,000 each, which even in 1985 was very good value.

Despite this welcome addition, our need for yet further accommodation continued to be pressing. A provisional plan had been drawn up earlier which would involve demolition of a small and unattractive lodge standing by the college's vehicle entrance, with a view to replacing it by a major residential block. It was also proposed to extend the existing office block towards that entrance, thus providing more office space and visitor accommodation and enclosing the area of grass and trees to the south of the stables block and Observer's house to form another quadrangle. The cost of this development, even in 1985, was estimated to be at least half a million pounds. We therefore decided to mount a major appeal in the hope of proceeding with this ambitious plan and invited Michael Harrison of the University Surveyor's office (with Jack Lankester, now retired, as a consultant) to draw up revised plans. We also decided to excavate the site deeply below the proposed new residential block so as to provide a lecture theatre with 80–100 seats, since the Ida Green Seminar Room in the Observer's house, increasingly needed for meetings and conferences, could only accommodate up to 50 people (and then with some discomfort). Additional teaching accommodation was plainly needed to complement that in the committee room in the office block. We also realized that our popular library was soon likely to burst its seams and so planned in the basement not only a lecture theatre which could be used for musical recitals, but also a book stack. In the basement of the extended office block, we included a much-needed wine cellar and store for students' trunks.

Clearly the first step was to recruit an appeal committee of which fortunately Mr John Raisman, then Chairman of Shell (UK) and subsequently Deputy Chairman of British Telecom, agreed to become Chairman. Several local dignitaries and some notable medical colleagues from London and elsewhere also agreed to become members. The appeal was launched at a ceremony in the Merck Sharp and Dohme Room of the Royal Society of Medicine in late 1985 in the presence of many fellows of the college and student officers. We also designed an attractive but inexpensive appeal brochure which I sent out to a large number of companies, trusts, foundations and wealthy individuals. The initial response was frankly disappointing, though we did receive some reasonably substantial donations from industry. Sir Edward Abraham produced a very generous contribution from the E.P.A. Cephalosporin Trust and the Rhodes Trustees again came to our aid, as did our old friend Per Saugman of Blackwell Scientific Publications, who produced a substantial covenant towards the cost of the book stack. Hence we decided to call the lecture theatre the E.P. Abraham Theatre and the book stack the Blackwell Book Stack (we had already honoured Per, honorary fellow of the college, by naming the library reading room the Saugman room). Later still, Edwin and Kathleen Stevens, major benefactors of Jesus College of which he was an alumnus and of the Royal Society of Medicine, produced a major contribution, as did my good friend Alexander Patrick through his Patrick Trust of Birmingham. Thus a visitor suite in the office block became the Patrick Room. After six months, however, we were still far short of our target, having raised just over £250,000 from all sources. Throughout the exercise I had kept Cecil and Ida Green fully informed of our intentions and progress but had never formally requested a contribution, as when I first met Cecil a remark of his which I always remembered was 'My boy, never ask for money but tell people what you're doing in the hope that they might be interested!'. Naturally, therefore, we were thrilled when Cecil wrote to say that in the light of what he and Ida had read about our appeal, they would give us a million dollars, so that we were virtually 'home and dry'.

Just when we thought we could go full steam ahead, another cloud appeared on the horizon and soon assumed menacing proportions. Preliminary and tentative enquiries by Michael Harrison and consultations with the City's Planning Department and Conservation Officer had suggested that we would be unlikely to encounter any problem in obtaining planning consent, particularly since we planned to construct the new development in attractive stone and in the same architectural style as the original buildings designed by Jack Lankester. To our astonishment, our planning application was opposed by the Oxford Victorian Society on the grounds that the small, stark and unattractive lodge which would have to be demolished was, as they put it, a part of Oxford's architectural heritage as it had been designed in the office of Sir Hubert Worthington. The fact that it was built in 1935 did not seem to deter them from raising formal objections. To our even greater astonishment the City's Planning Committee supported them and refused planning permission, suggesting that we should redesign the new development so as to integrate the lodge into the new scheme. This seemed to us in the college and to our advisers to be complete architectural nonsense. After briefing the University's solicitors, we clearly had no alternative but to appeal and to brief counsel to present our case. In the meantime, we obtained many letters in support of our case, including one from Sir Michael Manser, President of the Royal Institute of British Architects, and another from my old friend Professor Douglass Wise, former Professor of Architecture in Newcastle, later head of a postgraduate school of architectural design in York. I recall with especial pleasure the letter which Douglass sent me, contrasting the elegant simplicity of the new buildings we planned with what he called the 'tweedy vernacular' of the lodge. Our appeal was heard on 1 and 2 July 1987; soon afterwards we learned with pleasure and relief that the inspector had agreed entirely with our submission. Hence after a delay of many months and at a total cost of approximately £25,000, we were finally able to proceed. I was also thrilled when Lord (Edwin) McAlpine of Moffat, whom I had come to know well through his support of the Royal Society of Medicine, generously agreed to persuade his company, Sir Robert McAlpine & Sons, to build the new buildings for us at very competitive cost. In acknowledgement of his generosity and that of his company, we decided to call the quadrangle which would be enclosed by the new development the McAlpine Quad. Even then all was not totally straightforward as we had to be careful not to refer to the new building adjacent to the office block, which abutted upon it but did not communicate, as an extension because an extension to an existing building would have attracted 15% VAT, whereas a new building did not.

In February 1988 the lodge was quickly demolished, the ground excavated and progress thereafter was uninterrupted. When our friend and benefactor Cecil Green paid us a brief visit in March 1988 on his way to Saudi Arabia he laid a commemorative foundation stone to acknowledge his and Ida's generosity. Everything then went smoothly and the buildings were ready for occupancy in May 1989. Fortunately their completion came just in time for us to arrange to celebrate the tenth anniversary of the founding of the college along with a formal opening by the new Chancellor of the University, Lord Jenkins of Hillhead, in the presence of Cecil Green, the Vice-Chancellor and innumerable other benefactors and dignitaries, as well as fellows, students and staff of the college, in Encaenia week in June. This was an exceptionally moving and memorable week for us, first because my life peerage had been announced a week earlier in the Queen's Birthday Honours List (Betty and I had given a garden party for fellows and student officers to celebrate that event), secondly because the sun shone throughout and the Oxford weather was gloriously warm and windless, thirdly because many old friends like Bill Gibson and his wife from Canada, were able to be with us, and fourthly because the Governing Body had decided to honour us both by calling the new residential block the Walton building. The innumerable events we arranged, including the usual run of dinners and lunches, a symposium in the new lecture theatre, a concert and a dinner-dance in a marquee on the lawn, all went swimmingly and Cecil enjoyed himself hugely, as did we, as for Betty and me this represented the last series of formal college events in which we would be involved since my Wardenship was drawing to a close. The only problem for Betty was that she felt distinctly unwell, experiencing queasy abdominal symptoms for much of the week (though no-one else would have noticed it); after the wonderful if exhausting week was over and Cecil had winged his way back to Dallas, her nausea, anorexia and weight loss increased so alarmingly that we had no alternative but to seek medical advice. After investigation it proved that she had picked up giardiasis during our splendid Swan Hellenic cruise in the Mediterranean, probably when we called at Cairo for lunch. Treatment was quickly prescribed and was soon effective, so that when July came round and our move to 13 Norham Gardens (see below) was completed, she was restored to health and able to enjoy our August retreat to Detchant before we returned to Oxford for our last month in college.

Innumerable happy memories of these remarkable six years continually recur, not least the surprise party in 1A Observatory Street which Betty, completely without my knowledge, had arranged in September 1987 for my 65th birthday and for our daughter Ann's 40th. I came back from London after an exhausting GMC meeting and called at my office to sign my letters. After I had done so, Rosemary, a part of the conspiracy, telephoned Betty in Observatory Street to say that I was on my way. I was anticipating changing into dinner jacket in order to attend a major reception organized by the Nuffield Department of Orthopaedic Surgery at Blenheim Palace, a commitment which had been in my diary for some months. Little did I know that instead of accepting that invitation, as I had thought, Rosemary had sent our apologies for absence! When I entered the kitchen the television was on and Betty was watching athletics. I sat with her for a few minutes; she then said that she was reluctant to trouble me when I had had a hard day, but that the builder had come to repair a slight leak in the roof and one of his men had put his foot through the ceiling in a bedroom on the top floor. I tore out of the room and up the two flights of stairs to inspect the damage; on flinging open the bedroom door I found the entire family there, Ann, Judy, Christopher, their spouses and all the grandchildren, singing 'Happy birthday to you'. This was an indescribable emotional experience (I should have been forewarned, having arranged a similar event in Newcastle for Betty's 60th birthday). We ate at 1A that evening with food provided splendidly by Bo Simmons. Next day the party spirit continued, after golf at Frilford, as friends and relatives arrived from throughout the country, including Donald and Betty Webster, Rex and Pat Belas, Jack and Joan Phillips, Austin and Peggy Laws and several of Ann's old friends from London. They massed in Observatory Street for drinks; we then enjoyed a splendid dinner in college (for which I paid later!), and I used my new video camera, something which I had long wished to acquire and which the family had bought for me to commemorate that never-to-be-forgotten occasion.

Early in my Wardenship I received a pressing invitation, sponsored by Cecil and Ida, to be the Green Visiting Professor at the University of Texas Medical Branch in Galveston, Texas. Betty and I agreed to spend a week there in June 1984, when the irrepressible Andy Suttle was our host and where for the first time we really got to know well Cecil and Ida. Cecil had clearly been a vigorous, thrusting, entrepreneurial businessman who had made a tremendous success of his scientific and professional life and of the companies which he founded. And Ida, despite his and her regrets that they had never had children of their own, had given him unstinting support and had always kept a weather eye upon the nature and extent of the benefactions which the two of them together had lavished upon worthy causes in medicine and science in the USA, Canada, Australia and, of course, Green College. Though Galveston is not the most attractive of places, we had a happy and friendly week enjoying the hospitality of the Greens and of Andy Suttle, Bill Willis and their associates in the University. My lectures and clinical demonstrations seemed to go quite well and we also had a little spare time for bird-watching along the coast. This was not the hurricane season, though we noted with some apprehension that all the houses along the sea-front were built on stilts because of the regular violent flooding to which the area was subjected. During this brief visit we also met the remarkable Jack McGovern, founder of the McGovern Allergy Clinic in Houston, a major founder and supporter of the American Osler Society, whose interest in Osler and medical history was profound. Later he was to be instrumental, through his foundation, in giving substantial financial support towards the restoration of Osler's former home at 13 Norham Gardens (see below).

On our return to Oxford I set out to try to acquire for Cecil an honorary doctorate of Oxford University to add to the many that he had already received in his own country and in Canada and Australia. I knew that I must tread carefully as Oxford, like all other UK universities, has an aversion, fully justified, to any proposal which might suggest that honorary degrees were conferred upon benefactors solely because of the magnitude of their donations. The case for Cecil therefore had to be based upon his scientific contributions to geophysics and I was happy to obtain the support of my former Newcastle colleague Professor Keith Runcorn, an internationally known geophysicist, who enthusiastically supported the submission. Fortunately my friend John Potter, GMC member, former neurosurgeon and Director of Postgraduate Medical Studies in Oxford was a member of the Hebdomadal Council and was able to submit the proposal; happily it was accepted. Sadly, before the degree could be conferred at Encaenia in June 1986, Cecil and Ida were involved in a car accident when it seems that Cecil fell asleep at the wheel and the car he was driving ran off the road, colliding with a tree. Cecil suffered only minor bruises but Ida was more seriously injured and had to be admitted to hospital. Unfortunately, too, she had been under treatment for some years for a blood disorder; the combined effects of her illness and of the accident meant that she was unable to join Cecil in Oxford. The occasion, nevertheless, was moving and impressive; once again we enjoyed glorious hot weather and Cecil, though in his late eighties, stood up remarkably well to the events of the week, including the usual lunches and dinners in Green College, Lord Crewe's Benefaction (champagne with strawberries and cream) on the morning of Encaenia followed by the degree ceremony, the magnificently sumptuous lunch in the Codrington Library of All Souls which Betty and I invariably enjoyed, the garden party in the afternoon and even the Christ Church gaudy in the evening. We made a video recording of the events of the day and Ida was able to enjoy watching it with Cecil when he returned to La Jolla.

Sadly we did not see Ida again as her health declined steadily and on Boxing Day, 26 December 1986, as Betty and I were preparing in Observatory Street to drive north to spend the New Year at Detchant, the sad news came that Ida had died that morning. I decided that I must, of course, fly to California for the funeral, but before doing so we drove to Detchant as we had planned a dinner party for friends there on New Year's Eve and felt that we must go ahead with the arrangements. I therefore returned to London by train and flew to California on the 29th in time to act as a pall-bearer with some of Cecil's friends at a moving funeral service conducted by the Bishop of San Diego in the stately white episcopalian church at La Jolla, close to Cecil's home. Later we saw Ida laid to rest alongside Cecil's parents, Charles and Maggie Green, in a massive mausoleum where a place was also prepared for Cecil when his time came. Happily, however, when he came over to lay the foundation stone of the new buildings in 1988 and returned yet again for the opening ceremony in 1989, he was as vigorous, sharp and charming as ever, if a little harder of hearing. He, like us, was much amused by a minor incident, fortunately discovered a few days before the opening ceremony, which might otherwise have marred it. When the foundation stone had been laid in 1988, it was then removed and carefully wrapped in opaque polythene before being inserted at an appropriate point in the new building when under construction. The polythene was left in place to protect it and was only removed a few days before the ceremony when, to our horror, we found that it had been laid upside down. Fortunately stonemasons were able easily to extract it and to replace it the right way up; this incident enabled me to say during my speech that the builders had clearly inserted the stone under the mistaken impression that our benefactor, Dr Green, was an Australian rather than an American. Yet again the indefatigable Cecil returned to Oxford for Encaenia week in June 1991, when once more Betty and I were able to entertain him in our flat at 13 Norham Gardens; although he was a little more stooped and a little more deaf, the vigour, the humour, charm and interest were as lively as ever. As he told us, he was continuing to travel extensively, if only to try to assuage the loneliness which he had felt after 61 years of marriage to his beloved Ida. As the obituary in the *San Diego Union* had said of them after Ida's death: 'Without fanfare and sometimes in secrecy, Cecil and Ida Green donated with enormous generosity to worthy causes around the world, after carefully researching them. Theirs was a rare partnership in giving. The world is a much better place because Ida and Cecil Green passed by.'.

For Betty, much of the pleasure she derived from Green College resulted not just from her contacts with the students but also from her involvement in the work of the Art Committee and above all the Music Society. The college had gradually acquired a collection of good-quality watercolours and prints and a few oil paintings. In 1984 we were particularly pleased to receive an early watercolour of Christ Church by J. M. W. Turner, generously given by Mr Eric Towler, former Chairman of the Board of Governors of the Radcliffe Infirmary. Later still, our friend the late Arthur Williams, gynaecologist, loaned us a painting by Paul Nash, and these two treasures still adorn the Fellows' Room. The splendid little stables gallery was also an excellent venue for exhibitions by local artists who found the ambience delightful and many succeeded in selling some of the their works. Once a year, too, members of the college displayed for two weeks examples of their own artistic and photographic work; Betty herself was a regular exhibitor. We were all charmed by the supremely skilful artistic work of a common room member, Dr Irvine Loudon, and by the photographic skills of Andrew Markus and Charles Warlow, among others. Students and Phil Whittaker, our head porter, were also regular contributors. It is a sad commentary upon the age in which we live to have to report that some pictures displayed by the Oxford Print Makers Cooperative were stolen and that we also lost an Ogden Nash work from our own collection in the Smoking Room. Remarkably, too, a complete set of curtains was stolen from the landing in the office block and the committee room; in consequence, our insurance had to be revised and our security tightened considerably.

Before we arrived, the Music Society had confined its activities to arranging biannual concerts by visiting artists and to arranging occasional performances by string quartets from within the college and Osler House Club; Sara Tunnicliffe was a very capable organizer. However, with the support of an enthusiastic committee which soon elected Betty as President of the Society, and through the energy of college fellows and members like Brian and Christine Bower, Tom Patterson, Terence Ryan, David Millard and Ruth Wynne-Davis, it was decided to form a college choir. This began quietly but once Peter McKenzie, a common room member and consultant anaesthetist, and his wife had joined and Peter had agreed to be conductor, the choir prospered and Betty served throughout as regular accompanist during rehearsals, ably assisted by Christine Bower. While she was also anxious to sing whenever possible and did so when an orchestral accompaniment was available, she also accompanied the choir in many private and public performances. Among the many concerts given over the years, often with imported soloists and sometimes with an enthusiastic, locally recruited, amateur orchestra, were Purcell's 'Dido and Aeneas', the concert version of 'Die Fledermaus', and Mendelssohn's 'Hymn of Praise' (which Betty accompanied on the piano in the newly-refurbished St Paul's Church in Walton Street). Later still, when additional members were recruited from other colleges and from the Oxford hospitals, the choir became even more ambitious. Nevertheless, there were some traumatic occasions when, because of the shifting student population and the clinical responsibilities of the medics, attendance at rehearsals was less good than Peter McKenzie would have wished. Sometimes he was seriously alarmed lest the actual performances which he was to conduct would be of inadequate quality. Usually all turned out well, but nevertheless after a few years Peter decided to give up and the choir had to find a new conductor. Fortunately they quickly identified Francis Knights, a postgraduate student of music at Christ Church who proved to be enthusiastic and unflappable. Under his tutelage performances of Vivaldi's 'Gloria' and of the Fauré 'Requiem' were given, for example, at St Barnabas Church before a relatively large and enthusiastic audience and even attracted a favourable review in the Oxford Times. The choir's repertoire was nothing if not catholic, as on another occasion they performed some Russian church music and on yet another Betty accompanied them in a performance of 'Captain Noah and his

Floating Zoo' at the John Radcliffe Hospital, assisted by double bass and drums.

With the enthusiastic support of the College Chaplain, David Cook, who became a fellow in our second year, we arranged college services at the beginning and end of each academic year in the Radcliffe Infirmary Chapel, where Betty played the organ and the choir provided an anthem. David Cook, a PhD of Edinburgh with a background of training in classics, also once delivered the annual Latin Sermon, on my nomination, in the University Church of St Mary; Betty and I attended loyally, though we understood very little. That occasion was also marked by the fact that I hung up my coat and precious fur hat in the church vestibule before the service, only to find afterwards that the hat had been stolen. Later David, at my request, wrote a short college grace—*Pro bono cibo et sodalitate huius collegii te deum laudamus*—which Francis Knights later set to music. That musical version was sometimes performed on college dining-in nights and especially, followed by carols, at the fellows' Christmas dinner. Betty's musical pedigree had been established quite early when, at our first college Christmas dinner, she and Terence Ryan played 'The Arrival of the Queen of Sheba' as a duet for four hands on the splendid college Yamaha grand, while others like Brian Bower performed, he on his oboe and Richard Wood (subsequently to leave us on being appointed to a chair of surgery in London) also demonstrating his instrumental expertise. Later still, Betty and I thought that it would be pleasant to have a college hymn. One Easter at Detchant she composed the music and prevailed upon me to write the words. The hymn has subsequently been performed regularly (it was sung for the first time when we held a service to celebrate the opening of our new buildings in June 1989); it has now been published in the College Record.

Three other musical matters deserve mention. First, through the good offices of Larry Bachmann, an old friend of his from California, Richard Colburn, came each summer to give a recital with his string quartet in the splendid tower room. He is an enthusiastic amateur viola player; each year when he comes to his London home to look after his UK business interests, he brings with him three professional musicians from the USA whose fares and expenses he covers personally, and they always delight in entertaining us at Green College. Mr Colburn has been a regular benefactor of the college and through his family trust helped us to buy an upright practice piano so that the college grand, previously housed in the Music Room, is now kept permanently in the Common Room, no longer having to be moved backwards and forwards for concerts and other public occasions. More recently still, the practice piano has been moved to the E. P. Abraham Theatre as Joan and Richard Doll have generously donated a Broadwood grand which now sits in the Music Room for practice and rehearsal purposes.

In 1988 Betty and I were surprised to be visited by John Sear and Peter McKenzie with a peculiar request. They told us that the Nuffield Department of Anaesthesia was celebrating its 50th anniversary and intended to hold a weekend of celebrations, including some academic events and entertainment. They planned a musical evening in Green College and asked whether Betty and I might consider performing some Geordie songs. At first we were reluctant, not least because we were unsure as to how such a performance would be accepted by an Oxford audience and by international participants, many from far afield. In the end, however, we were persuaded; I gave an explanatory introduction with a flip-chart showing how to translate Geordie language into English, and vice versa. Betty contributed some pianistic flourishes and my performance of 'The Blaydon Races' and of 'The Lambton Worm', interspersed with some Geordie tales, seemed to go surprisingly well. Indeed there were some overseas visitors who had formerly worked in Newcastle as well as Oxford who found the occasion quite nostalgic and joined in lustily in the choruses. By request we gave a repeat performance in September 1989 when the Music Society kindly arranged a farewell concert in Betty's honour, with piano solos by Terence Ryan, Christine Bower and several students, a performance by the choir, solo vocal renderings by members of the common room and by students, and several instrumental performances; especially for Betty but also for me this was an exceptionally memorable and moving event. At the end Mona Britton, on behalf of the fellows' ladies, gave Betty a charming presentation and I have a much-treasured video recording of the whole occasion (apart from our own contribution), including Betty's little speech of acceptance at the end.

Before I end these comments on the cultural activities of the college, it would be an oversight not to mention the theatre trips organized so effectively each term by Dr James McWhinnie. Routinely we went to a London theatre in the autumn, to the English National Opera in the spring and to Stratford for a Shakespeare performance in the summer, travelling by coach from the college and almost always having a buffet meal on the way or in the coach before the performance. Performances I particularly remember were those of 'The Magistrate' by Pinero at the National Theatre with Nigel Hawthorne, and 'Les Miserables' in London, 'Julius Caesar' and 'Romeo and Juliet' (played as between mods on scooters and rockers on motorbikes) at Stratford, the Jonathan Miller production of 'The Mikado' and 'Don Carlos' at the ENO. While many fellows were regular supporters, our overseas students and visiting fellows seemed especially to enjoy these occasions.

I must not, of course, forget academic activities. Before we arrived, Richard Doll had arranged an annual series of four Green College Lectures on the first four Mondays of the Hilary Term; this was a tradition which

I willingly continued. We managed, I believe, to choose themes which invariably attracted a capacity audience. In 1984 the theme was 'Medicine abroad' and lectures were given by Roger Brearley on the EEC, Sir Gordon Wolstenholme on the USA, Professor John Webb on the third world and Professor Jan Brod on medicine behind the iron curtain. The theme in 1985 was 'Education for the caring professions'; I discussed basic medical education, followed by Philip Rhodes from Southampton on postgraduate education, Baroness McFarlane of Llandaff on educating the nurses, and Olive Stevenson of Nottingham who considered education of the social worker. We were fortunate that Stephen Lock, editor of the *British Medical Journal*, agreed to publish abbreviated versions of the lectures, which assured for them a wide audience. The tradition continued in 1986 when two Nobel Prize winners agreed to contribute to our series on 'The nature of discovery in medical science'. Sir Andrew Huxley talked about discoveries on muscle, Sir James Black on pharmacology, John Humphrey on immunology, and David Weatherall on molecular biology. The standard was maintained in 1987 when our topic was 'Social and environmental influences on human health' and the speakers were Alwyn Smith of Manchester, George Brown and Geoffrey Rose from London, and Sir Richard Southwood from Oxford. In 1988 Sir George Godber, Sir Patrick Nairne, Sir Richard Bayliss and Sir Christopher Booth each contributed inimitable talks on 'British medicine: yesterday, today and tomorrow', and finally in 1989 Eric Anderson, Headmaster of Eton College, discussed the responsibility of the educator, John Havard of the BMA the responsibility of the doctor, Lewis Wolpert that of the scientist, and Zelman Cowen, Provost of Oriel College and Chairman of the Press Council, the responsibility of the media. We also decided to commemorate the contributions of John Radcliffe to Oxford medicine by holding an annual Radcliffe Lecture to open the academic year each Michaelmas Term. The first, on John Radcliffe himself, was delivered in a refreshing and lively style by The Rt Hon Lord Quinton, President of Trinity College, the second by Sir Roger Ormrod, a medical graduate of Oxford and former Lord Justice of Appeal, who talked upon 'An aetiological approach to law'. The third was a stimulating commentary on 'Artist or administrator: challenge and change in the arts' by Sir Roy Strong, Director of the Victoria and Albert Museum, while the fourth, equally fascinating, by the Rt Hon. Lord Dainton in 1988 dealt with 'The British knowledge industry: nationalized, privatized or hybrid?'.

We were also pleased when many friends and admirers of the late Professor Brod, one of our Green College Lecturers in 1984 who sadly died in Germany shortly afterwards, decided to mount an appeal to establish a Jan Brod lecture on a topic relating to his life-long interest in hypertension and renal disease. Stephen Lock of the *BMJ*, along with several noted colleagues, led the campaign and eventually we attracted sufficient funds to support a biennial event. The first lecture was delivered in 1987 by Dr Arnold Relman, editor of the *New England Journal of Medicine*, who discussed differences in the management of end-stage renal disease as between the UK and the USA, and in 1989 Professor A. W. (Bill) Asscher, Dean of St George's Hospital Medical School in London, talked about preventing renal failure.

Of the many other seminars, lectures, conferences and other college academic events, it might be appropriate to mention only the outstanding annual series of seminars on the organization and delivery of health care planned by Alex Gatherer, those on the ethics of medical practice arranged by David Cook, and the academic seminars to which fellows, members and students themselves contributed.

College life was invariably enlivened by the presence of many junior research fellows and by a more limited number of stipendiary senior fellows. Among the latter was the Joan and Richard Doll Fellow, a post occupied with distinction for several years by David Matthews whose work on diabetes achieved for him international renown. We were also fortunate, through the good offices of Dr Francisco Kerdel-Vegas, an internationally-known dermatologist from Venezuela, later Venezuelan Ambassador to the UK, in being able to establish an Armando Planchart Fellowship through the Venezuelan foundation of that name, to enable a Venezuelan doctor of distinction to spend one or two years in the college and in an appropriate university or hospital department. The first was Pedro Grases, a senior and able pathologist, the second, Jesus Isea Perez, a vigorous young cardiologist who worked with Peter Sleight in cardiology. These two visitors and their wives were enthusiastic contributors to college life. Later, through Sir Walter Bodmer, Director of the Imperial Cancer Research Fund (ICRF) Laboratories in London, we established a permanent stipendiary fellowship with funds from the ICRF and through an endowment from Sir Walter and his family, for the Director of the ICRF research unit at the Radcliffe Infirmary, Dr Valerie Beral; this was named the Bodmer/Billigheimer Fellowship in memory of Sir Walter's parents. Later still, through my personal contacts with Professors Kiikuni and Kaketa of the Japan Medical Education Foundation, and through the generosity of Dr Kawasaki, founder of the Kawasaki Medical School, we created an annual Kawasaki/Green College fellowship to enable a Japanese doctor (chosen by the Japan Medical Education Foundation in collaboration with the British Council in Tokyo) to work in a relevant Oxford department. The payment of an adequate stipend to these young doctors was made possible by a supplementary five-year grant which I also negotiated with the Great Britain/Sasakawa Foundation. These appointments also proved to be a great success and we remember with particular affection the first incumbent Dr Yoko Nakasu, a female neurosurgeon from Shiga University Medical School whose impact upon the college was striking, not only because of her charming personality and her willingness to wear Japanese traditional dress on appropriate occasions but also because of the skill and expertise she displayed in her specialty, which greatly impressed Christopher Adams, head of neurosurgery and a fellow of the college.

We were also fortunate to receive a grant of £20,000 per annum for two years through the good offices of Sir Edgar Williams of the Nuffield Provincial Hospitals Trust and its Director, Gordon McLachlan, to enable us to appoint senior visiting fellows, each of whom could be offered accommodation, a modest honorarium and academic expenses so as to spend a period of between three and six months on sabbatical leave in the college. These appointments, which spanned the period from 1985–1987, enabled us to appoint for varying periods fellows as distinguished as Struther Arnott (Purdue University, Indiana— subsequently Principal of St Andrews University), Alan Emery (Professor of Human Genetics in the University of Edinburgh), Murray Forsyth (Reader in International Politics at Leicester University), Hugh Freeman (consultant psychiatrist from Hope Hospital, Salford, and editor of the *British Journal of Psychiatry*), Harvey Gochros (Professor and Chairman of the Medical Social Work Programme in the University of Hawaii), Jerold Taitz (Senior Lecturer in the Faculty of Law at the University of Cape Town), Paul Colinvaux (Department of Zoology, Ohio State University), A. C. Munday-Castle (Professor of Psychology in the University of Lagos) and W. F. H. M. Mommaerts (Professor of Physiology in the University of California, Los Angeles) who, as a noted amateur bass singer who had previously performed in the Superbowl at Los Angeles, also became an enthusiastic member of the choir.

Junior research fellowships were different. These competitive appointments, invariably attracting a large field of applicants, were established by endowment through major financial contributions from many different bodies and individuals to enable young men and women working in research in the University or its associated hospitals in non-established appointments to have a college attachment and so to enjoy its facilities and contribute to its academic and social programme. Before we arrived the college had already established a McAlpine fellowship in neurology and neuroscience and two E. P. Abraham fellowships. Subsequently, with the generous help of visiting fellows and supporters of the college, we were able to obtain funds from the Imperial Cancer Research Fund (for two ICRF fellowships), from the Wellcome Trust (for two fellowships in the history of medicine), from Cecil and Ida (to endow Charles and Maggie Green and William Carleton Gibson fellowships), from Richard and Joan Doll (for a fellowship in medical epidemiology and statistics), from the Institute of Nursing (for a fellowship in nursing studies), from Beecham, Glaxo, Unilever and the International Primary Aluminium Institute, and from the Girdlers Company, the latter funding a fellowship specifically limited to doctors from New Zealand or with New Zealand connections. Other fellowships were also established by the Health Education Council enabling two local general practitioners to work in health education. In view of the numerous individuals involved, it would be invidious to identify many who held these fellowships with such enthusiasm and distinction during my Wardenship, but I would mention particularly Dr Robin Irvine (later Sir Robin) the first Girdlers' Fellow, who spent a year with us on sabbatical leave from his appointment as Vice-Chancellor of the University of Otago in Dunedin, New Zealand. We were also able to acknowledge the many contributions to medicine, science and to the college itself made by senior colleagues in the UK and overseas by appointing them as visiting fellows. These included Arthur Buller (former Chief Scientist to the Department of Health), John Webb (former professor of Child Health in Newcastle), Richard Charkin (Managing Director of Academic Books, Oxford University Press), David Greer (Dean of Medicine at Brown University in the United States), Professors Kaketa and Kawasaki from Japan, Jack McGovern from Texas, Philip Porter from Unilever and John Raisman, who had masterminded our building appeal, along with many others. We also honoured Sir John Burnett (former Sibthorpian Professor of Rural Economy in Oxford and later Principal of the University of Edinburgh), Dr John Horder (former President of the Royal College of General Practitioners) and Dame Rosemary Rue (former Regional Medical Officer in Oxford and President of the Faculty of Community Medicine of the Royal College of Physicians) by electing them as honorary fellows.

A significant difference between Oxford and Cambridge and the major civic universities in Britain is the fact that Oxbridge colleges have so much power. Most are independent foundations with their own statutes giving them full control over their finances and admission procedures. The Conference of Colleges, which meets twice a term and is attended by heads of houses with one other officer from each college is, however, a body which simply has an advisory role in relation to the University, with no specific authority. Heads of houses, in other words, play no significant part in University administration unless they are elected to Council or to other major University committees. Admittedly, all are members of Congregation where they can vote on issues of importance, but unlike Deans of Faculties in the civic universities, they have no specific authority in university affairs. In the past all Vice-Chancellors of Oxford, serving for three or sometimes four years, were chosen from among the heads of houses, until the tradition was broken recently by the election of Sir Richard Southwood, the distinguished Professor of Zoology, who succeeded Sir Patrick Neill of All Souls. During my time in Oxford I rarely attended Congregation and refused to stand for Council, first because

I felt that if elected my service could only be brief, and secondly, I had frankly had enough of intimate involvement in major university administration during the 10 years that I was Dean in Newcastle.

However, with very many others I attended the historic Congregation at which the proposal to grant an honorary degree to Mrs Margaret Thatcher at Encaenia was voted down after several impassioned speeches had been made by many members of the University, including several medical colleagues. This came quite early in my Wardenship and I felt less confident about contributing to the debate than I should have been. Had I done so, I would certainly have disagreed vehemently with many close and valued medical friends, including David Weatherall, Peter Morris and others, who argued that if the University conferred an honorary degree upon Mrs Thatcher this would be tantamount to endorsing her policy towards the universities. I would have explained that I was as bitterly opposed to the Government's programme of cutting grants to the universities and to the Research Councils as were any of those who spoke. On the other hand, my experience on an Honorary Degrees Committee in Newcastle had confirmed my view that a university does not award honorary degrees to endorse policy but simply to acknowledge achievement. For a graduate of Oxford, a former student of Somerville, to have become one of the outstanding Prime Ministers of the UK this century, and the first woman premier to boot, was in itself a sufficiently major achievement to have justified the award, especially since all Oxford graduates who had achieved that high office had been so honoured in the past. In my view Congregation's decision was made for specious and invalid reasons and did Oxford untold harm. Many potential benefactors were deeply aggrieved. Mr Eric Towler, who had given us our Turner watercolour and who was considering further benefactions to Green College, was so infuriated that he refused to have anything more to do with the University or with the college; several other former supporters took the same view. Of course Mrs Thatcher should have received an honorary degree several years earlier; it was perhaps the timidity of Council (for fear, it is said, of *student* protest) in not proposing her when elected premier which led to this unfortunate decision. History will, I think, judge that this clumsy act of crass insensitivity will be almost as famous as was the vote of the Oxford Union in the 1930s that 'under no circumstances would this house fight for King and country'. I cannot but express surprise that so many close friends for whose opinions and intellectual and personal integrity I have the highest regard were among the many who voted against. In my capacity as BMA President and later as President of the GMC, I had been as openly critical both in oral presentations in several fora and in my writings about Government policy in relation to the support of medical research and the universities as had many colleagues. But these views in no way diminished my conviction that the decision of Congregation did Mrs Thatcher a grievous wrong which can never, of course, be undone.

Heads of houses, even if not involved in other major university decisions, were nevertheless invited to major social occasions such as the 90th birthday party for the Chancellor (formerly Mr Harold Macmillan), the Earl of Stockton, at Balliol. I walked in procession alongside Mr Edward Heath who shook with pleasure on hearing the organ scholar performing manfully, having been one himself. Throughout dinner we glanced with increasing apprehension at the Chancellor who seemed to slump forward over high table, eating rarely and just occasionally stretching out a shaky hand to lift a glass of amber liquid (his favourite Scotch) to his lips. But as usual, when the meal was over he rose unsteadily but delivered a racy, humorous and stimulating speech, without a note, revealing that he was intellectually as sharp as ever. Later some of us repaired to the Master's lodgings where the Chancellor was surrounded by an admiring throng until well into the night. Next morning I met Tony Kenny (Master of Balliol) walking slightly unsteadily down St Giles and complaining bitterly of a hangover as he had had to sit up till 2.30 a.m. with the Chancellor, trying to keep pace with him as the whisky flowed. Sadly, the Chancellor, well into his nineties, eventually died in office and I had the privilege of attending the magnificent memorial service held for him in the University Church of St Mary. There then followed the jolly business of electing his successor. At first it seemed that honours were relatively even as between Edward Heath, Lord Blake (of Queen's) and Lord (Roy) Jenkins of Hillhead, but Roy Jenkins romped home by a substantial majority and has proved to be an assiduous and excellent Chancellor.

Even though my involvement with the University was limited, I was occasionally called upon to give advice to the Campaign for Oxford which set out, admittedly rather late in the day in comparison with other universities, to raise private funds. Led by Sir Patrick Neill and directed by Henry Drucker, it has gained increasing impetus and within a very short time has made huge strides towards its ultimate target of £220,000,000. As I write, more than £190,000,000 has been raised. At the same time, I was also involved in the Radcliffe Medical Foundation appeal which aimed to achieve many long-awaited developments in the Oxford hospitals. Here again the target of £5,000,000 has now been raised under the inspired leadership of Baroness (Janet) Young, formerly Minister of State at the Foreign and Commonwealth Office in the House of Lords and a great supporter of Oxford medicine.

There were, however, three University committees which the Vice-Chancellor asked me to chair. The first, which I much enjoyed, was the Committee for Disabled People which set out to try to improve facilities in University departments and colleges for disabled students and staff. Despite the miniscule budget which Council allowed us, I believe that we made good progress in improving facilities and access. Not least, we attracted charitable funds and volunteer support to provide a reading service for blind students in the Bodleian Library. With the enthusiastic support of Charles Mould, the Secretary, and the dedicated volunteer efforts of Col. Baker, this was quickly established. I believe that the committee continues to prosper, now under the chairmanship of Sir Raymond (Bill) Hoffenberg.

The Vice-Chancellor also persuaded me to undertake a much less attractive assignment by chairing another committee of dons and students which was invited to develop a code of practice to deal with allegations of sexual harassment in the University. We laboured for several months, receiving at times some inaccurate and even unsavoury press publicity, not just in the local and national press but in other parts of the world (I received a few semi-abusive international telephone calls). The task was not easy, even though we had two lawyers and some very sensible members of staff and students on the committee. Eventually I believe we drafted a sound code of practice suggesting a three-stage procedure for dealing with such complaints. It was designed to protect the interests of the individuals making the allegations and those complained against. However, two members of the committee, Ruth Deech (soon to be Principal of St Anne's) and Margaret Rayner of Council, submitted a minority report preferring a much simpler mechanism. When I presented our report to Council, the minority report prevailed. My own view was that it was oversimplistic and unlikely to be effective in the long term; recently I understand that the issue has reared its head again and yet another working party has now reported, making recommendations of which several seem very familiar.

More pleasurable but equally demanding was the request that I should chair a local organizing committee charged with raising the necessary funds to support the national meeting of the British Association for the Advancement of Science which was to be held in Oxford in 1988. I was delighted to do so, particularly since my friend Sir Walter Bodmer was to be President. However, the fund-raising exercise proved far more arduous than we had anticipated, not least because we began our work at a time when local authorities were under serious financial constraint and neither Oxford City nor Oxfordshire were able to give us the grants which local authorities in major UK cities had given when the BA met in their respective universities. Nevertheless with the help of the outstanding local organizer, Lady (Wendy) Ball, wife of the Warden of Keble, and an enthusiastic group of helpers, plans materialized and money trickled in reasonably well. However, as the week of the meeting approached we became increasingly anxious. Early on I had approached Robert (Bob) Maxwell of Pergamon Press and he and his delightful wife, Betty, invited some of us to lunch at their home at Headington Hill Hall, which for many years they had rented from the Council (as Bob said, it was the most luxurious council house in the country!). Certainly we were impressed not only by its physical ambience but by the interest which Bob expressed in the activities of the BA, and thought we were on an excellent wicket. Indeed at one stage he suggested that he would be willing to give us £50,000 provided the BA accepted a number of suggestions about its future activities. I discussed these with the BA officers and all were acceptable. I then approached him again to confirm this, but found it increasingly difficult to make contact, either in Oxford or through his headquarters in the Mirror building in London. Eventually one morning I called on him at 8.00 a.m. in his London flat where, to my surprise, he said that it was unlikely that he would help us at all. I reminded him of his offer and he agreed to reconsider; since nothing came I went back to see him yet again. At last, after innumerable telephone calls and several further meetings we received his cheque for £10,000 as our last major contribution. This helped us almost to reach our target, though the University was compelled to make a contribution, fortunately far less than the sum it had originally agreed to underwrite. The meeting was immensely successful; and Wendy Ball and her helpers, including an enthusiastic band of students, made the delegates from the UK and from other parts of the world completely welcome. Patrick Moore's lecture, which I chaired, was especially enjoyable. Sir Walter's presidential address in the Sheldonian Theatre was also outstanding and I gave the vote of thanks. Little did I think then that three years later I would be involved with the BA again by being invited to chair the National Commission on Education which they had decided to sponsor and which was generously funded by the Paul Hamlyn Foundation.

Only one other major committee came my way and that was to join with Tony Epstein (subsequently Sir Anthony) and others in the Working Party on Bovine Spongiform Encephalopathy established by the Ministry of Agriculture, Fisheries and Food under the expert chairmanship of Sir Richard Southwood. I believe that our report, accepted and endorsed by Government, reassured the public that the chance of transmission of BSE to human subjects by eating beef was miniscule, and so I believe it has proved.

Another matter concerning our Oxford years remains to be mentioned and relates to 13 Norham Gardens, the former home of the great Sir William Osler, Regius Professor of Medicine in Oxford from 1905 to 1919. He lived at that address from 1907 until his death at the age of 70 in 1919; during that period the house became known as 'The Open Arms' because of the outstanding hospitality which he and his wife showed to doctors, medical students and visitors from the British Isles and the rest of the world. His teaching and example were so pervasive and long-lasting, building upon the image and reputation he had created at McGill

University in Montreal, in the University of Pennsylvania Hospitals at Philadelphia and as Foundation Professor of Medicine at Johns Hopkins University in Baltimore, that after his death his memory was hallowed by the creation of Osler Societies in many countries throughout the world. Some 19 were established and many still function, including the Osler Club of London, and the American, Japanese and Danish Osler Societies to quote but a few. 13 Norham Gardens is a huge Victorian house in which Lady Osler continued to live after Sir William's death. In her will she bequeathed the house, as Sir William had wished, to Christ Church as a permanent home for all future Regius Professors of Medicine. However, Sir William's successor did not wish to live there; for some time the house was used by the University as a student hostel, which eventually led to the establishment of St Anne's College. Much later, however, the house was occupied by two successive Regius Professors, Sir George Pickering and Sir Richard Doll, though it was modified in the interim by converting some accommodation at the north end of the building into self-contained flats.

When Sir Richard Doll retired as Regius Professor to become Warden of Green College and moved into 1A Observatory Street, the house again became vacant and the University decided to offer it on a 21-year full repairing and maintenance lease to Green College. The college carried out further refurbishment; four self-contained apartments for married students were retained to the north while three large rooms on the ground floor and a conservatory, as well as part of the basement, were leased to the University Newcomers Club. This club had been created to entertain and assist the wives and families of new members of staff and visitors to the University coming from other parts of the UK but more especially from other parts of the world. The substantial residual accommodation was converted first into a capacious apartment to be made available for any future Regius Professor of Medicine, while a separate suite of offices on the ground floor was provided in Osler's old library and in an adjacent room which had been the Oslers' drawing room. When we arrived at Green College the apartment and ground floor offices were occupied by Dr Philippe Shubik and his wife. Dr Shubik was a senior research fellow of Green College, carrying out work on toxicology with the support of grants from the United States where he had previously worked.

During my Wardenship, it soon emerged that the fabric of 13 Norham Gardens was in need of attention. Much of the stonework on the balustrades of the rear verandah, on the balconies around certain windows and on the steps leading to the front door was crumbling, the roof was in urgent need of repair and so, too, was much of the woodwork. An estimate revealed that not less than £50,000 was needed in order to repair the most obvious deficiencies and hence we embarked upon a 13 Norham Gardens appeal, seeking support from Osler Societies and from personal admirers of Osler the world over. Later still, we established the 'Friends of 13 Norham Gardens', of which Dr Alastair Robb-Smith, the retired Oxford pathologist and outstanding medical historian, agreed to become President while Jack McGovern of Houston, Texas, who had helped to pay for the original conversion of the building in Richard Doll's day became Honorary Life President. I was invited to be Chairman and many distinguished patrons were also recruited. Fortunately, after much correspondence and effort, funds were gradually accumulated and Jack McGovern was again exceptionally generous in giving us a major grant from his foundation. Some friends and supporters in the United States and Canada such as Paul Beeson and Jerry Barondess, among many others, persuaded organizations like McGill University, the Hannah Institute for the History of Medicine, Trinity College of the University of Toronto, the University of Toronto itself, Johns Hopkins Hospital, Johns Hopkins University and Jefferson Medical College in Philadelphia to give us major contributions. Many individuals in Britain, in the United States, in Canada and in Japan also contributed, so that in the end we embarked upon a major programme of repair and refurbishment which was finally completed in spring 1989.

We also set out to try to restore as best we could Osler's library to something like what it was in his day, even though Dr Shubik was continuing to use it as a working office. A copy of the triptych of Linacre, Harvey and Sydenham which had been installed above the fireplace by Osler was prepared through the efforts of Alastair Robb-Smith and a replica of the Pembroke portrait of Sir Thomas Browne, one of Osler's literary heroes, was also provided by him. It now hangs in state above one of the bookcases, as did the original in Osler's day. We also acquired innumerable books, reprints and other memorabilia, including, ironically, a silver cigarette case given to us by a Dr Ramsden who received it from his uncle, a friend of Osler's; it contains Osler's visiting card with the inscription 'Smoke and think of your friend, Sir William Osler'. We also received a generous contribution from the American Neurological Association, of which Osler was a member, through the intervention of Jim Toole of Winston-Salem (later a visiting scholar of the college), a copy of the Abraham Belsky Medal, a cast of Osler's head by Doris Appel (kindly donated by Dr McGovern), a picture of Osler's birthplace at Bond Head, Ontario, and a piece of Revere silver which had belonged to the Osler family, from Mr Campbell Osler, QC, and his wife from Toronto. The latter was particularly interesting because Grace Osler, née Revere, was the great grand-daughter of Paul Revere, the Boston silversmith, who undertook the famous ride to warn the colonists of the approach of British troops. Also proudly displayed in the hall, with a detailed commentary upon its complicated history, is Osler's Oxford DSc gown, given by Lady Osler after his death to Sir Walter Morley Fletcher, which later

528   The Spice of Life

came into the hands of Lord Brain who had it converted to a DM gown for use by his son Michael. When Lord Brain died and Michael (now Professor of Haematology at McMaster University, Hamilton, Ontario) acquired his father's gown, he donated the converted Osler gown to 'The Friends'.

As my Wardenship of Green College drew to a close, Betty and I were honoured by being invited to take on the tenancy of the regius Professor's flat once the Shubiks' lease had expired. This we were delighted to do; after some negotiation I was able to raise the necessary funding through my friend Alexander Patrick of Birmingham to enable me also to rent the ground floor offices, including the library, in order to continue with my professional work. I was also relieved to be awarded a Leverhulme Emeritus Fellowship which supported my continuing work and activities after my retirement and contributed towards the salary of my secretary, Rosemary. After my retirement she worked half-time for a year with me and half-time with the Acting Warden of Green College, Dr Trevor Hughes, who stood in ably during the inter-regnum before my elected successor Sir Crispin Tickell, former UK representative at the United Nations, was able to take office in 1990. Fortunately after my election as the President of the World Federation of Neurology in October 1984 and my acquisition of other responsibilities, I was able to find the additional resources needed to employ her full-time at 13 Norham Gardens, where she continues to work in the delightful office next door to Osler's library.

The move to 13 Norham Gardens in July 1989 went smoothly in that glorious hot summer, with the willing and strenuous assistance of our daughter Ann who flew over from Geneva to be with us for a week. Since then we have much enjoyed the ambience of Osler's former residence and its garden. I have been a life-long admirer of Osler ever since, as a medical student, I was introduced to his writings by Sir James Spence in Newcastle. I then read avidly many of his works, including *Aequanimitas and Other Essays*, *An Alabama Student and Other Essays*, *Counsels and Ideals* and also purchased and read Cushing's *Life of Osler* and then Fulton's *Life of Cushing*. The first semi-scientific paper that I wrote was published in the University of Durham *Medical Gazette* in 1944 and was entitled 'A great physician'; it dealt with Osler's life and work. And in 1982 when the BMA celebrated its 150th anniversary and I handed over the presidency at its annual meeting to His Royal Highness Prince Charles, Stephen Lock invited me and the other chief officers to write articles for the *British Medical Journal* on 'The medical book I would most like to have written'. I unhesitatingly chose Cushing's *Life of Osler*, while Tony (later Sir Anthony) Grabham chose *Aequanimitas*, as did, without any collusion, David Bolt, the Chairman of the Central Committee for Hospital Medical Services, not, as he said, so much because he would have liked to have written the book, but because he would like to have been the kind of man who could have written it.

During the past three years of our enjoyable residence in 13 Norham Gardens (as neither the present Regius, Professor Henry Harris, nor his successor, Sir David Weatherall, wish to occupy the apartment there) I have continued to collect, to catalogue and display various Osler memorabilia and have been delighted that so many Osler admirers from the UK and other parts of the world have come to visit the Osler shrine, which it is such a privilege to occupy. As I write I can almost feel the great man looking across the room from his bookcases and over my shoulder into the garden and through the blanket of trees into the University Parks.

CHAPTER 18

Lectures, Honours and Awards

That frisson of pleasure invariably aroused by receipt of an invitation to deliver an eponymous lecture is almost always followed by feelings of doubt and introspection. These may be eased a little if the invitation specifies a choice of topic of which one feels in reasonable command, but occasionally a subject is suggested so far out of one's field of personal expertise that it presents a real challenge. More often, however, the choice is left to oneself and innumerable questions then arise. What topic shall I choose? Should I (in the earlier days) stick to my principal research interests like the muscular dystrophies, polymyositis, or clumsy children, or would it be better to manufacture a more 'catchy' title, to be reasonably sure of attracting a good audience? Alternatively, should one try to bring the audience up to date with exciting developments in science which have nurtured and transformed the practice of clinical neurology by talking about 'The changing face of neurology'? How and when would it be wise to inject an element of humour, in the hope of keeping the audience awake? And what is the makeup of the audience to be? Will it be largely general practitioners and trainees in hospital medicine, will there be many consultants present or even some noted scientists who may well be more knowledgeable than oneself about the chosen topic? Inevitably these and many other factors influence one's choice of title and content, as does the question as to whether a manuscript is required for publication. If it is, in what format should it be prepared, how will the references be quoted, how many illustrations are likely to be needed, and to what extent will publication in any way conflict with, or duplicate, work which one has previously published in scientific papers in refereed journals? And when the time comes to give the talk, would it be sensible to try to follow the script which will be published, especially if it is a subject about which one has talked infrequently? Or would it be better to prepare a different speaking script or set of notes, appreciating that to read a text prepared for publication purposes can prove very dull? Whenever possible, except on the most prestigious occasions, I have tried to speak without a script and have used a profusion of slides, some illustrating the scientific content of the talk and others providing a series of headings which serve as my notes and as an *aide memoire* which one then shares with the audience.

The art of lecturing is a considerable skill. Some possess it as an innate trait based upon their verbal fluency, impeccable memory and extraverted personality, while others slowly improve their technique by painful and repetitive practice, either through speaking into, and subsequently playing back, their presentation on a tape-recorder or by rehearsing before their peers. My mentor Henry Miller used to say that there are two kinds of lecturers, those with slides and those with ideas; later in life he often used slides himself. I have found them an invaluable lecturing aid, though one must not dim the lights throughout the presentation; there must be periods between slides when the lights are raised so as to avoid undue somnolence in the audience.

As a registrar and junior consultant, I regularly lectured to medical students, to nurses and to other groups of professionals in the Newcastle region, and soon received invitations to talk to medical societies in the region and elsewhere. Feedback from students on the content and quality of my lectures was always helpful, as were the frank (often critical) opinions expressed by some professional colleagues who were in the audiences I addressed. And as Betty began to listen to some of my talks when we were able to travel together she became my staunchest supporter but also my sternest (and invaluable) critic.

The first eponymous lecture I was invited to deliver was the Goulstonian to the Royal College of Physicians in London in 1964, a privilege accorded to one of the four youngest Fellows of the College elected each year. I shall never forget the tension engendered by the anticipatory robing of myself, the President, Censors and College officers, followed by the slow, stately procession into the lecture theatre and the sight of the large audience including Betty, members of the family and many personal friends. But once I got going on my favourite topic of muscular dystrophy, all seemed to go smoothly. Delivering the Lumleian Lecture 15 years later in the same lecture theatre and the inaugural college regional lecture in Leeds in 1985 evoked less overt anxiety, but the profound emotions of 1964 surfaced again in 1990 when the College invited me to give its prestigious Harveian Oration, for which I chose the topic 'Method in medicine'. If that were not sufficient, at the Harveian Dinner afterwards before serried ranks of dinner-jacketed Fellows and distinguished guests (many of them benefactors) I was required to respond to the toast to the Harveian Orator and almost audibly sighed in exhausted relief once that further ordeal was over. The occasion was also historic for two reasons; first, Betty was invited and this was the first time that the lecturer's spouse, not being a Fellow of the College, attended a Harveian Oration and dinner; secondly, I learned that my friend Sir Raymond (Bill) Hoffenburg, who would deliver the 1991 oration, would not be required to respond to the toast. Hence I have the distinction of being the last Harveian Orator to be required to fulfil the dual responsibility.

1965 saw the Saville Lecture at the West End Hospital for Nervous Diseases in memory of the distinguished neurologist who was one of the founders of that hospital; I discussed other muscle diseases. In 1969, I reverted to my favourite topic of the muscular dystrophies in delivering the annual Osler Lecture to the Canadian Medical Association meeting in Halifax, Nova Scotia, beginning with a few sentences in French which seemed to please my hosts. In 1971 I was delighted to be able to pay tribute to Dr Bernard J. Alpers who many years before had presented me, as a young visiting neurologist, with a copy of his textbook when I first visited Philadelphia, by delivering the lecture named after him at the Jefferson Medical College. Later that year, through the generous invitation of Dr Dick Rischbieth of Adelaide, I talked there about 'Changing concepts of neuromuscular disease' when giving the Cairns Memorial Lecture; Hugh Cairns, later a distinguished neurosurgeon and foundation Nuffield Professor of Surgery in Oxford, had been brought up in Adelaide. I was equally pleased to be asked to give the Wilder Penfield Lecture to the Middle East Medical Assembly at the American University of Beirut in Lebanon, not least because of Penfield's kindness when I had first met him in Montreal, and subsequently when he accepted my invitation to talk to a scientific session at the BMA Annual Meeting in Newcastle. Fortunately, Betty and I had a wonderful few days in Beirut with my former research fellow Jean Rebeiz just one year before the troubles began. Peter Schurr, the lecturer a year later, had to be escorted from his plane to the lecture theatre by armed police and was then rapidly delivered to the airport for his return journey. The Middle East Medical Assembly has never subsequently been held in that once delightful but now tragic location.

I returned to the United States in 1975 to give Milton Shy Memorial Lectures in the University of Pennsylvania and in the other two centres in which he had worked, NIH in Bethesda and the New York Neurological Institute of the Columbia-Presbyterian Medical Center. Milton, in his short professional life made remarkable contributions to our knowledge of neuromuscular disease and his promising and productive career was tragically cut short when he died suddenly soon after becoming chairman of neurology at the latter centre. Giving the Wartenberg Lecture to the American Academy of Neurology in Los Angeles in 1978 was another remarkable experience and was the first time I had ever addressed an audience of about 2000. Fortunately they seemed attentive and appreciative of my offering on 'The science of clinical neurology' and Bob Joynt, then President of the Academy, was especially warm and welcoming.

During the next few years I was invited to commemorate the varied and manifold contributions made to neurology and neurosurgery by many notable figures in Britain, the USA and India. These included the Sutcliffe Kerr Lecture in Liverpool, the Esmond Rees Memorial Lecture in Swansea, the Paul Garvey Lecture in Rochester, New York, the T. S. Srinivasan Memorial Lecture in Madras, the E. P. Bharucha Memorial Oration in Bombay, the H. J. Mehta Memorial Oration in Bangalore and the Stanley Graveson Lecture in Southampton. It was also a singular honour to be asked to give two orations in memory of the great John Snow. He had first been apprenticed to an apothecary in Burnopfield, Co. Durham, near Pickering Nook, my first school. He later moved to Killingworth in Northumberland and made there some important observations on cholera, before moving to London to train for a time at the Westminster Hospital Medical School. His subsequent fame arose because he is said to have terminated a serious cholera epidemic in London by removing the handle of the Broad Street pump, and because in his subsequent career in anaesthesia he gave chloroform to Queen Victoria in childbirth. My first John Snow Lecture in 1982 was at the Westminster Medical School; the second, in 1983, in Newcastle at the annual meeting of the Association of Anaesthetists three days before we moved to Oxford.

Of the 57 eponymous lectures I have given to date, no fewer than 11 were delivered in 1983, the year of our move, which inevitably presented problems with respect to my choice of subject. While I was still able to discuss changing concepts of neuromuscular disease and the inflammatory myopathies, in which I continued to take a lively interest despite my personal detachment from laboratory research, it was inevitable that I should at times consider subjects more directly relevant to my educational and ethical interests in medicine arising out of my experiences as Dean in Newcastle and my GMC responsibilities. When I gave the annual Thomas Young Lecture at St George's Hospital in London, honouring the memory of that remarkable polymath, mathematician, scientist and physician (who described Young's modulus), scientific developments in neuromuscular disease seemed appropriate, and also for the Cavendish Lecture to the London West End Medical Society. For the Samuel Hyde Memorial Lecture to the Section of Rheumatology at the RSM inflammatory myopathy was the obvious choice. However, I discussed 'On training tomorrow's doctors', describing my experiences with curricular review in my Presidential address to the Newcastle and Northern Counties Medical Society in 1975 and this seemed a suitable topic for various talks elsewhere, including the Isle of Man Medical Society. For the Maudsley Lecture to the Royal College of Psychiatrists in late 1983 I chose 'Professional responsibility in a changing society', discussing the changing views and recommendations of the GMC about several medical ethical issues which seemed likely to be of particular interest to psychiatrists. Medical education, however, seemed more suitable for the bicentenary lecture at the Royal College of Surgeons in Dublin in 1984, while for the Percival J. Hay Memorial Lecture to the North of England Ophthalmological Society in the same year I dealt with the interface between neurology and ophthalmology. In 1985, however, I turned again to issues of professional responsibility and ethics, both in the Crookshank Lecture to the Royal College of Radiologists and in the Bradlaw Oration to the Faculty of Dental Surgery of the Royal College of Surgeons, attempting in the latter to draw some analogies between the ethical problems confronting doctors on the one hand and dentists on the other. I returned to that theme in 1988 when my friend Roy Storer invited me back to Newcastle to give the Founders and Benefactors lecture in the Dental School.

The Bishop Lecture to the Library Association, also in 1985, commemorating a notable medical librarian, offered a significant change of scene as I talked about planning and editing the *Oxford Companion to Medicine*. In the same year the Hughlings Jackson Lecture to the Section of Neurology at the Royal Society of Medicine, previously delivered every few years by many glitterati of British neurology and neuroscience, gave me the opportunity of paying a tribute to the seminal contributions of Hughlings Jackson on epilepsy and cerebral localization; I went on to sketch the historical development of neurology in Newcastle before discussing major recent contributions of neuroscientists to clinical neurology.

Yet another change of theme arose in 1986 when in my Darwin Lecture to the Institute of Biology, delivered at the Natural History Museum in London, I discussed in a semi-sentimental manner my personal introduction to, and subsequent increasing involvement in, neuro-muscular research in animals and man. This was a topic to which I again returned four years later when delivering the Stephen Paget Memorial Lecture to the Research Defence Society, by which time I was able to discuss developments resulting from localization and characterization of the Duchenne muscular dystrophy gene with especial reference to the potential therapeutic approaches resulting from the discovery of a similar dystrophin-deficient myopathy in mice and in dogs.

In 1987 I again discussed the science of clinical neurology in the Sir Isaac Gilchrist lecture in Aberdeen but later prepared a much modified talk on professional responsibility and medical ethics for the Sir Arthur Hall Memorial Lecture in Sheffield. This was given before a huge invited audience in the main hall of the University in the presence of the Chancellor, Lord Dainton, the Vice-Chancellor, many members of the university staff and local dignitaries. This was one of those stately occasions when academic dress was worn, as it was in 1988 when I gave the Astor Lecture on graduation day for newly qualified doctors at the combined University College and Middlesex Hospital Schools of Medicine.

New knowledge of neuromuscular disease was again my theme in the Fitzgerald Peel Lecture given in 1987 to the Scottish Society of Physicians in Paisley a few days after Betty and I had returned from India. Though we were still slightly jet-lagged, the hospitality we received was exceptional. For Betty, the opportunity of visiting the magnificent Burrell Collection (which I had seen before) during my lecture relieved her of the duty of listening yet again to one of my effusions but also enlivened an enjoyable visit.

An opportunity arose in 1988 of updating one of the subjects upon which I had often talked to medical societies and BMA divisions throughout the UK but had never published, namely that on illness in doctors and their families. I brought my talk up to date in order to prepare the Harben Lecture to the Royal Institute of Public Health and Hygiene, and it was then published. By now, my involvement with Green College and 13 Norham Gardens had resulted in my being asked to give several talks abut Osler and Oxford, the first being the Osler Lecture to the Society of Apothecaries and the second the McGovern Lecture to the American Osler Society in Birmingham, Alabama, in 1989 when I discussed 'The "Open Arms" reviving—can we rekindle the Osler flame?'. Medical history, too, was the theme of yet another university lecture embellished by the splendour and panoply of an academic procession when I gave the Lord Cohen History of Medicine Lecture on the history of the GMC in Liverpool and was delighted, in so doing, to pay a tribute to my much-admired predecessor as President.

1990 was another exceptional year with eight eponymous lectures, including the Harveian and Stephen Paget Orations, but began inauspiciously in the spring when I had agreed to give the Telford Memorial Lecture to the Manchester Medical Society. This was planned for 5.30 p.m. and as I had attended a dinner in London the previous evening and had stayed overnight, I spent the morning working in the RSM library and took a noon train to Manchester, due to arrive at 2.45 p.m. Regrettably, some 20 minutes out of Euston the train came to a juddering stop. After a prolonged, frustrating and unexplained delay, we learned sadly that while the train was travelling at about 100 miles an hour, a young man had thrown himself in front of the engine. The force of the impact had fractured all of its brake pipes so that the entire train was disabled. Fortunately I was able to telephone the Dean, Robert Boyd, from the train once British Rail provided portable telephones, explaining that I would be delayed. After several Manchester trains had passed by, we were eventually towed into a station and re-embarked. We arrived at Manchester Piccadilly at 5.25 p.m. in pouring rain, to find a large queue for taxis. However, I was eventually able to hail a taxi outside the station and arrived at the lecture theatre just after 6.00 to find my audience waiting patiently. Fortunately, Robert had sensibly arranged for wine to be served before the lecture instead of afterwards, so that perhaps my audience was in a better mood than might otherwise have been the case. Fortunately no such contretemps afflicted my Bayliss Lecture, sponsored by Private Patients Plan, given at the RCP London later in the year on 'Medicine in a changing society' to honour the manifold contributions of, as I said, that 'compleat physician', my friend Sir Richard Bayliss. And in September my Sasakawa Lecture on 'Osler, Oxford and "The Open Arms"' to the Japanese Osler Society in Tokyo, repeated a few days later to the branch of that society in Kyoto, went smoothly enough. In November, nostalgically, I dined at the Royal Army Medical College Headquarters Mess in Millbank and stayed overnight in those familiar surroundings of my TA days, after giving the Mitchiner Lecture to honour the great St Thomas' surgeon, subsequently Major-General Mitchener, late RAMC, whose Rabelaisian discourse to the medical unit of the Senior Training Corps in Newcastle I had so much enjoyed as a medical student in the 1940s.

Little did I think in earlier years that so many honours would later come my way but each, however unexpected (and undeserved) has brought great pleasure, tinged at times (I hope) with proper humility. In 1965 I received the Territorial Decoration (often described by TA colleagues as a reward for 12 years of undetected crime). When I later prefixed my medical qualifications with the letters TD on professional correspondence, I was teased unmercifully by Henry Miller who, in the presence of Hugh Garland (visiting Newcastle to give a lecture), asked me whether I really felt the addition was necessary. He was told briskly by Hugh that he, having been in the TA before the war, always quoted his own TD. A few weeks later Henry was further chastened when, as Dean, he was rebuked by the University's Chancellor, His Grace the Duke of Northumberland, for the fact that in an offical document the Duke's TD had been omitted.

Rather tentatively, in 1972 I submitted my publications to Newcastle University's DSc Committee in the hope that they might be thought to justify the award of that degree and was delighted when the submission was successful. The possibility of receiving an honorary degree had not, however, crossed my mind. In 1975 I was astonished but thrilled to receive a letter from Georges Serratrice of Marseille, for whom I had lectured several times in that city and whom we had appointed Vice-President of the Newcastle muscle congress in 1974, notifying me that the University of Aix-Marseille, of which he was then Premier Assesseur (and later its President), had agreed to confer upon me the honorary degree of Docteur de l'Université. From the information I received, the arrangements sounded very different from those with which I had become familiar in Newcastle in honorary degree congregations. I was told that I must take my own academic robes and that I would be required to speak in response to what Georges would say in presenting me; each honorary graduand would, it seemed, be presented by a different member of the University. After much thought, I decided to make my acceptance speech in French. I therefore wrote a suitable response in English; a Newcastle lecturer in

French generously translated the text and then rehearsed me, correcting as best she could my infelicities of pronunciation.

We set off for Marseille via Paris in keen anticipation, but were greatly alarmed on arriving in Marseille on the afternoon before the congregation to find that our luggage had not arrived. Mine, of course, contained my academic dress which would be essential for the ceremony. Fortunately it soon emerged that our bags had been sent from Paris to Lyon rather than Marseille; they were transferred to a flight arriving in Marseille early next morning, so that after a few hours of anxiety all was well. The ceremony was exceptionally moving. My speech seemed to go down well (at least the audience laughed in the appropriate places). I then realized why I had needed my own academic dress as the conferment of a French honorary doctorate involves the attachment to the left shoulder of a strip of red material running fore and aft and decorated by several transverse pieces of white ermine. This has been permanently attached to my Durham MD gown ever since and I wear it with pride. Being a graduate of Aix-Marseille gave me the privilege in 1982 of presenting (again in French) the distinguished physiologist and Nobel Prize winner, Sir Andrew Huxley, with whom I had been closely associated through our mutual interest in the Muscular Dystrophy Group, for an honorary degree during the International Congress on Neuromuscular Diseases splendidly organized by Georges Serratrice. Ray Adams and Sigvald Refsum from Norway were similarly honoured.

I was again surprised when in 1979 I learned from Derek Wood, GMC member and Dean of the Faculty of Medicine in the University of Leeds, that that university proposed to award me an honorary Doctorate of Science. Yet another moving ceremony ensued; the degree was conferred by the Duke of Kent, deputizing for the Chancellor, the Duchess, who was indisposed. That notable man of erudition, culture and encyclopaedic musical knowledge, the late Lord (Edward) Boyle, was then Vice-Chancellor. The Public Orator was generous with just the right amount of leg-pulling and I was greatly taken by the bright green facings of the gown which I wore. It fell to me to respond by offering thanks to the University on behalf of the honorary graduates, and yet again to speak after dinner, so that the occasion, though in every way delightful, was a little taxing and we returned to Newcastle by train next day in a glow of pleasure tinged by just a hint of fatigue.

Next year I was delighted yet again to receive a Doctorate of Science *honoris causa* from the University of Leicester, along with Sir Douglas Black, Dame Josephine Barnes and Sir Patrick Nairne (former Chief Civil Servant to the Department of Health whom we later came to know well as Master of St Catherine's College in Oxford) when the University graduated its first cohort of medical students. The only snag was that the ceremony took place the day after I had been installed as BMA

President in Newcastle, so that we had to make a very early start to drive to Leicester in time, still in the throes of an emotional peak which was reinforced yet again by the splendour of the ceremonial. This time the Public Orator was my old friend Sydney Brandon, formerly of Newcastle and an able professor of psychiatry whose prior knowledge of my Geordie roots proved slightly embarrassing, if totally accurate. That same knowledge surfaced yet again when I received an honorary MD in Sheffield in 1987. I was presented by a fellow Pilgrim, John Richmond, then Dean of the Medical School who later became President of the Royal College of Physicians of Edinburgh.

1988 was also exceptional as I was deeply touched when my former university of Newcastle decided to give me an honorary Doctorate of Civil Law, at the same time as Mr (later Sir) John Hall, creator of the magnificent Metro Centre in Gateshead, was similarly honoured, while Sir John Harvey-Jones, former Chairman of ICI, received a Doctorate of Science. The ceremony this time was more familiar but no less moving, and Max Sussman, the Public Orator, did us proud. Happily, too, several members of the family were there and Judy took a video recording which we shall always treasure. Then in July, after the annual BMA meeting in Norwich, Betty and I drove on through Lincolnshire to Hull where I was privileged to receive another honorary Doctorate of Science in that relatively young but burgeoning university, formerly governed by Sir Brynmor Jones of GMC memory but in 1988 being under the inspired leadership of Dr (later Sir) William Taylor. Here the individual honorary graduands were again presented by different individuals. In my case a special concession had been granted to allow Dr John Bennett, a noted gastroenterologist and an old friend from the GMC and Council of the RCP, who was not a member of the university staff but a member of its Council, to present me, as he did skilfully and wittily.

I am constantly interested and amazed by the variety, style and colour of the academic dress one sees in different parts of the UK and across the world and by the different procedures adopted by various universities in their honorary degree congregations. In Newcastle all honorary graduands are presented by the Public Orator and no-one is required to respond (except informally after dinner in the evening). The academic procession is organized with military precision by a Deputy Registrar who calls out the name of each individual member of staff who had agreed to process, who then fall in in strict order, so that seats in the hall are identified individually and there is no risk of anyone being without a place. In Oxford at Encaenia, by contrast, always a glittering and magnificent occasion (though one cannot but wonder whether the tradition of presenting all honorary graduands in Latin will continue indefinitely), the procession is, with respect, organized rather less well. Oxford doctors fall in first after the University's officers, and are then followed by heads of houses who are not doctors. All will previously have enjoyed Lord Crewe's Benefaction of champagne and strawberries and cream served at 11.00 before the noontime ceremony, its purpose being as defined in the will of the noted Lord Crewe, Lord Bishop of Durham, to sustain the participants throughout the gruelling performance which follows. Once at Encaenia I, as Warden of Green College, happened by chance to come at the end of the procession of 'heads of houses who are not doctors' (Oxford doctors, of course), along with Eric Heaton, Dean of Christ Church, and Lord (Asa) Briggs, Provost of Worcester. When we reached the appropriate seating area in the Sheldonian Theatre, all seats were taken and for an uncomfortable moment it seemed that we three would have to sit on the stairs. However, the Proctors made some rapid adjustments in the face of the huge assembled company and we were soon seated in fair comfort, if rather precariously.

Whereas the French (and Belgians) on conferring an honorary degree award an insignia to be attached to one's gown and which one then keeps, no such procedure occurs, so far as I am aware, in any UK university. However, when I became an honorary fellow of the American College of Physicians in New Orleans in 1980 (Betty and I enjoyed revisiting many old haunts) I was presented at that huge ceremony with a hood to keep and which, like the French insignia, I have often worn with my MD gown. Equally impressive but more intimate was the ceremony when I received an honorary fellowship of the Royal College of Physicians of Edinburgh in 1981. Afterwards I was given a latch key to the front door which would allow me access to the College at times when the staff were off duty so as to reach the limited residential accommodation which the College offers its fellows. When Betty and I went to Montreal in 1984 so that I could become an honorary fellow of the Royal College of Physicians of Canada, there was no such presentation but the College, with exceptional generosity, paid transatlantic fares for us both. Frankly, I know of few if any similar institutions which would do as much. We met there our friends Henry and Kay Barnett, paid a fleeting but enjoyable visit to the magnificent botanical gardens and also spent an hour or two, covered in oilskins, on a flat-bottomed boat shooting the Lachine rapids in the St Lawrence River, an event which I much enjoyed, though Betty and Kay, from the sounds they uttered, seemed less enthusiastic.

Each of those who presented me for honorary degrees had done their homework assiduously and had dug deep into my past, consulting without my knowledge friends and family members. One had somehow discovered that I had been dismissed twice in one innings when playing cricket! Syd Brandon described my professional progress under the influence of that 'intellectual rogue elephant' of British medicine, Henry Miller, and commented on my hole-in-one and Captaincy of Bamburgh Golf Club and upon the subsequent press report in the Berwick

Advertiser. In Sheffield, John Richmond contrasted me as a 'muscle man' with Henry as a 'brain man' and referred to my fondness for snooker, apologizing for the fact that the season on green baize at the Crucible Theatre in Sheffield had ended. Somehow or other, Max Sussman had disinterred a tale about a dispute over the use of microscopes in biology teaching at the Alderman Wraith Grammar School in Spennymoor, and also remarked upon the sense of shell-shock he felt on receiving from me a detailed reply to an importuning letter written to the Dean an hour earlier. And John Bennett, after sketching my clinical, scientific, administrative and quasi-political career in medicine, reverted to my North Eastern origins and what he alleged was my reputation as a raconteur and performer of Geordie songs.

Just as these honorary degrees were a source of great pleasure and pride, so too were the honorary memberships I received from neurological and other professional associations throughout the world. After becoming a corresponding member of the American Neurological Association in 1969 and of the American Academy of Neurology in 1974, I was later elected to honorary membership of both in 1983. A paper on polymyositis, carefully translated and equally carefully rehearsed in French before being delivered to the Société Française de Neurologie resulted in my election to honorary membership of that body in 1970, and in the same year I became an honorary member of the Deutsche Gesellschaft für Neurologie. During our visit to Australia in 1971 my colleagues there kindly elected me an honorary member of the Australian Association of Neurologists, while on two further overseas visits in 1974 honorary memberships of the Academia Brasileira de Neurologia and of the Spanish Neurological Society were conferred, each accompanied by the presentation of attractive parchments. Another overseas honour followed when in 1977 I became the first honorary foreign member of the Venezuelan Neurological Society, and in the same year, through the advocacy of Irena Hausmanowa-Petrusewicz, I was invited to the Polish Embassy in London to receive my parchment of honorary membership of the Polish Neurological Society from the Ambassador. Membership of the Société Belge de Neurologie followed in 1978, of the Neurological Society of India in 1984 and of the Italian Neurological Society in 1985. In 1978, after delivering a guest lecture, I felt especially honoured to become the first British honorary member of the Japanese Neurological Association, and in 1986, again during two overseas visits, I was similarly honoured by the Neurological Society of Thailand and by the Canadian Society of Neurological Sciences, while in 1987 the youthful Hong Kong Neurological Society made me its first honorary foreign member. Honorary membership of the Austrian and Russian neurological societies followed in 1991.

Several non-neurological distinctions also came my way. Particularly touching was my honorary membership of the British Paediatric

Association, no doubt acknowledging my early training with James Spence and my interest in paediatric neurology. In 1986, on the nomination of Paul Beeson (a co-editor of the Oxford Companion to Medicine) I became an honorary member of the Association of American Physicians and was congratulated by my long-standing friend Dick Johnson, Professor of Neurology at Johns Hopkins, who pointed out that I was one of only five neurologists then extant to be so honoured. My presidency of the Royal Society of Medicine was followed by election to the honorary fellowship of the Society and later of its Section of Neurology, while my growing involvement in Oslerian matters resulted in my becoming an honorary member of the Osler Club of London in 1986, of the American Osler Society in 1988 and of the Japanese Osler Society in 1990.

Totally unexpected was my election as a member of the Venezuelan Academy of Medicine in 1991 but I am sure that Francisco Kerdel-Vegas the dermatologist, Venezuelan ambassador to the UK and a good friend of Green College, had a hand in it. In 1987, also out of the blue, there came an invitation for Betty and me to travel to Oslo so that I could become a foreign member of the Norwegian Academy of Science and Letters. I described that splendidly moving occasion in chapter 14.

Another unexpected honour arose in 1979 through Alderman (later Sir) Ronald Gardner-Thorpe (as I mentioned earlier, his son, Christopher, was my senior registrar). When he discovered that I had never become a member of the Society of Apothecaries or of any other City livery company (such membership would automatically have carried with it the freedom of the City of London) he invited me to London to have the Freedom conferred at a delightful little ceremony. When expressing my thanks, I jokingly mentioned that no-one had ever suggested that I might become a freeman of Newcastle. A month or two later I remembered that remark when Councillor Jeremy Beecham, leader of Newcastle City Council, approached me and asked whether I would be willing to receive the honorary freedom of the city during the celebration in 1980 of the 900th anniversary of its founding. Naturally I was thrilled to be so honoured by the city which had nurtured me and which I held so dear, and eagerly accepted.

The ceremony of presentation took place in the magnificent Banqueting Hall of the Civic Centre on 4 July 1980, where I was one of nine to be similarly honoured. Five were former Lord Mayors of the City and the other four were myself, Jackie Milburn (the former Newcastle United and England centre forward), Col George Brown (one of the founding fathers of Newcastle Breweries) and last but not least Cardinal Basil Hume (formerly George Hume, son of Sir William, who before the war was a distinguished cardiologist and professor of medicine in Newcastle). Sir William had married a French woman and hence his children were brought up in the Roman Catholic faith. George (or Basil, his ecclesiastical name) had a distinguished career in the church, becoming Abbott of Ampleforth prior to his appointment as Cardinal at Westminster Cathedral. Although he had been a capable rugger player in his youth, his schooling and upbringing in Newcastle had made him a life-long Newcastle United supporter, like myself. The ceremony of the Freemen was moving and impressive, as were the parchments which we all received. The cardinal had been chosen to make the speech of acceptance on behalf of us all and caused great amusement by saying that it was the greatest day of his life as he had always wished to meet Jackie Milburn. Indeed Jackie's homespun Northumbrian charm shone through that day; I told him how marvellous it had been to be at Wembley to see the two magnificent goals he scored in Newcastle's second successive FA Cup victory in the 1950s. He came, of course, from a famous footballing family as his mother was a Charlton and his cousins were Bobby and Jackie. Every time I go back to the Civic Centre, I invariably sneak a glance at the point on the stone wall where my name is carved along with those of all other Honorary Freemen of the City created over the centuries. Mine, indeed, is engraved close to that of President Jimmy Carter of the USA who had been so well briefed when he visited Newcastle that he began his speech by saying 'Howway the lads'. Inevitably he also visited Washington Old Hall, a few miles away, the original home of the Washington family of which George, first US President, was a descendant.

However proud I was of these honours and distinctions, which often made me reflect upon how it had come about that a lad from Spennymoor found himself in such a position, I suppose that for any Englishman who loves his country (even if unalloyed patriotism may have become unfashionable in some quarters in the later 20th century), it is honours conferred by the Crown which give greatest pleasure. When I served on the MRC and as Chairman of the Education Committee of the GMC, it gradually dawned upon me that I might possibly receive such an award, but when my 12 years of involvement with the MRC ended I set this possibility aside. However, when I talked to a branch of the Friends of the Hebrew University of Jerusalem in Newcastle about my experiences as Henry Cohen Visiting Lecturer in Israel, I overhead a remark surely not intended for my ears when someone in the audience referred to 'the future Sir John Walton'. That comment in turn recalled Alan Ogilvie's comment in the letter he wrote when I ended my term as his registrar.

In our early years in Beechfield Road the morning post used to come at about 7.30 a.m., so that I was always able to deal with my correspondance on tape before leaving for work. After one of those innumerable reorganizations of our postal services, allegedly undertaken 'to improve efficiency', the morning delivery began to arrive much later.

I therefore established a routine, having defined his normal route, of walking along North Avenue in Gosforth at about 7.45 a.m. to meet the postman who always had my mail ready. One morning in November 1978, Jack, whom I had come to know well, said nothing but gave me a quizzical look. At the top of the pile he had placed a letter on which the top left-hand corner of the envelope said 'Prime Minister—urgent'. While hastening home I slit open the envelope, to find what I later learned to be a standard letter from the Prime Minister's Principal Private Secretary saying that the Prime Minister had it in mind to recommend on the occasion of the forthcoming New Year's Honours List that the honour of knighthood should be conferred upon me, but before making this recommendation he wished to know that this would be agreeable to me. I was invited to complete and return an enclosed form. When I burst open the kitchen door and showed this to Betty, she naturally shared my delight but expressed no surprise as she said frankly that she had been expecting it! Hurriedly I completed the form and returned it with a covering letter in which I expressed, I hope with due humility, my deep sense of honour and pride. I also learned that if I accepted, I might be accompanied at the investiture by Betty and no more than two other members of the family. With three children, we were immediately faced with a dilemma but then recalled that Judy had met the Queen at a Garden Party in Buckingham Palace just a few days before she was married, so that we nominated Ann and Christopher.

There followed a tense period of suspense and anticipation when we heard no more and during which we were at times assailed with doubt, even anxiety, lest my reply and the completed form had not been safely delivered. There was also the problem of keeping the news confidential, as one is invariably enjoined to do, though naturally we told Ann, Judy and Chris while swearing them to secrecy. A few days before Christmas we decided that we could properly break the news to a few others and held a little party at home for other family members and a few of our closest friends, not indicating our reasons for the party until Betty, with glass in hand, eventually spilt the beans. After an unusually enjoyable and exciting family Christmas in Gosforth, we went to Detchant for our usual New Year's break, intending, as I had become Captain of Bamburgh Castle Golf Club in the previous August, to enjoy the annual New Year's Eve dinner at the club and then to go to Bamburgh Church to hear the bells ring in the New Year. Knowing that my knighthood would be announced publicly on 30 December, (as New Year's Eve was a Sunday) we anticipated that the dinner that evening would be an exceptional occasion. But the fates determined otherwise.

No sooner had we settled in at Detchant when on 29 December snow fell steadily from leaden skies and soon we had a substantial covering. On the morning of the 30th we could not help wondering again, as was

I suppose inevitable, whether there was any possibility, in view of the total silence following my response to the original letter, that it had gone astray or whether the Prime Minister might have had a change of heart. I knew that honours lists were sent out confidentially in advance to newspapers and other branches of the media. Eventually I could restrain myself no longer and telephoned my friend Len Harton, Editor of the *Newcastle Journal*, simply to enquire in confidence whether or not my name was in the list. He delightedly confirmed that it was and indeed was glad that I had phoned as a member of his staff had been telephoning our Gosforth number without success to obtain some information, which I was glad to pass on to him.

Our friend Joan Dunford had invited us to a supper party in Bamburgh on 29 December, along with other friends. As the day wore on we became increasingly apprehensive about whether or not we would get there as snow fell steadily. Fortunately our neighbours, David and Joan Souter, were also invited and had a Land Rover, so that we reached Bamburgh without serious difficulty even though about six inches of snow (exceptional for the area) had fallen. We enjoyed a hilarious evening and as we all donned duffle coats, scarves and gumboots to return home late that night, our irrepressible friend and Belford GP, Denys Byers, who was also present, enfolded Betty in his arms, lifted her up and said loudly 'Take to the hills!'. Difficult though it had been, we had kept our personal news to ourselves, but when Denys telephoned his congratulations next morning, as did dozens of others, he said sheepishly that if he had known that next morning Betty was to become Lady Walton, he would have been a little less familiar! The snow continued to fall heavily and most minor roads in the area were impassable, though much of the A1 was being kept open by ploughs with difficulty. We consulted the golf club steward by phone as it was quite clear that in these weather conditions the dinner must be cancelled. We therefore faced the prospect of spending one of our most memorable and exciting New Year's Eves all alone, snow-bound in The Old Piggery. However, our other near neighbours, Wyndham and Oriel Rogers-Coltman from Grey Mare Farm up the hill behind us found that their plans for New Year's Eve had been similarly disrupted. Also having a Land Rover they joined us for drinks and a meal in a state of poorly suppressed hilarity since, as Wyndham said, he almost fell out of bed laughing at the thought of the knight in The Old Piggery. A most unusual New Year's Eve ended with our watching 'My Fair Lady' on television and retiring soon after we had seen in the New Year. Wyndham, suitably provided with money, a piece of coal and other traditional local requirements, acted as our 'first-foot' to bring us luck in 1979. Two or three days later Charles Bosanquet, the former Vice-Chancellor of Newcastle University, telephoned us to draw to our attention the headline in the *Berwick Advertiser* to which I referred earlier. I have often quoted it since in various after-dinner speeches, to such an extent that Betty has told me more than once that if I do it again she will disown me.

Once New Year was over, it was exceptionally difficult to settle down to normal life. Letters flooded in by every post from far and wide, totalling in the end nearly 800, which Betty kindly filed in alphabetical order. To all of those written by hand, I replied personally in longhand, while to those which were typed I dictated replies to Rosemary or Betty Dodds (or Nancy if they came to the Medical School), while 'topping and tailing' them and usually adding a personal postscript. Later we gave a little party at home for the three of them and for Doris Wilkinson (our faithful and long-serving daily 'help') and her husband. In addition, my neurological colleagues gave us a splendid dinner at Gosforth Park Hotel, hosted and organized by Jack Foster. Derek Nicholson and David Shaw arranged a party in the Medical School and my colleagues in the Regional Neurological Centre, including the Dystrophy Labs, organized another splendid event in the out-patients department, where I was forcibly attired by John Harris in a white coat, a black and white striped woollen hat and a Newcastle United scarf before being invited to respond to their congratulations. I was deeply touched by the obvious delight of all of my colleagues; as they said, they shared a little in reflected glory, and as I made clear, nothing I had achieved in medicine or in life would have been possible without the support of Betty, my family and my professional colleagues and friends.

After the announcement, several things inevitably ensued. First, I was invited to join the Imperial Society of Knights Bachelor, which I duly did, and bought Betty a brooch carrying the insignia of the inverted sword which can be worn by the wives of those enrolled in this Order of Chivalry. Secondly, I was approached by the College of Arms in London asking me to call there to sign the roll. When I did so, I was surprised to find that almost a third of those similarly honoured never respond to that request. However, my reaction was much less positive when Garter King of Arms, Colin Cole (later Sir Colin), asked me whether I would wish to have my own Coat of Arms (armorial bearings) prepared for the 'nominal sum of £750'. When I discussed this with Betty her view was the same as mine, that she saw no pressing reason for incurring that expense. However, when we casually mentioned this to the family, their response was quite different when I told them that such a Coat of Arms would remain in the family indefinitely; eventually they nagged us to have it done. I also happened to meet my friend Sir Alastair Currie, with whom I had served on the MRC and who was knighted at the same time as I. He told me that his family had applied similar pressure and that he too had given way. I admit that I was rather surprised to find that Lord Lyon in Scotland was prepared to have Coats of Arms prepared for a Scottish Knight for £500 and I was never able to discover the reason for the discrepancy. However, when I told Garter that I had changed my mind, I saw Chester Herald, Hubert Chesshyre, who was very helpful in explaining how armorial bearings were prepared in order to identify, within certain limits, the interests and background of the recipient. Eventually we settled upon the customary knight's vizor surmounted by a seahorse (the symbol of the city of Newcastle). Across the top of the shield we included three St Cuthbert's crosses for Lindisfarne and Durham on a background of palatinate purple for Durham University. Below that, within the shield, was a castle for Newcastle and Bamburgh Castles, with a background of red and white wavy lines which were supposed to signify muscles and nerves in view of my professional interest in neuromuscular disease. There remained the question of a motto, about which I consulted David West, Professor of Latin and Pro-Vice-Chancellor in Newcastle, who came up with the splendid idea of 'Disce, Doce, Medere' (to learn, to teach and to heal). Hence my armorial bearings were eventually prepared in that format and now, suitably framed, hang in Norham Gardens.

Having confirmed that I would be accompanied by Betty, Ann and Christopher at the investiture, we looked forward keenly to the event in March 1979. After staying overnight at the East India Club, we all changed—I into my morning suit (acquired, as mentioned earlier, for £5.00 from Captain French in my Army days)—and took a taxi from St James's Square to the Palace very early; this was just as well, as queues of traffic were building up in The Mall. In accordance with custom, we had a family group photograph taken in The Mall before entering the Palace. On arriving in the courtyard, a uniformed flunkey enquired discreetly 'Which honour are you receiving, sir?'. When I told him, I was conducted into a large anteroom with the few others who were to be similarly honoured, while Betty, Ann and Christopher were directed to the Great Hall in which the investiture was to take place. Fortunately they were early enough to be seated on the lateral tiers overlooking the centre of the hall, giving them an excellent view of the proceedings. I soon discovered why those of us receiving knighthoods and similar honours had been segregated, as a lieutenant-colonel of the Guards quickly appeared in dress uniform with a subaltern and announced that as certain gentlemen had had problems in the past in kneeling appropriately before Her Majesty to have their honour conferred, a rehearsal was necessary. His subaltern acted as marker; in brisk military tones the colonel indicated that on entering the hall one would wait by the marker until one's name was called by the Lord Chamberlain, when one would march briskly forward, turn and face Her Majesty, bow and then kneel on the stool with one's right hand on a wooden support, then being dubbed with the sword on both shoulders, after which one would again stand. At this stage he said that Her Majesty 'may or may not speak to you'. As, however, it was her custom normally to do so, one should wait to be spoken to before replying and then taking two paces backwards, bowing again, turning to the right and walking out of the hall to receive one's insignia. Afterwards one would then be conducted to an appropriate seat in the hall in order to watch the remainder of the proceedings.

For an ex-TA type this all seemed straightforward, but nevertheless as the moment of the ceremony approached, my heart began to pound, especially as we processed slowly along a series of corridors and as the music of the military band playing on the balcony in the main hall came closer and closer. As my turn came to wait by the marker at the entrance, the colonel's detailed instructions all seemed to fade from my memory but I am told that I performed appropriately. As I knelt and felt the gentle tap of the sword on both shoulders a lump came to my throat. Her Majesty was most gracious in asking me in what field I worked and where and in asking about Newcastle before I stepped backwards, bowed, turned and strode out, I trust in suitable military style. No-one who has not experienced such a ceremonial occasion could, I believe, fully appreciate its emotional impact and I was hardly aware of the noted individuals of stage and screen, such as Olivia Newton-John, who also received honours at the same investiture. Chris, however, took a lively interest throughout and he and Ann vied with one another in trying to spot celebrities. Yet again we posed in the courtyard for the official photographs, now taken with me wearing my insignia, and returned that evening by train to Newcastle glowing with pride and pleasure.

I trust it does not sound immodest, but when I was knighted I genuinely felt that I had reached a peak of achievement and would have no further honours to come. One advantage of the UK system is that when one is knighted, one's wife shares in the honour by acquiring the title of Lady. No-one could have deserved this more than Betty in view of the unstinting support she had given me, often in the face of the innumerable difficulties and pressures associated with the exceptional demands of my career. For overseas friends and correspondents, British titles are inevitably mysterious, and even in the UK some of today's youngsters, however well educated, do not learn early in life as we had done about the nuances and appropriate styles of address involved. All too often from abroad and very often from Britain (even occasionally from noted companies and academic institutions) I was addressed as Sir Walton. Attempting to explain that to call me Sir John did not demonstrate undue familiarity often, especially overseas, evoked looks of amazement. Regularly I, and Betty too, ignored the titles on our travels unless these were specifically mentioned on registration badges or documents and simply introduced ourselves as John and Betty Walton.

Having said that I did not anticipate further honours, I suppose in all honesty I must admit that when I became GMC President the possibility of the House of Lords did cross my mind, if only because the two most recent of my long-serving predecessors in that office, Henry Cohen and John Richardson, were both ennobled. However, when Margaret Thatcher became Prime Minister, for several reasons the medical profession became less than popular in her eyes. I believe that the comments regularly quoted about 'Is he one of us?' were not totally apocryphal. When she saw and heard the criticisms regularly expressed by doctors in all branches of the profession about the policies of her government towards the universities and the Health Service, it seems that she must have felt that doctors, who had traditionally been in the main conservative voters, were opposing the ideals and principles underlying the policies of her government. The fact that many doctors like myself, admired her personally, and endorsed many of her policies, save for those on health and education and still voted for her party, often seemed irrelevant. Whether or not this was the reason no-one can tell, but for many years no doctors were awarded life peerages after Lord (Bob) Hunter of Newington, former Vice-Chancellor of Birmingham University, had been ennobled in the latter years of the Labour Government. Previously a life peerage had been awarded to a member of the profession every two or three years and Bob Hunter went to the Lords soon after John Richardson in 1979. Many of us later tried hard, by writing regular letters of recommendation, to obtain peerages for some distinguished colleagues. However, our efforts in this regard were unsuccessful. During my BMA and GMC presidencies I was among the many who had publicly criticized government policy towards medical research, education and the NHS, and when my GMC presidency terminated in February 1989 I dismissed the prospect of entering the upper house. There had indeed been a nine-year gap without any doctor being ennobled with the single exception of Lord Trafford, a former Conservative MP for the Wrekin who was created a working peer and who soon afterwards became Minister for Health in the upper house. However, a possible change of heart was signified by the award of a life peerage to my friend John Butterfield, medical pilgrim, twice a vice-chancellor and former professor of physic in Cambridge, in the Birthday Honours of 1988. In May 1989 Betty and I went off on our splendid Swan Hellenic cruise to the Mediterranean. On our return Rosemary told us that in our absence she had taken a confidential telephone call from the Prime Minister's office asking to what address a personal letter from Mrs Thatcher should be sent. Rosemary explained that I was out of the country and so the letter had been sent to her in a second sealed envelope for safe keeping in the college until I returned. Inside the sealed envelope was another with the familiar 'Prime Minister—Urgent' in the top left-hand corner. This time the letter was signed by Mrs Thatcher herself and informed me that she had in mind to recommend to Her Majesty that in the forthcoming Birthday Honours List a life peerage of the United

Kingdom should be conferred upon me, etc., etc. Naturally I replied positively by hand and in haste, not (of course) including the words which weeks later I jokingly quoted to the family—'Well, if you insist!'. Seriously, I could not but feel yet again greatly honoured, recognizing that despite my retirement from the GMC and my imminent retirement from Green College, membership of the House of Lords would give me the opportunity, as I saw it, to continue at least in some way to serve my beloved medical profession and my country. And I could not but feel grateful also to Margaret Thatcher herself, whose charisma and staunch leadership I had so much admired, especially in the earlier years of her premiership, even if I had also at times criticized and even roundly condemned some of her policies.

Yet again there followed the same anxious interval of waiting for the list to be published, but in the light of our previous experience, we felt no significant apprehension as to whether or not my response had been received. In some ways it was even more difficult to keep this news confidential and indeed we decided, as before, with the same solemn vow of secrecy, to tell the immediate family. I also had to explain to Gerald Chambers why it was that on the weekend before Encaenia, Dr Green's visit, our tenth anniversary celebrations and the opening of the new college buildings we wished on the Saturday, when the honours list was to be published, to hold a drinks party in the college garden for the fellows, studer t officers and staff. The invitees were simply told that Betty and I wished to say a modest 'thank you' for their help and support over our years in the college. We explained that the date was chosen because of the impending summer vacation and because of our projected July move to 13 Norham Gardens. The weather was magnificent and some of our friends who arrived to be regaled with champagne and canapés had not read the morning papers, so that their surprise and delight added much to our enjoyment and ambience of the occasion.

This time I knew that there would be no investiture but that I would have to choose peers of a similar standing to myself who would ultimately introduce me on an appropriate date into the House of Lords. I also knew that whereas one may use the title of a knighthood immediately it is announced, a peerage is not formally conferred until published in the London Gazette. As Garter, now Sir Colin Cole, told me when I went to see him, that announcement could not be published until my title and full designation had been agreed with him. He pointed out that I could, if I so wished, keep my own name or I could choose any other name provided it had not been adopted by another peer. My response was immediate in saying that I wished to retain the name Walton as, for example, when the historian Hugh Trevor-Roper became Lord Dacre, many people were not sure who he was. Garter replied that on the assumption that I would make that decision, he had done a little research;

he had discovered that there had never been a Lord Walton but that there had been a Lord Watton, that there was then a Lord Walston (who sadly has subsequently died), a Lord Woolton and a Baroness Wootton. It was therefore his view that the possibility of confusion between my name and that of other peers might arise and it would thus be necessary to add, as he said, to my *nomen dignitatum* a geographical location. Again my response was immediate as Betty and I had discussed this and agreed that the geographical location should be Detchant, which we had loved for over 30 years. 'Detchant', said Garter, 'never heard of it'! I immediately pointed out its size and location, to which he responded that he must then be certain that it existed officially. He turned to a very large gazetteer on his desk and quickly found 'Detchant, Northumberland, in the parish of Belford, population 21'. My title was therefore approved, my *nomen dignitatum* being Baron Walton of Detchant, of Detchant in the county of Northumberland. In other words, my surname now is officially not just Walton but Walton of Detchant and it is in this form that I must sign all official documents.

By now I was beginning to think that Garter was just a trifle stuffy, but was soon disabused when he went on to discuss the question of whom I would choose to introduce me. Even though I had been a life-long Conservative voter (despite an occasional glance in the direction of the SDP when I felt disenchanted with some Tory policies) I decided, like many doctors, lawyers, academics and scientists, to be a cross-bencher (Independent), first so as not to be constrained by a party whip but more particularly to feel free to support whichever policy, whatever the party of origin, seemed to me most worthy. Cross-bench peers now number more than 260. I explained that I had already approached two cross-bench peers, John Richardson and Arthur Porritt—John as a past President of the BMA, GMC and RSM, and Arthur of the Royal College of Surgeons and RSM—both of whom I knew well and who enthusiastically agreed. The question of my robes then arose; Garter pointed out that I could buy these at a price then of £3000 plus VAT; my hesitation was *immediately* apparent so he went on to explain that I could hire them from Ede & Ravenscroft if I preferred, or, said he with a twinkle, 'Don't tell Black Rod that I told you so, but you can go to the House and borrow them from the quartermaster's store'. 'Done', I said, and so the arrangements were completed, my title was gazetted in early July and, as time was getting short before the summer recess, we planned (Chapter 21) that I would be formally introduced on a date to be decided in October.

The only matter then outstanding related yet again to my armorial bearings which, as Garter pointed out, should now be modified. The knight's vizor and helmet would be accompanied by a coronet and I was now entitled to have supporters on either side of the shield. With yet another twinkle, Garter explained that the necessary modifications could now be made at the 'nominal cost of £300' but if I waited until 1 July the price was going up to nearly £600. Once again we clinched the deal; I paid up and engaged in further discussions with Chester Herald, Hubert Chesshyre, suggesting to him very tentatively that as we lived in The Old Piggery at Detchant, something porcine might be appropriate. In the end we settled upon a boar (commonly used in heraldry) and a goose, in view of the huge numbers of greylag geese which regularly fly over Detchant to and from Lindisfarne in the winter.

This title, too, has inevitably produced problems at home and abroad. Officially, of course, as a peer I should be addressed either as 'Lord Walton' or 'my lord' which for old friends and associates both sound much more formal than Sir John, to which everyone had become accustomed. Strictly, Lord John is incorrect, but nevertheless I feel comfortable to be addressed as such, especially by those who, despite my insistence, refuse simply to call me John. But in this computerized world I find myself being variously called in correspondence Lord Detchant, Lord John de Detchant, Lord J. W. Detchant, Lord Walton de Detchant and innumerable other variations. Many colleagues, too, improperly pronounce Detchant as if it were a name of French derivation, whereas it is pure Anglo-Saxon, meaning 'ditch-end'. And the British Airways Air Miles computer which can only, it seems, cope with a limited number of digits, now rejects me as Lord Walton but cannot record Lord Walton of Detchant, so to them I am now Lord Walton of Detch! No doubt more variations are yet to come. I have to confess that I am still ambivalent about my signature which has always been John N. Walton but should now be Walton of Detchant. Improperly, but conveniently, I still use the former on cheques and credit cards but on other occasions ring the changes as the mood takes me.

CHAPTER 19

Writing and Publishing

Ever since my Spennymoor schooldays I have loved the English language, have tried to appreciate its more complex nuances and have enjoyed manipulating words even though in writing, as in many other activities, I feel that I have lacked originality and flair. Writing, however, has usually come easily, though like everyone who puts pen to paper I have suffered intermittently from those curious mental blocks when one stares either at a blank sheet of paper or at a stationary dictating machine, finding that the words simply fail to flow. Sometimes they have, however, flowed much more readily, no doubt with consequential prolixity. Nevertheless my love of, and enjoyment in, language has always made me impatient and intolerant of carelessness in its usage and in grammatical construction. Misspelling by the highly intelligent I can tolerate, accepting that this may be a specific, if minor, learning defect which is difficult to overcome, as in the case, it is said, of Dr Samuel Johnson (despite his lexicographic expertise) and Edgar Allen Poe. I have been compelled to tolerate 'forums' rather than 'fora' and 'angiomas' rather than 'angiomata', if only on the basis of common usage, but I cannot avoid a sense of surprise on learning that expensively educated and outstandingly intelligent young people now lack the grammatical knowledge which was drummed into us all in Spennymoor before the School Certificate examination.

I began to take some interest in writing in school and even for a time produced, with a few friends, a duplicated newspaper which did not, however, last long. One or two of my effusions were published in *The Wraithian* (the school magazine) and I even tried my hand, without success, at poetry. In medical school, as an officer of the Students' Representative Council (Chapter 3), I produced for a couple of years a wall newspaper discussing student affairs and included some short commentaries on medical history. That interest in history, stimulated by James Spence, led me to write the article on Osler which I mentioned earlier. As this seemed successful and attracted a £5 prize, I followed it up by writing another on 'The English Hippocrates', the life of Thomas Sydenham. In the meantime, with the support of Peter Dickinson who preceded me as President of the SRC, we conducted a major questionnaire exercise sounding student opinion on several political issues of the moment, including student health and the future of medical education.

Based upon the response we wrote two reports which we signed jointly and proudly presented to the Dean. One sought to persuade the University to establish a student health service and the other recommended, in the light of the Goodenough Report, some major changes in medical education. I can appreciate from my own subsequent experience as Dean that these must have been thought by R. B. Green to be somewhat presumptuous in those less liberal days. At least he received them civilly, even though he hinted rather darkly that it was perhaps inappropriate for students to comment upon such matters as whether or not medical schools should have full-time deans. It was about 10–15 years before the University did decide to establish a student health service; perhaps our report was a first step along the road. In my final year, despite the heavy responsibilities we all carried in those days in student house officer posts (Chapter 3) Alan Jenkins and I became very interested in some patients with various types of anaemia in pregnancy and collaborated in writing yet another article for the *Student Gazette*; this too brought a prize of £5, which we shared. And while I was working with James Spence as a student houseman for three months before qualifying, I became partly irritated and partly fascinated by the fact that intravenous drips which I had so carefully and, I thought, assiduously erected tended to slow down and stop of their own accord. I therefore mounted the research project which I described in Chapter 4 and which eventually led to a paper published by *The Lancet*.

Literary activities then ceased during my busy house officer year and remained in abeyance during my Army service, apart from the innumerable letters which I wrote to Betty and occasionally to friends. But when I later became a registrar to Alan Ogilvie and Henry Miller, some interesting clinical problems arose which I felt should be recorded, I wrote papers on medical subjects as diverse as phaeo-chromocytoma of the adrenal and bleeding Meckel's diverticulum. With the encouragement of R. B. Thompson, I was fascinated by haematology and was greatly struck by the problems encountered in treating aplastic anaemia, for which at that time the only form of treatment was repeated blood transfusion which often became exceptionally difficult as vein after vein became thrombosed. In Chapter 6 I described my experiences in looking after one young girl who eventually recovered spontaneously. As I said in that Chapter in relation to the paper I wrote with Tom Boon, the loss of the original manuscript taught me how crucial it was to keep a copy of any material being prepared for publication to avoid such a catastrophe happening again. Christopher Strang and I later collaborated in analysing the records of the RVI over a 10-year period relating to a large series of cases of carcinoma of the body and tail of pancreas; our paper was eventually published in the *Annals of Internal Medicine*.

Despite my love of paediatrics and my interest in haematology, I was, however, beginning to turn my attention more and more to neurology, partly inspired by my work as house physician to Fred Nattrass but more especially by Henry Miller's fascinatingly charismatic personality. I therefore decided that I should write my MD thesis on subarachnoid haemorrhage and that endeavour was also described in Chapter 6. As Sir Charles Symonds, the external examiner, had suggested in his report that the information which the thesis contained was sufficiently interesting to warrant publication, I extracted from it material relating to several specific topics. These dealt with, for example, subarachnoid haemorrhage in childhood, in pregnancy and the long-term sequelae of the condition and so I produced a series of papers based upon those individual components of the study. Nevertheless, the idea slowly crystallized that perhaps a monograph based upon the thesis might be published and hence I rewrote it in chapter format. While working in Boston I tried it on Harvard University Press, who said that they would only publish it if I could find a subsidy of £1000, but as this was out of the question I declined. On returning to the UK, however, on the recommendation of a friend, I approached Charles Macmillan of E. & S. Livingstone in Edinburgh who soon expressed enthusiasm for the work and agreed to take it on as I mentioned in Chapter 9. Naturally I was delighted and was prepared to sign any agreement in order to have work published. No question of royalties was ever considered and the book was published on a profit-sharing basis. In other words, it was agreed that if the book sold enough copies to make a profit, the profits would be shared one-third to myself and two-thirds to the company. Eventually, the monograph was published in 1956 at 30/-. It was well reviewed, both in the UK and in the United States, but in the end sold only some 1400 copies and failed to make a profit, so that although I probably gained professional prestige from it, I certainly did not gain financially.

Nevertheless, the relative success of that publication made Ray Adams feel that the work that we had done together on polymyositis when I was in the United States also justified a monograph, as my own cases from Newcastle put together with his from Boston (many of whom I had seen while I was there) seemed to us to constitute one of the largest series yet analysed. Hence we prepared jointly a work which Charles Macmillan was also pleased to publish and that appeared in 1958 on the same profit-sharing basis. This book sold a few more copies than *Subarachnoid Haemorrhage*, and when after five years Ray Adams and I each received a cheque for the magnificent sum of £2.3s. 4d. the publishers promptly remaindered both volumes so that no further income was generated from that source. I soon learned therefore that unless one was writing a book which was likely to have a major sale to medical students or nurses, the profit-sharing system (which has since been discarded by all publishers) was unlikely to be beneficial. If one wished to have even a modest financial return from such publications, it was essential to have a contract under which royalties would be paid. Nevertheless, I shall always be grateful to Charles Macmillan for enabling me to publish these two monographs early in my career. My error in not having my illustrations properly prepared before the blocks were made (Chapter 9) in the case of *Subarachnoid Haemorrhage* was compensated for to some extent by Livingstone's error in advertising that book and quoting me, the author, as a consultant neurologist to the RVI in Newcastle at a time when I was Henry Miller's first assistant. Henry was not unnaturally irritated when he saw the adveriesement as he had himself been appointed to the post only a few months earlier. Eventually we each received a handsome apology, but again I learned how important it was to check the accuracy of advertising material in relation to one's publications.

Encouraged by the comparative academic, if not financial, success of these two volumes, I was very receptive to the approach I received from Dr Clark-Kennedy, senior physician at the London Hospital, about the possibility of writing a student text on neurology in a series on *Essentials* which he was commissioning through the Pitman Medical Publishing Company. There were then relatively few competitor volumes on the market aimed specifically at medical students and young postgraduates. Walshe's *Diseases of the Nervous System* was becoming a little long in the tooth and Lord Brain's shorter text *Clinical Neurology* had not yet appeared, so it seemed to me that there would be a ready market for such a volume. Clark-Kennedy was the advisory editor and Dr Geoffrey Bourne, reader in anatomy at the London Hospital Medical College, was series editor of what was intended to be a large series of texts covering all medical specialties. *Essentials of Pathology* had already appeared and several others were commissioned. I therefore set to work in such spare time as I had, despite my newly-acquired and arduous consultant responsibilities. In planning the structure of the book I tried to follow the principles adopted by Ray Adams in *Harrison's Textbook of Internal Medicine* to which I had contributed two chapters (at his request) while in the States. I planned that 10 chapters of the book would deal with principles of neurology and cardinal symptoms, and a second 10 would cover specific diseases and treatment. My old friend Peter Nathan of the neurological research unit at Queen Square cast a critical and helpful eye over the manuscript before the book went to press and it eventually appeared to reasonable critical acclaim in 1961.

Further editions were then published in 1966, 1971, 1975, 1982 and 1989. The preparation of several of these was not without trauma. All went well with the second, even though the avuncular David Dickens had moved on to higher things, to be succeeded by Michael Jackson, a man of energy and considerable expertise. When Michael eventually left the company to become Managing Director of W. B. Saunders (UK) Medical Publications, he was succeeded by Ian Herbert who asked in 1969 for a third edition to be prepared as stocks were running low. Hence I set to work, but soon afterwards Ian Herbert was promoted and John Maitland took over. He was far from well at the time and sadly died in July 1970. In February 1970 I sent the manuscript of the third edition to Pitmans by registered mail and when I enquired a month later about the publication schedule they claimed not to have received it, even though a receipt had been signed! Eventually it was located in their office in mid-April, but even then there were long and unexplained delays in receiving answers to correspondence and proofs were late in coming. I therefore engaged in some spirited correspondence with David Dickens, who thankfully resumed overall control and appointed Stephen Neal to take charge of the medical division. Happily the third edition appeared at last in good order and some stability was re-established so that we continued to correspond with Stephen for about ten years before he too was promoted and was succeeded by Katharine Watts. With Stephen at the helm all went reasonably smoothly with the fourth and fifth editions until another problem arose.

For reasons which were never clear to me, Pitman discontinued its longstanding agreement with Lippincott in the United States and its agency there was taken over by a small American company of which I had never heard. When I learned that the book (which had formerly sold over 1000 copies of each edition in the USA) had actually sold 39 of the fifth edition in that country, and even though it had been translated into Spanish, Italian and Greek so as to encourage sales in those respective countries (and had also been adopted by the British Council in its ELBS series for developing countries), I felt that I should probably terminate my agreement with Pitmans. However, the company was taken over by Longman in 1985 so that the book now fell within the ambit of Churchill Livingstone. Hence the sixth edition, the last in which I will be involved, in the preparation of which I recruited the invaluable help of Dr Michael O'Brien of Guy's Hospital, my former registrar, was published by that company in 1989. I hope that he will take over responsibility for subsequent editions, thus keeping the book alive.

The next (and quite unexpected) publishing commitment arose in 1962 when Mr Rivers of J. & A. Churchill Ltd. asked me to consider editing a text on muscle disease in view of growing world-wide interest in the subject. At first, feeling that I had quite enough on hand, I was reluctant to accept. Nevertheless, with the encouragement of my colleagues working in Newcastle in the neuromuscular field I eventually accepted and set about recruiting a suitably international group of authors to write the individual chapters. Having read and admired the book *Diseases of Muscle* by Adams, Denny-Brown and Pearson, which was essentially a study in pathology, I decided to plan the book in four sections, dealing respectively with the basic structure and function of muscle, pathology and biochemistry, clinical descriptions and genetics, and electrophysiology. Fortunately most of those approached agreed to contribute and despite the inevitable delays which arise in any multi-author publication, *Disorders of Voluntary Muscle* appeared in 1964; a second edition appeared in 1969. Churchill then was merged with Livingstone and the third, fourth and fifth editions, appearing respectively in 1974, 1981 and 1989, were published under the imprint of that company. In general, work on that book has gone reasonably smoothly and I have much appreciated the invaluable support throughout of the many contributors who in the light of innumerable developments, have invariably updated their chapters efficiently. Some have given way to others, some new authors have been recruited and the content and character of the book have changed immeasurably over the years. Andrew Stevenson and Joan Morrison of the publishers have been most supportive. Only one major snag arose over the fourth edition when the publishers changed their house style in relation to references and the in-house editor changed in mid-stream, so that some of the chapters prepared from paste-ups of the previous edition had references in the old style, some in the new. Even though I had been assured that that discrepancy would be corrected 'in house' this was not done before printing, and when the proofs arrived massive corrections were needed. I was considerably put out to find that a large sum in acknowledgement of those changes was later debited against my royalties so that some tetchy correspondence ensued, but all in the end was settled amicably.

Having got the first edition of *Disorders of Voluntary Muscle* and the second of *Essentials* safely out of the way, in the mid 1960s I was ready for a breathing space, being 'between books' as it were. However, two further unexpected opportunities then arose. Lord Brain of Eynsham, a distinguished neurologist and former President of the Royal College of Physicians, died in 1966 and a few months later his son, Michael, approached me on behalf of the family, asking whether I would assume the authorship of Lord Brain's classical *Diseases of the Nervous System*, then in its sixth edition. This was one of the most successful textbooks of neurology ever written and the fourth and fifth editions had each sold about 25,000 copies world-wide. Before he died, Lord Brain had revised about one-third of the book towards the preparation of the seventh edition. Hence I knew that if I accepted, the seventh would be something of a hybrid, partly revised by him and partly by me. Michael and Lady Brain, whom I later visited at the family home, were exceptionally persuasive, and while I realized that the task would be massive and demanding I ultimately agreed and was given access, in consequence, to many of Lord Brain's literary papers and books which he had set aside to help him with the revision. Once the contract was signed and financial negotiations had been satisfactorily concluded (I was to receive one-third of the royalties on the seventh edition, 50% on the eighth and all on the ninth and subsequent editions), I set to work and found the task daunting but also enjoyable. I was not entirely happy that the seventh (hybrid) edition was as up-to-date as I would have wished (this may have been responsible for the fact that the Japanese translation was unsuccessful). However, for the eighth edition, published in 1977, I was able to undertake extensive revision and restructuring, while the ninth (appearing in 1985) was largely my own with relatively little of the original book remaining. While the book never achieved the substantial sales that the fourth and fifth editions had enjoyed, as there were by now many more major competitors on the market in Britain, Europe and the United States, it has nevertheless continued to enjoy reasonable success. It even appeared transiently for about six weeks on the Oxford University Press bestseller lists in 1985. This book, like *Essentials of Neurology*, was accepted by the British Council for publication in the English Language Book Society (ELBS) series, a little-known but invaluable form of overseas aid whereby modern educational books are made available in the developing world at heavily subsidized prices. In this way, many copies were sold in the third world. Soon after the ninth edition had appeared, a work which involved the immense labour of identifying and collating innumerable papers in order to update the various sections in the light of vast recent progress in neuroscience, I recognized that I would be incapable of preparing a further edition single-handed. When I approached several senior neurological colleagues asking whether they would join me as co-author with a view to taking over the book in due course, all quailed at the prospect. Eventually I decided, after consulting John Manger and Alison Langton of OUP, to recruit 11 co-authors, most of whom would revise two chapters of the book (apart from the four which I would revise myself). That tenth edition is now in an advanced stage of preparation and publication is planned in 1993. The question as to who will lead the team if an eleventh edition is called for is a matter which I must now leave to my colleagues.

The second interesting challenge which came in the mid 1960s was from Michael Jackson, then working with W. B. Saunders, who approached me along with Jack Hanley, then one of the leading lights in W. B. Saunders (Philadelphia). They told me that that company was launching a series of monographs to be entitled 'Major Problems in . . . .' and they wondered whether I would be willing to edit of a series of books on *Major Problems in Neurology*. My responsibility would be to identify subjects, commission authors and then to read and edit the manuscripts critically prior to publication. In acknowledgement I would receive an override on royalties payable to the authors (it was only many years later that I discovered that Dr Geoffrey Bourne, of the London Hospital, later of Emory University, Georgia, and subsequently Vice-Chancellor of St. George's Medical School in Grenada in the Caribbean, had been receiving over the years a 2½% override on the royalties on my own *Essentials of Neurology*!). This again seemed to be an attractive challenge which would not involve me in any personal writing, though plainly much correspondence was involved. Hence I again accepted as the series seemed likely to make an important contribution to postgraduate training and to the information explosion in neurology. The books were to be simultaneously marketed in the USA and Canada and in the UK and elsewhere under the Saunders imprint. It was also proposed to sell subscriptions to the series so that libraries and individuals could commit themselves in advance to purchasing each monograph as it appeared. I was delighted when my friend Henry Barnett from London, Ontario, agreed to collaborate with Jack Foster and Peter Hudgson from Newcastle in writing the first volume in the series on *Syringomyelia*. That book was eventually published to substantial critical acclaim so that the series was off to an excellent start and has continued with varying degrees of success ever since. W. B. Saunders subsequently merged with Baillière Tindall so that later monographs in the series were published by that company, now a part of Harcourt Brace Jovanovich. The successive takeovers and mergers which have occurred in British medical and scientific publishing over the last few years have been a continuing source, to me at least, of confusion and bewilderment. Nevertheless, under the expert guidance of Katharine Hinton (née Watts, formerly with Pitman), this series continues to prosper. I was pleased when Charles Warlow, former fellow of Green College and now Professor of Neurology in the University of Edinburgh, agreed to become joint editor of the series in 1989 and I hope that he will soon accept responsibility for it. Twenty-four monographs have now appeared, one of the last a splendid work on 'Huntington's Disease' by Professor Peter Harper of Cardiff and his colleagues; several others are now in preparation.

My association with Baillière Tindall proved fruitful in yet another way. As a trainee neurologist I had found the Medical Research Council's pamphlet on the investigation of peripheral nerve injuries an admirable guide to the innervation of muscles and segmental sensory organization. That pamphlet had been prepared and published by the Medical Research Council during the war under the guidance of an expert sub-committee. In 1972 I was invited by the MRC to join a new sub-committee under the chairmanship of Sir Herbert Seddon charged with the task of revising that pamphlet. Michael O'Brien of Guy's was a tower of strength and demonstrated a remarkable ability to collate new anatomical information and to obtain excellent photographs to replace those in the original pamphlet which were now beginning to look outdated. In 1973 Sir Herbert retired and the MRC asked me to take on the chair of the sub-committee; our revised edition was published in 1976. Its title was then changed to that of *Aids to the Examination of the Peripheral Nervous System* in that year. Subsequently, after numerous reprints and minor amendments, it seemed sensible that this best-seller should be handled by a commercial publisher rather than by HMSO. Baillière Tindall, by agreement with the MRC, took it over in 1984 under an arrangement whereby royalties would not go to the authors (the sub-committee) but to the Guarantors of the journal *Brain* in order to contribute to research in neurology and the support of young trainee neurologists. Michael O'Brien continues to play a major role in revising this pamphlet. The first edition published by Baillière Tindall appeared in 1986 and yet another has subsequently been published.

As if all these publishing activities were not enough, I and my colleagues tried in the latter years that I was in Newcastle to plan a two-volume Newcastle textbook of neurology, of which the first volume would deal essentially with pathophysiology and the second with more didactic descriptions of disease. Many meetings were held and much effort was devoted to planning. Our old friend Per Saugman of Blackwell Scientific Publications in Oxford was enthusiastic about the project but it ultimately foundered largely because some of those primarily involved, including Jack Foster and Niall Cartlidge, felt that Adams and Victor's *Principles of Neurology* was so excellent a text for young postgraduates that the book that we had in mind would in their view be unlikely to challenge it. My friendship with Per Saugman which had flowered over the years was such that I always regretted that I had never published with his company, particularly in the light of his generosity to Green College. I shared the pleasure felt by his family and friends, when in 1990 Per received, as a Danish citizen, an honorary OBE to acknowledge his outstanding contributions to British medical and scientific publishing. When Wally Bradley left for the United States he told us that he still had in mind the prospect of publishing a two-volume major text on neurology, in preparing which he hoped to make use of many of the abortive outlines we had prepared for the proposed two-volume Newcastle work. I was not therefore surprised when in 1991 a splendid two-volume work *Neurology in Clinical Practice* edited by Bradley, Daroff, Fenichel and Marsden appeared. I recently reviewed it and concluded that it is the best two-volume neurology text now on the market. It will clearly be a substantial competitor to the next edition of *Brain*.

As the 1970s wore on and as my commitments with the MRC and GMC, and my decanal responsibilities in Newcastle continued to escalate, I did not see how I could conceivably take on yet further writing and indeed refused many approaches from publishers who asked me to write or edit books. However, during a week that I spent in San Francisco in 1975 as

Robert Aird Visiting Professor of Neurology, I was approached by Dr
'Holly' Smith, a distinguished physician and chairman of the department
of medicine in the University of California there, to ask whether I would
be interested in a major new publishing project. It was intended that a
three-volume *International Textbook of Medicine* should be published in the
hope of achieving substantial sales not only in the West but also in the
developing world. The work would be published by W. B. Saunders but
would be heavily subsidized by the Shah of Iran so as to bring it within
the reach of doctors and medical students in developing countries. The
editors would be himself, Chuck Samiy from Iran, a US trained physician
who was a close friend and associate of the Shah, and Jim Wyngaarden
of Duke University Medical Center. The proposal was that Volume III
should be a slimmed-down version of Cecil and Loeb's *Textbook of Medicine*
jointly edited by Jim Wyngaarden and Holly Smith; Volume II, to be
edited by Abe Braude, would deal essentially with medical microbiology
and infectious disease, but Volume I, edited by Holly Smith and Sam
Thier of Yale, would be virtually a new work on pathophysiology while
including a few relevant sections extracted from the Cecil and Loeb
textbook. Most authors in the new pathophysiology text would be
American but three UK contributors were being approached. I was invited
to tackle neurology, Colin Dollery clinical pharmacology and David
Weatherall haematology. Yet again, though with considerable reluctance,
I accepted, first because the proposal was challenging and secondly, to
be frank, because the financial arrangements proposed seemed very
attractive. Although I had attempted to deal with the pathophysiology
of the nervous system in the opening chapters of *Essentials of Neurology*,
it was clearly necessary to expand greatly the type of information covered
in that book by including much more fundamental neuroscience and its
pathophysiological consequences. Many midnight hours of dictating and
redrafting ensued, but the task was eventually completed and Volume
I appeared in 1981. However, in the interim, the revolution in Iran had
deposed the Shah, the proposed financial subsidy largely evaporated and
the predicted sales of the book in the third world never materialized.
Indeed while I later found Volume I useful for reference, the project
proved to be something of a failure. It also had another unfortunate
consequence. My good friend Fred Plum, Professor of Neurology at
Cornell Medical School and at the New York Hospital, had been for many
years the author of the neurological chapters in Cecil and Loeb. When
he learned that I and not he had been asked by Holly Smith to write the
neurological pathophysiology in Volume I, he was upset and threatened
to withdraw from future editions of the textbook. When I accepted Holly
Smith's invitation, the possibility that I might cause offence to an old and
valued friend had never crossed my mind. Relationships for a time
between Fred, Holly and the publishers were less than cordial; they were

only repaired when the publisher and editors agreed that if the International Textbook went to further editions, Fred rather than I would contribute the pathophysiology chapters. I in turn felt unhappy about this decision, if only because I had assumed that having contributed to the first edition, I might well continue to do so if the book was subsequently revised. My own correspondence with Fred was amicable throughout and the situation was resolved, I believe to everyone's satisfaction, when Saunders and Baillière Tindall (now their UK agents) agreed that my chapters in Volume I, suitably revised, could be republished as a paperback entitled *Introduction to Clinical Neuroscience*. This book was reasonably successful and well reviewed when it appeared in 1983 and I was therefore asked to prepare a second edition in 1987. By this time, however, there were many competitors on the market and the book did not seem to fill an obvious niche. I do not anticipate that any further editions will be needed.

Just as writing and reading have always been pursuits which I have enjoyed, the derivation and structure of words has also held a continuing fascination for me. When Henry Miller was invited to write the neurological definitions for Collins's (subsequently Butterworth's) medical dictionary, he felt that this was a task for which, at the height of his private practice era, he was unable to spare the time. He therefore invited me as his registrar in 1949–51 to 'ghost' for him, and I did so happily as in those impoverished registrar days the fees made a welcome contribution to the family income. In the early 1980s, therefore, I was not unreceptive to an invitation from Dr E. Lovell Becker, supported by my friend John Butterfield, to help with the neurological definitions for a major new *International Dictionary of Medicine and Biology*. I was told (but should nevertheless have taken the comment with a pinch of salt) that the amount of work involved would not be great as it was proposed to base the work upon a translation of a major French dictionary published by Masson. When I received the French definitions, with which Mrs Heather Russell, part-time editorial assistant in the Department of Neurology was an enormous help, I soon recognized some significant disparities between French and British neurology. Many French definitions, if translated literally, would be unacceptable to an Anglo-American audience and others, especially in relation to epilepsy, were excessively lengthy and complex (many had clearly been written by the charming and ebullient Professor Henri Gastaut from Marseille). Much rewriting in order to change emphasis was needed and some definitions were outdated, others even inaccurate. Major omissions from the items listed were soon evident and before long the editors realized that the task they had taken on would be infinitely more time-consuming and complex than originally envisaged. Finally, with an expanded Editorial Board including not only Lovell Becker and John Butterfield but also Drs A. McGehee Harvey, Robert Heptinstall and Lewis Thomas, two expert executive editors in Sidney Landau and Ruth Koenigsberg were recruited and the massive project gathered impetus. The task, if demanding, was also interesting, occupying much spare time intermittently over several years. At last, the massive three-volume work, which I find invaluable for reference, published by John Wiley & Sons, appeared in 1986. Later we were each invited to identify within the original work those entries which could appropriately appear in a new medical dictionary. With further editorial advice and with the continuing expert guidance of Ruth Koenigsberg as managing editor, Churchill's *Medical Dictionary*, published in 1989, was born. Even since then my fascination with dictionaries has been refreshed by an invitation from Oxford University Press to check and, where necessary, revise medical definitions for the next edition of the *Oxford English Dictionary* (OED) and for the *Shorter Oxford English Dictionary* (SOED). The regular flow of material I now receive in relation to these two publications continues to enliven my waking hours.

Bibliographies also appeal to me; as a medical student I collected a few books on medical history, inspired by Osler, but this hobby fell by the wayside during my impoverished days as a junior doctor and barely revived until I had been a consultant for several years. Nevertheless I was a founder member of 'The Book Club' of medical bibliophiles in Newcastle which later became the Pybus Club for the study of medical history. I was also honoured to serve as a trustee of the Pybus Collection when we supervised the printing and production of the catalogue of that splendid collection of medical books and incunabula left by Professor F. C. Pybus to the University Library. However, the prospect of writing or editing anything other than a volume on neurology or neuromuscular disease was one I had not considered. Richard Charkin, Managing Director of the Academic Division at Oxford University Press with whom I had been closely associated during the successive revisions of *Brain's Diseases of the Nervous System*, approached me, on learning that I would be moving to Green College, to ask whether I might help with *The Oxford Companion to Medicine*. As long ago as 1976 he and Bruce Phillips of OUP had approached Paul Beeson, formerly Nuffield Professor of Clinical Medicine in Oxford (who had recently returned to his native USA), suggesting that he might edit a Companion to Medicine which would do for this subject what other Companions had successfully accomplished in other spheres. They intended that the book should depict the history and principles underlying the profession and practice of medicine, and that it would be aimed at the educated public but more especially at the medical, nursing and paramedical professions and administrators in the Health Service. Having by then accepted many new and diverse editorial responsibilities on his return to the United States, Professor Beeson declined and for a time the project lay fallow.

In 1978, however, Richard approached Sir Ronald Bodley Scott, the distinguished London physician and editor of *Price's Textbook of Medicine* published by OUP. Sir Ronald agreed to be senior editor and to plan and edit the book. When approached by him, in 1980 Paul Beeson reconsidered his earlier decision and agreed to be second editor. The proposal was that the volume would take the form of an encylopaedia with alphabetical entries, both long and short. Articles would be included on the origins, development and present state of medicine, surgery and the derived specialties, on community medicine, nursing and other health-care professions, as well as accounts of the academic, educational and administrative structure of the profession and of its relationship to government and to the law. It was also planned to include biographical notes about those who had made major contributions to medicine and about medically-qualified men and women no longer living who had achieved distinction or notoriety in other fields. The principle was accepted that in considering the various specialties brief mention would be made of diseases which are common, notorious or of general interest. Those of particular historical, social or general concern would be accorded special entries but the accounts would stress these aspects and would contain no clinical details beyond a brief description in terms comprehensible to the layman. It was also agreed that although the volume would be mainly concerned with medicine in the English-speaking world, there would be brief consideration of other countries and notes relevant to medicine in the third world. Nevertheless, the emphasis would remain unashamedly Anglo-American.

In 1980 a headword list of entries was drafted by Ronald Bodley Scott, agreed with Paul Beeson and work began on the biographies. Those relating to doctors in the UK were written by Sir Ronald and those in North America and in other parts of the world by Paul Beeson, with the agreement that no living individual would be listed.

Preparation and writing of the entries was gaining impetus, when, sadly, Sir Ronald Bodley Scott died suddenly at the wheel of a car when on holiday in Italy in May 1982 and work on the book came to a halt. A few weeks later Richard Charkin telephoned me in Newcastle and invited me, on behalf of the Delegates of the Press, to become senior editor and to collaborate with Paul Beeson. Richard, charmingly persuasive as ever, brushed aside my instant refusal when I told him that I simply did not have the time to accept a task of this magnitude. He assured me that most, if not all, of the major articles had been commissioned and that I would simply be involved in editing these as they were received and in commissioning a few more, so that the work would not be too onerous. This was, of course, the kind of comment (as I told him) that I had often heard before, but nevertheless the project did seem exciting and different;

it also seemed that my experience with dictionaries might come in handy so that, reluctantly, I agreed.

During the next year, therefore, I had several meetings with Richard Charkin and Bruce Phillips and with Paul Beeson who fortunately visited the UK at least twice. We soon discovered that the original headword list of entries, both short and long, amounted to some 3,000 items but that there were many important omissions both in relation to major articles and shorter entries. We therefore set about revising the headword list and decided to define the content, length and scope of articles yet to be commissioned relating to the individual topics we wished to include. Six different categories of entry were specified. Those on topics of major importance were classified as A and were allowed up to 10,000 words. These included contributions on the major medical specialties but also on matters like religion, philosophy and ethics in relation to medicine, nursing, art and medicine, and many more. Entries classified as B would be of up to 5,000 words and would include, for example, addiction, aerospace medicine, experimental method, nutrition, poisoning, sociology in relation to medicine, etc. Articles with about 2,500 words, classified as C, embraced subjects as diverse as clinical trials, computers in clinical medicine, diagnosis, health care economics, intensive care and music and medicine. D entries of between 500 and 1,000 words would cover items like blood transfusion or classification, while the overlapping E and F entries, varying from 40 or 50 up to 500 words in length, would deal with the remaining short entries, of which there were many. Some were comparable to dictionary definitions while others were short notes describing and identifying selected institutions such as individual universities, medical schools or hospitals of special historical and scientific interest. We also planned that the biographies should not exceed 500 words in length, but that many would be much shorter, depending upon the importance of the contributions made by the individuals in question.

As the headword list grew and the number of major entries to be commissioned expanded, much of the work of identifying and inviting authors devolved upon myself and I recognized that it would be impossible for me personally to undertake more than a limited amount of writing, even of the short entries, biographies and definitions. After consulting Paul Beeson and my friends at OUP, we therefore recruited as associate editors Dr S. G. (Griff) Owen, an old friend from Newcastle and until recently Second Secretary of the Medical Research Council, and Professor Philip Rhodes, Dean of Postgraduate Medicine at the University of Southampton. Philip Rhodes agreed to write many of the D entries now included in the much-expanded headword list, while Griff accepted the substantial task of writing the entries classified as E and F (well over half of those in the book). In the course of this task he identified many more important omissions; eventually we added 15 supplementary lists even to our revised headword stock, ultimately finding ourselves with about 7,000 entries and 1.25 million words. Heather Russell of Newcastle helped us by checking references in the bibliographies against the text and in correcting inconsistencies of style and format, while Rosemary skilfully constructed a detailed flow chart which helped us to see at a glance the state of play in relation to the individual entries. Later Sue Charkin (Richard's wife) and Christopher Riches, who took over from Bruce Phillips, also gave invaluable help but I edited each contribution personally. After reading the proofs three times (some long air and train journeys helped), once when first received, secondly when returned with corrections by the contributors, and thirdly when read and further corrected by Paul Beeson and Griff Owen, the book appeared in two handsome volumes in 1986. Richard arranged a major launch on its publication date at the Royal Society of Medicine, to which many literary editors of various newspapers and journals, as well as distinguished members of the profession, were invited. I must pay a very special tribute to Griff Owen for the enormous amount of work that he handled in connection with this work, not least in the invaluable cross-referencing signified by asterisks included in longer articles against terms which were separately defined within the book. He also prepared several invaluable appendices listing medical and scientific qualifications and their abbreviations, as well as definitions of many acronyms relevant to medicine.

My hope and that of my collaborators was that the book would prove invaluable to a doctor working in any specialty or any field of medical activity who might consult it, for example, to learn about the history, functions and responsibilities of another branch of medicine. We also hoped that our aim of making the articles interesting for reference by the intelligent layman and by members of professions allied to medicine had been fulfilled. Despite the enormous labour of editing this book, I was myself educated by it, often thrilled, invariably fascinated, sometimes amused, occasionally disturbed, rarely annoyed, but always interested.

The book received generally excellent reviews, not least in *The Times Literary Supplement*, but we were very disappointed that these volumes intended not just for a professional but also for a much wider audience were never reviewed in any of the quality daily or Sunday newspapers, despite repeated urging from myself, from Richard Charkin and from other members of staff at OUP. The view was repeatedly expressed that medicine was too specialized to interest the audience for whom the book had been at least in part intended. I cannot help but wonder (and the same complaints have been expressed by John Maddox, editor of *Nature* and the well-known scientific journalist Bernard Dixon, to quote but two examples) when literary editors will begin to recognize that science and medicine often fascinate the lay public. Surely works on these topics intended for the intelligent layman should be reviewed in their pages, alongside some of the literary exotica dealing with the many circumscribed and often abstruse subjects which in the arts seem all too readily to receive attention.

Although the book had a reasonable success, selling over a few years almost 9,000 copies, as it was priced at over £60 it was regarded by some as being too expensive when compared with some of the longer-established and more popular Companions. Now that Paul Beeson feels that he would not wish to be involved in a revision, a view shared by Griff Owen, I am delighted that Dr Stephen Lock, the noted medical editor, and Dr Jeremiah Barondess, President of the New York Academy of Medicine, will join me in a task through which we soon hope to produce a one-volume version, slimmed down considerably from the first edition. We hope it will be published as a cheaper paperback and might then, we trust, be brought to the attention of a wider audience.

It was, I suppose, inevitable that at some stage I should be invited to edit a neurological journal. For some years I served as a Guarantor of *Brain* and was on the editorial board of the *Journal of Neurology, Neurosurgery and Psychiatry* and indeed of many other journals. However, the invitation to be an editor came rather earlier than I had anticipated. In 1965 Dr Macdonald Critchley succeeded Professor Ludo van Bogaert of Antwerp as President of the World Federation of Neurology (Chapter 20). A few years earlier the World Federation had established its first international journal, called *World Neurology*, edited by Dr Charles Poser of Boston and published in the United States. Sadly it never really took off and because subscriptions did not increase as rapidly as the publishers had anticipated, they discontinued publication almost without warning less than two years later. Ludo van Bogaert, assisted by his eager collaborator, Armand Lowenthal, then negotiated a new contract with the Elsevier Publishing Company of Amsterdam and the *Journal of the Neurological Sciences* was born as the official journal of the WFN. Macdonald Critchley agreed to be the first editor, with Dr John Bates of the National Hospital, Queen Square, as his assistant, and the journal soon prospered. However, when Dr Critchley was elected President he felt that he could no longer continue as editor and invited me to succeed him, which again, after careful consideration, I agreed to do. Frankly, the journal then ran on a shoestring. It appeared every two months and the only financial support for the editorial office was an annual grant of US $500 from the funds of the WFN, with no contribution from the publisher. I was responsible for receiving manuscripts, for vetting these personally, for sending them out to colleagues for peer review, for deciding in the light of their comments and my own evaluation whether they should be accepted for publication, and then for making all of the necessary editorial corrections, assisted by the faithful Rosemary, before forwarding them to the publisher in Amsterdam.

We developed a close relationship with an in-house editor, Mr D. Klinkenberg, who was a careful and faithful proof corrector, but nevertheless in every issue which I read from cover to cover for proof correction purposes, I invariably identified some errors or inconsistencies or printers' errors which he, despite his practised eye, had missed. At first manuscripts came in slowly and our rejection rate was low, but the quality of the papers we received from all parts of the world increased steadily. In 1966 I received 43 papers and rejected six while by 1975 the number submitted had increased to 243 (86 rejected). The work involved in editing papers written in English by some of our Japanese colleagues was at times daunting, but nevertheless my editorial responsibility was an excellent source of postgraduate education in the neurological sciences. Like all Elsevier journals, this one was very expensive and indeed the cost, even in the early days, was so great that relatively few individuals in the UK or even in the United States subscribed, so that the circulation never exceeded 1000. However, as the number of papers received increased we moved after a few years to monthly publication and the work of editing and proof correction (both galley proofs and page proofs) grew even more substantial. I recruited Professor E. J. Field first as assistant editor, later deputy editor and then Wally Bradley became assistant from 1972–1974, deputy from 1975–1977 and was a great help with these tasks.

Whenever I went abroad for a professional lecture tour or even on holiday, I would quail on returning to my desk at the General Hospital to see correspondence in one pile and an ever-growing number of papers awaiting editorial attention in another. Perhaps I was naive but I did not realize then that editors of journals in other parts of the world, particularly in the USA, found that such work provided a substantial income. For seven or eight years my department subsidized the journal by covering most of the postal costs and neither I nor Rosemary received any payment in acknowledgement of our responsibilities. Eventually, after Rosemary and I visited the publishers in Amsterdam in order to discuss the future of the journal, we did obtain a financial subvention which contributed to departmental costs, postage and telephone and at last allowed me to pay Rosemary an honorarium in acknowledgement of her services. However, as my commitments continued to grow, I decided in the mid-1970s that this was a responsibility which I must discard, so that after 12 years in the editorial chair I handed over at the end of 1977, with the full agreement of the WFN, to my longstanding friend and colleague, Professor Bryan Matthews of Oxford. He carried the journal from strength to strength before handing over in turn to Professor George Bruyn of Amsterdam. In 1990 he was succeeded by Jim Toole from Winston-Salem under whose careful supervision and tutelage the journal has changed its format and seems to be prospering greatly, progressively improving its citation rating.

In 1977, therefore, when with a sigh of relief I gave up that responsibility, I was determined not to accept any further editorial commitments. However, yet another exciting opportunity came along in 1986 when Gower Academic Journals (subsequently Current Science) told me that they were launching a series of journals entitled 'Current Opinion in . . . .' and asked whether, with the aid of a distinguished editorial board which I could choose, I would be willing to edit one on *Current Opinion in Neurology and Neurosurgery*. As it seemed to me that the exponential growth in published information in all branches of medicine, not least in the basic and clinical neurosciences, had become so horrifying that, despite advances in information technology, no-one could conceivably be capable of keeping abreast with that published in even a limited scientific field, my first reaction was that no new journal was required. I had responded similarly to several publishers who had approached me about the possibility of starting a new journal on neuromuscular disease; my advice fell on deaf ears since each time it was ignored and first *Muscle & Nerve* and later *Neuromuscular Disorders* were launched on to the market and each seemed to find a niche. However, when I learned the method planned for 'Current Opinion', it seemed that this was a refreshingly original publishing venture which was well worthwhile. The proposal was to publish over a 12-month period six issues which would attempt to summarize developments across the whole field of clinical neuroscience. This was to be achieved by employing scanners who would review a large number of journals chosen by myself and the other members of the editorial board. They would identify in those journals important papers of which copies would then be sent out to invited reviewers in each section, so that they could in turn prepare short review articles based upon them. This has proved to be an invaluable publishing venture as the individual articles have proved in many different hands to offer succinct, readable and yet comprehensive summaries of recent advances in knowledge; I know of no other method which has proved to be as successful.

Following my retirement from Green College, I was pleased to be invited by Howard Croft and his colleagues in RSM Services Limited to edit their International Congress and Symposium Series, and more recently to be chairman of the editorial board of their Family Health Library. The latter project relates to the publication of a number of books on major medical topics of the moment for the lay public, books which will be launched through many outlets with the collaboration of Octopus Books (for whom Richard Charkin now works since leaving OUP).

Perhaps, therefore, the reader will understand how and why writing and editing have played so important a part in my life. While several major ventures are still to be completed, and while I shall continue at least for a time to write my fortnightly column for *Doctor* newspaper and to keep an avuncular eye on the Chapman and Hall series of major medical textbooks (prompted throughout by the urging of Dr Peter Altman and Dr John Moll) and on the proposed new *Journal of Medical Biography*, I hope that over the next year or two my literary activities will decline. Nevertheless, in my dotage perhaps I may find time to handle my one remaining publishing ambition—to produce a work on the history of 20th century neurology; who knows?

CHAPTER 20

The World Federation of Neurology

In the mid-1950s, several neurologists from the United States and Europe, following informal discussions at international meetings, concluded that there would be much to be gained by establishing a world-wide federation of national neurological societies and associations. It was hoped first that this would promote the dissemination of information and scientific knowledge in the neurosciences, secondly that it would foster collaborative international programmes of clinical and basic neurological research, and thirdly that it would enable neurologists in developed countries to assist their less fortunate colleagues in the third world to promote high standards of neurological care and to develop improved services. The prime movers were Dr Pearce Bailey from the United States and Professor Ludo van Bogaert from Antwerp in Belgium, but Georg Schaltenbrand (West Germany), Houston Merritt (USA), Macdonald Critchley and William McMenemy (UK) and Raymond Garcin (France) were also supportive. Pearce Bailey obtained the endorsement of the American Academy of Neurology; his influence then with the National Institutes of Health (NIH) was also substantial. Eventually, after he, Ludo van Bogaert and the others had together drafted a formal application, the NIH offered a grant of US $126,190 annually for five years in order to get the federation off the ground. The grant was awarded in order to establish an office and to cover secretarial, postal, telephone and all other administrative and travel costs. It was also agreed that a new journal should be launched in order to disseminate information about the activities of the federation world-wide. Ludo van Bogaert, distinguished in both neurology and neuropathology, was elected as founding President and Pearce Bailey as Secretary-Treasurer General; an office was established in Antwerp. The process of recruiting the national neurological societies world-wide then began and the World Federation of Neurology (WFN) was effectively launched in 1957 at the International Congress of Neurological Science held in Brussels in that year. Additional funds were raised by levying an annual subscription from each member society or association of US $2 per active member.

Under the charismatic leadership of Ludo van Bogaert, the Federation prospered; most of the neurological societies and associations throughout the world agreed to join. It was soon decided that if the Federation was to gain in international credibility, it should act not only as a sounding board for quasi-political neurological activities but should also promote, as originally envisaged, international collaboration in research. To that end, several problem commissions were established to deal with topics of fundamental importance to clinical neuroscience and founding members were recruited, wherever possible on a broad international basis, to form what were effectively their executive committees. The National Institute of Neurological Diseases and Blindness (a major division of NIH) gave a grant of US $214,108 to fund a research project on the geographical pathology of cerebral vascular disease organized by one such commission. Additional grants of between 25 and US $40,000 were given to support the International Congress of Neurology in Rome in 1961, the first Asian and Oceanian Congress of Neurology in Tokyo in 1962 and the first Pan-American Congress in Lima in 1963. Commissions were established covering topics as diverse as cerebrovascular disease, comparative neuropathology, cerebrospinal fluid, child neurology, geographical neurology, tropical neurology, neurochemistry, neuro-ophthalmology and neurogenetics, to name but a few. Prominent in the early days were Professor Frauchiger of Bern (the chairman and secretary of the commission on comparative neuropathology), Professor Franceschetti, the noted Geneva ophthalmologist, in the commission on neuro-ophthalmology, and his close friend and associate, Professor David Klein of Geneva, founding chairman and secretary of the commission on neurogenetics, with which neuro-ophthalmology collaborated closely. As mentioned in Chapter 19, *World Neurology* was founded as the official organ of the WFN but failed to stay the course; the *Journal of the Neurological Sciences* was established as its successor and was first published under the editorship of Macdonald Critchley in 1964.

By the time the 1961 International Congress in Rome took place, the WFN was firmly established and was beginning to demonstrate its strength in international neurology. Whereas the Constitution and By-laws of the Federation decreed that the President and Secretary-Treasurer General should each serve for four years, re-election for a second term was allowed and in 1961 Ludo van Bogaert was re-elected unanimously. Previously the International Congresses had been planned on an *ad hoc* basis. At each such congress individuals representing the national neurological societies and associations met towards the end of the meeting in order to determine where the next one would be held (on the basis of bids from individual societies) and then devolved the organizational responsibilities totally upon the national society concerned. Hence the local organizing committee in the host country had total freedom to organize the congress programe, though it normally took note of spoken and written input from colleagues world-wide. Nevertheless, no formal procedure existed whereby national bodies could nominate main themes for consideration at the International Congresses. Once the WFN came into being, however, the situation gradually changed in that at every such congress the Council of Delegates of the Federation invariably met and made proposals to the officers chosen to host the next meeting about possible themes, topics and rapporteurs who might be nominated to contribute to, and organize, the scientific programme. The Amsterdam congress in 1977 was the last at which such a partnership arrangement between the WFN on the one hand and the host society, the Dutch Society of Neurology, on the other, was agreed. From then onwards it became the agreed policy that the WFN would assume responsibility first for choosing the venue for subsequent World Congresses (from 1977 onwards, these were known as 'world' rather than 'international' congresses) and then for identifying main themes, symposia, rapporteurs and other details, in collaboration with the officers of the neurological society of the host country and those subsequently chosen to be members of the local organizing and programme committees. A pattern then emerged whereby the Council of Delegates at a World Congress, having chosen the site for the next such meeting, would then meet with the local organizing committee two years before the congress in order to finalize the arrangements, and that mechanism still prevails.

My personal involvement with the World Federation began in 1964 when, in the light of my interest in neuro-muscular research, I proposed to Professor van Bogaert, whom I had met at several scientific meetings, that a problem commission on neuromuscular disease should be created. In anticipation I was invited to attend a meeting of secretaries of Problem Commissions in Antwerp on 12 December 1964. This meeting was called because the financial resources of the WFN were running low and, recognizing that his second term as President would end in 1965, van Bogaert was becoming apprehensive about the future. A clamp-down by the US Treasury had reduced the income available to NIH and it was made clear that no further funding for WFN activities would come from US Government sources, especially since the original funds were given for 'pump-priming' purposes, to enable the WFN to establish itself and then to generate its own income. I was able to use departmental travel funds to enable me to attend the meeting. The President proposed what seemed at first sight to be a sensible and logical development. As he pointed out, since the subscriptions being paid by each national neurological society were limited, the income to the WFN from that source was not capable of sustaining the expenses of a Federation office and of giving grants to problem commissions to promote their activities. He therefore proposed that a quasi-independent organization called the World Association of Neurological Commissions should be established under the loose control of the WFN. He felt that the problem commissions and an association made up of them would be more likely to be successful in fund-raising so as to ensure the viability of their future activities than would a World Federation which appeared to have a purely administrative and co-ordinating role. There was general agreement that such a World Association (WANC) should be created. Klaus Zulch, the Chairman of the Commission on Neuro-oncology, and Professors Frauchiger and Franceschetti from Switzerland were foremost in their advocacy of that proposal. As a new boy I kept rather quiet, though I did have reservations about the idea as it seemed to me that the WFN was dependent for its future viability upon the existence of its research activities, at least so far as its international image was concerned. Nevertheless, the proposal was agreed and was then put to the officers of the WFN and to the member associations as a formal proposal. Then, in January 1965 at the Newcastle General Hospital, my Problem Commission on Neuromuscular Disease was formally established at a meeting chaired by the President and attended by Raymond Garcin (Paris), Irena Hausmanowa-Petrusewicz (Warsaw), Christian Coërs (Brussels) and Dr Trojaborg representing Fritz Buchthal (Copenhagen). I was elected chairman and secretary and after drinks at my home we enjoyed an uproarious dinner with Henry Miller in the Alnwick Room at the University.

At the International Congress of Neurology in Vienna in 1965 the Council of Delegates of the WFN elected Macdonald Critchley as President with Henry Miller as Secretary-Treasurer General, and, at first, the hand-over went smoothly. Unfortunately, however, Macdonald Critchley in his new presidential role began to have increasing reservations about the proposal to hive off the commissions from the WFN. He therefore consulted all the national delegates of the affiliated societies and associations. I shall never know how his letter of consultation was phrased as I did not see a copy. However, as I had by then agreed to succeed him as editor-in-chief of the *Journal of the Neurological Sciences*, I now became for the first time an officer of the Federation. Soon it became clear that there was increasing opposition on the part of many delegates to the proposal that a separate World Association of Neurological Commissions, only loosely related to the WFN, should be created. As Macdonald Critchley stressed, the Federation without its research arm would effectively be impotent. It was therefore agreed that this matter should be further explored at a meeting of past and present officers of the WFN, with chairmen and secretaries of the problem commissions; this was arranged in Geneva from 1–2 July 1966.

Geneva was a magnificent location for the meeting. Tempers which had been frayed and choler which had been rising before the event were each to some extent assuaged by the splendour of the surroundings and by the arrangements which Professors Franceschetti and Klein had made for our entertainment and edification. For those who had not visited Geneva before, a bus trip to Mont Salève on a glorious day with its superb views of the lake and the fully operative fountain was magnificent and compelling. The quality of food and drink provided in the warm surroundings of the Institute of Ophthalmology was such that even Henry Miller approved. Hence, by the time that the meeting began the spirit of confrontation which had seemed likely had been slightly tempered. Nevertheless, the temperature rose again when Critchley read out the list of those national delegates who had written opposing the formation of WANC. At this moment when Critchley and van Bogaert seemed in danger of almost coming to blows, what many later commended as my skill in achieving compromise may have emerged for the first time on an international scene. I proposed as a compromise that the WFN should create a Research Committee, subject to the firm supervision and control of the Federation but with its own Chairman and Secretary-Treasurer who should then be accepted as officers of the Federation but would remain under the authority of the President and the Secretary-Treasurer General of the WFN as a whole. I spent some time after dinner that evening in setting out my proposals on paper before presenting them to the adjourned meeting next morning. After much vigorous argument, contention dissolved, sweetness and light prevailed, my proposals were accepted and even van Bogaert on the one hand and Critchley and Henry on the other felt able to shake hands on 'a deal'.

Thus the Research Committee of the WFN was born; it subsequently devised its own statutes and the first Chairman was Professor Franceschetti, with David Klein as Secretary-Treasurer General. In order to assist financially, it was agreed that each problem commission (now to be called a research group) would in future charge a subscription not only to its founding members (the executive committee) but also to the associate members who would be recruited by each group on a world-wide basis. A central bank account was established by David Klein in Geneva in which these subscriptions were to be lodged. They would be used to cover the expenses of the Research Committee and it was hoped that small grants might subsequently be given to individual research groups, particularly those in the third world (e.g. tropical neurology) to help promote their activities. David Klein and his wife Jacqueline fulfilled this responsibility superbly and kept careful accounts. Unfortunately our hopes of achieving financial viability through this arrangement were never fulfilled as fewer than half of the members of the individual research groups ever paid their subscriptions and the income derived therefrom was inadequate even to cover the secretarial expenses of Professors Franceschetti and Klein. Fortunately, I was able to obtain through the Polio Research Fund in the UK (subsequently the National Fund for Research into Crippling Diseases) a substantial grant to enable me to run my own Research Group on Neuromuscular Diseases, with the agreement that a proportion of the sum awarded could go towards funding the Research Committee of the WFN as a whole. That major contribution achieved solvency for the committee for some years from 1970 onwards but later, as the capital sum invested began gradually to decline, it became clear that the annual subscription of US $12 per member would not be sufficient to maintain the activities of the committee and of its constituent groups on an indefinite basis.

In the meantime, the WFN itself was struggling along on the financial resources derived solely from subscriptions from the national neurological societies and associations. Nevertheless Macdonald Critchley, one of the most intelligent and articulate neurologists of his generation, was an outstanding leader, and Henry Miller, of the charismatic and ebullient personality, invariably succeeded when supporting Mac (as we called him) in enlivening any meeting and debate in which they were both involved. Hence in 1969 when the International Congress of Neurology was held in the Hilton Hotel in New York under the vigorous and efficient, if slightly eccentric, leadership of Houston Merritt, they were both re-elected to serve for a further four years. The World Federation then ticked over smoothly without any major crises but without any major initiatives either, until 1973 when we met in Barcelona. Before that meeting the usual consultations had taken place about whom the WFN would wish to nominate as its President. There was an extraordinary unanimity as almost everyone in Europe and in the United States plumped for the kindly, judicious and statesmanlike Sigvald Refsum of Oslo (formerly of Bergen). He had been the first to recognize and describe a rare but important disorder which he called *heredopathia atactica polyneuritiformis* but which later became generally known by the less informative if substantially simpler eponym of Refsum's disease. This disease, developing in childhood and causing retinal pigmentation, ataxia and polyneuritis, was later shown by Refsum and his colleagues to be due to an abnormal accumulation of phytanic acid in the central and peripheral nervous system. Before long, the primary enzymatic defect was discovered and an effective form of treatment was introduced by restricting chlorophyll intake in the diet (phytanic acid is a dietary derivative of chlorophyll). Sigvald and his delightful wife, Sigrid, subsequently became our very good friends. Of all the neurologists I have met, he was one of the most eminent while being at the same time a warm, gentle, considerate and judicious man, even though when the occasion desired he could be firm and decisive. He chose as his Secretary-Treasurer General the eminent Professor Bent de Fine Olivarius of Denmark (the WFN constitution, repeatedly revised, nevertheless required that the Secretary-Treasurer General should come from the same general region or country as the President). For a while this arrangement worked well, but Professor

Olivarius himself subsequently became ill and major problems then arose when it emerged that annual requests to member societies and associations for the payment of subscriptions had not been despatched and that important correspondence directed to the Secretary-Treasurer General had not elicited replies. For about a year, through no fault of the President, the affairs of the Federation were chaotic, but eventually Professor Olivarius, in view of his indisposition (happily temporary), resigned and was replaced by the efficient and capable, stately figure of Professor Palle Juul-Jensen of Aarhus in Denmark. Professor Juul-Jensen was not only a distinguished clinical neurophysiologist but also dean of his own medical school and soon he had brought the affairs of the Federation back under control, with improved financial management and administrative stability.

It was also becoming clear that Professor Franceschetti, a man of distinction in neuro-ophthalmology, was finding it increasingly difficult, on the grounds of age, to fulfil his responsibilities as Chairman of the Research Committee, though David Klein, despite his recent retirement from the chair of clinical genetics in the University of Geneva, was still a vigorous Secretary-Treasurer. In 1977, a meeting of the Research Committee was called, after informal consultations, during the Amsterdam World Congress. To my surprise and pleasure, I was elected Chairman of the Research Committee with Armand Lowenthal of Antwerp, a long-term friend and associate, as Secretary, while David Klein continued as Treasurer until 1985. In the latter year, David, who had served the Research Committee faithfully and well, became an honorary life member of the Research Committee and Armand Lowenthal became both Secretary and Treasurer.

In Amsterdam several minor but troublesome contentious issues emerged as the WFN was still struggling financially and no new prospects of increasing its income had been identified. Professor George Bruyn, secretary of the Amsterdam congress, ably presided over by the stately and distinguished Professor den Hartog Jager, proposed that the WFN should establish a Finance Committee in an effort to improve matters; this was approved and George was elected chairman. He pointed out, reasonably, that the amount of labour and effort involved in collecting subscriptions from individual members of Research Groups was substantial, that many members never paid, and that the income derived from these subscriptions was limited. The Finance Committee therefore proposed, and the Council of Delegates ultimately, though with reluctance, agreed that individual subscriptions collected centrally by the Treasurer of the Research Committee should be discontinued but that the research groups should attempt to raise funds for the support of their activities, of which 10% would be paid to WFN central funds to support the administrative costs of the Research Committee as a whole. Not unnaturally, David Klein, who had laboured long and hard on behalf of the Committee, protested vigorously about this proposal, which was nevertheless approved. Sadly, this exchange soured David's relationship with the WFN and the Research Committee, though when in 1985 we presented him with a parchment and diploma of honorary life membership he was delighted. I could fully understand his reaction, while accepting the logic and justification of the new policy which George Bruyn and others had proposed.

We now entered a new era when I as Chairman of the Research Committee, ably supported by Armand Lowenthal, attempted to encourage the research groups to raise funds of which a percentage would come to the WFN. While some groups, including my own, responded positively and effectively, this policy was never very successful. As many chairmen and secretaries of the groups pointed out, they did not themselves charge subscriptions to individual members but invariably promoted their activities through sponsorship from commercial companies such as drug firms in order to hold the symposia which from time to time they all promoted. As these funds were earmarked for a specific purpose, they were never able to fulfil the recommendations which the Research Committee as a whole had endorsed and which were enshrined in its statutes. Fortunately, however, an alternative mechanism began to emerge as a potential financial saviour. Several groups had been so successful that, through their activities, international societies were established to promote the very scientific issues in whose interest they had originally been founded. This certainly occurred with respect to the International Society for Neuropathology, the American and European Societies of Neurochemistry, the International Child Neurology Association and many more. We therefore decided that a major objective of the research groups of the WFN should be, wherever possible and appropriate, to nurture the establishment of new international societies for the promotion of individual specialties within the neurosciences. Later still, we invited these societies to become corporate members of the Research Committee with the payment of an annual subscription by virtue of which they could be represented by one or, if need be, two members on the Research Committee (but with a single vote). They would thereby be able to attend all organizing committee meetings of the WFN when proposals were being tabled for main themes and symposia at future World Congresses. This policy has paid off handsomely as many more international bodies, including, for example, the International Stroke Society, Behavioral Neurology International and many other similar bodies in neuroscience have willingly and eagerly accepted corporate membership.

When we met in Kyoto, therefore, in 1981 (that meeting was especially historic for me as it was there that I was approached about the possibility of becoming Warden of Green College) the Research Committee seemed to be firmly established on a satisfactory course of expansion and development. My own Research Group on Neuromuscular Diseases was flourishing with a much increased membership (some 150 world-wide) and had been accepted by other international organizations as the body responsible for organizing the International Congresses on Neuromuscular Disease every four years. Before the 1981 Congress in Kyoto, innumerable consultations had been undertaken by Sigvald Refsum as to whom it might be appropriate to recommend to the Nominating Committee as a future President of the WFN. I had considered the possibility of recommending Ray Adams and Sigvald Refsum's initial response was very supportive. Unfortunately, as I knew well, Ray had a reputation in the United States for being a less than assiduous correspondent. Many of his colleagues often complained that his total dedication to neurology and to research had meant that he sometimes ignored important letters. While everyone held Ray in the highest regard as a leader, teacher and clinical scientist, the feeling was that his administrative potential as President of the World Federation of Neurology might leave something to be desired. Attention then turned to alternative American candidates and after a short period of further consultation it emerged that the nomination of Richard (Dick) Masland, former Director of the Institute of Neurology in the New York Presbyterian Medical Center, would be universally acclaimed. He was elected unanimously.

As Chairman of the Research Committee I have worked closely with Dick and his charming wife, Mollie, whom both Betty and I came increasingly to admire. Dick ran his WFN office on a shoestring, dealing with correspondence from his own home without, so far as one could tell, significant secretarial support, but nevertheless with consummate efficiency. He was a wholly admirable President whose judgement, business acumen, scientific credibility and acknowledged clinical expertise made him a leader acknowledged as outstanding by all segments of the clinical neuroscience community. One of his first acts as President was to suggest a modification of the constitution and by-laws of the WFN whereby the Chairman of the Research Committee would automatically become First Vice-President or Deputy President of the Federation. This was an honour I was delighted to accept when the Council of Delegates accepted his proposal. The question then arose as to whom Dick would wish to nominate as Secretary-Treasurer General. His first choice was Pierre Dreyfus, a former resident and fellow at the Massachusetts General Hospital in Boston whom I had come to know well in 1953–54 and who subsequently became Professor of Neurology at the Davis Medical School of the University of California in Sacramento. This tentative proposal was accepted avidly by Pierre, with the warm support of Murray Goldstein of the National Institute for Neurological Diseases and Blindness of NIH (then the US delegate to the WFN) and Maynard Cohen (then President of the American Academy of Neurology), both of whom were in Kyoto. Sadly, a few weeks later Pierre ran into some administrative difficulties in his medical school and university and felt compelled to withdraw. After further rapid consultation, Dick nominated (to my great pleasure) another old friend, Professor James Toole, Professor of Neurology at the Bowman Gray School of Medicine in Winston-Salem, North Carolina, someone whose work in cerebral vascular disease I had long admired. He had been my host on a previous visit to North Carolina (even being generous enough to allow me to beat him on the golf course on our one free afternoon).

Dick Masland's team was then complete, with himself as President, myself as Chairman of the Research Committee and First Vice-President, Jim Toole as Secretary-Treasurer General and Armand Lowenthal as Joint or Adjunct Secretary-Treasurer General and Secretary of the Research Committee. Under Dick's leadership, with the outstanding secretarial support and financial management of Jim Toole, the WFN went from strength to strength. Jim recruited an able local secretary, in Dee-Dee Vernon, and soon began the massive task of computerizing the records of the Federation and its list of names and addresses of members of all the national member societies (amounting to some 23,000 names world-wide). The mechanism of collecting and collating annual subscriptions from the member societies was rationalized; the Research Committee accounts with the increasing income derived from corporate members was put on a sounder footing and budgets to cover office and secretarial expenses for the principal officers were agreed. A Management Committee consisting of the President, First Vice-President and the two Secretary-Treasurers General was established with the agreement that it should meet regularly. The management of the Federation thus became more professional and its financial control more precise.

When the World Congress of Neurology was held in Hamburg in 1985 under the inspired presidency of Professor Klaus Poeck of Aachen, its organization was in every respect superb. The planning of the WFN meetings, of its constituent committees and Research Committee was equally well planned through the expertise of Dick Masland and Jim Toole and we at last began to feel that the WFN was an established professional organization with a significant role in world neuroscience. This view was heightened when in 1987 a formal association was agreed with the Mental Health Division of the World Health Organization (WHO) directed by Dr Norman Sartorius (no neurological division existed). That association which WHO has, with a number of other comparable non-governmental organizations (NGOs) such as the World Federation of Neurosurgical Societies and the International League Against Epilepsy, to quote but two examples, has become increasingly fruitful. The WFN was consulted officially for the first time about revisions of the International Classification of Disease (ICD-10) and the International Nomenclature of Disease, to name but two developments in which its input was significant and, what is more, noted and acted upon (even if some of our proposals on classification were rejected). We objected roundly, for example, to the inclusion of cerebrovascular disease in the cardiovascular rather than the neurological chapter. Now, with the expert help of Walter Bradley of Miami and Jean-Marc Orgogozo of Bordeaux, the WFN is collaborating with WHO in the production of a neurological adaptation of ICD-10, to be called ICD-10 NA.

One advantage of the WHO association was that from 1987, each year Norman Sartorius has invited me and Armand Lowenthal to represent the WFN (with the agreement of Dick Masland and Jim Toole) at meetings with other NGOs in the neurosciences at WHO headquarters in Geneva. We have arranged these meetings in the week before Christmas, so it has been very convenient for Betty and me to fly over together so that I could attend the meeting and spend a few days, sometimes over Christmas, with Ann and her family in Founex. We have much enjoyed these annual visits and I have even managed several times to play golf daily over the Christmas period. On one notable occasion we even played (Ian, Drew and I) on Christmas Day when Betty and Ann insisted that we should leave the house to allow them to prepare the Christmas dinner unimpeded. I hope that this annual pattern will continue.

During this period proposals for the establishment of new research groups continued to emerge and gradually we developed a mechanism of handling such applications whereby any proposal was considered first by the Management Committee on the advice of myself as Chairman of the Research Committee. When it seemed that the proposal had sufficient broad international support to be viable, the Management Committee then recommended the proposal to the Research Committee as a whole. If that committee approved it in turn, then the Council of Delegates would invariably give approval at its next meeting, in accordance with the statutes of the Research Committee and the constitution and by-laws of the WFN as a whole. Occasionally these approaches were rejected solely on the grounds that the promoter of the proposed research group had not been able to achieve a sufficiently broad degree of international support. The proposal was then referred back with the comment that it would be reconsidered if a greater international spread of representation could be included in the founding members who would constitute the executive committee. Usually that objective was eventually achieved and in 1990 the WFN had 28 research groups and 10 corporate members, each of them engaged in promoting collaborative programmes of research world-wide. Just as new research groups began to emerge, so some declined in activity and were eventually disbanded, particularly if the responsibilities which they had originally carried were later subsumed by international societies which had rendered their existence no longer necessary.

Throughout these years my involvement with the WFN was always fruitful and exciting. Despite the many influences which continually diverted me from neurology towards administrative matters in the UK, my continuing association with developments in the specialty world-wide was always refreshing. Not only in the 1980s was I First Vice-President and Chairman of the Research Committee, but Dick Masland also invited me to chair the Committee on Constitution and By-laws with a view to revising those articles governing WFN activities which had become somewhat outdated. One ticklish problem that we had to consider was that of representation on the Council of Delegates. Whereas the United States and Japan, for example, with many neurologists enrolled as members of their national associations (in the USA we had both the American Neurological Association and the American Academy of Neurology), each had only a single delegate (the AAN and ANA had to decide between them whom to nominate, and did so amicably in rotation), we had to accept a proposal through which colleagues in developing countries could form a society if there were a minimum of five practising neurologists in the country in question. It could then, after forming a society, and being accepted by the Council of Delegates, have the right to appoint a delegate who would have the same voting power as would those from the long-established neurological associations in countries like the USA, Japan and the UK. Fortunately this has caused relatively little difficulty but we did have a problem in trying to define a country when, for example, some of the republics absorbed in the post-war era into the USSR claimed that they were independent countries *ipso facto* and had the right to nominate a delegate. That issue is now finally resolved and the neurological society of Estonia has been accepted. Of much greater difficulty and sensitivity is the problem relating to the two Chinas. The Republic of China (Taiwan) was accepted many years ago as a member of the WFN and regularly sends a delegate to its meetings. In the days of Mao Tse-tung, the Chinese People's Republic (Beijing) eschewed all international contacts and no problem arose, but when the cultural revolution ended and the government of China became more open, Chinese neurologists (some of whom had been trained in Britain and in the USA before the cultural revolution) began to look again towards the forging of international links and explored tentatively the possibility that they might become members. At the Kyoto Congress in 1981, unfortunately, when delegates from the Republic of China (Taiwan) were provided with name badges upon which the words 'Republic of China' appeared, some of those from mainland China, on seeing the badges, walked out and played no further part in the meeting. Later, after some delicate negotiations, in 1985 in Hamburg there were name badges listed either as ROC (Taiwan) or Chinese Republic (Beijing); this seemed to satisfy the delegates and there was no further political confrontation. But as yet the Chinese Neurological Society has not applied for membership, and our political problems are by no means over. Nevertheless, it has been a pleasure recently to see the many neurologists now coming to congresses from eastern Europe freed from the constraints which used to prevent many of them, for example, from the USSR and from Czechoslovakia from travelling to the west.

Throughout this period, however, the problem of finance continued to rear its ugly head. George Bruyn and his colleagues on the Finance Committee endeavoured in 1987 to establish a sub-committee with the objective of raising funds to support the WFN and its activities, but this never got off the ground. It had always been the policy of the Federation to offer a loan equivalent to US $30,000 to the local organizing committee of any World Congress in order to enable them to begin planning and to cover initial expenses. That loan is always given interest-free with the agreement that it must be repaid after the congress in question, along with an agreed percentage of any profits which the congress achieves. The Hamburg conference generated a modest profit which revitalized the Federation's funds. And the next congress in New Delhi in 1989, organized by the indefatigable Professor Jagjit Chopra and members of his department from Chandigarh with relatively little professional help, was an enormous success culturally, scientifically and financially. Despite the constraints of the Indian government upon the export of hard currency, the loan which the WFN made to that organization was soon repaid and a substantial profit generated by the congress is now being held in an Indian bank account with the agreement that 50% of that sum is available for the support of WFN activities in India, while the other 50% has accrued to the Indian Society of Neurology, the host organization which organized the meeting. The Federation is also grateful to Professor George Bruyn and his Finance Committee for their courage in proposing at the Delhi meeting in 1989 that the annual subscription payable by all neurological societies and associations for each paying member of their respective societies should be increased from $2 to $5 per head (the first such increase since 1957). Subsequently that figure has been revised to £3.00 sterling but the result has been the same. The income of the WFN has been substantially increased and at last the organization in the 1990s has achieved reasonable financial stability. While the constitution and by-laws of the Federation require that any national society not paying its dues should not be able to vote at meetings of the Council of Delegates, virtually all national societies now pay willingly and promptly, so that acute financial anxieties are now, we trust, behind us.

A major initiative which has, I believe benefited greatly the public image of the Federation has been the publication of its newsletter 'World

Neurology', begun with enthusiasm by Dick Masland and Jim Toole soon after Dick acceded to the presidency. Initially that newsletter, circulated with the aid of commercial sponsorship to 23,000 neurologists world-wide, did not impose a drain upon the finances of the WFN. However, the initial programme of sponsorship expired after two or three years and thereafter Jim Toole and his colleagues manfully produced, printed and circulated the newsletter from Winston-Salem. This was an enormous task; much material was provided by Dick Masland from his home after extensive world-wide correspondence, while Jim was finally responsible for the editorial content and production. Once sponsorship expired, the cost of publishing and distributing the newsletter fell upon WFN funds. Nevertheless, there was general agreement among neurologists world-wide that the publication was an invaluable means of bringing WFN activities to the attention of an international audience in the clinical neurosciences.

As the Delhi congress of 1989 approached, the usual lobbying began about whom the WFN would nominate as successors to Dick Masland and Jim Toole. Just as the organization had established a Constitution and By-Laws Committee, a Finance Committee and a Publications Committee, there was also a Steering Committee charged with the responsibility of predigesting material before its presentation to the Council of Delegates. In some respects that Committee's responsibilities had perhaps been eroded slightly by establishing a Management Committee but it continued to play an effective part under the chairmanship of Klaus Poeck. Of equal importance was the Nominating Committee, chaired by Professor Ted Munsat of Boston, as that committee was responsible for proposing to the Council of Delegates in Delhi a list of names of those whom it would wish to nominate as the new chief officers of the WFN. I realized that my name was likely to be proposed for the presidency and that, if elected I would then be allowed, in accordance with the constitution and by-laws, to nominate my own Secretary-Treasurer General. I had, however, been approached by the chairman of the Nominating Committee and had tentatively suggested the names of Klaus Poeck as First Vice-President and Chairman of the Research Committee and of Dr Frank Clifford Rose of London as Secretary-Treasurer General. When at the first meeting of the Council of Delegates in Delhi the report of the Nominating Committee arose, I asked to be excused. I knew from conversations and private correspondence that the issue was likely to be contentious and that the report of the Nominating Committee would be opposed for the first time in the history of the WFN. I had learned in preceding months that George Bruyn, Secretary of the Amsterdam Congress and subsequently Editor-in-Chief of the *Journal of the Neurological Sciences*, was making a serious bid for the presidency. He had indeed written to many delegates suggesting that the next President should not come from a country from which a previous President had been chosen. Knowing that Macdonald Critchley was a former president made the significance of that proposal very clear.

When the report of the Nominating Committee was presented by Ted Munsat to the Council of Delegates and when Dick Masland proposed formally that it should be approved, there was, therefore, some opposition within the Council which took the view that alternative nominations to those proposed by the Nominating Committee should be allowed. Alternative names were suggested for the presidency and for the post of Secretary-Treasurer General and some of the nominated Vice-Presidents were also challenged. The Council of Delegates was then compelled to recommend a new procedure whereby formal nomination and seconding of candidates for each office should be allowed prior to a second meeting of the Council later in the week when these nominations would be considered alongside those proposed by the Nominating Committee. At the second meeting, at which I was present, there was a secret ballot and I was greatly honoured to be elected President by 32 votes cast in my favour, with 17 for George Bruyn as the alternative candidate. My nomination of Frank Clifford Rose as Secretary-Treasurer General and of Klaus Poeck as first Vice-President was then accepted without dispute, but there was a competitive election for the other Vice-Presidents and two of those proposed by the Nominating Committee were discarded in favour of others. This was democracy in operation. In view of these developments, emerging for the first time in the history of the WFN, the Committee on Constitution and By-Laws and the Nominating Committee are now reconsidering the method through which future officers of the Federation will be elected.

Since I became President in October 1989, I have greatly enjoyed my new responsibilities. I was a guest of the Neurological Society of Thailand to celebrate the thirtieth anniversary of its establishment, I have been to Madrid to participate in celebrations of the life and works of the great Ramon y Cajal, to Valencia for a joint Anglo-Spanish neurological meeting, to the United States as a guest of the American Academy of Neurology, and to a number of other fascinating and exciting locations across the world where Betty, has usually been able to accompany me. My colleague Frank Clifford Rose has proved to be an exceptionally assiduous, efficient and hard-working Secretary-Treasurer General. He has established a WFN office in London and, with the help of his secretary, is gradually working on a total updating of the Federation's membership database. Jim Toole, now Editor-in-Chief of the *Journal of the Neurological Sciences* in succession to George Bruyn, has rejoined the Management Committee in his new capacity. We have also been successful in obtaining substantial commercial sponsorship for *World Neurology*, which Frank edits and which is now being published quarterly by Smith-Gordon and Company; we are delighted to learn that it has been generally welcomed throughout the world. I am particularly grateful to Professor Hiro Narabayashi for his help in achieving Japanese sponsorship for the Asian edition of the newsletter and to Howard Croft of the RSM whose intervention was undoubtedly crucial in obtaining sponsorship for the copies now distributed in Europe and in the Americas. With the exceptionally capable and efficient support of my secretary, Rosemary, who has been immersed in the affairs of our Research Group, of the Research Committee and of the WFN over many years, we have established a working office in William Osler's old home at 13 Norham Gardens, Oxford, from which I hope to continue to supervise the activities of the Federation for the next few years. I look forward to promoting further new initiatives which will, I hope, benefit world neurology.

Betty and I much enjoyed attending the Asian and Oceanian Congress of Neurology in Tokyo in September 1991 and the subsequent meeting of the Council of Delegates of the WFN in Vancouver at which, in collaboration with the Canadian local organizing committee led by Henry Barnett, Don Paty and Albert Aguayo, we planned the outline programme for the 1993 World Congress in Vancouver. Regional congresses such as the Pan-American (which we attended briefly in Uruguay in October 1991), the Asian and Oceanian, the Pan-Arab and the Pan-European, are all represented on the Council of Delegates of the WFN by their Presidents (who during their term of office are Vice-Presidents of the WFN *ex officio*). On my proposal the former Pan-European Society became a European Federation of Neurological Societies (EFNS) under the auspices of the WFN at the Pan-European Congress in Vienna in December 1991. It will now be able to plan for the future on the same firm and assured long-term basis as do the other regional congresses.

CHAPTER 21

The House of Lords

While, as I said in an earlier chapter, I felt overawed and apprehensive when first appointed to a committee of the Medical Research Council and those emotions revived when I first crossed the portals of the GMC, neither experience could quite compare with how I felt on first entering the House of Lords via the peers' entrance. I knew that I was not entitled to use my new title until it was formally gazetted, but this quickly followed my consultation with Garter. When, soon afterwards, I went tentatively to the House to look around, I was able to introduce myself as Lord Walton of Detchant, even though I knew that until such time as I was formally introduced, I was not strictly a member of the House. Nevertheless, on my first visit during the summer recess of 1989 I encountered unfailing courtesy from policemen, doorkeepers, attendants, officers of the House and secretaries alike. I had previously visited the House on a few occasions for receptions arranged on behalf of charities by various peers in the Cholmondeley Room and on the terrace, and during my time at the BMA and at the GMC I had given evidence to one or two Select Committee hearings. I had also been entertained, with Betty, to dinner by Lord and Lady Schon and later by Lord McAlpine, so that the surroundings of the House itself and the public rooms were not totally unfamiliar. I had even assumed, somewhat naively, when I first went there several years before that the gleaming individually-named coat hooks inside the peers' entrance might well be gold-plated, whereas I soon found that they were made of varnished brass. When I was provided with my own named place and coat-hook, as these were arranged in alphabetical order, I, being a W, found mine on one side of a large coat rack on the other side of which were those allocated to His Royal Highness the Prince of Wales, the Duke of Edinburgh and the other Royal Dukes.

One of my first tasks was to see Sir John Sainty, Clerk of the Parliaments, to discuss with him the arrangements for my formal introduction. Although my peerage had been announced in June, it seemed unlikely that I would be able to mobilize the family (who all wished to be there) and my supporters in time for me to be introduced in July, and hence, after full consultation, we agreed that the introduction should be in October. When I saw Sir John, he gave me all of the information which is provided for new peers, including booklets on *Lords Spiritual and Temporal: General Information, Regulations for Visitors, A Guide to the Line of Route through the Houses of Parliament, General Information for Peers* and *Companion to the Standing Orders and Guide to the Proceedings of the House of Lords*, a somewhat formidable booklet of well over 200 pages which nevertheless contained much fascinating information. Being familiar with official handbooks of many kinds from my previous TA experience, I opened this one feeling that it might perhaps be comparable to *Staff Duties in the Field*, some of which I had found to be couched in obscure military gobbledegook. In fact the House standing orders seemed eminently sensible, clear and well-written, even if also rapidly forgettable. I set out, however, determined not to put a foot wrong, while recognizing that the long tradition and complex protocol of the House would inevitably mean that I, like many new peers, would sometimes be guilty of unintentional error. That was not long in coming, for when I discussed with Sir John's staff and the Whips' Office a possible date for my introduction, we settled provisionally on 11 October. Accordingly I told the family and also Arthur Porritt and John Richardson that this was the likely date. Subsequently, when I received a letter of congratulation from Baroness (Janet) Young, recently Leader of the House, whom we had come to know well and to admire during our time in Oxford, I rashly replied mentioning that my introduction would be on 11 October, little realizing that the date was still purely provisional and could not be finalized until the programme of Government business could be determined when the House reassembled. The subsequent reprimand I received from the Whips' office, combined with a reminder that the date must remain provisional and confidential for some time, was my first warning to watch my step in future. In the event, all was well and that date was confirmed; this was just as well as Betty and I were due to depart on 14 October for the World Congress of Neurology in Delhi where the WFN Presidential election was to take place.

Accordingly, I booked a table for lunch in the dining room and invited not only the Porritts and the Richardsons, but also Garter and his wife. It seemed wholly appropriate that Sir Colin and Lady Cole should join us as I knew that he was intimately involved in the ceremony. Ann, Judy and Christopher and their respective spouses were all able to be there; the only two grandchildren missing were Drew, who had just started at Durham University and felt unable to come to London, and Angus who was a little too young (we had been unofficially advised that children of 8 years old and over would be welcome but that younger ones were discouraged). And so, on a lovely day in October, Betty and I were there very early as we had been generously invited to meet the Lord Chancellor in his office for a glass of champagne before the proceedings. We found him to be thoroughly charming and kindly, a Highland Scot of great

distinction in the law and, as I subsequently learned, an immensely articulate, thoughtful and clear-thinking man whose speeches on innumerable
difficult issues invariably filled me with admiration. I was delighted when
in the following year the University of Newcastle awarded him an honorary
Doctorate on the occasion when my longstanding friend Mr Justice (Peter)
Taylor (by then a Lord Justice of Appeal and now Lord Chief Justice) was
similarly honoured; Betty and I were delighted to be present.

Ann, Ian and Victoria had driven over from Geneva to combine the
occasion with a visit to some friends and to Ian's family in Carlisle. Chris
and Denise arrived from the north, leaving Angus with a friend in
London, and Andy, Judy, Nicholas and Lucy, all smartly attired, arrived
from Burford. I simply could not suppress my sense of excited anticipation
and this clearly had infected the rest of the family, all of whom were in
cheerful, even ebullient spirits. After gathering in the courtyard under
the magnificent statue of Richard Coeur de Lyon outside the peers'
entrance, we then made a short tour of the House. I showed them the
coats of arms of the heads of the defence services as we climbed the main
staircase, the portraits of Henry VIII with his six wives, along with many
other monarchs, in the splendid Prince's Gallery, the Royal Gallery with
its magnificent array of portraits of more recent sovereigns and the
imposing pictures of Nelson's death at Trafalgar and of Wellington and
Blücher meeting on the battlefield at Waterloo. We glanced at the Victorian
Throne Room (now the royal robing room) with its superbly ornate ceiling
rivalling even that of the Royal Gallery, and then looked quickly at
Westminster Hall, the oldest part of the Palace of Westminster, with its
magnificent beamed roof and the plates in the floor commemorating the
lying in state of many monarchs and other major events in British history.
On we went then to the Peers' Guest Room for some refreshing cold
drinks and it was then, after the introductions, that Garter and John
Richardson reminded me what I should already have realized but had
not, that in consequence of my ennoblement Christopher, Ann and Judy,
had each become 'The Honourable'. However, while Denise (Christopher's
wife) also became entitled to use that title by virtue of her husband's,
this did not apply to Ann and Judy's husbands.

A pleasant lunch then passed with just the right amount of wine and
a blur of conversation, of which I absorbed very little, though I was
delighted to see that the family, especially the children, seemed to get
on famously with the Porritts, the Richardsons and the Coles. As 2 o'clock
approached, Arthur Porritt, John Richardson and I were whisked away
by Garter, resplendent in his ceremonial garb, to the Moses Room where
our robes (borrowed from the 'Quartermaster's store') were awaiting us
in time for the rehearsal which is invariably regarded as essential. Suitably
robed, photographed and with mounting but, I trust, suppressed
apprehension, we were then led by Black Rod (Air Chief Marshal Sir John

Gingell, GBE, KCB), elegant, slim and ramrod straight, into the Chamber after the usual briefing. The introduction ceremony is one which has been used in the House of Lords ever since 1621. According to protocol I had to choose two peers of the same standing to accompany me; in other words, as a life baron I could not have invited a duke, a marquess, an earl or a viscount. Black Rod and Garter went first, followed by John Richardson, myself and then Arthur Porritt. As each of us entered the Chamber, we bowed to the Cloth of Estate. We then moved slowly down the right-hand aisle towards the table where the Clerks would be sitting, and bowed there; then on to the Woolsack with another bow, after which I would be required to kneel and to hand my Writ of Summons to the Lord Chancellor. We then returned, again bowing to the Woolsack and table on the way, before I paused at the table to hear the Writ of Summons being read out by the Clerk, swearing my oath of allegiance and then signing the Roll. We then moved on further to the rear row of seats on the cross-bench side of the House, where the three of us were faced by Garter who invited us to put on our hats, to sit down, then to rise, to remove our hats and make simultaneously a sweeping bow to the Lord Chancellor, repeating this procedure three times before following Garter again down the right-hand side of the Chamber so that before departing I could shake hands with the Lord Chancellor. The rehearsal seemed to go quite well and in the meantime, after prayers, while we waited outside, the family were swept up into the public gallery to watch the proceedings (though Betty, now a peeress, was conducted to the Peeresses' Gallery). I had been able to obtain several tickets for the public gallery for some friends, including Rosemary, Gerald and Hilary Chambers from Green College, Paul Walker and Alexander Patrick of the Muscular Dystrophy Group, who were all delighted to be there. We were also thrilled to find that Rex and Pat Belas and Jack and Joan Phillips had obtained tickets through other avenues and had made the long journey from the north to be present on this moving occasion.

The rehearsal was, of course, one thing but the actual introduction was quite another. I could feel my heart pounding and pulse racing as we all with stately tread entered the Chamber. For any such introduction the present Labour front benches are emptied, as are the cross benches, and all cross bench peers must find somewhere to sit with the Labour, Liberal Democrat or Conservative peers until the ceremony is over. What I did not know then was that it had become the custom of many peers to award marks for the performance of those involved, including the new peer and his supporters. All went smoothly except for the fact that after swearing the oath I was about to move away but was reminded by a gentle tug on the arm to sign the Roll. In consequence of that trivial hiccup, some colleagues later told me that I received nine out of 10!

I could not help being deeply moved, being, as I freely admit it, a patriot and a traditionalist, when I heard the Clerk read the Summons which said:

Elizabeth the Second by the Grace of God of the United Kingdom of Great Britain and Northern Ireland and of Our other Realms and Territories Queen Head of the Commonwealth Defender of the Faith To Our right trusty and well beloved John Nicholas Walton of Detchant in Our County of Northumberland Chevalier

Greeting **Whereas** Our Parliament for arduous and urgent affairs concerning Us the state and defence of Our United Kingdom and the Church is now met at Our City of Westminster We strictly enjoining command you upon the faith and allegiance by which you are bound to Us that considering the difficulty of the said affairs and dangers impending (waiving all excuses) you be personally present at Our aforesaid Parliament with Us and with the Prelates Nobles and Peers of Our said Kingdom to treat and give your counsel upon the affairs aforesaid And this as you regard Us and Our honour and the safety and defence of the said Kingdom and Church and dispatch of the said affairs in nowise do you omit **Witness** Ourself at Westminster the   twenty-fourth   day of   July   in the   thirty-eighth   year of Our Reign

OULTON

To ·JOHN NICHOLAS LORD WALTON OF DETCHANT

A Writ of Summons to Parliament

OULTON

When I subsequently swore the Oath myself, holding the testament in my right hand, I was almost too full for words but am told that I managed to speak in a suitably clear and resonant way. And when I shook hands with the Lord Chancellor and heard the chorus of 'Hear, hear' from all corners of the House, tears came to my eyes.

Once the introduction ceremony was over and we had left the Chamber, proud but hugely relieved, there were more photographs followed by disrobing. I was then conducted back into the Chamber to sit for the first, and very probably for the last time, among the cross benchers on their front bench where Lord Hunter of Newington (my old friend Bob Hunter) had kindly kept a place for me. I was much amused to hear later that Hilary Chambers had said excitedly to her husband, Gerald, in the gallery 'Oh, look, he's come back without his clothes on'! I then listened to question time and the first part of the afternoon's business for 20 minutes or so, before leaving to rejoin the family. They had shared in the excitement and in my feeling that we had participated in an item of British ceremonial of considerable antiquity which nevertheless seemed curiously relevant to today. Even the sceptical Ian McNeil was moved and impressed. I was distressed later, having been so impressed by the splendour and dignity of the occasion, to learn (I was not present personally) that when Mrs Barbara Castle became Baroness Castle of Blackburn and was introduced, she apparently refused to wear her hat or to kneel to the Lord Chancellor (or at least so I am told). I understand that her discussions with Black Rod were somewhat disputatious and I am uncertain how that sensitive issue was resolved. For myself I find it difficult to understand how anyone steeped in British traditions and in parliamentary procedure could fail to find the introduction a moving experience.

On that very afternoon I had been pressed to attend an all-party meeting of peers to discuss policy relating to several issues arising in the next parliamentary session dealing with matters as emotive as the Human Fertilisation and Embryology Bill and the National Health Service Bill. Hence the family returned to Oxford without me, but I followed a few hours later and we enjoyed a splendid family party at 13 Norham Gardens.

Since then I have been a regular attender in the House whenever my travels abroad and other commitments have permitted. I soon recognized the very high standard of debate in the House, only rarely contaminated by overt party political arguments, and also soon appreciated how many peers, whether hereditary or appointed for life, are experts in some specific field of activity. The House largely operates as a revising chamber, being able to re-examine in detail Bills which have passed through all of their stages in the House of Commons. Often in the light of their personal experience and expertise, peers identify defects or inconsistences in Bills which the Commons may not have recognized fully and are able to amend them. Only occasionally does the House come into conflict with the Commons, as was the case, for example, in the War Crimes Bill which passed the Commons with a large majority but which was rejected for several reasons, largely on the basis of legal arguments, in the Lords. Many law lords led the arguments against it despite the emotional, if wholly sincere, contributions of some of their Lordships, notably Lord Beloff, who had for deep personal reasons concluded that anyone proven to have been involved in war crimes during the Nazi era in Germany should, even after so many years, be made to answer for his or her actions. That was one of the few recent occasions when the Government had to evoke the Parliament Act in order to pass a Bill which the Lords had rejected.

Bills are handled in the Lords in the same way as they are debated in the Commons, with one notable exception (i.e. the Committee stage— see below). The First Reading is purely a formality in order that the title of the Bill should come before the House and that its text be then lodged in the Printed Paper Office. The Second Reading is a much more formal occasion; a date is defined a week or two in advance and peers then have to decide whether they wish to speak and if so, must set down their names in the Government Whip's Office. The Government then, in consultation with the opposition parties, decides upon who will open for the Government; the opener is followed by speakers on behalf of the Labour and Liberal Democrat benches and often by a cross-bencher. Other peers are then invited to speak in a specific order, but the 'batting' order is not prepared and presented until shortly before the debate. There is then an opportunity at the end for speakers on behalf of each of the parties to summarize before the Government spokesman winds up, Depending upon the content of the Bill, there are sometimes 10 to 15 speakers or even fewer, but sometimes 50 or more, so that the duration of the debate can never be estimated in advance; this can disrupt considerably one's personal programme. On more than one occasion during my first two years in the House I found myself listed to speak on a particular issue but soon recognized as the debate continued that it would be impossible for me to get back to Oxford that evening. Often, when forewarned, I would book a room at the Athenaeum, the Oxford and Cambridge Club, or the Royal College of Physicians, but on at least two occasions in my second year I was badly caught out and had to telephone the Athenaeum at about 8.30 p.m. to see whether a room was available. Mercifully, each time one was vacant and I eventually reached the club well after midnight (once at 1.30 a.m.) when the debate ended, in order to sleep in my underclothes before catching an early morning train back to Oxford. It is the custom of the House that if one is a participant in a debate, one is expected to listen to the opening and closing speeches and to stay for as much as possible of the debate (subject always to the needs of refreshment and calls of nature). If for any reason one participates in a debate and is then compelled to leave before the end, it is customary in advance to offer apologies to the House.

Another interesting tradition is that maiden speakers are invariably listened to with the utmost courtesy and it is improper for anyone to enter or to leave the Chamber during such a speech. It is also the custom that the speaker following should congratulate the maiden speaker upon the content and quality of his or her contribution; indeed, many subsequent speakers customarily add brief congratulations. This is a privilege which has now fallen to me on several occasions and is one which I have much enjoyed, not least when I was able to congratulate Baroness (Julia) Cumberledge upon her speech about the health service.

Quite apart from debates on Bills, regulations and other legislative measures, there are also debates on topics chosen by their Lordships. Five hour debates on Wednesdays are allocated in rotation according to an agreed formula between the political parties and the cross-benchers, following which topics and the opening speakers are chosen in consultation; the appropriate minister responds. There are also some two-and-a-half hour debates chosen by ballot from submissions by individual peers. I have not yet initiated such a debate but will certainly do so in the future. However, I have contributed to several, notably those on the

National Health Service, science and education. And whereas most Bills reach the House of Lords from the Commons, there are times when, in planning the legislative programme, Bills are introduced into the Lords and pass through all of their stages there before going to the Commons. Later they then return briefly to the Lords for consideration of the Commons amendments and the reverse process also applies (see below).

Once the Second Reading is over, then not less than a week later the House goes into Committee to consider amendments which may have been set down by peers after the Second Reading. Unlike the Commons, however, where relatively small all-party committees (in designated committee rooms) analyse and amend Bills, the Committee stage in the Lords involves the whole House; anyone may attend and speak (without prior notice) in order to debate amendments. Often these amendments are withdrawn after full discussion, but where an issue of major principle arises upon which there is significant difference of opinion in different parts of the House, the proposer may decide to 'seek the opinion of the House'. The Chairman of Committees or a deputy (who normally preside during the Committee stage) will invite those in favour to say 'Content', while those who oppose will say 'Not content'. Almost invariably each side persists, an attendant calls 'Clear the bar' and the House divides. The 'contents' go into one lobby where two nominated tellers (one from each side), perform the count after the individual peers have each passed a clerk who checks off their names against the Roll. A similar procedure is followed in the 'not contents' lobby, and the outcome is then announced on the floor of the House.

A similar debating procedure follows at the Report stage, again occurring not less than a week later, by which time the Bill will have been amended by the inclusion of any amendments passed in Committee. The most significant difference between the Report and Committee stages is that no-one is entitled to speak more than once at Report on any single amendment. Following further amendment on Report comes the last stage, the Third Reading, usually an occasion for those still opposed to various sections of the Bill to state or restate their case. Only occasionally are amendments set down and voted upon at Third Reading. Once this is over, the proposal is put that the Bill should now pass. Bills coming to the Lords from the Commons then return there for consideration (and acceptance or rejection) of Lords amendments, before finally returning to the Lords to receive the Royal Assent.

Invariably question time at the beginning of each afternoon sitting is lively and interesting. On first taking my seat I was touched to find that each sitting at 2.30 p.m. (3 o'clock on Thursdays) is preceded by a short session of prayers with all strangers excluded, conducted in the presence of the Lord Chancellor by one of the Bishops (i.e. one of the Lords Spiritual, of whom there are 26, including the two Archbishops who do

not, however, take prayers; the other 24 undertake this task in rotation).
Peers kneel on their seats facing outwards towards the walls while
listening and saying the responses, as appropriate. I enjoy these occasions,
reinforcing as they do my Christian upbringing in the Methodist Church.
Question time then lasts half an hour, with four 'starred' questions set
down by individual peers well in advance (they may choose the date).
A large number of other questions are put down for written answer (I
have put down several) and peers then receive written replies from
appropriate Ministers. The questions and answers are then printed in
Hansard. At question time the peer who has tabled each starred question
will stand and say 'My Lords, I beg leave to ask the question standing
in my name on the order paper'; the Government Minister concerned
then gives an answer. The peer who tabled the question will then ask
a supplementary, almost invariably saying something like 'While I thank
the Minister for that not very encouraging reply, may I further enquire
whether . . .'. There is then an opportunity for other peers to ask
supplementary questions on the topic under consideration. I have done
so several times but I have generally restricted my interventions to issues
relevant to medicine, science and education. Once I was gently reproached
afterwards by my old friend the Earl of Halsbury (a senior and
distinguished cross-bench peer with whom I had served on the MRC)
because I had seemed to be reading my supplementary question, which
is not by custom allowed (as I should have remembered). That, like many
more, was a lesson I quickly learned and subsequently spontaneity has
prevailed. The questions proposed are enormously varied, covering topics
as diverse, for example, as salmon fishing in Scotland, preservation of
bird life, the greenhouse effect, new road schemes, revolution in
Cambodia, the ills of London transport, and the design of Oxford's new
railway station. There are a few peers who in these sessions tend to ride
the same hobby-horse, but most questions are carefully prepared and the
answers are relevant, though on these occasions party political divides
surface more overtly than in many other sessions. Peers may also set down
an 'unstarred' question for debate, by agreement with the Chief Whip's
Office, when a matter of some urgency justifies a public airing. Here again
innumerable important topics have often been considered in such debates,
even though unstarred questions invariably come at the end of the day's
business, often late at night.

Most impressive is the remarkable efficiency of the men and women
who enter the Chamber throughout the hearings in relays, recording the
debates either in shorthand (the majority) or through various mechanical
devices (the minority). After about 10 minutes, one disappears upstairs
and another takes his or her place. In a hive of industry on the top floor
several secretaries are busily engaged in transcribing their script on to
discs, typescripts emerge from their word processors and are then edited

before being sent within an hour or two to the printers. The full record of the debate will then normally be available in print in Hansard next morning. Any peer who so wishes may interrupt this flow, if only briefly, by checking the transcript of his or her contribution before printing. This is something that I have done rarely; only occasionally have I been misquoted, as when I referred to St Mark's Hospital in London as a centre for research in coloproctology and this was printed, not totally inaccurately, as colon pathology.

After one's introduction one may not contribute to debates or ask questions on the floor of the House until after making one's maiden speech; this was the next hurdle I had to face. After consulting the Chief Whip and the Leader of the House, it was agreed that I should make mine on the Queen's Speech in November, after Betty and I had returned from India; I therefore put my name down to speak on 23 November. It is the convention that maiden speeches must not be controversial and must not last more than eight minutes. Time restrictions other than those relating to maiden speeches are often troublesome in the House; one may decide several days in advance to speak in a long or short debate, and may then carefully prepare an appropriate speech, only to find that because of the number of names set down, the opening speakers may be allocated 10 or 15 minutes, while all other speakers are allowed only seven or eight. Much hasty cutting and reconstruction of even a provisional draft may then be necessary even while sitting in the Chamber during the opening remarks. However, having been forewarned about the topics which would be mentioned in the Queen's Speech, I felt that without being controversial, it would be proper for me to mention first that I would hope to contribute more extensively to subsequent debates on the Human Fertilisation and Embryology Bill, on the NHS and Community Care Bill and upon those items in the gracious speech from the Throne which proposed to introduce mechanisms for improving educational standards. Trembling slightly, I therefore pointed out first that it was in my view crucial to the interests of the families of patients with many tragic inherited and as yet incurable diseases that, with very proper safeguards and restrictions, selective manipulation of the human conceptus or embryo up to the fourteenth day should be allowed to continue. Recent developments in molecular biology, including the isolation and characterization of individual genes, thought of as being almost in the realms of science fiction no more than 10 years ago, had raised genuine prospects of prevention, inducing lively and wholly justifiable hopes in such patients and their families. In relation to the NHS proposals, I expressed the hope that discussion and debate between Government and the medical profession could proceed in an atmosphere of constructive collaboration, exploration, trial and assessment, so that those proposals of demonstrable benefit to patient care and to the service as a whole could proceed expeditiously, while those shown by experience to be potentially detrimental could be modified according to the needs of the service. Finally, in welcoming the Government's commitment to the raising of educational standards, I urged that this commitment should acknowledge the need to repair the crumbling infrastructure in British universities upon which, under the dual support system, so much medical and scientific research depended. Happily, my speech was accepted as being non-controversial and I was warmly congratulated upon it, not just by Lord (Alastair) Kilmarnock, (whom I had come to know well as a Governor of the MSD Foundation) who followed me, but also from other corners of the House. Indeed the Leader, Lord Belstead, wrote me a charming note of congratulation afterwards. I was delighted that Betty was able to be there to share in the excitement and in the apprehension which we both felt. She, like I, was much relieved by the cries of 'Hear, hear' which came from all sides of the House after I spoke. We later left the Chamber (she from the Peeresses' Gallery) after listening to more of the debate, with a considerable sense of relief. I felt no sense of anticlimax, nor did I experience the emotion attributed to one noble Lord (who shall be nameless) who said that giving one's maiden speech in the Lords is like dropping a feather into a bottomless pit and waiting for the echo.

This daunting experience came towards the end of two delightful days that we had spent in London, staying at the Royal College of Physicians. On 21 November we had the privilege of attending the State Opening of Parliament. We had often seen that event on television and had hoped, when I knew I was to become a life peer, to be able to attend. We knew that all peers attending must be robed. Hence, as soon as we knew the date, I entered my name in the ballot in the hope of being able to borrow a set of robes from the 'quartermaster's store'. I knew that only some 24 sets were available and that competition would be intense, but I was successful (probably because I was a new peer). Although Betty felt rather uncomfortable in being arrayed in a ball gown and jewellery when leaving the Royal College at about 10.00 a.m., we nevertheless revelled in the pageantry, pomp and circumstance of the occasion. Being a new peeress (wives of male peers are peeresses, whereas women becoming life peers are baronesses), Betty was given a seat on the floor of the House with a splendid view of the proceedings. As we arrived early, I was able to choose where to sit and did so comfortably on one of the rear benches instead of being compelled, like some of the latecomers, to sit without a backrest on central seats facing the throne. The baronesses and peeresses present plainly vied with one another to bring out their most impressive gowns and jewels, along with a glittering array of varied tiaras. As I pointed out earlier to Lord Belstead and to Lord Denham (the Chief Whip), we did not happen to have a family tiara to grace my wife's coiffure. They jokingly replied that a similar situation would undoubtedly arise in many noble families, even some of great antiquity. When I explored with various London jewellers the possibility of hiring one for the occasion, I discovered that all those available for hire had been bespoken well in advance for that date. Nevertheless, there were many ladies present without similar adornment and we much enjoyed the ceremonial surrounding the arrival of members of the Royal Family, including the Queen and the Duke. The Queen, as always, spoke very clearly when reading her speech from the throne; the occasion was an exceptionally memorable one, though we shall not necessarily be too anxious to be there on another occasion. It is the kind of experience to enjoy and savour once in a life-time.

The social facilities of the House are splendid. There is a Peers' Guest Room and on many occasions Betty and I have invited friends and relatives to join us for drinks and lunch and occasionally for dinner. Dinner is only served in the main dining room when the House is sitting late but is always available in the splendid stone-vaulted Barry Room in the basement. On the principal floor (for peers only) is a small but comfortable bar (the Bishops' Bar) with a small annexe where sandwiches, toasted sandwiches, bacon and eggs, sausages, paté, salad and other delicacies such as one could obtain in innumerable unpretentious cafés throughout the land are available, at very reasonable cost. Peers are also able, if they so wish, to book the splendid Cholmondeley Room in the basement and the adjacent terrace either for personal parties or in order to hold events on behalf of charities, professional societies and associations, etc. They can also use the House of Commons cafeteria and other facilities including the barber's shop, where an excellent haircut can be obtained at the remarkably low price of £3.00. As I speak of financial matters, it is important to disabuse the reader of one common misconception to the effect that peers are paid a daily allowance as a salary. This is certainly not so but travelling expenses, whether by car, by train or by air, are reimbursed, including, for example, first-class rail fare (on a rail card for those of appropriate age) along with a modest daily subsistence allowance, the cost of overnight stay up to an agreed maximum and, in appropriate cases, another modest contribution for secretarial, postal, telephone and other expenses. However, these expenses can only be claimed on the days when one actually attends the House or stays overnight in order to participate in a debate or in the work of a committee. Informal meetings of all-party groups, for example, of which I have attended many, or meetings of cross-bench peers which are regularly held on Thursday afternoons when the House is in session, under the admirable chairmanship of their convenor, Baroness Hylton-Foster, do not qualify.

Having made my maiden speech on 23 November (my baptism of fire was more pleasant in retrospect than in anticipation), I began to prepare for what I knew was to come as the Human Fertilisation and Embryology

Bill was to be introduced into the Lords. Much advance newspaper speculation indicated clearly that vocal opponents of abortion and of embryo research, including many noted figures in the Roman Catholic Church, were launching a vigorous campaign to try to persuade Parliament not to accept many provisions of the Bill. Following my maiden speech, I was approached by Lord Henderson of Brompton, an officer of the Progress group, a body established to promote embryo research and to oppose the proposals of the Pro-Life group which seemed to be gaining support in both Houses of Parliament. I attended several of their meetings and received substantial briefing from them, from the MRC and from other research-based organizations, thus being reasonably prepared for the Second Reading of the Bill on 7 December. No fewer than 80 peers had put their names down to speak. The introduction of the Bill by the Lord Chancellor was in every respect a masterly performance. He explained its provisions in detail and set out the points for and against so-called embryo research in an exceptionally balanced and judicial way. Predictably, many opponents of the Bill, including the Duke of Norfolk, Lord Ashbourne, the Earl of Perth, the Earl of Lauderdale and many more, some but not all of them members of the Roman Catholic Church, made powerful speeches in opposition. Many others, including Lord McGregor of Durris, the Archbishop of York and Lord Henderson of Brompton, to quote but a few, spoke in favour.

My turn to speak came at about 7.00 p.m. and I gave my reasons for welcoming Clause 11, Subsection 1, of the Bill which set out the circumstances in which experiments outside the body, involving human embryos of not more than 14 days' gestation, could be allowed to continue, while specifying methods to be used in regulating and restricting their scope. I also welcomed the proposal to establish a statutory licensing authority with functions as clearly defined in the Bill. I expressed the view that no responsible scientist would wish to engage in trans-species fertilization, or germ cell manipulation and cloning, which would be specifically proscribed by the proposed legislation. I then went on to explain the embryological background relating to what was meant by a human embryo, pointing out that up to the fifth day many fertilized embryos (which, at this stage, I preferred to call a conceptus or pre-embryo) were present in the female womb after fertilization by sperms, and that at least 80% of these were discarded before, at the fifth or sixth day, one or possibly two might begin to attach to the uterine wall. By that stage the embryo would have formed a blastocyst with an outer layer of cells from which the membranes and placenta would ultimately develop and a basal group of cells, the basal cell mass, which would later form an embryo and subsequently a fetus. I explained how it would become possible to take a biopsy (a single cell) from the outer layer of cells without damaging the subsequent development of the embryo so as to determine whether the gene responsible, for example, for the severe X-linked Duchenne type of muscular dystrophy was present, subsequently discarding those in which the gene was identified, while implanting only those in which no such gene was present. I went on to explain how the aspirations of innumerable female carriers of the gene responsible for this and many other tragic X-linked diseases would be raised by such experiments and how their hopes would be dashed if such work were prevented by law. I also pointed out that countless children born by *in vitro* fertilization, like the famous Louise Brown, would never have been born had such experimentation been prevented. Finally, I drew attention to some of the moral, philosophical and religious considerations which had been discussed during the debate and in the media. I said that I was a member of the Methodist Church and that church had endorsed, after full consideration, the provisions of the Bill which would allow research to continue under strict control. That view was also supported by many prominent members of the Anglican community, not least the eminent moral theologian, the Revd Gordon Dunstan, and even by some of the Roman Catholic faith including Professor Norman Ford, the noted Australian theologian. Happily, my speech attracted widespread support and I was congratulated upon it publicly later in the debate by Lord Houghton of Sowerby (over 90 years of age, but as sharp, articulate and amusing as ever), and by many others. Later several peers told me that after hearing my arguments they had changed their minds and had decided to vote for research, having previously concluded that they would not. In an exceptionally full House in which there were at least three former Prime Ministers (Lords Wilson, Callaghan and Home), innumerable former Cabinet Ministers and well over 300 peers, the debate raged for several hours more but in the end the Second Reading was carried by 242 votes to 80, a far greater majority than we had anticipated.

The battle was by no means won, but we had a break during the Christmas recess until the Committee stage of the Bill continued on 6, 8 and 13 February, when innumerable amendments were considered in detail. Among the first of these was one proposed, predictably, by the Duke of Norfolk which, if passed, would have banned research. He proposed the amendment movingly and sincerely but on grounds which I regarded as being scientifically misguided and ill-founded. Immediately he had spoken I was pressed by colleagues to stand and contribute, but as the Archbishop of York had risen I gave way to him and listened carefully to his lucid declaration in favour of research. Whereas others then strove to intervene immediately afterwards, I was deeply touched when, on again being prodded by colleagues, I rose to my feet to hear calls of 'Lord Walton, Lord Walton' from several parts of the House. I am sure that in that very crowded House no-one but me could hear or feel the castanets on the inside of my knees as I again deployed and redeveloped many arguments in favour of research. Once more after prolonged debate, our views prevailed and the proposal to allow research up to 14 days was passed by a very large majority. However, much remained to be done, as other amendments, if passed, would have rendered illegal the long-established hamster test. This test involves the use of hamster eggs from which the outer capsule can readily be removed. On mixing such eggs with human sperm, the ability of those sperm to penetrate the egg can be assessed rapidly on a slide and the test has been found very useful as an index of male fertility. However, the details given relating to the test in the Bill raised in the minds of many peers the spectre of trans-species fertilization and powerful speeches were made by Lord Home of the Hirsel and by the Earl of Perth opposing it. Certainly the wording of the original clause in the Bill was open to misinterpretation. When I explained the exact significance of the test and pointed out that immediately after the sperm had penetrated the egg the resultant product was destroyed, and when I also made it clear that the 'organism' formed by the test could not conceivably be viable, several peers changed their minds. Eventually, after consulting the Earl of Perth in the House and later by telephone, I produced an alternative form of words, checked these with Parliamentary counsel, and proposed an amended clause at Report stage which happily was accepted. Even that wording was not totally favoured by Lord Zuckerman, the eminent biologist, as it included a phrase indicating that the test would assess the motility and normality of human sperm. He pointed out, reasonably, that tests could demonstrate abnormality but rarely, if ever, could they prove normality in strictly scientific terms. Although he was not persuaded, legal opinion and the Lord Chancellor's view favouring my wording prevailed. My amendment was eventually incorporated into the Bill, which after the Report stage on 6 March and the Third Reading on the 13th, completed its stages in the House of Lords before going on to the Commons. I and my colleagues were delighted to learn that it was accepted there as amended by the Lords, with only minor additional changes, again by a very large majority. Despite the many misconceived letters which I subsequently received as a consequence of press publicity, most of which were based upon total ignorance of the facts and/or prejudice (including one which said 'Come back Nazi Germany, all is forgiven'), the provisions of the Bill and the Statutory Licensing Authority now established will allow research to be conducted under licence and under careful supervision which will be of inestimable benefit to mankind, particularly to many members of families of those with tragic inherited diseases. Interestingly, throughout our prolonged debates, their Lordships did not divide wholly along religious lines as some Anglican peers voted against research and some Roman Catholics, including Lord (Dennis) Carter on the Labour bench, voted for it.

After that long series of debates was over, Betty and I went north for Easter for relief and relaxation, feeling that my contribution had had a significant influence on the passage of legislation which would benefit mankind. My break from the House routine was, however, relatively brief as the National Health Service and Community Care Bill soon loomed with its Second Reading, again with very many speakers, falling on 3 April. During the long series of debates which followed, with four days in Committee on 19, 24, 26 and 30 April, followed by the Report stage on 7 June, many medical peers, including myself, John Butterfield, John Richardson, Rodney Smith, Bob Hunter and Richard Adrian, contributed, splendidly supported throughout by some of our scientific and university colleagues who also had a major interest in medicine, including that redoubtable pair, Fred Dainton and Brian Flowers. We also received substantial support from some unexpected quarters on the Tory benches. Baroness (Janet) Young was most helpful in the debates about a university presence on the new Health Authorities, and Baroness Cox, originally trained as a nurse, also opposed Government policy in the Bill in relation to several issues about which she shared our concern. Many of us felt unhappy about the rapid introduction of the internal market and the freedom to be granted under the Bill to NHS Trusts. We were also concerned about the effects which the reforms would have upon scientific and medical research in our hospitals and universities, about the future of academic medicine and about proposals which would allow self-governing trusts to set their own salary scales. In our view this would disrupt the long-established process of national negotiation through Review Bodies relating to the salaries of doctors and nurses and could create unhealthy differentials. These debates were always lively, sometimes exciting, usually courteous (though Lord Ennals, who felt deeply about many issues, was at times ferocious in his condemnation of Government policy). On several occasions we were up very late at night. Indeed during the Report stage, when John Butterfield, Fred Dainton and I, with our wives, were invited to attend a magnificent dinner in the City to celebrate the 50th anniversary of the founding of the Nuffield Provincial Hospitals Trust, we changed rapidly into dinner jackets, collected our ladies and went to the dinner, leaving the debate but also a telephone number through which we could be recalled when crucial amendments arose. We left the dinner together at about 10.30 p.m., having just managed to hear the splendid speech made by the Chairman of the Trust, Sir Maurice Shock. We returned to the House just in time to meet Janet Young at the peers' entrance; she breathed a sigh of relief on seeing, as she put it, that three 'white knights' had arrived to relieve her of the responsibility of fighting the university corner, as her car was waiting to take her back to Oxford. John Butterfield, who had his car, nobly took Barbara Dainton back to the Goldsmiths, where she was staying, and deposited Betty at the Oxford and Cambridge Club in Pall Mall to which I eventually returned at the end of the debate at about 2.00 a.m. Anyone who believes that being in the House of Lords is a sinecure must be unaware of the stress engendered by such late-night sittings.

It would be inappropriate to discuss in detail the many fascinating debates in which I have subsequently engaged. Student loans, the effects of atomic explosions upon ex-servicemen, the Access to Health Records Bill, a major debate on education, another on no-fault compensation in medicine, a spirited discussion upon the wearing of seat belts in the rear seats of motor vehicles and on random breath testing for drivers have all exercised my attention. Many such occasions have been amusing, as when I spoke in favour of random breath tests for motorists, pointing out that under the present Road Traffic Act a policeman cannot stop a motor vehicle unless he detects evidence of a moving road traffic offence. Even then, it is not legal for him to require a breath test unless he has reasonable suspicion that the driver whom he has stopped has been drinking. Often these provisions of the present law seem to be flouted and I suggested that it would be more sensible and rational for all concerned if random testing were legalized, as it has been in New South Wales where the result has been a major reduction in drink-related driving offences. Lord Hailsham, however, pointed out that many friends would say that he was a very poor shot on the grouse moor; but even if that were so, it was his view that it was a better principle to aim at the bird rather than to fire randomly into the air. One could see the logic of his comment, but while I and the others who supported the proposal knew that we would lose, we pressed this particular amendment to a division. It was predictably lost, as was another proposing to reduce the legal limit from 80 to 50 mg of alcohol per 100 ml of blood. I am sure, nevertheless, that these provisions will eventually be accepted and that public opinion is gradually moving in their favour.

I also felt it necessary to speak at question time on the very last day of sittings in July 1991 before the summer recess in order to pose a supplementary question following one set down by the Duke of Norfolk relating to the use of mifepristone (RU486) for abortion. He and several other peers castigated the Government for its decision to license this drug which can induce abortion in early pregnancy, especially when combined with vaginal progesterone. They talked about the dangers associated with its use and felt that the trial period allowed before licensing was inadequate; however, I pointed out first that the pill has been used by more than 100,000 women world-wide, including more than 90,000 in France, without a single fatality due to its use and with remarkably few side-effects. And there was no evidence that it had ever produced fetal abnormality. It had been subjected to three years of extensive multi-centre trials in Great Britain. All the evidence indicated that, given appropriate safeguards through which it could only be prescribed in the National Health Service under careful hospital supervision, it represented a major advance and was likely to relieve much of the distress and discomfort associated with surgical methods of abortion. Yet again, I was gratified to hear a chorus of 'Hear, hear' from various parts of the House and to be congratulated afterwards by some of my colleagues upon my intervention. Sitting down in total silence after a carefully prepared speech (as one may often do) is never encouraging.

While some such experiences have been stimulating, even heart-warming, for any new peer learning the ropes there are inevitably occasions when one's interventions are less successful or when, through ignorance or oversight, one transgresses some hallowed and long-established rule. When I spoke on the Committee stage of the Student Loans Bill (having missed the Second Reading) I was fiercely interrupted from the Tory benches when I opposed the principle as I was told that the principle had been accepted at second reading and that I should have been discussing possible amendments instead of offering outright opposition (I suppose I *was* making a Second Reading speech). Once, too, I remained standing to cries of 'Order, order' when the Lord Chancellor had risen to his feet (when he does so, one is supposed to sit down at once, even if one is on one's way out of the Chamber). On yet another occasion, in my haste to reach the division lobby in order to vote (I had been out of the Chamber when the division bell rang) I almost committed the ultimate, unpardonable sin of walking in front of the Chairman of Committees as he sat on the Woolsack with the mace behind him before realizing the error of my ways and rapidly retracing my steps. As Ian McColl, who was sitting on the steps of the throne, said smilingly, 'Peers have been sent to the Tower for lesser offences'.

Throughout these exciting years I have made new friends, I have been received in the House with unfailing courtesy and with splendid support and advice from many colleagues; I have been constantly impressed by the dignity and quality of its proceedings. Betty's support, sitting among the peeresses during many debates, has also been a source of inspiration and comfort. While I can see the justice of the arguments of those who oppose the hereditary principle, many hereditary peers make outstanding, indeed invaluable, contributions to the work of the House. I am convinced that the country needs a second chamber with the revising authority and ability of the present House. Indeed I don't see too much wrong with the way it now operates, but then it will certainly be said 'He would say that, wouldn't he!'. My life has continually presented new challenges every few years and this has been one of the greatest, one which I enjoy and find deeply fulfilling. I have also been continually blessed by good fortune, as I hope my tale will have shown. Still, at times, in our lovely home in Detchant, in Osler's shadow at 13 Norham Gardens, on my travels overseas for the WFN and, above all, in the Palace of Westminster, I look around in wonderment and contemplation, asking myself—'How did a lad from Rowlands Gill, Middlestone Moor and Spennymoor get here?'. Variety is indeed the spice of life and my life has been full of it; but it would all have been impossible, certainly more empty and less rewarding, without the love and support I have been fortunate to have from my wife, family, friends and colleagues.

Index

Abbreviations used: BMA —British Medical Association
DCL —Doctorate in Civil Law
GMC—General Medical Council
MDG—Muscular Dystrophy Group
MGH—Massachusetts General Hospital
NMS —Newcastle Medical School
RSM —Royal Society of Medicine
RVI —Royal Victoria Infirmary
WFN —World Federation of Neurology

The Author is referred to throughout as JW

A

Aarli, Professor, 483
Abbott, John, 'old Bostonian', 192
Abortion advice, people under 16 years,
455
Abraham, Sir Edward, benefaction from
E.P.A. Cephalosporin Trust, 509
Academia Brasileira de Neurologia, JW
honorary member, 1974, 541
Academic dress, styles and colours world-
wide, 539
Acre, Betty and John visit, 1976, 375
Adams, Elinor (Raymond's wife), 199,
206, 348
Adams, George, golf, 265
Adams, Professor Raymond (Ray), 347
agrees to JW's application, 179
background, 200
home and hospitality, 199
honorary DSc, 303
Massachusetts General Hospital, 178
visits Europe, 211-212
Waltons invited to look after home,
212–213
work routine, 189–190
Adelaide
Betty and John visit, 1971, 369
golf, 262–263
Aden, HS 'El Nil' calls in for repairs, 136
Adlon Hotel, 334
Administrative and Planning Committee
see University Cabinet

Adrian, Lord (Richard), 604
Advisory Committee on Medical Education
in Europe, 444
Ahern, Donal, TA, 329
Ahern, Tim, TA, 329
Air-raid warden, JW at 17, 30
Air-raids on Tyneside, STC duties, 56
Aird, Professor Robert, and wife Elinor,
friendship, 210
Aix-Marseille, University honorary degree,
537
Akenside Terrace, Henry Miller's home,
305
Albert Einstein College of Medicine, 348,
349–351
Alberti, George, 251
Alderman Wraith Grammar School,
Spennymoor, JW 1933–1941, 13,
21–39
in the 1990s, 27
cricket, 245–246
House system, 28–29
Jack McManners, 500
Aldridge, Mark, 315
Alexander, Col Osmond, Chairman of
Council, 390
Alice Springs, 380
All-India Institute of Medical Sciences,
364
Allan, Rosemary, 405, 502
and the 65th birthday arrangements, 511
at JW's introduction, House of
Lords, 592

609

Astor Lecture, JW delivers, 1988, 535
Athens, Betty and John visit, 1967, 351–352
military coup, 351–353
Atkinson, Joe and Meta, sell house to
    Walton family, 269, 270
Attenborough, Richard (later Sir), 291
honorary DCL, 303
hosts event in aid of muscular
    dystrophy research, 290
opens extension to Muscular Dystrophy
    Research Laboratory, 292
President of MDG, 290
speaker, RSM, 473
Vice-Patron, ICND, 1974, 302
Audio-frequency spectrometry, RVI,
    173–174
Auschwitz, JW and Betty visit, 128,
    345–346
Australia
golf, 262–263
lectures and visits, 368–370, 380
Australian Association of Neurologists,
    JW honorary member, 1971, 541
Austrian Neurological Society, JW
    honorary member, 1991, 541
Avondale Hotel, 71
Ayers Rock, 380
Aynsley, Dorothy, clinical secretary,
    280
Ayyar, Ram, 353

B

BA Jockey Club, golf, 261
Bachelor of Medical Science examination
    (honours), 404
Bachmann, Bettina (wife of Larry), 500–501
Bachmann, Larry, 500–501, 516
Bacon, John, R.A., 487
Badenoch, Anne (wife of John), 498
Badenoch, John, 481, 484, 490
'Bailey and Love', Short textbook of surgery,
    72
Bailey, Pearce, WFN establishment, 573
Bailliere Tindall and Aids to the
    Examination of the Peripheral Nervous
    System, 560–561
Baird, Lt Gen Sir James, DGAMS,
    329
Ball, Lady (Wendy), organizer BAAS,
    1988, 524, 525
Ball, Major C.E. ('Cora'), 323
Ball, Staff Sergeant, chief clerk to EMO,
    107
Balla, John, career, 286
Ballantyne, Tom, neurosurgeon at MGH,
    193

Bamburgh Castle Cricket Club, 249
Bamburgh Castle Golf Club
fees, 256
floods, 258–259
John and Betty join, 255
JW Captain, 259
knighted, newspaper announcement,
    259
JW Chairman, 259
JW President, 259
vista from, 266
Band of King's African Rifles, 135–136
Bangalore, Betty and John visit, 1983, 377
Bangkok, Betty and John visit, 1971, 368
Banker, Betty, MGH, 190
Bannister, Roger (later Sir), 213, 265
Barber Surgeons Halls, 45
Barcelona
in 1973, golf, 261
Betty and John visit, 1968, 354–355
Barker, Allon, Consul, 198
Barlow, Charles, 214
Barnard Castle, description, 21
Barnes, Dame Josephine, 460, 461, 538
Barnetson, Jimmy, TA, 329
Barnett, Henry (Barney), 168, 405
career, 379
Christopher visits in Canada, 206,
    315
JW takes brick to Canada, 379
and Kay, hospitality and friendship,
    206, 316, 379, 473, 540
Baron, Hugh, 478
Barondess, Jeremiah (Jerry), President,
    New York Academy of Medicine, 474
Oxford Companion to Medicine, 568
Barwick, David, 286, 291, 293, 297
Baseball, 214
Basketball, 214
Bates, David, 234, 297, 298, 300, 495
Bates, John, at Queen Square 1954, 221
Batty Shaw, Major Tony, physician,
    Haifa and Norwich, 125
Bauwens, Phillippe
JW studies electromyography at
    St Thomas' Hospital, 162, 166
Bayliss Lecture, JW delivers, 1990, 536
Bayliss, Sir Richard, 518
Beadnell Hall Hotel
family holidays, 157, 181
Bearn, Professor Alick, 474
Becker, E. Lovell, 563
Beecham, benefactors, 520
9 Beechfield Road, Walton family home,
    269–270, 495
Beers, Robert, Deputy Registrar, GMC,
    435
Beeson, Professor Paul, 542
approached by Sir Richard Doll, 490